GE1

Rea

D0179325

9E 3-

CRC
LIBRARY

READING THE ENVIRONMENT

Cosumnes River College Library
8401 Center Parkway
Sacramento, CA 95823

LIBRARY

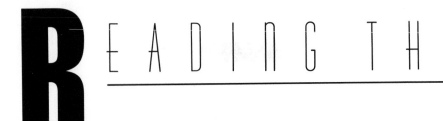

READING THE

This book is printed on

100% recycled paper.

W · W · NORTON & COMPANY

8401 Center Parkway

ENVIRONMENT

Melissa Walker

Emory University

NEW YORK • LONDON

Copyright © 1994 by W. W. Norton & Company, Inc.

Cover photograph: Tropical Atlantic rainforest at Serra Dos Órgãos National Park in Rio de Janeiro State, Southeastern Brazil, photograph by Luiz Claudio Marigo.

All rights reserved

PRINTED IN THE UNITED STATES OF AMERICA

The text of this book is composed in Galliard with the display
set in Helvetica Extra Condensed, Huxley Vertical, and Futura.
Composition and manufacturing by The Haddon Craftsmen, Inc.
Book design by Jack Meserole.

Library of Congress Cataloging-in-Publication Data
Reading the environment / [edited by] Melissa Walker.
        p.   cm.
    Includes bibliographical references (p.   ) and index.
    1. Environmental policy.   2. Environmental protection. I. Walker, Melissa.
  GE170.R4   1994
  363.7—dc20   93-29388

ISBN 0-393-96509-0

W. W. Norton & Company, Inc., 500 Fifth Avenue, New York, N.Y. 10110
W. W. Norton & Company Ltd., 10 Coptic Street, London WC1A 1PU

    4 5 6 7 8 9 0

CONTENTS

4 ECOSYSTEMS AND BIODIVERSITY   144

CHARLES DARWIN • CHRISTOPHER MANES • KIRKPATRICK SALE
BLACK ELK • EMILY DICKINSON

5 SPECIES AND EXTINCTIONS 214

KOYUKON RIDDLES • THEODORE ROOSEVELT • DAVID M. RAUP
LEWIS THOMAS

6 USING RESOURCES: CHOICES AND TRADE-OFFS 274

JOHN BURROUGHS • GIFFORD PINCHOT • BETSY HILBERT
DAVID BROWER

7 SIGNS OF TROUBLE   362

BRUCE BABBITT ◆ CESAR CHAVEZ ◆ JESSE JACKSON ◆ HELEN CALDICOTT

8   ROOTS OF THE CRISIS   440

MARY AUSTIN • GENESIS 1:28 • BARRY LOPEZ • KIRKPATRICK SALE

9 THE FUTURE: CHALLENGES AND SOLUTIONS 518

STEWART L. UDALL ◆ CHAIA HELIER ◆ HENRY D. THOREAU
JOHN LYON ◆ MURIEL RUKEYSER

RHETORICAL CONTENTS

DESCRIPTION

EXPOSITION

Essays That Compare and Contrast

Essays That Classify and Divide

Essays That Analyze Cause/Effect

PERSUASION/ARGUMENT

Essays That Present a Direct Argument

Essays That Imply an Argument

NARRATION

REFLECTIVE/AUTOBIOGRAPHICAL WRITING

IMAGINATIVE LITERATURE

Short Stories

TOPIC CLUSTERS/ARGUMENT PAIRS

PREFACE

The seeds of *Reading the Environment* were planted some three years ago when I visited the Monteverde rain forest in Costa Rica, where I'd traveled on a sabbatical semester to learn more about a region that concerned and fascinated me. Free of teaching responsibilities, I nonetheless thought about my students who over the years had become increasingly interested, as I had, in environmental issues. Given a chance, they were eager to work on papers and research projects ranging from rain forests to the greenhouse effect, from biodiversity to environmental racism.

I had begun the day under the rain forest canopy. Some time later, I walked out of the forest into a pasture where cows grazed on acres of sparse grass marred with the stumps of colossal trees. Still later, I headed down the mountain in an old bus whose diesel exhaust clouded the countryside. The further we descended—from rain forest to cattle pasture to eroded roadway—the more degraded the land became.

The journey, I realized, had been a "reading" experience—that of "reading the environment"—and it allowed me to contextualize the more literal reading of environmental writing that I had done before. Like many writing instructors, I've long believed that it is important for student writers to contextualize *their* reading—to learn about air pollution, for example, in the context of their own driving habits and the history of highway construction. The experience of a rain forest broadened my own sense of context and challenged me to think about how an anthology of readings on the environment could help students recognize and articulate the complexity of the issues and contexts—historical, political, and social.

Before a year had passed, *Reading the Environment* had taken shape as an idea: an anthology of essays, stories, and poems that would serve as a core reader in composition courses focused on environmental issues. The readings would, by design, deepen students' understanding of the specialized language of environmentalism—words like "biomass," "bioregionalism," "ecotage," and "monoculture." *Reading the Environment* wouldn't, however, preach to the converted, but would present complex problems from several points of view. Above all, it would be a gathering of excellent writing, and provide plenty of help for students working to become better writers and clearer thinkers.

THE BOOK

Reading the Environment is designed to help student writers analyze, understand, and communicate the complex forces that have shaped, and continue to shape, the environment and their lives: humanity's impact on the natural world; the ways different cultures interpret and make use of the world around them; the complexity and diversity of living communities and those forces that threaten life; the symptoms of health and sickness in living things; and the environmental consequences of the choices we make and how we live. Such diverse perspectives call for equally diverse writing. Authors include naturalists, corporate executives, developers, loggers, journalists, politicians, philosophers, economists, scientists, and historians. Selections include meditative writing about the natural world, science writing, and issues-oriented writing that provides students with opportunities for active debate. Because the extraordinary range of human response to the natural world can't be expressed in nonfiction alone, *Reading the Environment* includes six stories and seven poems as well. With more than three-quarters of its ninety-nine selections written since 1980, the emphasis of *Reading the Environment* is distinctly contemporary, but students will also learn something of the past and the future—to understand how we got here, as well as where we might go.

Chapter-by-Chapter

The nine chapters of *Reading the Environment* explore our evolving relationship with the natural world and present different approaches to environmental problems and their solutions. The selections in each chapter vary in length, formality, and difficulty; the most complex come at the end. A number of selections are also strategically positioned in topic clusters that look at different aspects of a single issue or theme (the human and economic costs of mining, or the costs of overreliance on cars, for example) or in argument pairs that square off on opposite sides of an issue.

Chapter 1, "Entering the Conversation," puts student writers in the thick of various environmental crises from the journalist's perspective. Fourteen concise, contemporary newspaper articles and editorials introduce the lightning-rod issues: overpopulation, air pollution, ozone depletion, species extinction, and global warming.

Chapter 2, "Wilderness and Nature," includes several classics of the American tradition of nature writing, as well as more recent nonfiction narratives and imaginative writing—all speaking to the individual's experience of nature, the qualities of "wildness," or the rationale for wilderness preservation.

Chapter 3, "People, Places, and Cultures," opens with Gary Snyder's beautiful meditation "The World Is Places," then goes on to explore the idea of place as a source of identity, with writings about places from Pennsylvania and North Dakota to Australia's New South Wales, Botswana's Kalahari Desert, and Malawi's Vwaza Marsh Game Reserve.

Chapter 4, "Ecosystems and Biodiversity," provides the context for Chapter 5, "Species and Extinctions"; students first consider the complex interactions of living things within communities of life, then turn to individual species and those forces that threaten them. The selections in Chapter 4, beginning with E. O. Wilson's brilliant "Storm over the Amazon," explore the richness of life that results from and relies on interdependency. Chapter 5 focuses on the particularities of specific species, from the celebrated (whales and wolves) to the lesser known (auks and limpets)—species saved, threatened, or lost as a result of human interference.

Chapter 6, "Using Resources: Choices and Trade-offs," looks at various ways human activity has impacted the environment and considers the price we pay for the way we use and abuse natural resources. The politics of development and conservation figure prominently in these selections. Who loses, we must ask, when conservation wins?

Chapter 7, "Signs of Trouble," looks beyond choices to consequences— declining bird populations, forests killed by acid rain, people poisoned by insecticides, and public confusion about environmental risks.

Chapter 8, "Roots of the Crisis," focuses on past attitudes and actions that have fostered the environmental problems we face today. A number of longer selections explore the values and implications of consumerism and environmentalism.

Chapter 9, "The Future: Challenges and Solutions," looks ahead for the means of change—global and national policy, corporate strategy, community action, and, underlying all these, individual ethics and behavior.

Apparatus

Reading the Environment's apparatus was designed with three purposes in mind: to spark student interest, to present a wealth of contextual information to help students navigate a complex subject, and to provide raw material for classroom debate, critical thinking, and writing.

The rhetorical table of contents on pages xiii–xix is a useful reference for organizing courses by modes, kinds, and genres of writing.

The Chronology at the beginning of the book situates historically significant publications, organizations, policy decisions, legislation, and catastrophes that have affected the environment and how we think about it. Students will find this a useful touchstone as they read particular selections.

At the start of each chapter are "vignettes"—prose paragraphs, brief poems, proverbs, quotations from a wide range of sources—as well as a photograph, designed to spark thinking, discussion, and writing on issues the chapter will cover. These are followed by a chapter introduction that provides students with an overview of the chapter's theme and selections.

Each selection in *Reading the Environment* is preceded by a brief biographical/bibliographic headnote. Sometimes knowing who authors are, when they were born, and where their voices come from helps us to understand where they stand on complex environmental issues.

Each selection is also followed by two sets of questions. "Understanding What You Read" questions are designed to reinforce students' grasp of content and help them analyze rhetorical strategies. "Writing About What You Read" questions suggest writing assignments—ranging from in-class activities to short-essay and research-paper topics—that go beyond the texts themselves. At the end of each chapter, "Making Connections" questions ask students to draw comparisons between various selections in the chapter—and sometimes elsewhere in the book.

Useful as a reference, a Glossary of more than a hundred key environmental concepts and terms that students will encounter repeatedly is included at the end of the book.

Finally, students can consult "A Selected List of Books for Further Reading" by authors included in *Reading the Environment* and others. This annotated list is a helpful starting point for research papers.

INSTRUCTOR'S HANDBOOK

An Instructor's Handbook for *Reading the Environment* begins with an "Environmental Literacy Quiz" (a useful diagnostic at the beginning and end of the course), with an answer key cross-referenced to selections in the text. The Handbook also provides, chapter by chapter, brief discussions of individual selections, writing and research suggestions, collaborative activities, and classroom debate topics.

ACKNOWLEDGMENTS

The love of the outdoors that went into making this book finds its origins in my grandmother's attachment to swamps and other wild places in middle Georgia, my mother's appreciation for wildlife, my father's deep knowledge of forestry, and my own experiences in the fields and woods of the rural South. This love was deepened in my teenage years by time spent in the national parks of the Pacific Northwest and in the Rocky Mountains of Colorado.

I have been fortunate both in rich experiences and the people I have known who directly and indirectly contributed to this book. For special help,

I would like to thank Jerome Beaty, Roberta Bondi, and Marjorie Shostak (all of Emory University), Mat Kayhoe (University of Virginia), Libby Miles (Purdue University), Jimmy Northup, Zak Sitter (Harvard University), Peter Vitousek (Stanford University), and Dan Zins (Atlanta College of Art).

For reading early stages of the manuscript and advising me about structure and selections, I would like to thank Linda Bergmann (Lewis College of Liberal Arts), Betsy Hilbert (Miami Dade Community College), Tom Kelly (Tufts University), Barbara Lounsberry (University of Northern Iowa), Sandra W. Stephan (Youngstown State University), and Fred Strebeigh (Yale University).

Many people have made suggestions and recommended material for this book. My mother, Pearl Graves, and my mother-in-law, Mary Jim Walker, regularly clipped relevant newspaper articles; my son, Richard, advised me about writings on tropical science; and my daughter, Laura, showed me places that helped me to understand environmental problems in Southern California. A number of scientists at the La Selva field station in Costa Rica were helpful, especially Antonio Nobre of the University of New Hampshire and Manaus, Brazil; David Clark, Deborah Clark, and Ronald Suarez (co-directors of La Selva); and Wes Jackson of the Land Institute in Kansas. My friends—including Cecelia Arzewski, Richard Bondi, Jingle Davis, Sandra Deer, Sue Dennard, Carol Light, Alex Redmountain, Virginia Ross, Wes Sanders, Sarah Steinhardt, and Suzanne Yaeger—have been enthusiastic about this book and continue to be supportive of my work. An incisive letter from Peter A. Fritzell of Lawrence University and a conversation with Janice L. Edens of Macon College helped to clarify my thinking early on. Marilyn Montgomery and Ernest Fokes provided me with a haven in their home in Idaho at a crucial stage in the process. For a place to stay in New York, I thank Rena Bulkin. Thanks also to Gay Kahn for her invaluable contribution to this project. My husband, Jerome Walker, read every word of the book, twice, and contributed significantly to its completion.

As a participant of the Santa Fe Environmental Council during the preparation of this book, I heard the concerns of people in leadership positions in industry, government, the legal profession, and education. Especially helpful were Dr. Robert P. Bringer, vice president for environmental engineering, 3M Company; Peter Corcoran, Bates College; Toni Cortese, dean of Environmental Programs, Tufts University; Tuss Erickson, director of policies and programs, Phillips Petroleum Company; Dee Fairbanks, Mille Lacs Band of the Ojibwe Indians, Onamia, Minnesota; Sarah Hayes, Applied Environmental Technology, Los Alamos Laboratories; Dr. Charles Hopkins, chairman of ECO-ED in Toronto, Ontario; Michael Last, founder of the Santa Fe Environmental Council; Ruth Musgrave, founder of the Center for Wildlife Law; Nancy Sanders of Cambridge, Massachusetts; Cornelius (Bud) Smith, Jr., ENVIRON Corporation, former vice president for health, safety, and environmental protection, Union Carbide Corporation; Claudine

Sneider, former congresswoman from Rhode Island; John Stokes of the Tracking Project; and Richard Warch, president of Lawrence University.

It is with profound gratitude that I acknowledge the core team at Norton—Susan Brekka, John Mardirosian, and Julia Reidhead—whose commitment to and involvement with the creation of this book has been extraordinary. Others who have contributed in important ways to the book include Laurie Dolphin and Hugh O'Neill for a beautiful cover, Deborah Gerish for sharp-eyed proofreading, Ted Johnson for excellent copyediting, Jack Meserole for the splendid design, Diane O'Connor for the crucial work of turning a manuscript into an attractive book in a timely fashion, and Anna Karvellas and Ann Tappert for attention to many last-minute details.

This book is lovingly dedicated to the memory of Barry Wade, my editor and dear friend at Norton for some ten years. It was under his inspired and skilled guidance that I learned how books are made. It was in conversation with him that *Reading the Environment* was conceived. For this book and many others at Norton, he made all the difference. Without him it would not have happened.

MELISSA WALKER

1735   Publication of Linnaeus' *Systema Naturae* establishes the modern system of classification of plants and animals.

1827–   Publication of John James Audubon's *The Birds of North America*,
1838   containing more than a thousand color illustrations and identifying more than five hundred species of birds.

1845   Publication of Henry David Thoreau's *Walden*, which commends the value of living simply and in harmony with nature.

1859   Publication of Charles Darwin's *On the Origin of Species by Means of Natural Selection*, which demonstrates that species are not unchangeable but have developed through time in relation to environmental factors.

1872   Yellowstone National Park established as the first of America's national parks.

1885   Development of a gas-burning internal combustion engine of the type now widely used in automobiles and other motor vehicles.

1890   Creation of Yosemite National Park as the result of the efforts of conservationist John Muir.

1892   John Muir and others found the Sierra Club, dedicated to the preservation and expansion of the world's parks, wildlife, and wilderness areas.

1902   Reclamation Act establishes a Bureau of Reclamation to administer dams and reclamation projects in western states.

1913   Bill passed authorizing the building of a dam that would flood Hetch Hetchy Valley, once part of Yosemite.

1916   National Park Service Act establishes National Park System, to preserve natural landscapes, historic landmarks, wildlife habitats, and wilderness areas.

1924   Establishment of the first wilderness reserve within a national forest in the Gila National Forest in New Mexico.

1934   Robert Marshall, Aldo Leopold, and others meet to found the Wilderness Society, which is committed to fostering the welfare of national forests, parks, wildlife reserves, and Bureau of Land Management areas.

1945 First atomic explosion near Alamogordo, New Mexico, followed by the bombing of Hiroshima and Nagasaki in Japan and by almost two decades of atmospheric testing of atomic weapons.

1949 Publication of Aldo Leopold's *Sand County Almanac,* calling attention to widespread abuse of the land and living things while urging a new respect for the earth and its wild places.

1956 First of many recognized cases of disfiguring disease caused by fish poisoned by mercury dumped in Minimata Bay in Japan.

1962 Publication of Rachel Carson's *Silent Spring,* which exposed the dangers of indiscriminate use of pesticides and caused a public outcry about such pollutants as DDT, one pesticide that was eventually banned.

1963 Clean Air Act (amended in 1970, 1977, and 1990) requires states to meet specified standards of air quality.

The United States and the Soviet Union sign a treaty that ends atmospheric testing of atomic weapons except for a few conducted by France and China.

1964 Passage of the Wilderness Act, authorizing the government to protect undeveloped tracts of public lands and defining wilderness as an area "where the earth and its community of life are untrammeled by man, where man himself is a visitor who does not remain."

1967 Publication of Roderick Nash's *Wilderness and the American Mind,* a landmark book that explores the meaning and importance of wilderness.

1968 Publication of Edward Abbey's *Desert Solitaire,* which celebrates the wonders of Arches National Monument while urging the development of sound policies to protect national parks and other wild places.

Wild and Scenic Rivers Act designates particular rivers or parts of rivers for protection.

1969 Passage of the National Environmental Policy Act, requiring that government agencies assess the environmental impact of proposed projects and produce an environmental impact statement.

1970 Celebration of first Earth Day by some twenty million people, who demonstrated for a better environment

Occupational Safety and Health Act (OSHA) authorizing establishment of strict standards to protect workers on the job.

Establishment of Environmental Protection Agency to regulate air and water quality, radiation and pesticide hazards, and solid-waste disposal.

Roadless Areas Review and Evaluation I (RARE I; RARE II, 1977) initiating a study to identify wilderness areas for protection and to open nonwilderness roadless areas to multiple-use management.

1972 Stockholm Conference on the Human Environment. Founding of United Nations Environmental Program (UNEP).

1973 Passage of the Endangered Species Act, setting up procedures for protecting endangered animals and plants (amended in 1982, 1985, and 1988).

Convention on International Trade in Endangered Species in Wild Flora and Fauna (CITES), an international agreement eventually ratified by 106 nations.

1974 Sherwood Rowland and Mario Medina publish results of their studies linking chlorofluorocarbons (CFCs) and stratospheric ozone depletion in volume 249 of *Nature*.

1976 National Forest Management Act legalizes clear-cutting on public lands, resulting in more monoculture, pesticide use, and animal control, and declining natural diversity.

1977 Clean Water Act changes the name of the Water Pollution Control Act of 1972 and requires that waters be "fishable and swimmable" by 1983.

Residents living near Love Canal near Niagara Falls, New York, discover that their water and soil and even the inside of their homes have been poisoned by industrial wastes buried years before.

1979 Release of radioactive material at Three Mile Island nuclear power plant.

1980 Comprehensive Environmental Response, Compensation, and Liability Act (the Superfund program) established a multibillion-dollar fund to clean up hazardous-waste dump sites.

1984 3,700 people die and 300,000 are injured at or near the Union Carbide pesticide plant in Bhopal, India, when highly toxic gas leaks from a storage tank.

1985 French secret service bombs a Greenpeace boat used to interfere in nuclear testing.

A team of British scientists announce that a large hole in the ozone layer has been appearing every spring since 1977, confirming the theories proposed by Rowland and Molina in 1974.

1986 Meltdown of Chernobyl nuclear power plant disperses radioactive material throughout much of the western Soviet Union and Europe.

1987 Montreal Protocol signatories agree to reduce CFC production. Amended 1990 to include more chemicals and to phase out all CFCs by the year 2000.

1988   Chico Mendes, organizer of rubber tappers and defender of rain forests, is assassinated by wealthy landowners in December in the doorway of his home in Brazil.

1989   Margaret Thatcher calls a meeting, attended by representatives of 123 nations, to discuss ozone depletion.

Exxon Valdez oil spill in Prince William Sound causes major damage to wildlife.

Time magazine's "Man of the Year" goes to the planet earth.

1991   Iraqi soldiers in the Persian Gulf War deliberately release massive amounts of oil into the sea from Kuwait's Sea Island terminal, causing untold environmental damage.

Eruption of Mount Pinatubo in the Philippines, cooling the earth and temporarily masking a warming tendency observed for some years.

1992   Publication of Al Gore's *Earth in the Balance* establishes Gore as a leading expert on environmental issues.

United Nations Conference on Environment and Development (UNCED) held in Rio de Janeiro, Brazil, in June results in worldwide publicity for many practices that threaten the environment.

1993   Oil spill from a grounded tanker in the North Atlantic damages wildlife on the Shetland Islands.

1 ENTERING THE

"Biologists Warn of Wholesale Extinction," *Boston Globe,* August 16, 1991.

♦

"Mexico City Tackles Herculean Pollution, Population Pressures," *Christian Science Monitor,* October 23, 1991.

♦

"War's Enduring Ecological Scars," *Los Angeles Times,* November 8, 1991.

♦

"Incinerators: Unwanted and Politically Dangerous: Supporting the Burning of Garbage These Days Is Something Politicians Dare Not Do," *New York Times,* December 12, 1991.

♦

"Novel Ideas to Remedy Global Warming and Ozone Loss Won't Work, Scientists Say," *Chronicle of Higher Education,* January 8, 1992.

♦

"Farmers in West May Sell Something More Valuable Than Any Crop: Water," *New York Times,* April 6, 1992.

♦

"Pollution-Weary Minorities Try Civil Rights Tack," *New York Times,* January 11, 1992.

♦

"Harm from Alaska Spill Goes on, Scientists Say," *New York Times,* February 6, 1993.

♦

"No More Pesticides for Dinner," *New York Times,* March 9, 1993.

♦

"Environmentalists Vie for Right to Pollute," *Wall Street Journal,* March 26, 1993.

CONVERSATION

Los Angeles Highways
(State of California Department of Transportation)

Introduction

Most of us have learned what we know about environmental issues in bits and pieces—a newspaper headline, a magazine article, a television program, a movie. You may remember reading about such problems as species extinction, the loss of biodiversity, the destruction of rain forests, global warming, ozone depletion, the population explosion, air and water pollution, toxic wastes, and acid rain. But chances are that you feel a little confused about these issues. You may feel even more confused by the frequently used phrase "environmental crisis," an umbrella term covering a variety of phenomena.

"Environmental crisis" is as broad and comprehensive as "the human condition," encompassing phenomena as varied as the erosion of topsoil, the contamination of the oceans, and the overconsumption of groundwater. Its many causes include overpopulation, unsustainable agriculture, excessive reliance on fossil fuels, and the wasteful habits of the affluent. Somewhere in the world, conditions justify using the word "crisis" for almost any environmental problem. At any given moment we could focus on particular countries or regions and find a water crisis, a population crisis, an energy crisis, a hunger crisis, an employment crisis, and on and on.

The environmental crisis is nothing less than all the undesirable consequences of the way humans impact this earth and its other living inhabitants. It is a river in Iowa contaminated with sewage and a child in Ethiopia dying of protein deficiency. It is a farmer in Costa Rica rendered sterile by exposure to pesticides and an asthmatic patient struggling for breath in smog-laden Los Angeles or Mexico City. It is found in the statistics about skin cancer in Australia and in landfills all over the world overflowing with garbage. It is a garbage heap full of plastic bottles and aluminum cans and a large car idling at a traffic light. It may be on the street where you live.

Walk out into your neighborhood, take a deep breath, and look around. You will probably encounter evidence of a degraded environment. If you examine your daily life, you might realize that you are contributing to what we call the environmental crisis.

While any one person could easily feel overwhelmed by the magnitude of this crisis, no one person has to solve it. Rather, solutions are being sought and found around the globe by people motivated by a variety of social conditions, ideas, and values. People whose survival depends on having a supply of firewood may be persuaded to plant trees; those who make a living selling ivory may be moved to protect elephants to ensure a steady supply; and people who love wilderness camping trips are likely to support movements to acquire more wilderness land. People who have the luxury of thinking about the world they want their grandchildren to live in may become involved in politics or join organizations that are committed to changing policies and practices that damage the environment.

The first step to becoming part of the solution rather than the problem is to learn just what that problem is and what the solutions might be. Equally important is to recognize the complexity of environmental issues and to avoid oversimplifying them.

If in the early nineties you scanned newspapers for articles on environmental issues, you would have encountered headlines like those at the beginning of this chapter. Reading articles like these is like entering a room full of people who have been talking for years about pesticides, oil spills, water shortages, species extinction, and other environmental concerns. Imagine that you enter such a room where people are chatting in small groups. Listening in, you hear references to the spotted owl, rain forests, pollution control devices, hazardous-waste cleanups, recycling, the ozone layer, global warming, and soil erosion. Joining this environmental conversation could be an exciting and important step, the start of a process that will last the rest of your life. To contribute effectively, however, you will need to understand the context and history of specific problems and to learn how one problem relates to others.

Regardless of what you already know about the environment, you will probably learn something new from the newspaper articles in this chapter. As you read them, jot down new facts, questions that arise, and points of confusion. Keep in mind, too, that no one in on the environmental conversation understands it all. Solving these problems is a global enterprise, and the work of generations.

But the news isn't all bad. For some decades now, people in many different contexts and countries have been working to prevent further damage to the environment and to change destructive policies and behaviors. As you read these words, political leaders are devising legislation to help preserve ecosystems, communities are setting up recycling centers, government officials are drafting proposals to reduce energy consumption, corporate leaders are discussing ways to reduce waste in the factory and workplace, teachers are talking to children about how living things are interconnected, biologists are developing ways to grow crops without chemical pesticides, and researchers are developing products that will replace ozone-depleting chlorofluorocarbons.

The environment is rapidly becoming everybody's business, ignored at everybody's peril. The number of professions that focus on environmental concerns is growing; more and more young people are studying to become environmental engineers, waste management consultants, pollution control managers, atmospheric scientists, and public health officers. Others study science so that they can later search for new drugs or new foods in rain forests, find and identify unknown species, or splice genes to improve the quality of our crops. There is work enough in the environmental arena to occupy many people for decades to come.

Concern with the environment, however, did not start with the discovery of the ozone hole or with the mounting fear of global warming. Some 150 years ago, long before Rachel Carson's *Silent Spring* warned of the dangers of pesticides or Barry Commoner warned of the risks of radiation exposure, there were people in North America protesting the exploitation of the land in the rush of settlement and urging a new way of thinking about wilderness and nature. The chronology at the front of this book traces some of the accomplishments and setbacks in the ongoing effort to find a balanced and sustainable relationship between human beings and the natural world.

BENJAMIN ZUCKERMAN

Two by Two, We'll Fill the Planet

HOW MANY angels can dance on the head of a pin? This is a type of question that people asked in the not so distant past when religion reigned supreme, and science and technology played a negligible role in everyday life. Now that the rise of science and technology has enabled enormous increases in the human population, we must face the question: How many people can live on the surface of the Earth?

The rate of growth, that is, the percentage increase per year, of the human population is at an all-time high. Many politicians, economists and religious leaders regard rapid population growth as "natural" and extol its virtues. For example, we often read that population growth stimulates the economy and is, therefore, good. This may be true if one's vision is expressed in units of four years and limited to a few decades at most. However, life has existed on Earth for at least 3.5 billion years and human beings for a few million years. So the very rapid population growth of the past 100 or so years is not natural.

If the current rate of growth of world population, about 2% per year, were continued into the year 3400, then each person now alive would have 1 trillion descendants and the total human population would be about 10,000,000,000,000,000,000,000 (10 sextillion). This is 10% of the total number of stars in the entire observable universe. Well before 3400, the average amount of land per person would have diminished to less than one square inch.

Broken down into shorter intervals, we are talking about a tenfold increase in just over a century. So by about the year 2100, at current rates, there would be 50 billion people on Earth. And 500 billion not long after the year 2200.

What about covering all the deserts and oceans with people? That would only delay the inevitable need for zero population growth by a century at the very most. How about shipping off the extra people (net difference between the number born and the number who die) to outer space? At current growth rates that would mean sending 10,000 people up every hour of every day. And we have trouble launching a few shuttles per year safely.

The issue is not whether an economy that is stimulated by population growth is good, bad or indifferent. The above calculations show that growth is impossible except in the very short run. The real issue is what kind of world will the people of the present and next few generations leave for the people and other creatures of the next few millennia.

FROM the *Los Angeles Times,* October 31, 1991.

According to UCLA professor and biologist Jared Diamond, the coming century will witness one of the worst extinctions in the history of life on Earth. Roughly one-half of the 30 million species that are estimated to exist will become extinct, courtesy entirely of human beings. If yet additional population and economic growth of the sort that some people espouse actually occurs, then the extinction rate will be even worse. A combination of far too many people, greed and unbridled technological power is destroying the natural world.

Each person plays a role in the population equation. If you and your spouse have two children and four grandchildren then you are reproducing at replacement levels (zero population growth). But if you have four children and they, in turn, each have four children so that you have 16 grandchildren, then that is roughly equivalent to the 2% per year growth rate that characterizes the world as a whole.

Each of us has his or her own system of values. For me, a planet with relatively few people, each of whom can live with dignity and a high quality of life, is far superior to a world where too many people, awash in pollution, stretch resources to the breaking point, and where billions struggle to survive at mere subsistence levels.

EDWARD CODY

Mexico City Family Oppressed by Pollution

MEXICO CITY, March 25—Since playing basketball with his teenage son over the weekend in the poisonous Mexico City air, Erick Alcantara has been swallowing aspirin tablets nonstop to combat a throbbing migraine.

His 6-month-old daughter, Irene, has suffered bronchial problems almost since birth in what the Alcantara family says is a reaction to the increasingly polluted atmosphere. School authorities this winter have forbidden the Alcantras' first-grader, Andres, and their 11-year-old daughter, Marycarmen, from running during school recess for fear they and their boisterous playmates will breathe in the befouled air too deeply.

"We can sit down in the playground, but we can't run," Andres, 6, complained. "Whoever runs is taken to the principal's office."

These have become the realities of everyday life for the Alcantaras and millions of other Mexico City families who reside in what is arguably the

FROM the *Washington Post*, March 26, 1992.

world's most polluted city, which in recent days has been going through what environmentalists and local authorities have classified as its worst air-quality emergency on record. Mexico City's problem is in part simple geography: It is ringed by mountains that trap pollution.

As ozone readings soared to record levels last week, President Carlos Salinas de Gortari's government imposed the most draconian antipollution measures so far on the city's 20 million inhabitants. Although some grumbled at the inconveniences and industrialists warned of slowing the economy, acceptance seemed widespread. After years of resignation many here have begun to demonstrate increasing impatience with the government's apparent inability to clean up the air they breathe.

"I am ready to use a bicycle, or even roller skates, if it will improve the pollution situation," Alcantara said in reaction to his inability to use the family car on Wednesday, Thursday and Saturday under the intensified restrictions.

A day-without-a-car program, in place for two years, was temporarily expanded to two days a week and weekends for some cars. That meant 40 percent of the city's nearly 3 million vehicles are kept off the road each day until conditions improve. Automobiles produce about 75 percent of the region's ozone.

Subway use jumped by about a million passengers to 5.5 million a day, stuffing an already crowded system. Executives in suits and ties were forced to garage their cars and ride alongside workers in the minibuses that swerve up and down the capital's main arteries.   8

In addition, the most polluting of the some 30,000 factories around Mexico City were forced to cut production 30 percent and Salinas announced a crackdown under which they will be forced to reduce contamination by 1994 or move out of the Valley of Mexico.

The government's emergency moves helped bring pollution down a bit. Also buoyed by favorable winds and atmospheric pressure, city antipollution officials said they were considering scaling back their restrictions, that is, until the next explosion of high readings.

But Mayor Manuel Camacho Solis and his environmental aides have acknowledged that, given political and economic realities, permanently reducing ozone levels will take at least a decade. Steps already in place have reduced other pollutants, such as lead and carbon monoxide, but increasing gasoline consumption, combined with Mexico City's 7,300-foot altitude, means only long-term hopes are realistic for getting ozone under control.

As a result, Carmina and Erick Alcantara and their four children have begun to talk of moving to a provincial city. So far, however, it has only been talk, since outside Mexico City employment opportunities are less numerous and schooling, particularly college preparatory classes for 16-year-old Erick Jr., is less prestigious.   12

In the meantime, they and their neighbors have been forced to play out their lives engulfed by pollution. Although the long-term effects on health have not been scientifically assessed, the Health Ministry has said contamination has become a major source of respiratory irritation, minor illnesses and debilitation.

"People here just live tired," Carmina said. "My kids are always coming home with headaches and stomach aches. And the baby is always having bronchial troubles."

*   *   *

EDITORIAL

Warning from the Stratosphere

OZONE LOSSES over the Antarctic have signaled for two decades the increasing chemical damage to the atmosphere. Now the National Aeronautics and Space Administration reports that last Sunday the ozone layer there was thinner than ever before in its 13 years of monitoring. Like all of these indicators, this one by itself is not conclusive. The ozone hole is produced by a highly complex interplay of man-made chemicals, chiefly the chlorofluorocarbons, or CFCs, and the weather. But this startlingly low reading is a part of an ominous pattern.

It is further evidence that ozone depletion is running faster than forecast—a warning that the process of depletion is not yet fully understood. There has been thinning over the Arctic as well, and NASA observed earlier this year that there has been a significant disappearance over the United States. Since the ozone layer blocks ultraviolet radiation, its deterioration will result in an increasing danger of skin cancer.

To this rising threat, the world has responded with a speed and intelligence that has created a model for worldwide environmental protection. Four years ago the countries producing most of these chemicals signed an agreement, the Montreal Protocol, to cut their output in half. When it developed that the layer was being eroded much faster than the negotiators at Montreal had anticipated, they returned to rewrite the protocol. The industrial world is now committed to ban all production of CFCs by the end of this decade and the developing countries by 2010. These latest findings will add force to the proposals to revise it once again and impose an even earlier ban.

Several useful lessons are contained in the case of the ozone layer. One

FROM the *Washington Post*, October 11, 1991.

is that environmental changes develop tremendous momentum and are very hard to stop or even to slow down once they begin. While governments will prevent the manufacture of more CFCs, the very large quantities of it produced in the past will continue to leak into the air for years to come. Another lesson is that the course of these changes, along with the speed at which they will take place, is very difficult to foresee. A third is that only time will reveal the full consequences.

All of these lessons apply to the challenge of global warming. Ozone and the CFCs are a much simpler case, for the chemical industry is already well advanced in developing alternatives to the CFCs. To cut emissions of carbon dioxide would be a much more disruptive and expensive proposition. But as it considers the prospect of global warming, the world will need to keep in mind its experience with the ozone layer.

JESSICA MATHEWS

Unfriendly Skies

M O R E B A D N E W S from the upper atmosphere. What is one to make of it?

First, the bare facts. A NASA-led team using satellites and aircraft has discovered unexpected, extremely high levels of the most potent ozone-destroying chemical, comparable to and even higher than levels found in the Antarctic ozone hole. Beneath them, however, were not penguins and phytoplankton, but London, Brussels, Berlin, Moscow and northern Maine. The results mean that the atmosphere is much less able than scientists previously thought to fend off the ozone-destroying effects of chlorofluorocarbons.

The discovery greatly increases the likelihood that an ozone hole will soon develop in the Arctic. Unlike the Antarctic hole, which stays put over the South Pole, an Arctic hole will slither around, periodically extending as far south as 45 degrees north latitude, north of which lies most of Europe and the former Soviet Union, Canada and several U.S. states.

In years when the hole lasted for a long time, pockets of very high ozone depletion would persist into May and June, when the sun is strongest, exposing heavily populated areas to very high levels of ultraviolet radiation, raising rates of melanoma and cataracts. Effects on nonhuman species are less clear but possibly worse for them, and indirectly, for us.

4

FROM the *Washington Post*, February 9, 1992.

The new findings confirmed earlier predictions that sulfates tossed into the stratosphere in the eruption of Mt. Pinatubu would accelerate ozone loss. This is another instance of a seemingly unrelated man-made change (chlorine in the atmosphere) turning an uncontrollable and otherwise relatively benign natural event (a volcanic eruption) into a severe result. Trees bathed in acid rain succumb to natural outbreaks of pests and disease they would otherwise resist. Deforestation on steep hillsides in the Philippines turned a moderate typhoon last year into a human catastrophe of death by mudslide. On this crowded planet even acts of God are becoming acts of man.

Happily, something can be done. Under the current terms of the Montreal Treaty, ozone loss will continue to grow until 2000. But revised terms requiring an accelerated phaseout of chlorofluorocarbons and tighter controls over related ozone-depleters can cut the inevitable loss significantly. Meanwhile, maximum diplomatic pressure needs to be exerted on India, the chief treaty holdout, to overcome its habitual antipathy to global problem-solving and join the effort.

There is a moral here for policymakers. The findings confirmed a hunch scientists had about a recently discovered mechanism of atmospheric chemistry. There are lots and lots (hundreds, maybe even thousands) of things of comparable significance that we don't know about this planet, because its study is a scientific frontier. Also, man is creating conditions that natural systems have never before encountered, which may trigger unpredictable shifts. For the next few decades, therefore, surprise will be a constant backdrop to decision-making. It has to be expected—and accommodated.

8   Waiting for scientific certainty, the administration's constant plea, is obviously a nonstarter. By that standard there would be no Montreal Treaty and no action possible even now. The only option is to learn to act in the presence of substantial doubt. The sensible way to do that is by taking relatively low-cost steps to reduce the risk of highly unpleasant outcomes—in the same spirit that we buy insurance.

*   *   *

WILLIAM BOOTH

So What If It's Getting Hot?

L A S T   W E E K, as eco-technocrats from a hundred countries bumped heads in Nairobi over how best to confront global warming, and as Washington wilted in a freak September heat wave, the National Academy of Sciences quietly issued a report with a remarkable conclusion: When it comes to the greenhouse effect, there's nothing to worry about.

If global warming is indeed a reality, if the temperature and the seas rise in the course of the next century, humans will adapt quite nicely, the report concludes. Stripped of its caveats, that is the gut-level impression of the dozen agronomists, economists, engineers and environmental scientists assembled to consider the matter by the Academy, the august body that advises the federal government.

The National Academy of Sciences has been wrestling with the greenhouse issue for years. In the spring, it issued another of its cautious reports, concluding the United States should adopt "effective but inexpensive" actions to slow down projected warming. That means reducing carbon dioxide and other gases produced by automobiles and industry, but doing so gradually, at least to begin with.

But this latest academy panel takes another approach. It *assumes* Earth is going to warm, and then dares to ask the politically incorrect question: So what? 4

A temperature rise of two or three or four degrees spread out over 50 or 60 years? No big deal, say these adaptationists. We'll crank up the AC and increase electric power generation by 12 to 22 percent. So what if it costs $400 billion? It all depends on how you discount the investment over time.

What about climatic refugees? It's happened before, say the adaptationists, and it'll happen again. The Irish fled the warm, moist summers of the 1840s that led to the potato blight. Midwesterners fled the Dust Bowl. This time around, Texans might move north to Minnesota. It costs, on average, $1,500 to transport the contents of a 450-square-foot apartment 400 miles to a six-degree-cooler climate. That's not going to break the bank.

A rise in sea level of one or two or three feet? The adaptationists envision dikes, levees, pumps and berms to hold it back. The Dutch had to build them, and they're doing okay. What's a seawall cost these days? In South Carolina, about $2,000 a foot, or about 6 percent of the value of the property the seawall is protecting.

Agriculture? If the greenhouse world is drier rather than wetter, which is entirely possible, we'll extend irrigation. We'll create genetically altered 8

FROM the *Washington Post*, September 22, 1991.

super-wheat. We've done it before. A new strain of cultivated plant, used these days for only about six years before it is replaced by another strain, costs about $1 million to develop. Farmers are among the most adaptable and ingenious of people in the pursuit of commerce.

The report has already attracted criticism for its complacent, almost breezy, even hopeful tone. Part of the reason is that the adaptationists rely for their analysis on economics and engineering, and not on ecology, a science that is still struggling valiantly to connect enough dots to present Earth's big picture.

It is precisely this difference in approach that will color every report and discussion of global warming and related environmental issues for years to come. Economists have not yet found a way to put a price tag on an acre of wetland or a species of warbler, and until they do, they will not enter the equation; there is not much salable meat on a warbler.

The report is also being criticized for its optimism. For the most part, the adaptationists see a very different future than do many environmental activists, who tend to be a more pessimistic bunch.

12   Look, for example, into the crystal ball of Michael Oppenheimer, a senior scientist with the Environmental Defense Fund, and his colleague Robert Boyle, the authors of the briskly selling book *Dead Heat*.

Here is an example of their vision of the mid-21st century: "In the Chesapeake Bay, Long Island Sound, Narragansett Bay and other coastal waters that once gave purpose and delight to sailors, swimmers, fishermen, and children building sand castles, the water is rankest in the summer. . . . Stimulated by warm, still weather, algal blooms deoxygenate the water below. Suddenly half a million menhaden, maybe a million, go belly up. After a week, the oily fish stink too much even for the gulls, but eels still burrow into the bloated fish to gorge on internal organs. Above the rotting carcasses washed up on shore, next to the shattered houses half tumbled into the water, the air is filled with the ceaseless buzzing of greenhead flies and the scurrying of rats' feet over broken glass."

No place to spend the weekend with the kids. To Oppenheimer and many others, including not a few scientists, the greenhouse world is no vacationland. It is downright terrifying.

The adaptationist panel's report was even too much for one of its own members. Jane Lubchenco, an ecologist from Oregon State University, issued a strong dissent, stating, "I disagree with the report's implicit message, that we can adapt with little or no problem."

16   Yet according to the majority of the panel, Lubchenco is overreacting, or rather reacting in the absence of good data. The results of a warming "will be no more severe, and adapting to them will be no more difficult, than for the range of climates already on Earth and no more difficult than for other changes humanity faces."

What about food riots and dust bowls, massive forest death and global economic chaos? What about melting polar ice caps and water lapping at the foot of the Washington Monument?

The panel is not so hysterical. It pleads for perspective. "Human adaptability is shown by people working in both Riyadh and Barrow and seeking out both Minneapolis and Galveston. Recent American migration has on average been toward warmth."

In fact, the adaptationists suggest we should be glad it's getting warmer and not colder, as some of the scientists who now predict warming once suggested would happen. If the world got nine degrees cooler, instead of nine degrees hotter, the upper midwestern United States would be crushed under a sheet of glacial ice. "None of the projected effects of the warming would make large areas uninhabitable."

The panel assumes the world will warm moderately and not all at once, as most computer simulations suggest. It notes that something weird and awful could happen, such as a reversal of the balmy Atlantic Ocean current that keeps Britain from freezing. But such an event is unlikely, it says. Better to monitor the situation than to react prematurely to nightmare scenarios.

20

*   *   *

Depending on how you view the world, the academy's report can be a little comforting, or extremely disturbing. It concludes, in essence, that the systems dominated by humans will, at worst, muddle along. There will be costs. There will be winners and losers. But the crops will grow. Industry will continue. Humans will adjust and adapt.

As for the warblers, elms and menhaden, the adaptationists say they'll have to fend for themselves.

GEORGE M. WOODWELL AND KILAPARTI RAMAKRISHNA

Forests, Scapegoats and Global Warming

W O O D S   H O L E ,   M A S S .—The earth's last great forests are being destroyed in this century, torn apart for trifling profits. Some destruction is deliberate—logging for lumber and pulp, burning to create pasture land. And some of it is collateral damage—assault by air and water pollution, the general toxification of an environment downwind of thousands of smokestacks.

But letting forests die is self-destructive. Their role as a filter of the

FROM the *New York Times,* February 11, 1992.

world's pollution, a sponge that absorbs carbon dioxide and slows global warming, is crucial to the life of the earth. Governments are only slowly recognizing the need for a global plan to manage the earth's forests. And the implications scare them.

Forest management is turning into one more issue over which industrialized and developing countries are fighting. In July 1990, the world's seven wealthiest nations endorsed the idea of an international agreement for managing the world's forests. Writing such a document is now on the agenda of the United Nations Conference on Environment and Development to be held in Brazil this June. The last of the meetings to arrange that conference are to be held in New York this month and in March.

4   But the discussions have not gone well. The world's poorer nations recognize that they are likely to be made the scapegoats of global warming.

Simply put, if the warming trend is to be slowed down, there need to be more trees and fewer exhaust pipes. Reducing pollution depends on energy efficiency and gradually switching from fossil fuels to renewable energy—an idea that is anathema to some industrialized nations, particularly the United States. In the eyes of developing nations, the developed countries are instead pushing strongly for saving forests because this would be less economically painful.

Certainly one aspect of the debate seems to suggest that the developing countries are right. Most of Canada, the eastern U.S. and Russia are covered by trees. But discussion of global warming has focused almost entirely on tropical forests. True, these forests are diverse and fascinating but they are also almost entirely in underdeveloped countries. And it is on those forests that developed nations are working hardest to impose their wills. But the north seems unable to live by the rules it wants to impose on the south: government-subsidized greed is allowing wide swaths of Canada and the northwestern U.S. to be clear-cut, and lumber companies are now maneuvering to make profits from the Siberian taiga.

As a result, a "convention on forests" has become unacceptable to many nations preparing for the Brazil conference. Now the best that seems possible is a "non-legally-binding authoritative statement of principles for a global consensus on the management, conservation and development of all types of forests." That promises little.

8   The scandal is the common assumption of these meetings: that forests are only valuable for their timber, pulp and fuel. All but dismissed are their intrinsic value as protectors of watersheds, safeguards against landslides, renewers of farm fertility, recreation areas and homes to diverse plants, animals and people. The discussions reveal ignorance of what forests do for the world and why international action to assure that they do not vanish is essential.

Deforestation is the second-biggest source of carbon dioxide, which traps the sun's heat in the atmosphere; only the burning of oil, coal and gas produces more. But scientists are beginning to recognize the possibility that the earth's warming will speed the decay of organic matter in soils, adding extra carbon dioxide and methane to the atmosphere. If this is to be slowed, the world must not only stop cutting and burning large forests, but replace many millions of acres that have been destroyed.

There is little immediate prospect of improvement without major changes in leadership and perspective. One promising suggestion is the creation of an International Commission on the Conservation and Utilization of World Forests to strengthen the scientific and economic analyses available and to draft an agreement for all countries to sign.

The project is urgent. The cost of the delay could be the world's forests, the biotic wealth they contain, the environmental services they perform and a possibly irreversible contribution toward making the earth too hot to live on.

BLAINE HARDEN

Poland Faces Communist Legacy of Pollution

W A R S A W—It spurts yellowish-brown from the tap, laced with heavy metals, coal-mine salts and organic carcinogens. It stains the sink, tastes soapy and smells like a wet sock that has been fished out of a heavily chlorinated swimming pool.

Given a few weeks, it will eat a hole in a steel pan. Better to wear rubber gloves while washing the dishes. Better to boil it before cooking. Best not to drink it.

Tap water drips daily into the collective consciousness of Warsaw as part of the pernicious legacy of four decades of communism. The water is a long goodbye from a totalitarian system that scorned environmental common sense and poisoned people in the name of the masses.

More than two years after Polish voters dumped communism, each morning's grungy dribble from the tap is a dispiriting reminder that political freedom and free-market economics offer no quick cure for a catastrophically fouled environment. Wretched tap water sends the same dismal message in Prague and Budapest.

Residents of these capitals need go no further than their kitchen sink to

4

FROM the *Washington Post*, December 15, 1991.

see—indeed, to taste and smell—that the old Eastern Bloc remains a poor, polluted and unhealthy appendage of the new Europe.

"When I washed my face with tap water, it caused little red blotches. My skin felt stretched and itchy. I felt like it might crack or split open if I spoke or laughed too much," said Barbara Matusevicz, 36, a secretary at Warsaw University's department of law.

Like many Warsaw residents whose skin hurts after washing with tap water, Matusevicz has experimented for years with boiled water, bottled water, skin lotions and home remedies. She finally settled on a cheap, if unorthodox, cure.

8   "I started making a facial mask out of porridge, the same stuff I serve my son for breakfast. It moisturizes and makes my skin feel smooth," Matusevicz said.

Jan Dojlido, head of the department of water chemistry and biology at the Polish Institute of Meteorology and Water Management, does not smear porridge on his face—but neither does he drink Warsaw water directly from the tap.

Strictly speaking, Dojlido said, the tap water is not "toxic." The water's tendency to irritate human skin, he said, is caused by its high concentration of chlorine, and heavy chlorination is required to defang the noxious cocktail of industrial and human waste that is present in river water as it is sucked into Warsaw's water-treatment plants.

For his own family's supply of drinking and cooking water, Dojlido runs tap water through an active-carbon filter and then boils it. He advises mothers to bathe their babies only in tap water that has been boiled for a full 15 minutes; this rids the water of cancer-causing organic compounds that he regularly measures in tap water at concentrations he said are more than twice as high as minimums set by the World Health Organization.

12   As a scientist who has been studying water quality for much of his adult life, Dojlido has a difficult time talking about Warsaw tap water without occasionally resorting to an unscientific adjective like "horrible."

"I came to Warsaw in 1948 and the water here is steadily getting worse. Warsaw is very unlucky when it comes to water," said Dojlido.

The causes of the pollution are many but the problem begins with Warsaw's principal source of drinking water, the Vistula River.

That river, Poland's longest, flows clean and drinkable out of the Carpathian Mountains in the south of the country. But about 150 miles before it reaches Warsaw, the Vistula soaks up the runoff from Silesia, Poland's industrial heartland. Few areas of the world are more polluted.

16   Using the river as a lifeline and a toilet, Communist central planners concentrated the nation's steel, chemical, fertilizer and pulp-and-paper plants in Silesia. People who live there have significantly higher rates of cancer, along with circulatory and respiratory diseases, than other Poles, according to

recent studies. Rates of mental retardation in Silesia have been described as "appalling" by the Polish Chemical Society.

Over the years, the Communists' central plan did not insist that Silesia's toxic waste be kept out of the river. The Ministry of Environmental Protection reported last month that about a quarter of Poland's big industrial plants either have no waste-water treatment or use devices of insufficient capacity. The ministry said half of the country's small industrial plants use no waste-water treatment.

Silesian factories seed the Vistula with pollutants including ammonia, phosphates and heavy metals such as lead and mercury. For example, the average concentration of mercury in the Vistula in 1990 was nine times higher than the Polish norm for safe drinking water.

Existing water treatment technology in Warsaw can do little to remove heavy metals from river water, according to Robert Latawiec, central waterworks manager.

Coal mines in Silesia are the biggest polluters of the Vistula. They dump about 6,600 tons a day of chlorides and sulfates into the river, according to the Ministry of Environmental Protection. These corrosive salts are the reason why Warsaw tap water can eat a hole in a baking pan and why rusted-out water pipes have to be dug up and replaced every 10 years. The ministry says corroded water pipes leak about one-third of the water they are supposed to carry.

The river is going to get even saltier. According to the Ministry of Environmental Protection, the amount of salt in the river will increase by about 70 percent over the next decade as coal mines continue to be exploited. Lacking oil, natural gas or nuclear-power plants, Poland needs the coal to produce electricity.

Salts are the major reason why 57 percent of the Vistula is classified as unfit for any purpose.

Polish cities and towns also contribute. About 40 percent of the country's sewage is untreated. A large proportion of it goes straight into the Vistula, both upstream and downstream from Warsaw. This city treats only about one-third of the waste it pumps into the river.

"The Vistula is a sewer for half the country," said Dariusz Jan Stanislawski, a scientist at the Polish Department of Water Economy and an adviser to the minister of environmental protection.

Cleaning up a national sewer that also happens to be Poland's main source of drinking water is a complex and costly project that environmental officials say will take at least 20 years.

*　　*　　*

JEREMY RIFKIN

Big, Bad Beef

In the U.S., beef is king. More than six billion hamburgers were sold last year at fast-food restaurants alone. The average American consumes the meat of seven 1,100-pound steers in a lifetime. Some 100,000 cows are slaughtered every 24 hours. In South America, the cattle population is approaching the human population. In Australia, cattle outnumber people.

Beef has been central to the American experience. Entrance into the beef culture was viewed by many immigrants as a rite of passage into the middle class. Commenting on the failure of European socialism to gain a foothold in America, Werner Sombart, the German economist, wrote, "On the shoals of roast beef and apple pie, all socialist utopias founder."

Now, the good life promised by the beef culture has metamorphosed into an environmental and social nightmare for the planet.

4   Cattle raising is a major factor in the destruction of remaining rain forests. Since 1960, more than a quarter of Central American forests have been razed to make cattle pastures. In South America, 38 percent of the Amazon forest cleared has been for ranching.

The impact of cattle extends well beyond rain forests. According to a 1991 report for the UN, as much as 85 percent of rangeland in the Western U.S. is being destroyed, largely by overgrazing. Nearly half the water used each year in the U.S. goes to grow feed for cattle and other livestock. A 1992 study by the California Department of Water Resources reported that more than 1,200 gallons of water are required to produce an eight-ounce boneless steak in California.

Cattle raising is even a significant factor in global warming. The burning of tropical forests to clear land for pasture releases millions of tons of carbon dioxide into the atmosphere each year. In addition, it is estimated that the earth's 1.28 billion cattle and other cud-chewing animals are responsible for 12 percent of the methane emitted into the atmosphere.

The beef addiction of the U.S. and other industrialized nations has also contributed to the global food crisis. Cattle and other livestock consume more than 70 percent of the grain produced in the U.S. and about a third of the world's total grain harvest—while nearly a billion people suffer from chronic under-nutrition. If the U.S. land now used to grow livestock feed were converted to grow grain for human consumption, we could feed an additional 400 million people.

8   Despite the grim facts, the government continues to pursue policies that support cattle production and beef consumption. For example, at the same

FROM the *New York Times*, March 23, 1992.

time the Surgeon General is warning Americans to reduce their consumption of saturated fat, the Agriculture Department's Beef Promotion and Research Board is trying to persuade Americans to eat more beef. This year, the board is expected to spend $45 million on advertising.

Equally troubling is the government's grading system to measure the value of beef. Established in 1927, the system grades beef on its fat content: the higher the fat "marbling," the better the beef. By favoring fat over lean beef, the Agriculture Department has helped promote greater amounts of saturated fat in the American diet and, in so doing, has contributed to rising health care costs.

Finally, the government has been virtually subsidizing Western cattle ranchers, providing them with cheap access to millions of acres of public land. Today, 30,000 ranchers in 11 Western states pay less than $1.92 a month per cow for the right to graze cattle on nearly 300 million acres of public land.

In 1986, the Reagan Administration estimated the market value for pasturing cattle on the same grasslands to be between $6.40 and $9.50 a month. This giveaway program has resulted in land erosion and the destruction of native habitats and wildlife.

The government's antiquated cattle and beef policies must be overhauled. The Agriculture Department needs to shift its priorities from promoting beef consumption to promoting a more balanced diet. Last year, the agency tried to do this by recommending a new "eating right" pyramid, which emphasized vegetables, fruit and grains. The effort was abandoned under pressure from the meat industry. The department's grading system should also be restructured, with new classifications that elevate the status of leaner cuts of beef.

In addition, Congress must pass legislation to insure that ranchers pay the market value for leased public lands. It should also reduce the public acreage available to ranchers, to help restore the Western grasslands and preserve the native wildlife and habitat.

If we reduce our beef consumption by at least 50 percent, we can help restore the global environment, free up arable land to grow food for hungry people, protect our own health and reduce the suffering of cattle and other animals.

MALCOLM W. BROWNE

Folk Remedy Demand May Wipe Out Tigers

ILLEGAL TIGER HUNTING to supply tiger bones for the Chinese folk medicine trade could bring about the extinction of an already endangered species, a leading conservationist says.

In a statement issued recently by the headquarters of the World Conservation Union in Gland, Switzerland, Peter Jackson, chairman of the organization's Cat Specialist Group, reported that poachers in one Indian game preserve alone killed 20 tigers in the last two years. Since there are only an estimated 7,000 tigers left in the wild throughout the world, the poaching trend could bring about their extinction, he said, despite a Chinese program that is breeding tigers in captivity for slaughter.

The rapidly rising price of tiger bone sold by traditional apothecaries in China and by druggists serving overseas Chinese communities has prompted the rise in poaching, Mr. Jackson said. The poachers are getting $170 to $250 per kilogram (2.2 pounds) of tiger bone smuggled to the border of China, where the bone is processed for retail sale. In Laos, which has a large Chinese population, tiger bone sells for $370 per kilogram. A small tiger yields about seven kilograms (15 pounds) of bone.

4

"It's a pretty safe assumption," Mr. Jackson said, "that conservationists and animal lovers are not going to persuade hundreds of millions of Chinese to abandon their ancient belief in the curative powers of tiger bone. The demand will be met only by poaching tigers in the wild. The rising price of tiger bone is bound to be an irresistible incentive for poachers. All this being true, wild tigers may indeed be doomed."

TIGER BREEDING PROGRAM

To partly meet the demand for bone, Mr. Jackson said, China has begun raising tigers in captivity to slaughter for their bones. Reporting on a trip he made to China in August, Mr. Jackson said he investigated a tiger-breeding farm in northeast China that started with 14 animals in 1986 and now has 62 Siberian tigers. With modern techniques, he said, it will be possible to breed 2,000 "industrial" tigers every seven years.

Mr. Jackson said that he had been tortured by the idea of breeding tigers in captivity for their bones, but added, "I do think that all of us who are interested in conserving tigers in the wild now have to address this question."

One of the worst recent outbreaks of poaching was at Ranthambhore National Park, India, a tiger preserve visited by many tourists. In 1989 there

FROM the *New York Times,* September 22, 1992.

were 44 tigers in the park, but a new census last May found only 15 left. Nine poachers were caught, but the tigers were gone. Since then, widespread tiger poaching has been discovered in other parts of India and Nepal.

Many Chinese believe that tiger bone, in powdered form or prepared as "tiger wine," soothes rheumatic pain and cures ulcers, malaria, burns and, according to one folk-medicine pharmacopeia, "eruptions under the toenail." Western medical experts discount all claims of any curative powers for tiger bone, as they do for rhinoceros horn, another popular Chinese medicine. Demand for rhinoceros horn has reduced the world rhinoceros population from 80,000 in 1972 to 10,000 today.   8

COLMAN MC CARTHY

Still Killing Whales

S O M E   M O D E R N Captain Ahabs, with Reykjavik, Iceland, as their home port and minke whales as their prey, are mad at the world. Claiming that their livelihoods are being threatened by international conservation meddlers, a group of Icelandic fishermen has announced it will defy the International Whaling Commission's six-year-old ban on hunting the endangered minkes.

A leader of the rebel whalers told a European newspaper: "We are not doing harm to anyone—just trying to earn a living. We can't allow foreigners to tell us what to do anymore. If anyone tries to stop us, there will be a bloodbath."

It's past bathings in blood—whales'—that enabled the world's environmental and conservation groups to rally international support that either shamed or pressured the whale-hunting nations to put away their harpoons. Most have, except for Iceland, Norway and Japan.

The history of commercial whaling, with the fictional Ahab aside, is one   4
of a scorched-earth policy applied to the high seas. That, combined with the overfishing of sea life, is leading to an oceanic desert.

The 19th-century image of brave New Englanders risking their lives in rowboats against leviathans has been replaced. Today's slaughter is done from factory ships using electronic explosive harpoons and guided by aerial tracking. Language is assaulted also: Whales are "harvested," not killed.

In the 1960s, when decimation peaked, Japan sent 10,000 workers to sea in more than 100 catcher boats and seven factory ships to kill as many as

FROM the *New York Times,* June 29, 1991.

15,000 whales annually. Humpback and blues, mammals slow to reproduce, were threatened with extinction. Japanese whalers then went after sei and fin. Those are now commercially extinct. The current prey is the smaller and less profitable minke.

The revolt of Iceland's whale hunters surfaced during last month's annual meeting in Reykjavik of the International Whaling Commission. The 36-nation group, which on notorious occasion has had as much spine as a jellyfish in making hard decisions, refused to lift the ban on commercial whaling. For another year, at least, it will be illegal.

8   Proposals are now before Iceland's legislature to pull out of the commission. This us-against-the-world stance might have a claim on public sympathy if Iceland's economy was even moderately dependent on whaling. It isn't.

The Icelandic whalers' self-description as oppressed working stiffs just hanging on economically deserves rejection. They are anything but subsistence fishermen, unlike some Eskimo communities.

"Iceland's whalers are earning incomes from other kinds of fishing," says Sally Shoup, a Greenpeace specialist on whaling who has attended the past three IWC meetings, including last month's in Reykjavik. "It's time they were a bit more candid about why they want to keep killing the minkes. It's for profit, which is how the problem was created in the first place. There's a small market in Iceland for whale meat, but the lucrative outlet is in Japan. It's a gourmet luxury food that can sell for over $100 a pound."

Iceland's whalers have sprung a major leak in their political boat. If they quit the IWC in a huff, they will lose the Japanese whale-meat market: Japan has domestic legislation forbidding the import of whale meat from non-IWC countries.

12   Instead of issuing blubbery threats to create "a bloodbath," Iceland's whalers ought to get in line with world opinion and stop the slaughter. They should be grateful that their coastal waters are not yet depleted of other stock.

If Iceland needs a model, the Soviet Union is available. Its whaling industry resisted joining the moratorium for years. In 1987, it did.

International pressure brought it around. Last year, some Soviet whalers came to the commission with a "research" proposal to kill 25–35 fin whales and 60–70 minkes, some from the protected waters in the Sea of Okhotsk. Scientists on the commission saw the proposal as having nothing to do with authentic research and rejected it.

*   *   *

That still leaves Japan prowling the seas, including Antarctica's, for "research whaling." Who's kidding whom? Last month in Tokyo, corpses of the scientific minke catch were served as deep-fried whale chunks, barbecued whale tail and slices of whale bacon at a banquet protesting the world's treatment of Japan's whaling industry.

16   The Japanese need to get with Icelanders and mutually try to wake each other up to the overwhelmingly strong arguments—environmental, ethical

and economic—against prolonging the killing. A thought of Herman Melville, Ahab's creator, stands like a lighthouse that warns against the destruction: "The moot point is whether Leviathan can endure so wide a chase and so remorseless a havoc; whether the last whale, like the last man, smoke his last pipe, then disappear in the final puff."

WILLIAM K. STEVENS

Loss of Genetic Diversity Imperils Crop Advances

THE FARMERS of the world, harvesting the abundant crops of the Green Revolution, have so far defied Malthusian predictions that population growth would outrun agricultural production and consign much of humanity to chronic famine.

But scientists say the diverse varieties of traditional crops and wild plants they need to breed more productive new strains are in jeopardy. In the field, farmers are abandoning them in favor of the new high-yield varieties. Wild strains of agricultural plants are disappearing as development destroys their habitat. And lack of funds, lack of care and political upheaval threaten the collections of seeds, in "banks" around the world, in which much of the remaining genetic diversity is stored.

The prospect of losing this genetic capital would be alarming under any conditions, scientists agree, but it is particularly threatening because of the way Green Revolution crops have changed the world's agriculture.

In the first phase of the revolution, high-yield strains of wheat and rice bred especially to accommodate and thrive on large amounts of synthetic fertilizer enabled harvest yields to double and triple in much of the third world. Famine caused by underproduction has largely disappeared; hunger today is mostly a product of political upheaval, bad administration of food supplies or the inability of the poor to buy food.

4

But this historic achievement has exacted a price: while the new crops are vastly more productive than traditional varieties, they are also much more vulnerable to catastrophic destruction by insects, fungi, bacteria and viruses. Genetically uniform crop strains have been adopted across wide stretches of the earth. As a result, pests or diseases that used to be local problems can race

FROM the *New York Times,* June 25, 1991.

across nations and continents, cutting a destructive swath through the world's food production.

To counter this threat, plant breeders must continually add new resistance traits to crops by crossing them with traditional and wild varieties. These same genetic techniques also allow scientists to confer on crops characteristics that contribute to higher yields—tolerance to drought, heat or cold, for instance. And they offer a benign alternative to synthetic pesticides and fertilizers and the environmental harm they can cause.

Some of the most recent results have been dramatic:

8   ♦ Scientists at Cornell University under contract to the International Potato Center in Lima, Peru, combined a nonedible wild potato from the Peruvian Andes with a conventional edible potato. Their offspring inherited a highly desirable characteristic from the wild plant: tiny hairs on leaves and stem that entrap insect pests. The hairs exude a substance that adheres to the insect's feet, immobilizing it. It also prevents egg-laying and feeding, and makes the plant highly resistant to all major potato pests, eliminating the need for pesticides. Cornell plans to test the potato in New York State fields this year.

♦ In another advance, scientists at the International Maize and Wheat Improvement Center in Mexico City are breeding wheat resistant to the Russian wheat aphid, an insect that costs the United States $300 million a year in lost production and insecticides. The scientists are crossing the modern wheat with traditional agricultural forms found in Turkey. Five more years of breeding cycles should achieve resistance, scientists say.

♦ Researchers at the International Center for Tropical Agriculture at Cali, Colombia, have identified wild bean plants containing antibiotics that keep bruchid bean weevils from reproducing. The weevils infest stored grains and destroy up to 15 percent of the total bean harvest of Latin America and 25 percent of the harvest in Africa. Insecticides cannot be used because they would poison the beans. The wild beans have been crossed with cultivated beans and are now being field-tested in Latin America and Africa.

Sounding the Alarms

The advances were described and alarms about the loss of genetic diversity were sounded last week by scientists at a symposium in Washington sponsored by the Washington-based Consultative Group on International Agricultural Research. This is a broadly based consortium that supports a worldwide network of research centers and gene banks in the forefront of the enterprise.

12   A similar warning was sounded earlier this month in Oslo, where an international group representing research organizations, foundations, governments and seed producers resolved to launch a global initiative aimed at

heading off the danger. If the erosion and deterioration of genetic resources continues, the group said in a statement of consensus, "genetic options for needed changes in agricultural production in the future will be lost forever." The group advocates a fivefold increase, to $300 million a year, in financing for preserving and developing genetic resources.

The Green Revolution itself is one contributor to the threat. As farmers increasingly adopt the new high-yield strains of rice and wheat, they abandon their traditional varieties. Traditional varieties of crops, scientists say, are the richest source of diverse genes. Unless the traditional varieties are collected and preserved as they are abandoned, their genes are lost. Wild strains are disappearing as development destroys ecosystems.

Collecting plants in the field is arduous and time-consuming, and there are few collectors with the necessary expertise. There are perhaps 15 of them in the Americas, Dr. H. Garrison Wilkes, a biologist at the University of Massachusetts at Boston, said at the Washington meeting.

Nearly half a million agricultural plant samples are now in international gene banks, and more in national collections. But many scientists agree that the condition of some of the collections is deteriorating. Many samples have been in storage for a quarter of a century, and must be regenerated by planting. Many seeds are probably already dead, scientists say, victims of inadequate manpower and money. Some gene banks, the conferees were told, are becoming "gene morgues."

Other gene collections are useless, researchers say, because their contents have not been identified, analyzed and catalogued, leaving them like a library without a card catalogue—or even any book titles. Often these seeds must also be planted so that they can be evaluated in the field.

Political strife threatens some collections, as in Ethiopia. At the Oslo meeting, said Dr. Don Plucknett, scientific adviser to the Washington-based research consortium, the Ethiopian representative "was really sweating every day" because of the potential threat that unrest in his country posed to the gene bank there. In Bolivia a few years ago, protesting workers at a gene bank ate the national collection of potato seeds. They were replaced from international stocks, but not all national stocks are duplicated elsewhere.

A BILLION MORE PEOPLE

All of this is especially unsettling, many scientists believe, given United Nations forecasts that the world's population will grow by nearly a billion people by the end of this decade.

World agriculture is not ready for that, Dr. Wilkes said. "We're losing our diversity" in genetic resources "and we don't have our gene banks in the best operating order," he said.

Even if the genetic resources were intact and in no danger, a number of scientists say, they would not enable farm productivity to keep up with population growth forever. Most of the Green Revolution's big gains have already been achieved, many experts say. The biggest leap forward came with the introduction, starting in the 1960s, of dwarf strains of grain. Breeders endowed them with stalks sturdy enough to hold up the fatter, heavier kernels produced by high doses of synthetic fertilizer. This was the key to their higher yields.

But now, food demand is expected to double in the next 25 years, Dr. Donald Winkelmann, director general of the maize and wheat center in Mexico City, said in Washington. Most of us, he said, believe that it will be possible to meet demand for some time, but at higher prices. Citing a World Bank estimate, he said that the real price of grain, now at historic lows, was expected to rise by 20 to 25 percent in the next decade as demand started to outpace supply.

The long-term prospects "could be quite bleak" unless population growth is brought under control, said Dr. Peter Day, an agricultural scientist at Rutgers University who heads a special National Academy of Sciences committee on global genetic resources, and who was chairman of the Washington conference. "The ability and resources of agricultural scientists and plant breeders are limited," he said in an interview. "All we can supply is some time for making more decisions."

The ability to supply that time, he said, is what is threatened by genetic erosion in crops.

By tapping the genetic resources, he said, it is also possible to create a more environmentally benign agriculture. Agriculture that relies on high applications of synthetic fertilizer and pesticides is "expensive and it's destructive," Dr. Day said. Nitrates from fertilizer contaminate water, for example, as do pesticides.

A FIVE-YEAR TURNOVER

One result of years of crossbreeding is that today's crops are miles away, genetically speaking, from those of even a few years ago. "We don't plant the same wheat we did in 1950," said Dr. Wilkes. Typically, he said, a crop strain is in the field only about five years before it is replaced, either because a new variety yields more or because it has become susceptible to pests or disease.

While there were fewer than 10 gene banks in the world 20 years ago, there are scores today, said Dr. Plucknett. But some countries, he said, "don't allocate the resources to run them; amazingly enough, some are not running because of the operating costs."

Scientists at the Washington meeting pointedly observed that the $300 million a year more that they believe is required is a fraction of the estimated $30 billion to $50 billion spent worldwide each year on seeds.

"I think what you heard at that meeting was a cry for a sensible level of investment in what is absolutely fundamental to life on earth," Dr. Day said. "And it's something we all too easily take for granted."

WILLIAM ALLEN

The Extinction Crisis

DESPITE REPORTS of a "mass murder" of dinosaurs, other animals and plants from a comet striking the Earth 65 million years ago, the world is now experiencing its first true catastrophic extinction of species, many scientists say.

The so-called extinction spasm at the end of the age of dinosaurs cannot be compared with the "present human destruction of the biosphere," said John C. Briggs, a biologist at the University of Georgia.

"Regrettably, a fairly common reaction to the current extinction crisis is, 'Well, we've had a great extinction in the past and got over it,' " Briggs said.

"But if you look into the extinctions of the past, you see that they took place gradually. They were not catastrophic. What is happening now is catastrophic because of the rate at which it's occurring." 4

Briggs detailed his views in a recent telephone interview from San Diego, where he addressed the annual meeting of the Geological Society of America. He also described them in the October issue of the scientific journal Bio-Science.

The debate about extinction is important because scientists are trying to assess and communicate to the public the magnitude of the current "bio-diversity crisis."

That's the term used to describe what researchers estimate will be the extinction of several million species in the next two to three decades. They are disappearing mainly because of tropical deforestation.

Scientists are so concerned about the rate of extinction that they are building a new version of Noah's ark. Rather than a boat, the new ark consists of a worldwide network of zoos, botanical gardens, seed banks and wild protected areas. 8

They are concerned that millions of species will go the way of the dinosaurs. They hope to preserve some animals and plants until—perhaps hundreds of years from now—the destruction ends and these organisms can be reintroduced into the wild.

"Scientists have the difficult task of making it clear to the public that the world is now undergoing its first genuinely catastrophic extinction," Briggs said. A burgeoning world population, especially in poor tropical countries, is destroying forests and their species at an increasing rate.

In September, United Nations researchers reported that tropical forests were yielding to the chainsaw and fire 50 percent faster than a decade ago. The world is now losing 1.3 acres of tropical forest a second.

If the human destruction continues for another 30 years, it "will result 12

FROM the *St. Louis Post-Dispatch,* January 19, 1991.

in an impoverished world that will not begin to recover until the human population pressure is relieved," he said. Even so, if such a recovery occurs, it would take millions of years and would not restore the animals and plants now being lost.

The biodiversity crisis is commonly described as the worst period of extinction since the death of the dinosaurs and other animals and plants some 65 million years ago, at the end of what scientists call the Cretaceous Period of Earth's history.

Many geologists say that the end of the Cretaceous Period was marked by a rapid, mass extinction when a giant asteroid crashed into the Earth. The massive explosion on impact altered climate to the point that many species died off, they argue.

Briggs and other scientists disagree, saying that a growing body of evidence from fossils shows that the extinctions were not sudden, but rather gradual.

16   Briggs has reported his detailed analysis of the fossil record and what it showed about the rates of extinction near the end of the Cretaceous Period and during other extinction events throughout geologic time.

Past periods of extinction lasted at least one million years, giving species and the ecosystems that they were a part of a chance to adjust to changing conditions by evolutionary processes, Briggs said.

"They may have died out as a species, but they gave rise to one or more other kinds of related species that had adapted," he said. "But what we have now is so rapid that there's no chance for adaptations," he said.

Because of the complex interactions within and between various ecosystems, human life eventually will suffer directly from these extinctions, several scientists say.

20   "What's being lost now isn't going to come back," he said. "You start dropping species out of an ecosystem and the ecosystem is going to go bust."

                    *   *   *

HARRY SAYEN

Sounding the Alarm on Threats to Earth

WHEN THE Union of Concerned Scientists (UCS) talk, we laypeople should listen—carefully.

Founded in 1969, the Cambridge, Mass—based nonprofit, nonpartisan group is dedicated to advancing responsible public policies in areas where technology plays a critical role. Arms control was an early issue of UCS concern, for example.

Now, the scientists have targeted our ability to sustain the Earth's natural resources. The warning signals of Earth's degradation have been too many, too obvious, and too widespread. Thus, Dr. Henry Kendall, chairman of UCS and a Nobel-winning physicist, is coordinating a worldwide appeal to reason, which includes 98 out of the 196 living Nobel laureates as well as senior officers from the most prestigious academies in Europe, North America, Asia, Africa and Latin America.

On Wednesday, Kendall and his team launched a Global Resources Campaign as a first step in combating the enormous threat to humanity's life-support system.

In the past, scientists, individually and in association, have spoken out on particular issues—such as the ozone problem, global warming and deforestation. Kendall's venture would incorporate existing UCS programs that promote sustainable use of resources. In Kendall's words:

"This kind of consensus is truly unprecedented. There is an exceptional degree of agreement within the international scientific community that natural systems can no longer absorb the burden of current human practices. The depth and breadth of authoritative support for the warning should give great pause to those who question the validity of threats to our environment."

Those *laissez faire* fellows who make fun of environmental "bozos" and "ozone" men had better listen. UCS represents, by far, the overwhelming majority of the world's scientific thinking.

What are the points of immediate stress? Kendall suggests the following areas are under critical pressure:

♦ The atmosphere. Stratospheric ozone depletion threatens us with enhanced ultraviolet radiation at the Earth's surface, which can be damaging or lethal to many life forms. Air pollution near ground level and acid precipitation are already causing widespread injury to humans, forests and crops.

♦ Water resources. Heedless exploitation of limited groundwater supplies endangers food production and other essential human systems. Heavy de-

FROM the *Trenton Times,* April 22, 1992.

mands on the world's surface waters have resulted in serious shortages in some 80 countries, which contain 40 percent of the world's population. Pollution of rivers, lakes and groundwater further limits the supply.

◆ Oceans. Destructive pressure on the oceans is severe, particularly in the coastal regions, which produce most of the world's edible fish. The total marine catch is now at or above the estimated maximum sustainable yield. Some fisheries have already shown signs of collapse.

12   ◆ Soil. Loss of soil productivity, which is causing extensive land abandonment, is a large-scale by-product of current practices in agriculture and animal husbandry. Since 1945, 11 percent of the Earth's vegetated surface has been degraded—an area larger than India and China combined.

◆ Forests. Tropical rain forests, as well as tropical and temperate dry forests, are being destroyed rapidly. At present rates, some critical forest types will be gone in a few years, and with them will go large numbers of plant and animal species.

◆ Living species. The irreversible loss of species, which by the year 2100 may reach one-third of all species now living, is especially serious. We are losing the potential they hold for providing medicinal and other benefits.

The root cause for all these pending disasters is a very simple fact of life: There are too many people and the world's population is expanding too fast.

16   In the words of UCS: "The Earth is finite. Its ability to absorb wastes and destructive effluent is finite. Its ability to provide food and energy is finite. . . ."

And what do the senior members of the scientific organization recommend? They say that "five inextricably linked areas must be addressed simultaneously":

(1) We must bring environmentally damaging activities under control to restore and protect the integrity of the Earth's systems we depend on. We must, for instance, move away from fossil fuels to more benign, inexhaustible energy sources to cut greenhouse gas emissions and the pollution of our air and water.

(2) We must manage resources crucial to human welfare more effectively.

20   (3) We must stabilize population by improving social and economic conditions and adopting effective, voluntary family planning.

(4) Reduce poverty.

(5) We must ensure sexual equality, and guarantee women control over their own reproductive decisions.

There's the challenge—a challenge ducked by George Bush but must be faced by President-elect Bill Clinton. The United States, as the largest user and waster of vital resources, had better lead the way and, in the doing, pay close heed to Kendall's words:

"No more than one or a few decades remain before the chance to avert   24
the threats we now confront will be lost and the prospects for humanity
immeasurably diminished."

Understanding What You Read

1. Newspaper articles often refer to people, places, and events that not all
   readers know about. After you have read the articles in Chapter 1, go
   back through them with a highlighter and mark anything you do not
   understand.
2. You may want to keep a notebook for listing items in your reading that
   you want to learn more about. As a way of starting your notebook, note
   the items you've highlighted in the newspaper articles, leaving room to
   identify each.
3. Choose one newspaper article that particularly interests you. Go to the
   library and find a newspaper published the same day. Browse through
   the news sections to find out what was going on in the world that day,
   and keep a record of references to other environmental issues.
4. Find a copy of *Time* or *Newsweek* published that week. Scan it to see
   what was newsworthy in the worlds of politics, culture, sports, science,
   and so on. Make a list of those events that have environmental consequences.

Writing About What You Read

1. You may find it useful to keep a notebook of environmental issues that
   make the news while you are using this book. Regularly reading a daily
   paper will help you keep up with the ongoing conversation about
   environmental concerns. Recording brief summaries of the articles you
   find will help you remember what you read and provide a record for
   future reference.
2. Make a list of what you consider the five most serious environmental
   problems. Choose the one you know the most about and write a short
   essay explaining the problem and arguing that it deserves immediate
   attention.

2 WILDERNESS AND

Pleasant it looked,
this newly created world.
Along the entire length and breadth
of the earth, our grandmother,
extended the green reflection
of her covering
and the escaping odors
were pleasant to inhale.
— "This Newly Created World" (Winnebago)

◆

And for the season it was winter, and they that know the winters of that country know them to be sharp and violent, and subject to cruel and fierce storms, dangerous to travel to known places, much more to search an unknown coast. Besides, what could they see but a hideous and desolate wilderness, full of wild beasts and wild men—and what multitudes there might be of them they knew not.
—WILLIAM BRADFORD, *Of Plymouth Plantation*

◆

If it's wild to your own heart, protect it. Preserve it. And fight for it, and dedicate yourself to it, whether it's a mountain range, your wife, your husband, or even (heaven forbid) your job. It doesn't matter if it's wild to anyone else: if it's what makes your heart sing, if it's what makes your days soar like a hawk in the summertime, then focus on it. Because for sure, it's wild, and if it's wild, it'll mean you're still free. No matter where you are.
—RICK BASS, *Wild to the Heart*

◆

The preservation of wilderness is not simply a question of balancing competing special-interest groups, arriving at a proper mix of uses on our public lands, and resolving conflicts between different outdoor recreation preferences. It is an ethical and moral matter. A religious mandate. Human beings have stepped beyond the bounds; we are destroying the very process of life.
—DAVE FOREMAN, *Confessions of an Ecowarrior*

NATURE

John Burroughs and John Muir, 1909
(Fred Payne Clatworthy)

Introduction

Imagine yourself abandoned in a wild place: the Sierra Nevada mountains in California, a remote area of the Adirondacks in New York, the Okefenokee Swamp in Georgia, the Rocky Mountain National Park in Colorado. You have no food or shelter and no prospect of being rescued. What would you be afraid of? Chances are that the greatest *natural* dangers you face would be dehydration and exposure—not poisonous snakes or wolves on the prowl. In fact, statistics tell us you would be far more likely to fall prey to a *manmade* danger—an automobile accident on the way to the wilderness.

But our ideas about wilderness don't have much to do with reason or reality. Many of our impressions of wild places come from movies and television programs that feature predatory animals in search of food. As children we learned from folk tales and songs to fear "untamed" creatures as enemies of people. Abandoned in the wilderness, you might imagine that wild animals were stalking you, but the most likely dangers are less dramatic. Would it occur to you to be afraid of contaminated water? Today, if you drank water from a stream in the Amazon rain forest, you might get sick from bacteria in the water. Or you might be poisoned by mercury dumped by mining operations farther upstream. Yet some people continue to think of wild places as "other," as separate from human activity.

Therein lies the power—and the paradox—of wilderness. Human beings have always observed and speculated about the natural world. For early humans, understanding how animals behaved and which plants were poisonous, which were curative, and which were edible was a matter of survival. Indigenous peoples around the globe still rely for their survival on their knowledge of the properties of plants and habits of animals—knowledge lost in industrial cultures as wilderness has been appropriated as a storehouse of raw materials for human use—for mining, logging, and hunting. This perception of wilderness has been changing, however. More and more people are learning to value wild places for their own sake as well as for what they can do for us. And more people are alert to the fact that our actions in the natural world have lasting consequences.

Only in the last century and a half have significant numbers of people in industrialized nations begun to view wild places as a resource in need of protection, and then only after much wilderness had disappeared. Before Europeans first explored the North American continent, Native Americans had long lived in harmony with the land, seeing as sacred the animals that provided their food, clothing, and shelter and the natural elements—land forms, weather, seasons—that defined their world. Contact with Indians did not, however, deter early explorers and settlers from their goal of conquest. When John James Audubon (1785–1851) was traveling the American frontier collecting the material for his great work *The Birds of North America,* hunters were routinely engaged in the wholesale slaughter of wildlife, and loggers were, as a matter of course, leveling ancient forests. Once-abundant species like the passenger pigeon were hunted to extinction. Vast areas of wilderness were destroyed before anyone had a chance to study the plants and animals that lived there. We now realize that the price of "taming" the North American continent was high.

Countering this legacy of destruction is a strong tradition in North America and, earlier, in England: that of fascination with, and writing about, wilderness. From the systematic studies and philosophical meditations of early naturalists—the botanist Linnaeus, Charles Darwin, Henry D. Thoreau—come the writing of scientists, nature writers, and environmental advocates today.

Though the tradition of nature writing is largely defined by British and North American writers, it was actually a Swiss botanist who originated the modern system of classification of plants and animals. Carl von Linné, known as Linnaeus (1707–1778), made it possible for nonscientists to understand that living things were related to each other and that studying these relationships as well as the interdependencies of different organisms was a fascinating and rewarding project. Establishing the framework for identifying and classifying all living things in *Systema Naturae* (1735) and *Species Plantarum* (1753), Linnaeus made the mysteries of nature seem accessible and orderly; every creature and every plant had its place. His works stimulated considerable interest in and controversy about the natural world—its plants and creatures—and the relationship of humans to that world.

A hundred years after Linnaeus, a profoundly new stimulus to thinking about nature appeared in the work of an Englishman, Charles Darwin (1809–1882). In 1831 the young Darwin set out as a naturalist on a scientific expedition to South America. On this sometimes perilous five-year voyage, Darwin studied rock formations, coral reefs, fossils of extinct animals, and many different but related living species. On the Galápagos Islands, six hundred miles west of Ecuador, he found strange forms of life that challenged everything he knew about natural history. Noting the considerable variety of characteristics within a single species, such as the ground finches of the Galápagos, Darwin began to suspect that species change through time and that such changes are correlated with environmental and climatic factors. These ideas became the basis of his theory of evolution. His study of fossils revealed that earlier systems of plants and animals had once occupied lands now inhabited by more familiar creatures. The more he observed natural phenomena, the more clearly he saw the dark and violent side of nature: animals at war with each other in a fierce battle for food and territory. Where Linnaeus had seen order and harmony, Darwin saw chaos and struggle. Throughout his travels he observed the damage done as humans invaded landscapes they did not understand.

During the same years that Darwin was exploring exotic places around the world collecting the data that would lead to his revolutionary book *On the Origin of Species* (1859), a seemingly less adventurous man was exploring a less exotic world. Henry David Thoreau (1817–1862) was an eccentric in his time, living in the thriving industrial center of America. He avoided regular employment and rejected the comforts of middle-class life. Yet his ideas about nature, his experiments with simple living, and the books he wrote about his observations and experiences—particularly *Walden* (1845)—have made him one of the most influential and admired of American philosophers and writers.

Thoreau lived most of his life in or near Concord, Massachusetts, and the natural world he observed was literally his own backyard. His few "extended" trips to unpopulated areas took him no farther than the Maine woods to the north and to Cape Cod, then an undeveloped part of the New England coast. In this familiar world Thoreau developed a sense of affinity with what he viewed as benevolent nature and a deep belief in the necessity of close relationship with the natural world, both for the well-being of individuals and for the survival of civilization.

Many of the concerns of contemporary environmentalists were expressed in the lives and work of naturalists and thinkers like Darwin and Thoreau. Those scientists today—E. O. Wilson prominent among them—who explore the diverse forms of life worldwide and who warn of the danger and recklessness of destroying biodiversity are the heirs of Darwin. Philosophers and writers—such as Wendell Berry, Bill McKibben, and Ann Zwinger—who closely observe the details of their worlds and who design ways of life consistent with the demands of nature might be seen as the heirs of Thoreau.

It was also in nineteenth-century America that a few people began to realize that studying nature and using it as a source of inspiration and recreation were not enough. Something had to be done to preserve the natural world or human activity would eventually destroy it.

Born some twenty years after Thoreau, John Muir (1838–1914) traveled as a young man by foot from Indiana to Florida and eventually migrated to eastern California, where he settled in the place that is almost synonymous with his name, the Yosemite Valley. Muir soon recognized that only by government protection could wilderness areas be saved from exploitation and overdevelopment. The struggle that Muir began was strenuous and often disappointing, but his victories offset his defeats. Without John Muir we might not have a National Park System today—or the Sierra Club, which he founded. More important than his specific accomplishments was the influence he had on others, such as his friend President Theodore Roosevelt, who laid the groundwork for the National Park System in 1906. Roosevelt was a conservationist in his own right, and his love of nature and outdoors adventure was deepened through his association with Muir.

Muir, of course, was not alone; he had counterparts all over the continent. But not all lovers of nature required the kind of wildness that attracted Muir. Unlike Muir, who spent much of his life in rugged and hazardous mountains of California and Alaska, John Burroughs (1837–1921) settled on a farm in Riverby on the Hudson River. He took quiet rambles in a relatively tame environment, without wandering far, and wrote descriptive essays of what he saw. A popular writer, Burroughs influenced large numbers of people to observe nature carefully and to appreciate their local environments through books such as *Locusts and Wild Honey* (1879) and *Bird and Bough* (1906).

Early in the twentieth century the establishment of schools of forestry and the growth of the biological and geological sciences created a new kind of conservationist. Aldo Leopold (1887–1948), a graduate of the Yale School of Forestry, worked within the federal government to acquire and preserve wilderness. As a ranger with the new U.S. Forest Service, founded in 1906, Leopold lobbied the government to set aside wild areas for preservation. In 1924 the Gila Wilderness in New Mexico became the first area designated for protection by the National Forest Service.

In recent decades, as the rate of destruction of wilderness has accelerated, concern and activism on behalf of treasured resources has intensified. Pioneers like John Muir and Aldo Leopold have been joined by hundreds of thousands of Americans who speak out and cast votes to bring about policies and practices that preserve wilderness before it is lost.

Most of us, however, share a certain ambivalence about the natural world. We want wilderness to be preserved, but we also expect to enjoy the amenities of civilization, some of which in turn threaten the wilderness. We want to live, for example, in air-conditioned comfort, even though the same fossil fuels that cool and heat our homes contribute to acid rain that in turn kills forests and sterilizes lakes. We plan wilderness vacations that take us from jet plane to rental car to a wilderness experience made comfortable by sophisticated outdoor gear made primarily from petrochemicals. In short, we want it both ways.

The words "wilderness" and "nature" are sometimes used interchangeably, but they often refer to very different kinds of places. Relatively few people have experiences in the wilderness—remote, unspoiled areas inaccessible by motorized vehicles. More people spend considerable time and money to visit "natural wonders"—canyons, mountains, waterfalls, caves, deserts, and glaciers. Most people have regular contact with Thoreau's version of nature: a shady spot in the backyard, a wooded lot in the neighborhood, a country lane, a pond, a hawk soaring above, a snake in the grass. For suburb and city dwellers, experiences of nature may be a squirrel in the neighbor's tree or pigeons in the park.

"Reading" nature, as the writers in this chapter do, is a first step in understanding the complexity of the environmental crisis.

HENRY DAVID THOREAU

Thoreau's (1817–1862) writings include travel narratives, natural history, and social criticism, as well as his highly original masterpiece *Walden* (1854). His other works include *A Week on the Concord and Merrimack Rivers* (1849) and a collection of essays about his travels in Maine published posthumously as *The Maine Woods* (1864). To support his travels around New England and his experiments in simple living, Thoreau gave lectures, mainly in small towns. These lectures often developed into essays. "Walking," considered one of the great American essays, began as a lecture called "The Wild," which Thoreau gave several times before publishing it in the *Atlantic Monthly* in 1862. The selection below is an excerpt from "Walking."

Walking

E V E R Y S U N S E T which I witness inspires me with the desire to go to a West as distant and as fair as that into which the sun goes down. He appears to migrate westward daily, and tempt us to follow him. He is the Great Western Pioneer whom the nations follow. We dream all night of those mountain-ridges in the horizon, though they may be of vapor only, which were last gilded by his rays. The island of Atlantis, and the islands and gardens of the Hesperides, a sort of terrestrial paradise, appear to have been the Great West of the ancients, enveloped in mystery and poetry. Who has not seen in imagination, when looking into the sunset sky, the gardens of the Hesperides, and the foundation of all those fables?

*　　*　　*

The West of which I speak is but another name for the Wild; and what I have been preparing to say is, that in Wildness is the preservation of the world. Every tree sends its fibres forth in search of the Wild. The cities import it at any price. Men plough and sail for it. From the forest and wilderness come the tonics and barks which brace mankind. Our ancestors were savages. The story of Romulus and Remus[1] being suckled by a wolf is not a meaningless fable. The founders of every State which has risen to eminence have drawn their nourishment and vigor from a similar wild source. It was because the children of the Empire were not suckled by the wolf that they were conquered and displaced by the children of the Northern forests who were.

I believe in the forest, and in the meadow, and in the night in which the corn grows. We require an infusion of hemlock-spruce or arbor-vitæ in our tea. There is a difference between eating and drinking for strength and from mere gluttony. The Hottentots[2] eagerly devour the marrow of the koodoo and other antelopes raw, as a matter of course. Some of our Northern Indians eat raw the marrow of the Arctic reindeer, as well as various other parts, including the summits of the antlers, as long as they are soft. And herein, perchance, they have stolen a march on the cooks of Paris. They get what usually goes to feed the fire. This is probably better than stall-fed beef and slaughter-house pork to make a man of. Give me a wildness whose glance no civilization can endure,—as if we lived on the marrow of koodoos devoured raw.

There are some intervals which border the strain of the wood-thrush, to which I would migrate,—wild lands where no settler has squatted; to which, methinks, I am already acclimated.

The African hunter Cummings tells us that the skin of the eland, as well as that of most other antelopes just killed, emits the most delicious perfume of trees and grass. I would have every man so much like a wild antelope, so much a part and parcel of Nature, that his very person should thus sweetly advertise our senses of his presence, and remind us of those parts of Nature which he most haunts. I feel no disposition to be satirical, when the trapper's coat emits the odor of musquash even; it is a sweeter scent to me than that which commonly exhales from the merchant's or the scholar's garments. When I go into their wardrobes and handle their vestments, I am reminded of no grassy plains and flowery meads which they have frequented, but of dusty merchants' exchanges and libraries rather.

A tanned skin is something more than respectable, and perhaps olive is a fitter color than white for a man,—a denizen of the woods. "The pale white

---

[1]Legendary founders of Rome, suckled by a she-wolf and raised by a herdsman.
[2]Name used by whites to refer to the Khoi-Khoi people in South Africa.

man!" I do not wonder that the African pitied him. Darwin[3] the naturalist says, "A white man bathing by the side of a Tahitian was like a plant bleached by the gardener's art, compared with a fine, dark green one, growing vigorously in the open fields."

Ben Jonson[4] exclaims,—

"How near to good is what is fair!"

So I would say,—

How near to good is what is *wild!*

Life consists with wildness. The most alive is the wildest. Not yet subdued to man, its presence refreshes him. One who pressed forward incessantly and never rested from his labors, who grew fast and made infinite demands on life, would always find himself in a new country or wilderness, and surrounded by the raw material of life. He would be climbing over the prostrate stems of primitive forest-trees.

Hope and the future for me are not in lawns and cultivated fields, not in towns and cities, but in the impervious and quaking swamps. When, formerly, I have analyzed my partiality for some farm which I had contemplated purchasing, I have frequently found that I was attracted solely by a few square rods of impermeable and unfathomable bog,—a natural sink in one corner of it. That was the jewel which dazzled me. I derive more of my subsistence from the swamps which surround my native town than from the cultivated gardens in the village. There are no richer parterres to my eyes than the dense beds of dwarf andromeda (*Cassandra calyculata*) which cover these tender places on the earth's surface. Botany cannot go farther than tell me the names of the shrubs which grow there,—the high blueberry, panicled andromeda, lamb-kill, azalea, and rhodora,—all standing in the quaking sphagnum. I often think that I should like to have my house front on this mass of dull red bushes, omitting other flower plots and borders, transplanted spruce and trim box, even gravelled walks,—to have this fertile spot under my windows, not a few imported barrow-fulls of soil only to cover the sand which was thrown out in digging the cellar. Why not put my house, my parlor, behind this plot, instead of behind that meagre assemblage of curiosities, that poor apology for a Nature and Art, which I call my front-yard? It is an effort to clear up and make a decent appearance when the carpenter and mason have departed, though done as much for the passer-by as the dweller within. The most tasteful front-yard fence was never an agreeable object of study to me; the most elaborate ornaments, acorn-tops, or what not, soon wearied and disgusted me. Bring your sills up to the very edge of the swamp, then, (though it may not be the best place for a dry cellar,) so that there be

8

---

[3]Charles Darwin (1809–1882), who had published *On the Origin of Species* three years before (1859).
[4](1572–1637), English poet and playwright.

no access on that side to citizens. Front-yards are not made to walk in, but, at most, through, and you could go in the back way.

Yes, though you may think me perverse, if it were proposed to me to dwell in the neighborhood of the most beautiful garden that ever human art contrived, or else of a dismal swamp, I should certainly decide for the swamp. How vain, then, have been all your labors, citizens, for me!

My spirits infallibly rise in proportion to the outward dreariness. Give me the ocean, the desert, or the wilderness! In the desert, pure air and solitude compensate for want of moisture and fertility. The traveller Burton[5] says of it,—"Your *morale* improves; you become frank and cordial, hospitable and single-minded. . . . In the desert, spirituous liquors excite only disgust. There is a keen enjoyment in a mere animal existence." They who have been travelling long on the steppes of Tartary say,—"On reentering cultivated lands, the agitation, perplexity, and turmoil of civilization oppressed and suffocated us; the air seemed to fail us, and we felt every moment as if about to die of asphyxia." When I would recreate myself, I seek the darkest wood, the thickest and most interminable, and, to the citizen, most dismal swamp. I enter a swamp as a sacred place,—a *sanctum sanctorum*. There is the strength, the marrow of Nature. The wildwood covers the virgin mould,— and the same soil is good for men and for trees. A man's health requires as many acres of meadow to his prospect as his farm does loads of muck. There are the strong meats on which he feeds. A town is saved, not more by the righteous men in it than by the woods and swamps that surround it. A township where one primitive forest waves above, while another primitive forest rots below,—such a town is fitted to raise not only corn and potatoes, but poets and philosophers for the coming ages. In such a soil grew Homer and Confucius and the rest, and out of such a wilderness comes the Reformer eating locusts and wild honey.

To preserve wild animals implies generally the creation of a forest for them to dwell in or resort to. So is it with man.

*   *   *

[5]Sir Richard Francis Burton (1821–1890), English explorer and writer.

Understanding What You Read

1. What does the sunset inspire Thoreau to do? Would it inspire you to do the same?
2. What do you think the statement "In wildness is the preservation of the world" means?
3. Do you agree that people need wildness?
4. What is the wildest place you know? What makes it wild? How far from human habitation does a place have to be for wildness?
5. Thoreau says that he prefers a wild place to a tame one, a swamp to a garden. Can you identify with this?

Writing About What You Read

1. Write a paragraph describing the wildest place you know.
2. If there is a wild place you like to visit, describe how it affects you to be there.

JOHN MUIR

Muir (1838–1914) was an an activist–adventurer first and a writer second. Born in Scotland, he migrated with his family in 1849 to Wisconsin, where he first began to explore the wonders of North America. Muir typically wrote letters and kept journals about his adventures, creating the raw material for his books, some published after his death. Among them are *The Mountains of California* (1894), *Travels in Alaska* (1915), and *A Thousand Mile Walk to the Gulf* (1916), about his trip from Indiana to the Gulf of Mexico. His great love and the focus of much of his work was the Yosemite Valley and the nearby Hetch Hetchy Valley, which he worked to save. "The Birds" is from his book *The Yosemite* (1912).

The Birds

T H E S O N G S of the Yosemite winds and waterfalls are delightfully enriched with bird song, especially in the nesting time of spring and early summer. The most familiar and best known of all is the common robin, who may be seen every day, hopping about briskly on the meadows and uttering his cheery, enlivening call. The black-headed grosbeak, too, is here, with the Bullock oriole, and western tanager, brown song-sparrow, hermit thrush, the purple finch,—a fine singer, with head and throat of a rosy-red hue,—several species of warblers and vireos, kinglets, flycatchers, etc.

But the most wonderful singer of all the birds is the water-ouzel that dives into foaming rapids and feeds at the bottom, holding on in a wonderful way, living a charmed life.

Several species of humming-birds are always to be seen, darting and buzzing among the showy flowers. The little red-bellied nuthatches, the chickadees, and little brown creepers, threading the furrows of the bark of the pines, searching for food in the crevices. The large Steller's jay makes merry in the pine-tops; flocks of beautiful green swallows skim over the streams, and the noisy Clarke's crow may oftentimes be seen on the highest points around the Valley; and in the deep woods beyond the walls you may frequently hear and see the dusky grouse and the pileated woodpecker, or woodcock almost as large as a pigeon. The junco or snow-bird builds its nest on the floor of the Valley among the ferns; several species of sparrow are common and the beautiful lazuli bunting, a common bird in the underbrush, flitting about among the azalea and ceanothus bushes and enlivening the groves with his brilliant color; and on gravelly bars the spotted sandpiper is sometimes seen. Many woodpeckers dwell in the Valley; the familiar flicker, the Harris woodpecker and the species which so busily stores up acorns in the thick bark of the yellow pines.

4 The short, cold days of winter are also sweetened with the music and hopeful chatter of a considerable number of birds. No cheerier choir ever sang in snow. First and best of all is the water-ouzel, a dainty, dusky little bird about the size of a robin, that sings a sweet fluty song all winter and all summer, in storms and calms, sunshine and shadow, haunting the rapids and waterfalls with marvelous constancy, building his nest in the cleft of a rock bathed in spray. He is not web-footed, yet he dives fearlessly into foaming rapids, seeming to take the greater delight the more boisterous the stream, always as cheerful and calm as any linnet in a grove. All his gestures as he flits about amid the loud uproar of the falls bespeak the utmost simplicity and confidence—bird and stream one and inseparable. What a pair! yet they are well related. A finer bloom than the foam bell in an eddying pool is this little bird. We may miss the meaning of the loud-resounding torrent, but the flute-like voice of the bird—only love is in it.

A few robins, belated on their way down from the upper meadows, linger in the Valley and make out to spend the winter in comparative comfort, feeding on the mistletoe berries that grow on the oaks. In the depths of the great forests, on the high meadows, in the severest altitudes, they seem as much at home as in the fields and orchards about the busy habitations of man, ascending the Sierra as the snow melts, following the green footsteps of Spring, until in July or August the highest glacier meadows are reached on the summit of the Range. Then, after the short summer is over, and their work in cheering and sweetening these lofty wilds is done, they gradually make their way down again in accord with the weather, keeping below the snow-storms, lingering here and there to feed on huckleberries and frost-nipped wild cherries growing on the upper slopes. Thence down to the vineyards and orchards of the lowlands to spend the winter; entering the gardens of the great towns as well as parks and fields, where the blessed wanderers are too often slaughtered for food—surely a bad use to put so fine a musician to; better make stove wood of pianos to feed the kitchen fire.

The kingfisher winters in the Valley, and the flicker and, of course, the carpenter woodpecker, that lays up large stores of acorns in the bark of trees; wrens also, with a few brown and gray linnets, and flocks of the arctic bluebird, making lively pictures among the snow-laden mistletoe bushes. Flocks of pigeons are often seen, and about six species of ducks, as the river is never wholly frozen over. Among these are the mallard and the beautiful woodduck, now less common on account of being so often shot at. Flocks of wandering geese used to visit the Valley in March and April, and perhaps do so still, driven down by hunger or stress of weather while on their way across the Range. When pursued by the hunters I have frequently seen them try to fly over the walls of the Valley until tired out and compelled to re-alight. Yosemite magnitudes seem to be as deceptive to geese as to men, for after circling to a considerable height and forming regular harrow-shaped ranks they would suddenly find themselves in danger of being dashed against the face of the cliff, much nearer the bottom than the top. Then turning in confusion with loud screams they would try again and again until exhausted and compelled to descend. I have occasionally observed large flocks on their travels crossing the summits of the Range at a height of 12,000 to 13,000 feet above the level of the sea, and even in so rare an atmosphere as this they seemed to be sustaining themselves without extra effort. Strong, however, as they are of wind and wing, they cannot fly over Yosemite walls, starting from the bottom.

A pair of golden eagles have lived in the Valley ever since I first visited it, hunting all winter along the northern cliffs and down the river cañon. Their nest is on a ledge of the cliff over which pours the Nevada Fall. Perched on the top of a dead spar, they were always interested observers of the geese when they were being shot at. I once noticed one of the geese compelled to leave the flock on account of being sorely wounded, although it still seemed to fly pretty well. Immediately the eagles pursued it and no doubt struck it down, although I did not see the result of the hunt. Anyhow, it flew past me up the Valley, closely pursued.

One wild, stormy winter morning after five feet of snow had fallen on the floor of the Valley and the flying flakes driven by a strong wind still thickened the air, making darkness like the approach of night, I sallied forth to see what I might learn and enjoy. It was impossible to go very far without the aid of snow-shoes, but I found no great difficulty in making my way to a part of the river where one of my ouzels lived. I found him at home busy about his breakfast, apparently unaware of anything uncomfortable in the weather. Presently he flew out to a stone against which the icy current was beating, and turning his back to the wind, sang as delightfully as a lark in springtime.

After spending an hour or two with my favorite, I made my way across the Valley, boring and wallowing through the loose snow, to learn as much as possible about the way the other birds were spending their time. In winter one can always find them because they are then restricted to the north side of the Valley, especially the Indian Cañon groves, which from their peculiar exposure are the warmest.

I found most of the robins cowering on the lee side of the larger branches of the trees, where the snow could not fall on them, while two or three of the more venturesome were making desperate efforts to get at the mistletoe berries by clinging to the underside of the snow-crowned masses, back downward, something like woodpeckers. Every now and then some of the loose snow was dislodged and sifted down on the hungry birds, sending them screaming back to their companions in the grove, shivering and muttering like cold, hungry children.

Some of the sparrows were busy scratching and pecking at the feet of the larger trees where the snow had been shed off, gleaning seeds and benumbed insects, joined now and then by a robin weary of his unsuccessful efforts to get at the snow-covered mistletoe berries. The brave woodpeckers were clinging to the snowless sides of the larger boles and overarching branches of the camp trees, making short flights from side to side of the grove, pecking now and then at the acorns they had stored in the bark, and chattering aimlessly as if unable to keep still, evidently putting in the time in a very dull way. The hardy nuthatches were threading the open furrows of the barks in their usual industrious manner and uttering their quaint notes, giving no evidence of distress. The Steller's jays were, of course, making more noise and stir than all the other birds combined; ever coming and going with loud bluster, screaming as if each had a lump of melting sludge in his throat, and taking good care to improve every opportunity afforded by the darkness and confusion of the storm to steal from the acorn stores of the woodpeckers. One of the golden eagles made an impressive picture as he stood bolt upright on the top of a tall pine-stump, braving the storm, with his back to the wind and a tuft of snow piled on his broad shoulders, a monument of passive endurance. Thus every storm-bound bird seemed more or less uncomfortable, if not in distress. The storm was reflected in every gesture, and not one cheerful note, not to say song, came from a single bill. Their cowering, joyless endurance offered striking contrasts to the spontaneous, irrepressible gladness of the ouzel, who could no more help giving out sweet song than a rose sweet fragrance. He must sing, though the heavens fall.

Understanding What You Read

1. Read an encyclopedia or magazine article about Yosemite. How do you suppose it has changed since Muir observed and wrote about the birds?
2. What features of the landscape does Muir describe in addition to the birds?
3. Which of the many species he writes about do you know?
4. What is special about the water-ouzel to Muir?
5. How does Muir give order and shape to his description of the birds of Yosemite? How many parts does it have and where do they begin and end?

Writing About What You Read

1. You may be familiar with a place where birds are found. If so, imagine sitting there watching the birds. Describe what you see.
2. Read what you have written and note whether there is a way to reorder your observations to give them more shape and meaning.

ALDO LEOPOLD

A conservationist, forester, writer, and teacher, Leopold (1876–1944) devoted himself to wilderness preservation and wildlife management. He was responsible for establishing the first designated wilderness area in the United States, which is located in the Gila National Forest in New Mexico. Leopold helped found the Wilderness Society in 1934, and led its efforts to preserve wilderness areas. And while Leopold was the author of a major textbook in wildlife management, it is for *A Sand County Almanac* (1949), that he is best known. A classic work of environmental writing, *A Sand County Almanac* was published shortly before Leopold died while helping to fight a forest fire on a neighbor's land. "Thinking Like a Mountain" is an excerpt from that book.

Thinking Like a Mountain

A DEEP chesty bawl echoes from rimrock to rimrock, rolls down the mountain, and fades into the far blackness of the night. It is an outburst of wild defiant sorrow, and of contempt for all the adversities of the world.

Every living thing (and perhaps many a dead one as well) pays heed to that call. To the deer it is a reminder of the way of all flesh, to the pine a forecast of midnight scuffles and of blood upon the snow, to the coyote a promise of gleanings to come, to the cowman a threat of red ink at the bank, to the hunter a challenge of fang against bullet. Yet behind these obvious and immediate hopes and fears there lies a deeper meaning, known only to the mountain itself. Only the mountain has lived long enough to listen objectively to the howl of a wolf.

Those unable to decipher the hidden meaning know nevertheless that it is there, for it is felt in all wolf country, and distinguishes that country from all other land. It tingles in the spine of all who hear wolves by night, or who scan their tracks by day. Even without sight or sound of wolf, it is implicit in a hundred small events: the midnight whinny of a pack horse, the rattle of rolling rocks, the bound of a fleeing deer, the way shadows lie under the spruces. Only the ineducable tyro can fail to sense the presence or absence of wolves, or the fact that mountains have a secret opinion about them.

4   My own conviction on this score dates from the day I saw a wolf die. We were eating lunch on a high rimrock, at the foot of which a turbulent river elbowed its way. We saw what we thought was a doe fording the torrent, her breast awash in white water. When she climbed the bank toward us and shook out her tail, we realized our error: it was a wolf. A half-dozen others, evidently grown pups, sprang from the willows and all joined in a welcoming mêlée of wagging tails and playful maulings. What was literally a pile of wolves writhed and tumbled in the center of an open flat at the foot of our rimrock.

In those days we had never heard of passing up a chance to kill a wolf. In a second we were pumping lead into the pack, but with more excitement than accuracy: how to aim a steep downhill shot is always confusing. When our rifles were empty, the old wolf was down, and a pup was dragging a leg into impassable slide-rocks.

We reached the old wolf in time to watch a fierce green fire dying in her eyes. I realized then, and have known ever since, that there was something new to me in those eyes—something known only to her and to the mountain. I was young then, and full of trigger-itch; I thought that because fewer wolves meant more deer, that no wolves would mean hunters' paradise. But after seeing the green fire die, I sensed that neither the wolf nor the mountain agreed with such a view.

*   *   *

Since then I have lived to see state after state extirpate its wolves. I have watched the face of many a newly wolfless mountain, and seen the south-facing slopes wrinkle with a maze of new deer trails. I have seen every edible bush and seedling browsed, first to anaemic desuetude, and then to death. I have seen every edible tree defoliated to the height of a saddlehorn. Such a mountain looks as if someone had given God a new pruning shears, and forbidden Him all other exercise. In the end the starved bones of the hoped-for deer herd, dead of its own too-much, bleach with the bones of the dead sage, or molder under the high-lined junipers.

8   I now suspect that just as a deer herd lives in mortal fear of its wolves, so does a mountain live in mortal fear of its deer. And perhaps with better cause, for while a buck pulled down by wolves can be replaced in two or three years, a range pulled down by too many deer may fail of replacement in as many decades.

So also with cows. The cowman who cleans his range of wolves does not realize that he is taking over the wolf's job of trimming the herd to fit the range. He has not learned to think like a mountain. Hence we have dust-bowls, and rivers washing the future into the sea.

*   *   *

We all strive for safety, prosperity, comfort, long life, and dullness. The deer strives with his supple legs, the cowman with trap and poison, the statesman with pen, the most of us with machines, votes, and dollars, but it all comes to the same thing: peace in our time. A measure of success in this is all well enough, and perhaps is a requisite to objective thinking, but too much safety seems to yield only danger in the long run. Perhaps this is behind Thoreau's dictum: In wildness is the salvation of the world. Perhaps this is the hidden meaning in the howl of the wolf, long known among mountains, but seldom perceived among men.

Understanding What You Read

1. When Leopold says in paragraph 4 that "I saw a wolf die" rather than "I killed a wolf," what aspect of the experience does he emphasize?
2. How does the absence of wolves lead to the destruction of the mountain?
3. Today there are projects underway to reintroduce wolves into habitats where they have been eliminated. What might be the effect of this?
4. How do you understand Leopold's statement that "too much safety" is dangerous?
5. What is meant by "objective thinking"?
6. How does one think like a mountain?

Writing About What You Read

1. Write down everything you know or think about wolves.
2. Compare the "green fire" of the dying wolf's eyes with the "song of the ouzel" in John Muir's piece on the birds of Yosemite.

EDWARD ABBEY

Abbey (1927–1989) was a park ranger, novelist, nature writer, storyteller, adventurer, and advocate of the wilderness and natural wonders. As an adviser to activists, Abbey believed that responsible individuals should defend endangered environments by whatever means necessary, except violence against life. Among his many books are *The Monkey Wrench Gang* (1976), a comic novel about four outrageous saboteurs who undermine the construction of dams and other projects that damage the environment, and *The Fool's Progress*

(1988). "The Serpents of Paradise" is an excerpt from Abbey's highly acclaimed book *Desert Solitaire* (1968), an account of his experiences as a ranger in Arches National Monument, near Moab in southeastern Utah.

The Serpents of Paradise

THE APRIL MORNINGS are bright, clear and calm. Not until the afternoon does the wind begin to blow, raising dust and sand in funnel-shaped twisters that spin across the desert briefly, like dancers, and then collapse—whirlwinds from which issue no voice or word except the forlorn moan of the elements under stress. After the reconnoitering dust-devils comes the real, the serious wind, the voice of the desert rising to a demented howl and blotting out sky and sun behind yellow clouds of dust, sand, confusion, embattled birds, last year's scrub-oak leaves, pollen, the husks of locusts, bark of juniper. . . .

Time of the red eye, the sore and bloody nostril, the sand-pitted windshield, if one is foolish enough to drive his car into such a storm. Time to sit indoors and continue that letter which is never finished—while the fine dust forms neat little windrows under the edge of the door and on the windowsills. Yet the springtime winds are as much a part of the canyon country as the silence and the glamorous distances; you learn, after a number of years, to love them also.

The mornings therefore, as I started to say and meant to say, are all the sweeter in the knowledge of what the afternoon is likely to bring. Before beginning the morning chores I like to sit on the sill of my doorway, bare feet planted on the bare ground and a mug of hot coffee in hand, facing the sunrise. The air is gelid, not far above freezing, but the butane heater inside the trailer keeps my back warm, the rising sun warms the front, and the coffee warms the interior.

4

Perhaps this is the loveliest hour of the day, though it's hard to choose. Much depends on the season. In midsummer the sweetest hour begins at sundown, after the awful heat of the afternoon. But now, in April, we'll take the opposite, that hour beginning with the sunrise. The birds, returning from wherever they go in winter, seem inclined to agree. The pinyon jays are whirling in garrulous, gregarious flocks from one stunted tree to the next and back again, erratic exuberant games without any apparent practical function. A few big ravens hang around and croak harsh clanking statements of smug satisfaction from the rimrock, lifting their greasy wings now and then to probe for lice. I can hear but seldom see the canyon wrens singing their distinctive song from somewhere up on the cliffs: a flutelike descent—never ascent—of the whole-tone scale. Staking out new nesting claims, I understand. Also invisible but invariably present at some indefinable distance are the mourning doves whose plaintive call suggests irresistibly a kind of seeking-out, the attempt by separated souls to restore a lost communion:

Hello . . . they seem to cry, *who . . . are . . . you?*

And the reply from a different quarter. *Hello* . . . (pause) *where . . . are . . . you?*

No doubt this line of analogy must be rejected. It's foolish and unfair to impute to the doves, with serious concerns of their own, an interest in questions more appropriate to their human kin. Yet their song, if not a mating call or a warning, must be what it sounds like, a brooding meditation on space, on solitude. The game.

Other birds, silent, which I have not yet learned to identify, are also lurking in the vicinity, watching me. What the ornithologist terms l.g.b.'s— little gray birds—they flit about from point to point on noiseless wings, their origins obscure.

As mentioned before, I share the housetrailer with a number of mice. I don't know how many but apparently only a few, perhaps a single family. They don't disturb me and are welcome to my crumbs and leavings. Where they came from, how they got into the trailer, how they survived before my arrival (for the trailer had been locked up for six months), these are puzzling matters I am not prepared to resolve. My only reservation concerning the mice is that they do attract rattlesnakes.

I'm sitting on my doorstep early one morning, facing the sun as usual, drinking coffee, when I happen to look down and see almost between my bare feet, only a couple of inches to the rear of my heels, the very thing I had in mind. No mistaking that wedgelike head, that tip of horny segmented tail peeping out of the coils. He's under the doorstep and in the shade where the ground and air remain very cold. In his sluggish condition he's not likely to strike unless I rouse him by some careless move of my own.

There's a revolver inside the trailer, a huge British Webley .45, loaded, but it's out of reach. Even if I had it in my hands I'd hesitate to blast a fellow creature at such close range, shooting between my own legs at a living target flat on solid rock thirty inches away. It would be like murder; and where would I set my coffee? My cherrywood walking stick leans against the trailerhouse wall only a few feet away but I'm afraid that in leaning over for it I might stir up the rattler or spill some hot coffee on his scales.

Other considerations come to mind. Arches National Monument is meant to be among other things a sanctuary for wildlife—for all forms of wildlife. It is my duty as a park ranger to protect, preserve and defend all living things within the park boundaries, making no exceptions. Even if this were not the case I have personal convictions to uphold. Ideals, you might say. I prefer not to kill animals. I'm a humanist; I'd rather kill a *man* than a snake.

What to do. I drink some more coffee and study the dormant reptile at my heels. It is not after all the mighty diamondback, *Crotalus atrox,* I'm confronted with but a smaller species known locally as the horny rattler or more precisely as the Faded Midget. An insulting name for a rattlesnake, which may explain the Faded Midget's alleged bad temper. But the name is apt: he is small and dusty-looking, with a little knob above each eye—the horns. His bite though temporarily disabling would not likely kill a full-grown man in normal health. Even so I don't really want him around. Am I to be compelled to put on boots or shoes every time I wish to step outside? The scorpions, tarantulas, centipedes, and black widows are nuisance enough.

I finish my coffee, lean back and swing my feet up and inside the doorway of the trailer. At once there is a buzzing sound from below and the rattler lifts his head from his coils, eyes brightening, and extends his narrow black tongue to test the air.

After thawing out my boots over the gas flame I pull them on and come back to the doorway. My visitor is still waiting beneath the doorstep, basking in the sun, fully alert. The trailerhouse has two doors. I leave by the other and get a long-handled spade out of the bed of the government pickup. With this tool I scoop the snake into the open. He strikes; I can hear the click of the fangs against steel, see the strain of venom. He wants to stand and fight, but I am patient; I insist on herding him well away from the trailer. On guard, head aloft—that evil slit-eyed weaving head shaped like the ace of spades—tail whirring, the rattler slithers sideways, retreating slowly before me until he reaches the shelter of a sandstone slab. He backs under it.

16 You better stay there, cousin, I warn him; if I catch you around the trailer again I'll chop your head off.

A week later he comes back. If not him, his twin brother. I spot him one morning under the trailer near the kitchen drain, waiting for a mouse. I have to keep my promise.

This won't do. If there are midget rattlers in the area there may be diamondbacks too—five, six or seven feet long, thick as a man's wrist, dangerous. I don't want *them* camping under my home. It looks as though I'll have to trap the mice.

However, before being forced to take that step I am lucky enough to capture a gopher snake. Burning garbage one morning at the park dump, I see a long slender yellow-brown snake emerge from a mound of old tin cans and plastic picnic plates and take off down the sandy bed of a gulch. There is a burlap sack in the cab of the truck which I carry when plucking Kleenex flowers from the brush and cactus along the road; I grab that and my stick, run after the snake and corner it beneath the exposed roots of a bush. Making sure it's a gopher snake and not something less useful, I open the neck of the sack and with a great deal of coaxing and prodding get the snake into it. The gopher snake, *Drymarchon corais couperi,* or bull snake, has a reputation as the enemy of rattlesnakes, destroying or driving them away whenever encountered.

20 Hoping to domesticate this sleek, handsome and docile reptile, I release

him inside the trailerhouse and keep him there for several days. Should I attempt to feed him? I decide against it—let him eat mice. What little water he may need can also be extracted from the flesh of his prey.

The gopher snake and I get along nicely. During the day he curls up like a cat in the warm corner behind the heater and at night he goes about his business. The mice, singularly quiet for a change, make themselves scarce. The snake is passive, apparently contented, and makes no resistance when I pick him up with my hands and drape him over an arm or around my neck. When I take him outside into the wind and sunshine his favorite place seems to be inside my shirt, where he wraps himself around my waist and rests on my belt. In this position he sometimes sticks his head out between shirt buttons for a survey of the weather, astonishing and delighting any tourists who may happen to be with me at the time. The scales of a snake are dry and smooth, quite pleasant to the touch. Being a cold-blooded creature, of course, he takes his temperature from that of the immediate environment— in this case my body.

We are compatible. From my point of view, friends. After a week of close association I turn him loose on the warm sandstone at my doorstep and leave for patrol of the park. At noon when I return he is gone. I search everywhere beneath, nearby and inside the trailerhouse, but my companion has disappeared. Has he left the area entirely or is he hiding somewhere close by? At any rate I am troubled no more by rattlesnakes under the door.

The snake story is not yet ended.

In the middle of May, about a month after the gopher snake's disappearance, in the evening of a very hot day, with all the rosy desert cooling like a griddle with the fire turned off, he reappears. This time with a mate. ₂₄

I'm in the stifling heat of the trailer opening a can of beer, barefooted, about to go outside and relax after a hard day watching cloud formations. I happen to glance out the little window near the refrigerator and see two gopher snakes on my verandah engaged in what seems to be a kind of ritual dance. Like a living caduceus they wind and unwind about each other in undulant, graceful, perpetual motion, moving slowly across a dome of sandstone. Invisible but tangible as music is the passion which joins them— sexual? combative? both? A shameless *voyeur*, I stare at the lovers, and then to get a closer view run outside and around the trailer to the back. There I get down on hands and knees and creep toward the dancing snakes, not wanting to frighten or disturb them. I crawl to within six feet of them and stop, flat on my belly, watching from the snake's-eye level. Obsessed with their ballet, the serpents seem unaware of my presence.

The two gopher snakes are nearly identical in length and coloring; I cannot be certain that either is actually my former household pet. I cannot even be sure that they are male and female, though their performance resembles so strongly a *pas de deux* by formal lovers. They intertwine and separate, glide side by side in perfect congruence, turn like mirror images of each other and glide back again, wind and unwind again. This is the basic pattern but there is a variation: at regular intervals the snakes elevate their heads, facing one another, as high as they can go, as if each is trying to outreach or overawe the other. Their heads and bodies rise, higher and higher, then topple together and the rite goes on.

I crawl after them, determined to see the whole thing. Suddenly and simultaneously they discover me, prone on my belly a few feet away. The dance stops. After a moment's pause the two snakes come straight toward me, still in flawless unison, straight toward my face, the forked tongues flickering, their intense wild yellow eyes staring directly into my eyes. For an instant I am paralyzed by wonder; then, stung by a fear too ancient and powerful to overcome, I scramble back, rising to my knees. The snakes veer and turn and race away from me in parallel motion, their lean elegant bodies making a soft hissing noise as they slide over the sand and stone. I follow them for a short distance, still plagued by curiosity, before remembering my place and the requirements of common courtesy. For godsake let them go in peace, I tell myself. Wish them luck and (if lovers) innumerable offspring, a life of happily ever after. Not for their sake alone but for your own.

28   In the long hot days and cool evenings to come I will not see the gopher snakes again. Nevertheless I will feel their presence watching over me like totemic deities, keeping the rattlesnakes far back in the brush where I like them best, cropping off the surplus mouse population, maintaining useful connections with the primeval. Sympathy, mutual aid, symbiosis, continuity.

How can I descend to such anthropomorphism? Easily—but is it, in this case, entirely false? Perhaps not. I am not attributing human motives to my snake and bird acquaintances. I recognize that when and where they serve purposes of mine they do so for beautifully selfish reasons of their own. Which is exactly the way it should be. I suggest, however, that it's a foolish, simple-minded rationalism which denies any form of emotion to all animals but man and his dog. This is no more justified than the Moslems are in denying souls to women. It seems to me possible, even probable, that many of the nonhuman undomesticated animals experience emotions unknown to us. What do the coyotes mean when they yodel at the moon? What are the dolphins trying so patiently to tell us? Precisely what did those two enraptured gopher snakes have in mind when they came gliding toward my eyes over the naked sandstone? If I had been as capable of trust as I am susceptible to fear I might have learned something new or some truth so very old we have all forgotten it.

They do not sweat and whine about their condition,
They do not lie awake in the dark and weep for their sins. . . .[1]

All men are brothers, we like to say, half-wishing sometimes in secret it were not true. But perhaps it is true. And is the evolutionary line from protozoan

[1] Lines from part 32 of Walt Whitman's *Song of Myself* (1881).

to Spinoza[2] any less certain? That also may be true. We are obliged, therefore, to spread the news, painful and bitter though it may be for some to hear, that all living things on earth are kindred.

[2]Dutch philosopher (1632–1677) who held that reality is beyond human perception.

Understanding What You Read

1. What do you think Abbey intends to communicate when he says "I'd rather kill a *man* than a snake"?
2. What reasons does he give for not killing the snake? Do you agree with his decision?
3. Abbey's encounters with the animals raise several questions and lead him to speculate about their nature and about his own incomplete understanding of them. What questions does he raise? Does he reach definite conclusions?
4. Mark those passages that use qualifying words or phrases to indicate incomplete understanding.
5. What is the significance of the title?

Writing About What You Read

1. If you have encountered animals in the wild, write an account describing the experience.
2. Observing domestic animals—cats, dogs, caged birds—sometimes leads us to wonder how they experience the world. If this has happened to you, write a short essay about it.
3. Certain animals inspire fear and awe in humans. If there is an animal, domestic or wild, that inspires strong feelings in you, write a paragraph or short essay in which you explore your reactions to it. If other animals come to mind, you may want to expand this essay to include one or more others.

PAM HOUSTON

Houston (b. 1962) has worked as a wilderness guide, teacher, and writer. A frequent contributor to such magazines as *Mirabella* and *Mademoiselle,* Houston is currently finishing her Ph.D. at the University of Utah and writing a novel. Her stories are funny and provocative, sensuous and serious. "A Blizzard under Blue Sky" is from her first book, *Cowboys Are My Weakness* (1992), a collection of twelve stories.

A Blizzard under Blue Sky

THE DOCTOR said I was clinically depressed. It was February, the month in which depression runs rampant in the inversion-cloaked Salt Lake Valley and the city dwellers escape to Park City, where the snow is fresh and the sun is shining and everybody is happy, except me. In truth, my life was on the verge of more spectacular and satisfying discoveries than I had ever imagined, but of course I couldn't see that far ahead. What I saw was work that wasn't getting done, bills that weren't getting paid, and a man I'd given my heart to weekending in the desert with his ex.

The doctor said, "I can give you drugs."

I said, "No way."

4 She said, "The machine that drives you is broken. You need something to help you get it fixed."

I said, "Winter camping."

She said, "Whatever floats your boat."

One of the things I love the most about the natural world is the way it gives you what's good for you even if you don't know it at the time. I had never been winter camping before, at least not in the high country, and the weekend I chose to try and fix my machine was the same weekend the air mass they called the Alaska Clipper showed up. It was thirty-two degrees below zero in town on the night I spent in my snow cave. I don't know how cold it was out on Beaver Creek. I had listened to the weather forecast, and to the advice of my housemate, Alex, who was an experienced winter camper.

8 "I don't know what you think you're going to prove by freezing to death," Alex said, "but if you've got to go, take my bivvy sack; it's warmer than anything you have."

"Thanks," I said.

"If you mix Kool-Aid with your water it won't freeze up," he said, "and don't forget lighting paste for your stove."

"Okay," I said.

12 "I hope it turns out to be worth it," he said, "because you are going to freeze your butt."

When everything in your life is uncertain, there's nothing quite like the clarity and precision of fresh snow and blue sky. That was the first thought I had on Saturday morning as I stepped away from the warmth of my truck and let my skis slap the snow in front of me. There was no wind and no clouds that morning, just still air and cold sunshine. The hair in my nostrils froze almost immediately. When I took a deep breath, my lungs only filled up halfway.

I opened the tailgate to excited whines and whimpers. I never go skiing without Jackson and Hailey: my two best friends, my yin and yang of dogs. Some of you might know Jackson. He's the oversized sheepdog-and-something-else with the great big nose and the bark that will shatter glass. He gets out and about more than I do. People I've never seen before come by my house daily and call him by name. He's all grace, and he's tireless; he won't go skiing with me unless I let him lead. Hailey is not so graceful, and her body seems in constant indecision when she runs. When we ski she stays behind me, and on the downhills she tries to sneak rides on my skis.

The dogs ran circles in the chest-high snow while I inventoried my backpack one more time to make sure I had everything I needed. My sleeping bag, my Thermarest, my stove, Alex's bivvy sack, matches, lighting paste, flashlight, knife. I brought three pairs of long underwear—tops and bottoms—so I could change once before I went to bed, and once again in the morning, so I wouldn't get chilled by my own sweat. I brought paper and pen, and Kool-Aid to mix with my water. I brought Mountain House chicken stew and some freeze-dried green peas, some peanut butter and honey, lots of dried apricots, coffee and Carnation instant breakfast for morning.

Jackson stood very still while I adjusted his backpack. He carries the dog food and enough water for all of us. He takes himself very seriously when he's got his pack on. He won't step off the trail for any reason, not even to chase rabbits, and he gets nervous and angry if I do. That morning he was impatient with me. "Miles to go, Mom," he said over his shoulder. I snapped my boots into my skis and we were off.

There are not too many good things you can say about temperatures that dip past twenty below zero, except this: They turn the landscape into a crystal palace and they turn your vision into Superman's. In the cold thin morning air the trees and mountains, even the twigs and shadows, seemed to leap out of the background like a 3-D movie, only it was better than 3-D because I could feel the sharpness of the air.

I have a friend in Moab who swears that Utah is the center of the fourth dimension, and although I know he has in mind something much different and more complicated than subzero weather, it was there, on that ice-edged morning, that I felt on the verge of seeing something more than depth perception in the brutal clarity of the morning sun.

As I kicked along the first couple of miles, I noticed the sun crawling higher in the sky and yet the day wasn't really warming, and I wondered if I should have brought another vest, another layer to put between me and the cold night ahead.

It was utterly quiet out there, and what minimal noise we made intruded on the morning like a brass band: the squeaking of my bindings, the slosh of the water in Jackson's pack, the whoosh of nylon, the jangle of dog tags. It was the bass line and percussion to some primal song, and I kept wanting to sing to it, but I didn't know the words.

Jackson and I crested the top of a hill and stopped to wait for Hailey. The trail stretched out as far as we could see into the meadow below us and beyond, a double track and pole plants carving though softer trails of rabbit and deer.

"Nice place," I said to Jackson, and his tail thumped the snow underneath him without sound.

We stopped for lunch near something that looked like it could be a lake in its other life, or maybe just a womb-shaped meadow. I made peanut butter and honey sandwiches for all of us, and we opened the apricots.

"It's fabulous here," I told the dogs. "But so far it's not working."

There had never been anything wrong with my life that a few good days in the wilderness wouldn't cure, but there I sat in the middle of all those crystal-coated trees, all that diamond-studded sunshine, and I didn't feel any better. Apparently clinical depression was not like having a bad day, it wasn't even like having a lot of bad days, it was more like a house of mirrors, it was like being in a room full of one-way glass.

"Come on, Mom," Jackson said. "Ski harder, go faster, climb higher."

Hailey turned her belly to the sun and groaned.

"He's right," I told her. "It's all we can do."

After lunch the sun had moved behind our backs, throwing a whole different light on the path ahead of us. The snow we moved through stopped being simply white and became translucent, hinting at other colors, reflections of blues and purples and grays. I thought of Moby Dick,[1] you know, the whiteness of the whale, where white is really the absence of all color, and whiteness equals truth, and Ahab's[2] search is finally futile, as he finds nothing but his own reflection.

"Put your mind where your skis are," Jackson said, and we made considerably better time after that.

The sun was getting quite low in the sky when I asked Jackson if he thought we should stop to build the snow cave, and he said he'd look for the next good bank. About one hundred yards down the trail we found it, a gentle slope with eastern exposure that didn't look like it would cave in under any circumstances. Jackson started to dig first.

Let me make one thing clear. I knew only slightly more about building snow caves than Jackson, having never built one, and all my knowledge coming from disaster tales of winter camping fatalities. I knew several things *not* to do when building a snow cave, but I was having a hard time knowing what exactly to do. But Jackson helped, and Hailey supervised, and before too long we had a little cave built, just big enough for three. We ate dinner quite pleased with our accomplishments and set the bivvy sack up inside the cave just as the sun slipped away and dusk came over Beaver Creek.

The temperature, which hadn't exactly soared during the day, dropped

---

[1]The whale in Herman Melville's novel *Moby-Dick* (1851).
[2]Captain of the *Pequod*, obsessed with killing Moby Dick.

twenty degrees in as many minutes, and suddenly it didn't seem like such a great idea to change my long underwear. The original plan was to sleep with the dogs inside the bivvy sack but outside the sleeping bag, which was okay with Jackson the super-metabolizer, but not so with Hailey, the couch potato. She whined and wriggled and managed to stuff her entire fat body down inside my mummy bag, and Jackson stretched out full-length on top.

One of the unfortunate things about winter camping is that it has to happen when the days are so short. Fourteen hours is a long time to lie in a snow cave under the most perfect of circumstances. And when it's thirty-two below, or forty, fourteen hours seems like weeks.

I wish I could tell you I dropped right off to sleep. In truth, fear crept into my spine with the cold and I never closed my eyes. Cuddled there, amid my dogs and water bottles, I spent half of the night chastising myself for thinking I was Wonder Woman, not only risking my own life but the lives of my dogs, and the other half trying to keep the numbness in my feet from crawling up to my knees. When I did doze off, which was actually more like blacking out than dozing off, I'd come back to my senses wondering if I had frozen to death, but the alternating pain and numbness that started in my extremities and worked its way into my bones convinced me I must still be alive.

It was a clear night, and every now and again I would poke my head out of its nest of down and nylon to watch the progress of the moon across the sky. There is no doubt that it was the longest and most uncomfortable night of my life.

But then the sky began to get gray, and then it began to get pink, and before too long the sun was on my bivvy sack, not warm, exactly, but holding the promise of warmth later in the day. And I ate apricots and drank Kool-Aid-flavored coffee and celebrated the rebirth of my fingers and toes, and the survival of many more important parts of my body. I sang "Rocky Mountain High" and "If I Had a Hammer," and yodeled and whistled, and even danced the two-step with Jackson and let him lick my face. And when Hailey finally emerged from the sleeping bag a full hour after I did, we shared a peanut butter and honey sandwich and she said nothing ever tasted so good.

We broke camp and packed up and kicked in the snow cave with something resembling glee.

I was five miles down the trail before I realized what had happened. Not once in that fourteen-hour night did I think about deadlines, or bills, or the man in the desert. For the first time in many months I was happy to see a day beginning. The morning sunshine was like a present from the gods. What really happened, of course, is that I remembered about joy.

I know that one night out at thirty-two below doesn't sound like much to those of you who have climbed Everest or run the Iditarod[3] or kayaked to Antarctica, and I won't try to convince you that my life was like the movies where depression goes away in one weekend, and all of life's problems vanish with a moment's clear sight. The simple truth of the matter is this: On Sunday I had a glimpse outside of the house of mirrors, on Saturday I couldn't have seen my way out of a paper bag. And while I was skiing back toward the truck that morning, a wind came up behind us and swirled the snow around our bodies like a blizzard under blue sky. And I was struck by the simple perfection of the snowflakes, and startled by the hopefulness of sun on frozen trees.

[3]The Alaskan dogsled race of some 1,100 miles ending in Nome, won several times by Susan Butcher.

Understanding What You Read

1. The narrator of this story reports that a doctor tells her she is "clinically depressed," a term that usually refers to severe, incapacitating depression. What is it that she is unable to do?
2. How do you understand the statement that the natural world "gives you what is good for you even if you don't know it at the time"? What aspects of the natural world does she observe?
3. What is the significance of referring to Hailey and Jackson as the "yin and yang" of dogs?
4. What is accomplished by reporting the conversations with the dogs?
5. How would the story be different if she ventured out alone and had an encounter with wolves?
6. What do the details of the story tell us about the narrator and what she knows?
7. What is the effect of using a comic tone for what is supposedly a serious depression?

Writing About What You Read

1. Imagine that you are depressed. Describe the outing you might plan to combat it.
2. If you have overcome bad feelings through an encounter with nature, write a narrative account of the experience.
3. If you suspect that the narrator is in fact not clinically depressed, but just unhappy about her boyfriend, write your version of what you think is on her mind.

ANNIE DILLARD

Dillard (b. 1945) achieved early success as a writer with the publication of *Pilgrim at Tinker Creek* (1974), a best-seller and winner of the Pulitzer Prize for nonfiction. Her other works include *An American Childhood* (1987), *The Writing Life* (1989), and *The Living* (1992), a novel about nineteenth-century life in Washington State, where Dillard lived for some years. Though she focuses in many of her works on the small details of nature in rural Virginia, Dillard has also written about her experiences in places as different as the Ecuadoran jungle and the Galápagos Islands. She teaches periodically at Wesleyan University in Connecticut. "Living Like Weasels," from *Teaching a Stone to Talk* (1982), is typical of Dillard's meditative mode, in which the observation of the natural world or an encounter with an animal leads her to an illumination about human nature or about how she herself intends to live.

Living Like Weasels

A WEASEL is wild. Who knows what he thinks? He sleeps in his underground den, his tail draped over his nose. Sometimes he lives in his den for two days without leaving. Outside, he stalks rabbits, mice, muskrats, and birds, killing more bodies than he can eat warm, and often dragging the carcasses home. Obedient to instinct, he bites his prey at the neck, either splitting the jugular vein at the throat or crunching the brain at the base of the skull, and he does not let go. One naturalist refused to kill a weasel who was socketed into his hand deeply as a rattlesnake. The man could in no way pry the tiny weasel off, and he had to walk half a mile to water, the weasel dangling from his palm, and soak him off like a stubborn label.

And once, says Ernest Thompson Seton[1]—once, a man shot an eagle out of the sky. He examined the eagle and found the dry skull of a weasel fixed by the jaws to his throat. The supposition is that the eagle had pounced on the weasel and the weasel swiveled and bit as instinct taught him, tooth to neck, and nearly won. I would like to have seen that eagle from the air a few weeks or months before he was shot: was the whole weasel still attached to his feathered throat, a fur pendant? Or did the eagle eat what he could reach, gutting the living weasel with his talons before his breast, bending his beak, cleaning the beautiful airborne bones?

I have been reading about weasels because I saw one last week. I startled a weasel who startled me, and we exchanged a long glance.

[1]Naturalist (1860–1946) who lived in Canada and was known for his books on wildlife.

4   Twenty minutes from my house, through the woods by the quarry and across the highway, is Hollins Pond, a remarkable piece of shallowness, where I like to go at sunset and sit on a tree trunk. Hollins Pond is also called Murray's Pond; it covers two acres of bottomland near Tinker Creek with six inches of water and six thousand lily pads. In winter, brown-and-white steers stand in the middle of it, merely dampening their hooves; from the distant shore they look like miracle itself, complete with miracle's nonchalance. Now, in summer, the steers are gone. The water lilies have blossomed and spread to a green horizontal plane that is terra firma to plodding blackbirds, and tremulous ceiling to black leeches, crayfish, and carp.

    This is, mind you, suburbia. It is a five-minute walk in three directions to rows of houses, though none is visible here. There's a 55-mph highway at one end of the pond, and a nesting pair of wood ducks at the other. Under every bush is a muskrat hole or a beer can. The far end is an alternating series of fields and woods, fields and woods, threaded everywhere with motorcycle tracks—in whose bare clay wild turtles lay eggs.

    So. I had crossed the highway, stepped over two low barbed-wire fences, and traced the motorcycle path in all gratitude through the wild rose and poison ivy of the pond's shoreline up into high grassy fields. Then I cut down through the woods to the mossy fallen tree where I sit. This tree is excellent. It makes a dry, upholstered bench at the upper, marshy end of the pond, a plush jetty raised from the thorny shore between a shallow blue body of water and a deep blue body of sky.

    The sun had just set. I was relaxed on the tree trunk, ensconced in the lap of lichen, watching the lily pads at my feet tremble and part dreamily over the thrusting path of a carp. A yellow bird appeared to my right and flew behind me. It caught my eye; I swiveled around—and the next instant, inexplicably, I was looking down at a weasel, who was looking up at me.

8   Weasel! I'd never seen one wild before. He was ten inches long, thin as a curve, a muscled ribbon, brown as fruitwood, soft-furred, alert. His face was fierce, small and pointed as a lizard's; he would have made a good arrowhead. There was just a dot of chin, maybe two brown hairs' worth, and then the pure white fur began that spread down his underside. He had two black eyes I didn't see, any more than you see a window.

    The weasel was stunned into stillness as he was emerging from beneath an enormous shaggy wild rose bush four feet away. I was stunned into stillness twisted backward on the tree trunk. Our eyes locked, and someone threw away the key.

    Our look was as if two lovers, or deadly enemies, met unexpectedly on an overgrown path when each had been thinking of something else: a clearing blow to the gut. It was also a bright blow to the brain, or a sudden beating of brains, with all the charge and intimate grate of rubbed balloons. It emptied our lungs. It felled the forest, moved the fields, and drained the pond; the world dismantled and tumbled into that black hole of eyes. If you and I looked at each other that way, our skulls would split and drop to our shoulders. But we don't. We keep our skulls. So.

He disappeared. This was only last week, and already I don't remember what shattered the enchantment. I think I blinked, I think I retrieved my brain from the weasel's brain, and tried to memorize what I was seeing, and the weasel felt the yank of separation, the careening splashdown into real life and the urgent current of instinct. He vanished under the wild rose. I waited motionless, my mind suddenly full of data and my spirit with pleadings, but he didn't return.

Please do not tell me about "approach-avoidance conflicts." I tell you I've been in that weasel's brain for sixty seconds, and he was in mine. Brains are private places, muttering through unique and secret tapes—but the weasel and I both plugged into another tape simultaneously, for a sweet and shocking time. Can I help it if it was a blank?

What goes on in his brain the rest of the time? What does a weasel think about? He won't say. His journal is tracks in clay, a spray of feathers, mouse blood and bone: uncollected, unconnected, loose-leaf, and blown.

I would like to learn, or remember, how to live. I come to Hollins Pond not so much to learn how to live as, frankly, to forget about it. That is, I don't think I can learn from a wild animal how to live in particular—shall I suck warm blood, hold my tail high, walk with my footprints precisely over the prints of my hands?—but I might learn something of mindlessness, something of the purity of living in the physical senses and the dignity of living without bias or motive. The weasel lives in necessity and we live in choice, hating necessity and dying at the last ignobly in its talons. I would like to live as I should, as the weasel lives as he should. And I suspect that for me the way is like the weasel's: open to time and death painlessly, noticing everything, remembering nothing, choosing the given with a fierce and pointed will.

I missed my chance. I should have gone for the throat. I should have lunged for that streak of white under the weasel's chin and held on, held on through mud and into the wild rose, held on for a dearer life. We could live under the wild rose wild as weasels, mute and uncomprehending. I could very calmly go wild. I could live two days in the den, curled, leaning on mouse fur, sniffing bird bones, blinking, licking, breathing musk, my hair tangled in the roots of grasses. Down is a good place to go, where the mind is single. Down is out, out of your ever-loving mind and back to your careless senses. I remember muteness as a prolonged and giddy fast, where every moment is a feast of utterance received. Time and events are merely poured, unremarked, and ingested directly, like blood pulsed into my gut through a jugular vein. Could two live that way? Could two live under the wild rose,

12

and explore by the pond, so that the smooth mind of each is as everywhere present to the other, and as received and as unchallenged, as falling snow?

16 We could, you know. We can live any way we want. People take vows of poverty, chastity, and obedience—even of silence—by choice. The thing is to stalk your calling in a certain skilled and supple way, to locate the most tender and live spot and plug into that pulse. This is yielding, not fighting. A weasel doesn't "attack" anything; a weasel lives as he's meant to, yielding at every moment to the perfect freedom of single necessity.

I think it would be well, and proper, and obedient, and pure, to grasp your one necessity and not let it go, to dangle from it limp wherever it takes you. Then even death, where you're going no matter how you live, cannot you part. Seize it and let it seize you up aloft even, till your eyes burn out and drop; let your musky flesh fall off in shreds, and let your very bones unhinge and scatter, loosened over fields, over fields and woods, lightly, thoughtless, from any height at all, from as high as eagles.

Understanding What You Read

1. What characteristics does a weasel have?
2. What does the story of the eagle with the skull of a weasel dangling from its neck suggest about weasels?
3. Paragraphs 4–7 describe the setting in which Dillard encountered the weasel. What natural details does she include in the scene? What details from the human realm? How do the two combine?
4. What is implied by the motorcycle tracks "in whose bare clay wild turtles lay eggs"?
5. Notice how often and in what way Dillard uses the word "wild." What is the significance of the "wild rose"? What is meant by the question beginning "Could two live under the wild rose"?
6. If you were to "grasp your one necessity and not let it go" (paragraph 17), what would it be?

Writing About What You Read

1. Write a paragraph or an essay in which you compare two ways of life: the animal living by necessity and the human being living by choice.
2. To write this essay, Dillard tells us that she did some reading about weasels. Choose another wild animal that interests you, do some research about its habits, and write an essay about what lessons its way of life might hold for humans.

BARRY LOPEZ

Lopez (b. 1945), who grew up in California and studied at Notre Dame and the University of Oregon, began writing shortly after graduation, and since then has mainly focused on the effects of human activity on the natural world. Much of his writing draws on his travels to far-flung places—including the Arctic, Antarctica, the Galápagos Islands, and Africa. Lopez periodically returns home to the Cascade Mountains of western Oregon to write. He is a contributing editor to *Harper's* and *North American Review* and the author of several outstanding books, including *Of Wolves and Men* (1978), a bestseller and winner of the John Burroughs Medal, and *Arctic Dreams* (1986), winner of the American Book Award. "Borders," first published in *Country Journal* in 1981, is found in *Crossing Open Ground,* a collection of essays published in 1989.

Borders

IN EARLY SEPTEMBER, the eastern Arctic coast of Alaska shows several faces, most of them harsh. But there are days when the wind drops and the sky is clear, and for reasons too fragile to explain—the overflight of thousands of migrating ducks, the bright, silent austerity of the Romanzof Mountains under fresh snow, the glassy stillness of the ocean—these days have an edge like no others. The dawn of such a clear and windless day is cherished against memories of late August snow squalls and days of work in rough water under leaden skies.

One such morning, a few of us on a biological survey in the Beaufort Sea set that work aside with hardly a word and headed east over the water for the international border, where the state of Alaska abuts the Yukon Territory. The fine weather encouraged this bit of adventure.

There are no settlements along this part of the Arctic coast. We did not in fact know if the border we were headed to was even marked. A northeast wind that had been driving loose pack ice close to shore for several days forced us to run near the beach in a narrow band of open water. In the lee of larger pieces of sea ice, the ocean had begun to freeze, in spite of the strong sunlight and a benign feeling in the air. Signs of winter.

As we drove toward Canada, banking the open, twenty-foot boat in graceful arcs to avoid pieces of drift ice, we hung our heads far back to watch migrating Canada geese and black brant pass over. Rifling past us and headed west at fifty miles an hour a foot off the water were flocks of oldsquaw, twenty and thirty ducks at a time. Occasionally, at the edge of the seaward ice, the charcoal-gray snout of a ringed seal would break the calm surface of the ocean for breath.

4

We drew nearer the border, wondering aloud how we would know it. I remembered a conversation of years before, with a man who had escaped from Czechoslovakia to come to America and had later paddled a canoe the length of the Yukon. He described the border where the river crossed into Alaska as marked by a great swath cut through the spruce forest. In the middle of nowhere, I said ruefully; what a waste of trees, how ugly it must have seemed. He looked silently across the restaurant table at me and said it was the easiest border crossing of his life.

I thought, as we drove on east, the ice closing in more now, forcing us to run yet closer to the beach, of the geographer Carl Sauer[1] and his concept of biologically distinct regions. The idea of bioregionalism, as it has been developed by his followers, is a political concept that would reshape human life. It would decentralize residents of an area into smaller, more self-suffi-cient, environmentally responsible units, occupying lands the borders of which would be identical with the borders of natural regions—watersheds, for example. I thought of Sauer because we were headed that day for a great, invisible political dividing line: 141 degrees western longitude. Like the border between Utah and Colorado, this one is arbitrary. If it were not actually marked—staked—it would not be discernible. Sauer's borders are noticeable. Even the birds find them.

On the shore to our right, as we neared the mouth of Demarcation Bay, we saw the fallen remains of an Eskimo sod house, its meat-drying racks, made of driftwood, leaning askew. Someone who had once come this far to hunt had built the house. The house eventually became a dot on U.S. Coast and Geodetic Survey maps. Now its location is vital to the Inuit,[2] for it establishes a politically important right of prior use, predating the establish-ment of the Arctic National Wildlife Refuge, within whose borders it has been included. I recall all this as we pass, from poring over our detailed maps the night before. Now, with the warmth of sunlight on the side of my face, with boyhood thoughts of the Yukon Territory welling up inside, the near-ness of friends, with whom work has been such keen satisfaction these past few weeks, I have no desire to see maps.

8   Ahead, it is becoming clear that the closing ice is going to force us right up on the beach before long. The wedge of open water is narrowing. What there is is very still, skimmed with fresh slush ice. I think suddenly of my brother, who lives in a house on Block Island, off the coast of Rhode Island. When I visit we walk and drive around the island. Each time I mean to ask him, does he feel any more ordered in his life for being able to see so clearly the boundary between the ocean and the land in every direction? But I am never able to phrase the question right. And the old and dour faces of the resident islanders discourage it.

[1]American geographer (1889–1975), author of *Morphology of Landscape* (1925).

[2]A people inhabiting northern Canada, Greenland, Alaska, and eastern Siberia—also known as Eskimos.

Far ahead, through a pair of ten-power binoculars, I finally see what appears to be a rampart of logs, weathered gray-white and standing on a bluff where the tundra falls off fifteen or twenty feet to the beach. Is this the border?

We are breaking ice now with the boat. At five miles an hour, the bow wave skitters across the frozen surface of the ocean to either side in a hundred broken fragments. The rumbling that accompanies this shattering of solid ice is like the low-throttled voice of the outboard engines. Three or four hundred yards of this and we stop. The pack ice is within twenty feet of the beach. We cannot go any farther. That we are only a hundred feet from our destination seems a part of the day, divinely fortuitous.

We climb up the bluff. Arctic-fox tracks in the patchy snow are fresh. Here and there on the tundra are bird feathers, remnants of the summer molt of hundreds of thousands of birds that have come this far north to nest, whose feathers blow inland and out to sea for weeks. Although we see no animals but a flock of snow geese in the distance, evidence of their residence and passage is everywhere. Within a few hundred feet I find caribou droppings. On a mossy tundra mound, like one a jaeger might use, I find two small bones that I know to be a ptarmigan's.

We examine the upright, weathered logs and decide on the basis of these and several pieces of carved wood that this is, indeed, the border. No one, we reason, would erect something like this on a coast so unfrequented by humans if it were not. (This coast is ice-free only eight or ten weeks in the year.) Yet we are not sure. The bluff has a certain natural prominence, though the marker's placement seems arbitrary. But the romance of it—this foot in Canada, that one in Alaska—is fetching. The delightful weather and the presence of undisturbed animals has made us almost euphoric. It is, after days of bottom trawls in thirty-one-degree water, of cold hours of patient searching for seals, so clearly a holiday for us.

I will fly over this same spot a week later, under a heavy overcast, forced down to two hundred feet above the water in a search for migrating bowhead whales. That trip, from the small settlement of Inuvik on the East Channel of the Mackenzie River in the Northwest Territories to Deadhorse, Alaska, will make this border both more real and more peculiar than it now appears. We will delay our arrival by circling over Inuvik until a Canadian customs officer can get there from the village of Tuktoyaktuk on the coast, though all we intend to do is to drop off an American scientist and buy gas. On our return trip we are required by law to land at the tiny village of Kaktovik to check through U.S. Customs. The entry through Kaktovik is so tenuous as to not exist at all. One might land, walk the mile to town, and find or not find the customs officer around. Should he not be there, the law requires we fly 250 miles south to Fort Yukon. If no one is there we are to fly on to Fairbanks before returning to Deadhorse on the coast, in order to reenter the

12

country legally. These distances are immense. We could hardly carry the fuel for such a trip. And to fly inland would mean not flying the coast to look for whales, the very purpose of being airborne. We fly straight to Deadhorse, looking for whales. When we land we fill out forms to explain our actions and file them with the government.

Here, standing on the ground, the border seems nearly whimsical. The view over tens of square miles of white, frozen ocean and a vast expanse of tundra which rolls to the foot of snow-covered mountains is unimpeded. Such open space, on such a calm and innocent day as this, gives extraordinary release to the imagination. At such a remove—from horrible images of human death on borders ten thousand miles away, from the press of human anxiety one feels in a crowded city—at such a remove one is lulled nearly to foundering by the simple peace engendered, even at the border between two nations, by a single day of good weather.

As we turn to leave the monument, we see two swans coming toward us. They are immature tundra swans, in steel-gray plumage. Something odd is in their shape. Primary feathers. They have no primary feathers yet. Too young. And their parents, who should be with them, are nowhere to be seen. They are coming from the east, from Canada, paddling in a strip of water a few inches deep right at the edge of the beach. They show no fear of us, although they slow and are cautious. They extend their necks and open their pink bills to make gentle, rattling sounds. As they near the boat they stand up in the water and step ashore. They walk past us and on up the beach. Against the gritty coarseness of beach sand and the tundra-stained ice, their smooth gray feathers and the deep lucidity of their eyes vibrate with beauty. I watch them until they disappear from view. The chance they will be alive in two weeks is very slim. Perhaps it doesn't exist at all.

16   In two weeks I am thousands of miles south. In among the letters and magazines in six weeks of mail sitting on the table is a thick voter-registration pamphlet. One afternoon I sit down and read it. I try to read it with the conscientiousness of one who wishes to vote wisely. I think of Carl Sauer, whose ideas I admire. And of Wendell Berry,[3] whose integrity and sense of land come to mind when I ponder any vote and the effect it might have. I think of the invisible borders of rural landscapes, of Frost[4] pondering the value of fences. I read in the pamphlet of referendums on statewide zoning and of the annexation of rural lands, on which I am expected to vote. I read of federal legislative reapportionment and the realignment of my county's border with that of an Indian reservation, though these will not require my vote. I must review, again, how the districts of my state representative and state senator overlap and determine if I am included now within the bounds of a newly created county commissioner's territory.

[3]See headnote on page 325.
[4]The poet Robert Frost (1874–1963) wrote mostly about rural life in New England.

These lines blur and I feel a choking coming up in my neck and my face flushing. I set the pamphlet on the arm of the chair and get up and walk outside. It is going to take weeks, again, to get home.

Understanding What You Read

1. Though this essay has the form of a personal narrative, it also raises larger questions. What are some of these questions?
2. How many different kinds of borders are there in this essay?
3. In paragraph 14, Lopez talks about being "at such a remove" from civilization. The very distance from human struggles serves as a border between simplicity and complexity. What kinds of unnecessary complexity does Lopez mention?
4. What is the significance of the two immature swans (paragraph 15) that pass by the boat and walk up the beach alone?

Writing About What You Read

1. Lopez makes a distinction between two kinds of borders: those imposed artificially on the land by political entities (states, nations) and those that occur naturally between different "bioregions." Describe the features of a distinct bioregion that is familiar to you.
2. Sometimes there are clear boundaries between one part of our lives and another. Other parts merge in imperceptible ways. Using Lopez's essay, write a paragraph or an essay in which you explore either clear borders (such as those of bioregions) or imperceptible borders (such as that between Alaska and Canada).
3. Compare an artificial border that you know with one that is defined by geographical features.

GARY SNYDER

Snyder (b. 1930) is a poet and essayist whose work explores the ways that human beings can live in harmony with the land and other living things. A student of mythology, Native American oral traditions, and of Buddhism, he draws on the wisdom of disparate cultures in his quest for an alternative to the imbalance and ignorance of contemporary civilization. While his commitments have taken him to remote places in the Far East and around the globe, he considers himself to belong in the Yuba River country in the Sierra Nevada of northern California. Snyder has lived most of his life on the West Coast, and currently teaches at the University of California, Davis. His books include *Regarding Wave* (1970); a collection of essays, *The Practice of the Wild* (1990); and *Left Out in the Rain: New Poems 1947–1985.* "The Call of the Wild," from his Pulitzer Prize—winning volume of poetry *Turtle Island* (1974), suggests connections between the wars people fight against animals and those fought against other human beings.

The Call of the Wild

The heavy old man in his bed at night
Hears the Coyote singing
          in the back meadow.
All the years he ranched and mined and logged.
A Catholic.
A native Californian.
        and the Coyotes howl in his
Eightieth year.
He will call the Government
Trapper
Who uses iron leg-traps on Coyotes,
Tomorrow.
My sons will lose this
Music they have just started
To love.

The ex acid-heads from the cities
Converted to Guru or Swami,
Do penance with shiny
Dopey eyes, and quit eating meat.
In the forests of North America,
The land of Coyote and Eagle,
They dream of India, of
        forever blissful sexless highs.
And sleep in oil-heated
Geodesic domes, that
Were stuck like warts
In the woods.

And the Coyote singing   28
    is shut away
    for they fear
    the call
    of the wild.   32

And they sold their virgin cedar trees,
    the tallest trees in miles,
To a logger
Who told them,   36

"Trees are full of bugs."
The Government finally decided
To wage the war   all-out. Defeat
    is Un-American.   40
And they took to the air,
Their women beside them
    in bouffant hairdos
    putting nail-polish on the   44
    gunship cannon-buttons.
And they never came down,
    for they found,
    the ground   48
is pro-Communist. And dirty.
And the insects side with the Viet Cong.
So they bomb and they bomb
Day after day, across the planet   52
    blinding sparrows
    breaking the ear-drums of owls
    splintering trunks of cherries
    twining and looping   56
    deer intestines
    in the shaken, dusty, rocks.
All these Americans up in special cities in the sky
Dumping poisons and explosives   60
Across Asia first,
And next North America,

A war against earth.
When it's done there'll be   64
    no place

A Coyote could hide.

envoy

68

I would like to say
Coyote is forever
Inside you.

But it's not true.

Understanding What You Read

1. In each of the poem's three parts, people are responsible for the destruction of some part of the natural world. Why do you think an old man wants the coyotes killed?
2. Who are the "ex acid-heads" of the second part? What is the significance of their selling the virgin trees?
3. How does the bombing of Vietnam in the third part relate to the poisoning of North America?

Writing About What You Read

1. In each of the three parts of the poem the lives of coyotes and other animals are threatened by human activity. Write three paragraphs in which you explain the three threats.
2. Write an imaginative piece from the point of view of the coyote, revealing how the coyote experiences the threats to life and habitat.
3. Write in whatever form you choose about the significance of the last four lines of the poem, the "envoy."

RODERICK FRAZIER NASH

Nash (b. 1939) is a renowned scholar, professor, and advocate for wilderness rights. The author of numerous books and over one hundred essays, Nash is an expert on the history of the concept of wilderness and the development of environmental ethics. Among his recent works is *The Rights of Nature: A History of Environmental Ethics* (1989). He is best known for *Wilderness and the American Mind*, first published in 1967 and revised in 1973 and 1982. "Why Wilderness?" was first given as a speech at the 4th World Wilderness Congress, held in Denver and Estes Park, Colorado, in 1987, and was published the next year in *For the Conservation of the Earth,* an edited and selected collection of the conference proceedings. Roderick Nash is professor of history and environmental studies at the University of California, Santa Barbara.

Why Wilderness?

T H I S I S a time of irreversible decision for wilderness on earth. As a species, our kind has followed with a vengeance the advice of the Old Testament prophet and "made the crooked straight and the rough places plain." The transformation of wilderness into civilization has taken on aspects of a religion and crusade and nowhere is this more than in the United States. Presently in the 48 continuous states, excluding Alaska, the amount of protected wilderness is approximately equal to the amount of pavement: about 2 percent of the total landmass is in each category.

* * *

Wilderness is indeed an endangered geographical species.

Today, not 1890, is the effectual end of the American frontier. Our generation is making the final decisions about the continuing presence of wildness in the environment. The limits of the earth are rapidly being reached, and what this means is that wilderness will no longer exist as left-over or forgotten land that nobody knows. It will either be consciously and deliberately preserved by policy and law or it will vanish. The future will hold us accountable for the quality of environment it inherits. Will we pass on an enduring legacy of wilderness or will we bequeath a totally modified earth?

Pioneering in the past involved the destruction of wilderness, and it has almost completely succeeded. Future pioneering should emphasize preservation. The mission of the new frontiersmen should be centered on restraining, not extending, civilization. The point is that we have conquered the wilderness; now we need to conquer ourselves and our appetite for growth and development. Axes and rifles, barbed wire and bulldozers were useful in a time when civilization was struggling for a foothold in the wild world. But now it is wilderness that is struggling for existence, and the need is for new tools. Research into and education about the value of wilderness are the appropriate tools for the new frontiersmen.

4

* * *

There is substantial wilderness left on parts of the planet. The polar regions are largely wild, so is the floor of the ocean and the moon. But for most of us these are not "meaningful" wildernesses. Like heaven, it is nice to know it exists, but most of us are never going to get there! More specifically, in the tropical and temperate latitudes, where most humans live, wilderness is melting away like a snowbank in the August sun. Extrapolating from the recent growth of science and technology, can we be certain that we will not have within our power in a few decades the ability to civilize the poles, the oceans and even the stars? The necessity, again, is for restraint. We need to understand that on a limited planet everything must have limits. This includes our numbers and our impact. It is time to understand that civilization can be ironic: some is undeniably good, but in excess it can destroy itself by its own "too much." Balance is the key. Wilderness should no longer be seen as a threat to civilization, but rather as a valuable part of a rich and full civilization—an asset and not an adversary. In time we might discover something the old-style pioneers could not have been expected to know: Wilderness is not the enemy of civilization, but a necessity if that civilization is to live up to its potential as a human habitat.

Just a century and a half ago, on the great plains of Colorado, buffalo thundered, wolves howled and grizzly roamed the creek bottoms. Humans living then were wilderness people. We called them Indians. In 1837 another kind of people, the mountain men, were entering Colorado, and the last thing on their minds was the preservation of wilderness. What concerned them, understandably, was the preservation and extension of the civilization of which they were vanguards. Yet ironically, these frontiersmen sowed the seeds of wilderness appreciation. Their success in extending civilization made wilderness rare and, according to the scarcity theory of value, appreciated. Whereas a century and a half ago it could be said that there was too much wilderness, now, as we look around Denver's smog-fouled air basin, there is too much civilization. We have come full circle from the plains where deer, antelope and buffalo played to a metropolis where we plan strategy for finding places for the buffalo to roam again.

Edward Abbey,[1] the writer, says that wilderness needs no defense, only more defenders. Respectfully, I disagree. There is a pressing need for elucidation of the underlying principles and values upon which an effective defense of wilderness can be built. Such a philosophy of wilderness has been notable for its absence in the U.S. preservation movement.

8   We have, rather, witnessed a series of frantic, subjective and highly emotional defenses of particular places. "Save the grizzly!" or "Save Grand Canyon!" we cry. If anyone asked, "Why?" there was a sharp intake of breath, a scowl and the reply that it was the *Grand Canyon*. But that is not enough. The questions remain: *Why* save a place like the Grand Canyon, *why* keep it wild?

The point is that wilderness appreciation has been a creed, a faith, something you felt in your bones, something that was almost sullied by analysis and explication. But that is not good enough, especially when the world's wild places are increasingly hard-pressed by demands for the expansion of civilization. There is a need for an articulation of wilderness values

[1]See headnote on page 51.

based on historical fact, contemporary experience and the projected future needs of human life and of all life. This is the vital philosophy of wilderness. It must lie behind the defense of particular wild places like the philosophy of human dignity lies behind defenses of human freedom. Philosophers have spent 2,500 years setting forth the liberal philosophy. So, when Thomas Jefferson wrote his famous Declaration, when Lincoln emancipated the slaves or when more recent protests of discrimination occurred, few needed to ask, "Why?" The value of liberty and equality is well defined. Not so with the value of wilderness. The appreciation of wild places and wild creatures is, after all, barely a century old.

We should pause for a moment to consider several ways *not* to defend wilderness, ways that do not make the best case for preservation. The first is *scenery*. The problem here is that wilderness is not about scenery; it is about the absence of technological civilization and its controlling influence. Now some people do find the absence of civilization "scenic," but many others find it strange, weird, harsh, frightening and decidedly unlovely. They value it not because it is beautiful but because it is wild. Basing a defense of this kind of country on scenic beauty is to leave the case open to all sorts of logical pitfalls. How, for instance, is fire to be justified as a natural part of a wilderness ecosystem? Using beauty to defend wilderness, in sum, is like saying that only beautiful people are to be accorded rights to exist. We abandoned that tactic long ago in defending human rights, and it is time to question its validity in making a case for wilderness.

Recreation is another sandy foundation for wild country because it is not wilderness-dependent, to use a concept developed by John Hendee, Robert Lucas and George Stankey. People can and do recreate and generally have fun outdoors in very nonwilderness settings. Camping can be had in KOA campgrounds, and excellent hunting and fishing is available in fenced and stocked compounds. We need to investigate what it is about *wilderness* recreation that is different and valuable.

A third way not to defend wilderness is *economics,* and I say this with the full realization that cost-benefit analyses and the expenditures of tourists have been used repeatedly to justify the existence of wildness. Generally, proponents of the economic argument are interested in offering a countervailing argument to the developers' calculations of the cash value of natural resources present in wilderness. The problem is that wilderness almost always loses in such figuring. Its "benefits" are invariably less than, say, that which timber or mineral extraction, or condominium building, would provide. And tourists utilizing hotels and restaurants always spend more than backpackers. Economic arguments are thus a dead end for wilderness. Moreover, there is the point that wilderness should be measured on a different scale of value, like the Parthenon or Chartres Cathedral or a beloved person. I am reminded here of an exchange I once had with a distinguished resource economist who was using the cost-benefit technique to evaluate wilderness. At the conclu-

12

sion of his remarks, I simply asked him, "What's the cost-benefit ratio of your 87-year-old mother?" Affronted, the economist blustered, "Well, that's different." So, I submit, is wilderness. It's our biological and cultural mother. The point is that wilderness defenders should have the courage to not go to the economic mat with their opponents. They should remember that economists are sometimes accused of knowing the price of everything and the value of nothing.

A corollary to this reasoning is that the wilderness we have protected around the world is generally worthless land. There are few designated wildernesses in Iowa or France. We have saved places that are high, dry, cold and remote. When an economic use is found for such a place, more likely than not, its wilderness value is forgotten. The classic instance in U.S. History is Yosemite National Park's once-spectacular Hetch Hetchy Valley. In 1913 San Francisco convinced Congress that the highest value of the region was as a municipal water reservoir and hydropower facility. It was removed from the national park and flooded, a reminder to our foreign guests that the U.S. example can demonstrate how not to care for wilderness as well as how to preserve it. The lesson is that those who lean too heavily on economic arguments for wilderness run the risk of having their leaning posts cut off at the roots.

Reviewing the liabilities of scenery, recreation and economics as defenses of wilderness, and thinking about the reasons why we love it, I thought about an analogy. May I address the men in the audience for a moment? Isn't it true, gentlemen, that we have all been asked by a woman at one time or another (usually, it seems, late at night), "Why do you love me?" I suggest that three reasons that won't be satisfactory are scenery, recreation and economics!

So how are we to answer the question "Why do we love wilderness?" I will sketch, briefly, seven reasons that are wilderness-dependent, historically valid and shaped by an understanding of both the realities of wilderness and the needs of civilization. They have been refined by our best wilderness philosophers and they constitute the granite philosophical bedrock in which the case for wilderness should rest.

16   1. The first might be called the *scientific value*. It rests on the idea that wilderness is a reservoir of normal ecological and evolutionary processes as well as a kind of biological safe-deposit box for the many forms of life. One variation of this value is quite utilitarian and might be called the "cure-for-cancer" argument. The wild places of the world harbor species presently and potentially important to human welfare and even survival. As David Brower[2] is fond of saying, "Wilderness holds the answers to questions we do not yet

[2]Head of the Sierra Club for 17 years, founder of Friends of the Earth and Earth Island Institute, which he currently chairs.

know how to ask." Norman Myers[3] prefers the metaphor of an ark: those who protect wilderness are like Noah. They make sure that nothing is lost from the full complement of genetic raw material evolved on earth. But on a less instrumental plane, the scientific argument suggests that humans have no right to disturb the evolutionary process. We have already modified the planet enough. When it comes to the existence of species, we should be careful about playing God in Yellowstone or anywhere else. Perhaps Aldo Leopold[4] put it best when he observed that the first law on successful tinkering is to save all the parts. Our own survival, and that of many other creatures, depends on wilderness environments far more than we think. And mistakes in this area are generally final. Extinction, as the Nature Conservancy likes to point out, is forever.

2. *Spiritual values* are the second important pillar in support of wilderness. For many people wilderness is as important as temple or church. We might start with the American Indians and other aboriginal people who regarded places, not just buildings with steeples, as sacred. Commonly, these sacred spaces were in the wilderness where the messages of divine powers seemed the clearest. Later generations, pursuing answers to the weightier problems in human existence, found wilderness to have religious significance. Some worshiped nature outright, some found evidence of God in the natural world and some simply turned to wilderness as an appropriate place to pray and reflect. Henry David Thoreau and Ralph Waldo Emerson, the American Transcendentalists, certainly believed that nature was the symbol of the spiritual world. And John Muir[5] regarded Hetch Hetchy Valley as a temple. Even Colorado's own John Denver sings about cathedral mountains. Around the world we find that the deserts and open spaces have been the source of many of the world's great faiths. Jesus was not the only religious leader to commune with deity in the wilderness.

The religious significance many find in wilderness raises the possibility of defending it on the grounds of freedom of worship. This is a basic right in U.S. culture and in many others. Even if wilderness is a church for a minority, do not they have a right to worship as they choose? Indians have been accorded this right under the Native American Religious Freedom Act of 1978. Although hitherto neglected, it could become a bulwark of non-Indian defense of wilderness.

3. Earlier I dismissed scenery as a basis for a wilderness philosophy, but there is an *aesthetic value* dependent on wild settings. The Romantic movement of the seventeenth and eighteenth centuries had a word for it: "sublimity." It involved awe in the face of large, unmodified natural forces and places such as storms, waterfalls, mountains and deserts. Some people find

[3]See headnote on page 202.
[4]See headnote on page 49.
[5]See headnote on page 45.

a beauty here that cannot be replicated in pastoral settings, cities or art museums. If the destruction of beauty is to be avoided, then wilderness should be preserved.

20   4. The *heritage value* of wilderness is grounded on the fact that wild country has been a major force in the shaping of character and culture. As a species, we have lived in the wilderness a thousand times longer than in civilization. In nations like the United States, Canada and Australia, wilderness has had a very recent and very strong formative influence. The U.S. historian Frederick Jackson Turner[6] pointed to one form when he argued in 1893 that the frontier experience built respect for the individual and, later, for democratic institutions. We need wilderness, Turner implied, if we are to understand the source of freedom. Wilderness nourishes it by permitting people to be different, to escape the controlling force of established institutions. The Puritans in Massachusetts Bay and the Mormons in Utah understood this association. So do contemporary freedom fighters who take to the hills to continue their rebellion if the hills exist. Parenthetically, the totalitarian regime that George Orwell described in his novel, *1984,* made its first concern the elimination of wilderness. Big Brother could not control thought in wild country.

Wilderness is also an historical document just as much as a collection of manuscripts or a bill of rights. Losing wilderness means losing the ability to understand our past; it is comparable to tearing pages from a book in the library. Could we go even further and say that people have a right to their heritage, their history? If so, the preservation of wilderness is incumbent on our generation.

5. Physical health is not wilderness-dependent. You can become very fit at an urban health club. But wilderness has *psychological value* based on the contrast it offers to the environments which most people occupy most of the time. When these civilized environments become repressive, to use a concept the psychologist Sigmund Freud popularized, wilderness offers a unique opportunity for psychological renewal—literally recreation. The reason is that our minds developed under wilderness conditions for millions of years. Suddenly in the last few hundred we have been propelled into a world of bewildering speed and complexity. For some people occasional relief is a vital mental necessity. They covet the chance to drop back into the older and more comfortable channels.

*   *   *

Primitivists from Jean-Jacques Rousseau with his "noble savage" to Edgar Rice Burroughs and Tarzan have argued that the wild world produces a superior human being. Overcivilization is a real and growing danger. Contemporary therapy programs, such as those of Outward Bound, use the challenges of wilderness to build self-reliance and self-respect. A wilderness

[6]American historian (1861–1932), author of *The Frontier in American History* (1920).

area may well have more psychological importance than hundreds of beds in a mental hospital.

6. Wilderness has *cultural value,* because in the words of Ralph Waldo Emerson, it permits an opportunity for an original relationship to the universe. The wild world is cultural raw material. Artists, musicians, poets and writers have turned to it repeatedly in their quest to shape a distinctive and distinguished culture. In the United States, cultural independence from the Old World did not come until writers such as James Fenimore Cooper and painters such as Thomas Cole began to use wilderness as a setting for their work. This has been true around the world. If we preserve it, wilderness can continue to inspire cultural creativity. Without it we will be reduced to making ever-fainter copies of copies, like a Xerox machine. Indeed, wilderness seems to be associated with the very roots of the creative process. It is no accident that artists and scholars use adjectives such as "pathbreaking" and "pioneering" to describe fresh work. They speak of the "frontiers" of knowledge. The unknown is the primary goal to discovery, and classic wilderness is the unknown. Its presence invigorates a culture, in Henry David Thoreau's terms, as fertilizer does a barren, sandy field. Perhaps this is what Thoreau had in mind when he wrote in 1851 that in wilderness is the preservation of the world.

7. The last and least anthropocentric wilderness benefit derives from the very recent idea that nonhuman life and even wild ecosystems themselves have *intrinsic value* and the right to exist. From this perspective wilderness is not *for* humans at all, and wilderness preservation testifies to the human capacity for restraint. A designated wilderness, in this sense, is a gesture of planetary modesty and a way of demonstrating that humans are members, not masters, of the community of life. In the last decade, environmental ethics and deep ecology have called attention to the idea that rights, and ethical obligations, do not end with human-to-human relationships but extend to the farthest limits of nature. Americans, especially, should not find this concept strange because the history of liberalism in the United States has been one of a selected group of white males; we now find the limits of liberalism extended to the rights of nature. In the course of this progression slavery disappeared and now the more radical environmentalists are calling for the end of *land* slavery. Wilderness is the best place to learn humility, dependency and reverence for all life.

From this nonanthropocentric point of view wilderness preservation is truly a radical act. It is indeed subversive to the forces that have accelerated modern civilization to power but now threaten its continuation: materialism, utilitarianism, growth, domination, hierarchy, exploitation. Development and the preservation of wilderness are *not* compatible. If we are going to really have enduring wilderness on earth, we must challenge the growth ethic. In a limited world everything must have limits including human population and civilization. Only cancer cells respect no limits, and in doing so they destroy their habitat and perish. Civilization has cancerous tendencies; wilderness protection is an antidote. Growth, it increasingly appears, is like a drug that can destroy the user. The antidrug slogan on the streets is "Just say NO." It is time to apply the same logic to growth. The existence of wilderness is the surest sign that mankind has understood this truth and that he is prepared to put his own legitimate demands into ecological balance with those of his fellow travelers on spaceship earth.

In conclusion, let me return to the analogy of the woman who asks, "Why do you love me?" Thinking about the values of wilderness outlined above, try telling her that you worship her, that you cherish the life you have lived together, that she is necessary for your mental welfare, that her presence in your life makes you different, that in her own special way she is beautiful, that she inspires you to be creative, and that she challenges you and offers you an alternative to the way most other women are in the world. Finally tell her your love is totally disinterested, that you love and value and respect her just because she exists and not for anything she does for you. You love her like the climbers say, "because she is there." You want to protect and nurture her because she has a right to exist. I believe, gentlemen, that this will be a successful response. In the 1980s I think it is called "being sensitive about relationships."

28   Wilderness appreciation is very new under the sun. The World Wilderness Congress would have been inconceivable a century ago or even 70 years ago when Gifford Pinchot[7] and Theodore Roosevelt called governors together at the White House to discuss the importance of conservation. They meant *utilitarian* conservation and the sustaining of growth and greatness. John Muir, who loved wilderness, was pointedly excluded from the 1907 gathering. Today wilderness has a major place in the world's conservation agenda and Muir's memory is honored, but we still have miles to go before wilderness has a secure, permanent place in all the representative latitudes of this planet. The final fruits of our efforts may not be harvested quickly, and in this connection it is well to recall a story that John F. Kennedy liked to tell when he was president of the United States. It concerned an ancient Chinese monarch who was planning an orchard. Informed that a particular tree would not bear fruit for a century, the wise monarch responded, "In that case, let us plant it this morning!"

In protecting wilderness we are also planting ideas and policies that will be slow in maturing. We should do well, then, to start the process immediately.

---

[7]American forester (1865–1946) who greatly influenced public policy regarding conservation and forest management.

Understanding What You Read

1. Nash rejects three common arguments commonly used to defend wilderness. What are they? On what grounds does he reject them?
2. Paragraph 5 says that there is "too much civilization." Based on your own experience and knowledge of places, write a paper agreeing or disagreeing.
3. In paragraph 13, Nash uses the analogy of what a man should never say to a woman who wants to know why he loves her. From your perspective, does this analogy work? That is, does it reinforce Nash's argument, or is a distraction?
4. What are the seven defenses for wilderness that Nash proposes?
5. When Nash returns to the analogy at the end, he equates each of the suggested responses to the woman's question about why she is loved with one of the defenses of wilderness. Do you find these comparisons appropriate? Is the analogy comic? If so, what is the value of interjecting laughter into the serious argument about preserving wilderness?

Writing About What You Read

Imagine that you heard Nash give this paper as a speech. Write a response to him, agreeing or disagreeing in part or entirely with what he says. You may include your own rationale for preserving wilderness areas.

Making Connections

1. Much has been said in the selections of this chapter about the value of wilderness. Compare and contrast Thoreau's views in "Walking" with those of Roderick Nash in "Why Wilderness?"
2. Both Pam Houston and Roderick Nash explore the psychological value of experiences in the wilderness (Nash) or a hostile and very cold environment (Houston). Using material from both of these selections, argue for (or against) the connection between wilderness and nature and the psychological well-being of people.
3. Annie Dillard and Edward Abbey write of intense encounters with animals to which they give special meaning. Compare and contrast Abbey's experience with the snakes with Dillard's confrontation with the weasel.

You know what home is. For many years, you've tried to be a modest and eager watcher of the skies, and of the Earth, whose green anthem you love. Home is a pigeon strutting like a petitioner in the courtyard in front of your house. Home is the law-abiding hickories out back. Home is the sign on a gas station just outside Pittsburgh that reads "If we can't fix it, it ain't broke." Home is springtime on campuses all across America, where students sprawl on the grass like the war-wounded at Gettysburg. Home is the Guatemalan jungle, at times deadly as an arsenal. Home is the pheasant barking hoarse threats at the neighbor's dog. Home is the exquisite torment of love and all the lesser mayhems of the heart.

—DIANE ACKERMAN, *A Natural History of the Senses*

◆

Once in his life man ought to concentrate his mind upon the remembered earth, I believe. He ought to give himself up to a particular landscape in his experience, to look upon it from as many angles as he can, to wonder about it, to dwell upon it. He ought to imagine that he touches it with his hands at every season and listens to the sounds that are made upon it. He ought to imagine the creatures there and all the faintest motions of the wind. He ought to collect the glare of noon and all the colors of the dawn and dusk.

—N. SCOTT MOMADAY, *The Way To Rainy Mountain*

◆

"You have to infer the whole dragon from the parts you can see and touch," the old people would say. . . . Dragons are so immense, I would never see one in its entirety. But I could explore the mountains, which are the tip of its head. . . . When climbing the slopes, I could understand that I was a bug riding on a dragon's forehead as it roams through space. . . . In quarries I could see its strata, the dragon's veins and muscles; the minerals its teeth and bone. . . . I had worked the soil, which is its flesh, and harvested the plants and climbed the trees, which are its hairs. I could listen to its voice in the thunder and feel its breathing in the winds, see its breathing in the clouds. . . . In the spring when the dragon awakes, I watched its turnings in the river.

—MAXINE HONG KINGSTON, *The Woman Warrior*

!Kung Women Gathering Nuts
(Marjorie Shostak)

Introduction

The places that people relate to most intensely are sometimes very ordinary. A tree in the backyard, a public park, the view of a setting sun, a kitchen window, a field of wheat, an open range, a baseball diamond on a corner lot, or an apartment house in Brooklyn—any of these might have special significance to some but would go unnoticed by others. There are those who feel that their very being is defined by a particular place and who are uncomfortable when separated from it; others are at home anywhere on the planet. In that sense they are "homeless," as Gary Snyder expresses it; they are not dependent on a particular landscape, a home, or material possessions for their well-being.

The writers in this chapter explore the sense of place and the way it affects actions in and on behalf of that place. The way people feel about places determines what they do to take care of them. Some, like Alice Walker and Annie Dillard, grew up in or near one place, and they leave it only to feel a constant longing for it, even a sentimental nostalgia that draws them home again, where they might, perhaps, recapture childhood and whatever was good about it. When Walker imagines the sheltering tree of her childhood feeling pain when people built fires in its hollow, she may be projecting on the tree her own pain at being disconnected from the place of her birth. When she imagines the tree grieving because it was not part of the family, she must surely be expressing her own sadness about being separated from place and kin. People want to take care of the places that nurtured them. Similarly, people who feel at home anywhere and who value the whole earth as home are likely to want to preserve the planet as a whole, not just their own backyards. On the other hand, those with no memories of "home," who have moved about and never felt connected to a place, may be careless with the places they encounter and thus dangerous to the earth as a whole. Such people may need to learn what Wallace Stegner's father never learned (see p. 479), that how we treat the earth affects not only the quality of our lives but the welfare of generations to come.

Some people who grow up lacking a strong sense of place find it later in life, as Ann Zwinger does in Colorado. The forty acres called Constant Friendship become her Walden Pond; she studies every detail of the landscape with the thoroughness that Thoreau brought to his observations. After years of wandering with her husband, who had a career in the military, Zwinger finds a place she can call home.

For others, like Donald Walker, Jr., the home place is where they have always been and where their parents and grandparents lived before them. The Walkers' tree farm in Oakridge, Oregon, is such a place. Kathleen Norris thinks of home as that of her ancestors, even though she never has lived there. Norris lived in diverse places—Virginia, Illinois, Hawaii, Vermont, New York—but when some twenty years ago she left New York for her grandparents' house on the border of North and South Dakota, she felt that she was discovering her "spiritual geography," and the raw material for her writing.

Some people are more passionate about adopted homes than they are about the places where they were born. For Gretel Ehrlich, a California native who went to school in the East, the vast open spaces of Wyoming captured her imagination. Her experiences working on ranches led to an attachment to the land, the people, and the culture of cowboys. Many of the settlers of Australia and North America left home by choice or by force for a new land of opportunity. Jill Ker Conway describes the ranching life in New South Wales—a place that attracted a tough group of men and women and toughened them even more as they tried to survive with little water, extreme temperatures, and few amenities of civilization.

Culture arises from the collective efforts of humans to adapt and respond to environment. People may be drawn to a place for its beauty, its history, or its myths, but daily life, once they're settled, revolves around specific features of the environment—soil quality, climate, water resources, vegetation, and wildlife. The complex set of behaviors and beliefs that we call "culture" develop to some degree as people interact with environmental conditions, and culturally dictated practices in turn influence the environment. The rugged terrain in western Australia, for example, helps create the culture of the people who live there, and their ranching and grazing practices then alter the land.

Three pieces in this chapter explore the needs of indigenous peoples in Africa who know the place of their birth not only from having always lived there but from the accumulated knowledge of generations before them. Marjorie Shostak explains how an intimate knowledge of plants and animals passed down through generations over many centuries makes it possible to survive in a seemingly barren place. Doris Lessing's story "No Witchcraft for Sale" dramatizes the obstacles that scientists may encounter searching for the secrets of folk medicine. In "Miles and Miles of Bloody Africa," Jonathan Adams and Thomas McShane tell the stories of two African men who share the same knowledge about a place, but choose very different paths for surviving there.

The interconnectedness of living things is determined not just by biological programming but by cultural, economic, political, and even religious factors. For example, consumption in North America—be it of hamburgers or cocaine—profoundly affects the daily lives of people in Central and South America and the environments in which they live. Similarly, manufacturing in Ohio affects the health of the forests and lakes in Canada. Understanding the environmental crisis requires that we consider how people—individually and in groups—think about and treat the places they live, how they use and misuse other places, and how cultural values and beliefs affect behavior.

GARY SNYDER

Snyder (b. 1930) is a poet and essayist whose work explores the ways that human beings can live in harmony with the land and other living things. A student of mythology, Native American oral traditions, and of Zen Buddhism, he draws on the wisdom of disparate cultures in his quest for an alternative to the imbalance and ignorance of contemporary civilization. While his commitments have taken him to many remote places in the Far East and around the globe, he considers himself to belong in the Yuba River country in the Sierra Nevada of northern California. He currently teaches at the University of California, Davis. His books include *Regarding Wave* (1970); *Turtle Island* (1974), which won the Pulitzer Prize for poetry; and *Left Out in the Rain: New Poems 1947 – 1985.* "The World Is Places" is from a collection of essays, *The Practice of the Wild* (1990).

The World Is Places

WE EXPERIENCE slums, prairies, and wetlands all equally as "places." Like a mirror, a place can hold anything, on any scale. I want to talk about place as an experience and propose a model of what it meant to "live in place" for most of human time, presenting it initially in terms of the steps that a child takes growing into a natural community. (We have the terms *enculturation* and *acculturation,* but nothing to describe the process of becoming placed or re-placed.) In doing so we might get one more angle on what a "civilization of wildness" might require.

For most Americans, to reflect on "home place" would be an unfamiliar exercise. Few today can announce themselves as someone *from* somewhere. Almost nobody spends a lifetime in the same valley, working alongside the people they knew as children. Native people everywhere (the very term means "someone born there") and Old World farmers and city people share this experience of living in place. Still—and this is very important to remember— being inhabitory, being place-based, has never meant that one didn't travel from time to time, going on trading ventures or taking livestock to summer grazing. Such working wanderers have always known they had a home-base on earth, and could prove it at any campfire or party by singing their own songs.

The heart of a place is the home, and the heart of the home is the firepit, the hearth. All tentative explorations go outward from there, and it is back to the fireside that elders return. You grow up speaking a home language, a local vernacular. Your own household may have some specifics of phrase, of pronunciation, that are different from the *domus,* the *jia* or *ie* or *kum,* down the lane. You hear histories of the people who are your neighbors and tales involving rocks, streams, mountains, and trees that are all within your sight. The myths of world-creation tell you how *that mountain* was created and how *that peninsula* came to be there. As you grow bolder you explore your world outward from the firepit (which is the center of each universe) in little trips. The childhood landscape is learned on foot, and a map is inscribed in the mind—trails and pathways and groves—the mean dog, the cranky old man's house, the pasture with a bull in it—going out wider and farther. All of us carry within us a picture of the terrain that was learned roughly between the ages of six and nine. (It could as easily be an urban neighborhood as some rural scene.) You can almost totally recall the place you walked, played, biked, swam. Revisualizing that place with its smells and textures, walking through it again in your imagination, has a grounding and settling effect. As a contemporary thought we might also wonder how it is for those whose childhood landscape was being ripped up by bulldozers, or whose family moving about made it all a blur. I have a friend who still gets emotional when he recalls how the avocado orchards of his southern California youth landscape were transformed into hillside after hillside of suburbs.

4   Our place is part of what we are. Yet even a "place" has a kind of fluidity: it passes through space and time—"ceremonial time" in John Hanson Mitchell's[1] phrase. A place will have been grasslands, then conifers, then beech and elm. It will have been half riverbed, it will have been scratched and plowed by ice. And then it will be cultivated, paved, sprayed, dammed, graded, built up. But each is only for a while, and that will be just another set of lines on the palimpsest.[2] The whole earth is a great tablet holding the multiple overlaid new and ancient traces of the swirl of forces. Each place is its own place, forever (eventually) wild. A place on earth is a mosaic within larger mosaics—the land is all small places, all precise tiny realms replicating larger and smaller patterns. Children start out learning place by learning those little realms around the house, the settlement, and outward.

One's sense of the scale of a place expands as one learns the *region*. The young hear further stories and go for explorations which are also subsistence forays—firewood gathering, fishing, to fairs or to market. The outlines of the larger region become part of their awareness. (Thoreau says in "Walking" that an area twenty miles in diameter will be enough to occupy a lifetime of close exploration on foot—you will never exhaust its details.)

The total size of the region a group calls home depends on the land type. Every group is territorial, each moves within a given zone, even nomads stay within boundaries. A people living in a desert or grassland with great visible spaces that invite you to step forward and walk as far as you can see will range across tens of thousands of square miles. A deep old-growth forest may rarely be traveled at all. Foragers in gallery forests and grasslands will regularly move broadly, whereas people in a deep-soiled valley ideal for gardens might not go far beyond the top of the nearest ridge. The regional boundaries were roughly drawn by climate, which is what sets the plant-type zones—plus soil type and landforms. Desert wastes, mountain ridges, or big rivers set a broad edge to a region. We walk across or wade through the larger and smaller boundaries. Like children first learning our homeland we can stand at the edge of a big river, or on the crest of a major ridge, and observe that the other side is a different soil, a change of plants and animals, a new shape of barn roof, maybe less or more rain. The lines between natural regions are never simple or clear, but vary according to such criteria as biota, watersheds, landforms, elevation. Still, we all know—at some point—that we are no

---

[1] From Mitchell's 1984 book *Ceremonial Time: Fifteen Thousand Years on One Square Mile*, about a patch of land 35 miles west of Boston.

[2] An old writing surface (such as a parchment or tablet) used again after earlier writing has been erased.

longer in the Midwest, say, but in the West. Regions seen according to natural criteria are sometimes called bioregions.

(In pre-conquest America people covered great distances. It is said that the Mojave of the lower Colorado felt that everyone at least once in their lives should make foot journeys to the Hopi mesas to the east, the Gulf of California to the south, and to the Pacific.)

Every region has its wilderness. There is the fire in the kitchen, and there is the place less traveled. In most settled regions there used to be some combination of prime agricultural land, orchard and vine land, rough pasturage, woodlot, forest, and desert or mountain "waste." The de facto wilderness was the extreme backcountry part of all that. The parts less visited are "where the bears are." The wilderness is within walking distance—it may be three days or it may be ten. It is at the far high rough end, or the deep forest and swamp end, of the territory where most of you all live and work. People will go there for mountain herbs, for the trapline, or for solitude. They live between the poles of home and their own wild places.

Recollecting that we once lived in places is part of our contemporary self-rediscovery. It grounds what it means to be "human" (etymologically something like "earthling"). I have a friend who feels sometimes that the world is hostile to human life—he says it chills us and kills us. But how could we *be* were it not for this planet that provided our very shape? Two conditions—gravity and a livable temperature range between freezing and boiling—have given us fluids and flesh. The trees we climb and the ground we walk on have given us five fingers and toes. The "place" (from the root *plat,* broad, spreading, flat) gave us far-seeing eyes, the streams and breezes gave us versatile tongues and whorly ears. The land gave us a stride, and the lake a dive. The amazement gave us our kind of mind. We should be thankful for that, and take nature's stricter lessons with some grace.

Understanding What You Read

1. What does it mean to have a "home-base" on earth?
2. Is there a particular place that you call home?
3. Whether you have lived in one, several, or many places, what do you know about the place or places you have lived?

Writing About What You Read

Imagine that you are a child between six and nine years old, reaching out beyond your home to explore the world outside. Describe yourself and what you see, hear, and smell. Whether the world you describe is a city block, an urban neighborhood, a small town, a mountain, a farm, a suburb, or a housing development, include as many details as possible to convey the special qualities of that place.

ANNIE DILLARD

Dillard (b. 1945) achieved early success as a writer with the publication of *Pilgrim at Tinker Creek* (1974), a best-seller and winner of the Pulitzer Prize for nonfiction. Her other works include *Teaching a Stone to Talk* (1982), *The Writing Life* (1989), and *The Living* (1992), a novel about nineteenth-century life in Washington State, where she lived for some years. Though she focuses in many of her works on the small details of nature in rural Virginia, Dillard has also written about her experiences in places as different as the Ecuadorian jungle and the Galápagos Islands. She teaches periodically at Wesleyan University in Connecticut. The piece below, the prologue to her autobiographical *An American Childhood* (1987), begins with her own very personal attachment to the landscape of her birth and is a meditation about the history of that land and what it was like before European men and women felled the first trees and plowed the first fields to grow corn.

Land Where the Rivers Meet

WHEN EVERYTHING ELSE has gone from my brain—the President's name, the state capitals, the neighborhoods where I lived, and then my own name and what it was on earth I sought, and then at length the faces of my friends, and finally the faces of my family—when all this has dissolved, what will be left, I believe, is topology: the dreaming memory of land as it lay this way and that.

I will see the city poured rolling down the mountain valleys like slag, and see the city lights sprinkled and curved around the hills' curves, rows of bonfires winding. At sunset a red light like housefires shines from the narrow hillside windows; the houses' bricks burn like glowing coals.

The three wide rivers divide and cool the mountains. Calm old bridges span the banks and link the hills. The Allegheny River flows in brawling from the north, from near the shore of Lake Erie, and from Lake Chautauqua in New York and eastward. The Monongahela River flows in shallow and slow from the south, from West Virginia. The Allegheny and the Monongahela meet and form the westward-wending Ohio.

Where the two rivers join lies an acute point of flat land from which rises 4
the city. The tall buildings rise lighted to their tips. Their lights illumine other
buildings' clean sides, and illumine the narrow city canyons below, where
people move, and shine reflected red and white at night from the black
waters.

When the shining city, too, fades, I will see only those forested mountains
and hills, and the way the rivers lie flat and moving among them, and the way
the low land lies wooded among them, and the blunt mountains rise in
darkness from the rivers' banks, steep from the rugged south and rolling from
the north, and from farther, from the inclined eastward plateau where the
high ridges begin to run so long north and south unbroken that to get
around them you practically have to navigate Cape Horn.

In those first days, people said, a squirrel could run the long length of
Pennsylvania without ever touching the ground. In those first days, the
woods were white oak and chestnut, hickory, maple, sycamore, walnut, wild
ash, wild plum, and white pine. The pine grew on the ridgetops where the
mountains' lumpy spines stuck up and their skin was thinnest.

The wilderness was uncanny, unknown. Benjamin Franklin had already
invented his stove in Philadelphia by 1753, and Thomas Jefferson was a
schoolboy in Virginia; French soldiers had been living in forts along Lake Erie
for two generations. But west of the Alleghenies in western Pennsylvania,
there was not even a settlement, not even a cabin. No Indians lived there, or
even near there.

Wild grapevines tangled the treetops and shut out the sun. Few songbirds 8
lived in the deep woods. Bright Carolina parakeets—red, green, and yellow—nested in the dark forest. There were ravens then, too. Woodpeckers
rattled the big trees' trunks, ruffed grouse whirred their tail feathers in the
fall, and every long once in a while a nervous gang of empty-headed turkeys
came hustling and kicking through the leaves—but no one heard any of this,
no one at all.

In 1753, young George Washington surveyed for the English this point
of land where rivers met. To see the forest-blurred lay of the land, he rode
his horse to a ridgetop and climbed a tree. He judged it would make a good
spot for a fort. And an English fort it became, and a depot for Indian traders
to the Ohio country, and later a French fort and way station to New Orleans.

But it would be another ten years before any settlers lived there on that
land where the rivers met, lived to draw in the flowery scent of June rhodo-
dendrons with every breath. It would be another ten years before, for the first
time on earth, tall men and women lay exhausted in their cabins, sleeping in
the sweetness, worn out from planting corn.

Understanding What You Read

1. The city that Dillard describes as "poured rolling down the mountain" is modern-day Pittsburgh. What is accomplished by removing the city from the hillsides and recreating the scene before humans arrived?
2. What do you know about the flora and fauna that inhabited the area before settlers moved in?
3. What is the significance of Dillard's mentioning the Carolina parakeet (paragraph 8), a bird that is now extinct? Would it be different if she had referred to robins here instead?
4. What is the significance of the first building being a fort?
5. Why do you think Dillard chooses to end the piece by referring to "tall men and women . . . sleeping in the sweetness, worn out from planting corn"? Why "tall"?

Writing About What You Read

1. Describe the special features of your particular region, beyond the home and neighborhood that you know: land type, climate, presence or absence of agriculture, wildlife, geological features (mountain, rivers, plains, marshes), plants and trees.
2. If there is a place whose history you know well enough, write an essay similar to this one. If not, choose a place, do some research about its history, and then write an essay using details that convey a sense of loss.

ALICE WALKER

Walker (b. 1944) is a poet, short-story writer, novelist, and essayist. Her novels include *The Color Purple* (1982, winner of the Pulitzer Prize and the American Book Award), *The Temple of My Familiar* (1989), and *Possessing the Secret of Joy* (1992). Born and raised in rural Georgia, Walker has since traveled widely, teaching at numerous universities and working for civil rights. Her experiences in Africa inform Walker's concern for the environment and her appreciation of landscape as a source of personal identity. Walker now runs a publishing company, Wild Trees Press. "The Place Where I Was Born" is the opening prose passage of "My Heart Has Reopened to You," from *Her Blue Body Everything We Know* (1991), a volume of poetry she subtitles *Earthling Poems 1965–90 Complete*.

The Place Where I Was Born

I AM a displaced person. I sit here on a swing on the deck of my house in Northern California admiring how the fog has turned the valley below into a lake. For hours nothing will be visible below me except this large expanse of vapor; then slowly, as the sun rises and gains in intensity, the fog will start to curl up and begin its slow rolling drift toward the ocean. People here call it the dragon; and, indeed, a dragon is what it looks like, puffing and coiling, winged, flaring and in places thin and discreet, as it races before the sun, back to its ocean coast den. Mornings I sit here in awe and great peace. The mountains across the valley come and go in the mist; the redwoods and firs, oaks and giant bays appear as clumpish spires, enigmatic shapes of green, like the stone forests one sees in Chinese paintings of Guilin.[1]

It is incredibly beautiful where I live. Not fancy at all, or exclusive. But from where I sit on my deck I can look down on the backs of hawks, and the wide, satiny wings of turkey vultures glistening in the sun become my present connection to ancient Egyptian Africa. The pond is so still below me that the trees reflected in it seem, from this distance, to be painted in its depths.

All this: the beauty, the quiet, the cleanliness, the peace, is what I love. I realize how lucky I am to have found it here. And yet, there are days when my view of the mountains and redwoods makes me nostalgic for small rounded hills easily walked over, and for the look of big leaf poplar and the scent of pine.

I am nostalgic for the land of my birth, the land I left forever when I was thirteen—moving first to the town of Eatonton,[2] and then, at seventeen, to the city of Atlanta.

I cried one day as I talked to a friend about a tree I loved as a child. A tree that had sheltered my father on his long cold walk to school each morning: it was midway between his house and the school and because there was a large cavity in its trunk, a fire could be made inside it. During my childhood, in a tiny, overcrowded house in a tiny dell below it, I looked up at it frequently and felt reassured by its age, its generosity despite its years of brutalization (the fires, I knew, had to hurt), and its tall, old-growth pine nobility. When it was struck by lightning and killed, and then was cut down and made into firewood, I grieved as if it had been a person. Secretly. Because who among the members of my family would not have laughed at my grief?

I have felt entirely fortunate to have had this companion, and even today remember it with gratitude. But why the tears? my friend wanted to know.

[1]A city in China (Kweilin or Kueilin) known for its oddly shaped mountain peaks, favorite subjects of Chinese landscape painters.
[2]The middle-Georgia town where Walker went to high school.

And it suddenly dawned on me that perhaps it *was* sad that it was a tree and
not a member of my family to whom I was so emotionally close.

O, landscape of my birth
because you were so good to me as I grew
I could not bear to lose you.
O, landscape of my birth
because when I lost you, a part of my soul died.
O, landscape of my birth
because to save myself I pretended it was *you*
who died.
You that now did not exist
because I could not see you.
But O, landscape of my birth
now I can confess how I have lied.
Now I can confess the sorrow
of my heart
as the tears flow
and I see again with memory's bright eye
my dearest companion cut down
and can bear to resee myself
so lonely and so small
there in the sunny meadows
and shaded woods
of childhood
where my crushed spirit
and stricken heart
ran in circles
looking for a friend.

Soon I will have known fifty summers.
Perhaps that is why
my heart
an imprisoned tree
so long clutched tight
inside its core
insists
on shedding
like iron leaves
the bars
from its cell.

You flow into me.
And like the Aborigine or Bushperson or Cherokee

who braves everything 40
to stumble home to die
no matter that cowboys
are herding cattle where the ancestors slept
I return to you, my earliest love. 44

Weeping in recognition at the first trees
I ever saw, the first hills I ever climbed and rested my
unbearable cares
upon, the first rivers I ever dreamed myself across,
the first pebbles I ever lifted up, warm from the sun, and put 48
into
my mouth.

O landscape of my birth
you have never been far from my heart.
It is *I* who have been far. 52
If you will take me back
Know that I
Am yours.

As a child I assumed I would always have the middle Georgia landscape to live in, as Brer Rabbit,[3] a native also, and relative, had his brier patch. It was not to be. The pain of racist oppression, and its consequence, economic impoverishment, drove me to the four corners of the earth in search of justice and peace, and work that affirmed my whole being. I have come to rest here, weary from travel, on a deck—not a Southern front porch—overlooking another world.

I am content; and yet, I wonder what my life would have been like if I 8 had been able to stay home?

I remember early morning fogs in Georgia, not so dramatic as California ones, but magical too because out of the Southern fog of memory tramps my dark father, smiling and large, glowing with rootedness, and talking of hound dogs, biscuits and coons. And my equally rooted mother bustles around the corner of our house preparing to start a wash, the fire under the black wash pot extending a circle of warmth in which I, a grave-eyed child, stand. There is my sister Ruth, beautiful to me and dressed elegantly for high school in gray felt skirt and rhinestone brooch, hurrying up the road to catch the yellow school bus which glows like a large glow worm in the early morning fog.

*   *   *

---

[3]Folk character popularized in the Uncle Remus stories by Joel Chandler Harris (1848–1908), also born in the country near Eatonton, Georgia.

Understanding What You Read

1. What details does Walker use to evoke the images of curling fog that looks like a dragon, a beloved tree, and the Southern fog of memory?
2. Why are there people in the Georgia sections of the essay but none in the California scenes?
3. What images does she associate with her father, her mother, and her sister Ruth?
4. What did the tree with a hollow big enough to build a fire inside mean to Walker? How do you respond to her suggestions that the tree suffered pain from the fire and that it might have grieved because it was not a part of her family?
5. What is the function of the references to Chinese paintings, Egyptian Africa, and "the four corners of the earth"?

Writing About What You Read

1. Write a paragraph about the place where you were born, and tell, in such detail that your reader gets a sense of it, what it felt like to live there.
2. Do you or have you ever felt like a displaced person in the sense that Walker does sitting on her deck in California thinking of Georgia? If so, communicate that feeling in a short essay, using details to evoke the two places.
3. If there is no one place that you think of as home, write a short piece about what you think the effect of having no sense of place has had on you.

ADRIENNE RICH

A major American poet, powerful prose writer, and feminist critic, Adrienne Rich (b. 1929) has published more than fifteen books of poetry since her first volume, *A Change of World,* was accepted by the Yale Series of Younger Poets in 1951. Rich's work explores the relationship between our selves—at their most personal and intimate—and the public and political world in which we move. Her recent works include *Your Native Land, Your Life* (1986) (from which Part I from "Sources" is taken), *An Atlas of The Difficult World: Poems 1988–1991* (1991), and *What Is Found There: Notebooks on Poetry and Politics* (1993).

Part I from "Sources"

Sixteen years.   The narrow, rough-gullied backroads
almost the same.   The farms: almost the same,
a new barn here, a new roof there, a rusting car,
collapsed sugar-house, trailer, new young wife   4
trying to make a lawn instead of a dooryard,
new names, old kinds of names: Rocquette, Desmarais,
Clark, Pierce, Stone.   Gossier.   No names of mine.

The vixen I met at twilight on Route 5   8
south of Willoughby: long dead.   She was an omen
to me, surviving, herding her cubs
in the silvery bend of the road
in nineteen sixty-five.   12

Shapes of things: so much the same
they feel like eternal forms: the house and barn
on the rise above May Pond; the brow of Pisgah;[1]
the face of milkweed blooming,   16
brookwater pleating over slanted granite,
boletus under pine, the half-composted needles
it broke through patterned on its skin.
Shape of queen anne's lace, with the drop of blood.   20
Bladder-campion veined with purple.
Multifoliate heal-all.

[1]According to the Bible, the mountain in ancient Palestine which Moses ascended to see
the Promised Land before his death.

Understanding What You Read

1. What kind of place does the first stanza of the poem describe? What is
   the function of the names and the phrase "No names of mine"?
2. What do you think the vixen was an omen for?
3. What is the function of the place names: Willoughby, May Pond, Pisgah?

Writing About What You Read

Paraphrase the poem, recasting it as a prose narrative using your own
voice and retaining the first person.

ANN ZWINGER

Zwinger (b. 1925) has written and illustrated more than ten books of natural history, including *Wind in the Rock* (1986), about the canyon country of Utah, and *Run River Run* (1975), about a journey down the Green River from its source in the Wind River Mountains of Wyoming to its end. Zwinger distinguishes herself from writers who focus on particular environmental problems, though she believes her goals are the same as theirs. Combining careful research with meticulous fieldwork, she collects the material that she uses to create the detailed descriptions of the natural environments she evokes lovingly in her writing. "The Lake Rock" is from Zwinger's first book, *Beyond the Aspen Grove* (1988), which paints in comprehensive detail the multitude of plants and animals that inhabit the forty acres she calls Constant Friendship. She currently holds an endowed chair in Southwestern Studies at Colorado College.

The Lake Rock

WHEN I need my sense of order restored, I sit on the lake rock. It sums up all I have learned about this mountain world. Connected to the shore by a narrow, somewhat unstable catwalk, the rock is just big enough to sit on comfortably. It is a pebble dropped into the water, the center of widening rings of montane life, beginning with the life of the lake itself and culminating in the evergreen forests, where the succession that is taking place is mapped in the communities that I can see. The rock is a place of order, reason, and bright mountain air.

Encircling the rock is the community of plants and animals which can survive only in the water. Small motes of existence, they float with its currents, cling to underwater supports, or burrow in the brown silt of the lake bottom. Some I can see as I sit here. Others have to be corralled under a microscope lens. I watch a fat trout lurking in the fringed shadows of the sedges. All around the edges of the lake, where water meets land, grow willows, sedges, and rushes, predicting a time when amber water will be green plant, the lapping sound of small waves the sly whisper of grass stems.

It is a busy place with a constant spin of insects, punctuated by the pursuing green arcs of leopard frogs. The south stream enters the lake through willows and cow parsnip and a pile of logs placed there when the lake was built to prevent silting. The north stream's entrance is hidden in elephant-foot-sized clumps of bulrush which change sheen in every breeze. Tangles of willows forecast spring in their catkins. Yellow or red branches identify them even in winter. The streams are the one constant in this landscape.

The circle widens. Behind the lake edge, to the north and west, the land rises into the lake meadow, drying as it slopes upward. Blue grass and brome grass crowd every square inch. I see chipmunk and ground-squirrel burrows, haloed with dandelions. Hundreds of wildflowers grow in this meadow, perennials whose coming I look for each year. A few aspens tentatively grow along its edge.

The established young aspen community between the two streams contains small slender trees, growing almost a foot a year. Still gangling and adolescent, they will in a short time obscure the view of the mature grove behind them. Leaves flicker celadon in spring, viridian in summer, clinquant in fall, tallying the sovereign seasons, graying and greening to reiterate the message of snow and sun.

Wider still, the north edge of the lake meadow steps upward over its granite base. Where it levels off, the ponderosas grow, big and sturdy and full of cones. They stand staunch, widely spaced, allowing sunlight to filter through for wild geranium and kinnikinnik and tiny wild candytuft that crosses the dusky duff.

The south slope of the lake curves away from the shore, becoming more spruce-shaded as it retreats. This area is the first to be snow-covered, the last to be clear. Shade-tolerant plants root in the precipitous hillside; from here I can see a few late orange-red Indian paintbrush and the stalks of monkshood and larkspur. Dark-red strawberry blite ties down an old log with the help of raspberry and rose bushes. A few last aspens mingle with the spruces, their trunks thin and pallid, most of their branches down from insufficient light. Above them the Douglas firs and spruces grow close together, presenting a solid wall of black-green.

The ever-widening circles of montane life culminate in these evergreens which intrude visually into the lake. Even in winter, when the India-ink reflections are gone, the uncompromising contrast of black and white still commands the eye. In the spring, when the air is heavy and laden with late snows, the lake reflects their pendent spires, solid as a German Expressionist woodcut. In the summer the reflections shimmer in the breeze, slotted with blue sky, an animate Monet. In the fall they form a moving mosaic with the aspen when the wind fragments the surface to create tesserae of emerald and gold leaf—a Byzantine pavement.

It is impossible to look at the land and not be aware of the evergreens. In all seasons they dominate, unchanging in color, towering in size. Their spires crenelate the sky. Their opacity of color, depth, and density create a background against which are measured the brightness of aspen leaf, iridescence of dragonfly wing, scarlet of gilia, and gleam of lake. The ponderosa, spruce, and Douglas fir are the reminders of an end point of succession for this land, for there is no other vegetation that will replace them, short of catastrophic climate change.

These trees change the environment to fit their needs, making an acid soil which is inhospitable to other plants, attracting rain by the massiveness of their own transpiration. At the beginning of succession, moss and lichen grow a few centimeters above the ground and a few below. At the end of succession, for this land, trees tower many feet into the air and send their roots through the ground, demanding the most that the environment can give. These conifers will be there in decades, in centuries, to come. They will shade out other trees and brighter flowers, intrude into the deepening soil of the meadows. Succession is an inexorable progression which may be altered or disrupted but which will eternally begin again and again to achieve the same end. No emotional pleas or moral inducements will change it; to understand this is to accept the irrevocableness of nature.

The knob of granite forming my tiny island rises three feet above the water on the lake side, stepping and sloping down to a few inches above on the land side. The surface breaks off and crumbles into sharp gravel in my hand with the ease of Pikes Peak granite. Near the waterline on the east, the plants grow in independent patches, on a nearly vertical face. On the rise and tread of the protected step they grow more thickly. Green pincushions of moss are softer to sit on than the gravel. At my feet, on top of one mat of moss, are a few square inches of blue grass, neatly trimmed by the wind. Through this nest of stolons and roots and rhizomes grow cinquefoils, wild strawberry, white clover, an ubiquitous dandelion, asters, wild chrysanthemum, rosettes of scarlet gilia and bright pink wild geranium.

12   Strawberry and geranium seeds may have arrived via the droppings of a gluttonous chickadee. The tiny leaves, replicas of normal-sized leaves on shore, bear the imprint of limitation. Composite seeds came on efficient parachutes, sometimes airborne, sometimes as a flotilla sailing across the water and snagging in a crack. Porter's asters and wild chrysanthemums give the final touch of yellow and white to the rock; golden asters are one of the most tolerant plants of the mountains, flourishing in a wide variety of habitats in a wide variety of altitudes.

Bush cinquefoil cliff-hangs at the southernmost edge of the rock; fully exposed, they set brilliant blooms against the darkness of the lake's pine-tree reflections. Although the bushes are small, their leaf and blossom size are the same as those of shore plants. Looking around the lake shore, I can see these same flowers and shrubs in the meadow or the aspen grove, usually where there is some protection and, at the very least, more soil.

I take a mental walk along the rim of the parent rocks of this island which form the south-facing slope at the edge of the lake. There, large boulders of Pikes Peak granite form a crumbling cliff with the ponderosa grove at the top and the lake at the base. Below the dam, the rim of granite drops sharply to the runoff stream. Facing almost due south, the slope receives the full intensity of mountain sunlight, especially in the winter when the low sun hits at a ninety-degree angle and keeps the slope snow-free.

In the weathered gravel which forms talus-like patches between the rocks, some plants have rooted. Water drains most quickly from a gravel slope, making colonization exceedingly difficult. Decomposed rock has little stability, and the steepness of the slope causes it to roll easily. Nonetheless there is a fairly even growth of penny-cress, shepherd's-purse, butter-and-eggs, amaranth, and buckwheat. Considered as being noxious weeds at lower elevations, they provide soil hold here, and even their propensity for forming myriads of seeds has not given them unchallenged progress. They simply find the growing conditions too difficult to make nuisances of themselves.

Towering over the annuals are the exclamation points of mullein, huge stalks of this year's green reiterated in the browned stalks of last year's pods. *Candelaria* is the descriptive Spanish name, and indeed they seem like huge candelabra, verdigris in summer, bronze in winter. With a few scarlet gilia, some small-flowered blue gilia, and white thistles, these are the only biennials. An early narrow-leafed mertensia is the only perennial herb. There are some rose twigs, but to call them shrubs would be presumptuous.

16

Farther down this same slope, on top of a large level rock which the children used to use for a stage, are a few pincushion cacti. Some also grow in the loose gravel nearby, tucked at the foot of another boulder near sprigs of pin cherry. Cacti have extremely shallow and spreading root systems, which cover such a large area that they can take full advantage of even a light rainfall. Leaves, like those of the conifers, have been narrowed to needles; stems are thickened to a sphere covered with a heavy cuticle. The stomata are closed during the day when evaporation is high and opened in the cool of the night. These devices hinder water loss so effectively that cacti are most common in desert areas. And this is very nearly just that: there is no shade, the rocks catch and radiate the full heat and glare of high-intensity altitude sunlight, and solid rock lies just beneath the surface. Growing conditions are hard indeed; the delicacy of the early pink flowers is almost incongruous.

Still farther down the slope, on another large rock table, is a cluster of stonecrop. Like the cactus, its succulent leaves are thickly cuticled and the root system is shallow and wide. Tolerant of a wide soil range, stonecrop grows on many montane rocks and dry slopes. It blooms profusely in June and July, brilliant six-pointed stars visible as puddles of yellow many feet away although no single blossom exceeds half an inch in diameter. Its vitality is in no way diminished by conditions other plants would find impossible.

To compare these rock environments with the lake rock is to see what water can do to alter the vegetational pattern. Cactus, stonecrop, and mullein could not grow on the lake rock, for they require a dry situation. Other conditions are the same: Pikes Peak granite base, exposed site, close enough to receive identical amounts of sun and rain. The difference in vegetation is caused by the surrounding water, and is indicated not only in the type but the increased variety of plants. The measured relative humidity on the rock is consistently nearly double that of the shore rocks. In the winter the rock is ice-locked and generally snow-covered over the plant line, protecting the plants from the extremes of thaw and freeze and desiccation that the shore plants must endure.

20   Water is the most important single factor in this succession. The lake has made possible a local condition with local vegetation, just as the stream running through the dry prairie makes possible the phalanx of trees along its banks. The two extremes exist side by side.

The lake-rock community has progressed as far, in terms of plant succession, as the meadow community, and in a measurably short time—since the lake was built some seventeen years ago. It had and still has many aspects of a pioneer community. Much of the growth is isolated, a hand-span or more apart. The soil is minimal and undifferentiated. Layering is narrow, and the environmental factors almost totally control the plant life. The predominant growth here is that of perennial herbs, characteristic of a more advanced stage of succession than that which exists on the shore rocks before me. None of these plants are limited in range or in need of special conditions on this rock. Tolerance and hardiness mark the pioneers.

A succession of animal life accompanies the succession of plant life. The animals who busy themselves by the lake rock are insects, mostly transients who can fly. No mice burrow here, no deer browse, no birds perch. The blue damselfly frequents the rock as a passerby. Flies make a noisy nuisance of themselves but lay their eggs elsewhere. Only wolf spiders leave dots of white cotton egg cases. The lake rock is isolated from the shore, the water as effective a barrier as if it were a mile across, and the sparse plant cover provides no shelter for larger animals.

But when the lake has finally been absorbed, and the rock is surrounded and covered by soil, then perhaps larger animals will come padding and pawing and nosing about, their ancestors even now roaming the woods. I would like to think so. But perhaps they will not, for by then they may already be gone from here, as the wolves, wolverines, and grizzly bears are already gone, pushed to extinction by man's narrowing of the wilderness.

24   We have tried to understand the patterns of the land at Constant Friendship. We have hoped to change it as little as possible. After all, we are only visitors to this mountain land. But to keep this land untouched has meant that we have had to partially fence it, with a fence almost as much psychological as physical. And this, incongruously, seems to be the only way in which wilderness lands can be saved. Only within the periphery of the fence is there time to learn, to understand, to cherish. My interest in the vast world of nature began when we came to this land, with the finding of a new world, a sense of discovery, a sharing. But somewhere in the learning came commitment,

the realization that in the understanding of this natural world comes the maintenance of it, that with knowledge comes responsibility.

At Constant Friendship we chop down a dead aspen that might fall on the cabin during a wind storm, destroying the chance for it to be home for bird or insect or weasel. It makes good firewood, we say, thinking of our creature comforts. But we have cut down no masses of trees, leaving open scars to erode. We have polluted no streams, shot no marauding bobcat for bounty, no deer for sport. But by our presence we do cause the balances of nature to be readjusted.

Because we can and do manipulate our environment, we are then charged with the responsibility of our acts, for if we are to survive we must insure that this best of all possible worlds survives with us.

The lake rock is a microcosm, and here I find stability and order, and an understanding of my own place in an impeccable design. From here I can reach out to my less orderly world beyond. From here I can see the seasons chain together in a continuity that runs through our lives. Each one of us has sat here, at one time or another, almost as much a part of the landscape as the lake rock itself, absorbing a sense of strength from the granite and a sense of freedom from the sky.

Understanding What You Read

1. Zwinger's description of the special view from the rock in her lake is full of details. What do you recall about the plants, animals, and geological features of the place? Can you see it in your mind's eye? Is it a scene that you would like to sit and observe?
2. Detailed, richly textured writing requires careful ordering. How does Zwinger organize the many details to give shape to her essay?
3. Why does Zwinger go to such lengths—and into such detail—to set the scene, before making her point that the lake rock is a microcosm?

Writing About What You Read

If there is a place in the natural world where you are familiar with the rock formations, plants, and animals, place yourself in the scene and describe what you see.

JILL KER CONWAY

Conway (b. 1934) lived in her native Australia until 1960, when she left for the United States to begin graduate studies in history at Harvard University. She has taught at the University of Toronto and served as its vice president from 1973 to 1975, when she became president of Smith College. Since 1985 she has been a visiting scholar and professor at the Massachusetts Institute of Technology. Conway's scholarly books include *The Female Experience in 18th and 19th Century America* (1982) and *Women Reformers and American Culture* (1987). "The West" is taken from the opening chapter of her autobiography, *The Road to Coorain* (1989).

The West

THE WESTERN PLAINS of New South Wales[1] are grasslands. Their vast expanse flows for many hundreds of miles beyond the Lachlan and Murrumbidgee rivers until the desert takes over and sweeps inland to the dead heart of the continent. In a good season, if the eyes are turned to the earth on those plains, they see a tapestry of delicate life—not the luxuriant design of a book of hours[2] by any means, but a tapestry nonetheless, designed by a spare modern artist. What grows there hugs the earth firmly with its extended system of roots above which the plant life is delicate but determined. After rain there is an explosion of growth. Nut-flavored green grass puts up the thinnest of green spears. Wild grains appear, grains which develop bleached gold ears as they ripen. Purple desert peas weave through the green and gold, and bright yellow bachelor's buttons cover acres at a time, like fields planted with mustard. Closest to the earth is trefoil clover, whose tiny, vivid green leaves and bright flowers creep along the ground in spring, to be replaced by a harvest of seed-filled burrs in autumn—burrs which store within them the energy of the sun as concentrated protein. At the edges of pans of clay, where the topsoil has eroded, live waxy succulents bearing bright pink and purple blooms, spreading like splashes of paint dropped in widening circles on the earth.

Above the plants that creep across the ground are the bushes, which grow wherever an indentation in the earth, scarcely visible to the eye, allows for the concentration of more moisture from the dew and the reluctant rain. There is the ever-present round mound of prickly weed, which begins its life a strong acid green with hints of yellow, and then is burnt by the sun or the frost to a pale whitish yellow. As it ages, its root system weakens so that on windy days the wind will pick it out of the earth and roll it slowly and

---

[1]A state in southeastern Australia.
[2]Lavishly illuminated medieval prayer book.

majestically about like whirling suns in a Van Gogh painting. Where the soil contains limestone, stronger bushes grow, sometimes two to three feet high, with the delicate narrow-leaved foliage of arid climates, bluish green and dusty grey in color, perfectly adapted to resist the drying sun. Where the soil is less porous and water will lie for a while after rain, comes the annual saltbush, a miraculous silvery-grey plant which stores its own water in small balloonlike round leaves and thrives long after the rains have vanished. Its sterner perennial cousin, which resembles sagebrush, rises on woody branches and rides out the strongest wind.

Very occasionally, where a submerged watercourse rises a little nearer the surface of the earth, a group of eucalyptus trees will cluster. Worn and gnarled by wind and lack of moisture, they rise up on the horizon so dramatically they appear like an assemblage of local deities. Because heat and mirages make them float in the air, they seem from the distance like surfers endlessly riding the plains above a silvery wave. The ocean they ride is blue-grey, silver, green, yellow, scarlet, and bleached gold, highlighting the red clay tones of the earth to provide a rich palette illuminated by brilliant sunshine, or on grey days a subdued blending of tones like those observed on a calm sea.

The creatures that inhabit this earth carry its colors in their feathers, fur, or scales. Among its largest denizens are emus, six-foot-high flightless birds with dun-grey feathers and tiny wings, and kangaroos. Kangaroos, like emus, are silent creatures, two to eight feet tall, and ranging in color from the gentlest dove-grey to a rich red-brown. Both species blend with their native earth so well that one can be almost upon them before recognizing the familiar shape. The fur of the wild dogs has the familiar yellow of the sunbaked clay, and the reptiles, snakes and goannas, look like the earth in shadow. All tread on the fragile habitat with padded paws and claws which leave the roots of grass intact.

On the plains, the earth meets the sky in a sharp black line so regular that it seems as though drawn by a creator interested more in geometry than the hills and valleys of the Old Testament. Human purposes are dwarfed by such a blank horizon. When we see it from an island in a vast ocean we know we are resting in shelter. On the plains, the horizon is always with us and there is no retreating from it. Its blankness travels with our every step and waits for us at every point of the compass. Because we have very few reference points on the spare earth, we seem to creep over it, one tiny point of consciousness between the empty earth and the overarching sky. Because of the flatness, contrasts are in a strange scale. A scarlet sunset will highlight grey-yellow tussocks of grass as though they were trees. Thunderclouds will mount thousands of feet above one stunted tree in the foreground. A horseback rider on the horizon will seem to rise up and emerge from the clouds. While the patterns of the earth are in small scale, akin to complex needlepoint on a vast tapestry, the sky is all drama. Cumulus clouds pile up over the center of vast continental spaces, and the wind moves them at dramatic pace along the horizon or over our heads. The ever-present red dust of a dry earth hangs in the air and turns all the colors from yellow through orange and red to purple on and off as the clouds bend and refract the light. Sunrise and sunset make up in drama for the fact that there are so few songbirds in that part of the bush. At sunrise, great shafts of gold precede the baroque sunburst. At sunset, the cumulus ranges through the shades of a Turner[3] seascape before the sun dives below the earth leaving no afterglow, but at the horizon, tongues of fire.

Except for the bush canary and the magpie, the birds of this firmament court without the songs of the northern forest. Most are parrots, with the vivid colors and rasping sounds of the species. At sunset, rosella parrots, a glorious rosy pink, will settle on trees and appear to turn them scarlet. Magpies, large black and white birds, with a call close to song, mark the sunrise, but the rest of the day is the preserve of the crows, and the whistle of the hawk and the golden eagle. The most startling sound is the ribald laughter of the kookaburra, a species of kingfisher, whose call resembles demonic laughter. It is hard to imagine a kookaburra feeding St. Jerome[4] or accompanying St. Francis.[5] They belong to a physical and spiritual landscape which is outside the imagination of the Christian West.

The primal force of the sun shapes the environment. With the wind and the sand it bakes and cleanses all signs of decay. There is no cleansing by water. The rivers flow beneath the earth, and rain falls too rarely. In the recurring cycles of drought the sand and dust flow like water, and like the floods of other climates they engulf all that lies in their path. Painters find it hard to capture the shimmer of that warm red earth dancing in the brilliant light, and to record at the same time the subtle greens and greys of the plants and trees. Europeans were puzzled by the climate and vegetation, because the native eucalyptus trees were not deciduous. The physical blast of the sun in hot dry summers brought plants to dormancy. Slow growth followed in autumn, and a burst of vigorous growth after the brief winter rainy season. Summer was a time of endurance for all forms of life as moisture ebbed away and the earth was scorched. Winter days were like summer in a northern climate, and spring meant the onset of unbroken sunshine. On the plains, several winters might go by without a rainy season, and every twenty years or so the rain might vanish for a decade at a time. When that happened, the sun was needed to cleanse the bones of dead creatures, for the death toll was immense.

[3]William Turner (1775–1851), British painter known for romantic seascapes and landscapes.
[4](341–420); lived as a hermit in the Syrian desert and was, according to legend, esteemed by wild animals.
[5](1181–1226); from Assisi in Italy. St. Francis was known for his affinity for the poor, animals, and the natural world.

The oldest known humans on the continent left their bones on the
western plains. Nomadic peoples hunted over the land as long as forty
thousand years ago. They and their progeny left behind the blackened stones
of ovens, and the hollowed flat pieces of granite they carried from great
distances to grind the native nardoo grain. Their way of life persisted until
white settlers came by bullock wagon, one hundred and thirty years ago, to
take possession of the land. They came to graze their flocks of sharp-hooved
sheep and cattle, hoping to make the land yield wealth. Other great inland
grasslands in Argentina, South Africa, or North America were settled by
pastoralists[6] and ranchers who used forced labor: Indian peons, Bantus, or
West African slaves. On Australia's great plains there were no settled native
people to enslave. The settlers moved onto the plains long after the abandonment of transportation from Great Britain, the last form of forced labor
available in the Antipodes. As a result, the way of life that grew up for white
settlers was unique.

A man could buy the government leasehold for hundreds of thousands
of acres of grassland at a modest price if he settled the land and undertook
to develop it. Others, beyond the reach of government scrutiny, simply
squatted with their flocks on likely-looking land. The scale of each holding
was beyond European dreams of avarice. Each settler could look out to the
vacant horizon knowing that all he saw was his. To graze the unfenced land
required a population of sheepherders, or, as they came to be called, boundary riders. A settler would need twelve to fifteen hands for his several hundred
thousand acres, but most would live out on the "run" (sheep run) at least
a day's ride from the main settlement. The hands were solitary males, a
freewheeling rural proletariat, antisocial, and unconcerned with comfort or
the domestic pleasures. Their leisure went in drink and gambling, and their
days in a routine of lonely and backbreaking work. The main house would
be spare and simple also, its roof of iron and its walls of timber laboriously
transported from the coast. The garden would be primitive and the boss's
recreations would be little different from his hands'. If he shared his life with
a wife and children, they lived marginally on the edge of his world of male
activity. There was no rain for orchards, no water for vegetable gardens, and
no society for entertaining. Women worked over wood stoves in 100 degree
heat and heated water for laundry over an open fire. There was little room
for the culinary arts, because everyone's diet was mutton and unleavened
bread, strong black tea, and spirits. The ratio of women to men was as
distorted in this wave of settlement as anywhere in the settlement of the New
World.

The bush ethos which grew up from making a virtue out of loneliness and
hardship built on the stoic virtues of convict Australia. Settled life and
domesticity were soft and demoralizing. A "real man" despised comfort and
scorned the expression of emotion. The important things in life were hard

[6]Herdsman.

work, self-sufficiency, physical endurance, and loyalty to one's male friends, one's "mates." Knowledge about nature, the care of animals, practical mechanics was respected, but speculation and the world of ideas were signs of softness and impracticality. Religion and belief in a benevolent deity were foolish because daily life demonstrated beyond doubt that the universe was hostile. The weather, the fates, the bank that held the mortgage, bushfires— disaster in some form—would get a man in the end. When disaster struck what mattered was unflinching courage and the refusal to consider despair.

Very few women could stand the isolation. When a settler prospered, his wife and children moved to a distant but comfortable rural town, where there were schools for the children and companionship for their mother. If he did not prosper, she was likely to be overwhelmed by loneliness. Nothing interrupted the relentless routine of hard labor, the anxiety of illness far from hope of help, the certainty of enervating summer heat, frosty winter cold, and the pervasive anxiety of disaster looming. Disaster could strike swiftly—some little-understood disease might wipe out the investment in the flock or the herd; a man or a child could die from snakebite, a tetanus-infected wound, a fall from a horse. Or disaster could set in slowly with the onset of drought. It was ever-present and a woman at home alone all day had time to think about it. Some took despairingly to drink, some fell into incurable depression, others told their husbands they could not endure it and left for the city.

The ideal woman was a good manager—no small task with only wood stoves, kerosene lamps, inadequate water, and the nearest store for canned goods fifty to a hundred miles away. She was toughened by adversity, laughed at her fears, knew how to fix things which broke in the house, and stifled any craving she might once have had for beauty. She could care for the sick, help fight a bushfire, aid a horse or cow in difficult labor, laugh and joke about life's absurdities and reverses, and like a man, mock any signs of weakness or lack of stoicism in her children. Everyone knew the most important gift to a child was an upbringing which would toughen him (her) up so as to be stoic and uncomplaining about life's pains and ready for its reverses. The sons of the outback made great soldiers in modern wars because they had been prepared for them since infancy. The daughters lacked such a calling.

The pattern of the year followed the seasons. If the rains came, they fell in the winter. Lambing was planned for the spring, when the grass was at its best, and the last winter showers might have left some tender growth for young lambs to nibble before their teeth developed. If seasons cooperated, the lambs were well grown, able to walk great distances for their food and water by the time the summer set in. In February, before the summer reached its peak, the lambs were shorn, and the faces and withers of the grown sheep were trimmed so that flies could not infest the places where sweat and urine soiled their fleeces. In June, in midwinter,[7] when it was less harmful to move

[7]The winter months in Australia are the same as the summer months in the northern hemisphere.

the animals over distances and hold them penned in yards, the grown sheep were brought to a shearing shed and shorn. If there had been an uninterrupted supply of nourishment through the year, their fleece would be seven inches thick, unstained by dust, and carrying an unbroken staple that meant it could be easily combed to spin the finest yarn. If the land they grazed did not carry enough herbage throughout the year, the staple of their fleeces would show a break to mark the point where the food supply had faltered. When the staple was broken it could not be so easily combed, and the yarn it produced, being of less high quality, sold for less. If there were too many breaks it might not repay the cost of producing it.

A pastoralist could follow several economic strategies. Fewer sheep could be grazed over a set area of land, moved to fresh pasture whenever their nourishment required, and thus produce smaller amounts of more valuable wool. More sheep could be grazed over land they would crop bare in a year, for a larger volume of less valuable wool. The land which was grazed out each year succumbed quickly to drought. The land which was grazed in careful rotation might not succumb for as long as four or five years, for the unbroken root systems of the plants would hold the ground. One thing was certain. If the drought was long enough, sheep and cattle would, in their hunger, drag up the roots of the herbage, their sharp hooves would loosen the topsoil, and it would begin to blow away in the wind. The grasslands the earliest settlers saw had never been cropped by ruminant animals. No sharp hooves had ever disturbed the soil. It looked rich and indestructible, but in reality it was one of the most delicately balanced environments on the planet.

*   *   *

Understanding What You Read

1. What is suggested in this piece about the relationship between a place and the people who live there?
2. The part of Australia that Conway describes was settled first by convicts and then by adventurous people lured there by the promise of thousands of acres. How were they changed by the harsh climate and unyielding land they found there?
3. What was life like for women in this environment?

Writing About What You Read

1. Imagine you are a woman living in the outback. Write a letter to your sister in England describing your life. Or imagine that you are a landowner in New South Wales writing to your younger brother who wants to come to Australia to acquire land and raise sheep. Write a letter to

him either encouraging or discouraging him, but in either case explaining what he will find if he comes.

2. Write an essay about a place (perhaps where you were raised) that helped shape your character.

GRETEL EHRLICH

Ehrlich (b. 1946) went to Wyoming to make a film about sheepherders in 1976, and she soon learned to brand, herd, calve, and lamb. Drawn to the sweeping Wyoming landscape and its people, she stayed and married a rancher. She and her husband now live on a ranch in northern Wyoming. Firsthand experience of the difficult work of a ranch hand was the inspiration for her first book, *The Solace of Open Spaces* (1985). "About Men," one of the twelve essays in that book, provides a new perspective on the men known as cowboys and how they relate to the harsh Western environment, to the people they work with, and to the animals they care for.

About Men

WHEN I'M in New York but feeling lonely for Wyoming I look for the Marlboro ads in the subway. What I'm aching to see is horseflesh, the glint of a spur, a line of distant mountains, brimming creeks, and a reminder of the ranchers and cowboys I've ridden with for the last eight years. But the men I see in those posters with their stern, humorless looks remind me of no one I know here. In our hellbent earnestness to romanticize the cowboy we've ironically disesteemed his true character. If he's "strong and silent" it's because there's probably no one to talk to. If he "rides away into the sunset" it's because he's been on horseback since four in the morning moving cattle and he's trying, fifteen hours later, to get home to his family. If he's "a rugged individualist" he's also part of a team: ranch work is teamwork and even the glorified open-range cowboys of the 1880s rode up and down the Chisholm Trail[1] in the company of twenty or thirty other riders. Instead of the macho, trigger-happy man our culture has perversely wanted him to be, the cowboy is more apt to be convivial, quirky, and softhearted. To be "tough" on a ranch has nothing to do with conquests and displays of power. More often than not, circumstances—like the colt he's riding or an unex-

---

[1]Route from Texas to the railheads in Kansas over which millions of cows were driven to market.

pected blizzard—are overpowering him. It's not toughness but "toughing it out" that counts. In other words, this macho, cultural artifact the cowboy has become is simply a man who possesses resilience, patience, and an instinct for survival. "Cowboys are just like a pile of rocks—everything happens to them. They get climbed on, kicked, rained and snowed on, scuffed up by wind. Their job is 'just to take it,' " one old-timer told me.

A cowboy is someone who loves his work. Since the hours are long—ten to fifteen hours a day—and the pay is $30 he has to. What's required of him is an odd mixture of physical vigor and maternalism. His part of the beef-raising industry is to birth and nurture calves and take care of their mothers. For the most part his work is done on horseback and in a lifetime he sees and comes to know more animals than people. The iconic myth surrounding him is built on American notions of heroism: the index of a man's value as measured in physical courage. Such ideas have perverted manliness into a self-absorbed race for cheap thrills. In a rancher's world, courage has less to do with facing danger than with acting spontaneously—usually on behalf of an animal or another rider. If a cow is stuck in a boghole he throws a loop around her neck, takes his dally (a half hitch around the saddle horn), and pulls her out with horsepower. If a calf is born sick, he may take her home, warm her in front of the kitchen fire, and massage her legs until dawn. One friend, whose favorite horse was trying to swim a lake with hobbles on, dove underwater and cut her legs loose with a knife, then swam her to shore, his arm around her neck lifeguard-style, and saved her from drowning. Because these incidents are usually linked to someone or something outside himself, the westerner's courage is selfless, a form of compassion.

The physical punishment that goes with cowboying is greatly under-played. Once fear is dispensed with, the threshold of pain rises to meet the demands of the job. When Jane Fonda asked Robert Redford (in the film *Electric Horseman*) if he was sick as he struggled to his feet one morning, he replied, "No, just bent." For once the movies had it right. The cowboys I was sitting with laughed in agreement. Cowboys are rarely complainers; they show their stoicism by laughing at themselves.

If a rancher or cowboy has been thought of as a "man's man"—laconic, hard-drinking, inscrutable—there's almost no place in which the balancing act between male and female, manliness and femininity, can be more natural. If he's gruff, handsome, and physically fit on the outside, he's androgynous at the core. Ranchers are midwives, hunters, nurturers, providers, and conservationists all at once. What we've interpreted as toughness—weathered skin, calloused hands, a squint in the eye and a growl in the voice—only masks the tenderness inside. "Now don't go telling me these lambs are cute," one rancher warned me the first day I walked into the football-field-sized lambing sheds. The next thing I knew he was holding a black lamb. "Ain't this little rat good-lookin'?"

So many of the men who came to the West were southerners—men

4

looking for work and a new life after the Civil War—that chivalrousness and strict codes of honor were soon thought of as western traits. There were very few women in Wyoming during territorial days, so when they did arrive (some as mail-order brides from places like Philadelphia) there was a stand-offishness between the sexes and a formality that persists now. Ranchers still tip their hats and say, "Howdy, ma'am" instead of shaking hands with me.

Even young cowboys are often evasive with women. It's not that they're Jekyll and Hyde creatures—gentle with animals and rough on women—but rather that they don't know how to bring their tenderness into the house and lack the vocabulary to express the complexity of what they feel. Dancing wildly all night becomes a metaphor for the explosive emotions pent up inside, and when these are, on occasion, released, they're so battery-charged and potent that one caress of the face or one "I love you" will peal for a long while.

The geographical vastness and the social isolation here make emotional evolution seem impossible. Those contradictions of the heart between re-spectability, logic, and convention on the one hand, and impulse, passion, and intuition on the other, played out wordlessly against the paradisical beauty of the West, give cowboys a wide-eyed but drawn look. Their lips pucker up, not with kisses but with immutability. They may want to break out, staying up all night with a lover just to talk, but they don't know how and can't imagine what the consequences will be. Those rare occasions when they do bare themselves result in confusion. "I feel as if I'd sprained my heart," one friend told me a month after such a meeting.

8　　My friend Ted Hoagland[2] wrote, "No one is as fragile as a woman but no one is as fragile as a man." For all the women here who use "fragileness" to avoid work or as a sexual ploy, there are men who try to hide theirs, all the while clinging to an adolescent dependency on women to cook their meals, wash their clothes, and keep the ranch house warm in winter. But there is true vulnerability in evidence here. Because these men work with animals, not machines or numbers, because they live outside in landscapes of torrential beauty, because they are confined to a place and a routine embel-lished with awesome variables, because calves die in the arms that pulled others into life, because they go to the mountains as if on a pilgrimage to find out what makes a herd of elk tick, their strength is also a softness, their toughness, a rare delicacy.

Understanding What You Read

1. What tasks traditionally performed by women do cowboys perform routinely?
2. In what sense is the cowboy androgynous?
3. How do cowboys relate to women?

[2]See headnote on page 238.

Writing About What You Read

Compare the image of the Marlboro man with Ehrlich's understanding of cowboys.

DONALD WALKER, JR.

Walker (b. 1939) lives in Oakridge, Oregon. The following is Walker's account of his experiences, submitted to the *Wall Street Journal* and published on May 15, 1992. At that time there was considerable controversy between loggers and environmentalists committed to saving the old-growth forests in the American Northwest, the habitat of the endangered spotted owl. Federal officials have since authorized logging in some areas there, and banned it in others. This compromise left both sides dissatisfied.

A Logger's Story

My name is Donald Walker, Jr.

For 30 years, I was an Oregon logger. I have been out of work since August 1989, when the company I worked for closed out its operations near Oakridge, where my wife and I live.

Times have been pretty tough since then, though I think we have been luckier than many woodworkers. We still have our home, where we raised our children. Many younger loggers, with small children at home, have lost everything as a result of the spotted owl controversy that has tied Congress in knots.

My wife has an office job with the same company I worked for, but she had to accept a transfer to another office a four-hour drive from home. Now we see each other only on weekends. 4

It gets pretty lonely here without her, but our faith in God has kept us strong, and we continue to hope for better days when we can be together again like a family should be.

After I lost my job I took some courses at a local community college, thinking that I might be able to make a new start in life. I figured my best hope was to learn enough to start some sort of small business that was related to my 30 years of woods experience.

I took welding, some small business classes and a couple of courses in interpersonal communications. Can you imagine a logger in an interpersonal communications class!

8   Community college helped me a lot personally, but starting over when you are 55 years old isn't easy. Since 1989 the only work I've been able to find is as a part-time caretaker on some private timber land near here.

I've also worked seasonally as a yew bark collector for an outfit that has a contract with a big drug company that is searching for a cure for cancer. They think Taxol, which comes from yew bark, might be a miracle cancer cure.

I also work on the family tree farm, and that is the other part of this story.

My dad and my grandad bought this farm in 1932. Our family has been logging it for 60 years. We've replanted as we've gone along, or converted the land to fields where we graze a few cattle.

12   Our land was burned badly in a fire in 1912, so we don't have any of the old growth timber Oregon is famous for. None of our trees are more than 80 years old.

One of the hopes I have held on to since I lost my job is that I could supplement our income by continuing to manage our tree farm as my father and grandfather did for so many years. But it doesn't look like this is going to pan out either.

Last November, I received a letter from an outfit called the Forest Conservation Council telling me that if I cut any more timber on our land it would sue me for violating the Endangered Species Act, which protects spotted owls, and makes it a crime to tamper with their habitat.

I have never seen a spotted owl on our place, and I have never met anyone from the Forest Conservation Council. So far as I know, it's never even been on our farm. But I do have a typewritten, single-spaced four-page letter from their lawyer saying that what we have been doing on our tree farm for 60 years is no longer legal.

16   I might have felt a little bit better about the letter if they had offered to buy the land, or at least pay the taxes, which we have also been doing for 60 years. But they didn't and I guess I'm not surprised. From what I've read about these people, they don't believe in private property rights.

About 200 Oregon tree farmers got the same letter I got. There are actually many more tree farmers in Oregon, but for some reason we were singled out. It got me to thinking about how what has happened to us could happen to any private property owner. In fact, the newspapers are filled with stories like ours. It's happening to people all over the United States.

There is even a Supreme Court case now, involving a fellow in South Carolina who paid almost a million dollars for a couple of beachfront lots he has been told he can't build on because somebody thinks the land should be left to nature.

A lot of news reporters have visited our place since we got our letter from the Forest Conservation Council. I think they're impressed with the beauty of our farm, but I'm afraid they don't grasp the significance of what is happening to us, or to other private landowners across the country. Do they understand that the right of ownership of private property is fundamental to our democracy? I don't think so. I think they are too busy collecting what are called six-second sound bites, and that is not something I am very good at.

Some people say we should cut down all our trees now, while we still can, before the Forest Conservation Council letter becomes a court case. But we don't want to. We're conservationists. This tree farm is our home, and the trees are a part of our way of life. We work with nature to grow a crop the nation needs. The crop is wood. It puts food on our tables. 20

In 26 years of married life, we have never been late on a bill we owed. The pressure on us now is hard to describe. My wife won't even read the newspaper anymore, because it's filled with stories about loggers losing everything, and preservationists filing more lawsuits.

Where does it all end? Do people count anymore? Do private property rights still have meaning in America? Who will compensate us for our loss? The public? The Forest Conservation Council? So far, I haven't heard from anyone except the property tax collector.

The problem isn't the owl, or even old growth for that matter. The problem is an out-of-control preservationist movement that doesn't care about people or their rights.

Our tree farm is our last hope. It is worth fighting for, and I intend to fight for it every way I know how. 24

Understanding What You Read

1. What details of Donald Walker, Jr.'s, story make you particularly sympathetic to his plight?
2. Is there anything he says that does not strengthen his case?
3. What is the effect of his mentioning the Supreme Court case in South Carolina?
4. Do you think he should be compensated for his losses? If so, who should pay?

Writing About What You Read

1. Write a proposal for compensating Donald Walker, Jr., and others like him for what they have lost because of changes in government policy.
2. Write an essay in which you argue that society does (or does not) have the responsibility for those who lose property or income because of government policies.

KATHLEEN NORRIS

Norris (b. 1947) has lived for some twenty years in Lemmon, South Dakota, and she has spent considerable time doing research at the Institute for Ecumenical Research in Collegeville, Minnesota. She is the author of two books of poetry, *Falling Off* (1971) and *The Middle of the World* (1981). "Rain" is from *Dakota: A Spiritual Geography* (1993).

Rain

> Above all, it is a land in serious need of rain.
> —WILLIAM C. SHERMAN, *Plains Folk*

UNTIL I MOVED to western South Dakota, I did not know about rain, that it could come too hard, too soft, too hot, too cold, too early, too late. That there could be too little at the right time, too much at the wrong time, and vice versa.

I did not know that a light rain coming at the end of a hot afternoon, with the temperature at 100 degrees or more, can literally burn wheat, steaming it on the stalk so it's not worth harvesting.

I had not seen a long, slow rain come at harvest, making grain lying in the swath begin to sprout again, ruining it as a cash crop.

4 Until I had seen a few violent hailstorms and replaced the shingles on our roof twice in five years, I had forgotten why my grandmother had screens made of chicken wire for all the windows on the west side of her house.

I had not seen the whimsy of wind, rain, and hail; a path in a wheatfield as if a drunken giant had stumbled through, leaving footprints here and there. I had not seen hail fall from a clear blue sky. I had not tasted horizontal rain, flung by powerful winds.

I had not realized that a long soaking rain in spring or fall, a straight-down-falling rain, a gentle, splashing rain, is more than a blessing. It's a miracle.

An old farmer once asked my husband and me how long we'd been in the country. "Five years," we answered. "Well, then," he said, "you've seen rain."

Understanding What You Read

1. How many kinds of rain does Norris mention?
2. What special significance does rain have in places where it is scarce or unpredictable?

Writing About What You Read

1. Choose a place that you are familiar with and write an essay about the patterns of rainfall and what rain means to the people who live there.
2. If you live in an urban area, describe the effects of a heavy rainfall on the people there.
3. If you have experienced drought, write an essay about how it affects daily life.

MARJORIE SHOSTAK

Shostak (b. 1945) is an anthropologist who has worked with the !Kung San (Bushmen), a semitraditional hunting and gathering people on the northern fringe of the Kalahari desert in Botswana. Over the course of several field trips, she has explored what it means to be a !Kung woman. "Life in the Bush" is from *Nisa* (1981), a highly acclaimed and widely read book about one remarkable woman and her fascinating world.

Life in the Bush

THE NORTHERN FRINGE of the Kalahari desert[1] is a capricious and demanding environment. Total rainfall of the wet season can vary from as much as forty to as little as five inches from one year to the next. Forty inches fills depressions in the land and forms pools that often remain full for weeks or even months. Travel to distant places is easy, and people are able to disperse in small groups over the area in search of game and other food. Lesser-known plants, seen only once in several years, flourish, but some of the more basic foods may drown. Continuous rains may even cause the fruit of the staple food, the protein-rich mongongo nut, to rot; even worse, rare heavy downpours early in the season may damage the mongongo flowers before they bear fruit.

Five inches of rain, in contrast, is a drought condition, and many of the edible plants gathered by !Kung women may not be found. Severe drought occurs in the Dobe area on the average of one year in four. Knowing where permanent water springs are located, being able to see the shriveled vines that signal large water-storing roots hidden several feet under the ground, remembering the partially enclosed recesses of the thick mongongo and morula tree

[1]Located in Botswana, South Africa, and Namibia.

trunks that hide trapped water, can mean survival. All of this is compounded by the geographical variability of rainfall within one season; one area may receive twice as much as another just a few miles away.

An untrained visitor set down in this sand-and-thorn scrub brush on a typical spring day (September to November) would first look for some shade, and would be grateful to find some where the temperature was only 100°F. The visitor might not see water anywhere, and might find little if anything to eat. Even in the middle of the nut groves, with hundreds of thousands of mongongo nuts lying on the ground, the newcomer might go hungry; it would be necessary to find stones strong enough to crack the quarter-inch shell, then to determine how to hold the nut between the stones and, without smashing a finger, to hit it with just enough power in just the right spot to make it crack along the fault line, releasing the filbert-sized nut inside.

4 Suppose an animal were sighted and suppose further that the visitor had had the foresight to have fashioned arrowheads from bone remnants, shafts for the arrows from a tall, reedlike grass, poison from the larvae of a certain beetle, a bow from a partly dried green branch, and a string from fibrous plant threads rolled into twine. Even for such a well-prepared visitor, it would take the most extraordinary luck to make a hit without years of training and experience in tracking, stalking, and shooting. And even then, how long might it take for the animal to die? Hours? Days? Would the visitor be able to follow its tracks? To find enough plant food to survive in the meantime?

Even the !Kung average only one kill for every four days of hunting. The hunter must know how to read animal tracks—to know when they were made and what species of animal made them, as well as the animal's age, size, and condition of health. The quarry must not only be tracked but stalked, and the hunter must understand the vagaries of the wind in order to get close enough for a clear shot. If the arrow strikes, he must determine how far the poisoned shaft has entered, how long the animal will take to die, and where it is likely to travel as it dies. If the animal is large, the hunter may go back to the village for the night, and return the next day with others to help. They will pick up the tracks again, find the animal, and, if it is not yet dead, kill it with spears. If already dead, the animal may have attracted lions, leopards, hyenas, jackals, wild dogs, or vultures, separately or in combination, and these will have to be chased away, sometimes at great risk. The carcass will then be butchered and the skin carefully removed to be tanned later and made into clothing or blankets. The liver will be roasted and eaten immediately and the rest of the meat prepared for carrying back. Nothing will be left behind or wasted.

A man's hunting skills and inclinations are fostered early in childhood, often beginning when he is only a toddler. Toy bows and arrows are typically given to small children, usually by children not much older than themselves. Stationary objects are their first targets. Soon moving ones, such as grasshoppers and beetles, are added. As boys get older, they improve their aim by throwing sticks and wooden spears. Their mastery of animal tracks, like their ability to identify the hundreds of plant and animal species in the environment, is a slow process, acquired through practice and observation. Much of the animal lore so necessary to success in the hunt is learned from discussions of present and past hunts. Around the age of twelve boys are given their first quivers—with small bows and arrows—by their fathers, and begin to shoot birds and rabbits. They may also be taught to set snares. The next step is to accompany their fathers, uncles, and older brothers when they go out to hunt.

Hunts are often dangerous. The !Kung face danger courageously, but they do not seek it out or take risks for the sake of proving their courage. Actively avoiding hazardous situations is considered prudent, not cowardly or unmasculine. Young boys, moreover, are not expected to conquer their fear and act like grown men. To unnecessary risks the !Kung say, "But a person could die!"

These attitudes became clear to me as I heard the description of a kill witnessed by Kashe, a boy about twelve years old, and his cousin. Prior to this, the two boys' experience with hunting had been only in play. This time they accompanied their fathers on a real hunt. When they returned, Kashe and his father came to our camp to give us a present of meat from a large gemsbok they had killed. As we celebrated their good fortune (and ours) and talked about the details of the hunt, a broad smile never left Kashe's face. His father reviewed the events—how, after they had struck it with an arrow and had run after it, the gemsbok had finally stood and fought, and how fiercely it had warded off their spears with its long, razor-sharp antlers. Kashe, listening, seemed beside himself with excitement and pride. I asked, "Did you help?" "No," he replied, "I was up in a tree!" His smile became an easy laugh. Puzzled, I asked again, and he repeated that he and his cousin had climbed a tree as soon as the animal had stopped running and had stood its ground. I teased him, saying everyone would have gone hungry if the animal had been left to him and his cousin. He laughed again and said, "Yes, but we were so scared!" There was no hint of embarrassment or of a need to explain what might have been seen, in our culture, as behavior lacking in courage. Nor was there any suggestion that his fear in this situation reflected anything about how he would act when he was fully grown. There would be plenty of time for him to learn to face dangerous animals and to kill them, and there was no doubt in his mind (or his father's, to judge from the expression on *his* face), that he would, one day. When I questioned the father, he beamed. "Up in the tree? Of course. They're only children. They could have gotten hurt."

A boy is likely to kill his first large animal between the ages of fifteen and eighteen. The culture recognizes this event as a milestone and performs two separate ceremonies to celebrate the killing of the first male and the first female animal. Small ritual tattoos are administered and additional small cuts

8

are made to ensure, symbolically, the strength and success of the boy's future as a hunter. Although now considered eligible for marriage, he may not actually marry for as long as ten years. These years will be spent refining his skills and knowledge of the hunt.

By the age of thirty a man enters the most productive period of his hunting career, which is likely to extend for at least fifteen years. During this time, he will walk between 1,200 and 2,100 miles a year in the pursuit of the fifty-five species of mammals, birds, reptiles, and insects considered edible. He will use various methods to capture animals living above and below the ground, including knocking them down with sticks, snaring them, chasing them with or without dogs, and hunting them in the classic style with poisoned arrows and spears. Relying on his own and other people's knowledge of environmental conditions, he will decide in which direction the hunters should go on a particular day. He may also pay close attention to magical sources—dreams and divination disks—that are thought to provide information on the whereabouts of animals. These sources will also help give him confidence, suggesting as they do that powerful forces of the "otherworld" are behind him. He may hunt alone or with others. When he hunts with others, he will use secret names to refer to animals being pursued, and the hunters will communicate by hand signals and whistles so as not to disturb the game.

If the hunter is successful in killing a large animal, it will be carefully butchered and brought back to the village. There the meat will be distributed according to well-established rules of precedence. Everyone will receive a portion, directly or indirectly. Meat is highly valued—people may speak of "meat hunger" even when other food is abundant—and meat well laced with fat is especially prized because most desert animals are lean. Since the availability of meat is so uncertain, distributions are emotionally charged events; the size of the portions depends not only on clear issues such as kinship, but on subtle ones such as contribution to the hunt. Matters are further complicated by the tradition that most hunters carry other people's arrows in their quivers alongside their own. The arrow that kills an animal may therefore not belong to the hunter who shot it. According to !Kung custom, the person who owns the arrow is considered the true "owner" of the meat, and the prestigious (and onerous) task of distributing the meat fairly is his (or hers—women sometimes own arrows, as well). Thus the distribution must be handled with great delicacy to insure against insults, real or imagined. Some of the meat may be dried for later consumption, but prodigious amounts will be enthusiastically consumed on the spot. If the hunter is not successful, he may collect some vegetable foods on his way home so as not to come back to the village empty-handed.

12 !Kung men vary widely in their skill at hunting, but different levels of success do not lead to differences in status. Self-deprecation and understatement are rigorously required of the hunter after a successful hunt. This

modesty is in evidence from the moment he enters the village to relay his news. Walking silently, he sits down by a fire—his own or someone else's. He greets people and waits. When they ask, he says, "No, I didn't see anything today. At least, nothing worth talking about." The others, well versed in the rules, press for details: "That nothing you saw . . . did you get close enough to strike it?" Thus the conversation slowly reveals that an eland, a gemsbok, or even a giraffe has been shot. Excitement ripples through the camp as the news spreads; meanwhile, the hunter sits as before, quietly describing the events leading up to the kill. If his demeanor is interpreted as boastful or if his accomplishment is not presented as a mixture of skill and luck, pointed jokes and derision may be used to pressure him back into line. Later, dramatic accounts of the hunt will be given, and other important hunts will be recalled.

The problem for the truly accomplished hunter (or gatherer, musician, healer, and so on) is to perform as well as possible without provoking envy or anger in others. This strain may be decreased by the custom of sharing arrows, which helps to diffuse responsibility for the kill. In addition, a less successful hunter may feel imbued with power when using a more successful hunter's arrows, and this may give him the confidence he needs to succeed. Most hunters also alternate hunting with long periods of inactivity, thereby affording others the opportunity to bring in meat and to receive the praise and attention of the group—for a while.

As he grows older, a hunter starts accompanying younger men on the hunt, helping them to learn the skills and knowledge he has accumulated during his approximately forty years of active experience. By the time he ends his hunting career in his early sixties, he will have killed between 80 and 120 (or more) large game animals as well as hundreds of smaller animals. If he stays in good health, he will eventually shift to setting snares, teaching young boys how to interpret bird and small animal tracks in the bush, and foraging in areas close to the village.

Understanding What You Read

1. What does the capriciousness of rainfall have to do with the necessity of hunting?
2. If you were lost in the Kalahari desert and you encountered a !Kung man and woman, what would you want to learn from each of them in order to survive?

Writing About What You Read

Imagine what your daily life would be like if you were living in the Kalahari desert. What changes do you think it might make in your values and attitudes?

DORIS LESSING

Lessing (b. 1919) lived in the British colony of Rhodesia (present-day Zimbabwe) from the time she was four years old until 1949, when she left for England, where she has lived ever since. Lessing has written highly acclaimed novels ranging in genre from realism to science fiction, as well as significant works of nonfiction. Her early novels, particularly the first volumes of the *Children of Violence* series, expressed concern with the relationship of Europeans to the strange land they attempted to settle through colonization. "No Witchcraft for Sale" is from *African Stories,* a collection of short fiction published in 1964.

No Witchcraft for Sale

THE FARQUARS had been childless for years when little Teddy was born; and they were touched by the pleasure of their servants, who brought presents of fowls and eggs and flowers to the homestead when they came to rejoice over the baby, exclaiming with delight over his downy golden head and his blue eyes. They congratulated Mrs. Farquar as if she had achieved a very great thing, and she felt that she had—her smile for the lingering, admiring natives was warm and grateful.

Later, when Teddy had his first haircut, Gideon the cook picked up the soft gold tufts from the ground, and held them reverently in his hand. Then he smiled at the little boy and said: "Little Yellow Head." That became the native name for the child. Gideon and Teddy were great friends from the first. When Gideon had finished his work, he would lift Teddy on his shoulders to the shade of a big tree, and play with him there, forming curious little toys from twigs and leaves and grass, or shaping animals from wetted soil. When Teddy learned to walk it was often Gideon who crouched before him, clucking encouragement, finally catching him when he fell, tossing him up in the air till they both became breathless with laughter. Mrs. Farquar was fond of the old cook because of his love for her child.

There was no second baby; and one day Gideon said: "Ah, missus, missus, the Lord above sent this one; Little Yellow Head is the most good thing we have in our house." Because of that "we" Mrs. Farquar felt a warm impulse towards her cook; and at the end of the month she raised his wages. He had been with her now for several years; he was one of the few natives who had his wife and children in the compound and never wanted to go home to his kraal, which was some hundreds of miles away. Sometimes a small piccanin[1] who had been born the same time as Teddy could be seen peering from the edge of the bush, staring in awe at the little white boy with

[1]Term used in South Africa to refer to an African child.

his miraculous fair hair and Northern blue eyes. The two little children would gaze at each other with a wide, interested gaze, and once Teddy put out his hand curiously to touch the black child's cheeks and hair.

Gideon, who was watching, shook his head wonderingly, and said: "Ah, missus, these are both children, and one will grow up to be a baas, and one will be a servant"; and Mrs. Farquar smiled and said sadly, "Yes, Gideon, I was thinking the same." She sighed. "It is God's will," said Gideon, who was mission boy. The Farquars were very religious people; and this shared feeling about God bound servant and masters even closer together.

Teddy was about six years old when he was given a scooter, and discovered the intoxications of speed. All day he would fly around the homestead, in and out of flowerbeds, scattering squawking chickens and irritated dogs, finishing with a wide dizzying arc into the kitchen door. There he would cry: "Gideon, look at me!" And Gideon would laugh and say: "Very clever, Little Yellow Head." Gideon's youngest son, who was now a herdsboy, came especially up from the compound to see the scooter. He was afraid to come near it, but Teddy showed off in front of him. "Piccanin," shouted Teddy, "get out of my way!" And he raced in circles around the black child until he was frightened, and fled back to the bush.

"Why did you frighten him?" asked Gideon, gravely reproachful.

Teddy said defiantly: "He's only a black boy," and laughed. Then, when Gideon turned away from him without speaking, his face fell. Very soon he slipped into the house and found an orange and brought it to Gideon, saying: "This is for you." He could not bring himself to say he was sorry; but he could not bear to lose Gideon's affection either. Gideon took the orange unwillingly and sighed. "Soon you will be going away to school, Little Yellow Head," he said wonderingly, "and then you will be grown up." He shook his head gently and said, "And that is how our lives go." He seemed to be putting a distance between himself and Teddy, not because of resentment, but in the way a person accepts something inevitable. The baby had lain in his arms and smiled up into his face: the tiny boy had swung from his shoulders and played with him by the hour. Now Gideon would not let his flesh touch the flesh of the white child. He was kind, but there was a grave formality in his voice that made Teddy pout and sulk away. Also, it made him into a man: with Gideon he was polite, and carried himself formally, and if he came into the kitchen to ask for something, it was in the way a white man uses towards a servant, expecting to be obeyed.

But on the day that Teddy came staggering into the kitchen with his fists to his eyes, shrieking with pain, Gideon dropped the pot full of hot soup that he was holding, rushed to the child, and forced aside his fingers. "A snake!" he exclaimed. Teddy had been on his scooter, and had come to rest with his foot on the side of a big tub of plants. A tree-snake, hanging by its tail from the roof, had spat full into his eyes. Mrs. Farquar came running when she heard the commotion. "He'll go blind," she sobbed, holding Teddy close against her. "Gideon, he'll go blind!" Already the eyes, with perhaps half an hour's sight left in them, were swollen up to the size of fists: Teddy's small white face was distorted by great purple oozing protuberances. Gideon said: "Wait a minute, missus, I'll get some medicine." He ran off into the bush.

Mrs. Farquar lifted the child into the house and bathed his eyes with permanganate. She had scarcely heard Gideon's words; but when she saw that her remedies had no effect at all, and remembered how she had seen natives with no sight in their eyes, because of the spitting of a snake, she began to look for the return of her cook, remembering what she heard of the efficacy of native herbs. She stood by the window, holding the terrified, sobbing little boy in her arms, and peered helplessly into the bush. It was not more than a few minutes before she saw Gideon come bounding back, and in his hand he held a plant.

"Do not be afraid, missus," said Gideon, "this will cure Little Yellow Head's eyes." He stripped the leaves from the plant, leaving a small white fleshy root. Without even washing it, he put the root in his mouth, chewed it vigorously, and then held the spittle there while he took the child forcibly from Mrs. Farquar. He gripped Teddy down between his knees, and pressed the balls of his thumbs into the swollen eyes, so that the child screamed and Mrs. Farquar cried out in protest: "Gideon, Gideon!" But Gideon took no notice. He knelt over the writhing child, pushing back the puffy lids till chinks of eyeball showed, and then he spat hard, again and again, into first one eye, and then the other. He finally lifted Teddy gently into his mother's arms, and said: "His eyes will get better." But Mrs. Farquar was weeping with terror, and she could hardly thank him: it was impossible to believe that Teddy could keep his sight. In a couple of hours the swellings were gone: the eyes were inflamed and tender but Teddy could see. Mr. and Mrs. Farquar went to Gideon in the kitchen and thanked him over and over again. They felt helpless because of their gratitude: it seemed they could do nothing to express it. They gave Gideon presents for his wife and children, and a big increase in wages, but these things could not pay for Teddy's now completely cured eyes. Mrs. Farquar said: "Gideon, God chose you as an instrument for His goodness," and Gideon said: "Yes, missus, God is very good."

Now, when such a thing happens on a farm, it cannot be long before everyone hears of it. Mr. and Mrs. Farquar told their neighbors and the story was discussed from one end of the district to the other. The bush is full of secrets. No one can live in Africa, or at least on the veld, without learning very soon that there is an ancient wisdom of leaf and soil and season—and, too, perhaps most important of all, of the darker tracts of the human mind—which is the black man's heritage. Up and down the district people were telling anecdotes, reminding each other of things that had happened to them.

"But I saw it myself, I tell you. It was a puff-adder bite. The kaffir's[2] arm was swollen to the elbow, like a great shiny black bladder. He was groggy after a half a minute. He was dying. Then suddenly a kaffir walked out of the bush with his hands full of green stuff. He smeared something on the place, and next day my boy was back at work, and all you could see was two small punctures in the skin."

This was the kind of tale they told. And, as always, with a certain amount of exasperation, because while all of them knew that in the bush of Africa are waiting valuable drugs locked in bark, in simple-looking leaves, in roots, it was impossible to ever get the truth about them from the natives themselves.

The story eventually reached town; and perhaps it was at a sundowner party, or some such function, that a doctor, who happened to be there, challenged it. "Nonsense," he said. "These things get exaggerated in the telling. We are always checking up on this kind of story, and we draw a blank every time."

Anyway, one morning there arrived a strange car at the homestead, and out stepped one of the workers from the laboratory in town, with cases full of test-tubes and chemicals.

Mr. and Mrs. Farquar were flustered and pleased and flattered. They asked the scientist to lunch, and they told the story all over again, for the hundredth time. Little Teddy was there too, his blue eyes sparkling with health, to prove the truth of it. The scientist explained how humanity might benefit if this new drug could be offered for sale; and the Farquars were even more pleased: they were kind, simple people, who liked to think of something good coming about because of them. But when the scientist began talking of the money that might result, their manner showed discomfort. Their feelings over the miracle (that was how they thought of it) were so strong and deep and religious that it was distasteful to them to think of money. The scientist, seeing their faces, went back to his first point, which was the advancement of humanity. He was perhaps a trifle perfunctory: it was not the first time he had come salting the tail of a fabulous bush-secret.

Eventually, when the meal was over, the Farquars called Gideon into their living-room and explained to him that this baas, here, was a Big Doctor from the Big City, and he had come all that way to see Gideon. At this Gideon seemed afraid; he did not understand; and Mrs. Farquar explained quickly that it was because of the wonderful thing he had done with Teddy's eyes that the Big Baas had come.

Gideon looked from Mrs. Farquar to Mr. Farquar, and then at the little boy, who was showing great importance because of the occasion. At last he said grudgingly: "The Big Baas want to know what medicine I used?" He

---

[2]Originally referred to Xhosa people of South Africa; now a derogatory term for all black Africans.

spoke incredulously, as if he could not believe his old friends could so betray him. Mr. Farquar began explaining how a useful medicine could be made out of the root, and how it could be put on sale, and how thousands of people, black and white, up and down the continent of Africa, could be saved by the medicine when that spitting snake filled their eyes with poison. Gideon listened, his eyes bent on the ground, the skin of his forehead puckering in discomfort. When Mr. Farquar had finished he did not reply. The scientist, who all this time had been leaning back in a big chair, sipping his coffee and smiling with sceptical good-humor, chipped in and explained all over again, in different words, about the making of drugs and the progress of science. Also, he offered Gideon a present.

There was silence after this further explanation, and then Gideon remarked indifferently that he could not remember the root. His face was sullen and hostile, even when he looked at the Farquars, whom he usually treated like old friends. They were beginning to feel annoyed; and this feeling annulled the guilt that had been sprung into life by Gideon's accusing manner. They were beginning to feel that he was unreasonable. But it was at that moment that they all realized he would never give in. The magical drug would remain where it was, unknown and useless except for the tiny scattering of Africans who had the knowledge, natives who might be digging a ditch for the municipality in a ragged shirt and a pair of patched shorts, but who were still born to healing, hereditary healers, being the nephews or sons of the old witch doctors whose ugly masks and bits of bone and all the uncouth properties of magic were the outward signs of real power and wisdom.

20   The Farquars might tread on that plant fifty times a day as they passed from house to garden, from cow kraal to mealie field, but they would never know it.

But they went on persuading and arguing, with all the force of their exasperation; and Gideon continued to say that he could not remember, or that there was no such root, or that it was the wrong season of the year, or that it wasn't the root itself, but the spit from his mouth that had cured Teddy's eyes. He said all these things one after another, and seemed not to care they were contradictory. He was rude and stubborn. The Farquars could hardly recognise their gentle, lovable old servant in this ignorant, perversely obstinate African, standing there in front of them with lowered eyes, his hands twitching his cook's apron, repeating over and over whichever one of the stupid refusals that first entered his head.

And suddenly he appeared to give in. He lifted his head, gave a long, blank angry look at the circle of whites, who seemed to him like a circle of yelping dogs pressing around him, and said: "I will show you the root."

They walked single file away from the homestead down a kaffir path. It was a blazing December afternoon, with the sky full of hot rain-clouds.

Everything was hot: the sun was like a bronze tray whirling overhead, there was a heat shimmer over the fields, the soil was scorching underfoot, the dusty wind blew gritty and thick and warm in their faces. It was a terrible day, fit only for reclining on a verandah with iced drinks, which is where they would normally have been at that hour.

From time to time, remembering that on the day of the snake it had taken ten minutes to find the root, someone asked: "Is it much further, Gideon?" And Gideon would answer over his shoulder, with angry politeness: "I'm looking for the root, baas." And indeed, he would frequently bend sideways and trail his hand among the grasses with a gesture that was insulting in its perfunctoriness. He walked them through the bush along unknown paths for two hours, in that melting destroying heat, so that the sweat trickled coldly down them and their heads ached. They were all quite silent: the Farquars because they were angry, the scientist because he was being proved right again; there was no such plant. His was a tactful silence.

At last, six miles from the house, Gideon suddenly decided they had had enough; or perhaps his anger evaporated at that moment. He picked up, without an attempt at looking anything but casual, a handful of blue flowers from the grass, flowers that had been growing plentifully all down the paths they had come.

He handed them to the scientist without looking at him, and marched off by himself on the way home, leaving them to follow him if they chose.

When they got back to the house, the scientist went to the kitchen to thank Gideon: he was being very polite, even though there was an amused look in his eyes. Gideon was not there. Throwing the flowers casually into the back of his car, the eminent visitor departed on his way back to his laboratory.

Gideon was back in his kitchen in time to prepare dinner, but he was sulking. He spoke to Mr. Farquar like an unwilling servant. It was days before they liked each other again.

The Farquars made enquiries about the root from their labourers. Sometimes they were answered with distrustful stares. Sometimes the natives said: "We do not know. We have never heard of the root." One, the cattle boy, who had been with them a long time, and had grown to trust them a little, said: "Ask your boy in the kitchen. Now, there's a doctor for you. He's the son of a famous medicine man who used to be in these parts, and there's nothing he cannot cure." Then he added politely: "Of course, he's not as good as the white man's doctor, we know that, but he's good for us."

After some time, when the soreness had gone from between the Farquars and Gideon, they began to joke: "When are you going to show us the snake-root, Gideon?" And he would laugh and shake his head, saying, a little uncomfortably: "But I did show you, missus, have you forgotten?"

Much later, Teddy, as a schoolboy, would come into the kitchen and say:

"You old rascal, Gideon! Do you remember that time you tricked us all by making us walk miles all over the veld for nothing? It was so far my father had to carry me!"

And Gideon would double up with polite laughter. After much laughing, he would suddenly straighten himself up, wipe his old eyes, and look sadly at Teddy, who was grinning mischievously at him across the kitchen: "Ah, Little Yellow Head, how you have grown! Soon you will be grown up with a farm of your own . . ."

Understanding What You Read

1. Why doesn't Gideon object when "Little Yellow Head" harasses his son and calls him a "picannin"?
2. Do the Farquars exhibit racist behaviors and attitudes?
3. What is implied by Gideon's refusal to show the root to the scientist?

Writing About What You Read

1. Indigenous people around the world know about medicinal powers of native plants. Write a paper in which you propose how scientists might go about learning what indigenous people know before their knowledge is lost.
2. Write a paper arguing for the importance of saving the cultures and threatened environments of indigenous peoples.

JONATHAN ADAMS AND THOMAS O. MCSHANE

Adams (b. 1961) and McShane (b. 1956) are both on the staff of the World Wildlife Fund. Adams has traveled extensively in Africa, Asia, and Latin America and written many articles on wildlife conservation. McShane is a forester and has lived and worked in Niger, Malawi, and Gabon. "Miles and Miles of Bloody Africa" is a chapter from their book *The Myth of Wild Africa* (1992).

> How can you tell me I don't belong in a place where I've lived my whole life?
> —JOSHUA NYIRENDA

Miles and Miles of Africa

THE SMALL HERD of elephants roaming Malawi's[1] Vwaza Marsh Game Reserve turned and headed north, perhaps smelling water nearby. A few hundred yards back, some game scouts patrolling the reserve on foot watched as the elephants crossed an opening and then disappeared again into the trees. Suddenly, the scouts heard a gunshot somewhere off in the distance: sound can carry up to three miles in the woodlands of southern Africa. Following such a noise over rough terrain like the Vwaza Marsh takes a great deal of skill and experience, but for the scouts this was familiar territory. Although remote, the Vwaza Marsh Game Reserve, a rich wildlife area in northwest Malawi, near the border with Zambia, is well patrolled.

Malawi's scouts are among the best trained in Africa, and their training paid off here; coming through the bush the scouts were surprised to find not just a dead elephant, an unfortunately common experience, but someone with a gun sitting on the elephant as well. The man was arrested, his weapon and the ivory were confiscated, and he was convicted and sentenced to two years' hard labor or a $200 fine—a substantial amount of money in rural Malawi.

The man the scouts captured was more than sixty years old, and his name was Joshua Nyirenda. He was of small stature, and by the time of his arrest he was a tired old man with a mantle of gray hair. Even faced with a jail term, however, there was still life in his eyes, and the sense that after almost forty years of living off the land in and around Vwaza Marsh Game Reserve, he knew something that the game scouts and the conservationists didn't. This wasn't a protected area, this was home.

The nature of the combatants in the war against poaching has been vastly misrepresented. Few poachers are efficient killing machines armed with automatic weapons, and not all scouts are poorly equipped and poorly trained. Poachers and scouts are more alike than they are different. Both are simply Africans trying to make the best of exceptionally difficult circumstances.

No one, not even Joshua Nyirenda, knows where the name "Vwaza" came from, though it has been suggested that it is the sound of pulling your foot out of the mud—and there is no shortage of mud in this area. Vwaza forms part of a vast expanse of woodland that covers the southern third of Africa, stretching 2,000 miles from Tanzania in the east to Angola in the west, and 1,000 miles from the equatorial rain forests in the north to the arid savannas in the south. This carpet of tall trees and sparse grass is known by its Bantu name, *miombo*, after the species of *Brachystegia* and *Julbernardia* trees—similar in appearance to the oaks of the American West—which

4

[1]A country on the eastern side of south-central Africa, bordering on Zambia, Tanzania, and Mozambique.

dominate the landscape. The miombo woodland is possibly the greatest dry forest on earth.

The miombo woodlands are not well known for their extensive herds of wildlife, nor are they renowned for beautiful landscapes. The woodlands are a flat, monotonous stretch of trees, green and lush during the approximately six-month wet season, but dry and lifeless (most often burnt black) during the dry season. Spotting wildlife in these woodlands can be a challenge: while traveling through miombo in what is now Zimbabwe in 1882, Frederick Selous complained: "There appeared to be no game whatsoever in this part of the country . . . in the course of the day we saw a wart hog and a small herd of zebra." Even animals as large as elephants and buffalo are often obscured behind a wall of vegetation in miombo forests. Perhaps the most common sight is an antelope charging off into the bush, its tail flashing. The back half of an antelope does not make for famous national parks or long stays by tourists. Even those people who have worked for long periods in Africa have little love for miombo—mention the word to a group of African conservationists and they will most likely roll their eyes and groan.

Driving through these woodlands demands nothing so much as the ability to endure numbing boredom; roads stretch on for hundreds of miles without even a curve. Occasionally a small village appears, a few square huts crowded next to the road as if the villagers were grasping for any diversion to break the monotony. Against this unchanging landscape, every mundane thing that happens in these villages seems magnified: the children scream louder, the goats and sheep bleat more insistently. If it wasn't for the fear of crashing into the livestock, or of breaking an axle in a pothole, nothing would keep a driver awake while crossing the miombo. It was the miombo that led an anonymous British official to coin the phrase "miles and miles of bloody Africa," and there is no better way to describe it.

8   The Vwaza region in most ways is typical of the miombo zone. A few hills break up the horizon, but in general its broad, flat terrain covered with forest stretches into the distance. Vwaza, however, has one feature that sets it apart from the surrounding uniformity: water. An extensive area of wetlands bisects Vwaza and provides water throughout the year. Animals for many miles depend on the water in the Vwaza Marsh during the long six-month dry season.

Natural forces and governmental decisions by both colonial and African administrators have for the most part kept man out of Vwaza. The combination of tsetse infestation, competition and crop damage from elephant, buffalo, and hippo, and poor soils mean that much of the region is untouched bush.

Vwaza falls within the great tsetse fly belt that stretches from the Luangwa Valley of Zambia northward into Malawi. Unlike the tsetse elsewhere in Africa, the species found in miombo—*Glossina morsitans*—does not require dense riverine thickets to survive. This species has spread throughout the miombo zone, and limits the number of people and livestock the area can support. Nagana, the cattle disease spread by tsetse, effectively removes any thoughts of rearing livestock, and sleeping sickness is endemic: 5 to 10 percent of the population living in the Vwaza region today tests positive for the disease, the highest prevalence in Africa. Tsetse can be so thick at times that they will cover the bed of a pickup truck traveling through the forest.

With a relatively healthy wildlife population and few people, Vwaza was an obvious choice for classification as a protected area. Colonial administrators first expressed interest in the region in 1956 when they reserved the Vwaza Marsh for themselves as a controlled hunting area. Boundary changes were made over time until 1975, when the government declared the area a game reserve and removed—with small compensation—the last of the small number of people living there.

The Vwaza Marsh Game Reserve now has three game scout camps and twenty scouts to patrol the 380 square miles of protected area. People living around the reserve, some of whom were removed from within, still consider the land theirs—land on which they can eke out a meager living. These are the people we routinely condemn as poachers, though they hardly fit the role we have created for them as the scourges of Africa's wildlife.

Joshua Nyirenda was born in northern Malawi sometime in the early part of this century. His family tended a small farm in an area rich with game. His father was the community hunter responsible for providing meat to his family and close relatives as a supplement to their own crops. The hunting skills and traditions passed from father to son; Joshua went on hunting trips with his father and learned how to trap small game with snares made of vegetable fiber, and how to operate a homemade rifle with hand-cast bullets. Eventually Joshua replaced his father as the primary provider for the family, and began passing the knowledge he had gathered about hunting in the Vwaza Marsh on to his own son.

Joshua, his family, and his neighbors lived in a remote, sparsely populated area on the southern boundary of the Vwaza Reserve. The few widely spaced villages contain mud-and-stick houses surrounded by maize and sweet potato fields. Joshua's extended family in this patriarchal society consisted of his brothers and his sons, and their families. When Joshua said he was hunting with his son, he might have been referring to anyone from a son to a cousin to a nephew to a grandchild. Joshua had the ultimate responsibility of providing for them all.

The importance of children in this society cannot be underestimated. One of the goals of the patriarch was to have as many children as possible, preferably boys as they carry on the family name, wealth, and lineage. "You must have as many children as you can rear; they help you with the work in the fields, they help around the house, they hunt with you, and they bring you joy," Joshua said. They also care for you as you get old. The point of work was to be able to share with your family and your children, and hunting in the reserve provided some of the means of meeting their needs. When he was caught, Joshua was waiting for his son and other members of the community to return to help carry the elephant meat back to the village.

16   The hunting methods Joshua used to bring down that elephant resemble those his great-grandfather might have used, as hunting in this part of Africa has hardly changed with time. Joshua's weapon when he was arrested was an 1844 Tower Musket, a relic of Arab ivory and slaving trips that is now in a museum. His entire hunting party could have stepped out of the 1840s: three men, one musket, one homemade muzzle-loader, no tent, no shoes, and little more than rags for clothing. They had tracked an elephant for days, covering more than 15 miles over rough country before getting a shot at it.

Hunting with old or homemade firearms is a dangerous business. Guns misfire or explode, and Joshua bore the scars of an African hunter: one look at his face was enough to prove that his type of hunting was not for amateurs. Joshua had a gun explode on him twice. He smiled when asked about his injuries. "The first time was with a gun I had made," he explained. "We were hunting and found *nyama* [game], I pulled the trigger and nothing happened—then bang, the back of the gun shot me." At this Joshua crinkled his eyes as though he found it funny. His face was such a patchwork of scars and holes that it was hard to believe he had survived.

Despite his injuries, Joshua remained a formidable man in the bush. His small but well-muscled frame carried him for miles. He knew when and where to burn the underbrush to stimulate a flush of green grass that would draw animals into the open for hunting, and he knew what areas held water throughout the dry season. His knowledge of the Vwaza Marsh and its animals was as detailed and specific as that of someone who has grown up in a small town and knows everybody by name.

Even a hunter as skilled as Joshua, however, could find the miombo a daunting place. In the miombo, unlike the savanna of East Africa, plants dominate over animals. Broad-leaved trees 20 feet high, their crowns touching, are the hallmark of the habitat. The grass can grow to twice the height of a man, but at times it is just ankle-deep scrub. During the dry season, villagers burn off the grass to facilitate movement of their meager cattle and livestock, to stimulate new grass as food for their animals, and to clear the underbrush so they can hunt more readily. These fires—if started when the land is bone dry—burn in immense conflagrations that scorch the trees and leave the land black, dry, and desolate until the next rains, which may not come for four months.

20   The plants have evolved to fill their ecological niches so perfectly that the animals rarely get ahead. Miombo plants are rich in secondary chemicals, tannins, and poisons which can be called up when animals attack. When an animal begins to eat a plant, the plant responds by mobilizing its chemical defense system, producing acidic or foul-smelling oils that drive the feeding

animal away. These chemicals remain in the animal's body for hours, so that in effect plants can limit how much and how often the animals eat.

With the plants full of chemical weapons, the animals do not stand much of a chance. Even so, several unique animals have evolved in the miombo woodland. Among those that Joshua Nyirenda hunted were two antelope species: Liechtenstein's hartebeest and sable antelope. Both have developed the ability to squeeze out their existence from the sparse grasses that grow under the woodland canopy, but there the similarity ends. Liechtenstein's hartebeest looks like an afterthought, a mixture of animal leftovers. The face is long and narrow, with close-set eyes, giving the creature a rather stupid appearance. The hartebeest's horns form a peculiar double curvature like the letter Z, and the animal always looks as though it is standing on a hill, since the front end is much higher than the back.

Even the name "hartebeest" does not fit. It was originally given the designation due to its apparent likeness to other animals that inhabit the savanna regions of the continent. It is now thought that this hartebeest is quite different—an archaic form possibly more closely related to the wildebeest, another animal that resembles something put together from spare parts. As a result, Liechtenstein's hartebeest recently has been reclassified in its own genus, *Sigmocerus.*

The sable antelope, on the other hand, ranks as one of the most graceful and beautiful animals in Africa. A large creature, named for its glossy black color, the sable antelope has long horns running parallel to each other in a graceful and pronounced curve sweeping backward, and a well-developed mane of long, stiff hairs that extends from the top of the neck to the shoulder. The sable antelope thus resembles a noble form of horse.

Both sable antelope and hartebeest are found throughout the miombo woodlands, though usually scattered in small herds. The low population density, and the need for a relatively large area of woodland to support each individual antelope, means that these animals are particularly sensitive to changes in their habitat. As man continues to expand his influence, the antelope have retreated into the most remote areas, often within national parks and protected areas.

24

The habitats for hartebeest and sable antelope were not so remote that they fell outside of Joshua Nyirenda's traditional hunting grounds. Joshua's arrest for killing the elephant was just a passing inconvenience. His extended family paid his fine and he returned home to resume his role as head of the household. A year or so later, another group of game scouts on patrol following up tips from the village and the sound of gunfire found Joshua and his son sitting at a waterhole waiting for animals to come and drink. Since his musket was now a museum piece, Joshua had constructed a muzzle-loading gun from a length of pipe, some carved wood, and a few small pieces of scrap metal. Despite this untrustworthy weapon, Joshua had killed two Liechtenstein's hartebeest, a warthog, a tiny antelope called a duiker, and a bushpig, when he was arrested for the second time. He displayed the same smile, the same acceptance of his fate as on the first occasion. Both times he said, "This is my home."

Joshua and his son were convicted of hunting in the game reserve. Since this was their second conviction, they were given stiffer sentences of $500 fines or five years' hard labor. The family could not afford to pay both fines, so Joshua went to prison while his son returned home to help clear the fields and begin planting the next year's crops. Though both Joshua and his son were skilled hunters, an important and respected position in their world, agriculture remained the focus of their lives. Joshua's age got him out early, and he continued hunting. But this time Malawi's Department of National Parks and Wildlife decided to change their attitude and to use his knowledge of the region to better understand the reserve and the needs of the people around it. So for the first time Joshua began to share his deep understanding of Vwaza with the department. For half a century Joshua Nyirenda was a hunter—some would consider him a poacher—and a provider to his family, but toward the end of his life he formalized something he had always been, a conservationist.

Joshua was educating conservationists who were obsessed with capturing men like himself, and he undoubtedly enjoyed the irony of the situation. Anti-poaching efforts now absorb the majority of the resources available for park management, and dominate popular perceptions about conservation. Such work is widely portrayed as a war—an image that people in and out of Africa perpetuate to raise money. Yet recent research indicates that anti-poaching patrols are less effective at controlling poaching than more basic, and considerably less expensive, investigative techniques.

28   The war on poachers will always fall just a little short of its goals, for no matter how well equipped the game scouts may be, with high-tech tents and camping equipment, radios, helicopters, and airplanes, it will never be enough. More often than not, these items, sophisticated but ill suited to the rigors of the African bush, become excuses for not getting the job done. An all too common complaint made by scouts to their commander is: "Sir, we can't go on patrol today, the radio is buggered." If current trends continue, the war on poaching may soon resemble the war in Vietnam: a massive, well-armed force struggles in vain against a poor but unyielding foe.

Conservationists are gradually recognizing the futility of waging constant war on poachers. The wisest approach may be to make a virtue out of necessity by using the hunting skills of local people. Richard Bell, for example, who worked in Malawi for years before moving to Zambia and co-directing the Luangwa Integrated Resource Development Project (LIRDP), advocates incorporating poaching into conservation. The suggestion, like others Bell has made, is anathema to many conservationists, but it makes sense to capitalize on knowledge and techniques of the local hunters. Bell's plan would encourage poaching for high cash value products—particularly ivory—at the expense of subsistence poaching. Under the plan, the conservation authority would buy the ivory, trophies, skins, and whatever meat is not used locally, and then resell it. Revenue as well as most of the meat thus would go directly to local communities; and the conservation authority would earn money to support its programs, and would be in a better position to control illegal hunting and generally to control the marketplace.

Such a plan obviously depends on the existence of a legal market for ivory. Bell would not only encourage the ivory trade, he would actually reduce the number of game scouts on patrol. Again, this is an idea guaranteed to send a shudder through most Western supporters of conservation. The image of the noble game scout has been repeated so often in the popular media that his effectiveness is taken for granted. The only problem, most people assume, is a lack of funds to send more scouts into the bush, so the idea of cutting the number of scouts seems like surrender.

Bell, however, has the numbers to support his contrary position. Two research efforts, first in Kasungu National Park and later in the area administered by LIRDP, revealed that the best way to stop illegal killing of large mammals, most notably elephants and rhinos, is to employ investigative methods, much like the police, in villages. Most hunting of animals with firearms is practiced by a few village professionals, and it is relatively easy to keep an eye on these people and monitor their movements once they are identified. Following Joshua Nyirenda's arrest, for example, the park authorities monitored his movements to and from the village, leading to his second arrest. The park warden knew when Joshua had entered the game reserve, and had a rough idea of where he had gone, so the anti-poaching patrol had a relatively easy job in catching him.

In the LIRDP area in Zambia, investigations led to nearly four times as many arrests as did patrols, and captured more than five times as many firearms. Given that scouts in the area spent less than one day per month investigating reports of poaching, compared to nearly seven days on patrol, the efficiency of investigations over patrols becomes even clearer. "In terms of arrests, one man-day spent investigating is worth twenty-eight days on patrol," Bell says. "And in terms of capturing firearms, one day spent investigating equals forty-four days on patrol." 32

The cost of carrying out investigations in the villages is much lower and shows better results than equipping a large number of anti-poaching patrols and expecting them to carry out the work themselves. While the patrols in the field still have a role to play, the myth that surrounds the end results of such actions dies slowly and at great expense. Unlike cops on the beat, anti-poaching patrols are not a deterrent by themselves.

Anti-poaching patrols certainly never deterred Joshua Nyirenda. Joshua saw numerous changes over the years in the miombo where he hunted, in animal populations and their distribution, and in the status of the land and those charged with its protection. In the widely accepted story of conservation in Africa, park scouts and poachers are sworn enemies, at opposite ends of the spectrum in terms of their relationship with wildlife. Yet scouts and poachers often live quite similar lives, blurring the line between those who protect wildlife and those who make use of it.

A scout named Henry Kachoyo was among those who heard Joshua's gunshots both times he was arrested. Like most of Malawi's wildlife scouts, Kachoyo was well trained. Scouts in Malawi (unlike those in other parts of Africa) are expected to be able to read and write, and usually must have finished, at least, primary school. They frequently undergo a period of apprenticeship as porters for the more experienced scouts, thereby weeding out those who might have an affinity for life in the bush from those who don't. The scouts are trained in police techniques, the law, and firearm use and safety, and are expected to spend up to twenty-four days a month in the field away from home, usually camping. Rangers, who lead scout groups, are expected to have a secondary school education, and most of them have been trained at one of Africa's wildlife colleges. This background and training makes Malawi's game scouts an effective force, experienced in working in the field and reporting back to their superiors on what they have seen and done.

36 Henry Kachoyo had been a member of Malawi's Department of National Parks and Wildlife for many years before being transferred to the northern part of the country to work in the department's research unit. The government provided him with a uniform, boots, housing, a World War II–vintage .303 rifle for protection, and training. Like Joshua Nyirenda, Henry Kachoyo's main concern was providing for his family. Unlike Joshua, he could not hunt or even collect plant material, since both are illegal in Malawi's protected areas. Henry and his family relied on the government for food and for transport to collect it, something that was not always available. This meant that Henry and his family often resorted to hunting and gathering, just like Joshua. Only instead of being out in the bush, Henry was required to hunt and gather in the local markets, often among people who resented his position and his role in their society. Sometimes food was not available at all, and sometimes the merchants made it available at a higher price.

Working for the government, the department staff usually live far from their friends and extended family, and thus lack the extensive support system to help plant crops, prepare food, and care for the sick. Families such as Henry's may not have the labor to cultivate enough land to feed themselves, and indeed may not cultivate any land at all. What crops they can grow are often damaged by animals. Oddly enough, this description sounds more like the stereotype of how a poacher lives—on the fringes of civilization, with limited contact with family, tribe, or nation.

Occasionally the bad feelings between game scouts and the local people turn especially nasty. One year shortly before Christmas, the scouts of Vwaza Marsh Game Reserve arrested a villager for hunting in the reserve. In the process of bringing him to park headquarters, he escaped back to his village.

Since the scouts know most of the people in the area, they knew where to find him. Crossing the large river which forms the southern boundary of the reserve, the scouts found themselves far outnumbered by an angry mob of villagers. Giving up any hope of trying to retake the man they had arrested, the scouts attempted to retreat. In the heat of the confrontation, someone began throwing stones, and the villagers attacked. Two of the scouts were badly injured and drowned trying to cross the river back into the reserve. When the park authorities found the bodies, they discovered that both had received skull fractures. "Why did it happen? Those were people we buy our food from," one scout who survived said after the incident. Another scout repeated the lament of police everywhere: "We were just doing our job."

Unfortunately, the job of a game scout sometimes means violent conflict between people who share the same history, culture, and values. Both Henry Kachoyo and Joshua Nyirenda grew up in small villages surrounded by family and friends. The difference for Henry was that he finished primary school and ended up not as a farmer in the village but as a game scout hired by the government to patrol Kasungu National Park, not far from his home. Henry had a bottomless curiosity about his natural surroundings, and through his work with a young Zimbabwean researcher he became the department expert in miombo flora. He surrounded himself with books in a constant effort to increase his knowledge. At the time he was posted to the Vwaza Marsh, he was in his mid-forties, a father of nine children. Just starting to turn gray, Henry could march for days in the bush without tiring. When offered a drink of water, he would smile and say, "I'll have a smoke, it kills the thirst," and would light up a cigarette.

Henry Kachoyo's commitment to his work knew no bounds, whether it was research expeditions or anti-poaching patrols. While Joshua Nyirenda's face would light up at the sight of an animal, Henry's would light up at the sight of a plant, practically any plant. At some point during most collecting trips, Henry would come up over a hill, his face breaking into a wide grin and his eyes growing wide, as if he'd just spotted an especially rare and beautiful species. Everyone else on the trail behind him would hurry up to see as well, only to find Henry looking at a rather nondescript tree and saying, "I've never seen that tree in the reserve, we must collect a sample for the office."

While Henry Kachoyo was committed to his work, he was also committed to his family. He never ceased in his efforts to educate his children; it is no mean feat to send nine children to school where school fees and books must be paid on a salary of approximately $175 a month, and of course they must be fed as well. Though his formal schooling was limited, Henry's great desire to learn whatever he could showed him the value of education. His knowledge of plants put him in a position to work around educated people, and his pride was his collection of books. "These are my teachers, and my children's teachers," he would say. He never stopped pushing his children or his colleagues.

By the time Henry Kachoyo was posted to northern Malawi he was the department's botanist, the man who knew the country's vegetation and who could teach it to the younger generation of staff coming up through the system. He was in demand everywhere. Following his work in the Vwaza, he was posted to three other parks and reserves to help with vegetation work before finally going back to Kasungu National Park to be near his home and prepare for retirement. He was even asked to stay on for an extra year or two to train people to follow in his footsteps. There is a small core of Malawians in the Vwaza who are now botanists because of Henry Kachoyo.

The growing expertise of Malawi's park managers is beginning to change conservation in the Vwaza. For the first time, conservation authorities are seeking out the villagers and asking for their opinions. In the village of Filimon Kumwenda, not far from where Joshua Nyirenda lived, the department is no longer just a police force but is becoming a force for development. With support from the German government and WWF, villages are going into the beekeeping and honey production business. Beekeeping is a traditional occupation in Malawi, but it had fallen off over the past 10 years as the human population grew and the forest receded. To revive the practice, Wildlife Department staff trained in beekeeping are working with villagers to help them establish hives in the reserve by forming beekeeping clubs. Before this effort began, the villagers were not allowed into the Vwaza Game Reserve to collect honey. However, they went in despite the law and ended up burning down trees to get at the hives. With improved extraction and marketing techniques, the villagers can now use the reserve without harming the ecosystem, and in return they have promised the Wildlife Department that they will not hunt or collect firewood within the reserve's boundaries.

44

Now that villagers have a stake in the Vwaza, interesting benefits are turning up. Not long ago an elephant was found dead in the reserve, shot by a local hunter. Village members of the Filimon Kumwenda Beekeeping Club provided the information that led to the arrest of the culprit. This success depended on a combination of goodwill toward the park authorities generated by working with the local community and intelligence work in the villages. As a honey cooperative member said: "We found an elephant that had been killed in our reserve. We asked questions in the nearby villages and found out who did it and where the gun was. We told this to the wildlife scouts so they could catch this man. If these people continue to do this, we will not have the reserve for our bees." The gun and ivory were recovered, and the hunter was arrested. It is their new benefits and involvement in decision-making that have brought these Malawians onto the side of conservation.

Joshua Nyirenda did not live to see the advances made by the beekeeping project. He finally ran out of steam and died in his seventies, a ripe old age for someone living in the bush. No doubt today his son, with the same appreciation for the land and what it can provide, is still trying to avoid anti-poaching patrols as he hunts the same land as his father and Joshua's father before him. His family continues to carve out whatever living the land can provide.

Henry Kachoyo retired from the Department of National Parks and Wildlife and returned to his plot of land and the home he had been preparing for some time. He moved back to the land, to a life little different from that of Joshua's family. After his retirement, Henry began suffering from pain in his eyes and headaches. The pain worsened, and suddenly Henry died at fifty-two, leaving a wife, nine children, and one grandchild. Henry died of sleeping sickness, a disease he had contracted from working in remote areas like the Vwaza. And what of his family? A letter from his daughter Joyce sums it up:

> I hope you are doing fine with the weather of U.S.A. moreover from this side, not so bad but cool and warm have accumulated us here.
>
> Actually, the aim of writing this kind of letter to you is to identify ourselves from problems which have occurred here due to the death of our father. Since in his absence I and Oliver Kachoyo left school due to the shortage of fees and clothes. This has been so because, support so that we should educate ourselves in order to help our younger brothers couldn't be found, and you already know the situation of our mother that she is growing older and older and no assistance can be obtained from her, and nine children have been left by our father. This gives our mother a great problem because everyone in our family is walking naked and it gives shame to those who are seeing us. We have no where we could arise our problem.
>
> Finally, I say goodbye and have a nice stay in the U.S.A. together with your family and comrades.

In the end, Henry Kachoyo's family is just like Joshua Nyirenda's, maybe worse off. Both these men loved the bush, both possessed intimate knowledge of the Vwaza, and both had a deep respect for its wildlife. The two men followed different paths, Henry choosing to finish his schooling and pursue a career in government service, but neither strayed far from village life. In the village, Henry and Joshua could have been the best of friends. This story has no heroes and no villains. Ultimately, both Henry and Joshua were just trying to survive.

Understanding What You Read

1. Describe the environment in the Vwaza Marsh Game Reserve. What are the trees like? How do the plants relate to animals?
2. Why do the men who live on the margins of this hostile land want to have many children?
3. How do the plants' chemical defenses affect first the animals and then the people?

4. What is the agriculture like in the villages near the reserve?
5. Explain how the beekeeping project contributed to conservation of the reserve.

Writing About What You Read

1. Make parallel columns listing everything you know about Joshua Nyirenda and Henry Kachoyo. Then write a point-by-point comparison, emphasizing what is similar and what is different about the two men.
2. Adams and McShane compare Joshua Nyirenda's detailed and specific knowledge of the Vwaza Marsh with that of "someone who has grown up in a small town and knows everybody by name" (paragraph 18). If you grew up in a small town, do you think this is a fair comparison? If so, write a paragraph about this aspect of small-town life.

Making Connections

1. Dillard and Walker both write about the place where they were born, but with very different purposes. Compare what you think the purpose of each piece is and how it is accomplished.
2. Explain the similarities and differences between the men who settled New South Wales in Australia ("The West") and those who went to the American West to be cowhands ("About Men").
3. Compare how the "whimsy" of the rain in Norris's South Dakota and the "capricious" rain of the Kalahari ("Life in the Bush") affects the people in the two places.
4. In what way is Joshua Nyirenda's story ("Miles and Miles of Bloody Africa") similar to that of Donald Walker ("A Logger's Story")?
5. The three pieces about Africa ("Life in the Bush," "No Witchcraft for Sale," and "Miles and Miles of Bloody Africa") all deal with "reading" the environment. How do native Africans read and understand their environments? How do foreigners read and misread their environments?

4

It is interesting to contemplate a tangled bank, clothed with many plants of many kinds, with birds singing on the bushes, with various insects flitting about, and with worms crawling through the damp earth, and to reflect that these elaborately constructed forms, so different from each other and dependent upon each other in so complex a manner, have all been produced by laws acting around us.

—CHARLES DARWIN, *The Origin of Species*

♦

The world is a web of interdependent living communities, not a department store.

—CHRISTOPHER MANES, *Green Rage*

♦

We may not become as sophisticated about the land we live upon and its resources as the original inhabitants, those who had forty words for snow or knew every tree in the forest. But any one of us can walk the territory and see what inhabits there, become conscious of the birdsongs and waterfalls and animal droppings, follow a brooklet to a stream and down a river, and learn when to set out tomatoes, what kind of soil is best for celery, and where blueberries thrive.

—KIRKPATRICK SALE, *Dwellers in the Land*

♦

My friend, I am going to tell you the story of my life. . . . It is the story of all life that is holy and is good to tell, and of us two-leggeds sharing it with the four-leggeds and the wings of the air and all green things; for these are children of one mother and their father is one Spirit.

—BLACK ELK, from *Black Elk Speaks*

♦

To make a prairie it takes a clover and one bee,
One clover, and a bee,
And revery.
The revery alone will do,
If bees are few.

—EMILY DICKINSON

BIODIVERSITY

Leaves, Mills College, Oakland, California, 1931
(Ansel Adams)

Introduction

You live in an ecosystem, but if you were asked to plot its boundaries and note all the living things within it, you would have a difficult job. Applying the concept of ecosystem to most parts of the world is, in fact, an imprecise matter, since the features of most landscapes are constantly changing, animals are migrating, and alien plants are replacing endemic ones. Yet we use "ecosystem," knowing the term is impossible to pin down and that its boundaries may well be arbitrary. We mean by it a community of species interacting with each other and the physical environment, even though that combination is never quite the same as it was yesterday or last year.

Many natural factors affect how ecosystems function. Changes in air temperature and content, alterations in rainfall, a volcanic eruption, a hurricane, or even a tornado might alter forever an island, a swamp, or a forest. But by far the most powerful agents of change overall are human beings. Humans have devised any number of ways to alter ecosystems—draining wetlands, fertilizing and spraying crops, developing land for housing and shopping malls, strip-mining for minerals, lumbering, damming, paving, and excavating, to name a few. The deliberate burning of millions of acres of rain forests in Brazil kills untold numbers of species, many of which have never even been identified. And we now know that life communities can be affected by activities many hundreds or even thousands of miles away. A meltdown in a nuclear power plant in Russia may contaminate crops in Europe, and the waste from coal-burning power plants in Ohio is certainly sterilizing lakes and killing trees in New York and Canada.

One of the greatest concerns of many scientists today is that the alteration and destruction of ecosystems are dramatically reducing the earth's biodiversity; species will be lost before their potential value both to humans and to the earth as a whole can be determined. Accelerating this loss of life is rapid growth of the human population, which contributes to all forms of environmental degradation.

No one knows how many species of plants and animals exist. To appreciate the magnitude of human ignorance on this subject, consider how many species you know. Make a list of all the plants, mammals, birds, fish, reptiles, insects, and bacteria that you have seen or know by name. You could stimulate your memory by thinking of smaller groups of animals—rodents, water birds, poisonous snakes, for example—or by thinking of the foods you like and the plants and animals they come from. And don't forget the animals you have seen in the zoo, in movies, and on television. If you take a prescription drug, the odds are one in four that it was derived from a plant. If you worked on it, your list might add up to several hundred species that you know by name. Now consider this: scientists to date have identified some 1.4 million kinds of organisms, and readily acknowledge that this is only a fraction of the total number. According to the evolutionary biologist E. O. Wilson, there are anywhere from five to thirty million plant and animal species. The word "biodiversity"—Wilson's term—encompasses them all.

It is not difficult to understand, in a general way, what biodiversity is. Understanding why it is important is another matter. That question is usually answered in terms of human welfare. For example, the rain forests destroyed today might well contain plants with chemicals that could cure cancer or AIDS, genetic material that could improve agricultural productivity, or substances that could be used to deter pests safely. These arguments are often made by scientists who see the tragedy of lost miracle drugs and new food sources. Others, who think of themselves as "deep ecologists," argue that all forms of life, plant and animal, have the same right to exist that humans do. Deep ecologists value biodiversity for its own sake and see humans simply as members of an ecosystem alongside other species. Not all people who argue for the rights of all living things share the view of the deep ecologists. For some, preservation of species is an ethical matter, a question of right and wrong, or a matter of religious conviction.

The selections in this chapter introduce the concept of interdependence of living things and describe specific ecosystems, some with enormous biodiversity. More than half of the earth's biodiversity is found in tropical rain forests, which cover only 6 to 7 percent of the earth's land surface. Two selections take you to two of the largest and most varied tropical forests on the planet—a rain forest of the Amazon basin and a dipterocarp forest in Borneo.

The beauty of the rain forests and the mystery of the vast variety of unknown species that inhabit them attract both scientists and nonscientists. First-time visitors have endless questions. Why are there so many ants? What are the howler monkeys communicating with their strange and protracted roars? How does a storm affect the structure of the forest? Why is biodiversity essential to the health of such a forest? E. O. Wilson proposes answers to these questions and raises still others in "Storm over the Amazon." And Norman Myers takes his readers on a tour of a rain forest in Borneo, pointing out its amazing diversity.

Farther north, the settling of the American prairie exacted an enormous environmental cost, reducing biodiversity and altering the face of America forever. The rich polyculture of perennial grasses and legumes that once covered the Great Plains was torn from the earth, roots and all, and gradually replaced with fields of corn, wheat, and other monocultures. Repeated plowing of the land has resulted in erosion, depletion of nutrients, vast reduction of biodiversity, and general degradation of the land. Just as there are those bringing the bison back to the American plains, so there are scientists working to restore the prairie by developing combinations of perennial plants that will hold the soil and renew nutrients without being plowed. One of these scientists is Wes Jackson, whose essay "Living Nets in a New Prairie Sea" explores the possibilities of restoring prairies. His short piece "Old *Salsola*" considers one plant's strategies for survival and speculates about its place in a larger ecosystem.

Other selections look at diverse ecosystems—the unique animal life of the Galápagos Islands, the self-renewing lava-rich land of Krakatau, the extraordinary Florida Everglades, a natural river of grass unspoiled when Marjory Stoneman Douglas wrote "Life on the Rock" and now threatened by real estate development, agricultural wastes, and the invasion of alien species such as the melaleuca tree, a highly combustible plant that can actually explode in a fire.

Two ecosystems examined in this chapter are in rather ordinary settings: Sue Hubbell's yard in Arkansas and a Nature Conservancy forest in New England. Yet what happens in each has implications beyond those settings, and raises the question of whether human actions of *any* sort can influence the environment over the long term. In "The Idea of a Garden" Michael Pollan argues that "the concept of an ecosystem is only a metaphor, a human construct imposed upon a much more variable and precarious reality." Faced with uncertainty, Pollan argues, controversially, *for* human alteration of particular ecosystems and, by implication, of the planet as a whole.

DONELLA MEADOWS

A systems analyst and international coordinator of research management institutions, Meadows (b. 1941) holds a Ph.D. in biophysics from Harvard University. She is coauthor of *The Limits to Growth* (1972), which stirred controversy in its insistence that we must limit consumption, and *Beyond the Limits: Confronting Global Collapse* (1992). Since 1982, Meadows has taught in the Environmental Studies Program at Dartmouth. "What Is Biodiversity and Why Should We Care About It?" is from her 1991 book *The Global Citizen.*

What Is Biodiversity and Why Should We Care About It?

M O S T   O F   U S have grasped the idea that there's a hole in the sky over the South Pole that could give us skin cancer. We are beginning to understand that a global warming could inundate Miami Beach and make New York even more unbearable in the summer. There is another environmental problem, however, that doesn't have a catchy name like "ozone hole" or "greenhouse effect," and that hasn't yet entered the public consciousness. It's the loss of biodiversity.

Bio-*what?*

Biodiversity sounds like it has to do with pandas and tigers and tropical rain forests. It does, but it's bigger than those, bigger than a single species or even a single ecosystem. It's the whole, all of life, the microscopic creepy-crawlies as well as the elephants and condors. It's all the habitats, beautiful or not, that support life—the tundra, prairie, and swamp as well as the tropical forest.

4 Why care about tundras and swamps? There's one good reason—self-interest. Preserving biodiversity is not something to do out of the kindness of our hearts, to express our fondness for fuzzy creatures on Sunday mornings when we happen to feel virtuous. It's something to do to maintain the many forms of life we eat and use, and to maintain ourselves.

How would you like the job of pollinating all trillion or so apple blossoms in the state of New York some sunny afternoon in late May? It's conceivable, maybe, that you could invent a machine to do it, but inconceivable that the machine could work as efficiently, elegantly, and cheaply as honeybees, much less make honey.

Suppose you were assigned to turn every bit of dead organic matter—from fallen leaves to urban garbage to road kills—into nutrients that feed new life. Even if you knew how, what would it cost? Uncountable numbers of bacteria, molds, mites, and worms do it for free. If they ever stopped, all life would stop. We would not last long if green plants stopped turning our exhaled carbon dioxide back into oxygen. The plants would not last long if a few beneficent kinds of soil bacteria stopped turning nitrogen from the air into fertilizer.

Human reckoning cannot put a value on the services performed for us by the millions of species of life on earth. In addition to pollination and recycling, these services include flood control, drought prevention, pest control, temperature regulation, and maintenance of the world's most valuable library, the genes of all living organisms, a library we are just learning to read.

8 Another thing we are just learning is that both the genetic library and the ecosystem's services depend on the integrity of the entire biological world. All species fit together in an intricate, interdependent, self-sustaining whole. Rips in the biological fabric tend to run. Gaps cause things to fall apart in unexpected ways.

For example, attempts to replant acacia trees in the Sahel at the edge of the Sahara desert have failed because the degraded soil has lost a bacterium called rhizobium, without which acacia trees can't grow. Songbirds that eat summer insects in North America are declining because of deforestation in their Central American wintering grounds. European forests are more vulnerable to acid rain than American forests because they are human-managed, single-species plantations rather than natural mixtures of many species forming an interknit, resilient system.

Biodiversity cannot be maintained by protecting a few charismatic megafauna in a zoo, nor by preserving a few greenbelts or even large national parks. Biodiversity can maintain itself, however, without human attention or expense, without zookeepers, park rangers, foresters, or refrigerated gene banks. All it needs is to be left alone.

It is not being left alone, of course, which is why biological impoverishment has become a problem of global dimensions. There is hardly a place left on earth where people do not log, pave, spray, drain, flood, graze, fish, plow, burn, drill, spill, or dump.

Ecologists estimate that human beings usurp, directly or indirectly, about 40 percent of each year's total biological production (and our population is on its way to another doubling in forty years). There is no biome, with the possible exception of the deep ocean, that we are not degrading. In poor countries biodiversity is being nickeled and dimed to death; in rich countries it is being billion-dollared to death.

To provide their priceless service to us, the honeybees ask only that we stop saturating the landscape with poisons, stop paving the meadows and verges where bee food grows, and leave them enough honey to get through the winter.

To maintain our planet and our lives, the other species have similar requests, all of which, summed up, are: Control yourselves. Control your numbers. Control your greed. See yourselves as what you are, part of an interdependent biological community, the most intelligent part, though you don't often act that way. Act that way. Do so either out of a moral respect for something wonderful that you did not create and do not understand or out of a practical interest in your own survival.

Understanding What You Read

1. What is biodiversity?
2. What is destroying it?
3. What is necessary to preserve it?

Writing About What You Read

Write a paragraph in which you explain three important services that could be lost through decreases in biodiversity.

E. O. WILSON

The evolutionary biologist Edward O. Wilson is one of America's most distinguished and influential scientists. He currently teaches at Harvard University. Wilson is author of, among other prize-winning books, the best-selling *Sociobiology: The New Synthesis* (1975), a work that aroused controversy for its assertion that genes determine behavior. An authority on social insects, Wilson has expanded a research interest in how ant communities function to a far-reaching considera- tion of how life became so diverse, how little we know about most species, and how human activity is destroying diversity. *Biophilia* (1984), a collection of Wilson's personal essays, reflects his belief that an affinity for life (biophilia) must be the ethical basis for human efforts to preserve diversity. Not content simply to sound the alarm about the threats to biodiversity, Wilson proposes in his most recent book, *The Diversity of Life* (1992), specific actions to preserve and enhance biodiversity. "Storm over the Amazon" is from the opening chapter of that book.

Storm over the Amazon

IN THE Amazon Basin the greatest violence sometimes begins as a flicker of light beyond the horizon. There in the perfect bowl of the night sky, untouched by light from any human source, a thunderstorm sends its pre- monitory signal and begins a slow journey to the observer, who thinks: the world is about to change. And so it was one night at the edge of rain forest north of Manaus, where I sat in the dark, working my mind through the labyrinths of field biology and ambition, tired, bored, and ready for any chance distraction.

Each evening after dinner I carried a chair to a nearby clearing to escape the noise and stink of the camp I shared with Brazilian forest workers, a place called Fazenda Dimona. To the south most of the forest had been cut and burned to create pastures. In the daytime cattle browsed in remorseless heat bouncing off the yellow clay and at night animals and spirits edged out onto the ruined land. To the north the virgin rain forest began, one of the great surviving wildernesses of the world, stretching 500 kilometers before it broke apart and dwindled into gallery woodland among the savannas of Roraima.[1]

Enclosed in darkness so complete I could not see beyond my out- stretched hand, I was forced to think of the rain forest as though I were seated in my library at home, with the lights turned low. The forest at night is an experience in sensory deprivation most of the time, black and silent as the midnight zone of a cave. Life is out there in expected abundance. The jungle teems, but in a manner mostly beyond the reach of the human senses. Ninety-nine percent of the animals find their way by chemical trails laid over the surface, puffs of odor released into the air or water, and scents diffused out of little hidden glands and into the air downwind. Animals are masters of this chemical channel, where we are idiots. But we are geniuses of the audiovisual channel, equaled in this modality only by a few odd groups (whales, monkeys, birds). So we wait for the dawn, while they wait for the

[1]Territory in the extreme northern part of Brazil.

fall of darkness; and because sight and sound are the evolutionary prerequisites of intelligence, we alone have come to reflect on such matters as Amazon nights and sensory modalities.

I swept the ground with the beam from my headlamp for signs of life, and found—diamonds! At regular intervals of several meters, intense pinpoints of white light winked on and off with each turning of the lamp. They were reflections from the eyes of wolf spiders, members of the family Lycosidae, on the prowl for insect prey. When spotlighted the spiders froze, allowing me to approach on hands and knees and study them almost at their own level. I could distinguish a wide variety of species by size, color, and hairiness. It struck me how little is known about these creatures of the rain forest, and how deeply satisfying it would be to spend months, years, the rest of my life in this place until I knew all the species by name and every detail of their lives. From specimens beautifully frozen in amber we know that the Lycosidae have survived at least since the beginning of the Oligocene epoch, forty million years ago, and probably much longer. Today a riot of diverse forms occupy the whole world, of which this was only the minutest sample, yet even these species turning about now to watch me from the bare yellow clay could give meaning to the lifetimes of many naturalists.

The moon was down, and only starlight etched the tops of the trees. It was August in the dry season. The air had cooled enough to make the humidity pleasant, in the tropical manner, as much a state of mind as a physical sensation. The storm I guessed was about an hour away. I thought of walking back into the forest with my headlamp to hunt for new treasures, but was too tired from the day's work. Anchored again to my chair, forced into myself, I welcomed a meteor's streak and the occasional courtship flash of luminescent click beetles among the nearby but unseen shrubs. Even the passage of a jetliner 10,000 meters up, a regular event each night around ten o'clock, I awaited with pleasure. A week in the rain forest had transformed its distant rumble from an urban irritant into a comforting sign of the continuance of my own species.

But I was glad to be alone. The discipline of the dark envelope summoned fresh images from the forest of how real organisms look and act. I needed to concentrate for only a second and they came alive as eidetic images, behind closed eyelids, moving across fallen leaves and decaying humus. I sorted the memories this way and that in hope of stumbling on some pattern not obedient to abstract theory of textbooks. I would have been happy with *any* pattern. The best of science doesn't consist of mathematical models and experiments, as textbooks make it seem. Those come later. It springs fresh from a more primitive mode of thought, wherein the hunter's mind weaves ideas from old facts and fresh metaphors and the scrambled crazy images of things recently seen. To move forward is to concoct new patterns of thought, which in turn dictate the design of the models and experiments. Easy to say, difficult to achieve.

The subject fitfully engaged that night, the reason for this research trip to the Brazilian Amazon, had in fact become an obsession and, like all obsessions, very likely a dead end. It was the kind of favorite puzzle that keeps forcing its way back because its very intractability makes it perversely pleasant, like an overly familiar melody intruding into the relaxed mind because it loves you and will not leave you. I hoped that some new image might propel me past the jaded puzzle to the other side, to ideas strange and compelling.

8 Bear with me for a moment while I explain this bit of personal esoterica; I am approaching the subject of central interest. Some kinds of plants and animals are dominant, proliferating new species and spreading over large parts of the world. Others are driven back until they become rare and threatened by extinction. Is there a single formula for this biogeographic difference, for all kinds of organisms? The process, if articulated, would be a law or at least a principle of dynastic succession in evolution. I was intrigued by the circumstance that social insects, the group on which I have spent most of my life, are among the most abundant of all organisms. And among the social insects, the dominant subgroup is the ants. They range 20,000 or more species strong from the Arctic Circle to the tip of South America. In the Amazon rain forest they compose more than 10 percent of the biomass of all animals. This means that if you were to collect, dry out, and weigh every animal in a piece of forest, from monkeys and birds down to mites and roundworms, at least 10 percent would consist of these insects alone. Ants make up almost half of the insect biomass overall and 70 percent of the individual insects found in the treetops. They are only slightly less abundant in grasslands, deserts, and temperate forests throughout the rest of the world.

It seemed to me that night, as it has to others in varying degrees of persuasion many times before, that the prevalence of ants must have something to do with their advanced colonial organization. A colony is a superorganism, an assembly of workers so tightly knit around the mother queen as to act like a single, well-coordinated entity. A wasp or other solitary insect encountering a worker ant on its nest faces more than just another insect. It faces the worker and all her sisters, united by instinct to protect the queen, seize control of territory, and further the growth of the colony. Workers are little kamikazes, prepared—eager—to die in order to defend the nest or gain control of a food source. Their deaths matter no more to the colony than the loss of hair or a claw tip might to a solitary animal.

There is another way to look at an ant colony. Workers foraging around their nest are not merely insects searching for food. They are a living web cast out by the superorganism, ready to congeal over rich food finds or shrink back from the most formidable enemies. Superorganisms can control and dominate the ground and treetops in competition with ordinary, solitary organisms, and that is surely why ants live everywhere in such great numbers.

I heard around me the Greek chorus of training and caution: *How can you prove that is the reason for their dominance? Isn't the connection just another shaky conclusion that because two events occur together, one causes the other? Something else entirely different might have caused both. Think about it—greater individual fighting ability? Sharper senses? What?*

Such is the dilemma of evolutionary biology. We have problems to solve, we have clear answers—too many clear answers. The difficult part is picking out the right answer. The isolated mind moves in slow circles and breakouts are rare. Solitude is better for weeding out ideas than for creating them. Genius is the summed production of the many with the names of the few attached for easy recall, unfairly so to other scientists. My mind drifted into the hourless night, no port of call yet chosen.

The storm grew until sheet lightning spread across the western sky. The thunderhead reared up like a top-heavy monster in slow motion, tilted forward, blotting out the stars. The forest erupted in a simulation of violent life. Lightning bolts broke to the front and then closer, to the right and left, 10,000 volts dropping along an ionizing path at 800 kilometers an hour, kicking a countersurge skyward ten times faster, back and forth in a split second, the whole perceived as a single flash and crack of sound. The wind freshened, and rain came stalking through the forest.

In the midst of chaos something to the side caught my attention. The lightning bolts were acting like strobe flashes to illuminate the wall of the rain forest. At intervals I glimpsed the storied structure: top canopy 30 meters off the ground, middle trees spread raggedly below that, and a lowermost scattering of shrubs and small trees. The forest was framed for a few moments in this theatrical setting. Its image turned surreal, projected into the un-bounded wildness of the human imagination, thrown back in time 10,000 years. Somewhere close I knew spear-nosed bats flew through the tree crowns in search of fruit, palm vipers coiled in ambush in the roots of orchids, jaguars walked the river's edge; around them eight hundred species of trees stood, more than are native to all of North America; and a thousand species of butterflies, 6 percent of the entire world fauna, waited for the dawn.

About the orchids of that place we knew very little. About flies and beetles almost nothing, fungi nothing, most kinds of organisms nothing. Five thousand kinds of bacteria might be found in a pinch of soil, and about them we knew absolutely nothing. This was wilderness in the sixteenth-century sense, as it must have formed in the minds of the Portuguese explorers, its interior still largely unexplored and filled with strange, myth-engendering plants and animals. From such a place the pious naturalist would send long respectful letters to royal patrons about the wonders of the new world as testament to the glory of God. And I thought: there is still time to see this land in such a manner.

The unsolved mysteries of the rain forest are formless and seductive. They are like unnamed islands hidden in the blank spaces of old maps, like dark shapes glimpsed descending the far wall of a reef into the abyss. They draw us forward and stir strange apprehensions. The unknown and prodigious are drugs to the scientific imagination, stirring insatiable hunger with a single taste. In our hearts we hope we will never discover everything. We pray there will always be a world like this one at whose edge I sat in darkness. The rain forest in its richness is one of the last repositories on earth of that timeless dream.

That is why I keep going back to the forests forty years after I began, when I flew down to Cuba, a graduate student caught up in the idea of the "big" tropics, free at last to look for something hidden, as Kipling[2] had urged, something lost behind the Ranges. The chances are high, in fact certain, of finding a new species or phenomenon within days or, if you work hard, hours after arrival. The hunt is also on for rare species already discovered but still effectively unknown—represented by one or two specimens placed in a museum drawer fifty or a hundred years ago, left with nothing but a locality and a habitat note handwritten on a tiny label ("Santarém, Brazil, nest on side of tree in swamp forest"). Unfold the stiff yellowing piece of paper and a long-dead biologist speaks: I was there, I found this, now you know, now move on.

There is still more to the study of biological richness. It is a microcosm of scientific exploration as a whole, refracting hands-on experience onto a higher plane of abstraction. We search in and around a subject for a concept, a pattern, that imposes order. We look for a way of speaking about the rough unmapped terrain, even just a name or a phrase that calls attention to the object of our attention. We hope to be the first to make a connection. Our goal is to capture and label a process, perhaps a chemical reaction or behavior pattern driving an ecological change, a new way of classifying energy flow, or a relation between predator and prey that preserves them both, almost anything at all. We will settle for just one good question that starts people thinking and talking: Why are there so many species? Why have mammals evolved more quickly than reptiles? Why do birds sing at dawn?

These whispering denizens of the mind are sensed but rarely seen. They rustle the foliage, leave behind a pug mark filling with water and a scent, excite us for an instant and vanish. Most ideas are waking dreams that fade to an emotional residue. A first-rate scientist can hope to capture and express only several in a lifetime. No one has learned how to invent with any consistent success the equations and phrases of science, no one has captured the metaformula of scientific research. The conversion is an art aided by a stroke of luck in minds set to receive them. We hunt outward and we hunt inward, and the value of the quarry on one side of that mental barrier is commensurate with the value of the quarry on the other side. Of this dual quality the great chemist Berzelius[3] wrote in 1818 and for all time:

[2]Rudyard Kipling (1865–1936), an English author born in India, who was known for stories and poems set in the exotic landscape of India.

[3]Baron Jöns Jakob Berzelius (1779–1848), a Swedish chemist who developed the modern system of symbols and formulas in chemistry.

All our theory is but a means of consistently conceptualizing the inward pro- 20 cesses of phenomena, and it is presumable and adequate when all scientifically known facts can be deduced from it. This mode of conceptualization can equally well be false and, unfortunately, presumably is so frequently. Even though, at a certain period in the development of science, it may match the purpose just as well as a true theory. Experience is augmented, facts appear which do not agree with it, and one is forced to go in search of a new mode of conceptualization within which these facts can also be accommodated; and in this manner, no doubt, modes of conceptualization will be altered from age to age, as experience is broadened, and the complete truth may perhaps never be attained.

The storm arrived, racing from the forest's edge, turning from scattered splashing drops into sheets of water driven by gusts of wind. It forced me back to the shelter of the corrugated iron roof of the open-air living quarters, where I sat and waited with the *mateiros*.[4] The men stripped off their clothing and walked out into the open, soaping and rinsing themselves in the torrential rain, laughing and singing. In bizarre counterpoint, leptodactylid frogs struck up a loud and monotonous honking on the forest floor close by. They were all around us. I wondered where they had been during the day. I had never encountered a single one while sifting through the vegetation and rotting debris on sunny days, in habitats they are supposed to prefer.

Farther out, a kilometer or two away, a troop of red howler monkeys chimed in, their chorus one of the strangest sounds to be heard in all of nature, as enthralling in its way as the songs of humpback whales. A male opened with an accelerating series of deep grunts expanding into prolonged roars and was then joined by the higher-pitched calls of the females. This far away, filtered through dense foliage, the full chorus was machine-like: deep, droning, metallic.

Such raintime calls are usually territorial advertisements, the means by which the animals space themselves out and control enough land to forage and breed. For me they were a celebration of the forest's vitality: *Rejoice! The powers of nature are within our compass, the storm is part of our biology!*

For that is the way of the nonhuman world. The greatest powers of the 24 physical environment slam into the resilient forces of life, and nothing much happens. For a very long time, 150 million years, the species within the rain forest evolved to absorb precisely this form and magnitude of violence. They encoded the predictable occurrence of nature's storms in the letters of their genes. Animals and plants have come to use heavy rains and floods routinely to time episodes in their life cycle. They threaten rivals, mate, hunt prey, lay eggs in new water pools, and dig shelters in the rain-softened earth.

On a larger scale, the storms drive change in the whole structure of the forest. The natural dynamism raises the diversity of life by means of local destruction and regeneration.

[4]Local people who earn their livelihood in the rain forest.

Somewhere a large horizontal tree limb is weak and vulnerable, covered by a dense garden of orchids, bromeliads, and other kinds of plants that grow on trees. The rain fills up the cavities enclosed by the axil sheaths of the epiphytes and soaks the humus and clotted dust around their roots. After years of growth the weight has become nearly unsupportable. A gust of wind whips through or lightning strikes the tree trunk, and the limb breaks and plummets down, clearing a path to the ground. Elsewhere the crown of a giant tree emergent above the rest catches the wind and the tree sways above the rain-soaked soil. The shallow roots cannot hold, and the entire tree keels over. Its trunk and canopy arc downward like a blunt ax, shearing through smaller trees and burying understory bushes and herbs. Thick lianas coiled through the limbs are pulled along. Those that stretch to other trees act as hawsers to drag down still more vegetation. The massive root system heaves up to create an instant mound of bare soil. At yet another site, close to the river's edge, the rising water cuts under an overhanging bank to the critical level of gravity, and a 20-meter front collapses. Behind it a small section of forest floor slides down, toppling trees and burying low vegetation.

Such events of minor violence open gaps in the forest. The sky clears again and sunlight floods the ground. The surface temperature rises and the humidity falls. The soil and ground litter dries out and warms up still more, creating a new environment for animals, fungi, and microorganisms of a different kind from those in the dark forest interior. In the following months pioneer plant species take seed. They are very different from the young shade-loving saplings and understory shrubs of the prevailing old-stand forest. Fast-growing, small in stature, and short-lived, they form a single canopy that matures far below the upper crowns of the older trees all around. Their tissue is soft and vulnerable to herbivores. The palmate-leaved trees of the genus *Cecropia*, one of the gap-filling specialists of Central and South America, harbor vicious ants in hollow internodes of the trunk. These insects, bearing the appropriate scientific name *Azteca*, live in symbiosis with their hosts, protecting them from all predators except sloths and a few other herbivores specialized to feed on *Cecropia*. The symbionts live among new assemblages of species not found in the mature forest.

28　　All around the second-growth vegetation, the fallen trees and branches rot and crumble, offering hiding places and food to a vast array of basidiomycete fungi, slime molds, ponerine ants, scolytid beetles, bark lice, earwigs, embiopteran webspinners, zorapterans, entomobryomorph springtails, japygid diplurans, schizomid arachnids, pseudoscorpions, real scorpions, and other forms that live mostly or exclusively in this habitat. They add thousands of species to the diversity of the primary forest.

Climb into the tangle of fallen vegetation, tear away pieces of rotting bark, roll over logs, and you will see these creatures teeming everywhere. As the pioneer vegetation grows denser, the deepening shade and higher humidity again favor old-forest species, and their saplings sprout and grow. Within a hundred years the gap specialists will be phased out by competition for light, and the tall storied forest will close completely over.

In the succession, pioneer species are the sprinters, old-forest species the long-distance runners. The violent changes and a clearing of space bring all the species briefly to the same starting line. The sprinters dash ahead, but the prolonged race goes to the marathoners. Together the two classes of specialists create a complex mosaic of vegetation types across the forest which, by regular tree falls and landslides, is forever changing. If square kilometers of space are mapped over decades of time, the mosaic turns into a riotous kaleidoscope whose patterns come and go and come again. A new marathon is always beginning somewhere in the forest. The percentages of successional vegetation types are consequently more or less in a steady state, from earliest pioneer species through various mixes of pioneer and deep-forest trees to stands of the most mature physiognomy. Walk randomly on any given day for one or two kilometers through the forest, and you will cut through many of these successional stages and sense the diversity sustained by the passage of storms and the fall of forest giants.

It is diversity by which life builds and saturates the rain forest. And diversity has carried life beyond, to the harshest environments on earth. Rich assemblages of animals swarm in the shallow bays of Antarctica, the coldest marine habitats on earth. Perch-like notothenioid fishes swim there in temperatures just above the freezing point of salt water but cold enough to turn ordinary blood to ice, because they are able to generate glycopeptides in their tissues as antifreeze and thrive where other fish cannot go. Around them flock dense populations of active brittlestars, krill, and other invertebrate animals, each with protective devices of its own.

In a radically different setting, the deep unlighted zone of caves around the world, blind white springtails, mites, and beetles feed on fungi and bacteria growing on rotting vegetable matter washed down through ground water. They are eaten in turn by blind white beetles and spiders also specialized for life in perpetual darkness.

Some of the harshest deserts of the world are home to unique ensembles of insects, lizards, and flowering plants. In the Namib of southwestern Africa, beetles use leg tips expanded into oarlike sandshoes to swim down through the shifting dunes in search of dried vegetable matter. Others, the swiftest runners of the insect world, race over the baking hot surface on bizarre stilt legs.

Archaebacteria, one-celled microorganisms so different from ordinary bacteria as to be candidates for a separate kingdom of life, occupy the boiling water of mineral hot springs and volcanic vents in the deep sea. The species composing the newly discovered genus *Methanopyrus* grow in boiling vents at the bottom of the Mediterranean Sea in temperatures up to $110°C$.

Life is too well adapted in such places, out to the edge of the physical envelope where biochemistry falters, and too diverse to be broken by storms and other ordinary vagaries of nature. But diversity, the property that makes resilience possible, is vulnerable to blows that are greater than natural perturbations. It can be eroded away fragment by fragment, and irreversibly so if the abnormal stress is unrelieved. This vulnerability stems from life's composition as swarms of species of limited geographical distribution. Every habitat, from Brazilian rain forest to Antarctic bay to thermal vent, harbors a unique combination of plants and animals. Each kind of plant and animal living there is linked in the food web to only a small part of the other species. Eliminate one species, and another increases in number to take its place. Eliminate a great many species, and the local ecosystem starts to decay visibly. Productivity drops as the channels of the nutrient cycles are clogged. More of the biomass is sequestered in the form of dead vegetation and slowly metabolizing, oxygen-starved mud, or is simply washed away. Less competent pollinators take over as the best-adapted bees, moths, birds, bats, and other specialists drop out. Fewer seeds fall, fewer seedlings sprout. Herbivores decline, and their predators die away in close concert.

36   In an eroding ecosystem life goes on, and it may look superficially the same. There are always species able to recolonize the impoverished area and exploit the stagnant resources, however clumsily accomplished. Given enough time, a new combination of species—a reconstituted fauna and flora—will reinvest the habitat in a way that transports energy and materials somewhat more efficiently. The atmosphere they generate and the composition of the soil they enrich will resemble those found in comparable habitats in other parts of the world, since the species are adapted to penetrate and reinvigorate just such degenerate systems. They do so because they gain more energy and materials and leave more offspring. But the restorative power of the fauna and flora of the world as a whole depends on the existence of enough species to play that special role. They too can slide into the red zone of endangered species.

Biological diversity—"biodiversity" in the new parlance—is the key to the maintenance of the world as we know it. Life in a local site struck down by a passing storm springs back quickly because enough diversity still exists. Opportunistic species evolved for just such an occasion rush in to fill the spaces. They entrain the succession that circles back to something resembling the original state of the environment.

This is the assembly of life that took a billion years to evolve. It has eaten the storms—folded them into its genes—and created the world that created us. It holds the world steady. When I rose at dawn the next morning, Fazenda Dimona had not changed in any obvious way from the day before. The same high trees stood like a fortress along the forest's edge; the same profusion of birds and insects foraged through the canopy and understory in precise individual timetables. All this seemed timeless, immutable, and its very strength posed the question: how much force does it take to break the crucible of evolution?

Understanding What You Read

1. What central concern of Wilson's does he introduce by using his observation of different species of wolf spiders?
2. Sitting on the edge of the Amazon rain forest, Wilson is comforted by the sound of an airplane overhead (paragraph 5). What does this detail contribute to the overall effect of the piece?
3. What are some of the unsolved mysteries of the rain forest that Wilson ponders?
4. How does the storm create change in the forest structure?
5. What causes an ecosystem to become degraded?

Writing About What You Read

Wilson uses a description of a night on the edge of a rain forest before, during, and after a violent storm to explain important features of the forest ecosystem, the development of biodiversity, and factors that threaten it. Write a long paragraph (or a short essay) in which you argue for the importance of biodiversity, using details from Wilson's piece to support your argument.

SUE HUBBELL

Hubbell (b. 1935) worked as a bookstore manager and librarian before becoming a beekeeper and writer. An important part of Sue Hubbell's life story is found in the book *A Country Year: Living the Questions* (1986), from which this selection is taken. After a life as a librarian, wife, and mother, Hubbell dared to do what many would find unthinkable when she gave up the security of her job and the comfort of a conventional life. First with her husband and then as a divorced woman alone, she lived simply on the fruits of the land and the money she earned from selling honey collected from her own hives in an isolated part of the Ozarks in Arkansas. She has recently published another book entitled *Broadsides from the Other Orders: A Book of Bugs* (1993).

Mites, Moths, Bats, and Mosquitoes

I A M an early riser, and now that the weather is warm I like to take a cup of coffee out under the oak trees in back of the cabin and get a feel for the kind of day it is going to be. Today the night creatures were still about when I went out there—katydids, whippoorwills, night-flying moths, owls and mosquitoes. By the time I had had a sip or two of coffee and my eyes had adjusted well enough to pick out the shapes of the trees, the mosquitoes had discovered me and gathered in an annoying buzz around my head. But before they had a chance to bite, a small furry shape appeared from nowhere. I heard the soft rush of wings beside my ear and the mosquitoes were gone. A few moments of silence. More mosquitoes, and once again a bat swooped in.

The arrangement was a pleasant one for both the bat and me. I don't like mosquitoes but the bat does. I served as bait to gather the mosquitoes in one rich spot, and the bat ate them before they bit me. For the mosquitoes the plan was not such a good one; they were kept from dinner and were turned into one instead. All this gives me a fine, friendly feeling toward bats. In their way, I suppose, they also approve of me.

The bats are quick, and in the dim light before dawn it is difficult to identify them, but I believe them to be *Myotis lucifugus,* more comfortably known as little brown bats. These, at least, are the ones I often see taking their daytime sleep hanging upside down from the rafters in the barn loft. They are common around here, and also sleep in caves or hollow trees. Like other bats, they belong to the order Chiroptera, which means wing-handed, a good word for an animal with wings made of a membrane of skin covering the hand and fingerbones. But I also like the old English name of flitter-mouse, an apt description of our only flying mammal.

4   Bats are mammals like we are. They suckle their young, and have such wizened ancient-looking faces that they seem strangely akin and familiar. Yet they find their way and locate their food by using sound that we cannot hear. They hunt by night, and in cold weather some migrate and others hibernate. They are odd and alien to us, too, so much so that we have made up fancies about them—that they are evil and ill-omened, or at the very least will fly into our hair. Anyone who has read *Dracula* will remember that young ladies should not moon around graveyards at night, or they will be in big trouble with bats.

The truth is that, from a human point of view, bats are beneficial. On the North American continent, the little brown bat and other temperate-zone bats have a diet made up almost exclusively of night-flying insects. Farther south, in tropical regions, there are bats that eat fruit, and even vampire bats, which have incisors that allow them to feed on the blood of large animals, but our northern bats have nothing to do with such fare, eating, instead, the kinds of insects that are often a bother to us.

Bats find their food by producing high-pitched sounds that echo against insects or other solid objects. The echos return to the bats' ears and give them a precise and vivid aural map of whatever is out there.

These cries are beyond our human range of hearing, but when translated to frequencies low enough for us they sound like a series of short clicks or chirps. The short ultrasound wavelengths allow bats to locate exactly even very small moving objects, such as mosquito-sized insects. They pluck the mosquitoes out of the air close to my head, and would never be so clumsy as to blunder into my hair.

What is more, the bats' discrimination is so fine that they can separate the echos of their own clicks from those of another bat. This is important, because they often fly and hunt in groups, and such accuracy allows them to do so without muddle or confusion. It may not be our way to get dinner, but it does strike me as wonderfully clever, efficient and simple. However, as with most things in life, it is not all that simple, and dinner is not always a sure thing.

Night-flying moths are one of the chief items in bat diet, and over a long time span of eating and being eaten, bat and moth have worked out a complex relationship.

My cousin Asher, whose academic specialty is moth ear mites, has during the course of a lifetime of work discovered a good deal about moths' ears, a structure that some of us never knew existed. He tells me that some moths who are night fliers and therefore potential bat dinners can hear the high-pitched noises made by bats and stand a good chance of escaping. What is even more remarkable is that certain moths have the ability to make sounds that the bats, in turn, can hear. In a sense, they can talk back to bats.

"And what," I asked Asher, "do they say?"

"They say, 'I am not good to eat,' " he replied.

This makes life harder for the bats and easier for the moths, but the moths' advantage is only preserved by a highly specialized relationship with yet another creature.

The moth ear mites Asher studies, the North American species, harm their hosts' ears, and if they were not careful, they would deafen them and make the moths and themselves easy prey. But they *are* careful.

The mites are tiny arachnids, scarcely visible to the naked eye. When they are ready to lay their eggs, they climb on the moth and make their way to the moth's ear, a safe and protected spot for their eggs. In the process of laying the eggs, they damage the delicate structure of the moth's ear. Since many mites may be present on a single moth, the moth would be deaf if they were to lay their eggs in both ears. So, in a stunning example of evolutionary respect, a case where courtesy and self-interest are one and the same, the first mite aboard makes a trail, in a manner not yet clearly understood, and all the mites who come later follow her trail, laying all their eggs in the same ear and leaving the opposite ear undamaged. This allows the moth to retain partial hearing, and may improve his chances of escaping bats during the time the mites' eggs hatch.

16   So there we are out under the oak trees in the dim light—the mites, the moths, the bats, the mosquitoes, and me. We are a text of suitability one for another, and that text is as good as any I know by which to drink my coffee and watch the dawn.

Understanding What You Read

1. How are mites beneficial to humans?
2. Sitting under the oak trees outside her cabin in rural Arkansas, Sue Hubbell becomes part of a web of interdependency among five organisms, including herself. Which animals are prey and which are predators?
3. What strategies do the moths have to protect themselves from predation?
4. What does the fact that Hubbell is enjoying her morning cup of coffee contribute to this piece?

Writing About What You Read

1. Imagine yourself going outdoors at dawn in a place you know well. You sit down with a cup of coffee and observe the life around you. Write about what you see.
2. Argue that Hubbell is part of an ecosystem. Describe that system.

WES JACKSON

A native of rural Kansas, Jackson (b. 1936) has lived in North Carolina, where he earned a Ph.D. in genetics, and in California, where he taught at Sacramento State University. He returned to Kansas in 1974, when he and his wife founded The Land Institute, a nonprofit research and educational organization committed to finding sustainable alternatives in agriculture, energy, waste management, and shelter. The institute has become an innovative center where students and professional researchers contribute to the project of developing perennial grains and legumes that can be grown without pesticides and fossil-fuel fertilizers. In 1980 Jackson published *New Roots for Agriculture*. "Old *Salsola*" and "Living Nets in a New Prairie Sea" are from *Altars of Unhewn Stone* (1987). In 1992, Wes Jackson received the prestigious MacArthur Foundation grant.

Living Nets in a New Prairie Sea

> The Grass was the Country as the Water is the Sea.
>
> —WILLA CATHER

AUTHOR Joseph Kinsey Howard[1] describes a spring day in 1883 in North Dakota when John Christiansen, a Scandinavian farmer, looked up while plowing a field to discover an old Sioux watching him. Silently the Sioux watched as the prairie grass was turned under. The farmer stopped the team, leaned against the plow handles, pushed his black Stetson back on his head, and rolled a cigarette. He watched amusedly as the Sioux knelt, thrust his fingers into the furrow, measured its depth, fingered the sod and the buried grass. Eventually the Sioux straightened up and looked at the immigrant. "Wrong side up," said the Sioux and went away.

Another writer in the mid-1930s described how his grandfather "broke prairie sod, driving five yoke of straining oxen, stopping every hour or so to hammer the iron ploughshare to a sharper edge. Some of the grass roots immemorial were as thick as his arm. 'It was like plowing through a heavy woven doormat,' grandfather said."

To many of us today it seems tragic that our ancestors should have so totally blasphemed the grasslands with their moldboards. But who among us, in their time, would have done otherwise? Nevertheless, it was one of the two or three worst atrocities committed by Americans that, for with the cutting of the roots—a sound that reminded one of a zipper being opened or closed—a new way of life opened, which simultaneously closed, probably forever, a long line of ecosystems stretching back thirty million years. Before the coming of the Europeans the prairie was a primitive wilderness, both beautiful and stern, a wilderness that had supported migrating water birds as well as bobolinks, prairie chickens, black-footed ferrets, and Native Americans. Never mind that the Europeans' crops would far outyield the old prairie for human purposes, at least in the short run. What is important is that the Sioux knew it was wrong, and that his words became regionally famous for the wrong reason. The story was often repeated precisely because farmer Christiansen, and the others who passed it on, thought it was amusing.

To their minds those words betrayed the ignorance of the poor Sioux. As far as the immigrant was concerned, "breaking the prairie" was his purpose in life.

Agriculture has changed the face of the land the world over. The old covering featured the top level of biological organization—the ecosystem. The new cover features the next level below, the population. For example, a piece of land that once featured a diverse ecosystem we call prairie is now covered with

4

---

[1]Historian and biographer (1906–1951) who wrote about the exploitation of Montana.

a single-species population such as wheat, corn, or soybeans. A prairie is a polyculture. Our crops are usually grown in monocultures. The next most obvious fact is that the prairie features perennial plants while agriculture features annuals. For the prairie, at least, the key to this last condition resides in the roots. Though the aboveground parts of the prairie's perennials may die back each year, the roots are immortal. For whether those sun-cured leaves, passed over by the buffalo in the fall migration, go quickly in a lightning-started prairie fire or, as is more often the case, burn through the "slow, smokeless burning of decay," the roots hold fast what they have earned from rock and subsoil. Whichever way the top parts burn, the perennial roots will soon catch and save most of the briefly free nutrients for a living future. And so an alliance of soil and perennial root, well adapted to the task of blotting up a drenching rain, reincarnates last year's growth.

Soil still runs to the sea in nature's system, as in the beginning before land plants appeared, but gravity can't compete with the holding power of the living net and the nutrient recharge managed by nosing roots of dalea, pasqueflower, and bluestem. Banks will slip. Rivers continue to cut, as they did before agriculture, before humans. The Missouri was called "Big Muddy" before the prairies were plowed, a matter of possible confusion to those untutored by the river. But it is essential to realize that the sediment load before agriculture could not have exceeded the soil being created by the normal lowering of the riverbed, and what was carved from the interior highlands. It is even more important to appreciate that the amount of soil from the prairie that wound up in the river could not have exceeded what the prairie plant roots were extracting from parent rock or subsoil. Otherwise there would have been no soil over much of the watershed. What should concern us is the extra sediment load running in the river today—the fertility, the nutrients hard-earned by nature's myriad life forms, which broke them free of their rocky prisons over the course of millennia, bathed them with chemicals, and made them fit for that freedom known only in the biota. The solar energy cost of mining these nutrients with root pumps is characterized by a slow payback period, an energy cost that only geologic time can justify.

Species diversity breeds dependable chemistry. This aboveground diversity has a multiple effect on the seldom-seen teeming diversity below. Bacteria, fungi, and invertebrates live out their lives reproducing by the power of sun-sponsored photons captured in the green molecular traps set above. If we could adjust our eyes to a power beyond that of the electron microscope, our minds would reel in a seemingly surrealistic universe of exchanging ions, where water molecules dominate and where colloidal clay plates are held in position by organic thread molecules important in a larger purpose, but regarded as just another meal by innumerable microscopic invertebrates. The action begins when roots decay and aboveground residues break down, and the released nutrients begin their downward tumble through soil catacombs to start all over again. And we who stand above in thoughtful examination, all the while smelling and rolling fresh dirt between our fingers and thumbs, distill these myriads of action into one concept—soil health or balance—and leave it at that.

Traditional agriculture coasted on the accumulated principal and interest hard-earned by nature's life-forms over those millions of years of adjustment to dryness, fire, and grinding ice. Modern agriculture coasts on the sunlight trapped by floras long extinct; we pump it, process it, transport it over the countryside as chemicals, and inject it into our wasting fields as chemotherapy. Then we watch the fields respond with an unsurpassed vigor, and we feel well informed on the subject of agronomics. That we can feed billions is less a sign of nature's renewable bounty and of our knowledge than a sign of her forgiveness and of our own discounting of the future. For how opposite could monoculture of annuals be from what nature prefers? Both the roots and the aboveground parts of annuals die every year; thus, throughout much of the calendar the mechanical grip on the soil must rely on death rather than life. Mechanical disturbance, powered by an ancient flora, imposed by a mined metal, may make weed control effective, but the farm far from weatherproof. In the course of it all, soil compacts, crumb structure declines, soil porosity decreases, and the wick effect for pulling moisture down diminishes.

Monoculture means a decline in the range of invertebrate and microbial forms. Microbial specialists with narrow enzyme systems make such specific demands that just any old crop won't do. We do manage some diversity through crop rotation, but from the point of view of various microbes, it is probably a poor substitute for the greater diversity that was always there on the prairie. Monoculture means that botanical and hence chemical diversity above ground is also absent. This invites epidemics of pathogens or epidemics of grazing by insect populations, which in monocultures spend most of their energy reproducing, eating, and growing. Insects are better controlled if they are forced to spend a good portion of their energy budget buzzing around hunting for the plants they evolved to eat among the many species in a polyculture.

Some of the activity of the virgin sod can be found in the human-managed fields, but plowing sharply reduced many of these soil qualities. Had too much been destroyed, of course, we would not have food today. But then who can say that our great-grandchildren will have it in 2080? It is hard to quantify exactly what happened when the heart of America was ripped open, but when the shear made its zipper-sound, the wisdom that the prairie had accumulated over millions of years was destroyed in favor of the simpler, human-directed system.

Where does all this leave us? Is there any possible return to a system that is at once self-renewing like the prairie or forest and yet capable of supporting the current and expanding human population? I think there is.

12   Much of our scientific knowledge and the narrow technical application of science has contributed to the modern agricultural problem. Nevertheless, because of advances in biology over the last half-century, I think we have the opportunity to develop a truly sustainable agriculture based on the polyculture of perennials. This would be an agriculture in which soil erosion is so small that it is detectable only by the most sophisticated equipment, an agriculture that is chemical-free or nearly so, and certainly an agriculture that is scarcely demanding of fossil fuel. We are fortunate in this country to have a large and sophisticated biological research establishment and the know-how to develop high-yielding, seed-producing polycultures out of some of our wild species.

At The Land Institute, we are working on the development of mixed perennial grain crops. We are interested in simulating the old prairie or in building domestic prairies for the future. Conventional agriculture, which features annuals in monoculture, is nearly opposite to the original prairie or forest, which features mixtures of perennials. If we could build domestic prairies we might be able one day to have high-yielding fields that are planted only once every twenty years or so. After the fields had been established, we would need only to harvest the crop, relying on species diversity to take care of insects, pathogens, and fertility.

This of course is not the entire answer to the total agricultural problem, much of which involves not only a different socioeconomic and political posture, but a religious dimension as well. But breeding new crops from native plants selected from nature's abundance and simulating the presettlement botanical complexity of a region should make it easier for us to solve many agricultural problems.

As civilizations have flourished, many upland landscapes that supported them have died, and desert and mudflat wastelands have developed. But civilizations have passed on accumulated knowledge, and we can say without exaggeration that these wastelands are the price paid for the accumulated knowledge. In our century this knowledge has restorative potential. The goal to develop a truly sustainable food supply could start a trend exactly opposite to that which we have followed on the globe since we stepped onto the agricultural treadmill some ten millennia ago.

16   Aldo Leopold lamented that "no living man will see the long-grass prairie, where a sea of prairie flowers lapped at the stirrups of the pioneer."[2] Many share his lament, for what are left are prairie islands, far too small to be counted as a "sea." Essentially all this vast region, a million square miles, was turned under to make our Corn Belt and Breadbasket. But now the grandchildren of pioneers have the opportunity to establish a new sea of perennial prairie flowers, the product of accumulated scientific knowledge, their own cleverness, and the wisdom of the prairie.

---

[2]From Aldo Leopold's "The Remnants," part of the longer essay "Wilderness" (see headnote on page 49).

Understanding What You Read

1. What does Jackson mean when he says that a prairie is a perennial polyculture?
2. Why does monoculture reduce biodiversity in the soil?
3. What does Jackson hope to accomplish by simulating the old prairie of mixed perennials?

Writing About What You Read

In a paragraph or essay: explain why the destruction of the prairie was a mistake; or argue for the importance of reestablishing the prairie; or argue that plowing the prairie was necessary for the development of the continent by large numbers of settlers.

Old *Salsola*

TEN A.M., January 2, 1986. Through the windows of John's cabin, perched on a low bluff, I look northward over the Cheyenne Bottoms near the Great Bend of the Arkansas River. A strong wind blows from the northwest. Between where I sit and the expanse of water in the bottoms lies a poor pasture, some alfalfa fields, and newly worked sorghum ground. Tumbleweeds of the genus *Salsola* roll across these fields like purposeful animals migrating to some destination beyond the horizon. They *look* purposeful anyhow. They look at least as purposeful as the skein of geese that rises out of the bottoms each morning, forming long poor V's and heading south to shop for breakfast in the fields of shattered sorghum. The wind that propels these weeds and the wingbeat that propels the geese are from the same source: transformed sunlight. Barbed wire fences have stopped some thousands of these weeds, but thousands more roll right over, *even* where their dead relatives have not accumulated against the wire. A moment ago, one particularly bouncy weed rolled right over a fence, bounding almost like a deer, but with one important difference: a dead *Salsola* mother will hug the same wire that a live deer clears. Free of the fence so briefly hugged, the cheerful dance of the dead continues. I wonder what is the average number of seeds dropped at each bounce. Surely less than one, but there are lots of bounces in this winter trip of a dead *Salsola* dispersing her children.

Was it she or the "larger system," an ancient ecosystem, that prepared her for this day of winter wind: Born in June, her branching pattern makes her round by fall, testimony to her ability to remember the past and foresee the coming season with each cell division. But there is more to this globular weed than her shape. For all through the summer, at the base of her stem, she formed an abscission, a knotted ring of cells for easy detachment at ground level in late fall. I don't know whether she or the larger ecosystem was most responsible for that knotted ring, but the wind does seem a fitting hearse for a last ride to a fenceline cemetery. What other plant could beat *Salsola* in this respect: that it is only in her death that the most energetic and widespread dispersal of her offspring could happen?

Understanding What You Read

1. What is the effect of referring to the tumbleweed as "she"?
2. What questions about ecosystems does this piece raise?

Writing About What You Read

Write a letter to Wes Jackson explaining your response to "Living Nets in a New Prairie Sea" and "Old *Salsola*." Indicate what you like, what is confusing, and what you would like to know more about.

MARJORY STONEMAN DOUGLAS

Douglas (b. 1890) has worked as a reporter, editor, college professor, and writer. Since serving in 1927 as an original member of the committee to establish the Florida Everglades as a national park, she has been committed to the preservation of that remarkable region. "Life on the Rock" is from her book *The Everglades: River of Grass* (1947).

Life on the Rock

THE SAW GRASS and the water made the Everglades[1] both simple and unique. Yet bordering and encroaching on that simplicity, fighting for foothold on its coasts and islands, a diversity of life lives upon the rock that holds it. The saw grass in its essential harshness supports little else. It repelled man. But on the rock the crowding forms made life abundant, so that between the two the chronicle is balanced.

One begins with the plants.

[1]Located in south Florida, south of Lake Okeechobee.

If the saw grass here is four thousand years old, many other of these plant associations may have been here almost as long.

In the time of which I write, toward the end of the past century when everything was as it had been, the southern vague watery rim of Okeechobee was bordered by a strange jungle. The crusted wave foam was washed down among windrows of dead reeds and branches and rotting fish. In that decay a wide band of jungle trees sprang up.

Southwest it was all custard apple, a subtropic, rough-barked, inconspicuous tree, with small pointed leaves and soft fruits. It grew fiercely, crowded on roots that became gnarled trunks or trunks twisted and arched into bracing roots in the drag of the water. The spilth and decay of the custard apple, the guano of crowds of birds that fed on them, whitening the leaves, built up in the watery sunlessness below them an area of rich black peat, denser than muck, two or three miles wide and six or eight feet deep.

The earliest Americans on the lake called this area "the custard apple bottoms." It was edged with tall leather ferns and Boston ferns and knotted with vines, which no man could get through without axes or dynamite. Lake water crept darkly below.

The southeast was edged with a less tropical jungle, scrub willow with its light-green pointed leaves and yellow catkins and the ropy brown bark of elderberries, bearing out of their lacy plates of white blossoms the purple-black fruit about which the blue jays and the mockingbirds, the great black-glinting Florida crows, the grackles and the red-winged blackbirds in their thousands set up a flapping and creaking and crowing and ker-eeing. Bees and bright flies and yellow butterflies hovered when the blossoms were sweet. Under their shadows ground rattlers moved sluggishly. Winds carried to them from the reedy lake clouds of feeble white insects lake people call "chizzle winks," which breed and die in myriads in a short few days.

These were the willow-and-elder bottoms, which fought shrewdly with the saw grass for every rocky space. The dark-brown peaty muck they left went east up the lake edge between the sand ridges and the saw-grass arms.

Over all this thick jungle region climbed and hung down in moving green curtains the heart-shaped leaves of moonvines. In the luminous unseen dark of the night the moonflowers opened acres after acres of flat white blossoms, cloud white, foam white, and still. Northward, lake water moved darkly under the tiny pointed reflections of the stars. Below the region the moonflowers and the moon made their own, with no man's eye to see them, moved the enormous darkness without light of the saw-grass river.

East along the curving Everglades borders and west by the farther coast stood everywhere in their endless ranks the great companies of the pines. Where they grew the rock was highest—"high pine land," people called it. Their ranks went off across an open slough in a feathery cliff, a rampart of trunks red-brown in the setting sun, bearing tops like a long streamer of green smoke. Their warm piny breaths blew in the sun along the salt winds. They covered here, as they did everywhere in Florida, interminable miles.

Some southern longleaf, "common yellow pine," with its taller trunk and bushier branches is scattered south from the Caloosahatchee[2] and down the east coast to the New River. But below there, wherever it could find foothold in high rock, and up behind the western mangrove to what is now Gordon Pass, which is the area of West Indian vegetation, grows the Caribbean pine. It stands everywhere about the borders of the Caribbean. It is called slash pine. But in Dade County from the first it was called Dade County pine.

12   Its trunks are set thick with rust and brown and grayish bark patches, which resist fire. The patterns of its skimpy branches people find strange, or beautiful. Dying alone, as they often do away from their great companies, killed by lightning or the borer that instantly finds injured bark, these pines stand dead a long time, rigid gray or silver, their gestures frozen. The young fluffy pines start up everywhere about them, bearing long pale candles in the new light of spring.

With the Caribbean pines, as they do with other pines of the South, always grow the palmettos. These are saw palmettos, silver-green, blue-green, or in dry times magnificent tawny-gold across vast open savannas. Their spiky fans cover all the ground beneath the pine trees, on unseen spiny trunks. If they are burned, with a great oily popping and seething, only the blackened trunks are left, writhing like heavy snakes.

The small brown Florida deer step neatly at the edge of pine forests like these. The brown wildcats know them. The clear light falls mottled through the branches faintly green over endless fan points. Inconspicuous wild flowers grow in the wiry grass between palmettos, faint blue chicory, or yellow tea bush, or the tiny wild poinsettias with their small brush strokes of scarlet. The quail pipe and their new-hatched young run like mice with their small cheeping, at the edge of such pineland, and the brown marsh rabbit with small ears and no apparent tail nibbles some bit of leaf.

A diamondback rattlesnake may push out here slowly after such a rabbit or the cotton mice, or lie after shedding his flaky old skin to sun the brilliant dark lozenge marks on his almost yellowish new scales, slow to coil or rattle unless angered. Then in a blur he draws back in quick angles that wide-jawed head with the high nose balanced over the coils, his slitted eyes fixed and following his object, the forked tongue flicking through the closed jaws, tasting the disturbed air. His raised tail shakes the dry rattle of its horny bells. His strength, his anger, engorges that thick muscular body, ruffles his barky scales. If he strikes it is at one-third of his length. The jaws open back so that the long fangs strike forward and deep. His recovery is quicker than the eye can see. Or he lifts tall that kingly head before he lowers it in retreat, holding himself grandly, with the same dignity that has made him the king among all these beasts.

[2]A river in southern Florida.

All the woodpeckers in south Florida yank and hitch and cluck and rap   16
their way up these great patched pine trunks, all with red heads, the downy,
the hairy, the red-bellied, and that diabolical creature with a red and white
and black head like a medieval battle-ax, the pileated, which the early settlers
called so truly "the Lord God Almighty." But in those early days the even
more impressive ivory-billed, which we shall never see again, startled these
pinewoods with his masterly riveting.

Even in the middle of the saw-grass river, where an outcrop of old rock
is the only evidence of preglacial times, the pines grow tall to show where the
rock lies. The buzzards and the black vultures, their ragged wing tips like
brush strokes of India ink, sail and sail and rise on the upcurrents and soar
in their pure flight, turning about some old roost they have always kept and
returned to year after year. Their piercing glances watch for the glint of flies'
wings over carrion they crave, the most valuable birds in the world. Or from
the muddy water holes about the pineland the brown-black water moccasins
slide their wet ridged scales. Startled, they coil to retract those open, white-
lined jaws, like a queer white flower to anything peering down. Death is there
too.

Where the pines are thin, the Indians found their first source of life. There
grow foot-tall, ferny green cycads, plants older than this rock, with yellow
and orange cones for flowers and great thick roots. This is the "coontie" of
the oldest Indian legend. Its root is grated and squeezed and sifted to flour
to make the thick watery gruel "sofkee," which was always the basis of the
Indians' diet here. The Indians' legend came partly from the Spanish fathers.
They say that once there was a great famine here in Florida. The Indians
prayed to the Master of Breath, who sent down His Son, God's Little Boy,
to walk about at the edge of the pinelands and the Glades. And wherever He
walked, there in His heel marks grew the coontie, for the Indians to eat and
reverence.

Sometimes it is called compte. The early white men learned of it and
grated it to make starch and knew it as arrowroot. By the pinelands north of
the Miami River, the Indians camped often, so that their women could gather
it in what was called the Coontie grounds.

The dragonflies on iridescent wings dart and hang in squadrons by the   20
open air of pinelands. Below among the grass roots stirs all the minute
dustlike activity of the ants.

In the summer hosts of big red-and-yellow grasshoppers, with heads
shaped like horses', will descend and eat holes in all the softer leaves. Walking
sticks fly like boomerangs. Shining brown leaf-shaped palmetto bugs scurry
like cockroaches. Spiders like tiny crabs hang in stout webs. The birds snap
at small moths and butterflies of every kind. A blue racer, the snake that
moves across the cleared sand like a whiplash, will with one flick destroy the
smooth, careful cup of the ant lion in the hot sand. The whole world of the
pines and of the rocks hums and glistens and stings with life.

But if, on these rocky outcrops, the pines and the palmettos were destroyed, by lightning or the old fires of Indians, another great tree took its place and gradually changed, with its own associated forms, the whole nature of the place. This was the live oak, the first of the hardwoods. They made the first hammocks at the edge of rivers or on the driest Everglades islands.

The warblers in their thousands migrate up and down the continents, spring and fall, South America to North America and back, enlivening the oaks with their small flitting shapes and tiny whisperings; palm and pine warblers, the myrtles, the black-throated blues, the amazing redstarts, the black-and-whites—oh, it is impossible to name all the warblers that pass here.

24 Dozens of other birds are there in their seasons in the live oaks, among the red splashes of air plants and the patches of lichens. Green lizards puff out their throats like thin red bubbles in some unhearable love call. The eternal cardinals raise their first trillings before dawn, "Pretty, pretty, pretty—sweet, sweet-sweet." A mocking bird, all one whirl of gray and white, flips through those aging branches chasing a small brown owl or flinging him in the sun from the topmost twigs to fling up his modulated lovely spray of words. The small tree-frogs pipe there in the gray before rain and the yellow-billed cuckoo croaks, and the almost invisible rain-crow. In the first tender dark the little owl comes out from his hole where the mocker chased him to begin his low, liquid bubbling, the velvet secret voice of the night.

South in the lower hammocks in a live oak, frowsy with dry Resurrection ferns that the first rain startles to green life, some pale green slender stalk with minute gold eyes will seem to grow along a branch, poking upward on its own thoroughfare, high and higher in the leafiness, a small green tree snake. Such little snakes achieve the sun among the topmost leaves to be spied on by one of the loveliest bird-shapes of all, the free-flying, easy-soaring, easy-turning swallow-tailed kite, that lifts and ranges and swings in whiteness above the tree-tops. One stoop and the free bird slides upward on the wind, dangling the small tender green thing in pure sunlight to its airy and exalted death.

A huge ancient line of live oaks stands along the westernmost rock edge of Okeechobee, deep with moss, looking out over miles and miles of shallow reeds between them and the mirage-like glitter of that inland sea. There in open, sunblasted country the black-and-white caracara, that the Mexicans take for their national eagle, cries harshly from a bush top, his round, gold glance avid for lizards on the ground. A king snake, brave in yellow and fine black in the dust, snaps back in zigzags the speed of his fighting body. Grackles in thousands, creaking their interminable wheels of sound, hang in the reeds their thousands of pouchlike nests. Life is everywhere here too, infinite and divisible.

The live oaks, like dim giants crowded and choked by a thrusting forest of younger hardwoods, made that great Miami hammock, the largest tropical jungle on the North American mainland, which spread south of the Miami River like a dark cloud along that crumbling, spring-fed ledge of rock. Here where the leaf-screened light falls only in moving spots and speckles to the rotting, leaf-choking mold, the hoary ruins of live oaks are clouded by vines and Resurrection ferns, their roots deep in the rotting limestone shelves among wet potholes green-shadowed with the richest fern life in the world— maidenhair and Boston ferns and brackens and ferns innumerable. At night the mosquitoes shrill in the inky blackness prickled through with fireflies.

About the live oaks is waged the central drama of all this jungle, the silent, 28 fighting, creeping struggle for sunlight of the strangler fig. It is one of those great trees people call rubber trees or Banyans. They are all *Ficus,* but the strangler is *Ficus aurea.* A strangler seed dropped by a bird in a cranny of oak bark will sprout and send down fine brown root hairs that dangle and lengthen until they touch the ground. There they grip and thicken and become buttresses. Over the small hard oak leaves the thick dark-green oily strangler's leaves lift and shut out the sun. Its long columnar trunks and octopus roots wrap as if they were melted and poured about the parent trunk, flowing upward and downward in wooden nets and baskets and flutings and enlacings, until later the strangler will stand like a cathedral about a fragment of tree it has killed, crowning leaves and vast branches supported by columns and vaultings and pilings of its bowery roots.

The stranglers are only the most evident and dramatic of all these crowding tropical jungle trees; smooth red-brown gumbo limbos, ilex, eugenias, satinwoods, mastic, cherry laurel, paradise trees, the poisonous manchineel, the poisonwood, the Florida boxwood and hundreds more which the hurricanes brought over from Cuba and the West Indies.

This was the jungle that people thought the Everglades resembled. Birds flit through it only rarely. The little striped skunk leaves its trail. The brilliant coral snake buries its deadly black nose in its loam. The false coral, the harlequin, with its yellow nose, is hardly less hidden. Spiders stretch their exquisite traps for pale insects. Small brown scorpions move on the rotting logs. And far up among the tufted air plants the small native orchids are as brown and pale yellow and faint white as the light they seek.

Everywhere among these branches moves imperceptibly one of the loveliest life forms of these coasts—the pale-ivory, pale-coral, pale-yellow and pale-rose, whorled and etched and banded shell of the *Liguus,* the tree snails. Their pointed shell bubbles are found chiefly on smooth-barked trees in the dry hammocks, but every Everglades island-hammock has its own varieties, subspecies developed in countless lifetimes in a single unique area, varying with an infinity of delicate differences. They came from the tropics. They are a world in themselves.

Moths move in and out of the light at the jungle edge, the twilight hawk 32 moth, seeking the pale-flowered vines, and the rose-colored tiger moth. There is a day in the spring when myriads of white butterflies drift over the whole land, moving out to sea inexplicably. They are caught and die in thousands against the jungles.

But here especially the strangest of the butterflies quivers silently in the bands of sun in the green light of leaves, the only one of its tropical kind on this mainland. It is the *Heliconius*, named for the sun, barred black and pale yellow as the light and shade, wavering always in companies, which no bird will touch. The *Heliconius* drowse of nights in colonies, delicately crowded and hanging on a single small tree. When bright moon light reaches them they have been seen to wake and drift about, filling a leafy glade with their quivering moon-colored half-sleep.

About the rivers of the west, north of the tropic vegetation line, grows the water oak. The water oaks grow taller and more regular than the live oaks. Their longer pointed leaves drop off the bare boughs in a brief winter and put on their new light green long before the rusty live oaks renew themselves, in that misty river country. Both crowd down to the glossy water and make landscapes like old dim pictures where the deer came down delicately and the cows stand, to drink among their own reflections.

In the great Miami hammock, along the banks of almost every river, bordering the salt marshes, scattered in the thinner pineland, making their own shapely and recognizable island-hammocks within the Everglades river, everywhere, actually, except in the densest growth of the saw grass itself, stands the Sabal palmetto. To distinguish it from the low shrubby saw palmetto, it is called the cabbage palm. With its gray-green fans glittering like metal in the brilliance, its round top bearing also branches of queer blossoms and hard dark berries, the cabbage palm grows singly or in dramatic clumps over stout round trunks. The basketwork of old fan hilts is broken off below as the trunk grows tall and smooth. Ferns and vines and air plants and lizards and spiders live in that basketwork. They are often engulfed by strangler figs. They bristle on the banks of fresh-water rivers among the oaks. They make dense islands in the sawgrass river.

36   They are a northern growth, unrelated to the tropical palms, to the coconut palms that rise above the outer beaches and are set everywhere in cities, or the great royal palms that tower among the Everglades keys and in a few magnificent hammocks of their own toward the west coast. The Spaniards introduced the coconuts to Panama from the Philippines, the royals are native West Indians. Their nuts were blown over from Cuba and germinated in the rain-washed debris of some tropical cyclone. Other delicate palms, like the silver palm of the lower mainland, came the same way.

Then there is the enduring cypress. There are many cypresses in the world but the Everglades region has two: the short, often dwarf, pond cypress and the tall fresh-water river cypress. It is the river cypress that is tall, to 125 feet, silver gray, columnar, almost pyramidal on its broad fluted base, whose curiously short branches lose their leaves in winter and stand ghostly and gaunt among the hanging Spanish moss and red-tongued air plants. Spring draws out from the ancient wood the tiny scratched lines of its thready leaves, the palest yellow-green darkening to emerald. It is a fine timber tree. White and green, over brown water, against an amazing blue and white sky, it is most strangely beautiful.

The cypress that grows in muddy water has that curious accompaniment, the rootlike extension into the air, like dead stumps, called cypress knees, which are thought to aerate the mudbound roots. The dry-land cypress does not need them. It grows up rivers of both coasts and about the lake. But in its greatest area, a vast dramatic association of river cypress and pond cypress marks the west bank of the saw-grass river, and forms the Big Cypress Swamp.

The Big Cypress extends south from the Devil's Garden, a wilderness of pine and scrubby stuff and bushes, near that dome of land in the angle of Caloosahatchee and the lake, south in great fingers which reach to the headwaters of the Turner River, as far down as the salt water and the mangrove. The rock below it is uneven and ridgy, all hollows and higher places. It is called "swamp" because in the rains the water stands in it and does not run off. It is not moving water, like the saw-grass Glades. It was called "the Big Cypress" because it covered so great an area.

The river cypresses stand there in wintertime in great gray-scratched heads, like small hills, towering above the dense and lower pond, or dwarf, cypress between, thinly set in the wetter hollows of wire grass, starred with white spider lilies and sedges and, in drier places, milkwort in saffron-headed swaths. Red-shouldered hawks cruise the low cypress and the marshlands, marsh hawks balance and tip, showing white rump marks, and far over at the edge of a thicket a deer feeds, and flicks his white-edged tail before he lifts his head and stares.

From high in a plane at that time of year the Big Cypress seems an undulating misted surface full of peaks and gray valleys changing to feathering green. East of it, sharply defined as a river from its banks, move the vast reaches of the saw grass.

The brown deer, the pale-colored lithe beautiful panthers that feed on them, the tuft-eared wildcats with their high-angled hind legs, the opossum and the rats and the rabbits have lived in and around it and the Devil's Garden and the higher pinelands to the west since this world began. The quail pipe and call through the open spaces. The great barred owls hoot far off in the nights and the chuck-will's-widows on the edge of the pines aspirate their long whistling echoing cries. The bronze turkeys, the most intelligent of all the birds or beasts, feed in the watery places and roost early in the thick cypress tops, far from the prowlers below. And the black Florida bear, which sleeps even here his short winter sleep, goes rooting and grumbling and shoving through the underbrush, ripping up logs for grubs and tearing at berries, scorning no mice.

The bears move to the beaches and, like the panthers, dig for turtle eggs.

They catch crabs and chew them solemnly and eat birds' eggs if they find them, and ripe beach plums. The panthers prey most on the range hogs of the settlers, and so they are hunted with dogs, and fight viciously, killing many before they leap into trees and, snarling, never to be tamed, are shot.

44   Here in the cypress pools—but for that matter, everywhere in the watery Glades, from lake to sea—lives the Glades' first citizen, the otter. Like the birds, he is everywhere. The oily fur of his long lithe body is ready for heat or cold, so long as it is wet. His webbed hands are more cunning than the raccoon's. His broad jolly muzzle explores everything, tests everything, knows everything. His quickness is a snake's lightning quickness. He has a snake's suppleness and recovery, but not the snake's timidity. His heart is stout and nothing stops him.

The otter has been seen to swim and flirt and turn among a crowd of thrashing alligators, from whose clumsy attack he has only to dive and flash away. He knows how to enjoy life in the sun better than all the rest of all the creatures. He is gay. He is crammed with lively spirit. He makes a mud slide down a bank, and teaches his cubs to fling themselves down it and romp and tumble and swim upside down in the frothing water. He is fond of his female and plays with a ball and has fun. His ready grinning curiosity and friendliness betray him to the hunter and trapper. This is his home.

On the scanty dwarf cypress the gray Ward's heron stands rigid. The big black-and-white wood ibis, like a stork, which flies so high and so far in such grave and orderly squadrons, slides downward on hollow wing and lights with a great flapping and balancing that makes the tree look silly under its teetering grip as it stares down its great curved beak for a frog there below. It is as though all the life of the Everglades region, every form of beast or bird or gnat or garfish in the pools, or the invisible life that pulses in the scum on the pools, was concentrated in the Big Cypress.

The dwarf cypress has its area, perhaps the most fantastic of all, far toward Cape Sable, south of the live-oak jungle that was called Paradise Key, where the royal palms stood high overhead like bursting beacons seen across the sloughs. Men have said they have seen panthers here, not tan, but inky black. There southward, under the even more brilliant light, as if already the clouds reflected the glare from the sea beyond, the small cypress, four or five feet tall, stands in the rock itself, barely etched with green. These trees seem centuries old, and they are very old indeed, in spite of fire and hurricane. Even in full leaf their green is scant. There are moccasins around their roots out of the standing clear water, and high, high over, a bald eagle lazily lifting, or an osprey beating up from the fishing flats.

48   Lake jungles, pine, live oak, cabbage palmetto, cypress, each has its region and its associated life. As the islands in the saw grass pointed southward in the water currents, their vegetation changes like their banks, from temperate to subtropic, to the full crammed tropic of the south.

*   *   *

Understanding What You Read

1. This piece about the Florida Everglades was first published in 1947. Of the many animals that Douglas mentions, which would you expect to see if you went there today?
2. Which animals do you think might be threatened?

Writing About What You Read

1. Write a letter inviting a friend to join you on a camping trip to the Everglades for spring break. Using specific details about what it will be like, persuade your friend to come along.
2. Do some research in the library to find out about the Everglades today. What species are endangered? What industrial and agricultural pollution is damaging this fragile ecosystem? What alien plants are killing off the native flora? What is being done to preserve the Everglades? Write a report of your findings.

ANNIE DILLARD

Dillard (b. 1945) achieved early success as a writer with the publication of *Pilgrim at Tinker Creek* (1974), a best-seller and winner of the Pulitzer Prize for nonfiction. Her other works include *An American Childhood* (1987), *The Writing Life* (1989), and *The Living* (1992), a novel about nineteenth-century life in Washington State, where Dillard lived for some years. Though she focuses in many of her works on the small details of nature in rural Virginia, Dillard has also written about her experiences in places as different as the Ecuadorian jungle and the Galápagos Islands. She teaches periodically at Wesleyan University in Connecticut. "Life on the Rocks: The Galápagos" is from *Teaching a Stone to Talk* (1982).

Life on the Rocks: The Galápagos

FIRST there was nothing, and although you know with your reason that nothing is nothing, it is easier to visualize it as a limitless slosh of sea—say, the Pacific. Then energy contracted into matter, and although you know that even an invisible gas is matter, it is easier to visualize it as a massive squeeze of volcanic lava spattered inchoate from the secret pit of the ocean and hardening mute and intractable on nothing's lapping shore—like a series of islands, an archipelago. Like: the Galápagos. Then a softer strain of matter began to twitch. It was a kind of shaped water; it flowed, hardening here and there at its tips. There were blue-green algae; there were tortoises.

The ice rolled up, the ice rolled back, and I knelt on a plain of lava boulders in the islands called Galápagos, stroking a giant tortoise's neck. The tortoise closed its eyes and stretched its neck to its greatest height and vulnerability. I rubbed that neck, and when I pulled away my hand, my palm was green with a slick of single-celled algae. I stared at the algae, and at the tortoise, the way you stare at any life on a lava flow, and thought: Well—here we all are.

Being here is being here on the rocks. These Galapagonian rocks, one of them seventy-five miles long, have dried under the equatorial sun between five and six hundred miles west of the South American continent; they lie at the latitude of the Republic of Ecuador, to which they belong.

4   There is a way a small island rises from the ocean affronting all reason. It is a chunk of chaos pounded into visibility *ex nihilo:* here rough, here smooth, shaped just so by a matrix of physical necessities too weird to contemplate, here instead of there, here instead of not at all. It is a fantastic utterance, as though I were to open my mouth and emit a French horn, or a vase, or a knob of tellurium. It smacks of folly, of first causes.

I think of the island called Daphnecita, little Daphne, on which I never set foot. It's in half of my few photographs, though, because it obsessed me: a dome of gray lava like a pitted loaf, the size of the Plaza Hotel, glazed with guano and crawling with red-orange crabs. Sometimes I attributed to this island's cliff face a surly, infantile consciousness, as though it were sulking in the silent moment after it had just shouted, to the sea and the sky, "I didn't ask to be born." Or sometimes it aged to a raging adolescent, a kid who's just learned that the game is fixed, demanding, "What did you have me for, if you're just going to push me around?" Daphnecita: again, a wise old island, mute, leading the life of pure creaturehood open to any antelope or saint. After you've blown the ocean sky-high, what's there to say? What if we the people had the sense or grace to live as cooled islands in an archipelago live, with dignity, passion, and no comment?

It is worth flying to Guayaquil, Ecuador, and then to Baltra in the Galápagos just to see the rocks. But these rocks are animal gardens. They are home to a Hieronymus Bosch[1] assortment of windblown, stowaway, cast-away, flotsam, and shipwrecked creatures. Most exist nowhere else on earth. These reptiles and insects, small mammals and birds, evolved unmolested on the various islands on which they were cast into unique species adapted to

---

[1]A Flemish painter (1450–1516) whose colorful paintings were filled with bizarre plants and animals as well as fantastic, monstrous, and diabolical figures.

the boulder-wrecked shores, the cactus deserts of the lowlands, or the elevated jungles of the large islands' interiors. You come for the animals. You come to see the curious shapes soft proteins can take, to impress yourself with their reality, and to greet them.

You walk among clattering four-foot marine iguanas heaped on the shore lava, and on each other, like slag. You swim with penguins; you watch flightless cormorants dance beside you, ignoring you, waving the black nubs of their useless wings. Here are nesting blue-footed boobies, real birds with real feathers, whose legs and feet are nevertheless patently fake, manufactured by Mattel. The tortoises are big as stoves. The enormous land iguanas at your feet change color in the sunlight, from gold to blotchy red as you watch.

There is always some creature going about its beautiful business. I missed the boat back to my ship, and was left behind momentarily on uninhabited South Plaza island, because I was watching the Audubon's shearwaters. These dark pelagic birds flick along pleated seas in stitching flocks, flailing their wings rapidly—because if they don't, they'll stall. A shearwater must fly fast, or not at all. Consequently it has evolved two nice behaviors which serve to bring it into its nest alive. The nest is a shearwater-sized hole in the lava cliff. The shearwater circles over the water, ranging out from the nest a quarter of a mile, and veers gradually toward the cliff, making passes at its nest. If the flight angle is precisely right, the bird will fold its wings at the hole's entrance and stall directly onto its floor. The angle is perhaps seldom right, however; one shearwater I watched made a dozen suicidal-looking passes before it vanished into a chink. The other behavior is spectacular. It involves choosing the nest hole in a site below a prominent rock with a downward-angled face. The shearwater comes careering in at full tilt, claps its wings, stalls itself into the rock, and the rock, acting as a backboard, banks it home.

The animals are tame. They have not been persecuted, and show no fear of man. You pass among them as though you were wind, spindrift, sunlight, leaves. The songbirds are tame. On Hood Island I sat beside a nesting waved albatross while a mockingbird scratched in my hair, another mockingbird jabbed at my fingernail, and a third mockingbird made an exquisite progression of pokes at my bare feet up the long series of eyelets in my basketball shoes. The marine iguanas are tame. One settler, Carl Angermeyer, built his house on the site of a marine iguana colony. The gray iguanas, instead of moving out, moved up on the roof, which is corrugated steel. Twice daily on the patio, Angermeyer feeds them a mixture of boiled rice and tuna fish from a plastic basin. Their names are all, unaccountably, Annie. Angermeyer beats on the basin with a long-handled spoon, calling, "Here AnnieAnnieAnnieAnnie"—and the spiny reptiles, fifty or sixty strong, click along the steel roof, finger their way down the lava boulder and mortar walls, and swarm round his bare legs to elbow into the basin and be elbowed out again smeared with a mash of boiled rice on their bellies and on their protuberant, black, plated lips.

The wild hawk is tame. The Galápagos hawk is related to North America's Swainson's hawk; I have read that if you take pains, you can walk up and pat it. I never tried. We people don't walk up and pat each other; enough is enough. The animals' critical distance and mine tended to coincide, so we could enjoy an easy sociability without threat of violence or unwonted intimacy. The hawk, which is not notably sociable, nevertheless endures even a blundering approach, and is apparently as content to perch on a scrub tree at your shoulder as anyplace else.

In the Galápagos, even the flies are tame. Although most of the land is Ecuadorian national park, and as such rigidly protected, I confess I gave the evolutionary ball an offsides shove by dispatching every fly that bit me, marveling the while at its pristine ignorance, its blithe failure to register a flight trigger at the sweep of my descending hand—an insouciance that was almost, but not quite, disarming. After you kill a fly, you pick it up and feed it to a lava lizard, a bright-throated four-inch lizard that scavenges everywhere in the arid lowlands. And you walk on, passing among the innocent mobs on every rock hillside; or you sit, and they come to you.

12   We are strangers and sojourners, soft dots on the rocks. You have walked along the strand and seen where birds have landed, walked, and flown; their tracks begin in sand, and go, and suddenly end. Our tracks do that: but we go down. And stay down. While we're here, during the seasons our tents are pitched in the light, we pass among each other crying "greetings" in a thousand tongues, and "welcome," and "good-bye." Inhabitants of un-crowded colonies tend to offer the stranger famously warm hospitality—and such are the Galápagos sea lions. Theirs is the greeting the first creatures must have given Adam—a hero's welcome, a universal and undeserved huzzah. Go, and be greeted by sea lions.

I was sitting with ship's naturalist Soames Summerhays on a sand beach under cliffs on uninhabited Hood Island. The white beach was a havoc of lava boulders black as clinkers, sleek with spray, and lambent as brass in the sinking sun. To our left a dozen sea lions were body-surfing in the long green combers that rose, translucent, half a mile offshore. When the combers broke, the shoreline boulders rolled. I could feel the roar in the rough rock on which I sat; I could hear the grate inside each long backsweeping sea, the rumble of a rolled million rocks muffled in splashes and the seethe before the next wave's heave.

To our right, a sea lion slipped from the ocean. It was a young bull; in another few years he would be dangerous, bellowing at intruders and biting off great dirty chunks of the ones he caught. Now this young bull, which weighed maybe 120 pounds, sprawled silhouetted in the late light, slick as a drop of quicksilver, his glistening whiskers radii of gold like any crown. He hauled his packed bulk toward us up the long beach; he flung himself with an enormous surge of fur-clad muscle onto the boulder where I sat. "Soames," I said—very quietly, "he's here because *we're* here, isn't he?" The naturalist nodded. I felt water drip on my elbow behind me, then the fragile scrape of whiskers, and finally the wet warmth and weight of a muzzle, as the creature settled to sleep on my arm. I was catching on to sea lions.

Walk into the water. Instantly sea lions surround you, even if none has been in sight. To say that they come to play with you is not especially anthropomorphic. Animals play. The bull sea lions are off patrolling their territorial shores; these are the cows and young, which range freely. A five-foot sea lion peers intently into your face, then urges her muzzle gently against your underwater mask and searches your eyes without blinking. Next she rolls upside down and slides along the length of your floating body, rolls again, and casts a long glance back at your eyes. You are, I believe, supposed to follow, and think up something clever in return. You can play games with sea lions in the water using shells or bits of leaf, if you are willing. You can spin on your vertical axis and a sea lion will swim circles around you, keeping her face always six inches from yours, as though she were tethered. You can make a game of touching their back flippers, say, and the sea lions will understand at once; somersaulting conveniently before your clumsy hands, they will give you an excellent field of back flippers.

And when you leave the water, they follow. They don't want you to go. They porpoise to the shore, popping their heads up when they lose you and casting about, then speeding to your side and emitting a choked series of vocal notes. If you won't relent, they disappear, barking; but if you sit on the beach with so much as a foot in the water, two or three will station with you, floating on their backs and saying, Urr.

16

Few people come to the Galápagos. Buccaneers used to anchor in the bays to avoid pursuit, to rest, and to lighter on fresh water. The world's whaling ships stopped here as well, to glut their holds with fresh meat in the form of giant tortoises. The whalers used to let the tortoises bang around on deck for a few days to empty their guts; then they stacked them below on their backs to live—if you call that living—without food or water for a year. When they wanted fresh meat, they killed one.

Early inhabitants of the islands were a desiccated assortment of grouches, cranks, and ships' deserters. These hardies shot, poisoned, and enslaved each other off, leaving behind a fecund gang of feral goats, cats, dogs, and pigs whose descendants skulk in the sloping jungles and take their tortoise hatchlings neat. Now scientists at the Charles Darwin Research Station, on the island of Santa Cruz, rear the tortoise hatchlings for several years until their shells are tough enough to resist the crunch; then they release them in the wilds of their respective islands. Today, some few thousand people live on three of the islands; settlers from Ecuador, Norway, Germany, and France make a livestock or pineapple living from the rich volcanic soils. The settlers themselves seem to embody a high degree of courteous and conscious humanity, perhaps because of their relative isolation.

On the island of Santa Cruz, eleven fellow passengers and I climb in an open truck up the Galápagos' longest road; we shift to horses, burros, and mules, and visit the lonely farm of Alf Kastdalen. He came to the islands as a child with his immigrant parents from Norway. Now a broad, blond man in his late forties with children of his own, he lives in an isolated house of finished timbers imported from the mainland, on four hundred acres he claimed from the jungle by hand. He raises cattle. He walks us round part of his farm, smiling expansively and meeting our chatter with a willing, open gaze and kind words. The pasture looks like any pasture—but the rocks under the grass are round lava ankle-breakers, the copses are a tangle of thorny bamboo and bromeliads, and the bordering trees dripping in epiphytes are breadfruit, papaya, avocado, and orange.

20   Kastdalen's isolated house is heaped with books in three languages. He knows animal husbandry; he also knows botany and zoology. He feeds us soup, chicken worth chewing for, green *naranjilla* juice, noodles, pork in big chunks, marinated mixed vegetables, rice, and bowl after bowl of bright mixed fruits.

     And his isolated Norwegian mother sees us off; our beasts are ready. We will ride down the mud forest track to the truck at the Ecuadorian settlement, down the long road to the boat, and across the bay to the ship. I lean down to catch her words. She is gazing at me with enormous warmth. "Your hair," she says softly. I am blond. *Adiós.*

Understanding What You Read

1. Dillard says she is not anthropomorphizing the sea lions when she describes their behavior. What evidence does she give that suggests that in fact she does just that when she looks at the hawk, elements in the landscape, and other details?
2. How does the story of the visit to the Norwegian household relate to the rest of the essay?

Writing About What You Read

Dillard's essay was written more than ten years ago. Look up articles about the Galápagos published since then and write an essay about what you learn.

E. O. WILSON

The evolutionary biologist Edward O. Wilson is one of America's most distinguished and influential scientists. He currently teaches at Harvard University. Wilson is author of, among other prize-winning books, the best-selling *Sociobiology: The New Synthesis* (1975), a work that aroused controversy for its assertion that genes determine behavior. An authority on social insects, Wilson has expanded a research interest in how ant communities function to a far-reaching considera- tion of how life became so diverse, how little we know about most species, and how human activity is destroying diversity. *Biophilia* (1984), a collection of Wilson's personal essays, reflects his belief that an affinity for life (biophilia) must be the ethical basis for human efforts to preserve diversity. Not content simply to sound the alarm about the threats to biodiversity, Wilson proposes in his most recent book, *The Diversity of Life* (1992), specific actions to preserve and enhance biodiversity. "Krakatau," the second chapter of that book, is about how life returned to an island where all life was snuffed out by a series of violent volcanic eruptions.

Krakatau

KRAKATAU, earlier misnamed Krakatoa, an island the size of Manhattan located midway in the Sunda Strait between Sumatra and Java, came to an end on Monday morning, August 27, 1883. It was dismembered by a series of powerful volcanic eruptions. The most violent occurred at 10:02 A.M., blowing upward like the shaped explosion of a large nuclear bomb, with an estimated force equivalent to 100–150 megatons of TNT. The airwave it created traveled at the speed of sound around the world, reaching the opposite end of the earth near Bogotá, Colombia, nineteen hours later, whereupon it bounced back to Krakatau and then back and forth for seven recorded passages over the earth's surface. The audible sounds, resembling the distant cannonade of a ship in distress, carried southward across Australia to Perth, northward to Singapore, and westward 4,600 kilometers to Rod- riguez Island in the Indian Ocean, the longest distance traveled by any airborne sound in recorded history.

As the island collapsed into the subterranean chamber emptied by the eruption, the sea rushed in to fill the newly formed caldera. A column of magma, rock, and ash rose 5 kilometers into the air, then fell earthward, thrusting the sea outward in a tsunami 40 meters in height. The great tidal waves, resembling black hills when first sighted on the horizon, fell upon the shores of Java and Sumatra, washing away entire towns and killing 40,000 people. The segments traversing the channels and reaching the open sea continued on as spreading waves around the world. The waves were still a meter high when they came ashore in Ceylon, now Sri Lanka, where they drowned one person, their last casualty. Thirty-two hours after the explosion, they rolled in to Le Havre, France, reduced at last to centimeter-high swells.

The eruptions lifted more than 18 cubic kilometers of rock and other material into the air. Most of this tephra, as it is called by geologists, quickly rained back down onto the surface, but a residue of sulfuric-acid aerosol and dust boiled upward as high as 50 kilometers and diffused through the stratosphere around the world, where for several years it created brilliant red sunsets and "Bishop's rings," opalescent coronas surrounding the sun.

Back on Krakatau the scene was apocalyptic. Throughout the daylight hours the whole world seemed about to end for those close enough to witness the explosions. At the climactic moment of 10:02 the American barque *W. H. Besse* was proceeding toward the straits 84 kilometers east northeast of Krakatau. The first officer jotted in his logbook that "terrific reports" were heard, followed by

> a heavy black cloud rising up from the direction of Krakatoa Island, the barometer fell an inch at one jump, suddenly rising and falling an inch at a time, called all hands, furled all sails securely, which was scarcely done before the squall struck the ship with terrific force; let go port anchor and all the chain the locker, wind increasing to a hurricane; let go starboard anchor, it had gradually been growing dark since 9 A.M. and by the time the squall struck us, it was darker than any night I ever saw; this was midnight at noon, a heavy shower of ashes came with the squall, the air being so thick it was difficult to breathe, also noticed a strong smell of sulfur, all hands expecting to be suffocated; the terrible noises from the volcano, the sky filled with forked lightning, running in all directions and making the darkness more intense than ever; the howling of the wind through the rigging formed one of the wildest and most awful scenes imaginable, one that will never be forgotten by any one on board, all expecting that the last days of the earth had come; the water was running by us in the direction of the volcano at the rate of 12 miles per hour, at 4 P.M. wind moderating, the explosions had nearly ceased, the shower of ashes was not so heavy; so was enabled to see our way around the decks; the ship was covered with tons of fine ashes resembling pumice stone, it stuck to the sails, rigging and masts like glue.

In the following weeks, the Sunda Strait returned to outward normality, but with an altered geography. The center of Krakatau had been replaced by an undersea crater 7 kilometers long and 270 meters deep. Only a remnant at the southern end still rose from the sea. It was covered by a layer of obsidian-laced pumice 40 meters or more thick and heated to somewhere between 300° and 850°C., enough at the upper range to melt lead. All traces of life had, of course, been extinguished.

Rakata, the ash-covered mountain of old Krakatau, survived as a sterile island. But life quickly enveloped it again. In a sense, the spinning reel of biological history halted, then reversed, like a motion picture run backward, as living organisms began to return to Rakata. Biologists quickly grasped the unique opportunity that Rakata afforded: to watch the assembly of a tropical ecosystem from the very beginning. Would the organisms be different from those that had existed before? Would a rain forest eventually cover the island again?

The first search for life on Rakata was conducted by a French expedition in May 1884, nine months after the explosions. The main cliff was eroding rapidly, and rocks still rolled down the sides incessantly, stirring clouds of dust and emitting a continuous noise "like the rattling of distant musketry." Some of the stones whirled through the air, ricocheting down the sides of the ravines and splashing into the sea. What appeared to be mist in the distance turned close up into clouds of dust stirred by the falling debris. The crew and expedition members eventually found a safe landing site and fanned out to learn what they could. After searching for organisms in particular, the ship's naturalist wrote that "notwithstanding all my researches, I was not able to observe any symptom of animal life. I only discovered one microscopic spider—only one; this strange pioneer of the renovation was busy spinning its web."

A baby spider? How could a tiny wingless creature reach the empty island so quickly? Arachnologists know that a majority of species "balloon" at some point in their life cycle. The spider stands on the edge of a leaf or some other exposed spot and lets out a thread of silk from the spinnerets at the posterior tip of its abdomen. As the strand grows it catches an air current and stretches downwind, like the string of a kite. The spider spins more and more of the silk until the thread exerts a strong pull on its body. Then it releases its grip on the surface and soars upward. Not just pinhead-sized babies but large spiders can occasionally reach thousands of meters of altitude and travel hundreds of kilometers before settling to the ground to start a new life. Either that or land on the water and die. The voyagers have no control over their own descent.

Ballooning spiders are members of what ecologists, with the accidental felicity that sometimes pops out of Greek and Latin sources, have delightfully called the aeolian plankton. In ordinary parlance, plankton is the vast swarm of algae and small animals carried passively by water currents; aeolian refers to the wind. The creatures composing the aeolian plankton are devoted almost entirely to long-distance dispersal. You can see some of it forming over lawns and bushes on a quiet summer afternoon, as aphids use their feeble wings to rise just high enough to catch the wind and be carried away. A rain of planktonic bacteria, fungus spores, small seeds, insects, spiders, and other small creatures falls continuously on most parts of the earth's land surface. It is sparse and hard to detect moment by moment, but it mounts up to large numbers over a period of weeks and months. This is how most of the species colonized the seared and smothered remnant of Krakatau.

The potential of the planktonic invasion has been documented by Ian

Thornton and a team of Australian and Indonesian biologists who visited the Krakatau area in the 1980s. While studying Rakata they also visited Anak Krakatau ("Child of Krakatau"), a small island that emerged in 1930 from volcanic activity along the submerged northern rim of the old Krakatau caldera. On its ash-covered lava flows they placed traps made from white plastic containers filled with seawater. This part of the surface of Anak Krakatau dated from localized volcanic activity from 1960 to 1981 and was nearly sterile, resembling the condition on Rakata soon after the larger islands' violent formation. During ten days the traps caught a surprising variety of windborne arthropods. The specimens collected, sorted, and identified included a total of 72 species of spiders, springtails, crickets, earwigs, barklice, hemipterous bugs, moths, flies, beetles, and wasps.

There are other ways to cross the water gaps separating Rakata from nearby islands and the Javan and Sumatran coasts. The large semiaquatic monitor lizard *Varanus salvator* probably swam over. It was present no later than 1899, feasting on the crabs that crawl along the shore. Another long-distance swimmer was the reticulated python, a giant snake reaching up to 8 meters in length. Probably all of the birds crossed over by powered flight. But only a small percentage of the species of Java and Sumatra were represented because it is a fact, curiously, that many forest species refuse to cross water gaps even when the nearest island is in full view. Bats, straying off course, made the Rakata landfall. Winged insects of larger size, especially butterflies and dragonflies, probably also traveled under their own power. Under similar conditions in the Florida Keys, I have watched such insects fly easily from one small island to another, as though they were moving about over meadows instead of salt water.

12   Rafting is a much less common but still important means of transport. Logs, branches, sometimes entire trees fall into rivers and bays and are carried out to sea, complete with microorganisms, insects, snakes, frogs, and occasional rodents and other small mammals living on them at the moment of departure. Blocks of pumice from old volcanic islands, riddled with enough closed air spaces to keep them afloat, also serve as rafts.

Once in a great while a violent storm turns larger animals such as lizards or frogs into aeolian debris, tearing them loose from their perches and propelling them to distant shores. Waterspouts pick up fish and transport them live to nearby lakes and streams.

Swelling the migration further, organisms carry other organisms with them. Most animals are miniature arks laden with parasites. They also transport accidental hitchhikers in soil clinging to the skin, including bacteria and protozoans of immense variety, fungal spores, nematode worms, tardigrades,[1] mites, and feather lice. Seeds of some species of herbs and trees pass live through the guts of birds, to be deposited later in feces, which serves as

---

[1]Eight-legged microscopic arthropods that live in water or damp moss.

instant fertilizer. A few arthropods practice what biologists call phoresy, deliberate hitchhiking on larger animals. Pseudoscorpions, tiny replicas of true scorpions but lacking stings, use their lobsterlike claws to seize the hairs of dragonflies and other large winged insects, then ride these magic carpets for long distances.

The colonists poured relentlessly into Rakata from all directions. A 100-meter-high electrified fence encircling the island could not have stopped them. Airborne organisms would still have tumbled in from above to spawn a rich ecosystem. But the largely happenstance nature of colonization means that flora and fauna did not return to Rakata in a smooth textbook manner, with plants growing to sylvan thickness, then herbivores proliferating, and finally carnivores prowling. The surveys made on Rakata and later on Anak Krakatau disclosed a far more haphazard buildup, with some species inexplicably going extinct and others flourishing when seemingly they should have quickly disappeared. Spiders and flightless carnivorous crickets persisted almost miraculously on bare pumice fields; they fed on a thin diet of insects landing in the aeolian debris. Large lizards and some of the birds lived on beach crabs, which subsisted in turn on dead marine plants and animals washed ashore by waves. (The original name of Krakatau was Karkata, or Sanskrit for "crab"; Rakata also means crab in the old Javanese language.) Thus animal diversity was not wholly dependent on vegetation. And for its part vegetation grew up in patches, alternately spreading and retreating across the island to create an irregular mosaic.

If the fauna and flora came back chaotically, they also came back fast. In the fall of 1884, a little more than a year after the eruption, biologists encountered a few shoots of grass, probably *Imperata* and *Saccharum*. In 1886 there were fifteen species of grasses and shrubs, in 1897 forty-nine, and in 1928 nearly three hundred. Vegetation dominated by *Ipomoea* spread along the shores. At the same time grassland dotted with *Casuarina* pines gave way here and there to richer pioneer stands of trees and shrubs. In 1919 W. M. Doctors van Leeuwen, from the Botanical Gardens at Buitenzorg, found forest patches surrounded by nearly continuous grassland. Ten years later he found the reverse: forest now clothed the entire island and was choking out the last of the grassland patches. Today Rakata is covered completely by tropical Asian rain forest typical in outward appearance. Yet the process of colonization is far from complete. Not a single tree species characterizing the deep, primary forests on Java and Sumatra has made it back. Another hundred years or more may be needed for investment by a forest fully comparable to that of old, undisturbed Indonesian islands of the same size.

Some insects, spiders, and vertebrates aside, the earliest colonists of most kinds of animals died on Rakata soon after arrival. But as the vegetation expanded and the forest matured, increasing numbers of species took hold. At the time of the Thornton expeditions of 1984–85, the inhabitants in-

16

cluded thirty species of land birds, nine bats, the Indonesian field rat, the ubiquitous black rat, and nine reptiles, including two geckos and *Varanus salvator*, the monitor lizard. The reticulated python, recorded as recently as 1933, was not present in 1984–85. A large host of invertebrate species, more than six hundred in all, lived on the island. They included a terrestrial flatworm, nematode worms, snails, scorpions, spiders, pseudoscorpions, centipedes, cockroaches, termites, barklice, cicadas, ants, beetles, moths, and butterflies. Also present were microscopic rotifers and tardigrades and a rich medley of bacteria.

A first look at the reconstituted flora and fauna of Rakata, in other words Krakatau a century after the apocalypse, gives the impression of life on a typical small Indonesian island. But the community of species remains in a highly fluid state. The number of resident bird species may now be approaching an equilibrium, the rise having slowed markedly since 1919 to settle close to thirty. Thirty is also about the number on other islands of Indonesia of similar size. At the same time, the *composition* of the bird species is less stable. New species have been arriving, and earlier ones have been declining to extinction. Owls and flycatchers arrived after 1919, for example, while several old residents such as the bulbul *(Pycnonotus aurigaster)* and gray-backed shrike *(Lanius schach)* disappeared. Reptiles appear to be at or close to a similar dynamic equilibrium. So are cockroaches, nymphalid butterflies, and dragonflies. Flightless mammals, represented solely by the two kinds of rats, are clearly not. Nor are plants, ants, or snails. Most of the other invertebrates are still too poorly explored on Rakata over sufficiently long periods of time to judge their status, but in general the overall number of species appears to be still rising.

Rakata, along with Panjang and Sertung, and other islands of the Krakatau archipelago blasted and pumice-coated by the 1883 explosion, have within the span of a century rewoven a semblance of the communities that existed before, and the diversity of life has largely returned. The question remains as to whether endemic species, those found only on the archipelago prior to 1883, were destroyed by the explosion. We can never be sure because the islands were too poorly explored by naturalists before Krakatau came so dramatically to the world's attention in 1883. It seems unlikely that endemic species ever existed. The islands are so small that the natural turnover of species may have been too fast to allow evolution to attain the creation of new species, even without volcanic episodes.

In fact the archipelago has suffered turbulence that destroyed or at least badly damaged its fauna and flora every few centuries. According to Javanese legend, the volcano Kapi erupted violently in the Sunda Strait in 416 A.D.: "At last the mountain Kapi with a tremendous roar burst into pieces and sunk into the deepest of the earth. The water of the sea rose and inundated the land." A series of smaller eruptions, burning at least part of the forest, occurred during 1680 and 1681.

Today you can sail close by the islands without guessing their violent history, unless Anak Krakatau happens to be smoldering that day. The thick green forest offers testimony to the ingenuity and resilence of life. Ordinary volcanic eruptions are not enough, then, to break the crucible of life.

Understanding What You Read

1. What were the effects of the Krakatau eruption worldwide?
2. What was the first form of life to reappear on Rakata and how did it get there?
3. What does Wilson mean when he says that the recolonization of Rakata was by happenstance?

Writing About What You Read

Imagine that you are part of a team of scientists returning to Rakata in the 1930s. Describe the experience.

MICHAEL POLLAN

Executive editor of *Harper's* magazine, Pollan (b. 1955) has written about gardens and nature for the *New York Times Magazine*, *Harper's*, *Orion Nature Quarterly*, and other publications. "The Idea of a Garden" is from *Second Nature: A Gardener's Education* (1991), a book that advocates considering some hard environmental questions in terms of a garden rather than "wilderness."

The Idea of a Garden

THE BIGGEST NEWS to come out of my town in many years was the tornado, or tornadoes, that careened through here on July 10, 1989, a Monday. Shooting down the Housatonic River Valley from the Berkshires, it veered east over Coltsfoot Mountain and then, after smudging the sky a weird gray-green, proceeded to pinball madly from hillside to hillside for about fifteen minutes before wheeling back up into the sky. This was part of the same storm that ripped open the bark of my ash tree. But the damage was much, much worse on the other side of town. Like a gigantic, skidding pencil eraser, the twister neatly erased whole patches of woods and roughly smeared many other ones, where it wiped out just the tops of the trees. Overnight, large parts of town were rendered unrecognizable.

One place where the eraser came down squarely was in the Cathedral Pines, a famous forest of old-growth white pine trees close to the center of town. A kind of local shrine, this forty-two-acre forest was one of the oldest stands of white pine in New England, the trees untouched since about 1800. To see it was to have some idea how the New World forest must have looked to the first settlers, and in 1985 the federal government designated it a "national natural landmark." To enter Cathedral Pines on a hot summer day was like stepping out of the sun into a dim cathedral, the sunlight cooled and sweetened by the trillions of pine needles as it worked its way down to soft, sprung ground that had been unacquainted with blue sky for the better part of two centuries. The storm came through at about five in the evening, and it took only a few minutes of wind before pines more than one hundred fifty feet tall and as wide around as missiles lay jackstrawed on the ground like a fistful of pencils dropped from a great height. The wind was so thunderous that people in houses at the forest's edge did not know trees had fallen until they ventured outside after the storm had passed. The following morning, the sky now clear, was the first in more than a century to bring sunlight crashing down onto this particular patch of earth.

"It is a terrible mess," the first selectman told the newspapers; "a tragedy," said another Cornwall resident, voicing the deep sense of loss shared by many in town. But in the days that followed, the selectman and the rest of us learned that our responses, though understandable, were short-sighted, unscientific, and, worst of all, anthropocentric. "It may be a calamity to us," a state environmental official told a reporter from the *Hartford Courant,* but "to biology it is not a travesty. It is just a natural occurrence." The Nature Conservancy, which owns Cathedral Pines, issued a press release explaining that "Monday's storm was just another link in the continuous chain of events that is responsible for shaping and changing this forest."

4   It wasn't long before the rub of these two perspectives set off a controversy heated enough to find its way into the pages of *The New York Times.* The Nature Conservancy, in keeping with its mandate to maintain its lands in a "state of nature," indicated that it would leave Cathedral Pines alone, allowing the forest to take its "natural course," whatever that might be. To town officials and neighbors of the forest this was completely unacceptable. The downed trees, besides constituting an eyesore right at the edge of town, also posed a fire hazard. A few summers of drought, and the timber might go up in a blaze that would threaten several nearby homes and possibly even the town itself. Many people in Cornwall wanted Cathedral Pines cleared and replanted, so that at least the next generation might live to see some semblance of the old forest. A few others had the poor taste to point out the waste of more than a million board-feet of valuable timber, stupendous lengths of unblemished, knot-free pine.

The newspapers depicted it as a classic environmental battle, pitting the interests of man against nature, and in a way it was that. On one side were the environmental purists, who felt that *any* intervention by man in the disposition of this forest would be unnatural. "If you're going to clean it up," one purist declared in the local press, "you might as well put up condos." On the other side stood the putative interests of man, variously expressed in the vocabulary of safety (the fire hazard), economics (the wasted lumber), and aesthetics (the "terrible mess").

Everybody enjoys a good local fight, but I have to say I soon found the whole thing depressing. This was indeed a classic environmental battle, in that it seemed to exemplify just about everything that's wrong with the way we approach problems of this kind these days. Both sides began to caricature each other's positions: the selectman's "terrible mess" line earned him ridicule for his anthropocentrism in the letters page of *The New York Times;* he in turn charged a Yale scientist who argued for noninterference with "living in an ivory tower."

But as far apart as the two sides seemed to stand, they actually shared more common ground than they realized. Both started from the premise that man and nature were irreconcilably opposed, and that the victory of one necessarily entailed the loss of the other. Both sides, in other words, accepted the premises of what we might call the "wilderness ethic," which is based on the assumption that the relationship of man and nature resembles a zero-sum game. This idea, widely held and yet largely unexamined, has set the terms of most environmental battles in this country since the very first important one: the fight over the building of the Hetch Hetchy Dam[1] in 1907, which pitted John Muir against Gifford Pinchot, whom Muir used to call a "temple destroyer." Watching my little local debate unfold over the course of the summer, and grow progressively more shrill and sterile, I began to wonder if perhaps the wilderness ethic itself, for all that it has accomplished in this country over the past century, had now become part of the problem. I also began to wonder if it might be possible to formulate a different ethic to guide us in our dealings with nature, at least in some places some of the time, an ethic that would be based not on the idea of wilderness but on the idea of a garden.

Foresters who have examined sections of fallen trees in Cathedral Pines think that the oldest trees in the forest date from 1780 or so, which suggests that the site was probably logged by the first generation of settlers. The Cathedral Pines are not, then, "virgin growth." The rings of felled trees also reveal a significant growth spurt in 1840, which probably indicates that loggers removed hardwood trees in that year, leaving the pines to grow without competition. In 1883, the Calhouns, an old Cornwall family whose property borders the forest, bought the land to protect the trees from the threat of

8

[1]Damming the Hetch Hetchy Valley, once part of Yosemite, was authorized by Congress in 1913 after a prolonged fight led by John Muir (see headnote on page 45).

logging; in 1967 they deeded it to the Nature Conservancy, stipulating that it be maintained in its natural state. Since then, and up until the tornado made its paths impassable, the forest has been a popular place for hiking and Sunday outings. Over the years, more than a few Cornwall residents have come to the forest to be married.

Cathedral Pines is not in any meaningful sense a wilderness. The natural history of the forest intersects at many points with the social history of Cornwall. It is the product of early logging practices, which clear-cut the land once and then cut it again, this time selectively, a hundred years later. Other human factors almost certainly played a part in the forest's history; we can safely assume that any fires in the area were extinguished before they reached Cathedral Pines. (Though we don't ordinarily think of it in these terms, fire suppression is one of the more significant effects that the European has had on the American landscape.) Cathedral Pines, then, is in some part a man-made landscape, and it could reasonably be argued that to exclude man at this point in its history would constitute a break with its past.

But both parties to the dispute chose to disregard the actual history of Cathedral Pines, and instead to think of the forest as a wilderness in the commonly accepted sense of that term: a pristine place untouched by white men. Since the romantics, we've prized such places as refuges from the messiness of the human estate, vantages from which we might transcend the vagaries of that world and fix on what Thoreau called "higher laws." Certainly an afternoon in Cathedral Pines fostered such feelings, and its very name reflects the pantheism that lies behind them. Long before science coined the term *ecosystem* to describe it, we've had the sense that nature undisturbed displays a miraculous order and balance, something the human world can only dream about. When man leaves it alone, nature will tend toward a healthy and abiding state of equilibrium. Wilderness, the purest expression of this natural law, stands out beyond history.

These are powerful and in many ways wonderful ideas. The notion of wilderness is a kind of taboo in our culture, in many cases acting as a check on our inclination to dominate and spoil nature. It has inspired us to set aside such spectacular places as Yellowstone and Yosemite. But wilderness is also a profoundly alienating idea, for it drives a large wedge between man and nature. Set against the foil of nature's timeless cycles, human history appears linear and unpredictable, buffeted by time and chance as it drives blindly into the future. Natural history, by comparison, obeys fixed and legible laws, ones that make the "laws" of human history seem puny, second-rate things scarcely deserving of the label. We have little idea what the future holds for the town of Cornwall, but surely nature has a plan for Cathedral Pines; leave the forest alone and that plan—which science knows by the name of "forest succession"—will unfold inexorably, in strict accordance with natural law. A new climax forest will emerge as nature works to restore her equilibrium—or at least that's the idea.

The notion that nature has a plan for Cathedral Pines is a comforting one, 12
and certainly it supplies a powerful argument for leaving the forest alone.
Naturally I was curious to know what that plan was: what does nature do with
an old pine forest blown down by a tornado? I consulted a few field guides
and standard works of forest ecology hoping to find out.

According to the classical theory of forest succession, set out in the
nineteenth century by, among others, Henry Thoreau,[2] a pine forest that has
been abruptly destroyed will usually be succeeded by hardwoods, typically
oak. This is because squirrels commonly bury acorns in pine forests and
neglect to retrieve many of them. The oaks sprout and, because shade doesn't
greatly hinder young oaks, the seedlings frequently manage to survive beneath the dark canopy of a mature pine forest. Pine seedlings, on the other
hand, require more sunlight than a mature pine forest admits; they won't
sprout in shade. So by the time the pine forest comes down, the oak saplings
will have had a head start in the race to dominate the new forest. Before any
new pines have had a chance to sprout, the oaks will be well on their way to
cornering the sunlight and inheriting the forest.

This is what I read, anyway, and I decided to ask around to confirm that
Cathedral Pines was expected to behave as predicted. I spoke to a forest
ecologist and an expert on the staff of the Nature Conservancy. They told me
that the classical theory of pine-forest succession probably does describe the
underlying tendency at work in Cathedral Pines. But it turns out that a lot
can go, if not "wrong" exactly, then at least differently. For what if there are
no oaks nearby? Squirrels will travel only so far in search of a hiding place for
their acorns. Instead of oaks, there may be hickory nuts stashed all over
Cathedral Pines. And then there's the composition of species planted by the
forest's human neighbors to consider; one of these, possibly some exotic
(that is, nonnative), could conceivably race in and take over.

"It all depends" is the refrain I kept hearing as I tried to pin down
nature's intentions for Cathedral Pines. Forest succession, it seems, is only
a theory, a metaphor of our making, and almost as often as not nature makes
a fool of it. The number of factors that will go into the determination of
Cathedral Pines' future is almost beyond comprehension. Consider just this
small sample of the things that could happen to alter irrevocably its future
course:

A lightning storm—or a cigarette butt flicked from a passing car— 16
ignites a fire next summer. Say it's a severe fire, hot enough to damage the
fertility of the soil, thereby delaying recovery of the forest for decades. Or say
it rains that night, making the fire a mild one, just hot enough to kill the oak
saplings and allow the relatively fire-resistant pine seedlings to flourish without competition. A new pine forest after all? Perhaps. But what if the
population of deer happens to soar the following year? Their browsing would

[2]See headnote on page 41.

wipe out the young pines and create an opening for spruce, the taste of which deer happen not to like.

Or say there is no fire. Without one, it could take hundreds of years for the downed pine trees to rot and return their nutrients to the soil. Trees grow poorly in the exhausted soil, but the seeds of brambles, which can lie dormant in the ground for fifty years, sprout and proliferate: we end up with a hundred years of brush. Or perhaps a breeze in, say, the summer of 1997 carries in seedpods from the Norway maple standing in a nearby front yard at the precise moment when conditions for their germination are perfect. Norway maple, you'll recall, is a European species, introduced here early in the nineteenth century and widely planted as a street tree. Should this exotic species happen to prevail, Cathedral Pines becomes one very odd-looking and awkwardly named wilderness area.

But the outcome could be much worse. Let's say the rains next spring are unusually heavy, washing all the topsoil away (the forest stood on a steep hillside). Only exotic weed species can survive now, and one of these happens to be Japanese honeysuckle, a nineteenth-century import of such rampant habit that it can choke out the growth of all trees indefinitely. We end up with no forest at all.

Nobody, in other words, can say what will happen in Cathedral Pines. And the reason is not that forest ecology is a young or imperfect science, but that *nature herself doesn't know what's going to happen here*. Nature has no grand design for this place. An incomprehensibly various and complex set of circumstances—some of human origin, but many not—will determine the future of Cathedral Pines. And whatever that future turns out to be, it would not unfold in precisely the same way twice. Nature may possess certain inherent tendencies, ones that theories such as forest succession can describe, but chance events can divert her course into an almost infinite number of different channels.

20   It's hard to square this fact with our strong sense that some kind of quasi-divine order inheres in nature's workings. But science lately has been finding that contingency plays nearly as big a role in natural history as it does in human history. Forest ecologists today will acknowledge that succession theories are little more than comforting narratives we impose on a surprisingly unpredictable process; even so-called climax forests are sometimes superseded. (In many places in the northern United States today, mature stands of oak are inexplicably being invaded by maples—skunks at the climax garden party.) Many ecologists will now freely admit that even the concept of an ecosystem is only a metaphor, a human construct imposed upon a much more variable and precarious reality. An ecosystem may be a useful concept, but no ecologist has ever succeeded in isolating one in nature. Nor is the process of evolution as logical or inexorable as we have thought. The current thinking in paleontology holds that the evolution of any given species, our

own included, is not the necessary product of any natural laws, but rather the outcome of a concatenation of chance events—of "just history" in the words of Stephen Jay Gould.[3] Add or remove any single happenstance—the asteroid fails to wipe out the dinosaurs; a little chordate worm called *Pikaia* succumbs in the Burgess[4] extinction—and humankind never arrives.

Across several disciplines, in fact, scientists are coming to the conclusion that more "just history" is at work in nature than had previously been thought. Yet our metaphors still picture nature as logical, stable, and ahistorical—more like a watch than, say, an organism or a stock exchange, to name two metaphors that may well be more apt. Chance and contingency, it turns out, are everywhere in nature; she has no fixed goals, no unalterable pathways into the future, no inflexible rules that she herself can't bend or break at will. She is more like us (or we are more like her) than we ever imagined.

To learn this, for me at least, changes everything. I take it to be profoundly good news, though I can easily imagine how it might trouble some people. For many of us, nature is a last bastion of certainty; wilderness, as something beyond the reach of history and accident, is one of the last in our fast-dwindling supply of metaphysical absolutes, those comforting transcendental values by which we have traditionally taken our measure and set our sights. To take away predictable, divinely ordered nature is to pull up one of our last remaining anchors. We are liable to float away on the trackless sea of our own subjectivity.

But the discovery that time and chance hold sway even in nature can also be liberating. Because contingency is an invitation to participate in history. Human choice is unnatural only if nature is deterministic; human change is unnatural only if she is changeless in our absence. If the future of Cathedral Pines is up for grabs, if its history will always be the product of myriad chance events, then why shouldn't we also claim our place among all those deciding factors? For aren't we also one of nature's contingencies? And if our cigarette butts and Norway maples and acid rain are going to shape the future of this place, then why not also our hopes and desires?

Nature will condone an almost infinite number of possible futures for Cathedral Pines. Some would be better than others. True, what we would regard as "better" is probably not what the beetles would prefer. But nature herself has no strong preference. That doesn't mean she will countenance *any* outcome; she's already ruled out many possible futures (tropical rain forest, desert, etc.) and, all things being equal, she'd probably lean toward the oak. But all things aren't equal (*her* idea) and she is evidently happy to let the free play of numerous big and little contingencies settle the matter.

24

---

[3]See headnote on page 243.
[4]Fossils preserved in the Burgess Shale of the Canadian Rockies include a variety of extinct species that defy modern schemes of classification.

To exclude from these human desire would be, at least in this place at this time, arbitrary, perverse and, yes, unnatural.

Establishing that we should have a vote in the disposition of Cathedral Pines is much easier than figuring out how we should cast it. The discovery of contingency in nature would seem to fling open a Pandora's box. For if there's nothing fixed or inevitable about nature's course, what's to stop us from concluding that anything goes? It's a whole lot easier to assume that nature left to her own devices knows what's best for a place, to let ourselves be guided by the wilderness ethic.

And maybe that's what we should do. Just because the wilderness ethic is based on a picture of nature that is probably more mythical than real doesn't necessarily mean we have to discard it. In the same way that the Declaration of Independence begins with the useful fiction that "all men are created equal," we could simply stipulate that Cathedral Pines *is* wilderness, and proceed on that assumption. The test of the wilderness ethic is not how truthful it is, but how useful it is in doing what we want to do—in protecting and improving the environment.

So how good a guide is the wilderness ethic in this particular case? Certainly treating Cathedral Pines as a wilderness will keep us from building condos there. When you don't trust yourself to do the right thing, it helps to have an authority as wise and experienced as nature to decide matters for you. But what if nature decides on Japanese honeysuckle—three hundred years of wall-to-wall brush? We would then have a forest not only that we don't like, but that isn't even a wilderness, since it was man who brought Japanese honeysuckle to Cornwall. At this point in history, after humans have left their stamp on virtually every corner of the Earth, doing nothing is frequently a poor recipe for wilderness. In many cases it leads to a gradually deteriorating environment (as seems to be happening in Yellowstone), or to an environment shaped in large part by the acts and mistakes of previous human inhabitants.

28   If it's real wilderness we want in Cathedral Pines, and not merely an imagined innocence, we will have to restore it. This is the paradox faced by the Nature Conservancy and most other advocates of wilderness: at this point in history, creating a landscape that bears no marks of human intervention will require a certain amount of human intervention. At a minimum it would entail weeding the exotic species from Cathedral Pines, and that is something the Nature Conservancy's strict adherence to the wilderness ethic will not permit.

But what if the Conservancy *was* willing to intervene just enough to erase any evidence of man's presence? It would soon run up against some difficult questions for which its ethic leaves it ill prepared. For what is the "real" state of nature in Cathedral Pines? Is it the way the forest looked before the settlers arrived? We could restore that condition by removing all traces of European man. Yet isn't that a rather Eurocentric (if not racist) notion of wilderness? We now know that the Indians were not the ecological eunuchs we once thought. They too left their mark on the land: fires set by Indians determined the composition of the New England forests and probably created that "wilderness" we call the Great Plains. For true untouched wilderness we have to go a lot further back than 1640 or 1492. And if we want to restore the landscape to its pre-Indian condition, then we're going to need a lot of heavy ice-making equipment (not to mention a few woolly mammoths) to make it look right.

But even that would be arbitrary. In fact there is no single moment in time that we can point to and say, *this* is the state of nature in Cathedral Pines. Just since the last ice age alone, that "state of nature" has undergone a thorough revolution every thousand years or so, as tree species forced south by the glaciers migrated back north (a process that is still going on), as the Indians arrived and set their fires, as the large mammals disappeared, as the climate fluctuated—as all the usual historical contingencies came on and off the stage. For several thousand years after the ice age, this part of Connecticut was a treeless tundra; is *that* the true state of nature in Cathedral Pines? The inescapable fact is that, if we want wilderness here, we will have to choose *which* wilderness we want—an idea that is inimical to the wilderness ethic. For wasn't the attraction of wilderness precisely the fact that it relieved us of having to make choices—wasn't nature going to decide, letting us off the hook of history and anthropocentrism?

No such luck, it seems. "Wilderness" is not nearly as straightforward or dependable a guide as we'd like to believe. If we do nothing, we may end up with an impoverished weed patch of our own (indirect) creation, which would hardly count as a victory for wilderness. And if we want to restore Cathedral Pines to some earlier condition, we're forced into making the kinds of inevitably anthropocentric choices and distinctions we turned to wilderness to escape. (Indeed, doing a decent job of wilderness restoration would take all the technology and scientific know-how humans can muster.) Either way, there appears to be no escape from history, not even in nature.

The reason that the wilderness ethic isn't very helpful in a place like Cathedral Pines is that it's an absolutist ethic: man or nature, it says, pick one. As soon as history or circumstance blurs that line, it gets us into trouble. There are times and places when man or nature is the right and necessary choice; back at Hetch Hetchy in 1907 that may well have been the case. But it seems to me that these days most of the environmental questions we face are more like the ambiguous ones posed by Cathedral Pines, and about these the wilderness ethic has less and less to say that is of much help.

The wilderness ethic doesn't tell us what to do when Yellowstone's ecosystem begins to deteriorate, as a result not of our interference but of our neglect. When a species threatens to overwhelm and ruin a habitat because

32

history happened to kill off the predator that once kept its population in check, the ethic is mute. It is confounded, too, when the only hope for the survival of another species is the manipulation of its natural habitat by man. It has nothing to say in all those places where development is desirable or unavoidable except: Don't do it. When we're forced to choose between a hydroelectric power plant and a nuclear one, it refuses to help. That's because the wilderness ethic can't make distinctions between one kind of intervention in nature and another—between weeding Cathedral Pines and developing a theme park there. "You might as well put up condos" is its classic answer to any plan for human intervention in nature.

"All or nothing," says the wilderness ethic, and in fact we've ended up with a landscape in America that conforms to that injunction remarkably well. Thanks to exactly this kind of either/or thinking, Americans have done an admirable job of drawing lines around certain sacred areas (we did invent the wilderness area) and a terrible job of managing the rest of our land. The reason is not hard to find: the only environmental ethic we have has nothing useful to say about those areas outside the line. Once a landscape is no longer "virgin" it is typically written off as fallen, lost to nature, irredeemable. We hand it over to the jurisdiction of that other sacrosanct American ethic: laissez-faire economics. "You might as well put up condos." And so we do.

Indeed, the wilderness ethic and laissez-faire economics, antithetical as they might at first appear, are really mirror images of one another. Each proposes a quasi-divine force—Nature, the Market—that, left to its own devices, somehow knows what's best for a place. Nature and the market are both self-regulating, guided by an invisible hand. Worshipers of either share a deep, Puritan distrust of man, taking it on faith that human tinkering with the natural or economic order can only pervert it. Neither will acknowledge that their respective divinities can also err: that nature produces the AIDS virus as well as the rose, that the same markets that produce stupendous wealth can also crash. (Actually, worshipers of the market are a bit more realistic than worshipers of nature: they long ago stopped relying on the free market to supply us with such necessities as food and shelter. Though they don't like to talk about it much, they accept the need for society to "garden" the market.)

36   Essentially, we have divided our country in two, between the kingdom of wilderness, which rules about 8 percent of America's land, and the kingdom of the market, which rules the rest. Perhaps we should be grateful for secure borders. But what do those of us who care about nature do when we're on the market side, which is most of the time? How do we behave? What are our goals? We can't reasonably expect to change the borders, no matter how many power lines and dams Earth First![5] blows up. No, the

---

[5]Environmental organization that uses aggressive tactics against machinery but that adheres to strict principles of nonviolence in its dealings with people.

wilderness ethic won't be of much help over here. Its politics are bound to be hopelessly romantic (consisting of impractical schemes to redraw the borders) or nihilistic. Faced with hard questions about how to confront global environmental problems such as the greenhouse effect or ozone depletion (problems that respect no borders), adherents of the wilderness ethic are apt to throw up their hands in despair and declare the "end of nature."

The only thing that's really in danger of ending is a romantic, pantheistic idea of nature that we invented in the first place, one whose passing might well turn out to be a blessing in disguise. Useful as it has been in helping us protect the sacred 8 percent, it nevertheless has failed to prevent us from doing a great deal of damage to the remaining 92 percent. This old idea may have taught us how to worship nature, but it didn't tell us how to live with her. It told us more than we needed to know about virginity and rape, and almost nothing about marriage. The metaphor of divine nature can admit only two roles for man: as worshiper (the naturalist's role) or temple destroyer (the developer's). But that drama is all played out now. The temple's been destroyed—if it ever was a temple. Nature *is* dead, if by nature we mean something that stands apart from man and messy history. And now that it is, perhaps we can begin to write some new parts for ourselves, ones that will show us how to start out from here, not from some imagined state of innocence, and let us get down to the work at hand.

Understanding What You Read

1. A tornado destroys a two-hundred-year-old pine forest in Cornwall, Connecticut, and people divide into factions about what has actually happened, how they should respond, and what is likely to happen if they do nothing. What are four suggestions that people make about what should be done?
2. If the fallen forest is left alone, what different scenarios are possible?
3. What does Michael Pollan mean by the "wilderness ethic"? How does he distinguish it from the "garden ethic"?

Writing About What You Read

1. Write a paper in which you explain what the author means in saying that nature is happy "to let the free play of numerous big and little contingencies settle the matter" (paragraph 24). What are these contingencies?
2. Write a proposal in which you argue that people should intervene to bring about a particular environmental outcome; that is, decide what you think would be the best outcome and how you think it should be achieved based on the information in this essay.

NORMAN MYERS

A world-renowned environmental scientist with special interest in tropical forests, species extinction, sustainable development, and population growth, Myers has done research and participated in projects in more than ninety countries, including the tropical regions of Africa, South America, and Asia. He has published more than two hundred articles and more than ten books, including *The Sinking Ark* (1973), *The Gaia Atlas of Planetary Management* (1984), and *Ultimate Security: How Environmental Concerns Affect Global Stability* (1993). "Nature's Powerhouse" is from *The Primary Source: Tropical Forests and Our Future* (1984, expanded and reissued 1992).

Nature's Powerhouse

I WELL remember the day I took a hike through a forest in Borneo. It sticks in my mind because that proved to be the most impressive patch of tropical forest I have encountered during twenty years of roaming around these exuberant expressions of nature.

I had joined a field trip of three Indonesian colleagues from the University of Samarinda, the largest port city on Borneo's east coast. These local scientists had kindly offered to show me a sector of their famous dipterocarp forests, named after the predominant tree type. In Southeast Asia and centered on Borneo there are more than five hundred species of the plant family Dipterocarpaceae—the Latin name referring to the fact that the tree's fruits have two "wings." Esoteric as this scientific designation might seem to some readers, we can reflect on the relevance of dipterocarps to our daily lives when we note the number of items around our homes that derive from those same forests of Southeast Asia: specialist hardwoods for our parquet floors, fine furniture, decorative screens, fittings and cabinets, and the like. A large share of international trade in hardwoods comes from the dipterocarp forests of Southeast Asia. Gazing around me, I could see why dipterocarp forests are so renowned in the world of biologists, conservationists, and foresters. If tropical forests are the richest and most complex ecosystems on Earth, the dipterocarp forests are surely the grandest and the most prolific, as well as the oldest, of them all.

On looking back, I feel that that forest represented a more striking spectacle than any other I have come across during my travels in almost one hundred countries. At other times and in other places, I have watched a wildebeest migration in the Serengeti Plains of northern Tanzania—half a million animals in a single stretch of savannah. Off Baja California, I have seen large groups of whales taking their ease in their calving grounds. In the Caribbean, I have enjoyed some of the most splendid skin-diving I could imagine, fishes of every shape, size, and subtle hue, all within a few meters of my face mask. In southern Greenland, I have looked out over glaciers of such size that a single blue-green crevasse could swallow up an apartment block. At Lake Nakuru in Kenya, I have looked out on two million flamingos; and I understood why ornithologists call this the greatest bird sight on Earth. But a dipterocarp forest is in a class of its own. It is akin to other super-size spectacles on Earth, such as the Grand Canyon and the Victoria Falls. However much you read about the scene, however many photographs or films you see of it, nothing prepares you for the phenomenon itself with its sheer scale and impact. You gaze on it and you feel your life has started on a new phase. Things will not be the same for you again after setting eyes on something that exceeds all your previous experience.

STATURE OF A DIPTEROCARP FOREST

So it was with this dipterocarp forest. In the main, I suppose, I was affected most by the trees, giants on every side. An above-average dipterocarp, by no means an outsize specimen, can measure 5 meters around, making it one of the bulkiest boles[1] anywhere. To encircle a large trunk, I and my three friends had to join hands and stretch as far as we could. Most dipterocarps are not that big, many measuring only half as much and many more even less than that. But a large dipterocarp is at least as big as a good Douglas fir, and a lot more stately. Dipterocarps are tall trees, and their trunks, if slender by some standards, are impressive growths, straight and unencumbered for dozens of meters, soaring sheer from the ground to the canopy that is so far overhead that it seems to belong to a different world.

Still more important, it was the entire community of dipterocarps that impressed me, so many of these giants towering in one area. Out of a total of 400 to 700 trees per hectare,[2] at least 50 were giant-sized, while one dozen out-towered the rest above the forest canopy. My imagination failed when I tried to picture these huge plants extending across the island of Borneo for 1,000 kilometers, a greater quantity of impressive trees than anywhere else. Moreover, as a tree is more than just wood, so a forest is more than just trees. On every trunk and branch I saw a variety of herbaceous (nonwoody) plants, and on some of these plants, still more plants. As for animals, the forest interior supported monkeys, birds, frogs, insects, and snakes, among many other kinds. Although I saw only a single snake that day, and generally I sight none at all, I am sure that dozens turned a beady eye toward me. The insects, by contrast, are not hard to find: I can well believe those scientists who tell me there are at least as many insect species in tropical forests, covering a mere one-sixteenth of the planet's land surface, as there are on the entire rest of the Earth.

[1] The trunk of a tree.
[2] 2.47 acres.

When my friends and I tried to encircle a tree with our arms, we could not choose just any tree. Many support buttresses at their base—"plates" of ultrahard wood that occupy the triangle between the bole and the main roots. A typical tree can have three or four such buttresses, and I found several with twice as many. Although a buttress is thin, it usually reaches at least a man's height up the trunk and sticks out as much along the ground. I have seen similar flanges in tropical forests of Africa and Amazonia, and never outside the moist tropics. My Indonesian friends explained that so many dipterocarps have these buttresses because their shallow roots must remain near the surface to scavenge such nutrients as come their way from above ground, there being next to no sustenance in the infertile soils of tropical forests. The shallow root system offers little anchorage for the vast trunk, especially when 100-kilometer-per-hour winds assault the tree's crown and send a whiplash down the bole to the base. Without the buttresses, the tree might be uprooted during one of the storms that sweeps over the forest.

Looking up, I could see what my friends meant. A typical dipterocarp soars 50 meters, making it as tall as a twenty-story building, taller than the Statue of Liberty. Occasionally one stands twice as high, or almost as tall as the highest redwoods. This makes the dipterocarp a sizable plant. Indeed, a 50-ton dipterocarp is not unduly large, and a 100-ton tree is not unknown. Again, we can note for comparison that an average dipterocarp weighs about as much as an average redwood—though a giant sequoia, the bulkiest tree in the world, can readily top 1,000 tons. But whereas the redwoods and sequoias of California are limited to an area of just a few thousand square kilometers, the dipterocarp forests of Southeast Asia cover at least 1 million square kilometers.

8   Through the columns of dipterocarp giants, I could just make out the topmost layer of the forest, the canopy. The trees generally grow for two-thirds of their height with no branches, presenting an uncluttered bole of striking simplicity before starting to sprout branches that themselves are as big as many trees I have seen in my native Britain. One particularly splendid dipterocarp seemed to reach well above its neighbors. This exceptional specimen, explained my Indonesian colleagues, could have a canopy extending dozens of meters across. Again, I thought, dipterocarps are no ordinary trees; they are an expression of plant life in a league of its own. A moderate-sized dipterocarp, with a girth of two meters or so, will be at least 100 years old, possibly 200, while an "emergent," such as the one I had noticed soaring above the canopy of the main forest, can be anywhere from 400 to 600 years old.

As I looked around the forest, I could scarcely grasp the fact that plant communities like this one, with similar architectural grandeur, still extend not only across Borneo but also across much of Southeast Asia. What a capacity, I thought, for growing wood, more wood, ever-more wood. Whereas a temperate forest generally represents a few sprouts, so to speak, of timber sticking above the ground, a tropical forest amounts to a veritable dynamo for generating wood. My colleagues told me they had measured the amount of "woody biomass" in typical patches of dipterocarp forest and often found 400 cubic meters per hectare, or between three and five times as much as we would expect to find in a similar-sized patch of average forest in New England or Great Britain. Occasionally a dipterocarp forest measures as much as 600 cubic meters of woody biomass per hectare, while record totals surpass 750 cubic meters. This is only the wood of the forest; when we include herbaceous plants as well, the total occasionally approaches 1,000 cubic meters. To put the measurement into perspective, 1 cubic meter of wood weighs, roughly speaking, rather less than 1 ton.

PROFUSION OF PLANTS

But these statistics, as is frequently the case, tell less than the entire tale. What matters more to the workings of a tropical forest is the variety of the parts that make up the community. The trees around me appeared, at first glance, to be more or less alike. They all had smooth bark, rather light in color. Freshly fallen leaves on the forest floor were all dark green, leathery to touch. Yet the sector of forest that we could take in with our eye, roughly half a hectare, contained dozens of different sorts of trees. My Indonesian guides pointed out at least twenty species within just a few strides, these all being plants that "officially" qualify as trees by virtue of having a diameter of at least 10 centimeters (about four inches).

I thought back to the forests of Britain that I knew as a youth; they have a mere three or four species in a similar-sized patch. In the Appalachian forests of the United States, among the richest in tree species of any temperate forest, one would find no more than 25 species. But, my Indonesian colleagues told me, a tropical forest has, including its few bushes and shrubs, at least 100 woody species per hectare—often as many as 150, sometimes even 180, and occasionally, in the wettest lowland areas, more than 200. In an area of 10 sq. km. we can certainly expect to find 300 species, often twice as many or even more. British ecologist Professor Peter Ashton, who once worked in a sector of Brunei on the northwestern coast of Borneo, checked some 30,000 trees in an area of only 45 hectares and found 760 species, while neighboring Sarawak, a composite area totaling less than 10 hectares, revealed more than 780 species. In Brunei and Sarawak together, a territory totaling 126,000 sq. km., there are at least 2,500 native tree species, whereas in Great Britain, with its 244,000 sq. km., there are only about 35 such species. Generally speaking, we find a far greater variety of woody species in a tropical forest than elsewhere. Almost every order of plants includes trees or treelike growths among its representatives. Bamboos, for example, which are strictly speaking grasses, often reach 20 meters in height, with so much woody tissue that a thicket of bamboos will turn aside a herd of elephants.

Milkworts appear in the form of tough twiners as tall as any true tree, and with strands so tough that the strongest man could not hope to break one off. Even violets, dainty growths in temperate lands, can look like trees.

12   As for nonwoody plants, we may expect to find 1,000 species within just a few hectares of dipterocarp forest. Especially numerous are climbers, as I learned by looking around me. Almost every tree, it seemed, was festooned with vines. Some of them were thin, clinging to tree trunks like ivy and having tiny aerial roots that grow along their stems. Others, more striking in appearance, were great woody vines called lianas, some of the larger ones being as thick as a football player's thigh and occasionally twisted together like ropes. Although I could not see the forest-top lianas, my Indonesian friends told me that a network of interlacing loops links the treetops to one another. Sometimes these canopy lianas form such tangled networks that they can even hold a tree upright after its base has been cut by a chainsaw.

This phenomenon of plants growing on plants is a common characteristic of tropical forests. It is not difficult to find at least 30 species growing on a single tree, including ferns, vines, epiphytes, bromeliads, nettles, orchids, and passion flowers. Among the epiphytes ("air plants", from the Greek *epi* for "upon" and *phyton* for "plant"), particularly prolific are the orchids, of which almost 50 species have been found blooming on a single tree. All told, there are a full 4,000 orchids in Southeast Asia, or one-quarter of the Earth's total. While other plants in the region are not so numerous and diverse, Southeast Asia supports one in ten of all plant species in just 3 percent of the planet's land surface. I noticed that plants occupy almost every crack and crevice of the forest. They flourish not only on trees but on the forest floor, on rotting logs, on rocks of every shape, wherever there is a cranny or rough surface to adhere to. In that Borneo forest, I found at my feet a plethora of ferns, mosses, liverworts, and lichens. There were few of the flowers that make a carpet on the floor of a temperate forest. But wherever there was enough light from shafts of sun penetrating the canopy, there was undergrowth aplenty.

Yet despite the variety of plants, the undergrowth was far from thick. There was hardly any of the tangled vegetation popularly associated with tropical forests. I and my companions could walk about almost as we pleased, and in many places we could have marched in a straight line for dozens of meters. We carried machetes in order to mark our trail but did not need them to hack away a single strand of vegetation. All this represented a far cry from the scene so often portrayed by writers and movie-makers—a tumult of vegetation where Tarzan could easily lose his mate. This type of undergrowth is caused by the amount of light at the forest floor, only one-tenth of the sun's brilliance above the canopy. What explains the junglelike accounts of tropical forests? Naturalist explorers from North America and Europe have traditionally roamed forest regions by boat along waterways, where the forest is exposed to lots of sunshine—which stimulates the dense curtains of foliage that the explorers saw along river banks. Hence the accounts of impenetrable masses of vegetation that presumably persisted through the forest interior—hence too the impressions portrayed by old-time movie-makers, who used the same waterways.

Far overhead, the canopy offers splendid scope for sun-loving plants of every kind. Especially plentiful are epiphytes, which, needing no soil, depend on their tree hosts for nothing more than support: they derive all their sustenance from the air. Many of them are small ferns and other nonflowering plants, but bromeliads, members of the pineapple family, can be more showy even than orchids, blossoming in every size and hue. Skimming above the canopy in an airplane, I am astounded at the color of the spectacle. This sector of the forest is far more than a mass of greenery. So diverse is the world of the forest canopy that it can be considered the last great frontier of biology. No other habitat sustains a greater abundance and concentration of species, both plants and animals. Nor does any other habitat remain so relatively unknown. Here an entire realm of life awaits our attention, with a richness that I could never have guessed from the forest floor. Around me I sighted about one dozen different kinds of birds during the course of the day, but my Indonesian friends told me that in the middle reaches of the forest there could be between 50 and 70 species, with well over 100, perhaps 130, flitting around at topmost level.

To date we have obtained only a few specimens, and our knowledge of the forest canopy remains scanty. Yet this, the greatest array of life known on Earth, is not so much on Earth as 30 to 50 meters above it—much too far overhead for the forest-floor observer to see in any detail, even with binoculars. Yet because forest trees generally rise sheer from the ground with no branches until their upper reaches, they offer no handholds for the would-be explorer. Moreover, the bole timber is often so hard that you cannot drive a climber's spike into it: the metal simply bends. And the higher the explorer climbs, the more he has to cope with insect attacks, not to mention vertigo. Fortunately, the last few years have seen a breakthrough in research techniques. There is now an assortment of rope slings, pulley systems, and other fancy gear to enable scientists to explore the canopy more freely than they dreamed of only a decade ago. We can confidently expect that, within the next few years, the pioneering research of the upper forest will surpass, in its rich findings, the probings of deep-ocean trenches and other recent advances in frontier biology.

One of the main conclusions we can already anticipate is the discovery of a great many species, almost all of them very sparse in number. Of the Borneo plants that have already been identified by science, my Indonesian colleagues told me that I would generally find only a few representatives in a whole hectare. In some instances, I would come across only one in 20 hectares. In a typical hectare of Amazonia, with its 100 or more tree species, as many as half may be different from those in another hectare only 1 kilometer away.

16

These distribution patterns mean that many tropical forest plants are comparatively rare, which makes some of them liable to local extinction when a forest is subject to intensive exploitation. So extremely rare are the individuals of certain plants species in these forests, notably orchids and legumes, that we know a few of them from only a single encounter several decades ago. In the Malay Peninsula, a begonia was discovered during the 1940s, and, because of its ornamental appearance, it has become a popular cultivated plant in Europe, with millions of specimens in gardens, nurseries, and so forth. But it has not been found in the wild again. In Amazonia, numerous tree species were identified between 50 and 100 years ago that have not been located since.

Much the same applies to butterflies and birds, among other animals. In the Corcovado Park in Costa Rica, there are eight species of *Heliconius* butterflies, which researchers hardly ever encounter at a rate of more than three adults per hectare, often only a single one. Many butterfly species, together with large numbers of other insect species, appear to occur still more rarely. As for birds, in Amazonia the black-chested, tyrant flycatcher recently appeared 800 kilometers from the nearest place it had hitherto been seen, while the red-shouldered parrot had been recorded only through sightings of seven isolated individuals in all the 6 million square kilometers of the Amazonia region before scientists recently encountered an entire flock.

This extreme sparseness contributes to the unexpected diversity amongst tropical forests. Contrary to popular impression, they are far from being one homogeneous mass from horizon to horizon with each patch of greenery much like any other. When I travel from Borneo to New Guinea, a mere 1,700 kilometers eastward, I know that I shall find far fewer dipterocarp species, only 15 instead of 262, with entirely different families of trees in their place. The same applies, of course, to associated plants, together with animal life. Something similar, moreover, happens in a single landmass. The director of research at the New York Botanical Garden, Dr. Ghillean T. Prance, has found that Amazonia has eight phytogeographic zones, or "plant areas," each with a distinctive assembly of plants and animals. This diversity of formations in tropical forests is in contrast to the pattern of forests elsewhere. In Alaska, for example, we find a type of forest that is virtually identical to one in northeastern Canada—4,500 kilometers away.

20   Such divergence between tropical and nontropical forests alerts us to the fact that what makes one tick is very different from what makes the other tick. If we are to keep tropical forests ticking at all, we shall have to recognize that the strategies we have developed in temperate zones, whether for exploitation or for management or for preservation, do not work nearly so well, if at all, in tropical forests. Our scientific surveys must be different, our logging practices must be different, our planning of parks must be different. In fact, we must operate differently from start to finish. The more I become acquainted with tropical forests, the more I believe that using the term "forest"

for a bunch of trees in the tropics and a bunch of trees elsewhere is misleading. The two categories may reveal a few immediate similarities, but from there on they go their separate ways. How much better we might understand tropical forests if we gave them a new name, indicating that they are a fundamentally different state of affairs from the forests with which we are more familiar.

THE FOREST ENVIRONMENT

The basic dissimilarity between tropical and nontropical forests was further apparent to me later that day in Borneo. By midafternoon, the atmosphere became heavy, while the rare glimpses of blue sky overhead gave way to dark clouds. I knew we could expect a thunderstorm—routine toward day's end in a tropical forest. I also knew that Borneo receives 5 meters of rainfall, spread more or less evenly throughout the year, or five times more than that in New York City. I knew, moreover, that a half-hour downpour could bring 50 millimeters, or twenty times as much water as an average shower in New York. But when the heavens opened over backwoods Borneo, I was surprised that the rain did not deluge us. Instead it came down in a warm film, leaving me feeling for all the world as if I were taking a fine-spray shower. Way above, in the canopy, I could see tree crowns being tossed by the wind, and when we briefly detoured along the bank of a stream, I noticed the surface roiled by sheets of rain. Yet within the interior of the forest, the foliage served to break the impact of the downpour. My colleagues told me that, according to their measurements, one-quarter of the rain was reaching the ground by trickling slowly down branches and tree trunks, the rest reaching us in a drizzle. Another revelation for me.

I was also surprised by the tranquillity of the forest while the storm raged above. On the forest floor, my colleagues told me, the wind speed would be only one-hundredth what it would be above the canopy—while in the canopy it would be only one-tenth what it would be a few meters higher. This insulation of the forest interior, I surmised, must help to maintain the equable climate, with its stable warmth and moisture levels throughout the day and night.

Following the thunderstorm, the forest released a smell of earthy fertility. A musty odor, like that in a greenhouse, it was strangely satisfying even though it spoke of decomposition. I had been vaguely aware of it earlier in the day, and the humid atmosphere seemed to make it stronger. I knew where it came from but scarcely thought it could be so pervasive, or so pleasant. Then I remembered that a forest is home to hosts of decomposers, notably organisms of the topsoil, such as mites, nematodes, ants, and termites. In 1 square meter of leaf litter, Professor Daniel Janzen, of the University of Pennsylvania, found 800 ants belonging to 50 species, while a similar square meter may contain as many as 2,000 termites. In the dipterocarp forests of the Gunung Mulu National Park in Sarawak, Dr. Mark Collins found between 4 and 7 grams of soil fauna per square meter, an amount twice the likely weight of all mammals and birds in the region put together. Of these creatures, at least one-third and sometimes one-half are termites; the weight of termites in some dipterocarp forests of Peninsular Malaysia can be even higher, up to 10 grams per square meter, or over half as much as in the greatest wildlife spectacle on Earth: the herds of Serengeti National Park in northern Tanzania with their four million wildebeest, zebras, and gazelles.

24 Perhaps more important still, the topsoil contains multitudes of fungi, especially the mycorrhizal fungi, which recover and recycle nutrients from fallen vegetation and dead creatures. When a tree, for instance, dies, and its decaying parts are made available to support the life-styles of other organisms, the mycorrhizae flourish. In other words, the smell of the fungi and other decomposers is the smell of life. My Indonesian friends added that when a patch of forest is cleared away, the smell disappears with it—as do the nutrients that the fungi and rootlets once garnered to maintain the healthy working of the ecosystem.

By the same token, I was struck to find only a meager amount of litter underfoot—and by "litter," I refer to fallen leaves and the like. A popular image of the tropical forest suggests that the ground is covered with age-old accumulations of decaying vegetation. Yet there was barely enough litter to conceal the soil—a result of the forest ecosystem. With its warm, moist climate, it provides a fertile environment for the multitudes of mini-organisms that, together with the fungi, break down the fallen leaves, logs, fruits, and other detritus far faster than would be the case in temperate zones. In fact, leaf litter can decompose within six weeks, as compared with one year in a temperate, deciduous forest, and seven years in a boreal, conifer forest.

As I tramped around the almost litterless forest floor, I reflected on other sterotypes of tropical forests: the green vastness of the "jungle," the lurking snakes, the choking vines, the clouds of mosquitoes, the crushing heat. In fact, I found the dipterocarp forest, like any other tropical forest I have visited, to be not only an extraordinarily interesting place to explore, but a very beautiful one to admire. I also found it a fairly pleasant place, and safer than the streets of the capital of Indonesia, Jakarta—or of Rio de Janeiro or Tokyo or New York.

While a visitor can readily see through the popular stereotypes of tropical forests, we still know next to nothing about what makes the forest continue on its quiet, complex way. Scientific researchers have barely made a start on their task of understanding this secluded world. We have probably not discovered more than 20 percent or so of the several million species that likely exist there. In the largest forest region of all, Amazonia, scientists have made a detailed study of no area larger than a few dozen hectares. Just recently we discovered several large tributaries of the Amazon River, and we now realize that we have drawn entire mountain ranges on our maps of Amazonia in places hundreds of kilometers away from their actual location. Moreover, as recently as the early 1970s, scientists noted the Tasaday tribe in the Philippines pursuing their Neolithic way of life, after having been cut off from the outside world by a strip of forest that is a mere 25 kilometers wide. Perhaps most telling of all, we do not have a precise idea of just how much tropical forest still exists—and how fast it is being cut down.

I ended my day feeling as I generally do after sojourns into tropical forests, sensing that I had picked up more basic biology in this patch of forest than possible during a day in any other ecological zone. I had achieved it in one of the few ways that really matter, through first-hand experience. At the same time, I was absorbing my biology "lesson" both through the scientific information that my Indonesian friends fed to me, and through a process of "imaginative osmosis" that I find stirs within me whenever I am confronted with a major phenomenon of nature. A day of field research in a tropical forest is not work for me; rather, it is recreation in the sense of re-creation.

28

Understanding What You Read

1. Find Borneo and Sarawak on a map.
2. What products found in homes come from dipterocarp forests?
3. What past experiences and specific details does Myers use to convince readers that the dipterocarp forest is truly an amazing phenomenon?
4. Myers focuses largely on plant material in this selection. What does he say about the diversity of species among trees in these forests of Borneo?
5. How does Myers explain the common misconception that the jungle floor is an impassable tangle of plants and vines?
6. What does he mean when he says that the forest canopy is "the last great frontier of biology"?

Writing About What You Read

1. Write a short essay comparing and contrasting this rain forest in Borneo with a temperate American forest.
2. Imagine that you take a student trip to a tropical rain forest with a biology professor. Write a letter to a friend about your experience.

Making Connections

1. Sue Hubbell in "Mites, Moths, Bats, and Mosquitoes," like Edward Abbey in "Serpents of Paradise" (Chapter 2), uses the device of coming outdoors with a cup of coffee to watch the dawn and observe wildlife. What does the dawn provide that other times of the day would not?

2. How do Michael Pollan ("The Idea of a Garden") and E. O. Wilson ("Storm over the Amazon") use a natural disaster to explore the question of whether nature has a plan?

3. Compare the differences in the kinds of observations made by Annie Dillard ("Life on the Rocks: The Galápagos") and E. O. Wilson ("Krakatau") when they describe life on volcanic islands.

4. You have learned about several different kinds of ecosystems in this chapter. Choose one and argue for the importance of its preservation (or restoration), emphasizing the role of individual species in the system. In support of your argument, draw on ideas found in more than one of the chapter selections.

5. Marjory Stoneman Douglas ("Life on the Rock") and Ann Zwinger (in Chapter 3) are skilled observers who note with meticulous detail everything they see in a given ecosystem. Choose a place outdoors that provides you with adequate detail, closely observe what you see, and describe the scene as completely as possible. If you do not know the names of plants and animals, identify them descriptively. You may want to include man-made objects in your depiction.

5

RIDDLE: Wait, I see something: It has taken the color of cloudberries.
ANSWER: The bill of the white-fronted goose.

RIDDLE: Wait, I see something: Far away yonder a fireflash comes down.
ANSWER: A red fox, glimpsed as it dashes brightly through the brush.
—Koyukon riddles

◆

When I hear of the destruction of a species I feel just as if all the works of some great writer had perished; as if we had lost all instead of part of Polybius or Livy.
—THEODORE ROOSEVELT, letter to Frank M. Chapman, president of the Audubon Society, February 6, 1899

◆

Almost all professional football players are still alive. The same is probably true for nuclear physicists, city planners, and tax consultants. . . . Not so for species! There are millions of different species of animals and plants on earth—possibly as many as forty million. But somewhere between five and fifty *billion* species have existed at one time or another. Thus, only about one in a thousand species is still alive—a truly lousy survival rate: 99.9 percent failure.
—DAVID M. RAUP, *Extinction: Bad Genes or Bad Luck?*

◆

This is a very big place, and I do not know how it works, nor how I fit in. I am a member of a fragile species, still new to the earth, the youngest creatures of any scale, here only a few moments as evolutionary time is measured, a juvenile species, a child of a species. We are only tentatively set in place, error-prone, at risk of fumbling, in real danger at the moment of leaving behind only a thin layer of our fossils, radioactive at that.
—LEWIS THOMAS, "The Art and Craft of Memoir"

EXTINCTIONS

Pelican, Point Lobos, 1941
(Edward Weston)

Introduction

To appreciate how intricately all aspects of the environment are related, we have only to think about how difficult it is to talk about ecosystems without mentioning species, or about the extinction of species without mentioning the loss of biodiversity. Yet the decision to bring the survival and extinction of species together in this chapter was not arbitrary. The finality of extinction can be most fully felt as we contemplate the unique qualities of particular animals and plants.

It is easy to inspire compassion and concern for the survival of certain large animals—what Donella Meadows calls "charismatic megafauna"—especially if their behavior resembles that of humans or they demonstrate superior intelligence. People readily join the cause to save animals that are most like themselves or are most captivating to the human imagination. Primates, of course, attract concern worldwide, especially when they are the subjects of popular books and movies based on the work of well-known scientists. Scores of people have heard of the chimpanzees of Gombe, and many could be persuaded to send money to save them. Similarly the gorillas of Rwanda, the elephants of Kenya, the Bengal tiger of India, and the humpback whale with its haunting song—all these charismatic animals have their champions. But often those who work to protect these animals do not extend that protection to their habitats, which must be sufficiently large and rich in resources to support enough members of a species to preserve genetic diversity. However diminished a world without chimpanzees or tigers may seem, their loss may be of lesser consequence than that of the genetic diversity that is diminished daily as habitats of all kinds are destroyed.

The cumulative effect of large and small human projects and activities worldwide is immense. A golf course, a condominium, a dam across a river, a bayside resort, a drained swamp, a clear-cut forest are all intended to enhance human life; they all also contribute to species extinction. Though we cannot pinpoint one cause of extinction, our knowledge of causes and effects is increasing. Government agencies and nonprofit organizations in the United States, Canada, Germany, and other countries are now monitoring species and habitats to identify the forces that threaten them and contribute to extinctions. While Chapter 6 examines the cost of change—the compromises and trade-offs involved in safeguarding species—in this chapter you will learn about a number of species themselves: the great auk, whose extinction Peter Matthiessen dramatizes in "The Outlying Rocks," wolves and whales, the humble limpet, and, perhaps surprisingly, prairie grasses.

While it is easy to recruit people in the cause of protecting animals, it is harder to kindle the same passion for saving plants. Can you imagine asking people to give money to save the cutleaf Silphium? Probably not, and neither could Aldo Leopold, whose project was more modest. His goal in "Prairie Birthday" is to call readers' attention to what is lost in the clearing of a meadow and to inspire us to care about "one episode in the funeral of the floras of the world."

Wolves, however, have always gotten attention—from hunters, conservationists, and ranchers, to small children who still know by heart the story of Little Red Riding Hood (told here with a twist in Angela Carter's "The Company of Wolves") and adults who worry about "the wolf at the door" or respond, with a smile or a slap, to a well-timed "wolf whistle." Edward Hoagland's "Howling Back at the Wolves" explores the mysterious connection between wolves and human beings, a relationship based largely on centuries of bad press (witness Hollywood's fascination with werewolves) and misunderstanding. Farley Mowat spent months studying wolves in the Canadian Arctic to find their behavior defied every expectation, as he relates in "Of Mice and Wolves."

Wolves continue to be in the limelight of controversy, the subject of laws and protests. A recent controversy concerns whether the state of Alaska should institute a program to shoot wolves from helicopters to safeguard caribou populations for hunters. The fight has intensified because of conflicting views of predator/prey relations; while wolves kill and eat caribou, studies demonstrate that they prey on weak and unhealthy animals, leaving the strong animals to breed and strengthen the herd. In the balance, then, are the lives of wolves and the size of the caribou herd; human decisions will determine the outcome.

Not all animals threatened with extinction are victims of human activity. Stephen Jay Gould's "Losing a Limpet" tells the history of an extinction resulting from nonhuman forces. Depleted food supplies, loss of habitat, and dwindling genetic diversity are factors that can and do bring about extinctions over time. In "The Beautiful and Damned," David Quammen searches history for the cause of the genetic impoverishment of the South African cheetah and explains why a depleted gene pool leaves organisms at risk. Paul Colinvaux's "Every Species Has Its Niche" speculates about *Homo sapiens* as a species and explains how breeding stragies affect its odds for survival; for, even when the conditions of life are ideal, the numbers of a given species are limited by the size of its niche. Finally, striking a lively counterpoint, Thomas Palmer argues for the importance of the unique qualities of *Homo sapiens* and suggests that humans are not solely "intruders, tramplers, and destroyers."

PETER MATTHIESSEN

A prolific writer, Matthiessen (b. 1927) has written novels as well as numerous works of nonfiction based on extensive travel to remote regions of the five continents. Concerned with the devastating effects that humans have had on their environments worldwide, Matthiessen has written about environmental issues ranging from endangered species to threatened rain forests. His novels include *At Play in the Fields of the Lord* (1965), *Far Tortuga* (1975), and *Killing Mr. Watson* (1990), about a murder in the Florida Everglades. His many works of nonfiction include *The Snow Leopard* (1978) and *In the Spirit of Crazy Horse* (1983). "The Outlying Rocks" is the opening part of his 1959 book *Wildlife in America*, a case-by-case story of the decline, recovery, extinction, and vulnerabilities of specific North American animals.

The Outlying Rocks

These Penguins are as bigge as Geese, and flie not
. . . and they multiply so infinitely upon a certain
flat Iland, that men drive them from thence upon
a boord into their Boates by hundreds at a time; as
if God had made the innocencie of so poore a
creature to become an admirable instrument for
the sustenation of man.

—RICHARD WHITBOURN (1618)

IN EARLY JUNE of 1844, a longboat crewed by fourteen men hove to off
the skerry called Eldey, a stark, volcanic mass rising out of the gray wastes of
the North Atlantic some ten miles west of Cape Reykjanes, Iceland. On the
islets of these uneasy seas, the forebears of the boatmen had always hunted
the swarming sea birds as a food, but on this day they were seeking, for
collectors, the eggs and skins of the garefowl or great auk, a penguinlike
flightless bird once common on the ocean rocks of northern Europe, Iceland,
Greenland, and the maritime provinces of Canada. The great auk, slaughtered indiscriminately across the centuries for its flesh, feathers, and oil, was
vanishing, and the last birds, appearing now and then on lonely shores, were
granted no protection. On the contrary, they were pursued more intensively
than ever for their value as scientific specimens.

At the north end of Eldey, a wide ledge descends to the water, and,
though a sea was running, the boat managed to land three men, Jon Brandsson, Sigourour Isleffson, and Ketil Ketilsson. Two auks, blinking, waddled
foolishly across the ledge. Isleffson and Brandsson each killed a bird, and
Ketilsson, discovering a solitary egg, found a crack in it and smashed it. Later,
one Christian Hansen paid nine pounds for the skins, and sold them in turn
to a Reykjavik taxidermist named Möller. It is not known what became of
them thereafter, a fact all the more saddening when one considers that, on
all the long coasts of the northern ocean, no auk was ever seen alive again.

The great auk is one of the few creatures whose final hours can be
documented with such certainty. Ordinarily, the last members of a species die
in solitude, the time and place of their passage from the earth unknown. One
year they are present, striving instinctively to maintain an existence many
thousands of years old. The next year they are gone. Perhaps stray auks
persisted a few years longer, to die at last through accident or age, but we
must assume that the ultimate pair fell victim to this heedless act of man.

One imagines with misgiving the last scene on desolate Eldey. Offshore,
the longboat wallows in a surge of seas, then slides forward in the lull, its stem
grinding hard on the rock ledge. The hunters hurl the two dead birds aboard
and, cursing, tumble after, as the boat falls away into the wash. Gaining the
open water, it moves off to the eastward, the rough voices and the hollow
thump of oars against wood tholepins unreal in the prevailing fogs of June.
The dank mist, rank with marine smells, cloaks the dark mass, white-topped

4

with guano, and the fierce-eyed gannets, which had not left the crest, settle once more on their crude nests, hissing peevishly and jabbing sharp blue bills at their near neighbors. The few gulls, mewing aimlessly, circle in, alighting. One banks, checks its flight, bends swiftly down upon the ledge, where the last, pathetic generation of great auks gleams raw and unborn on the rock. A second follows and, squalling, they yank at the loose embryo, scattering the black, brown, and green shell segments. After a time they return to the crest, and the ledge is still. The shell remnants lie at the edge of tideline, and the last sea of the flood, perhaps, or a rain days later, washes the last piece into the water. Slowly it drifts down across the sea-curled weeds, the anchored life of the marine world. A rock minnow, drawn to the strange scent, snaps at a minute shred of auk albumen; the shell fragment spins upward, descends once more. Farther down, it settles briefly near a *Littorina*,[1] and surrounding molluscs stir dully toward the stimulus. The periwinkle scours it, spits the calcified bits away. The current takes the particles, so small as to be all but invisible, and they are borne outward, drifting down at last to the deeps of the sea out of which, across slow eons of the Cenozoic era, the species first evolved.

For most of us, its passing is unimportant. The auk, from a practical point of view, was doubtless a dim-witted inhabitant of godforsaken places, a primitive and freakish thing, ill-favored and ungainly. From a second and a more enlightened viewpoint, the great auk was the mightiest of its family, a highly evolved fisherman and swimmer, an ornament to the monotony of northern seas, and for centuries a crucial food source for the natives of the Atlantic coasts. More important, it was a living creature which died needlessly, the first species native to North America to become extinct by the hand of man. It was to be followed into oblivion by other creatures, many of them of an aesthetic and economic significance apparent to us all. Even today, despite protection, the scattered individuals of species too long persecuted are hovering at the abyss of extinction, and will vanish in our lifetimes.

The slaughter, for want of fodder, has subsided in this century, but the fishes, amphibians, reptiles, birds, and mammals—the vertebrate animals as a group—are obscured by man's dark shadow. Such protection as is extended them too rarely includes the natural habitats they require, and their remnants skulk in a lean and shrinking wilderness. The true wilderness—the great woods and clear rivers, the wild swamps and grassy plains which once were the wonder of the world—has been largely despoiled, and today's voyager, approaching our shores through the oiled waters of the coast, is greeted by smoke and the glint of industry on our fouled seaboard, and an inland prospect of second growth, scarred landscapes, and sterile, often stinking, rivers of pollution and raw mud, the whole bedecked with billboards, neon lights, and other decorative evidence of mankind's triumph over

---

[1] A genus of small, heavy-shelled snails of the intertidal zone which includes periwinkles.

chaos. In many regions the greenwood not converted to black stumps no longer breathes with sound and movement, but is become a cathedral of still trees; the plains are plowed under and the prairies ravaged by overgrazing and the winds of drought. Where great, wild creatures ranged, the vermin prosper.

The concept of conservation is a far truer sign of civilization than that spoliation of a continent which we once confused with progress. Today, very late, we are coming to accept the fact that the harvest of renewable resources must be controlled. Forests, soil, water, and wildlife are mutually interdependent, and the ruin of one element will mean, in the end, the ruin of them all. Not surprisingly, land management which benefits mankind will benefit the lesser beasts as well. Creatures like quail and the white-tailed deer, adjusting to man, have already shown recovery. For others, like the black-footed ferret and the California condor, it is probably much too late, and the grizzly bear dies slowly with the wilderness.

* * *

"Everybody knows," one naturalist has written, "that the autumn landscape in the north woods is the land, plus a red maple, plus a ruffed grouse. In terms of conventional physics, the grouse represents only a millionth of either the mass or the energy of an acre. Yet subtract the grouse and the whole thing is dead."

The finality of extinction is awesome, and not unrelated to the finality of eternity. Man, striving to imagine what might lie beyond the long light years of stars, beyond the universe, beyond the void, feels lost in space; confronted with the death of species, enacted on earth so many times before he came, and certain to continue when his own breed is gone, he is forced to face another void, and feels alone in time. Species appear and, left behind by a changing earth, they disappear forever, and there is a certain solace in the inexorable. But until man, the highest predator, evolved, the process of extinction was a slow one. No species but man, so far as is known, unaided by circumstance or climatic change, has ever extinguished another, and certainly no species has ever devoured itself, an accomplishment of which man appears quite capable. There is some comfort in the notion that, however *Homo sapiens* contrives his own destruction, a few creatures will survive in that ultimate wilderness he will leave behind, going on about their ancient business in the mindless confidence that their own much older and more tolerant species will prevail.

* * *

Understanding What You Read

1. What details provoke an emotional response in the story of extinction of the great auk?

2. Why does Matthiessen refer to man as the highest predator?
3. What is his purpose in predicting that "the scattered individuals of species too long persecuted are hovering at the abyss of extinction, and will vanish in our lifetimes" (paragraph 5)?

Writing About What You Read

1. Write a paper in which you explain why the passing of the great auk is an important loss.
2. Using Matthiessen's piece as a model, consider another species that is endangered—African elephants, gray wolves, whooping cranes, or grizzly bears—and imagine the scene in which the last of one of these species dies. You may want to do some research.

ALDO LEOPOLD

A conservationist, forester, writer, and teacher, Leopold (1876–1944) devoted himself to wilderness preservation and wildlife management. He was responsible for establishing the first designated wilderness area, in the Gila National Forest in New Mexico. Leopold helped found the Wilderness Society in 1934, and led its efforts to preserve wilderness areas. And while Leopold was the author of a major textbook in wildlife management, it is for A Sand County Almanac (1949) that he is best known. A classic work of environmental writing, A Sand County Almanac was published shortly after Leopold died while helping to fight a forest fire on a neighbor's land. "Prairie Birthday" is from that book.

Prairie Birthday

DURING EVERY WEEK from April to September there are, on the average, ten wild plants coming into first bloom. In June as many as a dozen species may burst their buds on a single day. No man can heed all of these anniversaries; no man can ignore all of them. He who steps unseeing on May dandelions may be hauled up short by August ragweed pollen; he who ignores the ruddy haze of April elms may skid his car on the fallen corollas of June catalpas. Tell me of what plant-birthday a man takes notice, and I shall tell you a good deal about his vocation, his hobbies, his hay fever, and the general level of his ecological education.

Every July I watch eagerly a certain country graveyard that I pass in driving to and from my farm. It is time for a prairie birthday, and in one corner of this graveyard lives a surviving celebrant of that once important event.

It is an ordinary graveyard, bordered by the usual spruces, and studded with the usual pink granite or white marble headstones, each with the usual Sunday bouquet of red or pink geraniums. It is extraordinary only in being triangular instead of square, and in harboring, within the sharp angle of its fence, a pinpoint remnant of the native prairie on which the graveyard was established in the 1840s. Heretofore unreachable by scythe or mower, this yard-square relic of original Wisconsin gives birth, each July, to a man-high stalk of compass plant or cutleaf Silphium, spangled with saucer-sized yellow blooms resembling sunflowers. It is the sole remnant of this plant along this highway, and perhaps the sole remnant in the western half of our country. What a thousand acres of Silphiums looked like when they tickled the bellies of the buffalo is a question never again to be answered, and perhaps not even asked.

This year I found the Silphium in first bloom on 24 July, a week later than usual; during the last six years the average date was 15 July. 4

When I passed the graveyard again on 3 August, the fence had been removed by a road crew, and the Silphium cut. It is easy now to predict the future; for a few years my Silphium will try in vain to rise above the mowing machine, and then it will die. With it will die the prairie epoch.

The Highway Department says that 100,000 cars pass yearly over this route during the three summer months when the Silphium is in bloom. In them must ride at least 100,000 people who have "taken" what is called history, and perhaps 25,000 who have "taken" what is called botany. Yet I doubt whether a dozen have seen the Silphium, and of these hardly one will notice its demise. If I were to tell a preacher of the adjoining church that the road crew has been burning history books in his cemetery, under the guise of mowing weeds, he would be amazed and uncomprehending. How could a weed be a book?

This is one little episode in the funeral of the native flora, which in turn is one episode in the funeral of the floras of the world. Mechanized man, oblivious of floras, is proud of his progress in cleaning up the landscape on which, willy-nilly, he must live out his days. It might be wise to prohibit at once all teaching of real botany and real history, lest some future citizen suffer qualms about the floristic price of his good life.

Thus it comes to pass that farm neighborhoods are good in proportion to the poverty of their floras. My own farm was selected for its lack of goodness and its lack of highway; indeed my whole neighborhood lies in a backwash of the River Progress. My road is the original wagon track of the pioneers, innocent of grades or gravel, brushings or bulldozers. My neighbors bring a sigh to the County Agent. Their fencerows go unshaven for years on end. Their 8 marshes are neither diked nor drained. As between going fishing and going forward, they are prone to prefer fishing. Thus on weekends my floristic standard of living is that of the backwoods, while on weekdays I subsist as best I can on the flora of the university farms, the university campus, and the adjoining suburbs. For a decade I have kept, for pastime, a record of the wild plant species in first bloom on these two diverse areas:

Species First Blooming in	Suburb and Campus	Backward Farm
April	14	26
May	29	59
June	43	70
July	25	56
August	9	14
September	0	1
Total visual diet	120	226

It is apparent that the backward farmer's eye is nearly twice as well fed as the eye of the university student or businessman. Of course neither sees his flora as yet, so we are confronted by the two alternatives already mentioned: either insure the continued blindness of the populace, or examine the question whether we cannot have both progress and plants.

The shrinkage in the flora is due to a combination of clean-farming, woodlot grazing, and good roads. Each of these necessary changes of course requires a larger reduction in the acreage available for wild plants, but none of them requires, or benefits by, the erasure of species from whole farms, townships, or counties. There are idle spots on every farm, and every highway is bordered by an idle strip as long as it is; keep cow, plow, and mower out of these idle spots, and the full native flora, plus dozens of interesting stowaways from foreign parts, could be part of the normal environment of every citizen.

The outstanding conservator of the prairie flora, ironically enough, knows little and cares less about such frivolities: it is the railroad with its fenced right-of-way. Many of these railroad fences were erected before the prairie had been plowed. Within these linear reservations, oblivious of cinders, soot, and annual clean-up fires, the prairie flora still splashes its calendar of colors, from pink shooting-star in May to blue aster in October. I have long wished to confront some hard-boiled railway president with the physical evidence of his soft-heartedness. I have not done so because I haven't met one.

The railroads of course use flame-throwers and chemical sprays to clear the track of weeds, but the cost of such necessary clearance is still too high

12

to extend it much beyond the actual rails. Perhaps further improvements are in the offing.

The erasure of a human subspecies is largely painless—to us—if we know little enough about it. A dead Chinaman is of little import to us whose awareness of things Chinese is bounded by an occasional dish of chow mein. We grieve only for what we know. The erasure of Silphium from western Dane County is no cause for grief if one knows it only as a name in a botany book.

Silphium first became a personality to me when I tried to dig one up to move to my farm. It was like digging an oak sapling. After half an hour of hot grimy labor the root was still enlarging, like a great vertical sweet-potato. As far as I know, that Silphium root went clear through to bedrock. I got no Silphium, but I learned by what elaborate underground stratagems it contrives to weather the prairie drouths.

I next planted Silphium seeds, which are large, meaty, and taste like sunflower seeds. They came up promptly, but after five years of waiting the seedlings are still juvenile, and have not yet borne a flower stalk. Perhaps it takes a decade for a Silphium to reach flowering age; how old, then, was my pet plant in the cemetery? It may have been older than the oldest tombstone, which is dated 1850. Perhaps it watched the fugitive Black Hawk[1] retreat from the Madison lakes to the Wisconsin River; it stood on the route of that famous march. Certainly it saw the successive funerals of the local pioneers as they retired, one by one, to their repose beneath the bluestem.

I once saw a power shovel, while digging a roadside ditch, sever the "sweet-potato" root of a Silphium plant. The root soon sprouted new leaves, and eventually it again produced a flower stalk. This explains why this plant, which never invades new ground, is nevertheless sometimes seen on recently graded roadsides. Once established, it apparently withstands almost any kind of mutilation except continued grazing, mowing, or plowing.

Why does Silphium disappear from grazed areas? I once saw a farmer turn his cows into a virgin prairie meadow previously used only sporadically for mowing wild hay. The cows cropped the Silphium to the ground before any other plant was visibly eaten at all. One can imagine that the buffalo once had the same preference for Silphium, but he brooked no fences to confine his nibblings all summer long to one meadow. In short, the buffalo's pasturing was discontinuous, and therefore tolerable to Silphium.

It is a kind providence that has withheld a sense of history from the thousands of species of plants and animals that have exterminated each other to build the present world. The same kind providence now withholds it from us. Few grieved when the last buffalo left Wisconsin, and few will grieve when the last Silphium follows him to the lush prairies of the never-never land.

---

[1]Chief of the Sauk and Fox Indians, Black Hawk (1767–1838) refused to move his people west of the Mississippi in compliance with an 1804 treaty.

Understanding What You Read

1. Like Matthiessen in "The Outlying Rocks," Leopold uses details to stimulate feelings in his readers. What are the details?
2. What factors contribute to the diminishing number of plant species (flora) in the part of Wisconsin Leopold describes? What could be done to reverse this process?
3. Why is the railway right-of-way a place of significant species diversity?
4. What is the point of emphasizing that "few will grieve" when the Silphium is gone?

Writing About What You Read

1. Find a place in your part of the world—a cemetery, a highway or railroad right-of-way—that is not regularly plowed, mowed, grazed, or trampled. Count the plant species you find there and write a paragraph or more describing the experience.
2. Find out who on your campus or in your community knows about the local flora. Schedule an interview with that person to find out about the common plants as well as endangered species in your region. Write a report on what you have found.

ANGELA CARTER

Carter (1940–1992) was a journalist, a medieval scholar, a poet, and most prominently a writer of highly original fiction. Her journalistic writings were widely published in major British publications. Her early, award-winning novels include *The Magic Toyshop* (1967) and *Several Perceptions* (1968). Also highly acclaimed were *The Infernal Desire Machines of Doctor Hoffman* (1972) and *Nights at the Circus* (1984). "The Company of Wolves" is from *The Bloody Chamber* (1979), a collection of adult fairy tales and short stories.

The Company of Wolves

ONE BEAST and only one howls in the woods by night.

The wolf is carnivore incarnate and he's as cunning as he is ferocious; once he's had a taste of flesh then nothing else will do.

At night, the eyes of wolves shine like candle flames, yellowish, reddish, but that is because the pupils of their eyes fatten on darkness and catch the light from your lantern to flash it back to you—red for danger; if a wolf's eyes reflect only moonlight, then they gleam a cold and unnatural green, a mineral, a piercing colour. If the benighted traveller spies those luminous, terrible sequins stitched suddenly on the black thickets, then he knows he must run, if fear has not struck him stock-still.

But those eyes are all you will be able to glimpse of the forest assassins as they cluster invisibly round your smell of meat as you go through the wood unwisely late. They will be like shadows, they will be like wraiths, grey members of a congregation of nightmare; hark! his long, wavering howl . . . an aria of fear made audible.

The wolfsong is the sound of the rending you will suffer, in itself a murdering.

It is winter and cold weather. In this region of mountain and forest, there is now nothing for the wolves to eat. Goats and sheep are locked up in the byre,[1] the deer departed for the remaining pasturage on the southern slopes—wolves grow lean and famished. There is so little flesh on them that you could count the starveling ribs through their pelts, if they gave you time before they pounced. Those slavering jaws; the lolling tongue; the rime[2] of saliva on the grizzled chops—of all the teeming perils of the night and the forest, ghosts, hobgoblins, ogres that grill babies upon gridirons, witches that fatten their captives in cages for cannibal tables, the wolf is worst for he cannot listen to reason.

You are always in danger in the forest, where no people are. Step between the portals of the great pines where the shaggy branches tangle about you, trapping the unwary traveller in nets as if the vegetation itself were in a plot with the wolves who live there, as though the wicked trees go fishing on behalf of their friends—step between the gateposts of the forest with the greatest trepidation and infinite precautions, for if you stray from the path for one instant, the wolves will eat you. They are grey as famine, they are as unkind as plague.

The grave-eyed children of the sparse villages always carry knives with them when they go out to tend the little flocks of goats that provide the homesteads with acrid milk and rank, maggoty cheeses. Their knives are half as big as they are, the blades are sharpened daily.

But the wolves have ways of arriving at your own hearthside. We try and try but sometimes we cannot keep them out. There is no winter's night the cottager does not fear to see a lean, grey, famished snout questing under the door, and there was a woman once bitten in her own kitchen as she was straining the macaroni.

Fear and flee the wolf; for, worst of all, the wolf may be more than he seems.

There was a hunter once, near here, that trapped a wolf in a pit. This wolf

---

[1]Barn.
[2]Coating of frost.

had massacred the sheep and goats; eaten up a mad old man who used to live by himself in a hut halfway up the mountain and sing to Jesus all day; pounced on a girl looking after the sheep, but she made such a commotion that men came with rifles and scared him away and tried to track him into the forest but he was cunning and easily gave them the slip. So this hunter dug a pit and put a duck in it, for bait, all alive-oh; and he covered the pit with straw smeared with wolf dung. Quack, quack! went the duck and a wolf came slinking out of the forest, a big one, a heavy one, he weighed as much as a grown man and the straw gave way beneath him—into the pit he tumbled. The hunter jumped down after him, slit his throat, cut off all his paws for a trophy.

12 And then no wolf at all lay in front of the hunter but the bloody trunk of a man, headless, footless, dying, dead.

A witch from up the valley once turned an entire wedding party into wolves because the groom had settled on another girl. She used to order them to visit her, at night, from spite, and they would sit and howl around her cottage for her, serenading her with their misery.

Not so very long ago, a young woman in our village married a man who vanished clean away on her wedding night. The bed was made with new sheets and the bride lay down in it; the groom said, he was going out to relieve himself, insisted on it, for the sake of decency, and she drew the coverlet up to her chin and she lay there. And she waited and she waited and then she waited again—surely he's been gone a long time? Until she jumps up in bed and shrieks to hear a howling, coming on the wind from the forest.

That long-drawn, wavering howl has, for all its fearful resonance, some inherent sadness in it, as if the beasts would love to be less beastly if only they knew how and never cease to mourn their own condition. There is a vast melancholy in the canticles of the wolves, melancholy infinite as the forest, endless as these long nights of winter and yet that ghastly sadness, that mourning for their own, irremediable appetites, can never move the heart for not one phrase in it hints at the possibility of redemption; grace could not come to the wolf from its own despair, only through some external mediator, so that, sometimes, the beast will look as if he half welcomes the knife that despatches him.

16 The young woman's brothers searched the outhouses and the haystacks but never found any remains so the sensible girl dried her eyes and found herself another husband not too shy to piss into a pot who spent the nights indoors. She gave him a pair of bonny babies and all went right as a trivet until, one freezing night, the night of the solstice, the hinge of the year when things do not fit together as well as they should, the longest night, her first good man came home again.

A great thump on the door announced him as she was stirring the soup for the father of her children and she knew him the moment she lifted the latch to him although it was years since she'd worn black for him and now he was in rags and his hair hung down his back and never saw a comb, alive with lice.

"Here I am again, missus," he said. "Get me my bowl of cabbage and be quick about it."

Then her second husband came in with wood for the fire and when the first one saw she'd slept with another man and, worse, clapped his red eyes on her little children who'd crept into the kitchen to see what all the din was about, he shouted: "I wish I were a wolf again, to teach this whore a lesson!" So a wolf he instantly became and tore off the eldest boy's left foot before he was chopped up with the hatchet they used for chopping logs. But when the wolf lay bleeding and gasping its last, the pelt peeled off again and he was just as he had been, years ago, when he ran away from his marriage bed, so that she wept and her second husband beat her.

They say there's an ointment the Devil gives you that turns you into a wolf the minute you rub it on. Or, that he was born feet first and had a wolf for his father and his torso is a man's but his legs and genitals are a wolf's. And he has a wolf's heart.

Seven years is a werewolf's natural span but if you burn his human clothing you condemn him to wolfishness for the rest of his life, so old wives hereabouts think it some protection to throw a hat or an apron at the werewolf, as if clothes made the man. Yet by the eyes, those phosphorescent eyes, you know him in all his shapes; the eyes alone unchanged by metamorphosis.

Before he can become a wolf, the lycanthrope[3] strips stark naked. If you spy a naked man among the pines, you must run as if the Devil were after you.

It is midwinter and the robin, the friend of man, sits on the handle of the gardener's spade and sings. It is the worst time in all the year for wolves but this strong-minded child insists she will go off through the wood. She is quite sure the wild beasts cannot harm her although, well-warned, she lays a carving knife in the basket her mother has packed with cheeses. There is a bottle of harsh liquor distilled from brambles; a batch of flat oatcakes baked on the hearthstone; a pot or two of jam. The flaxen-haired girl will take these delicious gifts to a reclusive grandmother so old the burden of her years is crushing her to death. Granny lives two hours' trudge through the winter woods; the child wraps herself up in her thick shawl, draws it over her head. She steps into her stout wooden shoes; she is dressed and ready and it is Christmas Eve. The malign door of the solstice still swings upon its hinges but she has been too much loved ever to feel scared.

Children do not stay young for long in this savage country. There are no toys for them to play with so they work hard and grow wise but this one, so

[3]Werewolf.

pretty and the youngest of her family, a little late-comer, had been indulged by her mother and the grandmother who'd knitted her the red shawl that, today, has the ominous if brilliant look of blood on snow. Her breasts have just begun to swell; her hair is like lint, so fair it hardly makes a shadow on her pale forehead; her cheeks are an emblematic scarlet and white and she has just started her woman's bleeding, the clock inside her that will strike, henceforward, once a month.

She stands and moves within the invisible pentacle of her own virginity. She is an unbroken egg; she is a sealed vessel; she has inside her a magic space the entrance to which is shut tight with a plug of membrane; she is a closed system; she does not know how to shiver. She has her knife and she is afraid of nothing.

Her father might forbid her, if he were home, but he is away in the forest, gathering wood, and her mother cannot deny her.

The forest closed upon her like a pair of jaws.

28   There is always something to look at in the forest, even in the middle of winter—the huddled mounds of birds, succumbed to the lethargy of the season, heaped on the creaking boughs and too forlorn to sing; the bright frills of the winter fungi on the blotched trunks of the trees; the cuneiform slots of rabbits and deer, the herringbone tracks of the birds, a hare as lean as a rasher of bacon streaking across the path where the thin sunlight dapples the russet brakes of last year's bracken.

When she heard the freezing howl of a distant wolf, her practised hand sprang to the handle of her knife, but she saw no sign of a wolf at all, nor of a naked man, neither, but then she heard a clattering among the brushwood and there sprang on to the path a fully clothed one, a very handsome young one, in the green coat and wideawake hat of a hunter, laden with carcasses of game birds. She had her hand on her knife at the first rustle of twigs but he laughed with a flash of white teeth when he saw her and made her a comic yet flattering little bow; she'd never seen such a fine fellow before, not among the rustic clowns of her native village. So on they went together, through the thickening light of the afternoon.

Soon they were laughing and joking like old friends. When he offered to carry her basket, she gave it to him although her knife was in it because he told her his rifle would protect them. As the day darkened, it began to snow again; she felt the first flakes settle on her eyelashes but now there was only half a mile to go and there would be a fire, and hot tea, and a welcome, a warm one, surely, for the dashing huntsman as well as for herself.

This young man had a remarkable object in his pocket. It was a compass. She looked at the little round glass face in the palm of his hand and watched the wavering needle with a vague wonder. He assured her this compass had taken him safely through the wood on his hunting trip because the needle always told him with perfect accuracy where the north was. She did not believe it; she knew she should never leave the path on the way through the wood or else she would be lost instantly. He laughed at her again; gleaming trails of spittle clung to his teeth. He said, if he plunged off the path into the forest that surrounded them, he could guarantee to arrive at her grandmother's house a good quarter of an hour before she did, plotting his way through the undergrowth with his compass, while she trudged the long way, along the winding path.

I don't believe you. Besides, aren't you afraid of the wolves?   32
He only tapped the gleaming butt of his rifle and grinned.

Is it a bet? he asked her. Shall we make a game of it? What will you give me if I get to your grandmother's house before you?

What would you like? she asked disingenuously.

A kiss.   36

Commonplaces of a rustic seduction; she lowered her eyes and blushed.

He went through the undergrowth and took her basket with him but she forgot to be afraid of the beasts, although now the moon was rising, for she wanted to dawdle on her way to make sure the handsome gentleman would win his wager.

Grandmother's house stood by itself a little way out of the village. The freshly falling snow blew in eddies about the kitchen garden and the young man stepped delicately up the snowy path to the door as if he were reluctant to get his feet wet, swinging his bundle of game and the girl's basket and humming a little tune to himself.

There is a faint trace of blood on his chin; he has been snacking on his   40
catch.

He rapped upon the panels with his knuckles.

Aged and frail, granny is three-quarters succumbed to the mortality the ache in her bones promises her and almost ready to give in entirely. A boy came out from the village to build up her hearth for the night an hour ago and the kitchen crackles with busy firelight. She has her Bible for company, she is a pious old woman. She is propped up on several pillows in the bed set into the wall peasant-fashion, wrapped up in the patchwork quilt she made before she was married, more years ago than she cares to remember. Two china spaniels with liver-coloured blotches on their coats and black noses sit on either side of the fireplace. There is a bright rug of woven rags on the pantiles. The grandfather clock ticks away her eroding time.

We keep the wolves outside by living well.

He rapped upon the panels with his hairy knuckles.

It is your granddaughter, he mimicked in a high soprano.   44

Lift up the latch and walk in, my darling.

You can tell them by their eyes, eyes of a beast of prey, nocturnal, devastating eyes as red as a wound; you can hurl your Bible at him and your apron after, granny, you thought that was a sure prophylactic against these infernal vermin . . . now call on Christ and his mother and all the angels in heaven to protect you but it won't do you any good.

His feral muzzle is sharp as a knife; he drops his golden burden of gnawed   48 pheasant on the table and puts down your dear girl's basket, too. Oh, my God, what have you done with her?

Off with his disguise, that coat of forest-coloured cloth, the hat with the feather tucked into the ribbon; his matted hair streams down his white shirt and she can see the lice moving in it. The sticks in the hearth shift and hiss; night and the forest has come into the kitchen with darkness tangled in its hair.

He strips off his shirt. His skin is the colour and texture of vellum. A crisp stripe of hair runs down his belly, his nipples are ripe and dark as poison fruit but he's so thin you could count the ribs under his skin if only he gave you the time. He strips off his trousers and she can see how hairy his legs are. His genitals, huge. Ah! huge.

The last thing the old lady saw in all this world was a young man, eyes like cinders, naked as a stone, approaching her bed.

52 The wolf is carnivore incarnate.

When he had finished with her, he licked his chops and quickly dressed himself again, until he was just as he had been when he came through her door. He burned the inedible hair in the fireplace and wrapped the bones up in a napkin that he hid away under the bed in the wooden chest in which he found a clean pair of sheets. These he carefully put on the bed instead of the tell-tale stained ones he stowed away in the laundry basket. He plumped up the pillows and shook out the patchwork quilt, he picked up the Bible from the floor, closed it and laid it on the table. All was as it had been before except that grandmother was gone. The sticks twitched in the grate, the clock ticked and the young man sat patiently, deceitfully beside the bed in granny's nightcap.

Rat-a-tap-tap.

Who's there, he quavers in granny's antique falsetto.

56 Only your granddaughter.

So she came in, bringing with her a flurry of snow that melted in tears on the tiles, and perhaps she was a little disappointed to see only her grandmother sitting beside the fire. But then he flung off the blanket and sprang to the door, pressing his back against it so that she could not get out again.

The girl looked round the room and saw there was not even the indentation of a head on the smooth cheek of the pillow and how, for the first time she'd seen it so, the Bible lay closed on the table. The tick of the clock cracked like a whip. She wanted her knife from her basket but she did not dare reach for it because his eyes were fixed upon her—huge eyes that now seemed to shine with a unique, interior light, eyes the size of saucers, saucers full of Greek fire,[4] diabolic phosphorescence.

What big eyes you have.

60 All the better to see you with.

[4]A flammable substance used in warfare by Byzantine Greeks; it reputedly burst into flames when wet.

No trace at all of the old woman except for a tuft of white hair that had caught in the bark of an unburned log. When the girl saw that, she knew she was in danger of death.

Where is my grandmother?

There's nobody here but we two, my darling.

Now a great howling rose up all around them, near, very near, as close as the kitchen garden, the howling of a multitude of wolves; she knew the worst wolves are hairy on the inside and she shivered, in spite of the scarlet shawl she pulled more closely round herself as if it could protect her although it was as red as the blood she must spill.

Who has come to sing us carols, she said.

Those are the voices of my brothers, darling; I love the company of wolves. Look out of the window and you'll see them.

Snow half-caked the lattice and she opened it to look into the garden. It was a white night of moon and snow; the blizzard whirled round the gaunt, grey beasts who squatted on their haunches among the rows of winter cabbage, pointing their sharp snouts to the moon and howling as if their hearts would break. Ten wolves; twenty wolves—so many wolves she could not count them, howling in concert as if demented or deranged. Their eyes reflected the light from the kitchen and shone like a hundred candles.

It is very cold, poor things, she said; no wonder they howl so.

She closed the window on the wolves' threnody and took off her scarlet shawl, the colour of poppies, the colour of sacrifices, the colour of her menses, and, since her fear did her no good, she ceased to be afraid.

What shall I do with my shawl?

Throw it on the fire, dear one. You won't need it again.

She bundled up her shawl and threw it on the blaze, which instantly consumed it. Then she drew her blouse over her head; her small breasts gleamed as if the snow had invaded the room.

What shall I do with my blouse?

Into the fire with it, too, my pet.

The thin muslin went flaring up the chimney like a magic bird and now off came her skirt, her woollen stockings, her shoes, and on to the fire they went, too, and were gone for good. The firelight shone through the edges of her skin; now she was clothed only in her untouched integument of flesh. This dazzling, naked she combed out her hair with her fingers; her hair looked white as the snow outside. Then went directly to the man with red eyes in whose unkempt mane the lice moved; she stood up on tiptoe and unbuttoned the collar of his shirt.

What big arms you have.

All the better to hug you with.

Every wolf in the world now howled a prothalamion[5] outside the window as she freely gave the kiss she owed him.

64

68

72

76

[5]Song celebrating marriage.

What big teeth you have!

80 She saw how his jaw began to slaver and the room was full of the clamour of the forest's Liebestod[6] but the wise child never flinched, even when he answered:

All the better to eat you with.

The girl burst out laughing; she knew she was nobody's meat. She laughed at him full in the face, she ripped off his shirt for him and flung it into the fire, in the fiery wake of her own discarded clothing. The flames danced like dead souls on Walpurgisnacht[7] and the old bones under the bed set up a terrible clattering but she did not pay them any heed.

Carnivore incarnate, only immaculate flesh appeases him.

84 She will lay his fearful head on her lap and she will pick out the lice from his pelt and perhaps she will put the lice into her mouth and eat them, as he will bid her, as she would do in a savage marriage ceremony.

The blizzard will die down.

The blizzard died down, leaving the mountains as randomly covered with snow as if a blind woman had thrown a sheet over them, the upper branches of the forest pines limed, creaking, swollen with the fall.

Snowlight, moonlight, a confusion of paw-prints.

88 All silent, all still.

Midnight; and the clock strikes. It is Christmas Day, the werewolves' birthday, the door of the solstice stands wide open; let them all sink through.

See! sweet and sound she sleeps in granny's bed, between the paws of the tender wolf.

[6]Song of love and death from Richard Wagner's opera *Tristan and Isolde*.
[7]Eve of May Day on which witches are said to ride to an appointed rendezvous.

Understanding What You Read

1. What are the two parts of this story?
2. What myths about wolves are incorporated into the first part?
3. What animals does the little girl notice when she enters the woods?
4. What is the effect of describing details of the grandmother's house?
5. In what ways does the story reverse the traditional story of Little Red Riding Hood?
6. Read an encyclopedia article about werewolves and analyze how the story uses beliefs about werewolves.

Writing About What You Read

1. Find a version of the Little Red Riding Hood story and compare it with Carter's story.
2. Discuss how this story satirizes myths and folktales about wolves.

FARLEY MOWAT

Mowat (b. 1921) has lived most of his life in his native Canada, but has traveled widely. High-risk expeditions—notably to the Arctic and other regions where conditions are harsh—have provided material for more than twenty-five books, some written for children. Mowat's work has been widely translated and read around the globe. His best-known books include *A Whale for the Killing* (1972) and *Sea of Slaughter* (1984). After going to the frozen tundra of the Canadian Arctic to study the impact of the wolves on the caribou population, Mowat wrote *Never Cry Wolf* (1963), which was made into a popular movie. "Of Mice and Wolves" is from this book.

Of Mice and Wolves

AFTER SOME WEEKS of study I still seemed to be as far as ever from solving the salient problem of how the wolves made a living. This was a vital problem, since solving it in a way satisfactory to my employers was the reason for my expedition.

Caribou are the only large herbivores to be found in any numbers in the arctic Barren Lands. Although once as numerous as the plains buffalo, they had shown a catastrophic decrease during the three or four decades preceding my trip to the Barrens. Evidence obtained by various Government agencies from hunters, trappers and traders seemed to prove that the plunge of the caribou toward extinction was primarily due to the depredations of the wolf. It therefore must have seemed a safe bet, to the politicians-cum-scientists who had employed me, that a research study of wolf-caribou relationships in the Barrens would uncover incontrovertible proof with which to damn the wolf wherever he might be found, and provide a more than sufficient excuse for the adoption of a general campaign for his extirpation.

I did my duty, but although I had searched diligently for evidence which would please my superiors, I had so far found none. Nor did it appear I was likely to.

Toward the end of June, the last of the migrating caribou herds had passed Wolf House Bay heading for the high Barrens some two or three hundred miles to the north, where they would spend the summer.

Whatever my wolves were going to eat during those long months, and whatever they were going to feed their hungry pups, it would not be caribou, for the caribou were gone. But if not caribou, what *was* it to be?

I canvassed all the other possibilities I could think of, but there seemed to be no source of food available which would be adequate to satisfy the appetites of three adult and four young wolves. Apart from myself (and the

4

thought recurred several times) there was hardly an animal left in the country which could be considered suitable prey for a wolf. Arctic hares were present; but they were very scarce and so fleet of foot that a wolf could not hope to catch one unless he was extremely lucky. Ptarmigan and other birds were numerous; but they could fly, and the wolves could not. Lake trout, arctic grayling and whitefish filled the lakes and rivers; but wolves are not otters.

The days passed and the mystery deepened. To make the problem even more inscrutable, the wolves seemed reasonably well fed; and to baffle me to the point of near insanity, the two male wolves went off hunting every night and returned every morning, but never appeared to bring anything home.

8 As far as I could tell, the whole lot of them seemed to be existing on a diet of air and water. Once, moved by a growing concern for their well-being, I went back to the cabin and baked five loaves of bread, which I then took to Wolf House Bay and left beside one of the hunting paths. My gift was rejected. It was even scorned. Or perhaps Uncle Albert, who discovered them, simply thought the loaves were some new sort of boundary posts which I had erected, and that they were to be treated accordingly.

About this time I began having trouble with mice. The vast expanses of spongy sphagnum bog provided an ideal milieu for several species of small rodents who could burrow and nest-build to their hearts' content in the ready-made mattress of moss.

They did other things too, and they must have done them with great frequency, for as June waned into July the country seemed to become alive with little rodents. The most numerous species were the lemmings, which are famed in literature for their reputedly suicidal instincts, but which, instead, *ought* to be hymned for their unbelievable reproductive capabilities. Red-backed mice and meadow mice began invading Mike's cabin in such numbers that it looked as if *I* would soon be starving unless I could thwart their appetites for my supplies. *They* did not scorn my bread. They did not scorn my bed, either; and when I awoke one morning to find that a meadow mouse had given birth to eleven naked offspring inside the pillow of my sleeping bag, I began to know how Pharaoh[1] must have felt when he antagonized the God of the Israelites.

I suppose it was only because my own wolf indoctrination had been so complete, and of such a staggeringly inaccurate nature, that it took me so long to account for the healthy state of the wolves in the apparent absence of any game worthy of their reputation and physical abilities. The idea of wolves not only eating, but actually thriving and raising their families on a diet of mice was so at odds with the character of the mythical wolf that it was really too ludicrous to consider. And yet, it was the answer to the problem of how my wolves were keeping the larder full.

[1]To force Pharaoh to free the Israelites from bondage, Moses called down plagues on the people of Egypt.

Angeline tipped me off.   12

Late one afternoon, while the male wolves were still resting in preparation for the night's labors, she emerged from the den and nuzzled Uncle Albert until he yawned, stretched and got laboriously to his feet. Then she left the den site at a trot, heading directly for me across a broad expanse of grassy muskeg, and leaving Albert to entertain the pups as best he could.

There was nothing particularly new in this. I had several times seen her conscript Albert (and on rare occasions even George) to do duty as a babysitter while she went down to the bay for a drink or, as I mistakenly thought, simply went for a walk to stretch her legs. Usually her peregrinations took her to the point of the bay farthest from my tent where she was hidden from sight by a low gravel ridge; but this time she came my way in full view and so I swung my telescope to keep an eye on her.

She went directly to the rocky foreshore, waded out until the icy water was up to her shoulders, and had a long drink. As she was doing so, a small flock of Old Squaw ducks flew around the point of the Bay and pitched only a hundred yards or so away from her. She raised her head and eyed them speculatively for a moment, then waded back to shore, where she proceeded to act as if she had suddenly become demented.

Yipping like a puppy, she began to chase her tail; to roll over and over   16
among the rocks; to lie on her back; to wave all four feet furiously in the air; and in general to behave as if she were clean out of her mind.

I swung the glasses back to where Albert was sitting amidst a gaggle of pups to see if he, too, had observed this mad display, and, if so, what his reaction to it was. He had seen it all right, in fact he was watching Angeline with keen interest but without the slightest indication of alarm.

By this time Angeline appeared to be in the throes of a manic paroxysm, leaping wildly into the air and snapping at nothing, the while uttering shrill squeals. It was an awe-inspiring sight, and I realized that Albert and I were not the only ones who were watching it with fascination. The ducks seemed hypnotized by curiosity. So interested were they that they swam in for a closer view of this apparition on the shore. Closer and closer they came, necks outstretched, and gabbling incredulously among themselves. And the closer they came, the crazier grew Angeline's behavior.

When the leading duck was not more than fifteen feet from shore, Angeline gave one gigantic leap towards it. There was a vast splash, a panic-stricken whacking of wings, and then all the ducks were up and away. Angeline had missed a dinner by no more than inches.

This incident was an eye-opener since it suggested a versatility at food-   20
getting which I would hardly have credited to a human being, let alone to a mere wolf. However, Angeline soon demonstrated that the charming of ducks was a mere sideline.

Having dried herself with a series of energetic shakes which momentarily hid her in a blue mist of water droplets, she padded back across the grassy swale. But now her movements were quite different from what they had been when she passed through the swale on the way to the bay.

Angeline was of a rangy build, anyway, but, by stretching herself so that she literally seemed to be walking on tiptoe, and by elevating her neck like a camel, she seemed to gain several inches in height. She began to move infinitely slowly upwind across the swale, and I had the impression that both ears were cocked for the faintest sound, while I could see her nose wrinkling as she sifted the breeze for the most ephemeral scents.

Suddenly she pounced. Flinging herself up on her hind legs like a horse trying to throw its rider, she came down again with driving force, both forelegs held stiffly out in front of her. Instantly her head dropped; she snapped once, swallowed, and returned to her peculiar mincing ballet across the swale. Six times in ten minutes she repeated the straight-armed pounce, and six times she swallowed—without my having caught a glimpse of what it was that she had eaten. The seventh time she missed her aim, spun around, and began snapping frenziedly in a tangle of cotton grasses. This time when she raised her head I saw, quite unmistakably, the tail and hindquarters of a mouse quivering in her jaws. One gulp, and it too was gone.

24 Although I was much entertained by the spectacle of one of this continent's most powerful carnivores hunting mice, I did not really take it seriously. I thought Angeline was only having fun; snacking, as it were. But when she had eaten some twenty-three mice I began to wonder. Mice are small, but twenty-three of them adds up to a fair-sized meal, even for a wolf.

It was only later, by putting two and two together, that I was able to bring myself to an acceptance of the obvious. The wolves of Wolf House Bay, and, by inference at least, all the Barren Land wolves who were raising families outside the summer caribou range, were living largely, if not almost entirely, on mice.

*   *   *

Understanding What You Read

1. Why was it important to Mowat to demonstrate that wolves have a source of food other than the caribou?
2. What myths about wolves are inconsistent with their surviving on a diet of mice?
3. Why does Mowat conclude that during the summer months the wolves he observes are subsisting mainly on mice?

Writing About What You Read

Imagine you are a government official who believes wolves are responsible for the dramatic decline in the caribou population. Write a paper arguing for the importance of extirpating the wolves. You may want to go to the library to do more reading about wolves and caribou.

EDWARD HOAGLAND

Though he began his writing career as a novelist, Hoagland (b. 1932) is primarily known for his beautifully crafted personal essays, many of which focus on the relationship between humans and animals. An urbanite who also loves wild places, he splits his time between New York City and rural Vermont. Hoagland's love of the wild has taken him to many remote places. His most recent collection, *Balancing Acts* (1992), includes essays on the Okefenokee Swamp, the rain forests of Belize, the mountains of Yemen, and the Arctic circle. "Howling Back at the Wolves," first published in the December 1972 *Saturday Review,* is collected in *Heart's Desire: The Best of Edward Hoagland* (1988).

Howling Back at the Wolves

WOLVES HAVE marvelous legs. The first thing one notices about them is how high they are set on their skinny legs, and the instant, blurred gait these can switch into, bicycling away, carrying them as much as forty miles in a day. With brindled coats in smoky shades, brushy tails, light-filled eyes, intense sharp faces which are more focused than an intelligent dog's but also less various, they are electric on first sighting, bending that bushy head around to look back as they run. In captivity when they are quarreling in a cage, the snarls sound guttural and their jaws chop, but scientists watching pet wolves in the woods speak of their flowing joy, of such a delight in running that they melt into the woods like sunlight, like running water.

*　　*　　*

Wolves *would* be more of a loss to us than some exotic mouse, because they epitomize the American wilderness as no other animal does, and fill both the folklore of childhood and that of the woods—folklore that would wither away if they all were to die, and may do so in any case. We know that the folklore was exaggerated, that generally they don't attack man, which is a relief, but we treasure the stories nonetheless, wanting the woods to be woods. In the contiguous states the gray wolf's range is less than 1 percent of what it used to be, and that patch of Minnesota wilderness, twelve thousand square miles where they live in much the same density as in primeval times, is greatly enriched by the presence of wolves.

Wisconsin didn't get around to granting its wolves protection until they had become extinct, but Mech[1] got the Minnesota bounty removed and almost single-handedly turned local thinking around, until there is talk of declaring the wolf a "state animal" and establishing a sanctuary for it in the Boundary Waters Canoe Area. Mech is a swift-thinking, urbane, amused man, bald, round-faced, not a bit wolflike in appearance, although he is sharp in his rivalry with other scientists. As an advocate he knows how to generate "spontaneous" nationwide letter-writing campaigns and can gather financial support from the National Geographic Society and the New York Zoological Society, from Minneapolis industrialists and the federal government. He has a soul-stirring howl, more real than reality, that triggers the wolves into howling back when he is afoot trying to locate them, but his ears have begun to dim from a decade or more of flying all winter in flimsy planes to spot them against the snow. Sometimes he needs an assistant along to hear whether a pack at a distance is answering him.

4   That wolves do readily answer even bad imitations of their howl may have a good deal of significance. Observers have noticed the similarities between the intricate life of a wolf pack and the most primitive grouping of mankind, the family-sized band. Often there is a "peripheral wolf," for instance, which is tolerated but picked on, and as though the collective psyche of the pack required a scapegoat, if the peripheral wolf disappears another pack member may slip down the social ladder and assume the role, or a stray that otherwise might have been driven off will be adopted. The strays, or "lone wolves," not being bound by territorial considerations, range much farther and frequently eat better than pack wolves do, but are always seeking to enroll themselves.

What seems so uncanny and moving about the experience of howling to wolves, then hearing them answer, may be the enveloping sense of déjà vu,[2] perhaps partly subliminal, that goes right to one's roots—band replying to band, each on its own ground, gazing across a few hundred yards of meadow or bog at the same screen of trees. The listener rises right up on his toes, looking about happily at his human companions.

Wolf pups make a frothy ribbon of sound like fat bubbling, a shiny, witchy, fluttery yapping, while the adults siren less excitably, without those tremulous, flexible yips, although they sometimes do break pitch into a yodel. The senior wolf permits the response, if one is made, introducing it with his own note after a pause—which is sometimes lengthy—before the others join in. Ordinarily pups left alone will not answer unless the adult closest to them does so, as he or she returns to protect them. Wolves howl for only a half-minute or so, though they may respond again and again after a cautious intermission, if no danger is indicated from their having already betrayed their position. Each wolf has a tone, or series of tones, of its own that blends into

[1] L. David Mech, a scientist working to protect wolves in Minnesota.
[2] "Already seen." A feeling that what one is experiencing has happened before.

an iridescent harmony with the others, and people who howl regularly at a wolf rendezvous soon acquire vocal personalities too, as well as a kind of choral sequence in which they join together—cupping their mouths to the shape of a muzzle on cue.

I went out with a student of Mech's, Fred Harrington, who records and voice-prints wolf howls. His wife was along, doing the puppy trills, and so was the trap-line crew, who attach radio collars to the wolves they catch. We stood at the edge of a cutover jack-pine flat, with a few tall spruces where the wolves were. The sun was setting, the moon was rising, squirrels and birds were chitting close by, and we knew that a radio-collared bear was digging its winter den just over the rise. Howling is not a hunting cry and does not frighten other animals. The wolves howled as if for their own edification, as a pleasurable thing, a popular, general occasion set off by our calls to them, replying to us but not led by our emphasis or interpretation. If they had been actively scouting us they would have kept silent, as they do in the spring when the pups are too young to travel. To us, their chorus sounded isolated, vulnerable, the more so because obviously they were having fun, and we all felt the urge to run toward them; but they didn't share that feeling. A pack needs at least ten square miles for each member, as well as a deer every eighteen days for that individual, or a deer every three days for a pack of six. The figure for moose is one every three days for a pack of fifteen, Mech has calculated. Thus, howling between packs does not serve the function of calling them to confabulate. Instead, it seems to keep them apart, defining rough boundaries for their separate ranges, providing them mutually with a roster of strength, though by howling, mates in a pack do find one another and find solidarity.

In Algonquin Provincial Park in Ontario thousands of people howl with the wolves in the early autumn. Whether or not it is a high point for the wolves, it certainly is for the people. I've gone to one of the favorite locations, where the ground is littered with cigarette butts, and tried, except the day was rainy and the wolves couldn't hear me. Nobody who has had the experience will fail to root for the beasts ever after. Glacier National Park in Montana is next to Canada, like Mech's country, and they may manage to become reestablished there; Yellowstone Park has a small vanguard. In East Texas a few survive, hiding in the coastal marshes. These are red wolves—relic relations of the gray wolf that inhabited the Southeast and lower Mississippi Valley and are probably now doomed, pushed up against the sea, with no reservoir such as the wildlands of Canada provide from which to replenish their numbers.

Apparently a special relationship can exist between men and wolves which is unlike that between men and any of the bears or big cats. One might have to look to the other primates for a link that is closer. It's not just a matter of howling; owls with their hoots and loons with their laughter also interact with wolves. Nor is it limited to the mystery of why dogs, about fifteen thousand years back, which is very recent as such events go, cut themselves away from other wolves by a gradual, at first "voluntary" process to become subservient to human beings as no other domestic creature is, running with man in packs in which *he* calls the tune. Another paradox is that the wolves which remained wolves, though they are large predators that might legitimately regard a man-shaped item as prey, don't seem to look upon him as such; don't even challenge him in the woods in quite the same way that they will accost a trespassing cougar or grizzly.

In the campaign to rescue the wolf from Red Ridinghood status, some scientists, including Mech, have overdone their testimonials as to its liberal behavior, becoming so categorical that they doubt that any North American wolf not rabid has ever attacked a human being. This does violence to scientific method, as well as to the good name of countless frontiersmen who knew more about the habits of wilderness animals than it is possible to learn today. (What these scientists really mean is that none of their Ph.D. candidates doing field work has been attacked by a wolf so far.) Such propaganda also pigeonholes the wolf in a disparaging way, as if it were a knee-jerk creature without any options, like a blowfish or a hog-nosed snake.

But the link with man remains. Douglas H. Pimlott, who is Canada's wolf expert, explores this matter in *The World of the Wolf.* He mentions behavioral patterns that are shared by man and wolf, and by indirection might have come to influence wolves. Both hunt cooperatively in groups and are nearly unique in that respect; both have lived in complex bands in which the adults of either sex care for the young. He mentions the likelihood that there are subconscious attributes of the human mind that may affect wolves. After all, the bonds between a man and dog penetrate far beyond the awe of the one for the other—are more compulsive, more telepathic than awe—and cannot be fully explained under the heading of love. Wolves, like dogs, says Pimlott, are excellent readers of signs because of their social makeup and their cruising system of hunting, which does not depend as much on surprise as the habits of most other predators do: "They instinctively recognize aggression, fear, and other qualities of mind which are evidenced in subtle ways by our expressions and actions. . . . In hunting we stalk deliberately, quietly . . . in winter we move through the woods and across lakes and streams deliberately, as a wolf does in traveling over his range, hunting for prey."

12   These movements indicate to wolves that we are superior predators—superior wolves—and not prey. It could be added that wolves, like dogs, take a remarkable delight in submissive ritual, ingratiating themselves, placating a bigger, more daring beast—this part of their adaptation through the millennia to life in a pack, in which usually only one or two members are really capable of killing the sizable game that will feed many mouths; the rest dance attendance upon them. Of course not only the stew-hunter prowling in the woods is predatory. In the city, when much more driving and successful men

emerge on the street for a business lunch, their straight-line strides and manner, "bright-eyed and bushy-tailed," would bowl over any wolf.

Understanding What You Read

1. What details does Hoagland use in his description of wolves to make them seem attractive?
2. What does Hoagland mean when he says that people "want their woods to be woods" and what do wolves have to do with that desire?
3. Can you imagine yourself enjoying an expedition to howl with the wolves? Why or why not? What would you think of people who do?
4. What do we know about the behavior of wolves toward humans?

Writing About What You Read

1. Imagine that you are a wolf howling with people. Describe your experience.
2. Imagine that the last wolves in North America have been exterminated. Write an obituary for the wolf in a newspaper or magazine, using details that will help others understand what has been lost.

STEPHEN JAY GOULD

A renowned paleontologist, Gould (b. 1941) has, for twenty-six years, taught biology, geology, and history of science at Harvard University. His works have been read by millions around the world. For twenty years he has been regularly publishing essays in *Natural History* magazine under the general title "This View of Life." The six collections of these essays include *Ever Since Darwin* (1979) and *Bully for Brontosaurus* (1991). Gould's other works include the best-selling *Wonderful Life: The Burgess Shale and the Nature of History* (1989). "Losing a Limpet" is taken from his most recent collection, *Eight Little Piggies* (1993).

Losing a Limpet

D A R W I N   M A R V E L E D at the abundance of giant Galápagos tortoises when he visited the islands in September 1835, but he also noted a marked decline based on ease of human exploitation for food. (Ships would often take tortoises away by the hundreds, stacking them live in the hold to provide months of fresh meat "on the hoof." The tortoises were essentially defenseless. As a single barrier to capture, Darwin notes that ships usually sent out hunting parties in pairs, and two men could not lift the largest animals.) Darwin wrote in the *Voyage of the Beagle:*

> It is said that formerly single vessels have taken away as many as seven hundred of these animals and that the ship's company of a frigate some years since brought down two hundred to the beach in one day.

The species, though not threatened as a whole, is much depleted today, and several distinctive forms, once limited to single islands, have disappeared. I saw the saddest story of this legacy—Lonesome George, last survivor of the saddle-backed race from Pinta Island. No mate has been found for George, though the island has been scoured. He has been moved, for safekeeping (and in apparently vain hope for salvation of his kind), to a research station on Santa Cruz Island, where I saw him several years ago. He is well fed and surely pampered, and he may live for another century or more; but his lineage, at least as a pure pedigree, is already extinct.

4   Every George must have his Martha. The last passenger pigeon, also a mateless vestige of a doomed race, died in the Cincinnati Zoo on September 1, 1914. Martha's body was taken to the Cincinnati Ice Company, suspended in a tank of water, frozen into a three-hundred-pound block of ice, and sent for extrication and stuffing to the Smithsonian Institution, where she resides today.

Galápagos tortoises were vulnerable and restricted in geography; their extreme reduction and partial extinction merits no special surprise. But how could the superabundant and widespread passenger pigeon crash and die within a century? By some estimates, they were once the most common bird in America. They migrated in huge flocks over most of eastern and central North America. Pioneer ornithologist Alexander Wilson estimated one such aggregation as containing more than 2 billion birds. One colony in Wisconsin spread out over 750 square miles. The famous testimony of Audubon himself, made in Ohio just one hundred years before Martha's death, not only identifies human rapacity as the cause of eventual decline, but also depicts the fabulous abundance:

> As the time of the arrival of the passenger pigeons approached, their foes anxiously prepared to receive them. Some persons were ready with iron pots containing sulphur, others with torches of pine knots; many had poles, and the rest, guns. . . . Everything was ready and all eyes were fixed on the clear sky that could be glimpsed amid the tall tree-tops. . . . Suddenly a general cry burst forth, "Here they come!" The noise they made, even though still distant, reminded me of a hard gale at sea, passing through the rigging of a close-reefed vessel. The birds arrived and passed over me. I felt a current of air that surprised me. Thousands of the pigeons were soon knocked down by the polemen, whilst more continued to pour in. The fires were lighted, then a magnificent, wonderful, almost terrifying sight presented itself. The pigeons, arriving by the thousands, alighted everywhere, one above another, until solid masses were formed

on the branches all around. Here and there the perches gave way with a crack under the weight, and fell to the ground, destroying hundreds of birds beneath. . . . The scene was one of uproar and confusion. . . . Even the gun reports were seldom heard, and I was made aware of the firing only by seeing the shooters reloading. . . .

The picking up of the dead and wounded birds was put off till morning. The pigeons were constantly coming and it was past midnight before I noticed any decrease in the number of those arriving. The uproar continued the whole night. . . .

Towards the approach of day, the noise somewhat subsided. Long before I could distinguish them plainly, the pigeons began to move off. . . . By sunrise all that were able to fly had disappeared. . . . Eagles and hawks, accompanied by a crowd of vultures, took their place and enjoyed their share of the spoils. Then the author of all this devastation began to move among the dead, the dying and the mangled, picking up the pigeons and piling them in heaps. When each man had as many as he could possibly dispose of, hogs were let loose to feed on the remainder.

In 1805, passenger pigeons sold for a penny apiece in markets of New York City. By 1870, birds were reproducing only in the Great Lakes region. Hunters used the newly invented telegraph to inform others about the location of dwindling populations. Perhaps the last large wild flock, some 250,000 birds, was sighted in 1896. A gaggle of hunters, alerted by telegraph, converged upon them; fewer than 10,000 birds flew away. The last wild passenger pigeon was killed in Ohio in 1900. The few zoo colonies dwindled, as keepers could never induce the birds to breed regularly. By 1914, only Martha remained.

These sad, oft-told tales are canonical stories of the extinction saga: defenseless populations composed of individuals that are easy to find and profitable to kill. Restricted compass on an island is the surest path to destruction—the dodo or tortoise model. But even a large, continental spread will not save a vulnerable population—the passenger pigeon model.

One environment, however, has been seen as a refuge for at least most kinds of organisms—the open ocean. Here, or so the argument goes, geographic ranges are usually large enough, and ecological tolerances sufficiently broad, to prevent rapacious humanity (or any other agent of extinction) from getting every last one. Populations may be beaten way back, but a few survivors will always find a refugium.

This claim is as old as modern biology itself. In the first great document of evolutionary theory, published in 1809, Lamarck[1] tried to deny extinction altogether. (In his theory of creative response to perceived needs, and inheritance of characters thus acquired, organisms should evolve fast enough to overcome any environmental danger.) But Lamarck did allow an exception for conspicuous species on land. Even "Lamarckian" response cannot be quick or extensive enough to overcome the most powerful and efficient

[1]Jean Baptiste Lamarck (1744–1829), a French naturalist who classified invertebrates.

agency of environmental disturbance—human depredation. Lamarck wrote: "If there really are lost species, it can doubtless only be among the large animals which live on the dry parts of the earth; where man exercises absolute sway, and has compassed the destruction of all the individuals of some species which he has not wished to preserve or domesticate." But small inconspicuous oceanic species should be immune from our influence: "Animals living in the waters, especially the sea waters, . . . are protected from the destruction of their species by man. Their multiplication is so rapid and their means of evading pursuit or traps are so great, that there is no likelihood of his being able to destroy the entire species of any of these animals."

We would downplay Lamarck's optimism about the oceans today. Conspicuous species of large organisms with small populations are vulnerable— and several fish and marine mammals, including Steller's sea cow, have succumbed. But Lamarck's distinction and prognostication has held. The ledgers of death in historic times do not include marine invertebrates.

Extinction has certainly received its fair share of attention in our newspapers and TV specials. We are so used to tales of destruction, so inured or even numbed, that we expect almost any species, anywhere in the world, to be the next victim. We have engraved the notion of fragility upon our souls.

But step back from all these accounts of death and think for a moment: Have you ever heard about the extinction of a marine invertebrate species, even among widely exploited lobsters, scallops, or conchs? We may drive a local population of marine invertebrates to death, but never an entire species. In *The Panda's Thumb,* a previous volume in this series published in 1980, I told the sad story of *Cenobita diogenes,* a large Bermudian hermit crab, now apparently doomed because the only shell large enough to hold its body, the whelk *Cittarium pica,* was eaten to destruction on Bermuda. (The crabs now eke out a tenuous existence within fossil *Cittarium* shells eroded from Bermudian hillsides.) I was deluged with suggestions for salvation. One man offered to design a plastic *Cittarium* and to ship them by the thousands for distribution on Bermudian beaches. I was touched by his ingenuity and generosity, but a much simpler and more effective solution exists. *Cittarium pica* is extinct on Bermuda, but not elsewhere. This species is eaten with gusto on most West Indian islands, and piles of empty shells are stacked on beaches and roadsides. Any enterprising savior of *Cenobita* could easily fill a boat and bring the real McCoy back to Bermuda.

16   In short, Lamarck was right, and his distinction of sea and land has much to teach us about the general phenomenon of species death. By our records and reckoning, no marine invertebrate species has become extinct during historic times. (Geological extinctions, of course, occur at characteristic rates over millions of years—thus illustrating the immensity of difference between our time and earth time). Geerat Vermeij, a leading expert on oceanic life and its vulnerability, wrote in 1986 that "marine invertebrates are relatively immune from extinction." So Lamarck was right—that is, until 1991.

The first issue of the *Biological Bulletin* for 1991, the technical journal published by the Marine Biological Laboratory at Woods Hole, contains the following article by James T. Carlton and four other authors (including my good friend Gary Vermeij who must now eat his words or be happy that he wrote the disclaimer *"relatively* immune from extinction"): "The first historical extinction of a marine invertebrate in an ocean basin: The demise of the eelgrass limpet *Lottia alveus."*

Limpets are snails with an unusual mode of growth. Snail shells are cones that expand slowly and wind around an axis during growth, producing the conventional corkscrew of increasing width. But the limpet cone expands so rapidly that the shell never winds around its axis for more than a fraction of a whorl. Thus, a limpet shell looks like a Chinese hat of the old caricatures. The large open end clamps tightly down upon a rock, or a food source, and this power of adhesion has made the limpet a symbol of tenacity and stubbornness in many languages and cultures. In England, for example, limpets are (according to the *OED*) "officials alleged to be superfluous but clinging to their offices."

Lottia alveus, the eelgrass limpet of the western Atlantic, once lived in fair abundance from Labrador to Long Island Sound. Although this geographic range might have been broad enough to win the usual marine immunity from extinction, two peculiar features placed the eelgrass limpet into a rare category of vulnerability. First, as its name implies, the eelgrass limpet lived and fed only on a single species of plant, *Zostera marina.* (*Zostera,* a fascinating biological oddity in its own right, is one of the few marine genera of angiosperms, or ordinary flowering plants. Most people assume that all marine plants are algae, but a few "advanced" flowering land plants have managed to invade the oceans, usually forming beds of "sea grass" in shallow waters.)

Lottia alveus had a long and narrow shell, just wide enough to fit snugly over a *Zostera* blade. The limpet fed exclusively on epithelial cells of the sea grass. The fate of *Lottia* therefore depended upon the health of *Zostera.* Moreover, *Lottia* had an unusually narrow range of physiological tolerance, particularly for changes of salinity. This limpet could not survive any marked departure from normal oceanic salinity of some thirty-three parts per thousand, whereas *Zostera* spans a much broader range and can live in brackish waters of much reduced salinity.

Both *Zostera* and *Lottia* originated in the Pacific Ocean and invaded the North Atlantic in late Tertiary times (just before the ice ages), as many other species did, through the Bering Strait and along the Arctic Ocean. Populations of *Lottia* remain in both the eastern and western Pacific, so the entire genus is not lost. (Taxonomists are still debating the status of *Lottia.* Some regard the three populations—eastern Pacific, western Pacific, and extinct Atlantic—as fully separate species, others as subspecies of a single, coherent group. In either case, the Atlantic populations were distinct in form and color, and clearly represent some degree of genetic differentiation.)

Atlantic specimens of *Lottia* were reported as abundant by all collectors from first extensive descriptions of the mid-nineteenth century through the 1920s. The last living specimens were reported in 1933. The five authors have searched diligently for *Lottia alveus* throughout its former range from the early 1970s through 1990. They also looked in fourteen major museum collections for specimens gathered during the past fifty years—and found none that could be verified. They even searched through several herbarium collections of *Zostera*, hoping that dried limpet shells might be found on the pressed sheets. (Museums often preserve reference collections of plants by flattening them onto sheets of paper then bound into books.) Again, no *Lottia* could be found. This diligence certainly wins our assent to their preliminary conclusion that *Lottia alveus* is truly extinct in the Atlantic.

But why did *Lottia* gain the dubious honor of first marine invertebrate to disappear during historic time? Carlton and coauthors have also provided a coherent and satisfying explanation that neatly combines a specific historical event with the general biology of *Lottia*. Between 1930 and 1933, *Zostera* virtually disappeared from both the eastern and western Atlantic Ocean. (This species of sea grass has suffered numerous declines throughout its recorded history, but none nearly so severe as this accidental correlate with economic depression on adjacent lands.) The cause of this near wipe-out has been debated for years, with disease and environmental fluctuation as leading contenders. A series of articles published during the 1980s has decisively implicated a marine protist, the slime mold *Labyrinthula* (a unicelled creature that aggregates to form temporary colonies), as chief culprit. Infestation by the pathogenic species of *Labyrinthula* leads to formation of small black patches on *Zostera* leaves. The patches spread, eventually causing death and detachment of the entire blade.

This massive die-off of *Zostera* led to marked changes in associated ecosystems, including great reduction in migratory waterfowl populations and loss of commercial scallop fisheries. But neither *Zostera* nor any of these ecological dependents became entirely extinct. *Zostera* itself tolerates a much wider range of salinities than does the pathogen *Labyrinthula*. All populations of normal marine salinity were completely destroyed, but *Zostera* can also live in brackish water, while *Labyrinthula* cannot. Thus, relict *Zostera* populations hunkered down in low-salinity refugia, and the species survived. Other species associated with *Zostera* also pulled through, either because they could also tolerate the low salinities of *Zostera* refuges, or because they could live on other resources, though often with much smaller populations, while *Zostera* was absent. When *Zostera* returned after the *Labyrinthula* epidemic subsided, these other species reflowered as well.

But consider the cruel fate of poor *Lottia alveus*. This limpet lacked the flexibility of all other species associated with *Zostera*. *Lottia* could not hunker down with *Zostera* in the low-salinity refugia because this limpet could only live in normal marine waters. And *Lottia* could not switch to another host species because it ate only the epithelial cells of *Zostera* blades. For *Lottia*, the total disappearance of *Zostera* in waters of normal salinity spelled complete destruction. *Zostera* returned, but no *Lottia* remained to greet the renewed bounty.

Does the story of *Zostera* and *Lottia* bear a message for our chief parochial concern with the subject of extinction—anthropogenic assault on the biosphere and consequent loss of biodiversity? In a literal sense, the answer must be "rather little." *Lottia* was no Galápagos tortoise or passenger pigeon—creatures hounded to death by human hunters. *Lottia* didn't even fall victim to some unintended consequence of human disruption in natural habitats. In fact, *Homo sapiens* probably played no role whatsoever in the death of *Lottia* (I doubt that one person in a million ever laid eyes on the creature). *Lottia*'s extinction was an ordinary natural event, the kind that, summed through geological ages, produces the basic pattern of life's history. Epidemics are as intrinsic as water and sunshine in the history of life. They don't usually wipe out a species entirely (as the *Labyrinthula* epidemic spared *Zostera*). Yet species clearly have differential susceptibility to extinction, and some factors of weakness enhance the possibility of death in epidemics. Natural selection can only work for immediate reproductive advantages and cannot overtly protect a species against unexpected vicissitudes of time. Many strengths of the moment engender a potential for later extinction as an unintended and detrimental side consequence. So long as *Zostera* bloomed and seas stood at normal salinity, intense specialization may have aided individual *Lottia*. But such narrowly committed forms are usually the first to go when unusual circumstances wipe out a highly specific habitat, even temporarily. Marine species are "relatively immune" from extinction because few have such narrow commitments, but *Lottia*, as an exception for its intense specialization, paid the ultimate price.

Lottia does bear a symbolic message for the anthropogenic theme, how- ever. As the first species to die (during historic times) in the one habitat that, from Lamarck to 1991, seemed free of such danger, *Lottia* must stand as a warning and an emblem—as the Crispus Attucks[2] of a potential wave in the most protected arena, if our environmental assaults worsen. Didn't British power laugh at the ragtag rebellion when Attucks and four others died in the Boston Massacre of 1770? Most crises start with something small, something virtually beneath notice. But whispers soon grow to whirlwinds. Limpets, with their low profiles and large apertures (often serving as suction cups for attachment), are metaphors for tenaciousness, for hunkering down in times of trouble. How appropriate, then, as a warning against complacency, that a real version of this symbol should be the first species to die in a realm of supposed invulnerability.

[2](1723?–1770), a runaway slave shot in a Boston riot, thereby becoming the first martyr of the American Revolution.

Understanding What You Read

1. How did humans bring about the extinction of some giant Galápagos tortoises and the passenger pigeon?
2. What do the stories of these extinctions contribute to that of the eelgrass limpet?
3. What does the story of the limpet *Lottia alveus* suggest about the possibility of future extinctions?
4. Explain how the limpet became extinct for lack of food—though its single food source, the eelgrass, did not become extinct.

Writing About What You Read

Summarize the story of the extinction of the limpet in your own words, stressing the interdependency of species and the fragility of ecosystems.

DAVID QUAMMEN

A Rhodes scholar with a background in science, Quammen (b. 1948) is widely known for the science column "Natural Acts" in *Outside Magazine,* and he has published novels, stories, and two volumes of essays. "The Beautiful and Damned" is included in the collection *The Flight of the Iguana: A Sidelong View of Science and Nature* (1988).

The Beautiful and Damned

BEAUTY IS one of the lies we live by. The joys of success is another. God knows, we have been offered enough minacious parables over the centuries to discourage both of these stubborn delusions—from the *Iliad* and *Oedipus Rex* to *The Picture of Dorian Gray* and "Richard Cory"[1]—but still they survive, eternal inverities. Evidently we need them at least as much as we need mere truth. The latest increment of counterevidence against that pair of sleek cheery falsehoods came and went recently as an article in the journal *Science,* and unless you were watching closely, you may have missed it.

[1]Literary works: the *Iliad* is an epic poem attributed to the Greek poet Homer; *Oedipus Rex* is a tragedy by the Greek playwright Sophocles (496–406 B.C.); *The Picture of Dorian Gray* (1891) is a novel by the Irish writer Oscar Wilde (1854–1900); "Richard Cory" is a poem about the suicide of a successful man by the American poet Edwin Arlington Robinson (1869–1935).

Based on the experimental work of a team led by S. J. O'Brien, a geneticist from the National Cancer Institute, this article presents a technical assessment of the unusually low genetic diversity within a certain species. O'Brien's study is noteworthy to a broad audience not so much because of its results ("we found a total absence of genetic polymorphism in forty-seven allozyme loci and a low frequency of polymorphism in proteins") as because of the test subject in question. That species was *Acinonyx jubatus,* the cheetah.

Every schoolchild in America knows that the cheetah is the world's fastest mammal. Anyone who has seen and studied these creatures in the field is liable also to argue that they are the most beautiful of all carnivores, and the most successful of all wild cats. A dozen years ago I spent one lucky hour watching four cheetahs stalk game on the East African savanna, and I still haven't begun to forget their gorgeous, prepossessing grace. But the cheetah today, despite appearances, is not well. It is genetically depauperate.

Though there may still be as many as 20,000 cheetahs at large on the plains of Africa, the gene pool of *A. jubatus* appears to be much smaller than it should be for that number—too small, perhaps, to carry the species through any sudden adversities. Insufficient genetic options equals insufficient adaptability. So far, admittedly, only one of the two remaining large populations has been investigated: the South African cheetah, not the East African. In the course of O'Brien's study, blood tests were done on fifty-five animals, some of those from the Transvaal, some from Namibia, a few that had previously been exported to zoos in the United States. This scattered group of cats turned out to have all the genetic diversity of a palace full of incestuous Romanovs.[2]

Cheetahs are currently an endangered species. Twenty thousand is not such a large total, and the real number may be much less, possibly as low as 1,500. No one really knows, because the elusive habits of these animals make them very hard to count. Though officially protected in some of the countries where they occur, they are still occasionally threatened by fur poachers and stock-raising peoples. They are threatened even more by habitat loss. But the worst threat they face may be the genetic one. They are just dangerously short on genetic variety.

And that's one threat that we humans can't rectify. All we can do is give them time. A depleted population of animals can sometimes recover quickly. A depleted gene pool cannot. Thousands of new generations must be born and grow and achieve successful reproduction themselves, before the slow process of mutation will have restored a previous level of gene variations. Populations fall and rise again at geometric rates but, like some morbidly hurtful memory, genetic impoverishment lingers afterward.

4

---

[2] The ruling dynasty of Russia from 1613 to 1917.

Where did those missing cheetah genes go?

O'Brien and his coauthors are cautious about offering speculation, but their work, together with what is known of the history of this species in both the recent and the distant past, suggests a couple of sad possibilities.

The cheetah evolved independently of the other big cats and arrived at its modern form much earlier. Today it stands separate from all other living representatives of the cat family, a lonesome anomaly that in some ways shares more in common with dogs. Besides being faster, it is far more delicate, more slender, and less imposingly armed than any lion or leopard. Its teeth are shorter. Its jaws are rather weak. Other cats can voluntarily retract their claws into claw sheaths, thereby preserving the sharp points for piercing and slashing; the claws of the cheetah, in contrast, are not fully retractile and grow dull from being walked on. A cheetah's footprint, consequently, looks more like the print of a wolf than like the great soft ominous pug of a tiger. Though it may travel in small social groups (a mother with kits, a mixed trio of adults, even a pair of bachelor males), the cheetah seems most often to perform the act of killing solitarily. As slight of build as it is, as poorly equipped with lethal weapons, it would have little chance of winning a meal at all, if not for speed.

Speed it has, of course—unequaled speed—as well as a nicely matched set of anatomical adaptations that make that speed possible. The femur bone of the cheetah's leg is elongated, unusual among cats. The spine is long and flexible, and it bows dramatically with each stride, giving still greater reach to the legs. Those short, blunted claws are good for traction and quick turns. The nasal openings are especially large, as are the bronchi and the lungs, invaluable for an animal that needs huge volumes of oxygen for burning huge amounts of energy in very brief stretches of time. The heart is also large. The tail is long and held straight out, for balance, while the cheetah screams along at seventy miles per hour. Even the arteries are exceptionally muscular. *A. jubatus* is born to run.

More specifically, born to chase. The cheetah shows a few curious behavioral patterns that become comprehensible only in light of its anatomical assets and limitations, and one among these is perhaps the most intriguing: According to reliable observation, a cheetah will almost never attack a potential prey animal that does not bolt and run.

Its favored prey species are modest-sized grazers like the impala and the Thomson's gazelle, generally taken at weights less than the cheetah's own. But let an impala stand its ground (either from stupid daring or because it's paralyzed by fear) and the cheetah will pass it right by, focusing instead on one of the other herd members that has taken flight. For two or three hundred yards the cheetah will pursue at top speed, until (on a successful chase) it has pulled up beside the chosen impala's rear flank. Then it will do what is, to my mind, a charmingly roguish thing: It will swing out a paw (in mid-stride now, remember, at seventy miles per hour) and *trip* the impala.

The impala goes head-over-teakettle. The cheetah slams on its own brakes, and pounces. The actual killing is then accomplished with a throat bite—which must be held as long as it takes for the impala to strangle, since the cheetah's jaw muscles and teeth are too meager for chomping through the spine or ripping out the jugular. But what about that other brazen impala, the one left standing back at the start? Why did the cheetah choose to ignore it? No one can be sure, but the most plausible answer is that, without a high-velocity chase, without a well-timed trip, the speedy-but-weak cheetah simply has no means of knocking an impala off its feet.

The cheetah's hunting technique, with that long stealthy stalk followed by that sudden heart-shocking sprint, seems specifically designed to in-duce—rather than to preempt—a panicky bolt by the prey. That induced panic makes a gazelle or an impala vulnerable to the cheetah's modest killing tools in a way neither animal would otherwise be. The successive stages (spook-chase-overtake-trip-pounce-strangle) are all linked together with fine economy. The method is highly dramatic and highly successful.

It is so successful that the cheetah, lacking defensive weaponry in a fiercely competitive habitat, can afford to be (and is) frequently robbed of its own fresh-killed prey by lions and leopards and hyenas; yet the cheetah still survives quite well on the portion of kills left unstolen. And it is so dramatic that, for almost five thousand years, human potentates on three continents kept tamed cheetahs for sport hunting.

The possession of coursing cheetahs has been a self-flattering perquisite of royalty, in fact, for almost as long as the possession of gold. The Sumerian rulers used cheetahs on their hunts around 3000 B.C. The Pharaohs had captive cheetahs. So did the Assyrian kings. In the Caucasus a burial mound dated to 2300 B.C. has yielded a silver vase decorated with the figure of a cheetah—and this cheetah is wearing a collar. In Italy cheetahs were prized and collected from the fifth century onward. Russian princes hunted with them in the eleventh and twelfth centuries. Charlemagne enjoyed running cheetahs after game, as did William the Conqueror, and also Emperor Leo-pold I of Austria, who used his for deer hunting in the Vienna Woods.

Marco Polo reported that Kublai Khan had a stable of cheetahs, possibly as many as a thousand, at his summer palace in Karakorum. Those animals were kept hooded and subdued like falcons until the moment of being released for the chase; when a victim was taken away from them by their human handlers and they were rewarded with the viscera, they seem to have accepted that bad bargain with the same equanimity as if they had lost the whole meal to a pack of hyenas. The later Mogul emperor Akbar also had a thousand captive cheetahs, according to an account left by his son. What Akbar's son especially recalled was that, one time, a male cheetah slipped its collar and found a female to mate with, which union produced three kits who survived to adulthood. It was remarkable, said the son, because it never happened again.

16

Indeed: That accidental litter in Akbar's stables seems to be the only such case of captive breeding recorded from Sumerian times up to 1960. Though cheetahs can be chased to the point of exhaustion by horsemen and then lassoed, though they tame rather easily, they almost never (until recently) have been persuaded to reproduce in captivity.

All those thousands and thousands of regal pets, all those hunting cheetahs, had been taken straight from wild breeding populations. And it was a one-way trip. Their genes came out of the reproductively active gene pool, and we can safely assume that very few ever went back.

20   O'Brien's study reveals that those fifty-five members of the South African cheetah population are just too similar to each other, biochemically, for their own good. One startling bit of evidence was that their bodies failed to reject skin grafts traded surgically between different cheetahs—even their own immune systems couldn't distinguish among them. Another form of evidence came from electrophoresis, a technique whereby genetic differences can be deduced through the measuring of small electrical differences among enzymes and other proteins. Again, by this standard, the South African population was found to contain "10 to 100 times less genetic variation than other mammalian species." In addition, the male cheetahs had a drastically low sperm count and a drastically high proportion of abnormally shaped sperm in what they did have, two symptoms common among inbred livestock and inbred populations of lab mice. They also showed a disastrous vulnerability to disease (for instance, when eighteen cheetahs at a wildlife park in Oregon died suddenly from a virus that seldom threatens other cats). O'Brien and his colleagues concluded that "the catastrophic sensitivity of this genetically uniform species does provide a graphic natural example of the protection afforded to biological species by genetic variability." Without that protection, the same sort of epidemic die-off that happened in Oregon could also strike the wild African populations.

And still there's the unanswered question: Where did those missing genes go?

Possibly, alas, to the entertainment of seigneurial humans, back in the days when coursing cheetahs were such a vogue.

The O'Brien group hypothesize what they call a *population bottleneck* in the cheetah's recent (two hundred years) or less recent (two thousand years) past. This bottleneck could have been any situation where for one reason or another the number of breeding cheetahs was dramatically reduced—to a low point from which the population level subsequently recovered, but from which the gene pool so far has not. The American bison went through that kind of bottleneck during its near brush with human-caused extinction a century ago. So did the northern elephant seal at about the same time. The elephant seal survived in only a tiny population on one remote island off Baja, then rebounded prolifically when humankind stopped killing it, but today the seal still shows a severe shortage of genetic diversity. And if the California condor survives at all, squeezing through its present perilous bottleneck, it can look forward at best to the same sort of lingering genetic deficiency for a thousand years.

The next big question in cheetah research, meanwhile, is whether the East African population (of the Serengeti[3] and the high Kenyan plains) shares the genetic depauperacy of the South African group.

If the East African population is genetically robust, then it will seem that the South African cheetah's bottleneck was a recent and localized situation, possibly attributable to killing by skin hunters and ranchers of the Boer period. But if the East African cheetah is similarly impoverished, then the problem is likely much broader and much older.

It might be as old as Xanadu[4] and Karakorum,[5] as old as the pyramids, as old as that silver vase from a burial mound in the Caucasus. And it might be equally the consequence of a certain implacable, greedy human impulse: the impulse, not only to admire the embodiment of beauty, but to capture and possess it.

---

[3]The Serengeti plains in northwestern Tanzania, where large numbers of animals migrate every year.

[4]In Samuel Taylor Coleridge's poem "Kubla Khan" (1816), site of a fantastic "pleasure-dome."

[5]Capital of Mongol empire and site of Genghis Khan's residence.

Understanding What You Read

1. Does the introductory paragraph contribute to the overall effectiveness of the essay?
2. What characteristic of the cheetah gives it an advantage over other animals?
3. How does a cheetah capture and kill its prey?
4. What are the possible explanations for genetic impoverishment of the East African cheetahs?
5. What does Quammen suggest may be the consequence of trying to reestablish species that are down to a few members?

Writing About What You Read

Compare the life of a captured cheetah in one of the royal courts of the past with the life of a cheetah in the wilds of Africa.

MARY OLIVER

Volumes of Oliver's (b. 1935) poetry include *The River Styx, Ohio and Other Poems* (1972); *Twelve Moons* (1979); and *Dream Work* (1986). Her volume *American Primitive* won the 1984 Pulitzer Prize, and *New and Selected Poems* won the National Book Award in 1992. Both "In the Pinewoods, Crows and Owl" and "Humpbacks" are from *American Primitive*.

In the Pinewoods, Crows and Owl

Great bumble. Sleek
slicer. How the crows
dream of you, caught at last
4   in their black beaks. Dream of you
leaking your life away. Your wings
crumbling like old bark. Feathers
falling from your breast like leaves,
8   and your eyes two bolts
of lightning gone to sleep.
Eight of them
fly over the pinewoods looking down
12   into the branches. They know you are
there somewhere, fat and drowsy
from your night of rabbits and rats. Once
this month you caught a crow. Scraps of him
16   flew far and wide, the news
rang all day through the woods. The cold
river of their hatred roils
day and night: you are their dream, their waking,
20   their quarry, their demon. You
are the pine god who never speaks but holds
the keys to everything while they fly
morning after morning against the shut doors. You
24   will have a slow life, and eat them, one by one.
They know it. They hate you. Still
when one of them spies you out, all stream
straight toward violence and confrontation.
28   As though it helped to see the living proof.
The bone-crushing prince of dark days, gloomy
at the interruption of his rest. Hissing
and snapping, grabbing about him, dreadful
32   as death's drum; mournful, unalterable fact.

Humpbacks

*

There is, all around us,
this country
of original fire.

You know what I mean.   4

The sky, after all, stops at nothing, so something has to be holding
our bodies
in its rich and timeless stables or else
we would fly away.   8

*

Off Stellwagen
off the Cape,
the humpbacks rise. Carrying their tonnage of barnacles and joy
they leap through the water, they nuzzle back under it   12
like children
at play.

*

They sing, too.   16
And not for any reason
you can't imagine.

*

Three of them
rise to the surface near the bow of the boat,
then dive   20
deeply, their huge scarred flukes
tipped to the air.

We wait, not knowing
just where it will happen; suddenly   24
they smash through the surface, someone begins
shouting for joy and you realize
it is yourself as they surge
upward and you see for the first time   28
how huge they are, as they breach,
and dive, and breach again
through the shining blue flowers
of the split water and you see them   32
for some unbelievable
part of a moment against the sky—

like nothing you've ever imagined—
36   like the myth of the fifth morning[1] galloping
out of darkness, pouring
heavenward, spinning; then

*

they crash back under those black silks
40   and we all fall back
together into that wet fire, you
know what I mean.

*

I know a captain who has seen them
44   playing with seaweed, swimming
through the green islands, tossing
the slippery branches into the air.

I know a whale that will come to the boat whenever
48   she can, and nudge it gently along the bow
with her long flipper.

I know several lives worth living.

*

Listen, whatever it is you try
52   to do with your life, nothing will ever dazzle you
like the dreams of your body,

its spirit
longing to fly while the dead-weight bones

56   toss their dark mane and hurry
back into the fields of glittering fire

where everything,
even the great whale,
60   throbs with song.

[1]In Genesis, the first book of the Bible, God creates the great sea monsters and other sea life on the fifth day of creation.

Understanding What You Read

1. What does the narrator say the crows dream of? What do they do when they spot an owl?

2. What do you learn about the narrator from what she imagines the crows are thinking?
3. Why are these two species more appropriate for this poem than others?
4. What is special about whales?
5. What is the effect of attributing joy, play, and song to the whales?

Writing About What You Read

1. Write a paragraph or an essay expressing the feelings the crows and/or owls evoke for you.
2. Compare and contrast how Oliver gives meaning to what she imagines about the crows and the owl in the one poem and what she sees the whales do in the other.

PAUL COLINVAUX

Colinvaux (b. 1930) is professor of zoology at Ohio State and is author of the textbook *Introduction to Ecology*. He has done research in the history of climate change recorded in fossils in the mud of ancient lakes, the environmental history of the Galápagos, and the way of life of the people who settled the ancient plainsland now drowned by the Bering Sea. "Every Species Has Its Niche" is from *Why Big Fierce Animals Are Rare: An Ecologist's Perspective* (1978).

Every Species Has Its Niche

EVERY SPECIES has its niche, its place in the grand scheme of things.

Consider a wolf spider as it hunts through the litter of leaves on the woodland floor. It must be a splendid hunter; that goes without saying for otherwise its line would long since have died out. But it must be proficient at other things too. Even as it hunts, it must keep some of its eight eyes on the lookout for the things that hunt it; and when it sees an enemy it must do the right thing to save itself. It must know what to do when it rains. It must have a life-style that enables it to survive the winter. It must rest safely when the time is not apt for hunting. And there comes a season of the year when the spiders, as it were, feel the sap rising in their eight legs. The male must respond by going to look for a female spider, and when he finds her, he must convince her that he is not merely something to eat—yet. And she, in the fullness of time, must carry an egg sack as she goes about her hunting, and later must let the babies ride on her back. They, in turn, must learn the various forms of fending for themselves as they go through the different moults of the spider's life until they, too, are swift-running, pouncing hunters of the woodland floor.

Wolf-spidering is a complex job, not something to be undertaken by an amateur. We might say that there is a profession of wolf-spidering. It is necessary to be good at all its manifold tasks to survive at it. What is more, the profession is possible only in very restricted circumstances. A woodland floor is necessary, for instance, and the right climate with a winter roughly like that your ancestors were used to; and enough of the right sorts of things to hunt; and the right shelter when you need it; and the numbers of natural enemies must be kept within reasonable bounds. For success, individual spiders must be superlatively good at their jobs and the right circumstances must prevail. Unless both the skills of spidering and the opportunity are present, there will not be any wolf spiders. The "niche" of wolf-spidering will not be filled.

"Niche" is a word ecologists have borrowed from church architecture. In a church, of course, "niche" means a recess in the wall in which a figurine may be placed; it is an address, a location, a physical place. But the ecologist's "niche" is more than just a physical place: it is a place in the grand scheme of things. The niche is an animal's (or a plant's) profession. The niche of the wolf spider is everything it does to get its food and raise its babies. To be able to do these things it must relate properly to the place where it lives and to the other inhabitants of that place. Everything the species does to survive and stay "fit" in the Darwinian sense is its niche.

The physical living place in an ecologist's jargon is called the *habitat*. The habitat is the "address" or "location" in which individuals of a species live. The woodland floor hunted by the wolf spiders is the habitat, but wolf-spidering is their niche. It is the niche of wolf-spidering that has been fashioned by natural selection.

The idea of "niche" at once gives us a handle to one of those general questions that ecologists want to answer—the question of the constancy of numbers. The common stay common, and the rare stay rare, because the opportunities for each niche, or profession, are set by circumstance. Wolf-spidering needs the right sort of neighbors living in the right sort of wood, and the number of times that this combination comes up in any country is limited. So the number of wolf-spiders is limited also; the number was fixed when the niche was adopted. This number is likely to stay constant until something drastic happens to change the face of the country.

Likening an animal's niche to a human profession makes this idea of limits to number very clear. Let us take the profession of professing. There can only be as many professors in any city as there are teaching and scholarship jobs for professors to do. If the local university turns out more research scholars than there are professing jobs, then some of these hopeful young people will not be able to accept the scholar's tenure, however *cum laude* their degrees. They will have to emigrate, or take to honest work to make a living.

Likewise there cannot be more wolf spiders than there are wolf-spider jobs, antelopes than there are antelope jobs, crab grass than there are crab-grass jobs. Every species has its niche. And once its niche is fixed by natural selection, so also are its numbers fixed.

This idea of niche gets at the numbers problem without any discussion of breeding effort. Indeed, it shows that the way an animal breeds has very little to do with how many of it there are. This is a very strange idea to someone new to it, and it needs to be thought about carefully. *The reproductive effort makes no difference to the eventual size of the population.* Numerous eggs may increase numbers in the short term, following some disaster, but only for a while. The numbers that may live are set by the number of niche-spaces (jobs) in the environment, and these are quite independent of how fast a species makes babies.

But all the same each individual must try to breed as fast as it can. It is in a race with its neighbors of the same kind, a race that will decide whose babies will fill the niche-space jobs of the next generation. The actual number of those who will be able to live in that next generation has been fixed by the environment; we may say that the population will be a function of the *carrying capacity* of the land for animals of this kind in that time and place. But the issue of whose babies will take up those limited places is absolutely open. It is here that natural selection operates. A "fit" individual is, by definition, one that successfully takes up one of the niche-spaces from the limited pool, and the fitness of a parent is measured by how many future niche-spaces her or his offspring take up. "Survival of the fittest" means survival of those who leave the most living descendants. A massive breeding effort makes no difference to the future population, but it is vital for the hereditary future of one's own line. This is why everything that lives has the capacity for large families.

Yet there are degrees of largeness in wild families, and these degrees of largeness make sense when looked at with an ecologist's eye. The intuitively obvious consequence of a law that says "Have the largest possible family or face hereditary oblivion" is the family based on thousands of tiny eggs or seeds. This seems to be the commonest breeding strategy. Houseflies, mosquitoes, salmon, and dandelions all do it. I call it "the small-egg gambit." It has very obvious advantages, but there are also costs, which the clever ones with big babies avoid.

For users of the small-egg gambit, natural selection starts doing the obvious sums. If an egg is made just a little bit smaller, the parent might be able to make an extra egg for the same amount of food eaten, and this will give it a slight edge in the evolutionary race. It is enough. Natural selection will therefore choose families that make more and more of smaller and smaller eggs until a point of optimum smallness is reached. If the eggs are any smaller than this, the young may all die; if they are any larger, one's neighbor will swamp one's posterity with her mass production. The largest number of the smallest possible eggs makes simple Darwinian sense.

But the costs of the small-egg gambit are grim. An inevitable consequence is that babies are thrown out into the world naked and tiny. Most of them as a result die, and early death is the common lot of baby salmon, dandelions, and the rest. In the days before Darwin, people used to say that the vast families of salmon, dandelions, and insects were compensations for the slaughter of the young. So terrible was the life of a baby fish that Providence provided a salmon with thousands of eggs to give it a chance that one or two might get through. It seems a natural assumption, and one that still confuses even some biologists. But the argument is the wrong way round. A high death rate for the tiny, helpless young is a consequence of the thousands of tiny eggs, not a cause. A selfish race of neighbor against neighbor leads to those thousands of tiny eggs, and the early deaths of the babies are the cost of this selfishness.

There is this to be said for the small-egg gambit, though: once you have been forced into it, there are the gambler's compensations. Many young scattered far and wide mean an intensive search for opportunity, and this may pay off when opportunity is thinly scattered in space. Weed and plague species win this advantage, as when the parachute seed of a dandelion is wafted between the trunks of the trees of a forest to alight on the fresh-turned earth of a rabbit burrow. The small-egg gambits of weeds may be likened to the tactics of a gambler at a casino who covers every number with a low-value chip. If he has enough chips, he is bound to win, particularly if big payoffs are possible. He does have to have very many chips to waste, though. This is why economists do not approve of gamblers.

To the person with an economic turn of mind, the small-egg gambit, for all its crazy logic, does not seem a proper way to manage affairs. The adherents of this gambit spend all their lives at their professions, winning as many resources as possible from their living places, and then they invest these resources in tiny babies, most of whom are going to die. What a ridiculously low return on capital. What economic folly. Any economist could tell these animals and plants that the real way to win in the hereditary stakes is to put all your capital into a lesser number of big strong babies, all of which are going to survive. A number of animals in fact do this. I call it "the large-young gambit."

In the large-young gambit one either makes a few huge eggs out of the food available, or the babies actually grow inside their mother, where they are safe. Either way, each baby has a very good chance of living to grow up. It is big to start with and it is fed or defended by parents until it can look after itself. Most of the food the parents collect goes into babies who live. There is little waste. Natural selection approves of this as much as do economists. Big babies who have a very good chance of long life mean more surviving offspring for the amount of food-investment in the end. This prudent outlay of resources is arranged by birds, viviparous snakes, great white sharks, goats, tigers, and people.

Having a few, large young, and then nursing them until they are big and strong, is the surest existing method of populating the future. Yet the success of this gambit assumes one essential condition. You must start with just the right number of young. If you lay too many monster hen's eggs or drop too many bawling brats, you may not be able to supply them with enough food, and some or all will die. You have then committed the economic wastefulness of those of the tiny eggs. So you must not be too ambitious in your breeding. But the abstemious will also lose out, because its neighbor may raise one more baby, may populate the future just that little bit better, and start your line on a one-way ride to hereditary oblivion. You must get it just right; not too many young, and not too few. Natural selection will preserve those family strains which are programmed to "choose" the best or optimum size of family.

Many ecologists have studied birds with these ideas in mind, and they have found that there is often a very good correlation between the number of eggs in a clutch and the food supply. In a year when food is plentiful a bird may lay, on the average, one or two eggs more than in a lean season. The trend may be slight but sometimes is quite obvious. Snowy owls, which are big white birds of the arctic tundra, build vast nests on the ground. They feed their chicks on lemmings, the small brown arctic mice. When lemmings are scarce, there may be only one or two eggs in each owl's nest, but when the tundra is crawling with lemmings, the nests may well have ten eggs each. The owls are evidently clever at assessing how many chicks they can afford each year.

But people are cleverer than snowy owls and have brought the large-young gambit to its perfection. They can read the environment, guess the future, and plan their families according to what their intelligence tells them they can afford. Even the infanticide practiced by various peoples at various times serves the cause of Darwinian fitness, rather than acting as a curb on population. There is no point in keeping alive babies who could not be supported for long. Killing babies who could not be safely reared gives a better chance of survival to those who are left, and infanticide in hard times can mean that more children grow up in the end.

Thus, every species has its niche, its place in the grand scheme of things; and every species has a breeding strategy refined by natural selection to leave the largest possible number of surviving offspring. The requirement for a definite niche implies a limit to the size of the population because the numbers of the animal or plant are set by the opportunities for carrying on life in that niche. The kind of breeding strategy, on the other hand, has no effect on the size of the usual population, and the drive to breed is a struggle to decide which family strains have the privilege of taking up the limited numbers of opportunities for life. Every family tries to outbreed every other, though the total numbers of their kind remain the same. These are the principles on which an ecologist can base his efforts to answer the major questions of his discipline.

20

Understanding What You Read

1. Why do common species remain common and rare species remain rare?
2. Define the niche of a wood spider.
3. Why is there a limit to the population size of every species?
4. List several species with which you are familiar that use the small-egg gambit and several that use the large-young gambit.

Writing About What You Read

1. What profession or career do you intend to pursue? Is there likely to be a niche available when you are ready to go to work? Write an essay about your plans to prepare yourself for a niche and how you expect to fill it.
2. Colinvaux explains that a niche is "everything an animal does to get its food and raise its babies." Choose an animal (do some research if you need to) and write about what is required for it to fill its niche and what might happen that would make that impossible.

THOMAS PALMER

Palmer (b. 1955) grew up in Connecticut and attended Wesleyan University. He began his writing career with two novels, *The Transfer* (1983) and *Dream Science* (1990), but turned to nonfiction in *Landscape of Reptile: Rattlesnakes in the Urban World* (1992). This book, about a region outside Boston where the rattlesnake is endangered, grew out of Palmer's compulsion for the plight of this snake, which he sees as fitting the profile of a fictional hero—glamorous, feared, and surrounded by danger. "The Case for Human Beings," published in the January 1992 issue of the *Atlantic Monthly*, is adapted from this book. At the request of the *Atlantic Monthly*, Palmer deleted all references to rattlesnakes from the piece, except for the first paragraph.

The Case for Human Beings

AN ARGUMENT, a human argument, maintains that we ought to be concerned about the disappearance of individual animal species. If it could be directed at the objects of its solicitude, it would go approximately as follows: "You lesser beasts had better watch your step—*we'll* decide when you can leave." It recognizes that once chromosome patterns combine at the species level, they become unique and irreplaceable—one cannot make a rattlesnake, for instance, out of anything but more rattlesnakes. It looks at the speed at which such patterns are disappearing and shudders to think how empty our grandchildren's world might become, patternwise.

In the past twenty years this argument has conquered much of the world; it may soon become part of the thinking of nearly every school child.

Perhaps because we ourselves are a species, we regard the species level as that at which deaths become truly irreversible. Populations, for instance, can and do fade in and out; when a species dies, however, we call it extinct and retire its name forever, being reasonably certain that it will not reappear in its old form.

Students of evolution have shown that species death, or extinction, is going on all the time, and that it is an essential feature of life history. Species are adapted to their environments; as environments change, some species find themselves in the position of islanders whose islands are washing away, and they go under. Similarly, new islands (or environments) are appearing all the time, and they almost invariably produce new species.

What alarms so many life historians is not that extinctions are occurring but that they appear to be occurring at a greater rate than they have at all but a few times in the past, raising the specter of the sort of wholesale die-offs that ended the reign of the dinosaurs. Do we want, they ask, to exile most of our neighbors to posterity? Exactly how much of our planet's resources do we mean to funnel into people-making? Such questions are serious; they involve choosing among futures, and some of these futures are already with us, in the form of collapsing international fisheries, rich grasslands gnawed and trampled into deserts, forests skeletonized by windborne acids, and so forth. Thus high rates of extinction are seen as a symptom of major problems in the way our species operates—problems that may, if we're not careful, be solved for us. A new word has been coined to define the value most threatened by these overheated rates: "biodiversity." As species disappear, biodiversity declines, and our planet's not-quite-limitless fund of native complexities—so some argue—declines with it.

The process described above is indeed occurring. Human beings tend to change environments; when they do, species vanish. The Puritans, for example, though famous for their efforts to discipline sexuality, imposed upon Massachusetts an orgy of ecological licentiousness: they introduced dozens of microbes, weeds, and pests foreign to the region, some of which played havoc with the natives. Human beings tend to travel everywhere, and to bring their cats, rats, and fleas with them, so that hardly any environment is truly isolated today, and creatures that evolved in isolated environments have paid a high price. Of the 171 species and subspecies of birds that have become extinct in the past 300 years, for example, 155 were island forms.

Since extinction is a particularly final and comprehensive form of death, species preservation and its corollary, habitat protection, are now seen as the most important means available to stem the erosion of biodiversity. So far, so good—but I wonder if these ideas, which emphasize diversity at the species level, fail to give an adequate picture of recent biological history. If, for instance, biodiversity is regarded as the chief measure of a landscape's richness, then the American continents reached their peak of splendor on the day after the first Siberian spearmen arrived, and have been deteriorating ever since. More recent developments—such as the domestication of maize, the rise of civilizations in Mexico and Peru, and the passage of the U.S. Bill of Rights—are neutral at best, and are essentially invisible, since they are the work of a single species, a species no more or less weighty than any other, and already present at the start of the interval. But what kind of yardstick measures a handful of skin-clad hunters against Chicago, Los Angeles, and Caracas, and finds one group no more "diverse" than the other?

8   A considerable amount of pessimism is built into this species-based notion of diversity. Nearly all change on such a scale is change for the worse—especially human-mediated change. Change involves stress, and stress causes extinctions; each extinction is another pock in the skin of an edenic original. This original is frozen in time; more often than not, it is defined as the blissful instant just prior to the arrival of the first human being. In fact, the only way to re-create this instant, and restore biodiversity to its greatest possible richness, would be to arrange for every human being on earth to drop dead tomorrow.

This is not to say that cities are better than coral reefs, or that binary codes are an improvement on genetic ones, but only that "biodiversity" cannot adequately account for the phenomenon of *Homo sapiens.*

Maybe it's time to give up the notion of human beings as intruders, tramplers, and destroyers. We are all of these, there's no doubt about it, but they are not all we are. And yet the same mind-set that interprets human history as little more than a string of increasingly lurid ecological crimes also insists that our species represents the last, best hope of "saving" the planet. Is it any wonder that the future looks bleak?

Here we have the essential Puritan outlook disguised as science—human beings, the sinners, occupy center stage, and cannot move a muscle without risking the direst consequences in a cosmic drama. At stake is the fate of the world; thousands of innocents (other species) rely on the shaky powers of human foresight. One false step—and our ancestors, as we know, have taken almost nothing but false steps—and our dwelling place may be mutilated beyond redemption.

12   This outlook is realistic in its recognition that our species is different in kind from all others, as any visitor from outer space would admit; it is obnoxious in the limits it places on the organic experiment. Human consciousness—whether in the form of Bach chorales, three-masted schooners, or microwave communications—cannot, in this view, contribute to biodiversity, except by staying as far out of the picture as possible, so as to avoid

tainting still-intact landscapes with unnatural influences. The possibility that chorales and schooners might represent positive contributions to biotic richness—that they might, just as much as any rain-forest orchid, embody the special genius of this planet—is never admitted. Somehow an agreement has been reached to exclude whatever is human from the sum of biodiversity—as if the Apollo landings, for example, do not represent an astonishing breakthrough *in strictly biological terms.*

This view has a certain legitimacy as long as its definition of diversity is narrowly chromosomal, or species-based. Those environments richest in species—the tropical forests and the warmwater seas—are, from its perspective, the most diverse and complex. But I would argue that this definition, though accurate enough for most of the history of life, became obsolete about a half million years ago, when *Homo sapiens* came on the scene. This creature released organic change from its age-old dependence on genetic recombination and harnessed it to new energies—culture, symbolic language, and imagination. As is becoming more and more evident, nothing has been the same since.

Being reluctant to acknowledge this fact, ecologists, biologists, and environmentalists have had fits trying to introduce our species into their models of the natural world. These models are based on the idea of balance, or equilibrium, wherein each variety of plant or animal plays a limited, genetically prescribed role in the cycling of materials and energy. The roles are not absolutely fixed—natural selection, by sorting and resorting chromosomes, can adapt lines of descent to new ones—but change, by and large, is assumed to be gradual, and millions of years can pass without any notable restructuring of communities.

Human beings cannot be worked into such models. One cannot look at human beings and predict what they will eat, or where they will live, or how many of their children a given landscape will support. If they inhabit a forest, they may burn it down and raise vegetables, or flood it and plant rice, or sell it to a pulp-and-paper manufacturer. They may think of anything; the life their parents led is not a reliable blueprint, but merely a box with a thousand exits. Moralists in search of instructive contrasts will sometimes idealize primitive societies, claiming that they deliberately live "in balance" with their environments, but these examples don't stand up to scrutiny. The Massachuset Indians, for instance, though sometimes presented as sterling conservationists, were the descendants of aboriginal American hunters who appear to have pursued a whole constellation of Ice Age mammals to extinction (including several species of horses). When, in historical times, they were offered metal fishhooks, knives, and firearms, they didn't say, "Thanks, but we prefer rock-chipping."

The revelation that we are not like other creatures in certain crucial respects is an ancient one, and may be nearly as old as humanity; it probably

16

contributed to the idea, central to several major religions, that we inhabit a sort of permanent exile. Until recently, however, we could still imagine ourselves encompassed by, if not entirely contained in, landscapes dominated by nonhuman forces—weather, infectious illness, growing seasons, light and darkness, and so forth. This is no longer so; today most human beings live in artificial wildernesses called cities, and don't raise the food they eat, or know where the water they drink fell as rain. A sort of vertigo has set in—a feeling that a rhythm has been upset, and that soon nothing will be left of the worlds that made us. This feeling is substantiated by population curves, ocean pollution, chemical changes in the earth's atmosphere, vanishing wildlife, mountains of garbage, and numerous other signs that anyone can read. The nineteenth-century conservation movement, which sought to preserve landscapes for largely aesthetic reasons, has become absorbed in the twentieth-century environmental movement, which insists that more is at stake than postcard views. We are, it argues, near to exceeding the carrying capacity of our planet's natural systems, systems whose importance to us will become very obvious when they begin to wobble and fail.

These are not empty warnings. Human communities can and occasionally do self-destruct by overstraining their resource bases. Historical examples include the Easter Islanders,[1] the lowland Maya,[2] and some of the classical-era city-dwellers of the Middle East and North Africa. But if we set aside the equilibrium-based models of the ecologists, and do not limit ourselves to species-bound notions of diversity—in other words, if we seek to include human beings in the landscape of nature, rather than make them outcasts— what sort of picture do we get of the phenomenon of life?

The difference between life and nonlife, according to the biologists, is a matter of degree. A glass of seawater, for instance, contains many of the same materials as a condor (or a green turtle). What makes one alive and the other not are the varying chemical pathways those materials follow. The glass of water contains few internal boundaries, and gases diffuse freely across its surface. In the condor, in contrast, a much more complex array of reactions is in progress, reactions that maintain certain molecular-energy potentials in an oddly elevated state, even though the bird as a whole shows a net energy loss. In other words, both the condor and the glass of water cycle energy, but in the condor the energy goes to support a level of complexity not present in the water.

Perhaps the condor is more like a candle flame—both burn energy, and that burning keeps certain patterns intact. The condor, like the candle, can burn out. But although one can relight the candle, one cannot relight the condor—it is too delicately tuned, too dependent on various internal continuities.

[1]Inhabitants of an island in the South Pacific, where plant life is limited to grasses and shrubs because of deforestation.

[2]Central American Indians whose highly advanced civilizations may have declined in part because of agricultural practices that exhausted the soil.

As useful as these distinctions are, they tend to blur under increased   20
magnification. A virus, for instance, is more condorlike than flamelike, because the energy and materials it draws from its surroundings reappear not
primarily as heat, light, and simple oxides but as viral protein and nucleic
acids—complex substances that the flame cannot construct but only disas-
semble. And yet most students agree that viruses are not alive, because they
cannot build these substances without the aid of the machineries inside a
living cell. A certain level of independence is necessary—living things, according to this definition, not only must transform simple compounds into
more varied and characteristic ones but also must be able to do so in an
atmosphere of nonlife.

Life, for the biologists, is an uphill or retrograde process—it adds order and
complexity to environments whose overall tendency is toward diffusion and
disorder. It captures energies released by decay and exploits them for growth
and rebirth. It is startlingly anomalous in this respect: so far as we know, it
occurs nowhere but on the surface of this planet, and even here its appearance
seems to have been a one-time-only event; though many lifelike substances
have been produced inside sterile glassware, none has ever quickened into
veritable beasthood.

The evidence suggests that life continued to fructify and elaborate itself
for several billion years after its appearance. The milestones along the way—
the nucleated cell, photosynthesis, sexual reproduction, multicellularity, the
internal skeleton, the invasion of the land and sky, and so forth—are usually
interpreted as advances, because they added additional layers of complexity,
interconnection, and ordered interaction to existing systems. This drama did
not proceed without crises—photosynthesis, for instance, probably wiped
out entire ecosystems by loading the atmosphere with a deadly poison, free
oxygen—but life as a whole laughed at such insults, and continued on its
protean way.

If we believe that all life—in contrast to rocks and gases—shares a certain
quality of sensitivity, or self-awareness, then *Homo sapiens* was an astonishing
and wholly unpredictable leap forward in this respect, because human beings
manifested an idea of personhood never before achieved. The exact moment
of this discovery is of course problematic, as are most events in evolution, but
I would date it from early summer about 60,000 years ago, when a group
of Neanderthals living in present-day Iraq lost one of their members, dug a
grave for him in the Shanidar Cave of the Zagros Mountain highlands, placed
his body inside, and covered it with yarrow blossoms, cornflowers, hyacinths,
and mallows. Here, in a gesture of remarkable grace, a group of living
creatures betrayed an awareness that creatureliness is a pose, a pose that can't
be held forever.

The poignancy of this moment is profound. Though the idea is startling   24
to consider, all the evidence suggests that most of life's history has unfolded
unobserved, so to speak. I would bet that the dinosaurs, for instance, did not

know that they were reptiles, or that they had faces like their neighbors, or that they once hatched from eggs like their offspring.

Consciousness. Mind. Insight. Here are qualities that, if not exclusively human, seem appallingly rudimentary elsewhere. Primitive peoples distributed them throughout their worlds; we moderns hold to stricter standards of evidence. Does a cloud yearn, for instance, to drop rain? Is a seed eager to sprout?

The irruption of thoughtfulness that our species represents is not inexplicable in Darwinian terms. Once our apelike and erect ancestors began using weapons, hunting large animals, and sharing the spoils, the ability to develop plans and communicate them acquired considerable survival value, and was genetically enhanced. This ability, and the tripling in brain weight that accompanied it, turned out to be one of the most revolutionary experiments in the history of gene-sorting. It was as if Nature, after wearing out several billion years tossing off new creatures like nutshells, looked up to see that one had come back, and was eyeing her strangely.

The distance between that moment and today is barely a hiccup, geologically speaking. We are genetically almost indistinguishable from those bear-roasters and mammoth-stickers. But the world is a different place now. Grad students in ecology, for instance, are expected to do a certain amount of "fieldwork," and many of them have to travel hundreds and even thousands of miles before they consider themselves far enough from classrooms to be in the field.

28 Plainly, our planet contained vast opportunities for creatures willing to shape it consciously toward their ends. The way was clear; we know of no other species that has divined what we've been up to, or has a mind to object. What seems simple to us is far beyond them; it's almost as if we move so fast that we are invisible, and they are still trying to pretend—without much success—that the world is the same as it was before we arrived.

This speed on the uptake appears to be the chief advantage that cultural adaptation has over genetic. When human beings encounter new circumstances, adaptation rarely depends on which individuals are genetically best suited to adjust, passing on their abilities more successfully than others and producing subsequent generations better adapted to the new order. No, human beings tend to cut the loop short by noticing the new, puzzling over it, telling their friends, and attempting to find out immediately whether it is edible, combustible, domesticable, or whatever. In this way we develop traditions that are immaterial, so to speak, in that they evolve on a track largely disengaged from the double helix.[3]

This talent for endless jabber and experiment, and the pooling of useful knowledge it makes possible, means that human beings, unlike orangutans or condors, operate not primarily as individuals scattered over a landscape but

---

[3]The shape of the DNA molecule, the basis of genetic inheritance. As used here, "double helix" refers to genetically programmed behaviors.

as shareholders in a common fund of acquired skills, many of them the work of previous generations. This fund is extraordinarily deep and sophisticated, even among the most isolated bands of hunter-gatherers; when, as in recent times, it has included experience accumulated by thousands or even millions of forebears, it has enabled our species to become the quickest-acting agent of change in life's history. In fact, we might sensibly think of the human species not as five billion distinct selves but as five billion nodes in a single matrix, just as the human body is more commonly considered a unit than an accumulation of cells.

If life, as before noted, is a paradoxical chemical process by which order arises from disorder, and a movement toward uniformity produces more-complex local conditions, then human enterprise, though full of disasters for other species, is clearly not outside the main line of development. Equatorial rain forests, for instance, are probably the most diverse and multifaceted communities of species on earth. But are they more densely stuffed with highly refined codes and labels than, say, the Library of Congress? Long ago certain moths learned to communicate over as much as two miles of thick woods by releasing subtle chemicals that prospective mates could detect at levels measured in parts per million; today a currency broker in Tokyo can pick up a phone and hear accurate copies of sounds vocalized a split second earlier by a counterpart on the other side of the world. Which system of signals is more sensitive and flexible?

I am concerned, as is obvious, with an image—the image of our species as a vast, featureless mob of yahoos[4] mindlessly trampling this planet's most ancient and delicate harmonies. This image, which is on its way to becoming an article of faith, is not a completely inaccurate description of present conditions in some parts of the world, but it portrays the human presence as a sort of monolithic disaster, when in fact *Homo sapiens* is the crown of creation, if by creation we mean the explosion of earthly vitality and particularity long ago ignited by a weak solution of amino acids mixing in sunlit waters. Change—dramatic, wholesale change—is one of the most reliable constants of this story. To say that the changes we have brought, and will continue to bring, are somehow alien to the world, and are within a half inch of making its "natural" continuance impossible, displays some contempt, I think, for the forces at work, along with a large dose of inverted pride. Who are we, for instance, to say what's possible and what isn't? Have we already glimpsed the end? Where exactly did things go awry? It's useful to remember that just yesterday our main concern was finding something to eat.

I prefer to suppose that we will be here awhile, and that such abilities as we have, though unprecedented in certain respects, are not regrettable. The human mind, for instance, could never have set itself the task of preserving rare species if earlier minds had not learned how to distinguish light from

32

---

[4]The destructive beasts (who look like men) in Jonathan Swift's *Gulliver's Travels* (1726).

darkness, or coordinate limbs, or identify mates. Now that we think we know something about our immediate neighborhood, we are beginning to realize what a rare quality life is, and if we think of its multibillion-year history on earth as a sort of gradual awakening of matter, we must conclude that the dawning of human consciousness represents one of the most extraordinary sunrises on record. Is it any wonder, then, that the world is changing?

Perhaps because we have become so expert at interrogating our surroundings, we tremble a little at our own shadows. God, for instance, has become almost a fugitive. We have disassembled the atom; we have paced off the galaxies; He doesn't figure in our equations.

Maybe it would be useful at this point to compare our common birthplace to a fertile hen's egg. Nearly everyone has seen the delicate tracery of blood vessels that begins to spread across the yolk of such an egg within a few hours of laying. Before long a tiny pump starts to twitch rhythmically, and it drives a bright scarlet fluid through these vessels. The egg doesn't know that it is on its way to becoming a chicken. Chickens, for the egg, lie somewhere on the far side of the beginning of time. And yet the egg couldn't be better equipped to make a chicken out of itself.

36   I would argue that our planet, like the egg, is on a mission of sorts. We don't know what that mission is any more than the nascent nerve cells in the egg know why they are forming a network. All we know is that things are changing rapidly and dramatically.

Today many believe that these changes are often for the worse, and represent a fever or virus from which the body of life will emerge crippled and scarred. We look back with longing on a time, only a moment ago, when the human presence barely dimpled the landscape—when the yolk, so to speak, was at its creamiest, and no angry little eye-spots signaled an intent to devour everything.

I'm not persuaded by this picture—I think it arises from a mistaken belief that the outlines of earthly perfection are already evident. It has inspired a small army of doomsayers—if we burn the forests of the Amazon, we are told, our planet's lungs will give out, and we will slowly asphyxiate. Surely we have better, more practical reasons for not burning them than to stave off universal catastrophe. I can easily imagine similar arguments that would have required the interior of North America to remain empty of cities—and yet I don't think this continent is a poorer place now than it was 20,000 years ago. The more convinced we are that our species is a plague, the more we are obliged to yearn for disasters.

Students of historical psychology have noticed that the end of the world is always at hand. For the Puritan preachers it was to take the form of divine wrath, and they warned that the Wampanoag war was only a foretaste. The Yankees saw it coming in the flood of nineteenth-century immigrants, who meant to drown true Americanism. Today we are more likely to glimpse it in canned aerosols, poisoned winds, and melting ice caps.

40   Curiously enough, the end of the world always *is* at hand—the world

dies and is reborn on a daily basis. A fertile hen's egg is never today what it was yesterday, or will be tomorrow. Few would deny that the effort to preserve and protect as many as possible of the millions of species now existing represents a fresh and heartening expansion of human ambitions. But to suppose that earthly diversity is past its prime, and that a strenuous program of self-effacement is the best contribution our species has left to offer, is neither good biology nor good history.

Understanding What You Read

1. What does Palmer mean when he says that biodiversity does not adequately account for human beings?
2. How does Palmer undermine the argument of environmentalists that human beings are thoughtless destroyers of the natural world?
3. What specific evidence does he give that humans are different from other species?
4. Does the argument for human beings undercut the position of those who are concerned about loss of biodiversity?

Writing About What You Read

1. In your view, what qualities make humans superior to other animals? What qualities make us inferior? Be specific.
2. Write an essay arguing that humans are indeed responsible for the loss of species, or one arguing that they have the capacity to reverse the decline in biodiversity.

Making Connections

1. Based on what you have learned about wolves, write a short, objective encyclopedia entry about wolves. Alternatively, write an article entitled "Wolves: Facts and Fictions."
2. People place value on contact with or observation of wild animals. If there is a species that has special meaning to you, write an essay about it.
3. If you could be another species, what would it be? Write an essay about your life as a _____.

6 USING RESOURCES:

What unthinking people call design in nature is simply the reflection of our inevitable anthropomorphism. Whatever they can use, they think was designed for that purpose—the air to breathe, the water to drink, the soil to plant. It is as if they thought the notch in the mountains was made for the road to pass over, or the bays and harbor for the use of cities and shipping.

—JOHN BURROUGHS, "The Natural Providence"

◆

The first great fact about conservation is that it stands for development. There has been a fundamental misconception that conservation means nothing but the husbanding of resources for future generations. There could be no more serious mistake. . . . The first principle of conservation is the use of the natural resources now existing on this continent for the benefit of the people who live here now.

—GIFFORD PINCHOT, *Breaking New Ground*

◆

None of us knows the final outcome of any action, the endless chain of ripples that we start with every movement. We walk in the world blindly, crashing into unidentified objects and tripping over rough edges. We human beings are too big for our spaces, too powerful for our understanding. What I do today will wash up somewhere far beyond my ability to know about it.

—BETSY HILBERT, "Disturbing the Universe"

◆

A Grizzly Bear snuffling along Pelican Creek in Yellowstone National Park with her two cubs has just as much right to life as any human has, and is far more important ecologically. All things have intrinsic value, inherent worth. Their value is not determined by what they will ring up on the cash register of the gross national product, or by whether or not they are *good*. They are good because they exist.

—DAVID BROWER, *Confessions of an Eco-Warrior*

CHOICES AND TRADE-OFFS

Brazilian Gold Mine
(Sebastiao Salgado)

Introduction

One of the qualities that makes *Homo sapiens* different from all other species is our unpredictability, our freedom to choose a path different from the one taken by our parents. Wolf spiders, as we have learned, have no choice but to take up the career of wolf-spidering. They could never, under any circumstances, choose to live like leaf-cutting ants. Similarly, wolves have no choice but to be carnivores, and whatever they may be communicating when they howl to each other at night, they are almost certainly not grieving for the death of the caribou or the mice they eat. Human beings, by contrast, choose what to eat, where to live, what kind of transportation to use, what kinds of energy to produce, and what crops to grow.

The choices people have made in just the last hundred years are largely responsible for what we call the environmental crisis. These include producing millions of automobiles and the fossil fuels needed to run them; damming rivers for hydroelectric power; building expressways; using vast amounts of underground water, pesticides, and fertilizers to increase crop yields; using comparably vast amounts of land and grain to fatten cattle for market; and developing chemical products without reckoning their effects on air quality. All of these were made—and advertised—in the name of progress, comfort, and convenience. All of them had costs, some hidden for a time. No one dreamed that the freedom of movement a car provided would ultimately be paid for by breathing dirty air. Nor did people in the Northwest suspect that the cheap electric power generated by hydroelectric plants would deplete their rivers of millions of salmon. Nor did the homesteaders turning Midwestern prairies into farmland imagine the dust bowl their plowing would create.

Some choices, however, are made with full awareness of the consequences. In 1913 the United States Congress passed a bill authorizing the building of a dam across the Tuolumne River in the

Hetch Hetchy Valley in what was then part of Yosemite National Park. The trade-off? One of the most beautiful spots in the American West was covered with two hundred feet of water so that the city of San Francisco could have water and power. In this case there were other possible choices: valleys with less scenic value could have been flooded, but not as easily and cheaply as Hetch Hetchy. In spite of the naturalist John Muir's years of struggle to stop the dam, the project was completed in 1923.

These extremes notwithstanding, many of our choices are made in the gray area between ignorance and awareness. When in 1928 the chemist Thomas Midgeley invented chlorofluorocarbons (CFCs) for use as a refrigerant, he never imagined that his product could destroy ozone, but he did realize that he did not know what effect CFCs would have on the environment. In the interest of "progress," he was willing to proceed without a clear understanding of the consequences of using this new chemical.

When the Genofile family chose to build a house in the San Gabriel Mountains ("Los Angeles Against the Mountains"), they were willing to trade safety for scenery. They knew that they were at risk from debris slides, but as John McPhee makes clear, they did not know what it would feel like to watch as debris invaded their home and threatened their children's lives.

The willingness to *not* know, to not even question, has been common—for farmers using pesticides and fertilizers, for logging companies clear-cutting old-growth forests, for mining operations washing toxic metals into streams and rivers, for all of us who drive automobiles instead of using public transportation. But the consequences of uninformed choices are so widespread that laws have been passed to force people to find out just what it is they are trading for their convenience. The National Environmental Policy Act of 1969 requires federal agencies to file environmental impact statements for any proposed legislation or project that may significantly affect environmental quality. Other federal acts, such as the Clean Air Act (1963) and the Clean Water Act (1977), require commercial developers to assess the consequences of their projects. Most states also have comparable laws, and many countries, cities, and towns have ordinances—all intended to raise the level of environmental accountability of both private developers and government agencies as well as to protect the environment. But even these studies have environmental costs, as Barry Lopez reveals in "The Lives of Seals."

Of course, accountability on an individual level is harder to bring about; not everyone wants to know about the consequences of his or her actions. Some residents of Phoenix, Arizona, a city with less than eight inches of annual rainfall, fill their swimming pools and hot tubs and water their grass without ever considering that the water they use will not be available for their grandchildren. In "An Illusion of Plenty," Sandra Postel argues that individuals, like industrial leaders and farmers, need to make wiser choices about water use.

Corporations, too, face difficult choices to ensure that they are producing environmentally safe products manufactured in nonpolluting ways at the same time that they generate profits and safeguard jobs—a balancing act of enormous political and practical complexity. Currently, businesses, environmentalists, government agencies, and consumers are working in a compromise mode, allowing that a certain amount of damage is acceptable. Industrial societies operate on the assumption that industries pollute, and many people are willing to accept the cost of that pollution in exchange for the material benefits provided by such industries. Thus executives at DuPont, the world's main producer of CFCs, can argue without fear of mass public protest that they will gradually phase out these ozone-depleting chemicals and that they will wait for a public mandate to decide when to end their production altogether. If and when laws become too restrictive, some corporations simply move their manufacturing operations to countries that are eager for capital.

Developers, according to Wallace Kaufman, quickly learn that there is no such thing as risk-free development; those who plan "environmentally conscious" houses in a wooded area will find themselves compromising their environmental standards for the requirements of the building trade. Trade-offs, Kaufman makes clear, are essential to almost all human activities, especially those that require a chain saw.

Richard Schroeder ("The Butterfly Problem"), whose lifetime dream was to build a golf course, did not allow that dream to take precedence over the Oregon Silverspot Butterfly, a rare species protected by the Endangered Species Act. The difficult choices facing administrators of the Endangered Species Act put the basic question in sharp focus: how much protection, and at what cost?

A trio of very different pieces on mining looks at its costs and consequences. Wendell Berry, in "Mayhem in the Industrial Paradise," forces us to see the high price paid for the convenience of light switches that receive energy from coal-driven power plants in terms of despoiled earth; Muriel Rukeyser's poem "Alloy" sees the human cost of lungs poisoned by silica dust. William Cronon's history of the rise and fall of the copper-mining town of Kennecott uncovers the complex web of choices and trade-offs that created a boomtown in a wilderness inhabited by a small indigenous population. He then traces the more rapid process by which that community was abandoned and returned to wilderness.

The balance sheet shows that human beings have made unfortunate choices, but also some very good ones—to establish national parks and wilderness areas, to ban dangerous chemicals, to clean up rivers, to set limits to pollution, to establish laws that force us to be accountable, and to create agencies and found organizations that administer these laws and monitor their effects on the environment. The future provides an opportunity to make *Homo sapiens'* distinction—the capacity to make choices—its greatest strength.

JOHN MCPHEE

A consistent characteristic of McPhee's (b. 1931) writing on environmental topics is his refusal to oversimplify complex motives and
relationships. McPhee has written about the Alaskan wilderness in
Coming into the Country (1977); about David Brower, the influential
and vocal environmentalist and onetime head of the Sierra Club, in
Encounters with the Archdruid (1971); and about human attempts to
intervene in natural processes in *The Control of Nature* (1989), from
which "Los Angeles Against the Mountains" comes. Many of the
pieces gathered in his books first appeared in *The New Yorker*.

Los Angeles Against the Mountains

I N   L O S   A N G E L E S versus the San Gabriel Mountains, it is not always clear
which side is losing. For example, the Genofiles, Bob and Jackie, can claim
to have lost and won. They live on an acre of ground so high that they look
across their pool and past the trunks of big pines at an aerial view over
Glendale and across Los Angeles to the Pacific bays. The setting, in cool dry
air, is serene and Mediterranean. It has not been everlastingly serene.

On a February night some years ago, the Genofiles were awakened by a
crash of thunder—lightning striking the mountain front. Ordinarily, in their
quiet neighborhood, only the creek beside them was likely to make much
sound, dropping steeply out of Shields Canyon on its way to the Los Angeles
River. The creek, like every component of all the river systems across the city
from mountains to ocean, had not been left to nature. Its banks were
concrete. Its bed was concrete. When boulders were running there, they
sounded like a rolling freight. On a night like this, the boulders should have
been running. The creek should have been a torrent. Its unnatural sound was
unnaturally absent. There was, and had been, a lot of rain.

The Genofiles had two teenage children, whose rooms were on the uphill
side of the one-story house. The window in Scott's room looked straight up
Pine Cone Road, a cul-de-sac, which, with hundreds like it, defined the
northern limit of the city, the confrontation of the urban and the wild. Los
Angeles is overmatched on one side by the Pacific Ocean and on the other
by very high mountains. With respect to these principal boundaries, Los
Angeles is done sprawling. The San Gabriels, in their state of tectonic youth,
are rising as rapidly as any range on earth. Their loose inimical slopes flout
the tolerance of the angle of repose. Rising straight up out of the megalopo-
lis, they stand ten thousand feet above the nearby sea, and they are not
kidding with this city. Shedding, spalling, self-destructing, they are disintegrating at a rate that is also among the fastest in the world. The phalanxed
communities of Los Angeles have pushed themselves hard against these

mountains, an aggression that requires a deep defense budget to contend with the results. Kimberlee Genofile called to her mother, who joined her in Scott's room as they looked up the street. From its high turnaround, Pine Cone Road plunges downhill like a ski run, bending left and then right and then left and then right in steep christiania turns for half a mile above a three-hundred-foot straightaway that aims directly at the Genofiles' house. Not far below the turnaround, Shields Creek passes under the street, and there a kink in its concrete profile had been plugged by a six-foot boulder. Hence the silence of the creek. The water was now spreading over the street. It descended in heavy sheets. As the young Genofiles and their mother glimpsed it in the all but total darkness, the scene was suddenly illuminated by a blue electrical flash. In the blue light they saw a massive blackness, moving. It was not a landslide, not a mudslide, not a rock avalanche; nor by any means was it the front of a conventional flood. In Jackie's words, "It was just one big black thing coming at us, rolling, rolling with a lot of water in front of it, pushing the water, this big black thing. It was just one big black hill coming toward us."

In geology, it would be known as a debris flow. Debris flows amass in   4
stream valleys and more or less resemble fresh concrete. They consist of water mixed with a good deal of solid material, most of which is above sand size. Some of it is Chevrolet size. Boulders bigger than cars ride long distances in debris flows. Boulders grouped like fish eggs pour downhill in debris flows. The dark material coming toward the Genofiles was not only full of boulders; it was so full of automobiles it was like bread dough mixed with raisins. On its way down Pine Cone Road, it plucked up cars from driveways and the street. When it crashed into the Genofiles' house, the shattering of safety glass made terrific explosive sounds. A door burst open. Mud and boulders poured into the hall. We're going to go, Jackie thought. Oh, my God, what a hell of a way for the four of us to die together.

The parents' bedroom was on the far side of the house. Bob Genofile was in there kicking through white satin draperies at the paneled glass, smashing it to provide an outlet for water, when the three others ran in to join him. The walls of the house neither moved nor shook. As a general contractor, Bob had built dams, department stores, hospitals, six schools, seven churches, and this house. It was made of concrete block with steel reinforcement, sixteen inches on center. His wife had said it was stronger than any dam in California. His crew had called it "the fort." In those days, twenty years before, the Genofiles' acre was close by the edge of the mountain brush, but a developer had come along since then and knocked down thousands of trees and put Pine Cone Road up the slope. Now Bob Genofile was thinking, I hope the roof holds. I hope the roof is strong enough to hold. Debris was flowing over it. He told Scott to shut the bedroom door. No sooner was the door closed than it was battered down and fell into the room. Mud, rock, water poured in. It pushed everybody against the far wall. "Jump on the bed," Bob said. The bed began to rise. Kneeling on it—on a gold velvet spread—they could soon press their palms against the ceiling. The bed also moved toward the glass wall. The two teenagers got off, to try to control the motion, and were pinned between the bed's brass railing and the wall. Boulders went up against the railing, pressed it into their legs, and held them fast. Bob dived into the muck to try to move the boulders, but he failed. The debris flow, entering through windows as well as doors, continued to rise. Escape was still possible for the parents but not for the children. The parents looked at each other and did not stir. Each reached for and held one of the children. Their mother felt suddenly resigned, sure that her son and daughter would die and she and her husband would quickly follow. The house became buried to the eaves. Boulders sat on the roof. Thirteen automobiles were packed around the building, including five in the pool. A din of rocks kept banging against them. The stuck horn of a buried car was blaring. The family in the darkness in their fixed tableau watched one another by the light of a directional signal, endlessly blinking. The house had filled up in six minutes, and the mud stopped rising near the children's chins.

*   *   *

It was assumed that the Genofiles were dead. Firemen and paramedics who came into the neighborhood took one glance at the engulfed house and went elsewhere in search of people needing help. As the family remained trapped, perhaps an hour went by. They have no idea.

"We didn't know why it had come or how long it was going to last."

They lost all sense of time. The stuck horn went on blaring, the directional signal eerily blinking. They imagined that more debris was on the way.

"We didn't know if the whole mountain was coming down."

As they waited in the all but total darkness, Jackie thought of neighbors' children. "I thought, Oh, my gosh, all those little kids are dead. Actually, they were O.K. And the neighbors thought for sure we were all gone. All our neighbors thought we were gone."

At length, a neighbor approached their house and called out, "Are you alive?"

"Yes. But we need help."

As the debris flow hit the Genofiles' house, it also hit a six-ton truck from the LACFCD,[1] the vigilant bureau called Flood. Vigilance was about all that the LACFCD had been able to offer. The patrolling vehicle and its crew of two were as helpless as everyone else. Each of the crewmen had lived twenty-six years, and each came close to ending it there. Minutes before the flow arrived, the truck labored up Pine Cone Road—a 41 percent grade, steep enough to stiff a Maserati. The two men meant to check on a debris basin at the top. Known as Upper Shields, it was less than two years old, and had been built in anticipation of the event that was about to occur. Oddly

---

[1]Los Angeles County Flood Control District.

enough, the Genofiles and their neighbors were bracketed with debris basins—Upper Shields above them, Shields itself below them, six times as large. Shields Debris Basin, with its arterial concrete feeder channels, was prepared to catch fifty thousand tons. The Genofiles' house looked out over Shields as if it were an empty lake, its shores hedged about with oleander. When the developer extended Pine Cone Road up into the brush, the need for Upper Shields was apparent. The new basin came in the nick of time but—with a capacity under six thousand cubic yards—not in the nick of space. Just below it was a chain-link gate. As the six-ton truck approached the gate, mud was oozing through. The basin above had filled in minutes, and now, suddenly, boulders shot like cannonballs over the crest of the dam, with mud, cobbles, water, and trees. Chris Terracciano, the driver, radioed to headquarters, "It's coming over." Then he whipped the truck around and fled. The debris flow came through the chain-link barrier as if the links were made of paper. Steel posts broke off. As the truck accelerated down the steep hill, the debris flow chased and caught it. Boulders bounced against it. It was hit by empty automobiles spinning and revolving in the muck. The whole descending complex gathered force with distance. Terracciano later said, "I thought I was dead the whole way." The truck finally stopped when it bashed against a tree and a cement-block wall. The rear window shattered. Terracciano's partner suffered a broken leg. The two men crawled out through the window and escaped over the wall.

Within a few miles, other trapped patrols were calling in to say, "It's coming over." Zachau went over—into Sunland. Haines went over—into Tujunga. Dunsmuir went over—into Highway Highlands. As bulldozers plow out the streets after events like these, the neighborhoods of northern Los Angeles assume a macabre resemblance to New England villages under deep snow: the cleared paths, the vehicular rights-of-way, the parking meters buried within the high banks, the half-covered drift-girt homes. A street that is lined with palms will have debris berms ten feet up the palms. In the Genofiles' front yard, the drift was twelve feet deep. A person, without climbing, could walk onto the roof. Scott's bedroom had a few inches of space left at the top. Kimberlee's had mud on the ceiling. On the terrace, the crushed vehicles, the detached erratic wheels suggested bomb damage, artillery hits, the track of the Fifth Army. The place looked like a destroyed pillbox. No wonder people assumed that no one had survived inside.

There was a white sedan under the house eaves crushed to half its height, with two large boulders resting on top of it. Near the pool, a Volkswagen bug lay squashed. Another car was literally wrapped around a tree, like a C-clamp, its front and rear bumpers pointing in the same direction. A crushed pickup had boulders all over it, each a good deal heavier than anything a pickup could carry. One of the cars in the swimming pool was upside down, its tires in the air. A Volkswagen was on top of it. Bob Genofile—owner, contractor, victim—walked around in rubber boots, a visored construction cap, a foul-weather jacket, studying the damage, mostly guessing at what he couldn't see. A big, strongly built, leonine man with prematurely white hair, he looked like a middle linebacker near the end of a heavy day. He wondered if the house was still on its foundation, but there was no telling in this profound chaos, now hardening and cracking like bad concrete. In time, as his house was excavated from the inside, he would find that it had not budged. Not one wall had so much as cracked. He was uninsured, but down in the rubble was a compensation of greater value than insurance. Forever, he could say, as he quietly does when he tells the story, "I built it, man."

16   Kimberlee's birthday came two days after the debris. She was a college student, turning nineteen, and her father had had a gift for her that he was keeping in his wallet. "I had nineteen fifty-dollar bills to give her for her birthday, but my pants and everything was gone."

Young Scott, walking around in the wreckage, saw a belt sticking out of the muck like a night crawler after rain. He pulled at it, and the buried pants came with it. The wallet was still in the pants. The wallet still contained what every daughter wants for her birthday: an album of portraits of U.S. Grant, no matter if Ulysses is wet or dry.

The living room had just been decorated, and in six minutes the job had been destroyed—"the pale tangerines and greens, Italian-style furniture with marble, and all that." Jackie Genofile continues the story: "We had been out that night, and, you know, you wear your better jewelry. I came home like an idiot and put mine on the dresser. Bob put his on the dresser. Three weeks later, when some workers were cleaning debris out of the bedroom, they found his rings on the floor. They did not find mine. But—can you believe it?—a year and a half later Scott was down in the debris basin with one of his friends, and the Flood Control had these trucks there cleaning it out, and Scott saw this shiny thing, and he picked it up, and it was my ring that Bob had given me just before the storm."

Before the storm, they had not in any way felt threatened. Like their neighbors, they were confident of the debris basins, of the concrete liners of the nearby stream. After the storm, neighbors moved away. Where Pine Cone Road swung left or right, the debris had made centrifugal leaps, breaking into houses. A hydrant snapped off, and arcing water shot through an upstairs window. A child nearly drowned inside his own house. The family moved. "Another family that moved owned one of the cars that ended up in our pool," Jackie told me. "The husband said he'd never want to live here again, you know. And she was in real estate."

20   After the storm, the Genofiles tended to wake in the night, startled and anxious. They still do. "I wake up once in a while really uptight," Bob said. "I can just feel it—go through the whole thing, you know."

Jackie said that when rain pounds on a roof, anywhere she happens to be, she will become tense. Once, she took her dog and her pillow and went to sleep in Bob's office—which was then in Montrose, down beyond Foothill Boulevard.

Soon after the storm, she said, "Scotty woke up one night, and he had a real high temperature. You see, he was sixteen, and he kept hearing the mud and rock hitting the window. He kept thinking it was going to come again. Kim used to go four-wheeling, and cross streams, and she had to get out once, because they got stuck, and when she felt the flow of water and sand on her legs, she said, she could have panicked."

Soon after the storm, the family gathered to make a decision. Were they going to move or were they going to dig out their house and rebuild it? Each of them knew what might have happened. Bob said, "If it had been a frame house, we would be dead down in the basin below."

But it was not a frame house. It was the fort. "The kids said rebuild. So we rebuilt." 24

As he sat in his new living room telling the story, Bob was dressed in a Pierre Cardin jumper and pants, and Jackie was beside him in a pale-pink jumpsuit by Saint Germain. The house had a designer look as well, with its railings and balconies and Italianate marbles under the tall dry trees. It appeared to be worth a good deal more than the half-million dollars Bob said it might bring. He had added a second story and put all bedrooms there. The original roof spreads around them like a flaring skirt. He changed a floor-length window in the front hall, filling the lower half of it with cement block.

I asked what other structural changes he had made.

He said, "None."

The Genofiles sued Los Angeles County. They claimed that Upper 28 Shields Debris Basin had not been cleaned out and that the channel below was improperly designed. Los Angeles settled for $337,500.

From the local chamber of commerce the family later received the Beautification Award for Best Home. Two of the criteria by which houses are selected for this honor are "good maintenance" and "a sense of drama."

Understanding What You Read

1. How could the Genofiles claim to have lost in their struggle with the mountains? How could they claim to have won?
2. What other examples of beautiful but dangerous places to live do you know about?
3. Should the risk of property loss be borne exclusively by individuals who choose to live in such places or should society assume some of the risk, for example by building expensive debris basins or subsidizing insurance costs (as the federal government does for beachfront property)?

4. How do you feel about the fact that the landslides and debris flows put not only the residents at risk, but also public servants such as those who work for the flood control bureau in Los Angeles?

Writing About What You Read

1. Write an essay explaining why you either would or would not choose to live in a beautiful but dangerous setting.
2. Write an essay arguing that communities should or should not pass ordinances forbidding building in such places.

BARRY LOPEZ

Lopez (b. 1945) grew up in California and studied at Notre Dame and the University of Oregon. He began writing shortly after graduation and since then has mainly focused on the effects of human activity on the natural world. Much of his writing draws on his travels to far-flung places—including the Arctic, Antarctica, the Galápagos Islands, and Africa. Lopez periodically returns home to the Cascade Mountains of western Oregon to write. He is a contributing editor to *Harper's* and *North American Review* and the author of several outstanding books, including *Of Wolves and Men* (1978), a best-seller and winner of the John Burroughs Medal, and *Arctic Dreams* (1986), winner of the American Book Award. "The Lives of Seals," first published in a slightly different form in November 1982 in *Science/82*, is included in *Crossing Open Ground*, a collection of essays published in 1989.

The Lives of Seals

IN MY heavy clothing it is hard to move with any grace. I bend over awkwardly to retrieve shells from a nameless island at the edge of the Arctic Ocean, with an intention that is clear but for reasons difficult to articulate. At my feet are a startling variety—residue of the lives of surf clams, Greenland cockles, razor clams, whelks. Seeded among the shells are bits of shattered bone, an occasional tooth—residue of Eskimo hunting camps. In the wind is the smell of decay; a beach-cast walrus lies a hundred yards away where the Chukchi Sea[1] rasps and hammers at the sand. I lay back into its frozen pocket on the beach a primitive tool—seal bone, weathered smooth as polished wood, carved by hands long dead.

I pick up three or four of the most striking shells and cross back to the far side of the barrier island, where two friends wait. The lagoon is called Kasegaluk. In pale, flat light, against the memory of beating our way in here through heavy seas in a small boat, its still waters seem apparitional. The gray heads of spotted seals break its surface full of curiosity, then disappear abruptly, a snap of the fingers.

We sit back against a piece of driftwood with a simple lunch, a meal prepared that morning by people working on an oceanographic research vessel now waiting several miles to sea in deeper water. A mother ship. As isolated as we are on this barrier island, beneath somber skies, we feel attached, agreeably, to the ship. To some of those aboard what we are about to do is enigmatic, nearly arcane—or simply wrong, for we are about to take the lives of these seals. But other threads draw us together, the biologists I am with, myself, the ship's crew. It is for the people on the ship that I have picked up the shells. We eat the sandwiches now, the thick homemade soup prepared for us; at the end of the day the deck crew will snatch us again from the dead-cold water. If what we are about to do is to have any transcendent meaning it must in the end be meaningful to these cooks and mates and engineers. It must make sense not only to those acquainted with marine science, to those who comprehend the threat that oil development poses to life in these waters; it must also be comprehensible to the ones who clearly perceive only that certain shells are stunningly beautiful. That, at least, is the ideal of this kind of science—to enhance the life, somehow, of each human being.

On this particular fall day, as we prepare to kill the seals, the ideal is only vaguely with us. It is as distant as the violent image of an oil blowout, or the racket of automobiles stifled in traffic, or the slick-sell commerce of politics. We eat here in a remote and vast stillness, watching the seals appear and disappear in the glassy water; the moral ambiguities of such field science, even when death comes at the hands of decent and thoughtful men, are a perpetual ache.

I would like to pretend that the seals don't die. But they do. To pretend no animal dies in our efforts to take the measure of life—here at this lagoon, so the country can develop its energy reserves—is to ignore the responsibility inherent in committing the act.

No one thinks this out very well. Sipping my coffee, I wonder more about the rough water beyond the barrier island, whether the seas will come down before late afternoon and make the trip back easier. Safer. And I stare

4

---

[1]A region of the Arctic Ocean just north of the Bering Strait, between Siberia and Alaska.

at the shells resting on a strip of wind-crusted snow by my foot, which glow with a pearling light.

This part of the Alaskan coast, southwest of Icy Cape, is only vaguely known to biologists. The two I am with, Lloyd Lowry and Bob Nelson of the Alaska Department of Fish and Game, have spent the past month (and several months in the previous year) conducting a marine mammal reconnaissance along these coasts and examining food-chain relationships in the nearshore waters. The daily work entails bottom trawls and vertical plankton tows, collecting seals to examine stomach contents and to determine general state of health, and pinpointing areas habitually used by seals to rest and feed. The work is rote, but never monotonous. Each sampling of the water column with a fine-mesh, half-meter-wide net brings up a rich, translucent, writhing mass of copepods and other zooplankton—we hold them up in clear plastic Whirl-Paks against the light of the sky and marvel at the radiance and energy of this life. From otter trawls at five-, ten-, and fifteen-meter depths come the creatures that feed on this zooplankton—shrimps, mysids and euphausids, crabs and sculpins, eelpout, arctic and saffron cod, Alaska plaice, yellowfin sole, and dozens of others. And from the stomachs of seals come the remains of these creatures, and with that some crude sense of the food web here. The time and place of the trawls, the number of seals feeding at a particular lagoon entrance, air temperatures, water temperatures—everything is written down in a waterproof notebook. In the evening these raw notes are refined and in a shipboard laboratory a more thorough analysis of the trawls is made. Seal stomach contents and certain internal organs and representative organisms from the trawls and plankton tows are prepared for later analysis.

8   The work of Lowry and Nelson and their colleagues is funded by the Outer Continental Shelf Environmental Assessment Program and meant to complement the work of other biologists, geologists, ornithologists, and ecologists to create a reasonably clear picture of this region, one that, among other things, will be substantial enough to direct the process of offshore oil and mineral exploration along the least harmful course.

Such abstract ideas, the uncluttered logic of it all, seem impossible and amusing on this barrier island. Logistical support here is complicated and horrendously expensive. The work is arduous, the weather frequently harsh, and on some days we shoot poorly or struggle with fouled nets and broken lines and have nothing to show. Our daily operations are conducted from a twenty-foot open boat with outboard engines. It must be attended to each day. Freezing temperatures, salt spray, the abrading sea ice, and rough water exact a toll: combined with cutting snow squalls and navigating in dense fog banks these impediments also take a toll on us. Our daily regimen of inspection and repair is strict, and includes ourselves, an attentiveness to our sense of humor and perspective.

Before the three of us came aboard the NOAA[2] ship *Oceanographer* at Barrow, Alaska, a rumor was circulating on board that several marine biologists—I was a writer accompanying them—were going to be killing seals every day and hauling them back to the ship to butcher on the fantail. This news disturbed some members of the crew, who thought carefully about their objections to the killing and later expressed them. Why, they asked, did the seals have to die?

The second evening aboard ship, Lowry—chief scientist in a group that also included two ornithologists, a woman studying walrus biology, and a technician servicing water-current meters along the coast—addressed the crew. He explained how the work would be carried out from the small boat every day; he spoke about trophic, or food web, relationships and their complexity; and he indicated how these data could be used to guide oil and mineral development. He said nothing about the killing of seals beyond the fact that seals would be "collected" as part of this process. He urged the crew and officers, finally, to visit the lab whenever they wished and to ask the scientists about anything that was on their minds. Anyone who wanted to help, he said, in the sometimes tedious business of sorting the contents of the trawls (for which we were using Russian taxonomic guides, there being no suitable American guides for that part of the world) would be welcome. Lowry spoke extemporaneously, ingenuously, without self-importance or scientific distance. In the days that followed people visited the lab with growing frequency.

Most of the crew aboard the *Oceanographer* were based in Seattle. Few   12
had ever been to the Arctic Ocean. Over a period of weeks their, and our, cumulative experience of the region—immense flocks of migrating waterfowl, the open pack ice, pods of feeding gray whales, the long lingering of orange and purple light at dusk, the piggish odor of walrus, the sudden appearance of a polar bear in the water on a foggy morning—all this nourished a sense of the biological richness of the region. And its separateness. These feelings were enhanced in the lab. People marveled at the variety of the species the trawls brought up, at the diversity of anatomical design, at the vitality of an ocean they knew to be frigid, even at its sunlit surface.

A fragile camaraderie began to grow in these evening conversations with the crew, a sense of affinity, a sense of the privilege of exotic circumstances. One or two of the ship's engineers took to visiting the lab regularly to help sort specimens. The ship's carpenter, a man with many years at sea in a variety of ships, became fascinated with the fine details of seal anatomy. In this way, some of what was learned each day (and a certain amount of what was collected, for shrimp often ended up in the ship's kitchen) found its way out of the laboratory.

[2]National Oceanic and Atmospheric Administration.

One can be fooled by the casualness of such moments, by the informality of the conversations, the exchanges. As certain crew members became more adept at distinguishing taxonomic details, however, you could see that they carried themselves somewhat differently. And the desires that some scientists have—that their work be appreciated, that they be understood simply as other human beings trying to grasp the meaning of some part of the universe—those desires were also met in the laboratory each evening.

Because we do not readily share the private reaches of ourselves with each other, little of the pleasure we take in such encounters is ever articulated. During those weeks, however, in the evenings when I spoke with members of the crew, I discovered the far side of the rumor that had been there in the beginning, that faceless men whose life was killing seals were coming aboard. I sensed, when I stood in the companionway chatting with a Filipino steward about the taste of shrimp, or discussed seal biology with a ship's technician, or listened to an engineer explain, ardently and with confidence, the operation of the Fairbanks Morse engines that drove the ship, I sensed in those moments an aura of mutual regard. The dignity of each person's task, the dignity of their occupations, emerged.

16   The intuition one has that these things are present is as intangible as light. The feeling reached me directly and suddenly when a ship's officer, a man always somewhat aloof, stopped abruptly in a stairwell and said self-consciously that they had never had a finer group of scientists aboard. Or when a member of the crew beamed with surprise and pleasure at our remembering to bring back one of the common shells of the barrier beach. On our last day a sort of wistful exuberance pervaded the ship; something subtly affirming was so obviously over.

I know of few grounds more delicate to speak of than these. The hope of each human being to have a sense of value in his or her life is squarely before you. The desire to carry out fatal work honorably. The dream of fathoming the biology of seals. The notion of a rational and humane development of energy in the Arctic. The wordless euphoria in a person touched by the fecundity and resoluteness of the natural world, the vague belief that one is, or could be, a part of this. Such hopes are too deeply wished to be expressed; we convey them obliquely in our gestures, in our cultivation of an atmosphere of tolerance.

The afternoon I sat on the beach at Kasegaluk Lagoon, at an ancient Eskimo hunting site, eating food prepared by stewards for people they had come to like, I thought hard about killing seals. I understood some of the extenuating circumstances, and that, ironically, environmentalists would have these data to stand on in a court of law. But I had no finished answer. I stood uncomfortable, like so many, in the middle of the question.

We took their lives with as much dispatch and skill and respect as possible. Every bit of useful information was carefully written down, all the measurements and observations. We took the contents of the stomachs and various organs. And we let what remained slide quietly into the sea. We washed the blood from our clothes and off the boat. We never came back to the ship with signs of blood, not because we wished to obscure the seals' deaths but because it would have been so abjectly callow. One young woman, initially upset about the seal killings, said that though she came to understand the context and so would not condemn it, she would not countenance it. It was out of respect for such opinion that we brought no obvious sign of death back. From such small considerations, and with the hard thought of moral philosophers, it is possible to imagine that people will find some better answer to the animals' deaths than that they must die for the sake of an advancing civilization.

As a journalist I have listened to biologists complain that their work is used by politicians to advance technologies they don't believe in. I've been with Eskimo hunters who are dumbfounded by what people say about their way of life, that it is barbaric because it includes the hunting of animals. And aboard the *Oceanographer* I heard officers speculate about the propriety of killing animals for science, and members of a deck crew wonder that any sense could be made of a churning mass of animals dying in a trawl net. In each of these moments you could hear someone struggling to grasp another's point of view, to assess it. 20

One can adopt any of several attitudes toward what took place between a scientific party and a ship's crew aboard a research vessel one fall in the Chukchi Sea, precisely because what happened was without design. You could be cynical and say that the atmosphere aboard ships is romantic. You could be circumspect and say it is naive to believe that any such goodwill can extend very far beyond the moment. You could be grave and say that beside the death of seals, let alone copepods in a Whirl-Pak of formalin, any notion of a redeeming introspection or ultimate value is an evasion, a gloss, worthless to consider. But in each of these ways you crush something precious, as precious as knowledge of the behavior of pi-mesons or the orders of human personality. And you deny something fundamental: our acts, the consequences of our seemingly dissimilar lives, are irrevocably intertwined.

The marine survey of the Alaskan coast that Lowry and the others conducted will find its way to the desks of industrialists and environmentalists and scientists and lawyers, and they will discuss what is to be done at places like Kasegaluk Lagoon. And if they drill for oil at Kasegaluk, in land that has known only hunting and fishing camps for eight thousand years, and the seals and the polar bears and the nesting birds go away, it may be argued that nothing much has changed. But it will have changed. The members of a scientific party and the people aboard a ship will know it changed, and that they had a part in it. And they will tell their children, and their neighbors. And they will know one, inescapable thing—the hard questions about death and propriety and human acquisition never go away. And that you have to stay far into the night to comprehend, let alone answer them. And that in the end it is madness to answer them as though everyone lived alone, to answer them as if there were no seals.

Understanding What You Read

1. What does the ship's crew think at first about the marine biologists' killing of seals?
2. Why and how does their opinion change?
3. Are you convinced that this seal-killing project could "enhance the life, somehow, of each human being"?
4. How might the knowledge obtained through the killing of these seals aid in the preservation of this and other species?

Writing About What You Read

Explain your position on whether offshore oil and mineral exploration in Alaska is desirable. If not, what are the alternative ways to meet energy needs? What choices and trade-offs do these alternatives require?

JULIE TITONE

Titone (b. 1952) is a reporter who covers water and wildlife issues for the *Spokesman-Review* and *Spokesman-Chronicle* in Spokane, Washington. "The Balance of Power" was published in the September/October 1992 issue of *Earthwatch*.

Balance of Power: Can Endangered Salmon and Hydroelectric Plants Share the Same Rivers?

AT THE TURN of the century, thousands of sockeye salmon swam back to their central Idaho spawning grounds at Redfish Lake every year. So many crowded the creek that drains the lake, in fact, that they spooked the mounts of riders trying to cross. By last year, however, their numbers had shrunk dramatically: only four sockeye salmon made it to Redfish Lake, only one of them a female.

The sockeye earned the dubious distinction of becoming a federal endangered species last November. They are far from alone in their predicament. This spring, the Snake River stocks of spring, summer, and fall chinook salmon were listed as endangered, and biologists have identified 214 Northwest populations of wild-spawning salmonids threatened with extinction.

In the early 1900s, as many as 16 million wild salmon traveled up the Columbia River and its tributaries each year. Today there are only 2 million, all but 300,000 of which are from hatcheries. As salmon sport-fishing declined in recent decades, many Idaho riverside communities lost an important source of income. Now the misery is flowing downstream, as fishing communities on the Lower Columbia and along the Pacific coast face up to tough new harvest restrictions. The fish just aren't there anymore.

Genetically weaker hatchery fish, overharvesting, and degraded spawning habitat share some of the blame for the dwindling runs. But biologists say the biggest culprits are the dams, which are blamed for up to 95 percent of the deaths of young salmon making their way from their spawning beds to their adult homes in the Pacific Ocean. 4

There are 30 major dams in the Columbia Basin. Some of them, such as Grand Coulee Dam, have no fish passage facilities at all, and have blocked entire drainages to oceangoing fish. Eight of them—four on the Lower Snake, four on the Lower Columbia—provide a 460-kilometer obstacle course for such fish as the Snake River sockeye. The turbines in each of these dams kill up to 15 percent of the young fish that pass through them.

Young salmon, or smolts, are particularly vulnerable during their journey from spawning grounds to the ocean because the transformation from freshwater fish into saltwater creatures, "smoltification," appears to make them lethargic. Without natural spring freshets to push them downstream, the young salmon must find their way through a series of slackwater reservoirs. The journey from spawning grounds to ocean, which once took a week before the dams were built, now takes up to six weeks.

To help juvenile salmon through the slow, predator-filled reservoirs, since 1977 the U.S. Army Corps of Engineers has collected millions of fish at the first of the eight dams, then barged or trucked them downstream. Critics of that elaborate transportation system note that it has not resulted in an increase in the number of adults coming back upstream to spawn. Quite the opposite has happened.

The Endangered Species Act gives the National Marine Fisheries Service final say in recovering the wild salmon. But the Northwest Power Planning Council has significant authority in managing the Columbia River system, thanks to the Northwest Power Act of 1980. That Act required that fish and wildlife get equal attention with hydropower and other industrial uses of the Columbia. After more than a decade that hasn't happened. The Power Council set a goal of doubling the total salmon population. Instead, the total numbers dropped and numbers of wild species plummeted. 8

Balancing the loss of these fish against the costs of modifying dozens of dams has put the Pacific Northwest into an all-too-familiar predicament. In 1990, when conservation groups first petitioned for endangered status for some salmon species, the region was already deadlocked over spotted owl protection. Comparisons between the salmon and owl were inevitable and frightening. Protecting the spotted owl and its ancient forest habitat has dealt a major blow to the timber industry, which will have a ripple effect on the economies of Oregon, Washington, and northern California.

Salmon protection will involve tampering with the very lifeblood of the four-state region: the Columbia River and its tributaries. Improving fish passage could mean blasting new fish tunnels through the dams. It means changing the amount of water that goes through hydropower turbines, and the timing of that water's release from reservoirs. For example, allowing spring "drawdowns" will turn reservoirs into rivers and flush the fish to the ocean. Such changes could have a dramatic impact on reservoir levels, which would drop as much as 11 meters during the drawdowns. That eliminates barge traffic, leaves marina docks high and dry, and can cause embankments to slough and crack.

Salmon protection would thus raise utility rates for residents and industries, such as aluminum factories, grown reliant upon cheap hydropower. It would affect inland ports and the businesses that depend on them, because the reservoirs would no longer be high enough year-round to float barges. It would force irrigators to lengthen pipes they use to suck water from the rivers.

12   At first glance, the salmon may seem to have even more sociopolitical cards stacked against it than the spotted owl.

But unlike the spotted owl, the salmon has economic value. More than one far-reaching law protects it and no one says salmon are expendable. There's no fish equivalent of the bumper sticker "Save a logger. Eat an owl."

Efforts to recover the endangered salmon would boost all salmon and steelhead populations, both in the wild and in hatcheries (wild populations supply the varied genetic stock that keeps hatchery populations healthy). Therefore, salmon protection could actually be an enormous boon to the economy. Furthermore, the impact of more salmon for canning or as a lure for tourists has not been calculated. The focus has been on the short-term costs of recovering the endangered populations, not the long-term benefits of bolstering all the salmon runs. According to the Northwest Resource Information Center, one conservative 1982 estimate held that 44 million adult salmon and steelhead trout were lost to Northwest fisheries in the years 1960–1980. The estimated commercial and recreational loss to the region: $6.5 billion.

Annual drawdowns could well be part of the Snake River sockeye recovery plan currently being written by a team of biologists for the National Marine Fisheries Service. The team is building upon work done by the

Northwest Power Planning Council. Last December the Power Council gave a qualified endorsement to drawdowns as part of its own complex plan for reestablishing salmon runs.

Officials of the Bonneville Power Administration, which markets most of the region's hydropower, often note that the effort to restore salmon runs has cost its ratepayers a billion dollars in lost power sales and physical improvements to the river system. But they no longer contend that annual drawdowns to help the fish would increase consumer's power costs by a third; that estimate is down to about 4 percent. The Northwest would still have some of the cheapest electricity in the country.   16

This March the U.S. Army Corps of Engineers took its first reluctant but well-orchestrated step toward changing river operations. The corps conducted a month-long experiment to see how the reservoir system would respond to lower, faster flows. It dramatically dropped the reservoirs behind Lower Granite and Little Goose dams, the first ones that young Idaho salmon confront on their way down the Snake River. Official results of the drawdown test are still being written, but no major physical failures were observed. The dams' turbines didn't vibrate wildly when their power generation was cut in half; the levees protecting the upstream city of Lewiston, Idaho, didn't collapse.

Hydropower interests and communities that would suffer most from drawdowns demand proof that drawdowns, by pushing the juvenile salmon downstream, will result in more adults coming up to spawn. Biologists have no proof, only strong evidence.

Unfortunately, because the dams haven't been renovated to pass fish through at low water levels, the test had to be done before juvenile fish were actually traveling to the sea. So the March experiment does not prove that drawdowns would actually move fish quickly through the reservoirs.

According to a new report prepared for Idaho Governor Cecil Andrus,   20
drawdowns would be 5 to 20 times cheaper than the other salmon protection plans that have been proposed. Although there is no guarantee that drawdowns will save any of the Columbia Basin's wild salmon, they remain an expensive gamble worth taking. Without help, the Northwest's remaining wild salmon—and eventually the hatchery fish that depend on those wild stocks for genetic diversity—will surely swim to extinction.

Understanding What You Read

1. What clues in the article suggest ways that the salmon crisis could have been avoided?
2. How does the Endangered Species Act conflict with the Northwest Power Act of 1980?
3. Which government agencies are involved in this controversy over

whether the endangered salmon and hydroelectric plants can share the same rivers?

Writing About What You Read

Using the figures given in this article, argue for the economic benefits of saving the salmon from extinction; or do research about hydroelectric power and argue that the benefits of this energy source justify the loss of salmon.

SANDRA POSTEL

Postel (b. 1956) is vice president for research of the Worldwatch Institute in Washington, D.C. During her years there she has written numerous Worldwatch Papers and served as associate project director for several annual *State of the World* reports. She is coauthor of *Saving the Planet: How to Shape an Environmentally Sustainable Global Economy* (1991) and author of *Last Oasis: Facing Water Scarcity* (1992), in which "An Illusion of Plenty" appears.

An Illusion of Plenty

LIFE COULD HARDLY be more different in the east African town of Lodwar, Kenya, and the western U.S. metropolis of Phoenix, Arizona. At the touch of a tap, a child in Phoenix has ample water for drinking, bathing, even swimming in a backyard pool. His family probably uses some 3,000 liters of water on a typical day, enough to fill their bathtub 20 times over. A child living on the outskirts of Lodwar, on the other hand, daily treks several hours to a well or spring to help her mother bring home a couple of jugs of water. Her family uses barely 5 percent as much water as the Phoenix household, just enough to satisfy their most basic needs.

Yet when it comes to the amount of water nature makes available, Lodwar and Phoenix are "sister cities." Each gets a meager 16–18 centimeters of rainfall a year. And in each place human numbers have outstripped the ability of local water supplies to sustain a moderate standard of living.

Lodwar and Phoenix exhibit two very different faces of water scarcity. In Lodwar, people experience scarcity in its rawest form—it adds drudgery and insecurity to their everyday lives. And their plight is exacerbated, as it is in many developing regions, by the poor's lack of access to even the limited supplies available. In Phoenix, however, scarcity is masked by the damming, diverting, and pumping of water from near and far to make the city not only livable but lush. An illusion of plenty has been created in water-scarce Phoenix—which leads to overconsumption and adverse consequences for the environment and for future generations.

In a sense, masking scarcity is a principal aim of water development, the collection of engineering projects and technologies that give people access to and control over nature's supply. But all too often it has proceeded without regard for harmful side effects. We build ever more and larger projects to meet spiraling demands wherever they arise, but pay little mind to the ecological services of rivers, lakes, and wetlands that are lost in the process. And we deplete groundwater reserves to meet today's needs and desires, with no thought of the consequences for generations down the line.

For most of us, water scarcity conjures up visions of drought, those temporary dry spells that nature inflicts from time to time. But while droughts capture headlines and grab our attention, the far greater threat posed by our escalating water consumption goes largely unnoticed. In many parts of the world, water use is nearing the limits of natural systems; in some areas, those limits have already been surpassed. A number of areas could enter a period of chronic shortages during this decade, including much of Africa, northern China, pockets of India, Mexico, the Middle East, and parts of western North America.

Signs of water stress abound. Water tables are falling, lakes are shrinking, and wetlands are disappearing. Engineers propose "solving" water problems by building mammoth river diversion schemes, with exorbitant price tags and untold environmental effects. Around Beijing, New Delhi, Phoenix, and other water-short cities, competition is brewing between city-dwellers and farmers who lay claim to the same limited supply. And people in the Middle East have heard more than one leader voice the possibility of going to war over scarce water.

In the quest for better living standards and economic gain, modern society has come to view water only as a resource that is there for the taking, rather than a living system that drives the workings of a natural world we depend on. Harmonizing human needs with those of a healthy environment will require new ways of using and managing water. And it will require adjusting our production and consumption patterns so as to remain within ecological limits.

In each major area of water use—agriculture, industry, and cities— demands have risen markedly since 1950. At that time, both population and material consumption began a steep climb, driving water use rapidly upward. By and large, those pressures continue today, as worldwide needs for food, industrial products, and household services expand.

Agriculture claims the lion's share of all the water taken from rivers, lakes, and aquifers, accounting for an estimated 65 percent of global water use. As opportunities to extend cropland area have dwindled, augmenting food production has come to depend more on coaxing higher yields from existing farmland, which often requires irrigation. Over the course of this century, as the number of people to feed swelled from 1.6 billion to more than 5.4 billion, agriculture's water use increased fivefold. The really rapid rise began around mid-century, when water development entered its heyday, and continued as the Green Revolution—involving fertilizers and pesticides, high-yielding seeds, and irrigation—took hold and spread.

Industries make the second-largest claim on the world's water bodies, accounting for a fourth of global water use. Generating electricity in thermal power plants (nuclear and fossil fuel) takes copious amounts of water, as does making the paper, steel, plastics, and other materials we use every day. Spurred by droughts and strict pollution control requirements, industries in the richer countries have shown that they can reduce their water use dramatically by recycling and reusing their supplies. Yet these technologies remain greatly underused, particularly in the developing world, where industry's water use is now rising rapidly.

Water deliveries to households, schools, businesses, and other municipal activities account for less than a tenth of global water use today. Nonetheless, meeting these needs is no easy task. Drinking water must be treated to a high level of quality and supplied with a high degree of reliability, which makes it expensive. As cities expand, planners reach out to capture ever more distant and costly sources. Tapwater in many homes in Los Angeles, for instance, originates hundreds of kilometers away in northern California or the Colorado River basin. By the end of this decade, some 22 cities worldwide will have populations of 10 million or more, and 18 of them will be in the Third World. Serving these dense population centers will in many cases take more water, capital, and energy than is available or affordable.

12   Already today, there remains a large unmet demand for household water. Nearly one out of every three people in the developing world—some 1.2 billion people in all—do not have access to a safe and reliable supply for their daily needs. Often they resort to shallow wells or stagnant pools that are easily contaminated with human and animal waste. As a result, waterborne diseases account for an estimated 80 percent of all illnesses in developing countries. And women and children walk several kilometers each day just to collect enough water for drinking, cooking, and cleaning, a drudgery that saps time and energy from more productive activities.

Added up, total human demands for water—including agriculture, industries, and cities—still seem comfortably below the amount nature makes available each year. But this, too, is illusory. Much rainwater runs off in floods, falls in places too remote for us to capture it, or is needed to support the myriad other species and ecosystems with which we share the planet, and on which we depend.

Moreover, in many places, pollution is rapidly diminishing the usable supply. Each liter of polluted wastewater contaminates many additional liters in the water body that receives it. In Poland, for example, the share of river water of highest quality for drinking has dropped from 32 percent to less than 5 percent during the last two decades.[1] Some three quarters of that nation's river water is now too contaminated even for industrial use. Similar situations increasingly can be found in developing countries, where unchecked pollution poses a mounting threat during industrialization.

Although water is part of a global system, how it is used and managed locally and regionally is what really counts. Unlike oil, wheat, and most other important commodities, water is needed in quantities too large to make it practical to transport long distances. No global water crisis is likely to shake the world the way the energy crisis of the seventies did. But with key crop-producing regions and numerous metropolitan areas showing signs of water scarcity and depletion, global food supplies and economic health are in jeopardy. Moreover, global warming from the buildup of greenhouse gases could greatly complicate regional water problems by shifting the patterns of rainfall and runoff that agriculture and urban water systems are geared to.

Without question, water development has been a key to raising living standards, and it needs to be extended to the one fifth of humanity who have largely missed out on its benefits. But in our rush for economic growth, food sufficiency, and material well-being we have repeatedly ignored nature's limits—depleting underground aquifers, deforesting watersheds, and diminishing streamflows to ecologically damaging levels.

Achieving water balance will not be easy. The policies, laws, and practices that shape water use today rarely promote all three basic tenets of sustainable resource use—efficiency, equity, and ecological integrity. Even a casual glimpse around the world shows water allocation and use to be in a chaotic state. While farmers in California's Central Valley were spreading copious amounts of inexpensive irrigation water on cotton and rice, Los Angeles was draining the streams feeding fragile Mono Lake to fill swimming pools and wash cars. Sugarcane growers in the Indian state of Maharashtra take 50 percent of available irrigation supplies even though they occupy only 10 percent of the cropland. And from the Everglades to the Aral Sea,[2] aquatic habitats unravel from the siphoning off and pollution of rivers and streams.

Taking heed of water's limits, and learning to live within them, amounts to a major transformation in our relationship to fresh water. Historically, we have approached nature's water systems with a frontier philosophy, manipulating the water cycle to whatever degree engineering know-how would permit. Now, instead of continuously reaching out for more, we must begin to look within—within our regions, our communities, our homes, and

[1]For more information on Poland's pollution problem, see page 17.

[2]The Aral Sea is a large inland sea in the Central Asian region of the former Soviet Union, destroyed by poorly planned irrigation projects; for more information on the Everglades, see pages 170–79.

ourselves—for ways to meet our needs while respecting water's life-sustaining functions.

Doing more with less is the first and easiest step along the path toward water security. By using water more efficiently, we in effect create a new source of supply. Each liter conserved can help meet new water demands without damming another stretch of river or depleting more groundwater. With technologies and methods available today, farmers could cut their water needs by 10–50 percent, industries by 40–90 percent, and cities by a third with no sacrifice of economic output or quality of life. Most investments in water efficiency, recycling, reuse, and conservation yield more usable water per dollar than investments in conventional water supply projects do. But they will not materialize until policies, laws, and institutions begin to foster such measures rather than hinder them.

20   New technologies and better policies have much to offer toward the goal of achieving a secure water future, but they will take us only so far. They alone cannot avert conflicts and shortages where populations are expanding faster than efficiency measures can release new supplies. Any hope for balancing the water budgets of most Middle Eastern countries, for instance, rests as much on lowering birth rates as it does on modernizing irrigation systems. And in many water-short African countries, slowing population growth appears to be the only way of meeting minimal per capita needs in the near future.

A new water era has begun. In contrast to earlier decades of unfettered damming, drilling, and diverting to gain ever greater control over water, the next generation will be marked by limits and constraints—political, economic, and ecological. Yet numerous opportunities arise as well. Exploiting the market potential of new water-saving technologies is an obvious one. And in many cases, achieving better water management will require decentralizing control over water, and moving from top-down decisionmaking to greater people's participation—a shift necessary for better human and economic development overall.

Most fundamentally, water scarcity challenges us to adopt a new ethic to guide our relationship to the earth's natural systems, to other species, and to each other. Recognizing ourselves as part of the life-support network we depend on and learning to live within water's limits are integral aspects of creating a society that is sustainable in all respects. Measures to conserve water and use it more efficiently are now the most economical and environmentally sound water supply options available for much of the world—and they have barely been tapped. Together, they constitute our "last oasis."

Understanding What You Read

1. What are the three major areas of water use and what percentage of global water use does each account for?

2. How many people on the planet lack safe drinking water?
3. What steps does Postel propose to achieve water security?

Writing About What You Read

1. Describe your own water use and discuss ways that you might reduce it.
2. Discuss why we need (or don't need) to do something about our personal water use, even though "water deliveries to households, schools, businesses, and other municipal activities account for less than a tenth of global water use today."

GREENPEACE/PUBLIC MEDIA CENTER

This ad appeared in the *New York Times* on October 5, 1992.

Ozone Shock: Tell DuPont to Stop Destroying the Ozone Layer Now!

The world's leading atmospheric scientists, including those from NASA, are agreed: The ozone layer that protects life on Earth from excessive ultraviolet radiation has been dangerously depleted by CFCs and other chemicals, and it's getting worse. The Director of the United Nations Environmental Program has called it, "A danger as big as humanity has ever faced." The Canadian government has already begun daily ultraviolet alerts, due to dangerous depletion of the ozone shield over Canada. The U.S. is vulnerable, too. Before long ALL LIFE ON EARTH WILL BE IN FOR A TERRIFYING SHOCK. At a time like this, can you believe that DuPont Corporation and its

major shareholder, Seagram,
continue to profit from these deadly
products? Don't let them get away
with it. Please read below:

I. FUTURE LIFE

When DuPont advertised that it brings "better things for better living," it did not say this meant "better living" in fear of the sun, staying indoors, or donning ultraviolet radiation suits. For that's what the future may hold.

DuPont is the world's largest producer of chlorofluorocarbons (CFCs), the main culprit that causes ozone destruction. The chemicals work their way slowly to the stratosphere, break apart, and release ozone destroying chlorine. When this occurs, the ozone layer thins, and sunshine becomes increasingly toxic to life. In many parts of the southern hemisphere, Canada, Europe and the U.S., the problem has gone beyond the danger point.

According to NASA scientists, the ozone problem is worse than was ever predicted, and is accelerating. Here's why: it takes about 20 years for CFCs to rise to the ozone layer and cause damage. CFC production did not peak until the 1980s, so the majority of CFCs produced to date have not yet begun to reach the ozone layer. When they do, an already terrible crisis will get much worse. The whole Earth will be affected, and the danger will last for more than a century.

Even if all production stopped today, the damage could not be undone. The Environmental Protection Agency has predicted that 12 million Americans will suffer skin cancers over the next 50 years due to ozone depletion. 200,000 will die. It will also mean increased cataracts and blindness, and a serious weakening of the human immune system for millions of people, which, in turn, will increase vulnerability to infectious diseases.

Overall, it may mean that neither you, nor your children, nor theirs will, in their lifetime, go safely again to beaches or parks. In some places it could be dangerous to *ever* go outdoors without 100% skin coverage. *Normal life could be interrupted for generations.*

II. CORPORATE DENIAL

Scientists first linked CFCs with ozone destruction in 1974. DuPont denied these links and fought efforts to regulate CFCs. In 1978, when CFCs were finally banned for use in aerosol sprays, DuPont promoted these chemicals for auto air conditioning, refrigeration, industrial cleansers and foams. Eventually DuPont had to admit the problem, dubbed itself a champion of the environment, and proudly announced it would stop *some* production of *some* ozone destroying chemicals by 1996. *Some production by 1996?* Given that millions of additional people will get cancer and cataracts, and experience immune suppression, by what standard is the continued production warranted? *Corporate profit.*

It turns out that in 1996 DuPont will partly convert to hydrochlorofluorocarbons (HCFCs) which are only marginally better, since they *also* destroy the ozone layer, albeit somewhat less. Alternative technologies do exist, but DuPont does not profit from them, so it does not promote them. So much for your "green" corporation.

As for Seagram Corporation (Tropicana juices, Chivas Regal, Crown Royal), it owns 24.5% of DuPont and has seven members on DuPont's Board of Directors. Seagram's Chair, Edgar Bronfman Sr., has said, "We think DuPont is doing a superb job environmentally." Here's the question: if you were a Director of Seagram, sitting on DuPont's Board, would you say such a thing? Wouldn't you demand the company stop producing this horrible stuff *now?*

III. Effects on Non-Human Life

We have emphasized the effects on human beings: increased rates of skin cancer deaths, cataracts, blindness, and suppression of the immune system. These only begin to tell the story. We humans, at least, can try to cover ourselves. *Animals, plants, crops, and trees cannot do this.* They remain totally exposed to increased ultraviolet radiation. In southern Chile, for example, where the ozone hole has been open for over a decade, there has been increased incidence of rabbits and sheep with malformed eyes and impaired vision, as well as deformed tree buds, among other occurrences.

Even worse, however, are the apparent effects on oceanic phytoplankton, which live near the surface of the sea. These creatures are the base of the marine food chain. When plankton populations decline, so will the populations of the fish that eat plankton, and the mammals that eat the fish: seals, dolphins, whales *and human beings.* When you combine this effect with the fact that soybean and rice crops—which are the staple food for most of the Earth—are especially vulnerable to ultraviolet radiation, we may be looking at the greatest starvation the world has ever seen. And the greatest destruction of wild nature as well. This is why the U.N. calls it, "a danger as big as humanity has ever faced."

IV. Four Point Action Plan

The full effects of ozone destruction will be upon us in our lifetime. There is no way around this. But we *can* try to minimize the effects on our children and the Earth. Here are a few ways to start:

1. *Demand that DuPont immediately halt all production or licensing of CFCs and HCFCs, as well as the global warming gases, HFCs.* Continued

production of these deadly substances condemns your children and theirs to even more terrible problems. Write the DuPont and Seagram Chairmen and telephone them. (DuPont: 1-800-441-7515; Seagram: 212-572-7000).

2. *Demand that DuPont and Seagram put all the profits they have made from these ozone depleting chemicals into a new fund to:* 1) provide a transition to environmentally safe alternatives; 2) recapture and recycle existing CFCs, to prevent their release to the atmosphere; 3) assist non-industrial countries in procuring safe alternatives and avoid the deadly dependence on CFCs.

3. *Demand that DuPont and Seagram, and individual directors of these companies, be held accountable to the fullest extent of the law* for damages to people who develop disease caused by ozone depletion, as well as damage to property and the environment.

4. *Change your consumption habits.* Do not buy polystyrene foam, or any products packaged with polystyrene foam. Demand that your local appliance dealer sell only safe alternatives like helium, or water and alcohol refrigerators, and air conditioners that run on evaporation. If your home or office air conditioners or refrigerators require servicing, insist that all CFCs and HCFCs be recaptured rather than vented to the air. Demand that your community establish local CFC recapture and recycling centers. And, bring back windows that open.

*   *   *

Finally, of course, we must face a basic fact. With ozone destruction and global warming, it is obvious that human life is just as endangered as the rest of nature. Uncontrolled, industrial society is no longer enhancing human life, it is beginning to destroy it. We cannot pollute our own nests forever. *It is not a question of jobs vs. environment. There will be no jobs on a dead, scorched Earth, and no people either.*

You can help. Join the Greenpeace campaign to save the ozone layer from further destruction. In turn, we will send you more information, and tell you how you can participate in further actions. Please do this today. Thank you.

F. A. VOGELSBERG

This letter, dated December 18, 1992, was written by Vogelsberg, environmental manager for DuPont Fluorochemicals, in response to consumers' concern about the continued production of chlorofluoro-carbons.

Letter from DuPont

IN RESPONSE to your letter regarding the ozone issue, we welcome the opportunity to provide some facts on the importance and challenges for society to comply with the rapid and total phaseout of man-made compounds that can impact the stratospheric ozone layer.

DuPont is committed to phase out of CFC production as soon as possible. We are fully supportive of the U.S. Government's objectives in this regard and are committed to phase out CFC production for sale in the United States and other developed countries no later than the end of 1995. The Company has provided leadership in responding to the scientific and technical developments surrounding CFCs and, in our opinion, has made extraordinary efforts to hasten the worldwide elimination of CFCs and to find suitable replacements. We believe our progress has been impressive; DuPont CFC production in 1992 will be less than half the level produced in 1986 and substantially below the levels permitted by Montreal Protocol and the U.S. Clean Air Act.

We would cease production of CFCs immediately if substitute products and equipment were broadly available to make it practical to do so. To cease manufacture of CFCs would have no meaningful impact on our financial results. But we, along with the governments of the world who could mandate immediate cessation of production of CFCs, recognize that these materials are required to meet vital societal needs. These needs, such as refrigeration to protect the perishable food supply from production through distribution to consumption are, in our opinion, vital to the immediate health and well-being of the peoples of the world.

Similarly, cooling systems are required, not a luxury, for large portions of the world to operate manufacturing processes, factories, office buildings, supermarkets, hospitals and government buildings—the majority of which would be unusable without the coolants. [4]

It is our belief that the disastrous disruptions to commerce, medical care and the food supply resulting from a precipitous elimination of CFCs are among the reasons why the governments of the world have not banned CFCs immediately until suitable alternatives are available and equipment to use them has been developed and is in place.

DuPont regularly assesses its phaseout program for CFCs and will continue to review its phaseout goals as new information develops. We believe that it is the responsibility of the governments of the world and the users of CFCs to make the decision whether CFCs continue to be essential to societal needs. In the company's opinion, it would be irresponsible to disregard the considered positions of international bodies and world governments through a unilateral decision to cease production.

I hope these points clarify the challenges to achieve a total CFC phaseout.

Understanding What You Read

1. What alternatives to air conditioning can you think of?
2. What did people do to keep cool before air conditioning was invented?
3. Name several alternatives to polystyrene foam cups, food containers, and foam insulation.
4. Examine the strategies both the ad and letter use to frighten readers.

Writing About What You Read

Compare and contrast the persuasive tactics used in the ad and the letter.

WALLACE KAUFMAN

A writer and business consultant in countries around the globe, Kaufman (b. 1939) has written about the American shoreline, housing, and the Amazon Valley. He is concerned with the best ways to develop land with minimal damage to the natural environment. His book *The Beaches Are Moving: The Drowning of America's Shoreline*, coauthored with Orrin H. Pilkey, Jr., was first published in 1979. "Confessions of a Developer" is from *Finding Home* (1992), a collection of writings from *Orion* magazine. Kaufman lives in North Carolina.

Confessions of a Developer

I am a member of a persecuted minority. It's one whose story you haven't heard. Nobody has written poignantly about the daily personal abuse, the exile within society, the injustices we suffer. We haven't been eloquent in our own behalf either. A literary tradition has not emerged yet among developers.

I try not to be ashamed of who I am, but that is hard when I go to meetings with my friends in the environmental community. I often feel as if I were Italian and through the whole meeting people have been talking about the Mafia; I feel as if I were black and the talk is about nothing but crime and drugs and Willie Horton.[1] Developers, too are victims of stereotypes.

Like most minorities I can point to the past and say, "See, I come from

[1] A figure used by the 1988 Republican campaign to play on white fears, Horton was a black prisoner who committed a violent crime while on furlough from a Massachusetts prison.

a people with a rich history. Look how we raised ancient Sumer[2] in the desert. How about that 'rose-red city half as old as time'[3] in Egypt? What about the road we built over the scenic peaks of the Andes—the Inca trail[4]—and the great market squares and shopping centers our Mayans built in the rain forest of Yucatán?"

People look, but they still don't see. Revisionists have already eliminated my forerunners from history. Sumer, Alexandria, Chichén Itzá,[5] the Inca Trail, Venice—these are celebrated as triumphs in the life of civilization, but no one celebrates their developers. America is awash in monuments to soldiers, politicians, musicians, poets, civil rights leaders, teachers, conservationists, athletes, Indian chiefs, dinosaurs, and dogs, but how many monuments do you see to a real estate developer?

Who has raised a statue to Elmer Harmon, who in 1887 created the first planned suburb, which indeed was "the best chance ever offered in America for a poor man to acquire good property"? Harry Black brought skyscrapers like the Flatiron Building to Manhattan, and millions of Americans send postcards celebrating the skyline he inspired, but not even a stubby obelisk bears his name. Why is there no monument to Bill Levitt, whose housing innovations after World War II provided homes for tens of thousands of struggling veterans?

The truth is Americans associate real estate development more with wealth than courage or genius. Despite a reputation for materialism, Americans keep a cautious distance from people whose fame is inseparable from cutting trees, paving, wrecking, laying sewage discharge pipes, and spending large sums of money. It is not the money that is feared. It is the power. Those large sums endow the user with the power to change the face of the earth, the character of a city.

In the mind of an America that loves convenience, cars, technology, comfort, farms, parks, and wilderness, developers occupy a secure but lonely corner. We are what Jewish moneylenders were in the mind of medieval Europe, which craved and hated interest-bearing loans. Development is to the course of civilization what libido is to courtship.

I understand how people feel about development. Give me five minutes and I'll prove it faster than a bulldozer flattens a dogwood. In me parts of humanity are at war with each other. I am a developer and a conservationist. I love bulldozers, and I've never met a tree I didn't like. I would rather walk around a farm than a shopping center, but I believe that in many communities, shopping centers are a good substitute for a "downtown."

---

[2]Site of ancient civilization (circa 3000 B.C.) located in what is now southern Iraq. Sumerians produced abundant crops by irrigating the desert.

[3]From "Petra," a poem by Dean Burgon (1813–1888): "Match me such marvel save in Eastern clime,/A rose-red city half as old as Time!"

[4]Trail built by pre-Columbian Incas extending some 3,250 miles through the Andes.

[5]Mayan city in the central Yucatán of Mexico occupied from around 600 to 1400 A.D.

I am not so different from most Americans. All of us are by nature developers. When I visit a day-care center I don't see two kinds of kids—one growing plants and feeding fish while the other piles up blocks and pushes model trucks and bulldozers around the sandbox. (Neither toy manufacturers nor the Sierra Club offers a wilderness kit alternative.) Almost all the kids are making skyscrapers, building railroads, making Lego mansions. There we are, the developer animals.

Most kids never grow up to develop anything beyond the living room rug or the sandbox. Perhaps in some of us the developer perspective becomes dominant, while a nature preference prevails in others. Maybe some day someone will locate the development and nature preferences on opposite sides of the brain. In any case, a few people accept the development imperative and learn to build subdivisions, roads, shopping centers, and cities. Along the way they have to learn to destroy woods and prairies, orchards and farms, marshes and meadows.

I propose that if we understand and accept the development urge, we will come closer to solving our land-use problems. We should no more repress the development part of our psyche because some developers pillage nature than we should repress our sexuality because some men and women are pornographers and prostitutes.

12   I became a developer because I didn't like developers. I thought I could do it better. In 1966 there were five of us young English professors at the University of North Carolina at Chapel Hill who wanted to live in the country and have a little land.

I found an eighty-acre "mountain" overlooking the town water supply. We could have four or five acres each for a grand total of $5,000. For months we talked about what we would do. Finally, time came to buy in or drop out. "Too far out," said the James Joyce scholar. "What about snakes?" asked the man who taught about the courage of hunters in Faulkner's fiction. "Can we get a road in there?" wondered the Dos Passos biographer. The whole thing became an excursion into pastoral fantasy. I even said to myself, "Well, maybe the mountain is better off just the way it is."

I was learning my first important lesson in development: no development in the world can pass all the safety tests that concern even a small number of people. Certainly if we lived on the outskirts of Eden and Moses proposed the modest city of Jerusalem, he could not have written a satisfactory environmental impact statement. We certainly couldn't have done it for the irrigation projects of the Nile, or the Tigris and Euphrates. Most people would rather analyze risks than take them. There is no risk-free development. Development is the process of taking risks—financial, environmental, social, and personal.

As an academic myself, I should have known that scholars are not trained to take risks. I came, though, from a blue-collar family where new ideas were few but firmly attached to action. What I had started to do for myself and my colleagues in the English department, I now decided to do on speculation—for all those people who wanted to live in the country in peace with nature. With the help of a graduate student friend whose only expertise was an exhaustive study of the Icelandic Eddas,[6] I put a small down payment on 330 acres of trees that had taken over abandoned farms or grew in untillable valleys and rocky soil.

I was moving too fast to think about what I was doing and why, but I know now. My idea may have been different from other developments, but my inspiration was all-American. The concept had come in a straight line out of the tin double bed in a poor section of Queens where my brother and I used to lie awake at night telling each other how we would get out of the city and live on a jungle farm where we would tame panthers and boa constrictors and the only domestic animal would be a coal-black stallion. This was a child's version of what we often call "The American Dream," the place where we really want to live. Americans have been searching for it for four hundred years. Some Americans, call them developers, have been building places they hope will satisfy the searchers.

16

Like every other developer I offered my development as one of those places. I said to myself (and probably to a few others), I can provide homes for people without messing up the landscape the way other developers do. What's more I can do it cheaper and give people several acres where they can really appreciate what goes on in nature. While this wasn't a panther farm in the Colombian jungle, it was to be a Peaceable Kingdom[7] of the Piedmont.

What I planned and began to advertise didn't seem like development but the realization of my environmental and social ideals. The principles were simple: (1) make homesites five acres or larger where one person's way of life wouldn't interfere with a neighbor's; (2) write covenants to prevent people from cutting too many trees, polluting the streams, and leaving junk in the woods; (3) keep costs low by bypassing the realtors and paying for development from sales instead of debt; (4) finance the lots so that anyone with a steady job in the local mill could afford to buy.

Realtors assured me the idea was nice, but people really wouldn't want to live in the woods thirteen miles away from town. My friend who read the Eddas nevertheless believed in me. "Don't pay any attention to them," he said, and went on to finish his thesis on Mohammed in medieval literature. The month after we signed the mortgage, he expressed his regrets and moved to the Bronx to explain the terrible justice of Iceland's Snorri[8] to slum kids.

---

[6]Old Norse name for two Icelandic books, mainly about Norse cosmology and mythology.

[7]Isaiah 9 prophesies a kingdom of peace, and Isaiah 11 tells of a time when domestic animals and wild animals will lie down in peace together. Edward Hicks (1780–1849) depicted this prophecy in numerous paintings called *Peaceable Kingdom*.

[8]Icelandic historian and poet of the thirteenth century, author of the *Younger Edda* and reputed to have been unscrupulous and involved in deadly political intrigues.

20   In a way my critics were right. For a year and a half I guided prospective buyers down the little logging road into the property. I thought people would like the design-your-own-lot approach. They could choose how long and how wide the lot would be and what hills and trees might be on it. But even trail-seasoned country lovers arrived expecting to see some kind of development. All they saw was woods. There were no roads cleared, no lots laid out. Sometimes I would meet people on the public road. If I arrived late, they would be standing by our little wooden sign as if it offered some necessary anchor in the wilderness. Some people showed up in dresses and ties, sandals and shorts; some with babies barely able to walk and too big to carry far. They went back to town and talked about their crazy afternoon in the wilds. They didn't buy anything.

I was learning development lessons two and three. People buy a sense of place. They want a recognizable order, a road that leads somewhere, driveways that tell where a house might go. They want electricity. Perhaps they have their ideas of an ideal lot and home, but most people want developers to go ahead and give them something about which they can say yea or nay.

I also learned that satisfying this desire for a sense of place and security means investing a lot of money before answering the first inquiry. This front money means more risk. That means investors expect more profit. It also means more interest expense. In sum, it means more expensive development.

Developers are willing to take risks, but they don't take many. One of the axioms of real estate economics is that success breeds competition. Developers try to minimize their risks by copying other successful developments. We can call developers timid, but many are risking not only their own money but family money, or their friends' money. If they are risking money put up by stockholders or banks, the law, not to mention a bunch of nervous strangers, is always looking over their shoulder.

24   I was lucky. America celebrated the first Earth Day in 1970. It reaffirmed the intuition that "out in the country" was a good place to live. In many minds the forest became the place where nature could exert its most healing powers. Thirty-three lots and 330 acres sold out by 1972, and our little company had made enough money to put aside some 45 acres of stream valley as common land.

As I said, my buyers were not ready to blaze any trails. I had to build a road. That was the end of my environmental virginity. I rented a little chain saw from the Rent All. I wasn't going to have any bulldozer pushing over my trees and piling them up. I'd carefully select a road line that avoided the big trees. What I had to cut, I would cut so someone could use the logs.

The rented saw was little because I only wanted to do a little damage. But no matter which way I tried to run the road, big trees stood in my way. There were a lot more than I had imagined. It was like trying to shovel a blizzard with a teaspoon. The next day I took a company check and went to town and bought a big Stihl 041 with a twenty-one-inch bar. I intended to execute each and every oak and hickory, holly, and loblolly pine myself. Why let some anonymous bulldozer be my surrogate? If I were going to build a road, I'd take the emotional responsibility as well as the legal.

I managed to curve the road around a few special trees, but I cut dozens that had been standing in place for 150 or 200 years. I rubbed my nose in the damage. I counted rings, learned the marks left by weather and animals and the fall of other trees. I severed grapevines as thick as my arms, and returning the next day saw their watery sap still bleeding from the stubs. I learned the licorice smell of a pine stump, the acid smell of red oak, and the musky tannin of white oak. It was a little like killing and dressing your own meat.

Within a week I had cleared the first half mile. Not too bad, I told myself. The canopy would soon grow back over the road and it would be a shady country lane. Buddy the bulldozer operator laughed when he came to grub the stumps. "Hell, I can't even turn around in that space."

I learned that a road fit for service according to the state of North Carolina has the following characteristics:

The roadbed must be twenty feet wide and paved.

Then there are shoulders. These may be soft. Add four feet on each side.

The shoulders must not be soggy, however, so they are accompanied by ditches. Add six feet each side.

The slopes on the ditches and the embankments must be gradual enough so grass will not fall off or the soil erode. If you have any embankment beyond the ditch add five or ten more feet.

Accommodating all of this kindness to man and nature requires cutting a swath through the forest that is fifty to sixty feet wide. This was no job for one man and a chain saw.

In one day the D-8 Caterpillar had piled up all the trees I had cut and a lot more in three big mounds that looked as though a giant beaver expected someone to turn a river down that roadway. In three or four places I had left an especially large tree near the edge of the road, something like Frost's "Tuft of Flowers"[9] left by the mower. Life, however, happens differently than poems, and most of the trees had to go or have their roots cut: you can't run a road ditch around a tree. The dozer simply lifted its blade eight or ten feet up the trunk of a two-foot-thick oak and pushed until the tree's own whiplashing top helped break the roots' hold in the earth.

One weekend, while the piles were drying, I climbed over them looking for good logs and crotches to salvage for future woodworking. Everything was pinned at some point under something else. I did find a large hollow gum tree which I sectioned and split, intending to use the curved pieces for benches. When I scraped and pried the rot from inside the log, thousands of carpenter ants, beetles, and millipedes fell out and scattered in chaos on the

[9]A poem by Robert Frost (1874–1963).

ground. In that insignificant and dying tree a whole community of life had been carrying on confidently through years of darkness. By comparison the light-drenched roadbed was simple and lifeless.

On Monday Buddy arrived with a pickup load of old tires. We threw them on the piles, and he doused the pyres with gasoline. By evening the charred piles smoldered, not a tree or stump recognizable as oak, hickory, gum, or anything else. The next day the ashes were buried, and the road was clear—a red avenue of clay with big trees seeming to stand at numb attention on both sides. The dozer cut through the tops of hills until the roadbed had an acceptable incline. A pan roared up and down the road carrying the cutout earth to fill the low spots. The hills and valleys were being averaged into conformity.

Two days later, after scraping and graveling and grading, a car could drive from one end to the other at fifty miles per hour. Everything was slick and smooth.

I used to stand in that roadway, looking up and down and thinking, "God help me, did I do this?" I was like a man returning time and again to the scene of a hit-and-run accident. But there was no one to report to and not even a corpse to bury.

40   About that time Carolina Power and Light came along. They could not put their poles in the road right-of-way, so they cleared another fifteen feet alongside the road, felling trees, hacking away brush, and planting their poles.

Now people drove in with their Volkswagen bugs and Saabs and vans, and they began to buy. Nobody lamented the trees that had been cut and burned any more than cried about the destroyed forests of Manhattan Island.

Although each of them came praising the covenants that promised a peaceable and unpolluted kingdom, they approached their homes in the woods with a variety of styles that matched their paths through life. How did they love nature? Let me count the ways.

A young woman with milk goats and chickens allowed them to roam the woods, tearing up the forest floor and eating gardens as well as wildflowers. An insurance man with two Saint Bernards was happy his dogs had lots of room even though they walked through screen doors and knocked down a neighbor's eighty-year-old mother. Lou and Tammy's pack of hounds kept the ex-Marine next door awake. A dentist started a forest fire throwing out his wood-stove ashes. The ex-Marine cherished his privacy so much he wouldn't build a drive to his house and carried all his lumber in by hand; but he cleared part of the wildlife buffer for his garden. A stonemason who laid his stone in imitation of natural deposits drained his bathtub, sink, and washing machine into the woods near the creek. An Episcopal minister who built a log house to blend into the woods objected to the width of our roads that didn't blend in, but he controlled beetles in his natural house by periodically treating it with a toxic preservative.

44   I, the developer, had made a place bound to attract people who were sentimental about nature. They taught me lesson number four, a lesson that

ought to be one of the Ten Commandments of the environmental movement: sentimentality applied is just another form of development.

If I am going to be vilified as a polluter and destroyer, I want the
judgment to be applied impartially. I don't want someone spared because he
wears hiking boots, reads poetry, or milks cows.

For an example of nature sentimentality at its worst, look at our attitudes
toward farming. The notion that by preserving farmland we have fortified
ourselves against development and struck a blow for nature is nonsense.
From nature's point of view most farms are hugely destructive. What other
form of development routinely poisons its soils and devastates such vast areas,
exclusively to serve people? A farm murders natural diversity and extracts the
life force from nature's carcass to sell for profit. Most farming is voodoo
ecology that makes a walking zombie out of nature. So why do we celebrate
America's farmers with such a soft heart? Why do we find beauty in the
farmscape but not in the well-landscaped shopping mall or subdivision? It's
sentimentality.

When I did my first development back in 1968 I was fortunate to be free from
laws and regulations. I made my own decisions about erosion control, lot
size, water, sewers, curbs, gutters, electricity, open space, setbacks, traffic
flow, curb cuts, and who could do what on their land. In most high-growth
areas, including the Research Triangle area of North Carolina where I operate, all these things are now subject to approval by state, county, and city
governments.

As a citizen and conservationist I favor controls. I have stood up in   48
countless hearings and asked the planning board or county commissioners to
tighten regulations, to require more open space in a subdivision, or to deny
a permit for a shopping center. When Congress first considered a bill that
would prohibit development on some of our ocean beaches I went to
Washington and sat next to the head of the most powerful Political Action
Committee in the country, the Realtors PAC, and testified that my leader's
position was shortsighted, uninformed, and motivated by greed.

Developers, however, are just like a lot of writers, teachers, farmers, and
dancers. We think we can learn the business on our own, asking for help
when we think we need it and from the people who make us comfortable.
Although I see a legitimate role for the public in my development plans, I still
feel the way you do when someone looks over your shoulder as you write a
letter or knocks on your door when you're making love.

The public, of course, thinks developers need more attention than it gives
to people who merely create culture. There are several reasons for this. First,
development is an assault on our sensibilities. It's noisy and it's dirty, and it
changes our surroundings right before our eyes. Second, development destroys things we care about deeply—streams, trees, hills, animals. Finally, and
most important, development brings out greed.

My attempt to deal with greed taught me my fifth important lesson as a developer. The public is right that development tempts developers to do things they know are not right. It tempts everyone. Almost everyone has a price. In my first development, I began to see sellers who had gotten a good deal from us charging what the market would bear when they resold their lots. The kind of family I grew up in couldn't afford them anymore.

52   When I did my second development I wanted to protect everyone from greed. Into the covenants for this 225-acre community I wrote a clause that controlled resales. A seller could get the original purchase price of the land plus an amount equal to general inflation. For the house he could get the cost of replacing it. Half of anything over these figures had to be put in a landowners' trust fund to help lower-income people buy land.

Lawyers who undertook a closing on a resale here would call me up as if they could not read. They could read, but they couldn't believe what they were reading. Sometimes my covenant worked and owners sold at the formula price. Others got their neighbors to waive the profit restriction.

When it comes to money, I learned, there is no such thing as a liberal or a conservative. At the extremes are a few saints and Midases.[1] Everybody else wants as much as he or she can get. I once designed a small subdivision of a farm bought by a professor who specialized in Latin American land reform, a champion of redistributing wealth. He looked at the lot prices I proposed and said, "Aren't these very low? Can't we get much more than this?" I pointed out that after the road and survey costs, he would be doubling his money. And didn't he want as many people as possible to be able to afford his land? No, he wanted the same kind of money everybody else made on real estate.

When it comes to buying and selling real estate I've decided I too might as well make everything I can. If I forgo some profit someone else will grab it. They could be one of James Watt's Sagebrush Rebels[2] or one of my allies in conservation.

56   I made enough to free my house and land from mortgages and to devote more time to proving that the pen was mightier than the bulldozer. I dropped out of development for five or six years. Then at a conference on land use I ran into a conservative big-time realtor and developer who had grown wealthy on the Research Triangle's land boom. Some years earlier he and other investors had agreed to sell a seven-hundred-acre tract to a land trust that wanted to build a solar village on its south slopes overlooking the softly muscled waters of the Haw River. I had been president of the trust then, and we had failed to raise the money for a bargain price.

The price was higher now, but still a bargain. I sold new stock in my

[1]In Greek mythology, King Midas turned everything he touched to gold.

[2]Sagebrush Rebels refers to the ranchers and mine owners in western states whose interests Watt supported. Watt, secretary of the interior in the Reagan administration, increased mining, drilling, and logging on public lands in defiance of environmental laws and protests.

shrunken but still existing company, and we bought. I was back in business. Here were 720 acres full of beautiful beech and oak forests, silent stone chimneys surrounded by walnut and giant oaks, old fields once worked savagely by desperate family farmers and now lying quiet under a blanket of pine needles in the deep shade of big loblollies. The site was big enough to contain both the source and the mouth of several small creeks that ran clear. Wherever there was a soft stream bank or mud puddle, deer, raccoons, possums left their tracks. Turkeys thrived on the acorns and grubs in the leaf mold. It was a place that should have been preserved as a wilderness.

There was no one to preserve it, however, and the market was full of people more than willing to spoil it. If I had had a million dollars I would have bought it and left it for the animals and trees. It would have been the most natural and best-protected place left in this new Silicon Valley.[3] I didn't have enough money for a new pickup truck, much less the funds to pick up seven hundred acres of land. I knew I was once again going to go to war with myself.

I immediately began to write a peace treaty. Like most, it is full of compromises. I drafted a long set of covenants that reflected my accumulated frustrations with the way people use land as well as everything I know about how to protect wildlife, water, and air from people.

The building boom has begun. People have been moving in. Already I have problems. Owners don't want to keep their dogs and cats under control when the poor things could be enjoying such happy freedom of the woods. So there is now a little pack chasing deer and baying raccoons into the trees. I see an occasional cat prowling the roadside for rabbits, birds, lizards, mice, and voles.

There are days when I am ready to plow up the roads I've built and tear down the houses. I'm not alone in my regrets. In a recent issue of *North Carolina Wildlife*, a local conservationist and hunter lamented the changes development had brought to this place. Yet until I came along no one else had made a move to protect this land from the gathering forces of the market. No environmental group had even explored it, although it was one of the few big tracts left in the river valley.

Antidevelopers are fond of printing on their banners and posters Thoreau's declaration "In wildness is the preservation of the world." History and my own experience suggest the opposite: "In civilization is the preservation of wildness."

Real estate development doesn't pretend to be natural, but in the big picture it is kinder in quantity and often gentler in quality than other land uses. My road building has contributed its share of sediment to local streams and rivers, but not a fraction as much as the nearby dairy farmer's creekside feedlot. Acre

[3]Area in central California home to many high-tech companies.

for acre fewer toxic chemicals run into our rivers and streams from a subdivision or even a shopping center than from a farm.

64   Yet Americans are prejudiced for farmers and against developers. We are prejudiced for furry animals and against machines, for green plants and against concrete. The bias against developers and development finds many worthy targets, but like all prejudice, its driving force is irrational fear. We project onto others what we fear within ourselves.

Developers and environmentalists feel betrayed by each other. Betrayal, however, is possible only among people who share common values and commitments. Our dilemma is that as individuals and collectively as a society we have chosen both nature and development.

Almost anyone who drives a car, goes shopping, uses an airport, attends a school, wears factory-made clothing, or owns a musical instrument supports development somewhere. The real way to combat bad development is the same as the way to combat drugs. The users have got to say NO. I wouldn't have trundled my chain saw out to my first development if I had thought no one wanted to live there.

Development is not "unnatural." Nature made us the animal that imagines worlds more enjoyable than the world we were given. Then we develop that world. What human beings do to the planet is as much a part of nature as Yosemite Valley.

68   Knowing that won't help me the next time I set a bulldozer to work in a forest or channel a sparkling stream into a length of dark culvert. Just as we are the animal that imagines how things might be, we are also the one that remembers how things were. It is embarrassing and frustrating. Writing about it has helped me draw yet one more lesson from my life as a developer: none of us will succeed as either developers or environmentalists until we accept that we are both.

Understanding What You Read

1. What are the six lessons Kaufman learned in his career as a developer?
2. What does Kaufman mean when he says that people are both environmentalists and developers? Why does this require hard choices and trade-offs?

Writing About What You Read

From your own experience, identify and describe a development project undertaken with the intention of protecting the environment, or one that ignored environmental concerns.

CHARLES C. MANN AND MARK L. PLUMMER

Mann (b. 1955) and Plummer (b. 1954) are currently working on a book on biodiversity in America. They have coauthored articles as well as the book *The Aspirin Wars* (1991). Plummer is at the Discovery Institute in Seattle, Washington, and Mann is a contributing editor for the *Atlantic Monthly* and lives in Massachusetts. "The Butterfly Problem" was first published in the *Atlantic* in January 1992.

The Butterfly Problem

RICHARD SCHROEDER was five when he moved into the new house. It had a big back yard that opened up into the tall grass of the dunes—his own private slice of the Oregon coast. He played there almost every day until he was ten or eleven. Then his father began taking him to play golf. Richard loved the game, and was soon working as a caddy at the country club. In college he won several regional amateur tournaments. After graduation he went into the securities business, but he still played whenever he could. And he kept thinking about the land behind his parents' house. The rippling dunes, the smell of the surf—he could create a world-class golf course, eighteen holes as good as Pebble Beach,[1] right there in Gearhart, Oregon. People would come from thousands of miles away just to play on his course.

Dropping out of securities, he spent the mid-1970s working as a club pro, learning the golf trade. He also learned the development business. For the scheme to be profitable, the course had to be built in conjunction with a destination resort—a mixture of hotel and residential space. Schroeder was looking at a $100 million project. The acreage was split into a dozen parcels, each with a separate owner. Schroeder got them all behind the scheme and found a backer who would build it and a famous golf-course designer who would lay it out. All this took ten years—a long time, but Schroeder knew that dreams do not come true easily. Only in 1986, he says, did he learn about the "butterfly problem."

Schroeder was hardly planning to build on pristine wilderness. Part of the site is fenced off for cow pasture: the rest, to his annoyance, is strewn with beer cans and the tracks of four-wheel-drive vehicles. But the land is also one of the few remaining habitats for the rare Oregon silverspot butterfly *(Speyeria zerene hippolyta)*. A finger-sized reddish-brown insect, *S.z. hippolyta* is registered as a threatened species under the Endangered Species Act of 1973, which directs the U.S. Fish and Wildlife Service, a branch of the Department of the Interior, to maintain a list of species that are either endangered (in imminent peril of becoming extinct) or threatened (likely to become endangered in the near future) and to fine or imprison people who "harass, harm,

[1] A world-class golf course on the California coast near Carmel.

pursue, hunt, shoot, wound, kill, trap, capture, or collect" species on the list. Fines, jail—all at once Schroeder was in different territory. In addition to the usual obstacles facing developers (lawsuits, permits, bonding agents), he would now have to guarantee that his golf course could be built without killing a single Oregon silverspot butterfly.

4   The Endangered Species Act[2] first gained notoriety in 1978, when the Supreme Court stopped work on an almost finished dam in Tennessee because it menaced a little-known fish. Since then the act has reached its long fingers into many aspects of American life. The Fish and Wildlife Service has forced the cancellation of one dam, in Colorado, because it put whooping cranes at risk; pushed the Bureau of Reclamation to postpone expanding another, because it jeopardized the humpbacked chub; induced Massachusetts to close beaches just north of Boston at the height of summer, to protect the piping plover; started a lengthy political battle by proposing to settle packs of gray wolves in western states; sent a warning to 600 landowners in Polk and Highlands counties, Florida, spelling out the consequences if the development of their property harms the Florida scrub jay; and hauled the town of Ranchos Palos Verdes, California, into criminal court for inadvertently driving the endangered Palos Verdes butterfly into apparent extinction, in part by turning one of its major breeding grounds into a baseball field (the suit was thrown out on a technicality).

None of this comes cheap. Buying land for the Mississippi sandhill crane has cost more than $20 million. Riverside County, California, is spending an equal sum on the Stephens' kangaroo rat, and would have authorized an additional $100 million had voters not rejected the idea. Voters will not get the chance to refuse in the Pacific Northwest, where the Fish and Wildlife Service plans to save the northern spotted owl, a native of forests in Washington, Oregon, and California, by halting most logging on 8.2 million acres, an area nearly the size of Massachusetts and Connecticut combined. Some estimates of the cost of locking up the timber reach into the tens of billions of dollars. In the case of the California gnat-catcher, now proposed for the endangered-species list, the costs may rise even higher, for the bird lives in Los Angeles, and efforts to save it will require clamping down on the most powerful real-estate market in the nation.

Richard Schroeder worked diligently to accommodate *S.z. hippolyta*. He met with the silverspot recovery team, the group of scientists and Fish and Wildlife Service staffers in charge of the butterfly's future. He hired the world's expert on the insect, Paul Hammond, of Oregon State University, to put together an official lepidopterist-certified conservation plan for the Fish and Wildlife Service. But all came to naught. Last March, Hammond found an additional patch of butterfly habitat. Exasperated, Schroeder's financial backers pulled the plug—it seemed they would never know where

[2]See Chronology, pages xxvii–xxx.

the butterfly might turn up next. When we visited Schroeder last summer, he was a deeply frustrated man. "The whole thing's crazy," he said, shaking his head. He seemed to be trying to control his anger. Society had chosen an insect over the dream of a human being, and for the life of him Schroeder couldn't see the logic in it, or how anyone was better off for it.

THE NOAH PRINCIPLE

The Endangered Species Act is up for reauthorization this year,[3] and tales like Schroeder's are why a political brawl has already begun. Most Americans would be appalled if a shopping center wiped out the last bald eagle. And it is likely that they would be dismayed to learn the fate of the obscure Tecopa pupfish, which lost its sole habitat, a hot springs in Death Valley, to a bathhouse that could easily have been redesigned to save the fish. Instead, it became the first species to be removed from the endangered list by reason of extinction. But feelings are much less certain when it comes to canceling a $100 million golf course to save a bug nobody has ever heard of.

Perhaps fifty silverspots live on the land for Schroeder's project. How can anyone imagine that they are worth keeping in place of a multimillion-dollar resort? On the other hand, how can anyone sanction the elimination of a species from this earth to profit a few people? Would the decision be different if the land housed five insects, rather than fifty? Or if it held not butterflies but bald eagles? What if chemicals within butterflies turn out to have medical benefits, whereas eagles are useful only as a national symbol? And what if saving the eagle required canceling not one but ten resorts?

Until recent decades Americans were untroubled by such questions. The nation was still empty. It didn't seem possible that preserving a few animals could impose real hardship. There seemed no need to choose between a species and economic growth. But now the country's empty corners are filling up, and biologists warn that in the next decade or two the fate of thousands of species will be decided. In making those decisions, ordinary notions of balancing the benefits against the costs may seem inappropriate, inapplicable, or even immoral. Yet any time we decide that a course of action makes some entity "better off"—butterfly, golf-course builder, or society as a whole—we are perforce judging that whatever the benefits, they are greater than the costs. At present these decisions are governed by the Endangered Species Act. Unfortunately, the act fails to balance costs and benefits meaningfully. Indeed, it is put together in such a way that it explicitly avoids the terrible choices that must be faced.

Federal wildlife-protection laws go back to the end of the past century, when a famous poacher named Ed Howell slaughtered bison in Yellowstone National Park with impunity because no statute forbade it; public outrage at

[3]It was reauthorized in 1992.

Howell's cheeky remarks to the newspapers pushed Congress into passing the Yellowstone Park Protection Act of 1894. Other laws followed. Mostly aimed at poachers, they cost society little, and roused little opposition. In 1964 the Bureau of Sports Fisheries and Wildlife, the bureaucratic ancestor of today's Fish and Wildlife Service, compiled a "redbook" of sixty-three endangered species. Assembled informally by a panel of nine biologists, the redbook was the government's first endangered-species list. Laws passed in 1966 and 1969 directed the Department of the Interior to formalize the list and to protect the species on it by acquiring their habitats. These statutes were weak—they did not actually ban killing members of endangered species except in national wildlife refuges. When President Richard M. Nixon called for stringent legislation in 1972, the bid fell on receptive ears. Congress passed the Endangered Species Act by a large majority in December of 1973, and Nixon quickly signed it. Neither seems to have had a clue about what they were setting in motion.

"They thought they were writing a law about saving bald eagles and elk—what I call the 'charismatic megafauna,' " says Dennis Murphy, the director of the Center for Conservation Biology at Stanford. "Instead, they got a law protecting *species*"—a difference with unexpected implications. According to Edward O. Wilson, a renowned entomologist at Harvard, there are only a few thousand types of the mammals and birds that people like to anthropomorphize, but there may be something on the order of 100 million species, of which only about 1.4 million have been named. Creatures such as fungi, insects, and bacteria form the vast majority of this horde; mammals, birds, and other vertebrates are little but colorful epiphenomena. (Asked what years of research had taught him about God, J.B.S. Haldane, one of the founders of evolutionary biology, replied that the Creator had an "inordinate fondness for beetles.") Those not initiated into the ways of biological thought may equate "preserving global biodiversity" with saving whales and whooping cranes, but scientists who use the phrase are concerned with protecting organisms that most people wouldn't hesitate to step on.

12   Because the majority of species are unknown, no one can say with certainty how many are going extinct. Moreover, extinction itself is hard to observe—one can never be certain that a few specimens somewhere have not been overlooked. Thought for more than a decade to be extinct, the Shoshone pupfish, a cousin of the Tecopa pupfish, turned up in its native hot springs in 1986. The long-lost black-footed ferret was rediscovered accidentally a decade ago, when a ranch dog near Meeteetse, Wyoming, returned home with a dead one in its mouth; excited conservationists then found a small colony of the weasel-like creatures. But no one doubts that extinction occurs, and most biologists believe that it is now taking place at an accelerating rate. Worldwide, Wilson guesses, the rate may be 50,000 species a year. Figures for the United States are surprisingly uncertain, but Peter Hoch, of the Missouri Botanical Garden, has calculated what he calls a "rough but

defensible approximation": some 4,000 domestic species are at risk of extinction within five to ten years.

Biologists advance three arguments for avoiding this prospect. On a utilitarian level, living creatures are the source of almost all foods and many medicines; wiping out even the humblest mold might deprive humanity of the genes for a future penicillin. Wilson has calculated that the genetic information encoded in the DNA[4] from the common mouse, if represented as ordinary-size letters, would almost fill the fifteen editions of the *Encyclopaedia Britannica* printed since 1768. Who, conservationists ask, would like to see that information vanish, along with its potential benefit to humanity?

More generally, the web of species around us helps generate soil, regulate freshwater supplies, dispose of waste, and maintain the quality of the atmosphere. Pillaging nature to the point where it cannot perform these functions is dangerously foolish. Simple self-protection is thus a second motive for preserving biodiversity. When DDT[5] was sprayed in Borneo, the biologists Paul and Anne Ehrlich relate in their book *Extinction* (1981), it killed all the houseflies. The gecko lizards that preyed on the flies ate their pesticide-filled corpses and died. House cats consumed the dying lizards; they died too. Rats descended on the villages, bringing bubonic plague. Incredibly, the housefly in this case was part of an intricate system that controlled human disease. To make up for its absence, the government was forced to parachute cats into the area.

These reasons for protecting biodiversity are practical and anthropocentric. But the "foremost argument for the preservation of all nonhuman species," the Ehrlichs argue in *Extinction,* is neither. It is the "religious" belief "that our fellow passengers on Spaceship Earth . . . *have a right to exist.*" Far from being extreme, the "Noah Principle,"[6] as this argument was named by the biologist David Ehrenfeld, is shared by many scientists and conservationists. As a species, the Noah Principle says, the smallest grub has the same right to exist as the biggest whale; so does every species of cockroach, every species of stinging nettle (all plants are included in these arguments), and even the microorganisms that cause malaria and syphilis. Anthropologists refuse to categorize cultures as "higher" and "lower" civilizations, because all have intrinsic worth; biologists believe that there is no inherent difference in value between "higher" and "lower" organisms. All are precious, and human beings have a moral responsibility to each and every one. "It's a matter of stewardship," Wilson says.

The practical and moral costs of losing the nation's biological endowment may be enormous. But so may be the cost of saving it. To halt the

16

---

[4]The genetic substance of all living cells that stores and replicates hereditary information.

[5]Insecticide banned in the U.S. in 1972 and in some European countries in the 1960s. DDT is still used in developing countries (see page 374).

[6]Noah, at God's command, gathers pairs of each species before the great flood, recounted in chapters 7 and 8 of Genesis.

spasm of extinction, Wilson and Paul Ehrlich wrote in a special biodiversity issue of *Science* last August,

> the first step . . . would be to cease "developing" any more relatively undisturbed land. Every new shopping center built in the California chaparral, every hectare of tropical forest cut and burned, every swamp converted into a rice paddy or shrimp farm means less biodiversity. . . . [Even so,] ending direct human incursions into remaining relatively undisturbed habitats would be only a start. . . . The indispensable strategy for saving our fellow living creatures and ourselves in the long run is . . . to reduce the scale of human activities.

"To reduce the scale of human activities" implies telling people to make do with less: nations must choose between their natural heritage and the economic well-being of their citizens.

The Endangered Species Act is this country's response to that choice. It strongly favors preserving biodiversity—more strongly, conservationists say, than any other environmental law in the world. "Quite frankly," Murphy says, "it is the best weapon we have." It didn't start out that way. Indeed, few grasped the act's implications until its first test before the Supreme Court. On one side was the Tellico Dam, a Tennessee Valley Authority project frequently described as a boondoggle. On the other was the snail darter, a three-inch snail-eating fish that was first observed in 1973, six years after Tellico began construction and shortly before the act became law. Handed this unexpected weapon, Tellico's opponents petitioned the Fish and Wildlife Service to list the fish on an emergency basis in 1975. The amazed TVA complained that Tellico's environmental-impact statement had passed two federal court reviews, that $50 million in taxpayers' money had already been spent, that the dam would provide flood control, hydroelectric power, and recreational facilities (a lake). It claimed that the snail darter was found elsewhere, and thus was not endangered. Nonetheless the service listed the darter, and a civil action ensued, based on the Endangered Species Act. By 1978 the suit had wound its way up the legal trellis to the Supreme Court.

Attorney General Griffin Bell personally argued the case, attempting to demonstrate the snail darter's insignificance by displaying one to the justices. The tactic failed. In June of 1978 the Court ruled that "the plain intent of Congress" was to stop extinction *no matter what the cost.* The language of the act, the Court said, "shows clearly that Congress viewed the value of endangered species as 'incalculable' "—in practical terms, infinite. Obviously, a $100 million dam was worth less than an infinitely valuable fish. Simple logic dictated halting Tellico.

The decision had a "bombshell impact on Capitol Hill," says Donald Barry, of the World Wildlife Fund, who was then a staff attorney in the solicitor's office of the Department of the Interior. Even some of the law's most ardent congressional supporters were alarmed by its inflexibility, although that inflexibility, of course, endeared the act to environmentalists. Tellico's principal sponsor, Senate minority leader Howard H. Baker, Jr., of Tennessee, set out to change the act. The ensuing political maneuvering led to the establishment of a small escape hatch: a committee that could be convened when all other attempts had failed to resolve conflicts between protecting a species and building a project requiring federal funds or permits. Because it included several Cabinet members, the committee could not be summoned every time an endangered species was threatened. On the other hand, it could authorize the extinction of a species, as long as the benefits of the project strongly outweighed the benefits of actions aimed at saving the species. In its first meeting the "God Committee," as it was soon nicknamed, unanimously found in favor of the snail darter, though mostly because the group regarded Tellico as a waste of money.

Baker rammed through legislation exempting Tellico from the Endangered Species Act. The dam was built and, as predicted, proved to be less than an economic dynamo; a few years later more snail darters turned up in other rivers nearby. (The fish was downgraded to "threatened" in 1984.) But the whole affair set a pattern that has continued to the present. People who care little about the endangered species frequently invoke them as an excuse to stop projects; the science used to justify the actions of one side or another is often rushed, as it was for Tellico, and can be so incomplete that it verges on the fraudulent; and, most important, the law still insists that species must be saved no matter what the cost. 20

For the Fish and Wildlife Service, this set of circumstances has turned the Endangered Species Act into a bureaucratic horror. The agency, formerly a haven for guys who liked to work outdoors, is now a hot spot of sophisticated partisan arm-twisting. Hundreds of petitions flow in every year, and the service must evaluate them all, with litigious interest groups scrutinizing every move. Consequently, listing moves at a crawl. As of November, the most recent date for which official figures are available, 668 domestic species, more than half of which are plants and invertebrates, clung to their places on the list. Another 100 had been accepted for the list, but the service had not yet published a final notice about them in the *Federal Register,* the last step in listing. Some 500 species resided in a curious state of limbo called Category I: the Fish and Wildlife Service agreed that they merited listing but had not got around to accepting them officially. A further 3,000 occupied a *second* limbo, Category II: the service thought they might merit listing but had not yet investigated fully. At the current rate of progress, according to a 1990 report by the Department of the Interior's own Office of Inspector General, clearing today's backlog may take up to forty-eight years, during which time many more species will be menaced. Already, several species have vanished while the government was trying to decide whether they were endangered.

After listing a species, the Fish and Wildlife Service puts together a "recovery plan" for it. And here, too, the agency is behind, though the reasons are as much budgetary as political. It has approved 364 recovery plans, covering about half the listed species, but few have been implemented. In its 1990 report the Office of Inspector General estimated the recovery cost for all species currently listed or expected to be at $4.6 billion, spread over ten years. The service's 1990 budget for recovering species was $10.6 million. Other agencies pitch in, but even so, in 1990 the total state and federal budget for all aspects of endangered species—listing, research, land acquisition, and so on—was just $102 million, less than a fourth of the annual amount needed for recovery alone.

In reading these figures, one conclusion is inescapable: more species—many more—will be driven, like the Tecopa pupfish, to extinction. Few species are unsavable today; concerted human effort can save most of them. But we are unlikely to have the means to save them all. In this deficit-ridden age Fish and Wildlife Service budgets will not climb to the altitude necessary to save the few hundred species on the list, let alone the thousands upon thousands of unlisted species that biologists regard as endangered. Like cost-conscious Noahs, Americans will pick which creatures to bring with them and which to leave behind. The choice is inescapable—but the Endangered Species Act, in its insistence that we save every species, implicitly rejects this responsibility. As a result, the government is left with little guidance. It moves almost at random, with dismaying consequences.

*　　*　　*

Understanding What You Read

1. What are some of the difficult choices that protecting endangered species requires government officials to make?
2. Why is it so difficult to know all the endangered species and just what is threatening them?
3. What animals are more likely to be protected?
4. What animals do people tend to anthropomorphize?
5. How does this piece support the assertion that the Endangered Species Act is "a bureaucratic horror"?

Writing About What You Read

1. Based on your current knowledge, consider what criteria you would use to determine whether public funds should be spent protecting a species. Write a proposal specifying particular animals or kinds of animals that should be given the first priority, acknowledging that you are making difficult choices and that you understand you may be trading one species for another.
2. Discuss some of the difficult choices people may have to make to protect endangered species.

WENDELL BERRY

A farmer, teacher, essayist, novelist, and poet, Berry (b. 1934) grew up in rural Kentucky and attended the University of Kentucky, where he earned a B.A. and M.A. in English. After two years studying creative writing with Wallace Stegner in California, a year in Italy on a Guggenheim Fellowship, and three years teaching English at New York University, Berry went home to Kentucky, where he still lives, to farm, write, and teach. A mentor to environmentalists around the country, Berry is admired as a writer and thinker who lives by his convictions. His many books include *Unsettling of America* (1977), in which he argues for local small-scale farming and the repeopling of rural America. Other collections of essays are *The Gift of Good Land* (1981), *Home Economics* (1987), and *What Are People For?* (1990). "Mayhem in the Industrial Paradise" is from the collection *A Continuous Harmony* (1972).

Mayhem in the Industrial Paradise

> . . . they have made my pleasant field a desolate wilderness. . . .
>
> —Jeremiah 12:10

I HAVE just spent two days flying over the coal fields of both eastern and western Kentucky, looking at the works of the strip miners. Several times before, I had driven and walked to look at strip mines, mainly in the eastern part of the state, but those earlier, ground-level experiences did not prepare me at all for what I saw from the air. In scale and desolation—and, I am afraid, in duration—this industrial vandalism can be compared only with the desert badlands of the West. The damage has no human scale. It is a geologic upheaval. In some eastern Kentucky counties, for mile after mile after mile, the land has been literally hacked to pieces. Whole mountain tops have been torn off and cast into the valleys. And the ruin of human life and possibility is commensurate with the ruin of the land. It is a scene from the Book of Revelation.[1] It is a domestic Vietnam.

So far as I know, there are only two philosophies of land use. One holds that the earth is the Lord's, or it holds that the earth belongs to those yet to be born as well as to those now living. The present owners, according to this view, only have the land in trust, both for all the living who are dependent on it now, and for the unborn who will be dependent on it in time to come. The model of this sort of use is a good farm—a farm that, by the return of wastes and by other safeguards, preserves the land in production without

---

[1]The last book in the Bible; it prophesies the end of the world in a violent apocalypse.

diminishing its ability to produce. The standard of this sort of land use is fertility, which preserves the interest of the future.

The other philosophy is that of exploitation, which holds that the interest of the present owner is the only interest to be considered. The standard, according to this view, is profit, and it is assumed that whatever is profitable is good. The most fanatical believers in the rule of profit are the strip miners. The earth, these people would have us believe, is not the Lord's, nor do the unborn have any share in it. It belongs, instead, to rich organizations with names like Peabody, Kentucky River Coal, Elkhorn Coal, National Steel, Bethlehem Steel, Occidental Petroleum, The Berwind Corporation, Tennessee Valley Authority, Chesapeake & Ohio, Ford Motor Company, and many others. And the earth, they would say, is theirs not just for a time, but forever, and in proof of their claim they do not hesitate to destroy it forever—that is, if it is profitable to do so, and earth-destruction has so far been exceedingly profitable to these organizations.

4

The gospel of the strip miners is the "broad form deed," under which vast acreages of coal rights were bought up for as little as twenty-five and fifty cents an acre before modern strip-mine technology ever had been conceived. The broad form deed holds that the coal may be taken out "in any and every manner that may be deemed necessary or convenient for mining. . . ." Kentucky is one of the few coal states that still honor the broad form deed. In Kentucky, under the sanction of this deed, the strip miners continue to ravage other people's private property. They have overturned or covered up thousands of acres of farm and forest land; they have destroyed the homes and the burial grounds of the people; they have polluted thousands of miles of streams with silt and mine acid; they have cast the overburden of the mines into the water courses and into the public roads. Their limits are technological, not moral. They have made it plain that they will stop at nothing to secure the profit, which is their only motive. And in Kentucky they have been aided and abetted at every turn by lawmakers, judges, and other public officials who are too cowardly or too greedy to act in the interest of those they are sworn to protect. Though the violations of the inadequate strip-mine regulations passed by the legislature have been numerous and well publicized, the regulations have been weakly enforced.

If the model of good land use is to be found in a good farm, then it is a strange sort of farming indeed that is practiced by these strip miners, whose herds are not cattle eating grass, but machines devouring the earth. That sounds fantastical, but then strip mining is an industry *based* upon fantasy. It proceeds upon the assumption that there is no law of gravity, that no heavy rains will fall, that water and mud and rock will not move downhill, that money is as fertile as topsoil, that the wealthy do not ultimately share the same dependences and the same fate as the poor, that the oppressed do not turn against their oppressors—that, in other words, there are no natural or moral or social consequences. Such are the luxuries that our society affords to the warlords of the exploitive industries.

People who live nearer to the results of strip mining know better. Those whose homes and belongings have been destroyed, or who live beneath the spoil banks, or who inhabit the flood plains of mutilated streams and rivers, or who have been driven into ruin and exile—and there are now many thousands of them—they know that the costs are inconceivably greater than any shown on coal-company ledgers, and they are keeping their own accounts. They know that the figment of legality that sanctions strip mining is contrary to the laws of nature and of morality and of history. And they know that in such a contradiction is the seed of social catastrophe.

The most vicious fantasy of all is the endlessly publicized notion that the net profit of the coal companies somehow represents the net profit of the whole society. Historically, however, the enrichment of the coal interests in Kentucky has always involved the impoverishment of the people of the mining regions. And of all methods of mining, strip mining is the most enriching to the rich and the most impoverishing to the poor; it has fewer employees and more victims. The net profit is net only to the coal companies, only on the basis of an annual accounting. The corporate profit is reckoned on so short a term. But the public expenditure that supports this private profit is long-term; the end of it is not now foreseeable. By the time all the reclaimable mined lands are reclaimed, and all the social and environmental damages accounted for, strip mining will be found to have been the most extravagantly subsidized adventure ever undertaken.

An estimate of the public meaning of strip-mine profits may be made from the following sentences by James Branscome in the *New York Times* of December 12, 1971: "The Corps of Engineers has estimated . . . that it would cost the public $26-million to restore the extensively strip-mined Coal River watershed in West Virginia. This is an amount approximately equal to the private profit taken by the mining companies from the watershed." But even this may be too limited an accounting. It does not consider the environmental damage, or the property damage, that may have occurred outside the boundaries of the immediate watershed between the opening of the coal seam and the completion of reclamation. It does not attempt to compute the cost of what may have been the permanent degradation of the appearance and the fertility of the land. Nor does it consider the economic consequences of the social upheaval that must always accompany an upheaval of the environment. There is, then, every reason to believe that the large net profit of a strip-mine company will prove to be a large net loss to society.

This, as all Kentuckians should be aware, is largely the responsibility of absentee owners. Of the thirty-three largest owners of mineral rights in the Kentucky coal fields, as recently listed by the *Courier-Journal,*[2] only two are based in the state. But even those owners who live in the state are absentee owners in the strict sense of the term: they do not live with the consequences of what they do. As exploitive industrialists have done from the beginning,

8

---

[2]Louisville, Kentucky, newspaper.

they live apart, in enclaves of the well-to-do, where they are neither offended nor immediately threatened by the ugliness and the dangers that they so willingly impose upon others. It is safe, I think, to say that not many coal-company executives and stockholders are living on the slopes beneath the spoil banks of their mines; not many of them have had their timber uprooted and their farms buried by avalanches of overburden; not many of them have had their water supply polluted by mine acid, or had their houses torn from the foundations by man-made landslides; not many of them see from their doorsteps the death of the land of their forefathers and the wreckage of their own birthright; not many of them see in the faces of their wives and children the want and the grief and the despair with which the local people subsidize the profits of strip mining. On the contrary, the worries of the coal companies are limited strictly to coal. When the coal is gone they do not care what is left. The inescapable conclusion is that Kentucky has been made a colony of the coal companies, who practice here a mercantilism as heartless and greedy as any in history.

In this new year[3] the state's lawmakers have once again assembled in Frankfort. Again they have the opportunity to put a stop to this awful destruction, and to assure to the state the benefits of its own wealth, and to give to the people of the coal fields the same protections of the law that are enjoyed by people everywhere else. If the men in power will do these things that are so clearly right and just, they will earn the gratitude of the living and of the unborn. If they will not do them, they will be infamous, and will be unworthy of the respect of any honest citizen.[4]

Remembering the new deserts of this once bountiful and beautiful land, my mind has gone back repeatedly to those Bible passages that are haunted by the memory of good land laid waste, and by fear of the human suffering that such destruction has always caused. Our own time has come to be haunted by the same thoughts, the same sense of a fertile homeland held in the contempt of greed, sold out, and destroyed. Jeremiah would find this evil of ours bitterly familiar:

> I brought you into a fruitful land to enjoy its fruit and the goodness of it; but when you entered upon it you defiled it and made the home I gave you loathsome.

12   The damages of strip mining are justified in the name of electrical power. We need electrical power, the argument goes, to run our factories, to heat and light and air-condition our homes, to run our household appliances, our TV sets, our children's toys, and our mechanical toothbrushes. And we must have more and more electricity because we are going to have more and more gadgets that will make us more and more comfortable. This, of course, is the

---

[3]1972 [author's note].

[4]They did not do them, and they are as unworthy of respect as I said they would be [author's note].

reasoning of a man eating himself to death. We have to begin to distinguish between the uses that are necessary and those that are frivolous. Though it is the last remedy that would occur to a glutton or a coal company, we must cut down on our consumption—that is, our destruction—of the essential energies of our planet. We must use these energies less and with much greater care. We must see the difference between the necessity of warmth in winter and the luxury of air conditioning in the summer, between light to read or work by and those "security lights" with which we are attempting to light the whole outdoors, between an electric sewing machine and an electric toothbrush. Immediate comfort, we must say to the glutton, is no guarantee of a long life; too much now is, rather, a guarantee of too little later on. Our comfort will be paid for by someone else's distress. "We dig coal to light your tree," said a recent advertisement of the coal industry. That, we must realize, is not a Christmas greeting, but a warning of our implication in an immitigable evil.

In the name of Paradise, Kentucky, and in its desecrations by the strip miners, there is no shallow irony. It was named Paradise because, like all of Kentucky in the early days, it was recognized as a garden, fertile and abounding and lovely; some pioneer saw that it was good. ("Heaven," said one of the frontier preachers, "is a Kentucky of a place.") But the strip miners have harrowed Paradise, as they would harrow heaven itself were they to find coal there. Where the little town once stood in the shade of its trees by the riverbank, there is now a blackened desert. We have despised our greatest gift, the inheritance of a fruitful land. And for such despite—for the destruction of Paradise—there will be hell to pay.

Understanding What You Read

1. How is strip mining of coal conducted in Kentucky?
2. What choices on the part of the owners of mines lead to consequences for the poor who live near the mines?
3. Why does Berry say that coal mining may be a net loss to society?
4. What emotionally loaded words does Berry use to indict the owners of the coal mines?

Writing About What You Read

Imagine that you live in rural Kentucky where the quality of your life is diminished by nearby coal mining. Write a letter to the editor of your local paper outlining your complaints and arguing that something needs to be done to remedy the situation and compensate those whose lives and property have been damaged.

MURIEL RUKEYSER

Poet, activist, and biographer, Muriel Rukeyser's (1913–1980) writing life spanned forty-five years and over thirty-three works. She was born and raised in New York City and attended Vassar for two years, after which she left to support herself as a journalist. Rukeyser was twenty-one when she received the Yale Younger Poets Prize for *Theory of Flight* (1935), a work that revealed her lifelong concern for connecting personal experience with politics. Early in 1936, Rukeyser visited Gauley Bridge, West Virginia, to investigate unsafe working conditions in silica mines run by the New Kanawha Power Company. Weaving together documentary evidence—testimony, letters, interviews—from the hearings, Rukeyser wrote the multivoiced poem, "The Book of the Dead," from which "Alloy" comes.

Alloy

This is the most audacious landscape. The gangster's
stance with his gun smoking and out is not so
vicious as this commercial field, its hill of glass.

4   Sloping as gracefully as thighs, the foothills
narrow to this, clouds over every town
finally indicate the stored destruction.

Crystalline hill: a blinded field of white
8   murdering snow, seamed by convergent tracks;
the travelling cranes reach for the silica.

And down the track, the overhead conveyor
slides on its cable to the feet of chimneys.
12   Smoke rises, not white enough, not so barbaric.

Here the severe flame speaks from the brick throat,
electric furnaces produce this precious, this clean,
annealing the crystals, fusing at last alloys.

16   Hottest for silicon, blast furnaces raise flames,
spill fire, spill steel, quench the new shape to freeze,
tempering it to perfected metal.

Forced through this crucible, a million men.
20   Above this pasture, the highway passes those
who curse the air, breathing their fear again.

The roaring flowers of the chimney-stacks
less poison, at their lips in fire, than this
dust that is blown from off the field of glass;   24

blows and will blow, rising over the mills,
crystallized and beyond the fierce corrosion
disintegrated angel on these hills.

Understanding What You Read

1. What is the "Crystalline hill" Rukeyser refers to in line 7?
2. Why does Rukeyser suggest that fire is less dangerous than blowing dust?
3. What role do humans play in this poem?

Writing About What You Read

Write an essay about Rukeyser's "commercial field" (line 3). What are the "commercial" forces at stake in "Alloy"? What is the relationship between humans and machinery?

WILLIAM CRONON

A professor of history at the University of Wisconsin at Madison, Cronon (b. 1954) is a superb storyteller who brings an environmental perspective to the study of American history. In his acclaimed book *Nature's Metropolis: Chicago and the Great West* (1991), he explores how economic growth relates to the ecology of the land. He is also the author of *Changes in the Land: Indians, Colonists, and the Ecology of New England* (1983). "Kennecott Journey: The Paths Out of Town" is included in *Under Open Sky: Rethinking America's Western Past* (1992), a collection of essays by historians coedited by Cronon.

Kennecott Journey: The Paths Out of Town

KENNECOTT: It is one of the most unlikely ghost towns in the United States. The way there is long and hard, and you are not apt to stumble upon it by accident. About eighty miles north of Valdez in south-central Alaska, you turn east off the main Richardson Highway and drive thirty miles on deteriorating asphalt to the tiny hamlet of Chitina, with its bar, post office, and thirty-odd inhabitants. There, the pavement gives out altogether and you had better buy gasoline, for you will not get the chance to do so again. As you continue east across the Copper River, the roadbed suddenly narrows, changes to gravel, and shows increasing evidence of being exactly what it is: an abandoned railroad bed. The ties have been removed to make the going easier for cars, but each winter the frost still heaves up a few of the old spikes that once held rails and ties together. Locals will suggest that you check your spare tire before proceeding, lest one of these historical artifacts put a premature end to your journey.

You are on the McCarthy Road, which will carry you some 63 miles into the heart of the Wrangell Mountains. You will see few people or buildings along the way, but everywhere there are quiet indications that this corridor was once much busier than it is today. Despite its state of abandonment, the roadbed has obviously had great labor and capital expended upon it; although the countryside dips and rolls around you, the grade of the road is virtually a dead level, reflecting the engineering skill of its builders. At times decaying wooden trestles tower 50 or more feet above you, and you wonder who went to so much trouble to erect such structures in so remote a land. Your most exciting moment (some would say terrifying) is likely to come when the road crosses 283 feet above the gray-green waters of the Kuskulana River, on an eighty-year-old steel bridge that spans the narrow canyon with only the most casual of guardrails. That such a construction has survived the earthquakes and winter storms of three-quarters of a century is testimony to the care that went into building it. You can try to reassure yourself with this thought as you inch your car across it.

The McCarthy Road finally comes to an abrupt end at the foot of the Kennicott Glacier, where the dirty torrent emerging from beneath the ice has washed away all traces of the route. Your journey is still not over. Here you must leave your car behind and pull yourself across the river in a tiny hand-powered cable car suspended fifteen or twenty feet above the churning water. Once you've relocated the old railbed, it is a few hundred yards' walk to the village of McCarthy, where perhaps a dozen people still make their homes. You may want to pause before continuing, for the town is a rather haunting shadow of its former self. The streets have become little more than foot trails if you can find them at all beneath the dense foliage. Most of the buildings have not seen a coat of paint in half a century. More than a few are being actively reclaimed by the vegetation around them, as sagging roofs and collapsing walls return to the soil.

If you know the West, you have seen such abandonment before; it is all too familiar a place. As such, it conjures up the sorts of questions one often asks in the presence of romantic ruins. The people who built these empty structures, where did they come from? What sorts of lives did they lead, and why did they leave their homes in this sorry state? Why were they here, what did they do, where did they go? The solutions to such riddles lie like tracings in the landscape around you, for the past of these people is written in the marks they made upon this land.

To understand what happened to McCarthy, you must complete the final leg of your journey. The old railroad bed does not end here. It leads you yet another six miles north, skirting the edge of the vast dirty glacier, to your ultimate destination: Kennecott. Here, so the story goes, Jack Smith and Clarence Warner wandered up the valley in August 1900 and spied on a high hillside an outcropping of malachite so green that they mistook it for grass to feed their horses. In fact, it proved to be ore so pure that it assayed in at better than 70 percent copper, the richest vein the world has ever seen.

If McCarthy impresses one mainly with its state of collapse, Kennecott gives an opposite impression. The buildings and equipment that formed the heart of this company town have survived remarkably intact. At the center of everything is the enormous crushing mill and leaching plant, a sprawling structure that hugs the hillside as it drops in a series of steps 180 feet down toward the valley floor. Ore entered the mill via a tramway descending from the peaks above and then dropped through ever finer crushers and sifters until it spilled out the bottom into ammonia vats, where it was readied for shipment. The building's dozen or more stories reflect the multistaged refining process within, piled on top of each other in an oddly Gothic jumble like something out of a Charles Addams[1] cartoon. The red walls and white window trims have faded, but one gets little feeling of decay or collapse. It is a ghost factory in a ghost town, yet its haunting could almost have begun yesterday. In the bunkhouse where the millmen slept and ate, linen is still on the beds, and plates are still on the cafeteria tables. Open account books lie scattered about the storerooms and offices, protected from decay only by the coldness of the northern climate. Even the machinery is remarkably well preserved: Lift the cover of the sifting mechanisms, and beautifully clear oil still bathes the gears with lubricant.

Kennecott was once one of the greatest copper milling centers in the world, yet its rise and fall spanned less than three decades. It began as the brainchild of Stephen Birch, a young mining engineer just out of Columbia University, though the money for its development soon came from people

---

[1]Addams's (1912–1988) wittily depicted cartoons, regularly published in the *New Yorker,* focused on macabre subjects.

with names like Guggenheim and Morgan.[2] Their Alaska Syndicate, initially capitalized at ten million dollars, finally grew to an investment more than ten times that amount. Out of that money (and the labor it bought) came Kennecott's mines, crushing mill, company town, and railroad. The mines themselves, which were located 4,000 feet above the mill, eventually included 40 miles of underground tunnels, in rock so cold that the temperature at which men worked never rose more than a degree or two above freezing. An extensive network of aerial trams delivered ore to the mill, and the railroad then carried the concentrated product 196 miles to Cordova on the south coast, where a fleet of company-owned steamships carried it on to Tacoma, Washington. The first shipment arrived in that city on April 14, 1911, and was valued at a quarter of a million dollars. Over the next twenty-seven years Kennecott produced ore worth somewhere between two and three hundred million dollars, earning its owners approximately one hundred million dollars in profits.

8   And then it ended. Like so many other western colonies, Kennecott's days of promise and abundance were numbered. The depressed markets of the 1930s knocked the bottom out of world copper prices at the same time that Kennecott's fabulously wealthy veins finally began to give out. By 1938 Kennecott Copper Company (founded after the Alaska Syndicate had reorganized in 1915) had closed its Alaskan mines and shifted operations to Utah, Chile, and other more promising sites. Almost overnight, the machinery at Kennecott fell silent. Within a few months the population of the area had dwindled to a mere handful of people, so that not much remained but the buildings, the piles of blue-green tailings, and the deserted railroad. The Kennecott boom was over, though the corporation it had spawned would outlive its namesake to become the largest copper producer in the world. On November 11, 1938, the last locomotive completed its run from Kennecott to the coast, leaving behind it an abandoned pair of rails leading to an abandoned pair of towns in a remote but extraordinarily beautiful Alaskan valley.

What is one to make of this place and of the memories that lie so visibly on its landscape?

The thing that initially most strikes one about Kennecott is just how *western* it is. Despite its far northern location, nearly everything about it evokes the West. Its remote rocky valley, ringed by snow-capped peaks, could lie only on the sunset side of the Mississippi River. Although it inverts the dryness that characterizes large parts of the arid West, it shares with the rest of the region a more fundamental trait: a climate of extremes. It has too much cold, too much rain and snow, too much and too little sun to be mistaken for anywhere else on the continent. People living under these conditions must adopt very different survival strategies from those in the gentler East.

---

[2]American industrialists who built fortunes mining and refining mineral ores.

Because the climate is so severe, relatively few people can live here. Even at the height of its mining operations, the population density of the valley was minuscule, with virtually all its inhabitants clustering in two towns and four mines. This distribution of people mimicked in miniature the West as a whole, where large cities remain separated by vast stretches of relatively empty land. In much the same way Kennecott's resource-extractive economy mimicked that of many other parts of the region. Finally, these ruins evoke one of the most familiar patterns of western settlement, the boom-and-bust economy that can create and destroy communities almost overnight. If one wanted a case study for thinking about environmental change in the West as a whole, one could do a lot worse than to make the long journey to Kennecott.

What happened at this place, and the way it became connected to the rest of the world, provide a classic study in the environmental history of western North America. In exploring Kennecott's changing environment, we ask questions that have a significance beyond this place, for they point to new ways of thinking about the West as a region, new ways of approaching environmental history in other times and other places. In posing them, we seek to integrate three broad elements: the ecology of people as organisms sharing the universe with many other organisms, the political economy of people as social beings reshaping nature and one another to produce their collective life, and the cultural values of people as storytelling creatures struggling to find the meaning of their place in the world. Our goal in peering through these three lenses is to see how environmental change relates to other changes in human societies. The special task of environmental historians is to tell stories that carry us back and forth across the boundary between people and nature to reveal just how culturally constructed that boundary is—and how dependent upon natural systems it remains. As we seek to understand Kennecott, the questions we ask must show us the paths out of town—the connections between this lonely place and the rest of the world—for only by walking those paths can we reconnect this ghost community to the circumstances that created it.

One starting point, obviously, is the environment itself. It makes good sense to follow the geographer's lead and ask questions that map the natural features of the place called Kennecott. One looks at its climate to determine its temperatures (cold), its total precipitation (high), its annual growing season (short). One learns about its bedrock, its minerals, its soils. One identifies the plant species that make up its vegetation and the animal species that constitute its food chain. One gathers data about the microorganisms that infect the people and other creatures that live here. One maps out the flow of its rivers, the depth of its water table, the slopes of its topography, and all the other physical characteristics that might somehow be relevant to human life. The end product is a kind of atlas showing what is distinctive about the environment of this particular place.

The chief danger in this approach is that it all too easily produces an

12

endless accumulation of details with no order, no hierarchy, no analytical value beyond mere description. All too many regional histories and geographies, in the West and elsewhere, begin with a dry, dead chapter on "environment" that recites innumerable minutiae about climate, soil, and vegetation without the slightest indication of why they matter to history. Often they *don't* matter: the author forgets most of them as soon as the chapter is over, never bothering to explore their relevance to the rest of the narrative. The bankruptcy of such an approach should be self-evident. The chief innovation of environmental history has been to assert that discussions of natural context cannot be relegated to an isolated chapter but must be integral to the human history of which they are so fundamental a part.

Cataloging the environment, then, is only the beginning of our work. The deeper task is to connect it to the people who live within it. To do so, we might simply ask what those people eat. The food we put in our mouths, digest in our intestines, and excrete back into the environment is one of our most intimate ties to the natural world. Much of our social life is devoted to acquiring and consuming it. Our survival depends on it. Every article of food reaches our stomachs via a different route, and is thus a kind of pathway—out of town and back into nature—for an environmental historian to trace. Ecologists speak much of the energy flows and nutrient cycles that define an ecosystem, and these apply no less powerfully to human societies. Energy and nutrition are what food is all about. But because people inhabit cultures as well as ecosystems, the choice of what to eat has as much to do with filling the soul as with filling the gut. Two different communities inhabiting the same ecosystem can make radically different choices about which parts of it will enter their stomachs. In so doing, they say much about who they are and what they believe.

Take, for instance, the native people who inhabited the Copper River watershed before Kennecott ever existed. Called the Ahtnas—after the Russian name for the river itself—they relied entirely on local plants and animals for their survival. Salmon, caribou, and ground squirrels were among their most important foodstuffs. But to describe such creatures only as "food" would be to miss their most vital qualities, for they were also fellow beings who shared a complex moral universe with the people who hunted them. Long ago, in myth time, there had been no boundary between people and animals, so that beings could shift form from human to raven to fish and back again as suited their purposes. "Once all was man," the Ahtna storytellers said, and their tales of those former times reminded children of the essential qualities that people and animals shared with one another.

Even now the animals still had great power. They understood human speech and were always watching from just beyond the edges of the camp to see whether people were acting as they should. To understand the Ahtnas' environment—and the environment of most native peoples in North America—one has to see it as they did, as a moral space inhabited by spiritual beings. The forest was everywhere alive with eyes, all of them watching. "Good luck" and "bad luck" were no mere superstitions in such a place; rather, they defined success or failure in the hunt, which in turn marked the boundary between survival and death. One could kill and eat animals, but only after properly thanking them for acquiescing in their own deaths. Some were so powerful that to harm them at all brought great peril. Wolves, for instance, were among the greatest of animal hunters, and it was dangerous even to touch their tracks in the snow. If anyone was foolish enough to kill a wolf, the resulting bad luck was so strong that one would never kill anything else again. Unless one atoned for the death with a great gift to the animal, one would die a slow death oneself—by starvation.

Death by hunger is, of course, not merely a spiritual event but a profoundly material one. The Ahtnas had good reason to worry about it. For them, the threat of starvation was an annual affair. This suggests further questions we need to ask even about more forgiving environments. Any geographical description, no matter how static, can be set in motion by asking, "How does this place *cycle?*" As the planet rotates on its axis, how does the life of the day differ from that of the night? As the earth revolves around the sun, how does the flux of solar energy shift from month to month? During what period is life most exuberantly abundant, and for how long does the local world slumber in the winter cold? Most critically, at what time of year is sheer survival most at risk, and how do people respond to the dangers they face?

The Ahtnas dealt with the extreme seasonal cycling of their ecosystem in several ways. For one thing, they kept their total population very low, no more than a few hundred people in the entire Copper River valley south of Chitina. In the seventy-mile stretch of country between Chitina and Kennecott, perhaps thirty individuals made their homes. Even this small group could not always live together, for during the worst winter months the food supply was too sparse to feed so many people. The Ahtnas solved this difficulty by regularly shifting locations and changing the size of their settlements. Like most people and animals, they also stored surplus food to use when nature's larder would be nearly empty. In spring they lived in relatively large, permanent villages along the banks of rivers where they could fish the salmon runs, drying and storing their catch for later use. Toward midsummer they headed upslope to smaller meat camps where they could trap and hunt everything from caribou to squirrels. Fall found them back at their larger village sites to eat the stored salmon they had cached earlier in the year.

But the annual flow of solar energy is weak in Alaska, and even animals have difficulty storing enough summer fat in their bodies to make it through the long dark winter. Human beings faced the same problem, and their success or failure depended on that of the animals. By January or February Ahtna food caches usually began to give out and families were forced to disperse once again in search of whatever food remained. Late winter was always the hardest of times. If luck was good—if people were scrupulous in attending to their rituals and if the animals were generous in their gifts—a small band could capture enough ground squirrels and the occasional emaciated moose to make it through the winter without great suffering. If not, starvation was a constant possibility. In 1828 the winter failure of the caribou herds brought death to more than one hundred natives in the Copper River valley. When Lieutenant Henry Allen made the first American exploration through this country, during the late winter of 1885, he found hungry native families scrounging for food wherever he went. Allen's own group, dizzy with hunger and barely able to crawl, was eventually reduced to eating rotten moose meat, which they consumed as eagerly as the starving natives. As one member of the expedition reported, "it tasted good, maggots and all."

20   Not just food is affected by the seasonal cycling of the ecosystem. Virtually everything a human community does—its shelter, its clothing, its work, its rituals—reflects the wheel of the seasons. An environmental historian needs to track each of these elements and reconstruct their connections to the natural world. Take travel, for instance. Alaska's peculiar climate and soils make it extremely difficult to move through the interior during spring and fall, when mud, floods, and unreliable ice encourage everyone to stay at home. (In this it has much in common with other parts of the West; migrants on the famed Oregon and California trails faced many of the same seasonal problems.) Alaskan travel is easiest when rivers are open and not so flooded that boat travel becomes too dangerous, or in deep winter, when the rivers are frozen and can serve as highways for sled travel. This meant that groups like the Ahtnas could make extended journeys only at well-defined times of the year. When Lieutenant Allen set out from the mouth of the Copper River, traders there were expecting upstream natives to appear any day with their winter fur catch, taking advantage of the last reliable ice before the river broke up and travel became impossible.

Allen himself faced the same challenge. He and his men began their journey with nearly half a ton of supplies but quickly learned that there was no way to move so heavy a burden on sleds across the unreliable snow and ice of the March landscape. Within three days of starting, they had jettisoned nearly half their load. All that remained in the way of food were 150 pounds of flour, 100 pounds of beans, 40 pounds of rice, two sides of bacon, 15 pounds of tea, and small quantities of beef extract, deviled ham, and chocolate. The list of provisions is ecologically suggestive, for there is nothing Alaskan about it. Allen's food quickly gave out, so that he and his men soon found themselves, as Alaskans said, "living upon the country," but his original intention had been to survive on the stored food he had imported from Outside. This in turn opens up a profoundly important set of questions for environmental history and the history of the West.

Living upon the country or importing from Outside: These are the two most basic human choices about how to live in a particular place. From the many objects and organisms around them, people identify a certain subset as "resources," things to be drawn into the human community and turned to useful ends. Some become food, some are burned for warmth, some are fabricated into clothing and tools, some serve as markers of wealth and status, some express beauty, some become holy, and most become a mixture of these things. Asking how people partition an ecosystem into a resource base shows us the boundaries they draw between useful and useless things. Just so do they define a unique human place in nature, a unique way of being in the world.

Some of these resources are of interest to more than just local people. Among the many human actions that produce environmental change, few are more important than trade. When people exchange things in their immediate vicinity for things that can only be obtained elsewhere, they impose a new set of meanings on the local landscape and connect it to a wider world. In so doing, they invent what one might call new paths out of town. These increase the chance that the local environment will begin to change in response to outside forces, so that trade becomes a powerful new source of ecological change.

When transport systems and markets are limited, the resources that enter into them and travel farthest tend to be light, low in bulk, and highly valuable. It is no accident that early trade networks in many parts of the globe concentrated on spices, rare foods, precious metals, and furs. This was true throughout the West—one finds salt, coffee, alcohol, gold, and skins being traded everywhere—and it was true in the subarctic North. Natives from interior Alaska exchanged furs and fish with natives in coastal areas long before Europeans ever visited the region, thereby linking the resources of two broad ecological zones. Such exchanges were not necessarily peaceful. Coastal Chugach Eskimos from time to time made raiding expeditions nearly to the source of the Copper River to pillage Ahtna settlements, rob food caches, and kidnap women. Viewed ecologically, raids and conflicts of this sort often express many of the same values that underpin trade.

Although these "exchanges" might link communities hundreds of miles apart, native trade and its ecological consequences were limited because goods could move only in packs, sleds, or boats. When the Russians arrived in their sailing craft and sought to purchase furs, they pulled Alaska into a much larger Eurasian market. This meant that a certain share of Alaska's resources—particularly its fur-bearing mammals—began to be extracted from the region and shipped halfway around the planet to meet the demands of people with dramatically different cultural needs. Russian and native traders started operating along the coast and throughout interior Alaska. In response, the Ahtna made regular excursions to the mouth of the Copper River, traveling in boats made of caribou skins, which they dismantled, tanned, and sold after arriving at the trading post.

The ecological implications of such encounters were by no means simple.

24

The Russian demand for furs no doubt encouraged natives to kill animals for different purposes than before, putting new population pressures on species that were now being exported from the local ecosystem. A new market-oriented logic began to exist side by side with the older gift-giving rituals that previously characterized native relations with animals. But such changes were rarely absolute. Natives managed to respond to market demands without abandoning their older spiritual relationships with the world around them. As long as the fur trade depended for its work force solely on the small local population, hunting pressure on animals remained limited in scale.

This was less true on the coast. There marine mammals had special vulnerabilities that meant they could be exploited in much more intensive ways. Unlike other ocean dwellers, marine mammals had to breathe, opening themselves to human attack each time they surfaced for air. More important, several species—especially seals and sea otters—spent key periods of their reproductive cycles in coastal rookeries, where cows and calves could escape the attacks of predators. There they were easily slaughtered in the thousands by any human hunters who had clubs and the will to use them. To create that will, the Russians conquered native populations on the coast, especially the Aleuts, and reorganized them into a mobile labor force capable of exploiting seals and sea otters at levels far beyond their natural reproductive rates. By quite early in the nineteenth century market hunting was devastating marine mammals.

28   Trade linked the resources of one ecosystem with the human demands of another. Alaskan villages that had no sugar, alcohol, or tobacco obtained such things by trading with communities that had no furs. The net result was to redefine the resources of the Alaskan landscape, pushing them beyond the needs of local subsistence into the realm of the market, where any good could be transformed into any other. At the same time the act of economic consumption came to be increasingly separated from the place of ecological production, distancing people from the consequences of their own acts and desires. A kind of alienation from nature was the almost inevitable result.

In many parts of the world, one element in this process was simple population density. Trade redefined ecosystems by moving resources from places with few people to places with many. Certainly this happened in most parts of the American West. Natives of the Copper River valley had lived in relative balance with their fellow organisms partly because their numbers were small, and stayed so because a larger population would very likely have starved by winter's end. Local game animals were not likely to suffer serious depletion as long as they helped limit human numbers. Providing fur coats to the citizens of Moscow or Peking or New York City, on the other hand, was an entirely different matter. Wild game populations could hardly help failing in the face of such demand.

But population density by itself is almost never an adequate explanation for environmental change, for it leads willy-nilly to the much more complicated riddle of *why* human beings number as they do. Any environmental history must inevitably touch upon this question, if only implicitly. The answer has partly to do with the natural abundance of the ecosystem but has even more to do with social organization and political economy. Farming folk tend to be more numerous than hunting and gathering folk the world over. When farmers produce more food than they themselves consume, they can support individuals and groups that do not raise their own food. The result is not just greater human numbers but more elaborate human hierarchies. Agriculture thus supports the rise of cities, supplying their dense nonfarming populations with imported food. Although we too easily tend to forget this fact, every urban culture also farms. Industrial revolutions presuppose agricultural ones, so that city and country grow together.

Kennecott and the American West are hardly the places to explore human social evolution writ large, but they did supply distant cities whose inhabitants rarely gave a second thought to their existence. The process of linking sparsely populated regions with densely populated ones has been central to the entire course of western history. It takes little effort to write the history of the frontier West as a story of peripheral areas becoming ever more integrated into an urban-industrial economy. Because city dwellers were fed by an agricultural system that they themselves controlled and because they could look to so many different parts of the world to supply themselves, their needs were in no way limited by their local ecosystem. Indeed, no one place was essential to their survival, for they could always use their wealth and capital to look elsewhere if the resources of any one place began to run out. The same was true of frontier agriculture: If farmers exhausted the soil, they could move on to greener pastures and start again. The result was a dynamic, unstable system that constantly threatened to push beyond the limits of the ecosystems that supported it.

The story of Kennecott is a classic case in point. When Lieutenant Allen visited the area in 1885, the natives showed him copper knives, bullets, and jewelry, all of local manufacture. The Ahtna chief Nicolai explained that he and his people made these things from nuggets in a local river and that he knew of a vein of ore high above his settlement that he would be happy to show to his visitors after the snow melted. Ahtna villages had been trading copper goods south to the coast for generations. Although the local Indians clearly regarded their copper as valuable and depended on it for trade, their uses for it were limited. Weapons, tools, and jewelry were all they made with it, so their demand for the metal was considerably smaller than the supply. What made copper valuable was the human labor and skill that fashioned it into useful objects. The raw metal itself had much less intrinsic value, so the Ahtnas could afford to be generous in sharing it. "I do not believe," wrote Allen, "that the natives guard as a secret treasure the copper or other mineral beds, but think they would willingly reveal to the white man their knowledge in the matter." [32]

Allen, of course, saw the veins of blue-green ore with different eyes. For him, they had greater intrinsic value, for a reason that would have meant nothing to Nicolai: copper's ability to conduct electricity. The culture Allen represented was discovering a new need for this ability, and so began to draw Nicolai's world into its orbit. Allen's party embarked on its journey just as an increasing number of American prospectors were scouring the area for gold, a mineral they valued so highly that it could attract immigrants far in excess of the local ecosystem's ability to feed them. Already the increased numbers of people, armed with rifles and other weapons, were putting new pressure on local game species. In 1884 an army officer had issued clothing to natives on the Copper River because "it was quite plain to the casual observer that the immigration of so many white people into the Copper River Valley meant the driving out of the greater part of the large game. . . ." The long-term consequence was the same in the Copper River valley as in so many other parts of the West: Game disappeared.

Conflict seemed likely under such circumstances, and the army, remembering what had happened ten years before at Little Bighorn, was careful to make plans for winning any violent encounter that might occur. This was why Lieutenant Allen had been sent on his journey. The orders authorizing his expedition bluntly predicted that "the conflicting interests between the white people and the Indians of the Territory may in the near future result in serious disturbances between the two races. . . ." Allen's assignment was to explore what might be called the military ecology of the region. If the army invaded, it would bring a massive human influx to the region. Such a force would face the same choice as any other human population—living upon the country or importing from Outside—so army officials asked Allen to report on the local food sources and outside supply lines that would feed the troops. Although the Ahtna had heretofore been entirely peaceful in their dealings with Americans, the United States was planning for violence. It was an old frontier story. One way or another, an invasion was in the offing.

The ecological nature of Allen's reconnaissance is best suggested by the order that directed him to pay special attention to any grass species he encountered along the way. "You will examine," his superior told him, "especially as to the kind and extent of the native grasses, and ascertain if animals ordinarily used in military operations can be subsisted and made of service there." Did the Copper River valley contain enough grass to feed soldiers' horses? On the basis of their experiences elsewhere in the West, Allen's superiors were asking shrewd ecological questions, which historians would do well to emulate. Every human community depends for survival on its relationships with other species. If people migrate to a new location, other species do too. These in turn have all sorts of unexpected effects on ecosystems in which they gain a foothold.

36   The introduction of alien plants, animals, and diseases is one of the fundamental stories of environmental history throughout the American West.

Although the process was more limited in Alaska than elsewhere because of its harsh climates and soils, migration went on even in the Far North. The most famous instance in the nineteenth century was Sheldon Jackson's effort to encourage Eskimos living on the Bering Strait to start raising Siberian reindeer as a substitute for Alaskan caribou. Good missionary that he was, Jackson saw the reindeer as a way of introducing natives not just to a replacement source of food, but to a new pastoral way of life that would be more conducive to the Christian religion he sought to promote, proving again the intimate linkage of environment, economy, and cultural belief systems.

Most such introductions, however, occurred without the help of self-conscious missionaries like Jackson. When a Euroamerican community did finally develop at Kennecott, residents managed to supply part of their food needs with the alien species they brought with them. Inger Jensen Ricci, who spent her childhood in the town, remembered how her parents supplemented family meals with cabbages, onions, and turnips from a backyard garden. The Jensens kept chickens so as to have fresh eggs and raised rabbits for fresh meat. These mimicked in a small way the much more extensive migration of agricultural species in the West as a whole. But the Jensens' garden was hardly a farm. It contributed only a small share of the family's food because Kennecott's climate and terrain were poorly suited to the meat and grain crops of a typical American diet. The only viable alternative was for residents to import food from Outside.

The problem was how to do so. Lieutenant Allen's hardships in traveling across the Alaskan terrain demonstrated that no large-scale military movements were likely to be successful there, and none in fact ever took place. Instead, it was Nicolai's copper that finally brought a Euroamerican invasion to the region, enabling Outsiders to build a railroad that overcame the seasonal mud and ice of Alaskan travel to supply an urban-industrial colony by the side of the Kennicott Glacier. Fifteen years after Allen had visited the area, prospectors finally staked a claim to the blue-green vein that the Ahtna chief had described. In so doing, they introduced a new legal definition of property to the valley. Before Kennecott's copper could be used, before it could tempt anyone to pour millions of dollars into its development, it had first to be *owned*. Nicolai and his people claimed important rights of occupancy to the lands around their villages and when necessary defended them against intruders. But their shifting settlement patterns, and their reliance on the hunt, left them little concerned about drawing sharp property boundaries upon the landscape. When Jack Smith and Clarence Warner filed their claim to the copper vein that eventually became the Bonanza Mine, they had in mind a completely different way of owning and occupying the terrain. And therein lay the origin of the community called Kennecott.

Another group of questions about environmental history, then, has to do with property. How do people imagine they own the land and creatures around them? How does their legal system express this sense of ownership, and what consequences does it have for the environment? The legal history of the western economy, particularly as regards property, remains a largely unexplored field, badly in need of more theoretically sophisticated studies that will place the law in its cultural and ecological context. Law is the foundation on which property rests and is therefore the formal expression of a community's relationship to nature.

40 Kennecott came into being through a wide variety of legal mechanisms. Land laws enabled prospectors to claim ownership rights over any resources they "found." Laws of bankruptcy and limited liability allowed the Kennecott Copper Company to come into being and protected its owners from the full consequences of their actions. Contract laws governed trade and established the rules whereby managers and laborers worked together. Tort laws defined responsibility for accidents or environmental damages. Together they created a series of relationships between land and community that broke radically with the gift-giving spirituality of the Ahtnas. The law defined political and economic power in the West and is crucial to any systematic understanding of environmental change in the region.

Because Stephen Birch's Alaska Syndicate was able to buy up the legal rights to subsurface copper in the mountains above Kennecott, the company's owners knew they could sell and profit from that copper if only they could bring it to market. Toward that end they invested millions of dollars in the mining technology that brought ore out of the ground, the processing technology that purified it, and the transport technology that delivered it to the smelters where it finally became a commodity that people would buy. Collectively these technologies—along with the mineral in the ground and the money paid to workers—became the company's capital, which would henceforth determine the fate of the town it had called into being. The story is familiar to every mining community in every part of the American West.

Capital invested at Kennecott was driven by outside forces that had nothing to do with the local community or ecosystem of the Copper River valley. The syndicate's profits required it to earn the best rate of return on its investments. Those who capitalized the town knew from the beginning that its key resource would eventually be extracted so completely as to destroy the community's raison d'être. They could do this because their own survival in no way depended on conserving Kennecott's resources for the long run. Quite the contrary. Unlike the hunter-gatherer communities that preceded them, the owners of Kennecott had little interest in maintaining a self-sustaining relation to their resource base. Once it was used up, they could simply throw the remnants away.

In the Copper River valley a human population that depended almost entirely on the local landscape was invaded by a population that depended virtually not at all on that landscape. The same process happened to varying degrees throughout the nonagricultural West. Because the railroad liberated

Kennecott's miners from the seasonal food cycles of the local ecosystem, it permitted a much denser and more sedentary population to live there. Kennecott's inhabitants lived in Alaska by converting copper into cash. Market hunters might shoot wild game in the surrounding valleys, but the residents of Kennecott and McCarthy purchased their meat in local butcher shops without ever encountering the animals whose flesh they ate. Local gardens might yield onions, turnips, cabbages, and other northern produce, but such crops mainly supplemented a more southerly diet of rail-borne fish, grain, and meat from distant ports and farms.

Historians writing about the past of any particular western place would do well to remember that its history is tied to many other regions undergoing parallel changes at the same time. The canned salmon that Kennecott's workers consumed in their cafeteria presupposed the prior development of a commercial fishery along the Pacific coast and the creation of dozens of packing plants scattered up and down the Alaskan shoreline. The bread they ate came to them via Seattle from the vast agricultural areas of Washington and Oregon, where family farms followed the time-honored frontier practice of selling wheat—much as the mine owners sold copper—to buy supplies from the metropolitan economy. The coffee that the miners drank, and the sugar they used to sweeten it, reflected a broader international trade with tropical areas far to the south, each of which was undergoing its own peculiar encounter with the forces of capital and empire. Interregional trade networks such as these had been part of frontier history right from the beginning. Each trade linkage was also a new interface between ecosystems in remote parts of the world, and each raises possible lines of investigation—new paths out of town—for environmental historians seeking to place the history of the American West in its larger context.

But what of the smaller context? Kennecott was not simply the end of a trade route; it was also a world in its own right, a place where people made homes for themselves. Questions on a different scale suggest themselves here. Once people have chosen to call a place home, how do they arrange their lives within it? How does the physical form of their community reflect their relationships to each other and to the natural world? The shifting settlements of the Ahtnas responded to natural cycles of abundance and scarcity but also reflected the Ahtnas' sense that certain social groups should try to stick together. When a large summer village broke down into smaller camps, it did so along clearly defined lines of kinship, gender, and authority. Access to resources, political power, participation in rituals: all followed a carefully codified set of rules that expressed themselves as spatial patterns.

The same was true of Kennecott. Complex boundaries of class, gender, and ethnicity produced an intricate social geography between the mines on the ridgetops, the processing mill in the valley, and the private town of McCarthy at the foot of the glacier. Most ridgetop inhabitants were single men, wage employees of the company, who lived in bunkhouses where the ordinary domestic activities of eating, playing, and sleeping took place in an unusually public setting. Few of the men had families, and turnover was high. Miners came from widely different ethnic backgrounds and did not always speak the same language. Under such circumstances, "community" was a tenuous thing, defined partly by the corporation and partly in opposition to the corporation.

Mapping out the geography of gender, class, race, and ethnicity remains one of the most important but least studied aspects of environmental history. More questions to answer: Why do people live where they do? How do they declare their differences from one another in the locations and forms of their homes? How do their dealings with one another and with nature reflect their positions in society? What does it mean to be a single man in this place? A married woman? A middle-class child? A person of color? An immigrant who speaks no English? A tourist? How do the many categories into which people divide themselves define the ways they experience and affect the landscape? Who has power over whom in this place, and how does the land reflect that power?

48   In the Alaskan copper region a clear class hierarchy overlapped with gender to create the very different communities of Kennecott, McCarthy, and the mines. The mines were entirely male and working-class, save for the few foremen and managers—also male—who directed the mining process. The male world of the mines was matched by the more female world of McCarthy, although even there men constituted the larger share of the population. McCarthy was a "private" town, independent of the copper company, and it existed mainly as a market for the men on the ridgetops. A few miners had wives in McCarthy and conducted their family lives at long distance on an irregular cycle of meetings; the children of such unions might see their fathers only rarely. The rest of the miners visited McCarthy as well, but their relationships to the women of the town had a more commercial flavor. Sex and affection were usually filtered through the markets of the saloon and brothel. McCarthy had a middle class of store owners and their wives, but its customers made it a working-class town in which single men and women were a disproportionate share of the population.

This was less true of Kennecott, which residents knew simply as "camp." Camp had little to offer the miners, who rarely even stopped there on the trip down to McCarthy. Camp did not feel like nearly so working-class a place as McCarthy or the mines. The millworkers were single men much like the miners on the ridgetops, but they were more highly paid and had a higher status. More important, camp was where the company's manager and super-intendent lived. They, along with the doctor, teachers, nurses, and office workers, constituted the highest social class in the community. They had a separate dining hall for themselves and were provided with all the appurte-nances of middle-class life: comfortable single-family houses with leather furniture, fine china, silver service, wall hangings, and other markers of elite status. Somewhat below them in rank were the various foremen who oversaw the operations of the mill, but they too got houses that set them apart from the wageworkers in the bunkhouses.

The consequences of this class hierarchy were manifold. In Kennecott, to be working-class was to be single and male. To be a woman or child, on the other hand, was to be middle-class—very different from the situation in McCarthy. Women and children lived in the one-family dwellings that Americans saw as the ideal environment for middle-class life; indeed, children were told to stay away from the working-class bunkhouses "for fear of exposure to the hardened life." Then again, even the middle class had gradations; not all single-family dwellings were equal in status. The less desirable ones were a steep walk up the hillside next to the mill and did not have indoor plumbing. They had running water only until pipes froze in winter, whereupon a family had to carry its water in pails until spring. Only those in the most elegant buildings—and the workers in the bunkhouses—had the luxury of indoor toilets. Everyone else used outhouses. As Inger Jensen Ricci remembered it, "camp had a very definite class distinction."

Not surprisingly, camp's relation to the surrounding environment was very different from that of Nicolai's village. The whole point of this community, after all, was to carve a maze of tunnels beneath the slopes where men in heavy woolen clothing wearing carbide lamps worked in a constant icy fog to extract ore from the mountains' heart. Other than copper, little in the local ecosystem was essential to Kennecott's survival. Nature therefore became what it was for many other urban Americans: a place of outdoor recreation, in stark contrast with the mines' underground place of work. One symbol of this was the cantilevered tennis court perched on the hillside above camp, where those who had permission were allowed to play. (Unfortunately the mosquitoes became such a problem for the players that the court finally had to be covered over with netting.) Inger's father went hunting and maintained a trapline, but more as a hobby than anything else. He was an amateur taxidermist who enjoyed stuffing animals in his spare time—not something the Ahtnas would have thought to do with their animal neighbors. Some miners made a practice of drifting back and forth between underground wage work and "living upon the country" by hunting for part of the year, but most middle-class excursions from camp were more for play than anything else. Berry-picking time was a great favorite of the children, though the food it added to family tables was hardly a necessity of life. Come summer, families took their children on holiday to Long Lake, a modest middle-class tent resort about a dozen miles down the railroad from McCarthy. There, they could get out into "nature"—not the nature of the Ahtna hunters, but a nature of genteel leisure and romantic retreat, far from the noisy industrial world of Kennecott. It was as if a little bit of the Adirondacks had been transplanted to the Far North.

In the end, the abstract questions we ask about environmental history

52

resolve themselves into small human actions at very particular times and places: Ahtna hunters setting aside caribou meat as an offering by the fire, miners digging copper in frozen tunnels, middle-class families fishing by a lake. It is the details that matter. Imagine Inger Jensen as a ten-year-old Kennecott child out for a sunny walk along the railroad tracks to gather mountain cranberries so her mother could make pie—perhaps using an old Scandinavian recipe—as dessert for the family's dinner table. Then imagine an Ahtna girl doing much the same thing just a few years before—gathering the same favorite berry because it ripens so late in the year and stores so well through the winter months that it will still be nutritious when the snow melts, still provide color for dyes, still be useful as a medicine against sore throats and colds. Two children, both gathering food, both enjoying their useful play. Imagine the differences between them. Imagine their worlds.

Big questions, small answers.

The story of how Kennecott became a twentieth-century ghost town suggests much about the environmental history of the West. Like so many other historical sites in the region, what happened at Kennecott found its roots in the depths of the earth. Without the chalcocite and malachite that had concentrated copper in the fissures of Kennecott's dolomite, the human past of this place would have been entirely different. And yet the mere existence of these minerals did not in and of itself determine the events that took place here. Far from it.

For large-scale exploitation of Kennecott's copper to occur, a human community organized on an entirely different basis had first to find it. Before chalcocite and malachite could become significant "determinants" of human history, electricity had to be discovered as a form of energy capable of being transmitted over copper wire. Economic demand for electricity required that it have some practical application, so that the invention of electric lights, motors, and telecommunication devices went hand in hand with electrical generating stations in fostering the market for an inexpensive base metal capable of wiring them together. Just as necessary was the concentration of human populations into cities where economies of scale for the first time made it possible to sell lights, telephones, electricity—and therefore copper—at a profit.

56 To realize such profits, there had to be still other conditions. The community had to have people interested in reading past the ordinary hours of daylight and workers whose factories no longer closed at sunset or depended on belts and shafts for their primary power transmission. Scientists had to understand enough about geography, geology, and chemistry to know where copper occurred and how to extract it. Transportation systems had to be able to move heavy, low-priced metals cheaply over great distances from western mines to urban markets. Food supplies had to come from an agricultural system capable of moving foodstuffs to mines that were otherwise

incapable of feeding themselves. And not least, the economy required the capitalist social relations and corporations capable of mobilizing immense amounts of wealth to assemble the workers and equipment without which copper could neither be mined, turned into wire, nor installed in houses, offices, and factories.

Kennecott's emergence as a great copper-mining complex in the first two decades of the twentieth century was thus neither a historical accident nor a case of geographical determinism. At no prior moment in the history of the West would it have been possible for capitalists in New York to hire engineers and workers in Alaska to construct a railroad, mine, and crushing mill deep in the interior of that remote territory so that the nation's cities could purchase a metal they hardly knew they needed just half a century before. A particular vein of a particular mineral created an opportunity, and a particular culture with particular social and technical needs then seized that opportunity for its own purposes. Kennecott thus emerges as a near-perfect example of the environmental processes that scholars of western history most need to study and understand.

The mills at the end of the old railroad bed now stand silent, and the buildings are finally beginning to lean at crazy angles as the glacial till gradually shifts beneath them. The people who erected this vast complex inserted themselves into the local ecosystem, built a community, transformed the local economy, and extracted the only resource that mattered to them on behalf of urban markets thousands of miles away. Kennecott exists because a myriad of historical forces joined together to reshape the hillsides above a dirty glacier in an obscure Alaskan valley. It was called into being at the behest of such forces, and it was turned into a ghost town in much the same way. Its copper was used up, demand declined, markets disappeared, and there was no longer any reason to maintain so remote and expensive a colony in so cold and northern a place. And so, overnight, like so many western ghost towns before it, it all shut down.

The story, of course, does not quite end there. There is still the long drive over the abandoned railroad bed on which you began your journey to this place, and the reason you yourself bothered to come at all. Curiously, these too are among the central questions of environmental history in the American West. Your very presence is proof that Kennecott remains a kind of colony attached in a new but not altogether unfamiliar way to the outside world. The old mill now lies within the bounds of Wrangell–St. Elias National Park, the largest such park in the entire United States. The property has been deeded over to the federal government (though the corporation still retains subsurface rights to the copper—just in case). The old railroad bed has lost its ties, so that tourists can travel the seventy-odd miles from Chitina, across the Kuskulana River Bridge, by cable car across the river, and by foot from McCarthy to the red mills of Kennecott, to see this symbol of abandoned industrialism within one of the largest "wilderness" areas of the continent.

60   That this wilderness is honeycombed with underground tunnels, pock-marked by blue-green piles of tailings, and still shows traces of aerial tramways leading from mines to mills, hardly matters to the backpackers and mountain climbers who visit it today. For them, escapees from an urban world who are willing to pay dearly to travel to the outer edges of civilization, this place has become a symbol of romantic decay in the midst of deep wilderness. Your journey here has more than a little in common with the trip Kennecott families once made to the tent resort on Long Lake in their efforts to get away from town and closer to nature. As you scramble about the ruins of the place, admiring the icy sublimity of the mountains and reflecting on the more ambiguous beauty of the mill, you would do well to place yourself as one of the figures in this ghost landscape. You too are part of its environmental history, bringing with you—even as a reader—assumptions about nature and humanity that have led you to choose this particular place as the object of some desire. The paths out of town have brought you to Kennecott on the very road that once created it to send copper to the outside world. The end of the journey is also its beginning: in the wilderness that is culture's creature, the place where nature and history have met and turned, and turned again.

Understanding What You Read

1. What foods did the native people (the Ahtnas) of this area of south-central Alaska eat in the winter months?
2. What items did the Ahtnas first trade with the outside world?
3. In what ways did the development of trade affect the ecosystem of the Ahtnas?
4. How did the Ahtnas use copper?
5. List the conditions that were necessary before a profitable mine could be established.
6. What factors allowed the mining community to prosper in a place that could barely support a sparse population of hunter-gatherers?
7. What is the effect of inviting the reader to make an imaginary journey to Kennicott?

Writing About What You Read

1. Cronon makes the point that the Indians in Alaska depended on local resources for their food, clothing, and other necessities, while the industrialists who moved into the area used materials and supplies from thousands of miles away. Look around in your daily life at the food you eat, the clothes you wear, and the energy you consume and write an essay about where they came from and the cost—environmental and economic—of getting them to you.

2. Write an essay comparing and contrasting the life of an Ahtnas child with the life of a middle-class child of Kennecott.

SARAH ORNE JEWETT

Born in South Berwick, Maine, Jewett (1849–1909) moved as a child into her paternal grandfather's house, where she lived at least part of the year for the rest of her life. She began to publish stories and sketches in her twenties; *Deephaven* (1877), her first collection, established her reputation as a writer, and gave her the basis for friendships and correspondence with prominent writers such as John Greenleaf Whittier, Harriet Beecher Stowe, whose work influenced Jewett's, Mary E. Wilkins Freeman, and Willa Cather. Most of Jewett's books consist of loosely connected tales and sketches. Among them are *A White Heron and Other Stories* (1886) and *The King of Folly Island* (1888). *The Country of the Pointed Firs* (1896) is considered her masterpiece.

A White Heron

I

The woods were already filled with shadows one June evening, just before eight o'clock, though a bright sunset still glimmered faintly among the trunks of the trees. A little girl was driving home her cow, a plodding, dilatory, provoking creature in her behavior, but a valued companion for all that. They were going away from the western light, and striking deep into the dark woods, but their feet were familiar with the path, and it was no matter whether their eyes could see it or not.

There was hardly a night the summer through when the old cow could be found waiting at the pasture bars; on the contrary, it was her greatest pleasure to hide herself away among the high huckleberry bushes, and though she wore a loud bell she had made the discovery that if one stood perfectly still it would not ring. So Sylvia had to hunt for her until she found her, and call Co'! Co'! with never an answering Moo, until her childish patience was quite spent. If the creature had not given good milk and plenty of it, the case would have seemed very different to her owners. Besides, Sylvia had all the time there was, and very little use to make of it. Sometimes in pleasant weather it was a consolation to look upon the cow's pranks as an intelligent attempt to play hide and seek, and as the child had no playmates she lent herself to this amusement with a good deal of zest. Though this chase had been so long that the wary animal herself had given an unusual signal of her whereabouts, Sylvia had only laughed when she came upon Mistress Moolly at the swamp-side, and urged her affectionately homeward with a twig of birch leaves. The old cow was not inclined to wander farther, she even turned in the right direction for once as they left the pasture, and stepped along the road at a good pace. She was quite ready to be milked now, and seldom stopped to browse. Sylvia wondered what her grandmother would say because they were so late. It was a great while since she had left home at half past five o'clock, but everybody knew the difficulty of making this errand a short one. Mrs. Tilley had chased the hornèd torment too many summer evenings herself to blame anyone else for lingering, and was only thankful as she waited that she had Sylvia, nowadays, to give such valuable assistance. The good woman suspected that Sylvia loitered occasionally on her own account; there never was such a child for straying out-of-doors since the world was made! Everybody said that it was a good change for a little maid who had tried to grow for eight years in a crowded manufacturing town, but, as for Sylvia herself, it seemed as if she never had been alive at all before she came to live at the farm. She thought often with wistful compassion of a wretched dry geranium that belonged to a town neighbor.

" 'Afraid of folks,' " old Mrs. Tilley said to herself, with a smile, after she had made the unlikely choice of Sylvia from her daughter's houseful of children, and was returning to the farm. " 'Afraid of folks,' they said! I guess she won't be troubled no great with 'em up to the old place!" When they reached the door of the lonely house and stopped to unlock it, and the cat came to purr loudly, and rub against them, a deserted pussy, indeed, but fat with young robins, Sylvia whispered that this was a beautiful place to live in, and she never should wish to go home.

4 The companions followed the shady woodroad, the cow taking slow steps, and the child very fast ones. The cow stopped long at the brook to drink, as if the pasture were not half a swamp, and Sylvia stood still and waited, letting her bare feet cool themselves in the shoal water, while the great twilight moths struck softly against her. She waded on through the brook as the cow moved away, and listened to the thrushes with a heart that beat fast with pleasure. There was a stirring in the great boughs overhead. They were full of little birds and beasts that seemed to be wide-awake, and going about their world, or else saying good-night to each other in sleepy twitters. Sylvia herself felt sleepy as she walked along. However, it was not much farther to the house, and the air was soft and sweet. She was not often in the woods so late as this, and it made her feel as if she were a part of the gray shadows and the moving leaves. She was just thinking how long it seemed since she first came to the farm a year ago, and wondering if everything went on in the noisy town just the same as when she was there; the thought of the great red-faced boy

who used to chase and frighten her made her hurry along the path to escape from the shadow of the trees.

Suddenly this little woods-girl is horror-stricken to hear a clear whistle not very far away. Not a bird's whistle, which would have a sort of friendliness, but a boy's whistle, determined, and somewhat aggressive. Sylvia left the cow to whatever sad fate might await her, and stepped discreetly aside into the bushes, but she was just too late. The enemy had discovered her, and called out in a very cheerful and persuasive tone, "Halloa, little girl, how far is it to the road?" and trembling Sylvia answered almost inaudibly, "A good ways."

She did not dare to look boldly at the tall young man, who carried a gun over his shoulder, but she came out of her bush and again followed the cow, while he walked alongside.

"I have been hunting for some birds," the stranger said kindly, "and I have lost my way, and need a friend very much. Don't be afraid," he added gallantly. "Speak up and tell me what your name is, and whether you think I can spend the night at your house, and go out gunning early in the morning."

Sylvia was more alarmed than before. Would not her grandmother consider her much to blame? But who could have foreseen such an accident as this? It did not appear to be her fault, and she hung her head as if the stem of it were broken, but managed to answer "Sylvy," with much effort when her companion again asked her name.

Mrs. Tilley was standing in the doorway when the trio came into view. The cow gave a loud moo by way of explanation.

"Yes, you'd better speak up for yourself, you old trial! Where'd she tuck herself away this time, Sylvy?" Sylvia kept an awed silence; she knew by instinct that her grandmother did not comprehend the gravity of the situation. She must be mistaking the stranger for one of the farmer-lads of the region.

The young man stood his gun beside the door, and dropped a heavy game-bag beside it; then he bade Mrs. Tilley good-evening, and repeated his wayfarer's story, and asked if he could have a night's lodging.

"Put me anywhere you like," he said. "I must be off early in the morning, before day; but I am very hungry, indeed. You can give me some milk at any rate, that's plain."

"Dear sakes, yes," responded the hostess, whose long slumbering hospitality seemed to be easily awakened. "You might fare better if you went out on the main road a mile or so, but you're welcome to what we've got. I'll milk right off, and you make yourself at home. You can sleep on husks or feathers," she proffered graciously. "I raised them all myself. There's good pasturing for geese just below here towards the ma'sh. Now step round and set a plate for the gentleman, Sylvy!" and Sylvia promptly stepped. She was glad to have something to do, and she was hungry herself.

It was a surprise to find so clean and comfortable a little dwelling in this

New England wilderness. The young man had known the horrors of its most primitive housekeeping, and the dreary squalor of that level of society which does not rebel at the companionship of hens. This was the best thrift of an old-fashioned farmstead, though on such a small scale it seemed like a hermitage. He listened eagerly to the old woman's quaint talk, he watched Sylvia's pale face and shining gray eyes with ever growing enthusiasm, and insisted that this was the best supper he had eaten for a month; then, afterward, the new-made friends sat down in the doorway together while the moon came up.

Soon it would be berry-time, and Sylvia was a great help at picking. The cow was a good milker, though a plaguy thing to keep track of, the hostess gossiped frankly, adding presently that she had buried four children, so that Sylvia's mother, and a son (who might be dead) in California were all the children she had left. "Dan, my boy, was a great hand to go gunning," she explained sadly. "I never wanted for pa'tridges or gray squer'ls while he was to home. He's been a great wand'rer, I expect, and he's no hand to write letters. There, I don't blame him, I'd ha' seen the world myself if it had been so I could.

16   "Sylvia takes after him," the grandmother continued affectionately, after a minute's pause. "There ain't a foot o' ground she don't know her way over, and the wild creatur's counts her one o' themselves. Squer'ls she'll tame to come an' feed right out o' her hands, and all sorts o' birds. Last winter she got the jay-birds to bangeing[1] here, and I believe she'd 'a' scanted herself of her own meals to have plenty to throw out amongst 'em, if I hadn't kep' watch. Anything but crows, I tell her, I'm willin' to help support,—though Dan he went an' tamed one o' them that did seem to have reason same as folks. It was round here a good spell after he went away. Dan an' his father they didn't hitch,—but he never held up his head ag'in after Dan had dared him an' gone off."

The guest did not notice this hint of family sorrows in his eager interest in something else.

"So Sylvy knows all about birds, does she?" he exclaimed, as he looked round at the little girl who sat, very demure but increasingly sleepy, in the moonlight. "I am making a collection of birds myself. I have been at it ever since I was a boy." (Mrs. Tilley smiled.) "There are two or three very rare ones I have been hunting for these five years. I mean to get them on my own ground if they can be found."

"Do you cage 'em up?" asked Mrs. Tilley doubtfully, in response to this enthusiastic announcement.

20   "Oh, no, they're stuffed and preserved, dozens and dozens of them," said the ornithologist, "and I have shot or snared every one myself. I caught a glimpse of a white heron three miles from here on Saturday, and I have

[1]To loiter, tarry.

followed it in this direction. They have never been found in this district at all. The little white heron, it is," and he turned again to look at Sylvia with the hope of discovering that the rare bird was one of her acquaintances.

But Sylvia was watching a hop-toad in the narrow footpath.

"You would know the heron if you saw it," the stranger continued eagerly. "A queer tall white bird with soft feathers and long thin legs. And it would have a nest perhaps in the top of a high tree, made of sticks, something like a hawk's nest."

Sylvia's heart gave a wild beat; she knew that strange white bird, and had once stolen softly near where it stood in some bright green swamp grass, away over at the other side of the woods. There was an open place where the sunshine always seemed strangely yellow and hot, where tall, nodding rushes grew, and her grandmother had warned her that she might sink in the soft black mud underneath and never be heard of more. Not far beyond were the salt marshes and beyond those was the sea, the sea which Sylvia wondered and dreamed about, but never had looked upon, though its great voice could often be heard above the noise of the woods on stormy nights.

"I can't think of anything I should like so much as to find that heron's nest," the handsome stranger was saying. "I would give ten dollars to anybody who could show it to me," he added desperately, "and I mean to spend my whole vacation hunting for it if need be. Perhaps it was only migrating, or had been chased out of its own region by some bird of prey."

Mrs. Tilley gave amazed attention to all this, but Sylvia still watched the toad, not divining, as she might have done at some calmer time, that the creature wished to get to its hole under the doorstep, and was much hindered by the unusual spectators at that hour of the evening. No amount of thought, that night, could decide how many wished-for treasures the ten dollars, so lightly spoken of, would buy.

The next day the young sportsman hovered about the woods, and Sylvia kept him company, having lost her first fear of the friendly lad, who proved to be most kind and sympathetic. He told her many things about the birds and what they knew and where they lived and what they did with themselves. And he gave her a jack-knife, which she thought as great a treasure as if she were a desert-islander. All day long he did not once make her troubled or afraid except when he brought down some unsuspecting singing creature from its bough. Sylvia would have liked him vastly better without his gun; she could not understand why he killed the very birds he seemed to like so much. But as the day waned, Sylvia still watched the young man with loving admiration. She had never seen anybody so charming and delightful; the woman's heart, asleep in the child, was vaguely thrilled by a dream of love. Some premonition of that great power stirred and swayed these young foresters who traversed the solemn woodlands with soft-footed silent care. They stopped to listen to a bird's song; they pressed forward again eagerly, parting the branches,—speaking to each other rarely and in whispers; the

24

young man going first and Sylvia following, fascinated, a few steps behind, with her gray eyes dark with excitement.

She grieved because the longed-for white heron was elusive, but she did not lead the guest, she only followed, and there was no such thing as speaking first. The sound of her own unquestioned voice would have terrified her,—it was hard enough to answer yes or no when there was need of that. At last evening began to fall, and they drove the cow home together, and Sylvia smiled with pleasure when they came to the place where she heard the whistle and was afraid only the night before.

II

Half a mile from home, at the farther edge of the woods, where the land was highest, a great pine-tree stood, the last of its generation. Whether it was left for a boundary mark, or for what reason, no one could say; the woodchoppers who had felled its mates were dead and gone long ago, and a whole forest of sturdy trees, pines and oaks and maples, had grown again. But the stately head of this old pine towered above them all and made a landmark for sea and shore miles and miles away. Sylvia knew it well. She had always believed that whoever climbed to the top of it could see the ocean; and the little girl had often laid her hand on the great rough trunk and looked up wistfully at those dark boughs that the wind always stirred, no matter how hot and still the air might be below. Now she thought of the tree with a new excitement, for why, if one climbed it at break of day, could not one see all the world, and easily discover whence the white heron flew, and mark the place, and find the hidden nest?

What a spirit of adventure, what wild ambition! What fancied triumph and delight and glory for the later morning when she could make known the secret! It was almost too real and too great for the childish heart to bear.

All night the door of the little house stood open, and the whippoorwills came and sang upon the very step. The young sportsman and his old hostess were sound asleep, but Sylvia's great design kept her broad awake and watching. She forgot to think of sleep. The short summer night seemed as long as the winter darkness, and at last when the whippoorwills ceased, and she was afraid the morning would after all come too soon, she stole out of the house and followed the pasture path through the woods, hastening toward the open ground beyond, listening with a sense of comfort and companionship to the drowsy twitter of a half-awakened bird, whose perch she had jarred in passing. Alas, if the great wave of human interest which flooded for the first time this dull little life should sweep away the satisfaction of an existence heart to heart with nature and the dumb life of the forest!

There was the huge tree asleep yet in the paling moonlight, and small and hopeful Sylvia began with utmost bravery to mount to the top of it, with tingling, eager blood coursing the channels of her whole frame, with her bare

feet and fingers, that pinched and held like bird's claws to the monstrous
ladder reaching up, up, almost to the sky itself. First she must mount the
white oak tree that grew alongside, where she was almost lost among the dark
branches and the green leaves heavy and wet with dew; a bird fluttered off
its nest, and a red squirrel ran to and fro and scolded pettishly at the harmless
housebreaker. Sylvia felt her way easily. She had often climbed there, and
knew that higher still one of the oak's upper branches chafed against the pine
trunk, just where its lower boughs were set close together. There, when she
made the dangerous pass from one tree to the other, the great enterprise
would really begin.

She crept out along the swaying oak limb at last, and took the daring step [32]
across into the old pine-tree. The way was harder than she thought; she must
reach far and hold fast, the sharp dry twigs caught and held her and scratched
her like angry talons, the pitch made her thin little fingers clumsy and stiff as
she went round and round the tree's great stem, higher and higher upward.
The sparrows and robins in the woods below were beginning to wake and
twitter to the dawn, yet it seemed much lighter there aloft in the pine-tree,
and the child knew that she must hurry if her project were to be of any use.

The tree seemed to lengthen itself out as she went up, and to reach
farther and farther upward. It was like a great main-mast to the voyaging
earth; it must truly have been amazed that morning through all its ponderous
frame as it felt this determined spark of human spirit creeping and climbing
from higher branch to branch. Who knows how steadily the least twigs held
themselves to advantage this light, weak creature on her way! The old pine
must have loved his new dependent. More than all the hawks, and bats, and
moths, and even the sweet-voiced thrushes, was the brave, beating heart of
the solitary gray-eyed child. And the tree stood still and held away the winds
that June morning while the dawn grew bright in the east.

Sylvia's face was like a pale star, if one had seen it from the ground, when
the last thorny bough was past, and she stood trembling and tired but wholly
triumphant, high in the tree-top. Yes, there was the sea with the dawning sun
making a golden dazzle over it, and toward that glorious east flew two hawks
with slow-moving pinions. How low they looked in the air from that height
when before one had only seen them far up, and dark against the blue sky.
Their gay feathers were as soft as moths; they seemed only a little way from
the tree, and Sylvia felt as if she too could go flying away among the clouds.
Westward, the woodlands and farms reached miles and miles into the distance; here and there were church steeples, and white villages; truly it was a
vast and awesome world.

The birds sang louder and louder. At last the sun came up bewilderingly
bright. Sylvia could see the white sails of ships out at sea, and the clouds that
were purple and rose-colored and yellow at first began to fade away. Where
was the white heron's nest in the sea of green branches, and was this
wonderful sight and pageant of the world the only reward for having climbed

to such a giddy height? Now look down again, Sylvia, where the green marsh is set among the shining birches and dark hemlocks; there where you saw the white heron once you will see him again; look, look! a white spot of him like a single floating feather comes up from the dead hemlock and grows larger, and rises, and comes close at last, and goes by the landmark pine with steady sweep of wing and outstretched slender neck and crested head. And wait! wait! do not move a foot or a finger, little girl, do not send an arrow of light and consciousness from your two eager eyes, for the heron has perched on a pine bough not far beyond yours, and cries back to his mate on the nest, and plumes his feathers for the new day!

36 The child gives a long sigh a minute later when a company of shouting cat-birds comes also to the tree, and vexed by their fluttering and lawlessness the solemn heron goes away. She knows his secret now, the wild, light, slender bird that floats and wavers, and goes back like an arrow presently to his home in the green world beneath. Then Sylvia, well satisfied, makes her perilous way down again, not daring to look far below the branch she stands on, ready to cry sometimes because her fingers ache and her lamed feet slip. Wondering over and over again what the stranger would say to her, and what he would think when she told him how to find his way straight to the heron's nest.

"Sylvy, Sylvy!" called the busy old grandmother again and again, but nobody answered, and the small husk bed was empty, and Sylvia had disappeared.

The guest waked from a dream, and remembering his day's pleasure hurried to dress himself that it might sooner begin. He was sure from the way the shy little girl looked once or twice yesterday that she had at least seen the white heron, and now she must really be persuaded to tell. Here she comes now, paler than ever, and her worn old frock is torn and tattered, and smeared with pine pitch. The grandmother and the sportsman stand in the door together and question her, and the splendid moment has come to speak of the dead hemlock-tree by the green marsh.

But Sylvia does not speak after all, though the old grandmother fretfully rebukes her, and the young man's kind appealing eyes are looking straight into her own. He can make them rich with money; he has promised it, and they are poor now. He is so well worth making happy, and he waits to hear the story she can tell.

40 No, she must keep her silence! What is it that suddenly forbids her and makes her dumb? Has she been nine years growing, and now, when the great world for the first time puts out a hand to her, must she thrust it aside for a bird's sake? The murmur of the pine's green branches is in her ears, she remembers how the white heron came flying through the golden air and how they watched the sea and the morning together, and Sylvia cannot speak; she cannot tell the heron's secret and give its life away.

Dear loyalty, that suffered a sharp pang as the guest went away disappointed later in the day, that could have served and followed him and loved him as a dog loves! Many a night Sylvia heard the echo of his whistle haunting the pasture path as she came home with the loitering cow. She forgot even her sorrow at the sharp report of his gun and the piteous sight of thrushes and sparrows dropping silent to the ground, their songs hushed and their pretty feathers stained and wet with blood. Were the birds better friends than their hunter might have been,—who can tell? Whatever treasures were lost to her, woodlands and summer-time, remember! Bring your gifts and graces and tell your secrets to this lonely country child!

Understanding What You Read

1. How does the young ornithologist befriend Sylvia?
2. What does Sylvia fail to understand about him?
3. What does he offer in exchange for her assistance finding the white heron?
4. What does her refusal suggest?
5. What expressions and other details let you know that this story was written in the nineteenth century?

Writing About What You Read

1. Write an essay about Sylvia's choice to protect the bird. What does it suggest about her values and prospects for a future life. What is she giving up and what is she gaining?
2. Imagine that after the young man leaves, he writes a letter to the girl. Write that letter, affirming or criticizing her choice.

Making Connections

1. Both Mann and Plummer's "The Butterfly Problem" and Titone's "Balance of Power" are concerned with the Endangered Species Act. One species, a butterfly, has no known economic value; the other, the salmon, does. Should this make a difference?
2. Contrast the development of western Kentucky in Berry's "Mayhem in the Industrial Paradise" with that of the Piedmont of North Carolina described by Wallace Kaufman ("Confessions of a Developer").

3. In both Postel's "An Illusion of Plenty" and Cronon's "Kennecott Journey," resources (water and copper) are transported long distances to support a complex civilization. What are the choices and trade-offs involved in each case?

4. Compare the overall environmental damage (including that suffered by human beings) described in Berry's "Mayhem in the Industrial Paradise" and "Kennecott Journey."

5. Rukeyser's "Alloy" and Berry's "Mayhem in the Industrial Paradise" both explore the effects of mining on landscapes and communities. What concerns do they share? How do they differ in emphasis?

7 SIGNS OF TROUBLE

Public concern has at last driven political leaders to acknowledge what scientists have been telling us for years—that river-basin pollution, the burning of forests, acid rain, destruction of the ozone layer, and global warming transcend national boundaries and must have international solutions.

—Bruce Babbitt, *World Monitor*

◆

Children are still a big part of the farm labor force. Or they are taken to the fields by their parents because there is no child care. Pregnant women labor in the fields to help support their families. Toxic exposure begins at a very young age, often in the womb.

—Cesar Chavez

◆

Environmental destruction is an injustice visited upon the vulnerable—the poor, the young and elderly, red, yellow, black, brown, and white.

—Jesse Jackson

◆

Dangerous chemicals are found in almost every household article. Carcinogens are used to dry-clean clothes, and traces of chemicals often remain on the garments when we collect them from the shop—you can actually smell them. Paints and thinners are supplemented with toxic chemicals designed to discourage fungal growth or act as quick-drying agents. Cancer-causing chemicals are used to kill termites, cockroaches, and insects in homes, offices, schools, hospitals, and restaurants. Cleaners and deodorizers contain toxic chemicals, as do garden pesticides and fungicides. Toxic fumes emanate from synthetic carpets, furnishings, and curtains. Carcinogenic formaldehyde leaches into the air from certain types of insulation and fabrics used in walls and ceiling.

—Helen Caldicott, *If You Love This Planet: A Plan to Heal the Earth*

What Have We Done?
(Paul van Peenan)

Introduction

When the new factories and trains began to pour smoke into the heavy, wet air of nineteenth-century England, signs of trouble were made plainly visible. The Industrial Revolution that started there soon spread through much of Europe; and as the century progressed, more and more factories blackened the sky and fouled the water.

While factories polluted the air over England, a different kind of environmental degradation was under way in North America. As early as the seventeenth century, settlers on the Eastern seaboard were denuding coastal areas of old-growth forests, virtually exterminating some species of hardwood in the course of building settlements. Then, as they penetrated further inland, they cut down trees, again for building materials and firewood, but also to clear land for agriculture. Where Native Americans had used the resources of the forests for food, fuel, and shelter without significant damage to the environment, with the arrival of Europeans, the destruction of the landscape became equated with progress.

Animals, too, were not seen as solely a source of food and clothing, but a commodity. It was this attitude that led to the killings—of bison slaughtered by the millions, of the passenger pigeon to extinction, of huge numbers of seals and beaver whose pelts were exported for sale in Europe. It was this attitude that led to the defacement of mountains by miners in search of gold and to the waste of millions of barrels of oil by prospectors striking gushers that spewed oil across the landscape for days. First drilled for commercial use in Pennsylvania in 1859, oil was used to fuel kerosene lamps for more than twenty-five years before the development of the internal combustion engine in 1885 gave oil its coveted status of "black gold."

Few people saw these developments as signs of trouble. Nor did they realize that overgrazing the plains and plowing under the prairies would result in the massive disruption of fertile topsoil. Much of it was wasted, and what remained lay vulnerable to the inevitable droughts that would turn it into windblown dust. The Great Dust Bowl of the 1930s was finally a sign of trouble too large to ignore. A region in the Midwest of some 150,000 square miles was plagued first by drought and then by high winds that transformed the depleted dried soil into airborne dust and carried it many miles before depositing it over the eastern and southeastern United States. Many farmers left this impoverished land for California and other places where they thought life might be better. Federal agencies and local conservation groups rallied to rehabilitate the devastated lands of Kansas, Colorado, New Mexico, Oklahoma, and Texas. By 1941 the job was done, and farmers had learned soil-maintenance techniques still in use today—planting trees to break the wind, alternating drought-resistant crops with strips of fallow land, and contour-planting and terracing. Fundamentally, they learned that digging up the perennial prairie could have catastrophic consequences.

But by then the nation was at war, and no one was thinking of the environment. War industries were gearing up, notably the Manhattan Project which was mobilized to develop the atomic bomb. When World War II ended in 1945, Americans wanted to enjoy the peace and their attention was turned to the benefits of consumption, not its costs. The production and sale of consumer goods as well as the birthrate increased dramatically in the early fifties and sixties as Americans eagerly moved to newly built suburbs to raise their children (known as "baby boomers," and destined to become more voracious consumers than their parents). These families did not dream that the cars they were buying, the factories that produced their washing machines, the power plants that provided electricity to heat and cool their new homes, and the fertilizers and pesticides that made possible abundant food all would someday be blamed for acid rain and urban smog. Far from anyone's mind in the fifties and early sixties was the possibility that a miracle chemical used in plastic foams and refrigerators might someday deplete the ozone layer and thus increase the risk that a grandchild would contract skin cancer. Few people had ever heard of the ozone layer.

Following the war, atmospheric tests of nuclear weapons were conducted routinely, as Terry Tempest Williams recounts in "The Clan of One-Breasted Women." Few Americans saw these tests as a sign of trouble until, in the late fifties, a group of scientists and physicians, including Barry Commoner, organized the Committee for Nuclear Information to investigate the effects of radioactivity and to warn Americans that the consequences of these tests could be serious, even if the bombs were never again used in warfare. The sign of trouble came in the form of strontium 90, which showed up in the teeth of children who drank contaminated milk produced many miles from the test sites.

Throughout the fifties far more people worried about war with the Soviet Union than about our ongoing war with the planet. Just months before John F. Kennedy faced down Soviet premier Nikita Khrushchev over nuclear missiles in Cuba in the fall of 1962, Rachel Carson published *Silent Spring,* a book warning not just Americans but the entire world of the dangers of chemical pesticides, particularly DDT. Before the publication of this influential book, DDT had been considered a miracle chemical, capable of wiping out diseases by killing the insects that carry them and of increasing food production by destroying the pests that damage crops. The first selection in this chapter, taken from Carson's enormously influential book, compares the danger of excessive chemical use with that of radioactivity. Both are silent killers that invade organisms in ways that cannot be detected. Although DDT was banned in 1972 in the United States, it is still used in Latin American countries, sometimes on fruits exported to the United States. Carole Douglis's "Banana Split" surveys the damage done in Costa Rica by increasingly powerful new pesticides.

Carson's *Silent Spring* drew attention to a sign of trouble—the death of songbirds in Carson's backwoods—and also raised public awareness of the need to read the environment for such signs; however, much of the trouble can't be seen, smelled, or touched. A woman harboring a cancer caused by radioactive fallout does not necessarily know anything is wrong until a doctor tells her she has a potentially fatal disease; a man sitting beside a quiet lake in the Adirondack Mountains may not connect the silence around him or the clarity of the water with acid rain and the death of the lake. Many signs of trouble—declining bird populations and degraded rivers—are easily detected by careful observers. But even these detectable signs often require experts to explain their significance.

Why are there fewer birds? Why have frog populations disappeared? Why are the trees on the side of a hill turning brown in midsummer? Why is the sky not so blue as it seemed when you were a child? Why are the storms fiercer? The selections in this chapter answer some of these questions.

While exponential population growth is a hard concept to grasp, the population explosion is evident in everyday life. Even in America, signs are everywhere—on a crowded freeway at rush hour, on the beach in the middle of the summer, at a shopping mall during holidays. Paul and Anne Ehrlich make the essential connection between population and the major environmental problems; global warming, acid rain, depletion of ozone, soil impoverishment, declining water supplies. And Michael G. Coney's "The Byrds" is a futuristic fantasy set in a time when the pressures of population have reached such a point that people are encouraged to choose between life and "peace," a euphemism for death.

In the final selection in this chapter, Mark Schannon sees other signs of trouble in the breakdown of confidence between the public and industrial leaders. The crisis, for Schannon, is that citizens concerned about the environment don't trust those responsible for cleaning it up, and are more likely to get their information from movie stars than from scientific experts. We see the signs, but we don't know whom we can trust to interpret them.

RACHEL CARSON

Carson (1907–1964) was a marine biologist and writer. Awarded an M.A. degree from the Johns Hopkins University in 1932, a time when few women earned advanced degrees, she went on to write highly acclaimed books on sea life and wetlands: *Under the Sea Wind* (1941), *The Sea Around Us* (1951), and *The Edge of the Sea* (1954). During these years, Carson had worked full-time for the U.S. Fish and Wildlife Service, but in 1958 royalties from her books made it possible for her to give up her job to begin *Silent Spring*. Published in 1962, this influential book exposed the dangers of widespread use of pesticides, particularly DDT. At first attacked by the chemical industry, Carson was later vindicated by a panel of experts appointed by President John F. Kennedy. Because of the enormous influence of *Silent Spring*, Rachel Carson is considered by many to be the founder of the modern environmental movement. "The Obligation to Endure" is from *Silent Spring*.

The Obligation to Endure

THE HISTORY of life on earth has been a history of interaction between living things and their surroundings. To a large extent, the physical form and the habits of the earth's vegetation and its animal life have been molded by the environment. Considering the whole span of earthly time, the opposite effect, in which life actually modifies its surroundings, has been relatively slight. Only within the moment of time represented by the present century has one species—man—acquired significant power to alter the nature of his world.

During the past quarter century this power has not only increased to one of disturbing magnitude but it has changed in character. The most alarming of all man's assaults upon the environment is the contamination of air, earth, rivers, and sea with dangerous and even lethal materials. This pollution is for the most part irrecoverable; the chain of evil it initiates not only in the world that must support life but in living tissues is for the most part irreversible. In this now universal contamination of the environment, chemicals are the sinister and little-recognized partners of radiation in changing the very nature of the world—the very nature of its life. Strontium 90, released through nuclear explosions into the air, comes to earth in rain or drifts down as fallout, lodges in soil, enters into the grass or corn or wheat grown there, and in time takes up its abode in the bones of a human being, there to remain until his death. Similarly, chemicals sprayed on croplands or forests or gardens lie long in soil, entering into living organisms, passing from one to another in a chain of poisoning and death. Or they pass mysteriously by underground streams until they emerge and, through the alchemy of air and sunlight, combine into new forms that kill vegetation, sicken cattle, and work unknown harm on those who drink from once pure wells. As Albert Schweitzer[1] has said, "Man can hardly even recognize the devils of his own creation."

It took hundreds of millions of years to produce the life that now inhabits the earth—eons of time in which that developing and evolving and diversifying life reached a state of adjustment and balance with its surroundings. The environment, rigorously shaping and directing the life it supported, con-

---

[1]A philosopher, theologian, concert organist, and physician, Schweitzer (1875–1965) devoted his life to helping others, mainly as a medical missionary in Africa.

tained elements that were hostile as well as supporting. Certain rocks gave out dangerous radiation; even within the light of the sun, from which all life draws its energy, there were shortwave radiations with power to injure. Given time—time not in years but in millennia—life adjusts, and a balance has been reached. For time is the essential ingredient; but in the modern world there is no time.

The rapidity of change and the speed with which new situations are created follow the impetuous and heedless pace of man rather than the deliberate pace of nature. Radiation is no longer merely the background radiation of rocks, the bombardment of cosmic rays, the ultraviolet of the sun that have existed before there was any life on earth; radiation is now the unnatural creation of man's tampering with the atom. The chemicals to which life is asked to make its adjustment are no longer merely the calcium and silica and copper and all the rest of the minerals washed out of the rocks and carried in rivers to the sea; they are the synthetic creations of man's inventive mind, brewed in his laboratories, and having no counterparts in nature. 4

To adjust to these chemicals would require time on the scale that is nature's; it would require not merely the years of a man's life but the life of generations. And even this, were it by some miracle possible, would be futile, for the new chemicals come from our laboratories in an endless stream; almost 500 annually find their way into actual use in the United States alone. The figure is staggering and its implications are not easily grasped—500 new chemicals to which the bodies of men and animals are required somehow to adapt each year, chemicals totally outside the limits of biologic experience.

Among them are many that are used in man's war against nature. Since the mid-1940s over 200 basic chemicals have been created for use in killing insects, weeds, rodents, and other organisms described in the modern vernacular as "pests"; and they are sold under several thousand different brand names.

These sprays, dusts, and aerosols are now applied almost universally to farms, gardens, forests, and homes—nonselective chemicals that have the power to kill every insect, the "good" and the "bad," to still the song of birds and the leaping of fish in the streams, to coat the leaves with a deadly film, and to linger on in soil—all this though the intended target may be only a few weeds or insects. Can anyone believe it is possible to lay down such a barrage of poisons on the surface of the earth without making it unfit for all life? They should not be called "insecticides," but "biocides."

The whole process of spraying seems caught up in an endless spiral. Since DDT[2] was released for civilian use, a process of escalation has been going on in which ever more toxic materials must be found. This has happened because 8

[2]Insecticide banned in the U.S. in 1972 and in some European countries in the 1960s. DDT is still used in developing countries (see page 374).

insects, in a triumphant vindication of Darwin's[3] principle of the survival of the fittest, have evolved super races immune to the particular insecticide used, hence a deadlier one has always to be developed—and then a deadlier one than that. It has happened also because, for reasons to be described later, destructive insects often undergo a "flareback," or resurgence, after spraying, in numbers greater than before. Thus the chemical war is never won, and all life is caught in its violent crossfire.

Along with the possibility of the extinction of mankind by nuclear war, the central problem of our age has therefore become the contamination of man's total environment with such substances of incredible potential for harm—substances that accumulate in the tissues of plants and animals and even penetrate the germ cells to shatter or alter the very material of heredity upon which the shape of the future depends.

Some would-be architects of our future look toward a time when it will be possible to alter the human germ plasm by design. But we may easily be doing so now by inadvertence, for many chemicals, like radiation, bring about gene mutations. It is ironic to think that man might determine his own future by something so seemingly trivial as the choice of an insect spray.

All this has been risked—for what? Future historians may well be amazed by our distorted sense of proportion. How could intelligent beings seek to control a few unwanted species by a method that contaminated the entire environment and brought the threat of disease and death even to their own kind? Yet this is precisely what we have done. We have done it, moreover, for reasons that collapse the moment we examine them. We are told that the enormous and expanding use of pesticides is necessary to maintain farm production. Yet is our real problem not one of *overproduction*? Our farms, despite measures to remove acreages from production and to pay farmers *not* to produce, have yielded such a staggering excess of crops that the American taxpayer in 1962 is paying out more than one billion dollars a year as the total carrying cost of the surplus-food storage program. And is the situation helped when one branch of the Agriculture Department tries to reduce production while another states, as it did in 1958, "It is believed generally that reduction of crop acreages under provisions of the Soil Bank[4] will stimulate interest in use of chemicals to obtain maximum production on the land retained in crops."

12   All this is not to say there is no insect problem and no need of control. I am saying, rather, that control must be geared to realities, not to mythical situations, and that the methods employed must be such that they do not destroy us along with the insects.

The problem whose attempted solution has brought such a train of disaster in its wake is an accompaniment of our modern way of life. Long before the

[3]Charles Darwin (1809–1892), English naturalist who theorized that those organisms that adapt to their environments will survive and pass on adaptive genetic traits to their offspring.
[4]A federal program to divert farm land from production to conservation, begun in 1956.

age of man, insects inhabited the earth—a group of extraordinarily varied and adaptable beings. Over the course of time since man's advent, a small percentage of the more than half a million species of insects have come into conflict with human welfare in two principal ways: as competitors for the food supply and as carriers of human disease.

Disease-carrying insects become important where human beings are crowded together, especially under conditions where sanitation is poor, as in time of natural disaster or war or in situations of extreme poverty and deprivation. Then control of some sort becomes necessary. It is a sobering fact, however, that the method of massive chemical control has had only limited success, and also threatens to worsen the very conditions it is intended to curb.

Under primitive agricultural conditions the farmer had few insect problems. These arose with the intensification of agriculture—the devotion of immense acreages to a single crop. Such a system set the stage for explosive increases in specific insect populations. Single-crop farming does not take advantage of the principles by which nature works; it is agriculture as an engineer might conceive it to be. Nature has introduced great variety into the landscape, but man has displayed a passion for simplifying it. Thus he undoes the built-in checks and balances by which nature holds the species within bounds. One important natural check is a limit on the amount of suitable habitat for each species. Obviously then, an insect that lives on wheat can build up its population to much higher levels on a farm devoted to wheat than on one in which wheat is intermingled with other crops to which the insect is not adapted.

The same thing happens in other situations. A generation or more ago, the towns of large areas of the United States lined their streets with the noble elm tree. Now the beauty they hopefully created is threatened with complete destruction as disease sweeps through the elms, carried by a beetle that would have only limited chance to build up large populations and to spread from tree to tree if the elms were only occasional trees in a richly diversified planting.

Another factor in the modern insect problem is one that must be viewed against a background of geologic and human history: the spreading of thousands of different kinds of organisms from their native homes to invade new territories. This worldwide migration has been studied and graphically described by the British ecologist Charles Elton in his recent book *The Ecology of Invasions*. During the Cretaceous Period, some hundred million years ago, flooding seas cut many land bridges between continents and living things found themselves confined in what Elton calls "colossal separate nature reserves." There, isolated from others of their kind, they developed many new species. When some of the landmasses were joined again, about fifteen million years ago, these species began to move out into new territories—a movement that is not only still in progress but is now receiving considerable assistance from man.

16

The importation of plants is the primary agent in the modern spread of species, for animals have almost invariably gone along with the plants, quarantine being a comparatively recent and not completely effective innovation. The United States Office of Plant Introduction alone has introduced almost 200,000 species and varieties of plants from all over the world. Nearly half of the 180 or so major insect enemies of plants in the United States are accidental imports from abroad, and most of them have come as hitchhikers on plants.

In new territory, out of reach of the restraining hand of the natural enemies that kept down its numbers in its native land, an invading plant or animal is able to become enormously abundant. Thus it is no accident that our most troublesome insects are introduced species.

20   These invasions, both the naturally occurring and those dependent on human assistance, are likely to continue indefinitely. Quarantine and massive chemical campaigns are only extremely expensive ways of buying time. We are faced, according to Dr. Elton, "with a life-and-death need not just to find new technological means of suppressing this plant or that animal"; instead we need the basic knowledge of animal populations and their relations to their surroundings that will "promote an even balance and damp down the explosive power of outbreaks and new invasions."

Much of the necessary knowledge is now available but we do not use it. We train ecologists in our universities and even employ them in our governmental agencies but we seldom take their advice. We allow the chemical death rain to fall as though there were no alternative, whereas in fact there are many, and our ingenuity could soon discover many more if given opportunity.

Have we fallen into a mesmerized state that makes us accept as inevitable that which is inferior or detrimental, as though having lost the will or the vision to demand that which is good? Such thinking, in the words of the ecologist Paul Shepard, "idealizes life with only its head out of water, inches above the limits of toleration of the corruption of its own environment. . . . Why should we tolerate a diet of weak poisons, a home in insipid surroundings, a circle of acquaintances who are not quite our enemies, the noise of motors with just enough relief to prevent insanity? Who would want to live in a world which is just not quite fatal?"

Yet such a world is pressed upon us. The crusade to create a chemically sterile, insect-free world seems to have engendered a fanatic zeal on the part of many specialists and most of the so-called control agencies. On every hand there is evidence that those engaged in spraying operations exercise a ruthless power. "The regulatory entomologists . . . function as prosecutor, judge and jury, tax assessor and collector and sheriff to enforce their own orders," said Connecticut entomologist Neely Turner. The most flagrant abuses go unchecked in both state and federal agencies.

24   It is not my contention that chemical insecticides must never be used. I do contend that we have put poisonous and biologically potent chemicals

indiscriminately into the hands of persons largely or wholly ignorant of their potentials for harm. We have subjected enormous numbers of people to contact with these poisons, without their consent and often without their knowledge. If the Bill of Rights contains no guarantee that a citizen shall be secure against lethal poisons distributed either by private individuals or by public officials, it is surely only because our forefathers, despite their considerable wisdom and foresight, could conceive of no such problem.

I contend, furthermore, that we have allowed these chemicals to be used with little or no advance investigation of their effect on soil, water, wildlife, and man himself. Future generations are unlikely to condone our lack of prudent concern for the integrity of the natural world that supports all life.

There is still very limited awareness of the nature of the threat. This is an era of specialists, each of whom sees his own problem and is unaware of or intolerant of the larger frame into which it fits. It is also an era dominated by industry, in which the right to make a dollar at whatever cost is seldom challenged. When the public protests, confronted with some obvious evidence of damaging results of pesticide applications, it is fed little tranquilizing pills of half truth. We urgently need an end to these false assurances, to the sugar coating of unpalatable facts. It is the public that is being asked to assume the risks that the insect controllers calculate. The public must decide whether it wishes to continue on the present road, and it can do so only when in full possession of the facts. In the words of Jean Rostand,[5] "The obligation to endure gives us the right to know."

[5]French biologist (1894–1977) and author of important works on the place of biology in human culture.

Understanding What You Read

1. Carson's observations about the power of humans to alter the nature of the world were written in 1962. What further evidence of our power to alter the nature of the world has appeared since then?
2. What changes in agricultural practices does she recommend to reduce pesticide use?

Writing About What You Read

1. Carson concludes by quoting a French scientist's statement, "The obligation to endure gives us the right to know." Choose an environmental issue that you would like to know more about and write a detailed statement specifying what you want to know.
2. Go to the library and search for answers to these questions.

CAROLE DOUGLIS

Director of communications at Worldwatch Institute and a science writer, Douglis (b. 1955) has been published in the *Atlantic Monthly, National Geographic, Wilderness,* and *Harper's.* "Banana Split" is from the January/February 1993 *Worldwatch* magazine.

Banana Split

IN THE 1880s, when a young railroad baron from Brooklyn planted banana trees along the Atlantic coast of Costa Rica, he could hardly have known that he was sowing the destinies of entire economies.

Over the next century the banana trade boomed as the Old World transplant became the world's most widely consumed fruit. The business that Minor Cooper Keith started became the United Fruit Company—still the world's largest fruit producer—now known as Chiquita Brands. And, thanks too to the gunboat diplomacy that helped keep power in the hands of rulers friendly to the multinational fruit companies, Central American nations earned the epithet "Banana Republics."

What's good for bananas, though, isn't necessarily good for banana workers or the land. In Costa Rica and other banana-exporting countries, the sweet fruit has left behind a bitter legacy of environmental decline and pesticide-related health problems. But for the last year and a half, growers, government officials, workers, and environmentalists have come together in unprecedented—if sometimes uneasy—cooperation to devise ways of growing a more environmentally "friendly" banana.

4   Costa Rican environmentalists have long decried banana plantations for their abuse of the country's natural systems, from heavy pesticide doses to sloppily handled waste, rain forest toppling, and soil runoff. The rest of the world began to take notice in 1985, when a lawsuit was filed on behalf of some of the 2,000 banana workers allegedly sterilized by the pesticide dibromochloropropane (DBCP) in the 1970s. DBCP was used despite studies in the 1950s linking it to sterility in male lab animals. (Some of the *afectados,* as the workers call themselves, recently agreed to settle out of court.)

Costa Rica's plantation-grown banana crop is one of the most pesticide-intensive in the world. Unsafe methods of handling these chemicals cause hundreds of reported worker poisonings a year, as well as respiratory, skin, and eye problems among nearby residents. In fact, leading environmentalists point to pesticides as Costa Rica's top environmental problem.

The widespread criticism soon crescendoed into talk of an international boycott against Costa Rican bananas. In late 1991, the Costa Rican government and the multinational banana growers began to discuss the problems and to act on them. Bananas, after all, are the country's number one source of foreign exchange, earning $441 million in 1991 and employing 32,000 people.

The national growers' cooperative, Corbana, which includes the likes of Chiquita, Del Monte, and Dole, has directed its new environmental division to investigate pest-resistant banana strains and ways to reduce routine applications of pesticides. Checking banana trees carefully for pest problems can lead to spraying as needed, rather than on a set schedule. Such monitoring has already cut the number of aerial fumigations for black sigatoka, a common fungal disease, by more than a third. But airplanes still fog the plantations with chemicals about once every two weeks—down from about once a week.

Why so many chemicals in the first place? Growing in a monoculture—fields of a single variety—in a steamy tropical climate, banana plants are a prime, tasty target for all sorts of pests. The bulk of the chemicals are aimed at the leaves and roots savored by most pests, but the banana "fingers" are extraordinarily sensitive. The peels are easily scarred by insects, fungi, and touching—even by dust. So in addition to spraying, banana workers wrap each cluster of bananas in a bag of blue plastic doused with pesticides.

Only minuscule residues, if any, tend to linger on the edible part of the banana. But the bags, which are not reused, contribute to a massive waste disposal problem. In fact, each banana harvested leaves behind more than twice its weight in waste: the bags, cords, and plastic pesticide buckets, and organic waste, including rejected bananas and banana cluster stems.

Pieces of blue plastic litter the countryside and wash down irrigation ditches and rivers toward the coast; some rivers are said to "run blue" after a flood. Blue shreds, caught in branches when the water rises, hang from trees lining jungle canals. Strips of the plastic jam coral reefs. And pieces choke leatherback sea turtles that mistake the plastic for jellyfish.

Until recently, growers also let other garbage wash away into streams or burned it in the open air. As a result, growers and environmental groups have been looking into waste reduction and recycling techniques. Now some growers are composting the organic materials and simply picking up and storing the plastic bags while the industry decides what to do with them. Although there is talk of incinerating the bags, Corbana and other groups are also experimenting with recycling, which might turn bags into flower pots, building bricks, and prop-up poles for the banana plants.

Some growers, too, are beginning to reforest riverbanks to stem the high rates of erosion that afflict most banana fields. Costa Rican law mandates that at least 33 feet of forest be left bordering waterways. The law has been flouted for decades, however, and bananas often grow clear down to the water's edge. The resulting erosion of land and silting of water has killed fish populations and contributed to the decline of the country's Atlantic coast coral reefs.

In addition to Corbana's work is the ambitious Banana Amigo Project, sponsored by the U.S.-based Rainforest Alliance in partnership with the

Costa Rican groups Fundacion Ambio and Tsuli Tsuli/Audubon. Banana Amigo is helping all sides negotiate a code of conduct that covers waste disposal, use of water and agrochemicals, reforestation, and worker safety.

The Banana Amigo staff also hopes to promote environmental practices with a "reverse boycott." It plans to award a "Smart Banana" seal of approval to bananas grown in an ecologically improved manner and to persuade consumers to choose "Smart Bananas" even if they are blemished or smaller than other bananas. The first seals may appear in grocery stores at the beginning of 1993.

Even industry spokesmen admit that some of the changes in banana cultivation are long overdue. But the ecological improvements fail to address what is perhaps the most contentious issue of all: the amount of land—including rain forests—razed to make room for banana farms.

16   Hopeful of a larger European market, growers in recent years have been expanding their plantations. The area under production, currently 129 square miles in a country half the size of Tennessee, is expected to reach 193 square miles shortly. Some of this expansion has required leveling more rain forest, contributing to Costa Rica's dubious distinction of having the highest deforestation rate in Latin America over the last 30 years.

Critics also condemn the expansion of banana plantations because it disrupts Indian tribes and forces out small farmers growing food for local consumption.

While the banana industry's environmental plans do not include limiting its own growth, international politics and economics may apply the brakes instead. The European Community (EC) is now debating the possible use of tariffs to protect banana production in its countries, territories, and former colonies. Such a trade barrier could cut Costa Rica's banana exports to the EC by as much as 40 percent.

And an upstart industry—eco-tourism—is already second to bananas as a foreign exchange earner and may take the top spot in the next few years, according to the Ministry of Tourism. Eco-tourists, of course, value rain forest and a pristine environment more than plantations. Despite the alarming deforestation that has occurred over the years, Costa Rica is still home to an estimated 5 percent of the planet's biodiversity, most of that in its rain forests. If tourism manages to provide as many jobs as banana plantations have, it may prove the strongest incentive yet to clean up and limit banana production.

20   It is too early to tell how eagerly growers will carry out voluntary ecological guidelines. But, aided by sustained interest and gentle pressure from consumer nations, environmentalists and growers may manage to minimize the dark stains on the yellow fruit's reputation.

Understanding What You Read

1. What event in 1985 led to worldwide concern about pesticide use on bananas?
2. What harm to Costa Rica's environment has resulted from the way pesticides are applied to bananas?
3. What specific practices have been introduced to reduce the use of pesticides in Costa Rica?

Writing About What You Read

Write a paragraph about the possible undesirable consequences that might result if citizens in industrialized nations were to boycott Costa Rican bananas.

HOWARD YOUTH

Currently a free-lance writer living in Madras, India, Youth (b. 1956) previously specialized in avian behavior and population while at the Worldwatch Institute. "Birds Fast Disappearing" is from the World-watch publication *Vital Signs 1992: The Trends That Are Shaping Our Future.*

Birds Fast Disappearing

S O M E 9,000 bird species currently live in the world's forests, grasslands, deserts, wetlands, and other habitats. Through millions of years of evolution, each species has evolved a distinct set of living requirements. From a bee-sized hummingbird to an eight-foot-tall ostrich, each depends on adequate amounts of habitat in which to breed, feed, and rest. Extreme alteration to a particular habitat often elicits a quick drop or rise in that area's bird populations. Because of this sensitivity, and their high visibility, birds are barometers of environmental change.

Today, about 1,000 bird species—more than 11 percent—are at risk of extinction, while about 70 percent, or 6,300 species, are in decline. Habitat destruction is by far the most sinister threat to the majority of these birds, and to the other animals and plants that share their habitat. As the last large pockets of tropical forest—home to at least 3,500 bird species—fall to satisfy human needs for food, lumber, and minerals, even the freedom of flight cannot save birds.

Throughout history, human settlement has left behind a trail of bird extinctions. A wave of bird die-offs in Hawaii and other Pacific islands, for instance, resulted from overhunting by Polynesians even before Captain James Cook[1] arrived in 1778. Since then, exotic species introduced by western settlers have threatened most of the islands' remaining endemic species.

4   Similar effects have been felt on the mainland. From the mid-nineteenth century through the early twentieth, for example, virtually all large stands of virgin forest in the southeastern United States fell to loggers, while hunters took aim at birds for the plume trade and urban meat markets. By the twenties, the once-widespread ivory-billed woodpecker, Carolina parakeet, and passenger pigeon had become only museum memories.

Because they are easier to survey than other animals, birds are often accurate indicators of overall imbalances in a habitat that affect other species. The U.S. battle over the northern subspecies of spotted owl is, therefore, really over the future of old-growth forests in general, since not only the owl but also dozens of other species, from the red-backed vole to the Pacific yew tree, are in danger.

Judging from the health of certain avian populations, the health of the world's ecosystems is faltering. Many neotropical migrants, a group of about 150 songbirds, hawks, and shorebirds that winter in Central and South America but breed in North America, have shown alarming drops in population over the last 10–15 years (see Table 1), due primarily to deforestation in both the northern and southern parts of their ranges.

Common British woodland and farmland birds have been declining since the end of World War II, as 45 percent of the forests and 22 percent of the "natural boundary" hedgerows were plowed down to increase cropland size for larger, more modern machinery.

8   But birds do not reside only in forests, and their declines have been striking in other habitats as well. The disappearance of wetlands, mainly from conversion to farmland or industrial areas, has been marked by a sharp decline in duck species in North America as well as other water-dependent species. Overall, duck populations in the "prairie pothole" regions of the central United States and the southern half of Canada have dropped more than 30 percent since 1955.

The conversion of tidal flats in Japan to landfills, docking areas, and leisure resorts has severely reduced migrating bird concentration points. Along the U.S. East Coast, intense beachside recreation has eliminated from their only habitat the Snowy Plover (now listed as threatened) and other species, from ghost crabs to erosion-fighting beach grasses.

Birds are also reacting to changes humans cause in the earth's chemistry.

---

[1]An English explorer and navigator, Cook (1728–1779) circumnavigated the globe, charting the coasts of New Zealand and exploring much of the South Pacific.

Table 1: Declines in Some Widespread Neotropical Migrants, 1978–87	*Species*	*Annual Decline (percent)*
	Yellow-billed cuckoo	5
	Wood thrush	4
	Black-throated green warbler	3.1
	Northern oriole	2.9
	Canada warbler	2.7
	Northern Parula warbler	2.1
	Kentucky warbler	1.6
	Ovenbird	1

SOURCE: Chandler S. Robbins et al., "Population Declines in North American Birds That Migrate to the Neotropics," Proceedings of the National Academy of Sciences, Washington, D.C., June 29, 1989.

High levels of selenium resulting from chemical-laden agricultural water that washed into California's Kesterson National Wildlife Refuge and a number of other important wetlands resulted in failed nesting—due to embryo mortality and birth defects—of large numbers of common waterbirds.

Concentrations of organochlorine and heavy metals found in the tissue of shorebirds feeding in wetlands near Texas industrial sites indicate widespread danger of toxic contamination in wetlands. This buildup is an even greater danger to predators, which accumulate higher concentrations of toxins as they feed on contaminated shorebirds.

The population of the dipper, a semiaquatic bird that lives and feeds in rapidly flowing streams, has declined in Wales where pine plantations have replaced the native oak woods and made the water too acidic. The birds' increased scarcity is probably due to the fact that their prey, aquatic insects, cannot tolerate boosted acidity.

Pesticides are among the most difficult to track of all the dangers to birds. Numerous birds have been killed by the misuse of the insecticide Furadan on a variety of crops. In five incidents alone, this pesticide killed more than 5,000 ducks and geese that were feeding on or near sprayed alfalfa. Sprayings for locusts in Africa in 1986 and 1987 reportedly killed most birds unlucky enough to fall under the spray.

In the sixties, sharp declines in brown pelicans, ospreys, peregrine falcons, and bald eagles in North America led to a ban there of DDT, which caused birds to lay eggs with thinned shells that cracked prematurely during incubation. Since the ban, all four species have rebounded in varying degrees. Pesticide residues found in birds of prey in Africa and South America, where DDT is still widely used, indicate that the pesticide is taking a similar toll in the Third World.

12

Even harder to trace is the effect human activities have on the genetic makeup of species. As a species becomes rarer, its genetic pool narrows, reducing the genetic variability and health of species.

16   The ways in which humans coexist or choose to ignore other species will determine the biological diversity of the future. Currently, the most concentrated threat to bird—and other—species is in "biological hotspots," where unusually high numbers of endemic species, those unique to one location, are clustered in small areas. Recent studies of bird distribution reveal that 20 percent of all bird species occur in only 2 percent of the world's land. Most of this falls in tropical countries, the majority of which are still poorly studied and currently lack effective conservation programs.

The diminished health and disappearance of bird species worldwide indicates an environment at risk. Increasingly, it is becoming clear that the welfare of these winged indicators is inextricably tied to ours.

Understanding What You Read

1. Explain why birds are barometers of environmental change.
2. What has been the greatest threat to endemic species of the Hawaiian Islands?

Writing About What You Read

1. Summarize in your own words how the welfare of birds is linked to that of humans.
2. Find out about the bird populations where you live and write an essay about the prevalent species and what threatens them.

TERRY TEMPEST WILLIAMS

Born to a Mormon family in Utah, Williams (b. 1955) is the naturalist in residence at the Utah Museum of Natural History and sometimes teaches at the University of Utah. Her books include *Pieces of White Shell: A Journey to Navajoland* (1984) and *Coyote's Canyon* (1989), a collection of stories set in southern Utah. *Refuge: An Unnatural History of Family and Place* (1991), from which "The Clan of One-Breasted Women" is taken, weaves the story of her mother's battle with cancer with an account of the devastation to wildlife caused when the Great Salt Lake flooded the wetlands.

The Clan of One-Breasted Women

I BELONG to a Clan of One-Breasted Women. My mother, my grand-mothers, and six aunts have all had mastectomies. Seven are dead. The two who survive have just completed rounds of chemotherapy and radiation.

I've had my own problems: two biopsies for breast cancer and a small tumor between my ribs diagnosed as a "borderline malignancy."

This is my family history.

Most statistics tell us breast cancer is genetic, hereditary, with rising percentages attached to fatty diets, childlessness, or becoming pregnant after thirty. What they don't say is living in Utah may be the greatest hazard of all. 4

We are a Mormon family with roots in Utah since 1847. The "word of wisdom" in my family aligned us with good foods—no coffee, no tea, tobacco, or alcohol. For the most part, our women were finished having their babies by the time they were thirty. And only one faced breast cancer prior to 1960. Traditionally, as a group of people, Mormons have a low rate of cancer.

Is our family a cultural anomaly? The truth is, we didn't think about it. Those who did, usually the men, simply said, "bad genes." The women's attitude was stoic. Cancer was part of life. On February 16, 1971, the eve of my mother's surgery, I accidentally picked up the telephone and overheard her ask my grandmother what she could expect.

"Diane, it is one of the most spiritual experiences you will ever encoun-ter."

I quietly put down the receiver. 8

Two days later, my father took my brothers and me to the hospital to visit her. She met us in the lobby in a wheelchair. No bandages were visible. I'll never forget her radiance, the way she held herself in a purple velvet robe, and how she gathered us around her.

"Children, I am fine. I want you to know I felt the arms of God around me."

We believed her. My father cried. Our mother, his wife, was thirty-eight years old.

A little over a year after Mother's death, Dad and I were having dinner together. He had just returned from St. George, where the Tempest Com-pany was completing the gas lines that would service southern Utah. He spoke of his love for the country, the sandstoned landscape, bare-boned and beautiful. He had just finished hiking the Kolob trail in Zion National Park.[1] We got caught up in reminiscing, recalling with fondness our walk up Angel's Landing on his fiftieth birthday and the years our family had vacationed there. 12

Over dessert, I shared a recurring dream of mine. I told my father that

---

[1]Located in southwestern Utah, mainly in Washington County.

for years, as long as I could remember, I saw this flash of light in the night in the desert—that this image had so permeated my being that I could not venture south without seeing it again, on the horizon, illuminating buttes and mesas.

"You did see it," he said.

"Saw what?"

16 "The bomb. The cloud. We were driving home from Riverside, California. You were sitting on Diane's lap. She was pregnant. In fact, I remember the day, September 7, 1957. We had just gotten out of the service. We were driving north, past Las Vegas. It was an hour or so before dawn when this explosion went off. We not only heard it, but felt it. I thought the oil tanker in front of us had blown up. We pulled over and suddenly, rising from the desert floor, we saw it, clearly, this golden-stemmed cloud, the mushroom. The sky seemed to vibrate with an eerie pink glow. Within a few minutes, a light ash was raining on the car."

I stared at my father.

"I thought you knew that," he said. "It was a common occurrence in the fifties."

It was at this moment that I realized the deceit I had been living under. Children growing up in the American Southwest, drinking contaminated milk from contaminated cows, even from the contaminated breasts of their mothers, my mother—members, years later, of the Clan of One-Breasted Women.

20 It is a well-known story in the Desert West, "The Day We Bombed Utah," or more accurately, the years we bombed Utah: above-ground atomic testing in Nevada took place from January 27, 1951, through July 11, 1962. Not only were the winds blowing north covering "low-use segments of the population" with fallout and leaving sheep dead in their tracks, but the climate was right. The United States of the 1950s was red, white, and blue. The Korean War was raging. McCarthyism was rampant. Ike was it, and the cold war was hot.[2] If you were against nuclear testing, you were for a communist regime.

Much has been written about this "American nuclear tragedy." Public health was secondary to national security. The Atomic Energy Commissioner, Thomas Murray, said, "Gentlemen, we must not let anything interfere with this series of tests, nothing."

---

[2]Events and figures of the 1950s: the Korean War (1950–53) pitted the combined forces of the Republic of Korea and the United Nations against the invading armies of Communist North Korea; McCarthyism, after Republican senator Joseph S. McCarthy, refers to the Communist "witch hunt" led by the senator, which intensified a fear of Communism and in turn stimulated the buildup of nuclear weapons; "Ike" is the nickname of Dwight D. Eisenhower, president from 1953 to 1961; the Cold War refers to the power struggle from the end of World War II to the late 1980s between Communist countries under the influence of the USSR and the capitalist bloc represented by the United States and Western Europe.

Again and again, the American public was told by its government, in spite of burns, blisters, and nausea, "It has been found that the tests may be conducted with adequate assurance of safety under conditions prevailing at the bombing reservations." Assuaging public fears was simply a matter of public relations. "Your best action," an Atomic Energy Commission booklet read, "is not to be worried about fallout." A news release typical of the times stated, "We find no basis for concluding that harm to any individual has resulted from radioactive fallout."

On August 30, 1979, during Jimmy Carter's presidency, a suit was filed, *Irene Allen* v. *The United States of America*. Mrs. Allen's case was the first on an alphabetical list of twenty-four test cases, representative of nearly twelve hundred plaintiffs seeking compensation from the United States government for cancers caused by nuclear testing in Nevada.

Irene Allen lived in Hurricane, Utah. She was the mother of five children and had been widowed twice. Her first husband, with their two oldest boys, had watched the tests from the roof of the local high school. He died of leukemia in 1956. Her second husband died of pancreatic cancer in 1978.

24

In a town meeting conducted by Utah Senator Orrin Hatch, shortly before the suit was filed, Mrs. Allen said, "I am not blaming the government, I want you to know that, Senator Hatch. But I thought if my testimony could help in any way so this wouldn't happen again to any of the generations coming up after us . . . I am happy to be here this day to bear testimony of this."

God-fearing people. This is just one story in an anthology of thousands.

On May 10, 1984, Judge Bruce S. Jenkins handed down his opinion. Ten of the plaintiffs were awarded damages. It was the first time a federal court had determined that nuclear tests had been the cause of cancers. For the remaining fourteen test cases, the proof of causation was not sufficient. In spite of the split decision, it was considered a landmark ruling. It was not to remain so for long.

In April 1987, the Tenth Circuit Court of Appeals overturned Judge Jenkins's ruling on the ground that the United States was protected from suit by the legal doctrine of sovereign immunity, a centuries-old idea from England in the days of absolute monarchs.

28

In January 1988, the Supreme Court refused to review the Appeals Court decision. To our court system it does not matter whether the United States government was irresponsible, whether it lied to its citizens, or even that citizens died from the fallout of nuclear testing. What matters is that our government is immune: "The King can do no wrong."

In Mormon culture, authority is respected, obedience is revered, and independent thinking is not. I was taught as a young girl not to "make waves" or "rock the boat."

"Just let it go," Mother would say. "You know how you feel, that's what counts."

32   For many years, I have done just that—listened, observed, and quietly formed my own opinions, in a culture that rarely asks questions because it has all the answers. But one by one, I have watched the women in my family die common, heroic deaths. We sat in waiting rooms hoping for good news, but always receiving the bad. I cared for them, bathed their scarred bodies, and kept their secrets. I watched beautiful women become bald as Cytoxan, cisplatin, and Adriamycin[3] were injected into their veins. I held their foreheads as they vomited green-black bile, and I shot them with morphine when the pain became inhuman. In the end, I witnessed their last peaceful breaths, becoming a midwife to the rebirth of their souls.

The price of obedience has become too high.

The fear and inability to question authority that ultimately killed rural communities in Utah during atmospheric testing of atomic weapons is the same fear I saw in my mother's body. Sheep. Dead sheep. The evidence is buried.

I cannot prove that my mother, Diane Dixon Tempest, or my grandmothers, Lettie Romney Dixon and Kathryn Blackett Tempest, along with my aunts developed cancer from nuclear fallout in Utah. But I can't prove they didn't.

36   My father's memory was correct. The September blast we drove through in 1957 was part of Operation Plumbbob, one of the most intensive series of bomb tests to be initiated. The flash of light in the night in the desert, which I had always thought was a dream, developed into a family nightmare. It took fourteen years, from 1957 to 1971, for cancer to manifest in my mother—the same time, Howard L. Andrews, an authority in radioactive fallout at the National Institute of Health, says radiation cancer requires to become evident. The more I learn about what it means to be a "downwinder," the more questions I drown in.

What I do know, however, is that as a Mormon woman of the fifth generation of Latter-Day Saints, I must question everything, even if it means losing my faith, even if it means becoming a member of a border tribe among my own people. Tolerating blind obedience in the name of patriotism or religion ultimately takes our lives.

When the Atomic Energy Commission described the country north of the Nevada Test Site as "virtually uninhabited desert terrain," my family and the birds at Great Salt Lake were some of the "virtual uninhabitants."

One night, I dreamed women from all over the world circled a blazing fire in the desert. They spoke of change, how they hold the moon in their bellies and wax and wane with its phases. They mocked the presumption of even-tempered beings and made promises that they would never fear the witch

---

[3]Substances used in chemotherapy for cancer patients.

inside themselves. The women danced wildly as sparks broke away from the flames and entered the night sky as stars.

And they sang a song given to them by Shoshone[4] grandmothers: 40

Ah ne nah, nah	Consider the rabbits
nin nah nah—	How gently they walk on the earth—
ah ne nah, nah	Consider the rabbits
nin nah nah—	How gently they walk on the earth—
Nyaga mutzi	We remember them
oh ne nay—	We can walk gently also—
Nyaga mutzi	We remember them
oh ne nay—	We can walk gently also—

The women danced and drummed and sang for weeks, preparing themselves for what was to come. They would reclaim the desert for the sake of their children, for the sake of the land.

A few miles downwind from the fire circle, bombs were being tested. Rabbits felt the tremors. Their soft leather pads on paws and feet recognized the shaking sands, while the roots of mesquite and sage were smoldering. Rocks were hot from the inside out and dust devils hummedunnaturally. And each time there was another nuclear test, ravens watched the desert heave. Stretch marks appeared. The land was losing its muscle.

The women couldn't bear it any longer. They were mothers. They had suffered labor pains but always under the promise of birth. The red-hot pains beneath the desert promised death only, as each bomb became a stillborn. A contract had been made and broken between human beings and the land. A new contract was being drawn by the women, who understood the fate of the earth as their own.

Under the cover of darkness, ten women slipped under a barbed-wire fence and entered the contaminated country. They were trespassing. They walked toward the town of Mercury,[5] in moonlight, taking their cues from coyote, kit fox, antelope squirrel, and quail. They moved quietly and deliberately through the maze of Joshua trees. When a hint of daylight appeared they rested, drinking tea and sharing their rations of food. The women closed their eyes. The time had come to protest with the heart, that to deny one's genealogy with the earth was to commit treason against one's soul.

At dawn, the women draped themselves in mylar,[6] wrapping long streamers of silver plastic around their arms to blow in the breeze. They wore clear masks, that became the faces of humanity. And when they arrived at the edge 44

---

[4]Shoshonean Indians share a common linguistic heritage, and except for a few tribes, they live between the Rocky Mountains and the Sierra Nevada in semidesert, range, and sagebrush regions.

[5]Town in southern Nevada bordering the Nuclear Test Site.

[6]A filmy synthetic material.

of Mercury, they carried all the butterflies of a summer day in their wombs. They paused to allow their courage to settle.

The town that forbids pregnant women and children to enter because of radiation risks was asleep. The women moved through the streets as winged messengers, twirling around each other in slow motion, peeking inside homes and watching the easy sleep of men and women. They were astonished by such stillness and periodically would utter a shrill note or low cry just to verify life.

The residents finally awoke to these strange apparitions. Some simply stared. Others called authorities, and in time, the women were apprehended by wary soldiers dressed in desert fatigues. They were taken to a white, square building on the other edge of Mercury. When asked who they were and why they were there, the women replied, "We are mothers and we have come to reclaim the desert for our children."

The soldiers arrested them. As the ten women were blindfolded and handcuffed, they began singing:

> *You can't forbid us everything*
> *You can't forbid us to think—*
> *You can't forbid our tears to flow*
> *And you can't stop the songs that we sing.*

The women continued to sing louder and louder, until they heard the voices of their sisters moving across the mesa:

> *Ah ne nah, nah*
> *nin nah nah—*
> *Ah ne nah, nah*
> *nin nah nah—*
> *Nyaga mutzi*
> *oh ne nay—*
> *Nyaga mutzi*
> *oh ne nay—*

"Call for reinforcements," one soldier said.

"We have," interrupted one woman, "we have—and you have no idea of our numbers."

I crossed the line at the Nevada Test Site and was arrested with nine other Utahns for trespassing on military lands. They are still conducting nuclear tests in the desert. Ours was an act of civil disobedience. But as I walked toward the town of Mercury, it was more than a gesture of peace. It was a gesture on behalf of the Clan of One-Breasted Women.

As one officer cinched the handcuffs around my wrists, another frisked my body. She did not find my scars.

We were booked under an afternoon sun and bused to Tonopah,

Nevada. It was a two-hour ride. This was familiar country. The Joshua trees standing their ground had been named by my ancestors, who believed they looked like prophets pointing west to the Promised Land. These were the same trees that bloomed each spring, flowers appearing like white flames in the Mojave. And I recalled a full moon in May, when Mother and I had walked among them, flushing out mourning doves and owls.

The bus stopped short of town. We were released.

The officials thought it was a cruel joke to leave us stranded in the desert with no way to get home. What they didn't realize was that we were home, soul-centered and strong, women who recognized the sweet smell of sage as fuel for our spirits.

52

Understanding What You Read

1. What are the three parts of this essay?
2. What details about the Tempest family's experiences create an emotional response in readers?
3. What is the difference between the testing done in the 1950s and that carried out in the early 1990s?
4. Why were Americans building and testing nuclear weapons in the 1950s?
5. How does Williams's dream of women rebelling against what has happened to their bodies compare with her actual experience of joining a protest against nuclear testing?

Writing About What You Read

Imagine that you are a woman in Utah who has received a diagnosis of breast cancer, that you too remember seeing nuclear blasts as a child, and that you have just read Terry Tempest Williams's essay. Write a letter to your congressman explaining your experiences and request that the government take action. Be specific.

ANNE LA BASTILLE

LaBastille is an ecologist, consultant, wilderness guide, photographer, and writer. She holds a Ph.D. in wildlife ecology from Cornell University and has received many prestigious awards for her work in wildlife and wilderness conservation. Though she is widely known for her work in the Adirondack Mountains of New York and for the "simple" life she has chosen to live there, she has also spent more than twenty-five years researching an endangered water bird on Lake Atitlan in Guatemala. Her book *Mama Poc* (1990) tells that story. *Woodswoman* (1976) relates her experiences living alone in a cabin she built herself in the wilds of the Adirondacks. *Beyond Black Bear Lake* (1988), in which "Death from the Sky" appears, is the story of her life even deeper in the woods in a still smaller cabin she built in emulation of Thoreau's cabin at Walden Pond.

Death from the Sky

As I sat on my dock at Black Bear Lake of an evening, watching the sunset, I seldom saw the boats of fishermen anymore. The trout were disappearing. I also noticed fewer and fewer ospreys and kingfishers patrolling the shallows. During the early years I had often swum near otters, for they used to sit on the rocks crunching trout dinners. Now they seemed scarcer. Those few that frolicked and fished here carried only bullheads, frogs, crayfish, or nothing at all. Moreover, during the past five or six summers the mighty chorus of bullfrogs that once boomed over the lake had diminished. Finally I counted only five bullfrogs at Black Bear Lake. There were none at all around Birch Pond, Lilypad Lake, or Sunshine.

Loons, grebes, and herons have never nested here, to my knowledge, but usually one or two of these fish eaters fed or floated offshore in season. Lately they have been rare sights. Along with these water birds, the showy white water lilies on all three ponds have totally disappeared, although some cow lilies endure. Lilypad Lake is no longer a lily pad lake. My little lettuce garden down by the lakeshore no longer flourishes. I had to abandon it as the soil turned too acid. Mint and potatoes are about all that will grow.

At the same time that some plants and animals decreased, I could see that others throve. Water striders and boatmen were everywhere, and a green pondweed flourished. The bottom of Lilypad Lake became a solid, dense mat of sphagnum. Birch Pond was covered with a gray, feltlike carpet of filamentous algae.

4   Through all these subtle and not so subtle changes some things stayed the same. Blackflies prospered and fed on Condor[1] and me each spring. Swallows continued to flit over the lakes, picking off water striders and blackflies. And spring peepers still trilled.

At first I merely puzzled over these changes with a personal but casual concern. Then, in 1978, *Outdoor Life* magazine asked me to write a story on a brand-new environmental problem—acid rain. Scientific awareness of acid rain in the United States had started in the mid-1970s, but the popular press

[1]Her German Shepherd dog.

and public had paid little attention. I began researching the problem. Everything I read confirmed what was happening at Black Bear Lake. Waters in the western Adirondacks and other mountain lakes were becoming acidified and damaged by a chemical fallout in the form of polluted air, rain, frost, snow, fog, dew, and even dust.

After writing my article, I turned my professional attention to the acid rain problem around my cabin. First I bought a portable pH meter to measure the acidity of water. Housed in a briefcase-size plastic box, it contained a probe to dip into water. This was connected to a meter which registered on a scale of from 0 to 14, or very acid to very alkaline. The box also held a bottle of distilled water to rinse the probe after each use and two nine-volt batteries.

During every rainstorm and sometimes in snowfalls I collected water samples and analyzed them. Compared to a neutral pH of 7,[2] or a so-called normal rain and snow of pH 5.7, my readings were way low. Local ponds and lakes averaged pH 4.5 in summer, 4.1 in late fall and early spring after the autumn rains and April thaw. An average Adirondack rain registered around 4.3. Once I got as low as 3.2. That is almost as acidic as vinegar!

By luck, I found a report giving pH readings from Black Bear Lake in 1933. Then the water was pH 6.3. That meant my lake was roughly *a hundred times* more acidic in 1983 than it had been fifty years earlier!

Next, I started worrying about the otters and what their source of food would be now that fish life was disappearing. I examined their dried scats deposited on the rocks and found that they contained almost no fish bones or scales. Most were composed of small crayfish shells and frog skeletons. Presumably the otters were harvesting their food from deeper water and bottom mud. The acidity penetrated less there than at the surface. I stored the otter droppings in plastic containers (actually the Cool Whip ones used for my morning espresso) in order to assemble a record of otter food habit changes over the years.

As my anxiety about the Adirondack lakes grew, I started snorkeling to observe conditions underwater. Every time there was a heat wave, I would don my wet suit, mask, and flippers and check out a lake. The most dramatic was Brooktrout, way back in the West Canada Lakes Wilderness Area, lying at about twenty-two hundred feet. Long a traditional brook trout fishing lake, it lies five miles by trail from a dirt road, twelve miles more from a paved road, and another five from a town. Any conceivable source of pollution is more than thirty-five miles away.

I backpacked to Brooktrout with my gear and underwater camera and stayed overnight at the state lean-to. No night had ever seemed so still. From dusk to dawn, not a sound. Come morning, I scanned the shoreline with

---

[2]The pH scale ranges from 0 to 14, with 7 representing the value of pure water. The pH decreases from 7 as the level of acidity increases and rises above 7 as the alkalinity increases.

binoculars. No ripples broke the surface. There were no rising fish, stalking herons, swimming mergansers,[3] or plopping frogs. Brooktrout had the eerie feeling of a cemetery.

12   Underwater I discovered an unnaturally clear blue world, reminiscent of the Bahamas. Visibility was excellent. I gazed down at submerged spruces, which had fallen years back, were still intact, yet now were a ghostly gray, covered with slimy algae. Nothing lived underwater here. Most of the zooplankton was gone, accounting for the clarity of the water. The fish that had given the lake its name were gone, too, along with the freshwater mussels, frogs, and crayfish. I snapped several underwater shots of this disturbing, surrealistic world.

Next, I dived in lakes that were still healthy, where acid rain had not had an impact. These were *large* lakes at *lower* elevations which had extensive watersheds with few rocks, thick soils, and well forested shores. In direct contrast with Brooktrout Lake, their waters were brownish or greenish, alive with plankton. Visibility was limited to a few feet. Fish and amphibians moved about busily. White water lilies, cow lilies, pickerelweed, and other aquatic vegetation floated on the surface. Their long silvery stalks swayed gently in the waves, like beaded curtains in a doorway.

My underwater investigation clearly indicated that something was wrong with many high-elevation Adirondack lakes near my cabin. The New York State Department of Environmental Conservation claimed that close to six hundred lakes were threatened or "dead." And it appeared that more and more would be falling ill from the invisible "death from the sky" that was without taste, color, or smell.

In 1979, a year after my first article on acid rain, *National Geographic* approached me for another. The Adirondacks were fast becoming notorious as the "acid rain garbage dump" of our country as the result of air pollution on our prevailing winds, high elevations, thin, rocky soils, and heavy precipitation. Since I had lived in the area continuously, I could chronicle the environmental changes from personal experience.

16   I accepted the assignment from a sense of duty. My mountains and lakes were being hurt. Someone had to speak out, and to as many people as possible. Eleven million people subscribe regularly to *National Geographic,* and an estimated twenty to twenty-five million read the magazine at doctors' and dentists' offices and in school libraries.

At the same time I was apprehensive. It would be the most complicated piece I'd ever done, necessitating a working knowledge of chemistry, meteorology, geology, hydrology, physics, politics, biology, and more. The senior editor at *Geographic* encouraged me to attend conferences, interview scientists, and travel to other areas plagued by acid rain. Expenses were no

---

[3]Fish-eating, diving ducks.

problem. I had the backup of a marvelous photographer, Ted Spiegel, and two fine editors. Even so, the article took two years of research.

A trip to Scandinavia was essential. Its countries are harder hit by acidic deposition than the United States and Canada. Also, their scientists have been more deeply involved for a longer time in research than have North Americans. The "father of acid rain," Dr. Svante Odén, a soil scientist, is a Swede. With a stroke of genius he "discovered" the cause of this perplexing phenomenon in 1967. Over time, Dr. Odén reported an increasing pattern of acid deposition throughout much of Europe, including Scandinavia. He predicted many of the effects we see today. He compared acid rain to a "chemical warfare" among nations since such pollution honors no borders, no political powers.

Packing my pH meter, hiking boots, conference clothes, and a down parka, I headed for Scandinavia in October 1979. In Norway aquatic chemist Dr. Arne Henriksen guided me to a wild, rocky lake about three miles from the nearest road in the southern part of his country. "This is your classic acidified lake," he said. We arrived at midafternoon. The surface stretched mercury smooth, black as basalt, to a stony mountain backdrop. Gray cumulus clouds tinged with raspberry edged slowly overhead and were reflected in the still water. I listened. Not a sparrow sang. Not a cricket chirped. Not a squirrel chattered.

My colleague pulled a small rowboat from a shed and loaded it with scientific gear, food, and our camping stuff. Pulling away from shore, he dipped the probe of a pH meter into the lake. It read 4.3. Just like Black Bear and Brooktrout lakes!

"There are over sixty miles of green farms, forests, and fields from here to the sea," he said, gesturing south. "Then it's hundreds of miles over the ocean to the nearest sources of pollution in Great Britain and northern Europe. This acidity has to be blowing in long distances from *somewhere!*

"Our meteorological samples indicate that windborne dirty air emissions are coming from both places," he continued. "Scandinavia, especially southern Norway, is the long-range target; it's the same pattern as in your Adirondack Mountains that are dumped on by air pollution originating mainly in the midwestern United States, six hundred to eight hundred miles away."

We rowed to a rustic cabin under pines on a peninsula. Once it had been a private fishing lodge. Now it is a field station for acid rain research. A cold wind began sighing at sunset. Quickly we carried our gear inside and opened the heavy shutters of the cabin. Feeling right at home, I walked to the lake to fill buckets of water and out to the woodshed to tote in firewood. My companion laid a fire, using vertically stacked logs instead of horizontal ones. He touched a match to the kindling. Soon a ruddy glow was spreading over the hand-hewn log walls, where enormous brown trout trophies hung. Two were longer than my forearm with my fingers outstretched.

Pointing to the stuffed trout, Dr. Henriksen said, "Those fish were taken back in the 1930s. But not a fish has been caught here since 1945." He poured two small glasses of aquavit, pulled two chairs close to the hearth, and beckoned companionably to me. By now the fire was throwing its warmth out into the dank, cold room. We were able to stop moving around and sit down. Dr. Henriksen picked up a worn journal and thumbed through its yellowed pages. "Here it tells how the former owners tried restocking this lake several times. They introduced thousands of fish, yet none survived." His green eyes glinted in the firelight as he passed me the book. "In 1967 they suspected the problem might be acid rain. Finally, realizing their fishing lake was ruined, they offered the whole property to the Norwegian Acid Rain Project." He lapsed into silence and stared pensively into the flames.

It seemed so much like the sad situation at Black Bear Lake, except that in the States we were waking up ten years later. A strange feeling of déjà vu enveloped me. During our dinner a storm roared in, bringing rain. My colleague ran outside to collect a sample of water—pH 4.1. Later that night, as I lay on a rough-hewn bunk in my sleeping bag, I listened to the patter of raindrops on the roof. It felt exactly like my cabin home. The four thousand miles between lakes disappeared. Acid rain is a very leveling agent.

In Sweden two even more impressive experiences gave me additional material for my article. One of the researchers I interviewed, Dr. Hans Hultberg, drove me through rural lands west of Göteborg.[4] We bounced over rough roads, stopping frequently at tidy farmsteads that looked perfectly normal.

"You see that place over there?" The scientist pointed. "The babies had diarrhea off and on for months until we found that their well water was very acid and was leaching copper from the plumbing lines. This caused a high content of this heavy metal in the drinking water, hence into the food and milk of the babies. Once they were switched to pure bottled water, their diarrhea stopped."

Farther on we passed a small cottage and garden. "The lady who lives there," explained my colleague, "used to wash her hair in well water. As you see, most of us Swedes are blond, but *her* hair was *green*—tinted green by the copper sulfate leached into her well by acid rain. Green as a birch in spring!"

At still another homestead he described the owner as a kidney patient on dialysis. "This man is forced every week to travel a long way to a large hospital, where the water is highly filtered and distilled. If he tried to use the water at his home, he would be toxified. It is full of aluminum leached out of the soil by acid deposition."

At the end of our day Dr. Hultberg summarized by saying that the effects of acid rain itself will seem minor when compared to the toll of heavy metals and aluminum accumulation in the future.

[4]On the western coast of Sweden.

The high point of my investigation was a sailing trip on the Baltic Sea with Dr. Odén. At first I was perplexed why he wanted to go *there* for evidence of acid deposition since salt water neutralizes the sulfuric and nitric acids in acid precipitation. Yet he assured me that an interesting experiment lay ahead.

That October day was one of hammered gold and royal blue—a true Swedish fall day. The Baltic churned and flashed under a chilly wind. Suddenly it didn't much matter *what* we discovered. I had never seen such magical slanting light or been so far north before. We stashed a picnic in the galley and hoisted the sails. Then the small boat heeled over, and we were prancing toward low, rocky islands off to starboard.

The robust scientist stood at the helm, his blue eyes squinted into slits from the spray and sun, giving his face the look of a Lapp. He wore a pair of high rubber boots and a huge hand-knit white fisherman's sweater. His blond hair was tousled above a weather-beaten, tanned face. I felt as if a Viking had spirited me away.

We came into the lee of a point, and he dropped anchor close to shore. After jumping onto shore, he produced a pH meter and dipped its probe into the sea—pH 7.5, which is normal. Then he walked backward, stopping at tiny pools of rainwater left from the last storm and caught in clefts between rocks. The first read pH 6.5. It was about ten feet from shore and obviously subjected to salt spray from the waves. The second lay twenty-five feet from shore and read 5.5. The last, a good seventy-five feet away from the sea and its influence, was 4.5. Acid rain! It was a simple yet brilliant demonstration.

Beckoning me to follow, Dr. Odén walked toward some shrubby growth. "I've been sailing around these islands for several summers," he explained, "and have watched these plants sicken. Mark my words, the future of forests is at stake. After the lakes and fish go, after the soils are stripped of nutrients and trace metals, then the trees will start to die. It just takes them longer to respond to the poisoning than trout or salamanders."

The overall impact of these experiences was so strong that I decided to attend a high-level meeting on long-range transport of air pollution at the United Nations in Switzerland. I was anxious to hear what plans were being made to control emissions in Europe and compare them to U.S. strategies.

In the elegant halls of the UN the heads of environmental agencies and air pollution divisions from thirty-one of the thirty-three European nations were present. Sadly I listened to heart-rending appeals by the Norwegian and Swedish delegates to stop the pollution devastating their countrysides. Then, in astonishment, I heard expert testimony from the United Kingdom to the effect that there was *no* scientific evidence to link smoke from English electrical generating plants to fish and forest damage in Scandinavia. I was even more outraged to listen as West German officials refused to initiate emission controls on their steel plants and other factories because of the cost involved and insufficient evidence of damage then.

In simplest terms, certain upwind countries were dumping their pollution onto downwind countries and either neglecting to or refusing to clean up their mess. The Scandinavian situation bore a strong analogy to the Adirondack one. Yet, nation or state, it is *ethically* no different from a neighbor at Black Bear Lake flinging his garbage onto my land and turning his back, rather than driving to the dump, burning it, or burying it.

I returned home with a far greater understanding of the political and sociological forces at work in the acid rain arena—and with an appreciation of those Scandinavians I met. It was apparent to me that they were far more attuned to environmental health and nature than most Americans. The Swedes and Norwegians were sincerely trying to mitigate the acid rain problem. I did not sense there, as in America, a persistent paranoia about finances, political stances, and legalities. It seemed to me that Scandinavians believe the poisoning of their countryside is *wrong* and should be stopped. Solutions did not depend wholly on the monetary losses to fishing or tourism, the costs of scrubbers,[5] or the extra dollars that citizens might have to pay to clean up air pollution.

40

Moreover, the Scandinavians were not stalling cleanup actions by conducting more and more research, as our country has been doing. They were putting efforts into cleaning up their *own* mess, even though they are the victims. Of the acid deposition in Norway and Sweden 80 percent is "imported" from other European nations, whereas only 20 percent originates "at home." Already eighteen thousand of the eighty-five thousand Swedish lakes, plus many of the great Norwegian fishing rivers, have been affected in some degree by acid rain. Yet the Scandinavians have already eliminated 30 to 60 percent of their own dirty air.

At this writing it has been five years since publication of my *National Geographic* article. It seems to me the Adirondacks are in worse shape than before. I know of three scary things that have been happening right in my backyard. My old guide friend Rodney has had to replace the entire plumbing system of his house. The stout copper lines installed fifty years ago lasted for about thirty-five years. He replaced them. But in fewer than fifteen years the new lines pitted and corroded through. They are full of pinpricks where aggressive acidic water etched away the metal. Other neighbors are complaining of the same problem and expense.

Then an environmental health scientist from the New York State Department of Health sampled the groundwater of several Adirondack domestic wells and springs not long ago. I helped guide him to these locations, some of them back in the woods beyond human habitation. As in western Sweden, surprisingly high levels of aluminum and mercury showed up in springwater (leached by acid rain from the soils), and copper and lead in plumbing systems (leached from the lines). The scientist strongly urged that water which has lain overnight in metal (not plastic) plumbing systems be flushed

[5]Devices that reduce emission of pollutants from coal- or oil-burning power plants.

out by running the tap for two or three minutes before mixing frozen orange juice or making coffee.

Finally, right around my cabin there used to be sixteen enormous virgin red spruce trees. They were the ones that I worried would fall on my roof during windstorms and crush me in the sleeping loft. Of these sixteen, four have fallen harmlessly to high winds. The others started turning a peculiar yellow-green color and losing needles at the crowns. For several years they bore an extra-heavy crop of cones. Then all the foliage gradually dropped off. Only three trees are still alive. Many have snapped in two. When I pick up the shards of wood, they are as dry and brittle as papier-mâché. Useless!

To make sure this wasn't just an odd occurrence in the vicinity of my cabin, I paddled around the shoreline of Black Bear Lake, counting dead and live spruces. The results? Thirty-five percent of the big trees were dead or dying.

The same phenomenon is taking place on the upper slopes (at elevations of twenty-five to thirty-five hundred feet) of the High Peaks in the Adirondacks. An estimated 60 to 90 percent of the spruces are dead or in severe decline.

An even more extensive forest dieback has taken place in West Germany and several other European countries in the past decade. About five years ago West Germany reported a 34 percent reduction of firs, pines, spruces, and beeches in its mountainous areas. Today the die-off has affected 54 percent of these trees. Millions of acres of woodland are partially dead. The phenomenon is called *Waldsterben,* "forest death." Poland, East Germany, Czechoslovakia, along with Sweden, Norway, and the Netherlands, are reporting a similar tragedy.

Scientists strongly suspect that the culprit is acid deposition, acting in concert with certain weather and soil conditions. Acidic water leaches trace elements from soils, inducing nutrient loss and stress. Slowly the trees begin to starve and sicken. Acidic water also releases aluminum and heavy metals that kill fine root hairs. Slowly the trees die of thirst.

To combat *Waldsterben,* stringent air pollution controls began going into effect during 1986 in West Germany to cut emissions of sulfur dioxide and nitrous oxides from new power plants, vehicles, and factories. Older facilities will undergo abatement procedures of various kinds. The use of unleaded gas and lower speed limits on the autobahns are also being planned. West Germany has pledged a 33 percent reduction, or more, of these acid rain precursors by 1993. By contrast no Eastern European country appears to be addressing the problem.

I suppose I can console myself that in the space of five years I have had the bitter satisfaction of seeing the West German government do a complete about-face in its position toward acid rain and international pollution. After years of exporting vast quantities of unclean air to downwind nations (at least 50 percent of Sweden's acidic deposition comes from this highly industrialized nation) and believing itself immune to the problem, West Germany has bowed to the inevitable.

Political solutions clearly *are* possible. And Mother Nature may still repair the biological damage before it's irreversible. Unfortunately that is not the case in our country. Our federal government is no closer to reauthorizing, amending, and strengthening the Clean Air Act as of this writing than it was in 1980. It appears that each state may have to act if any cleanup is to happen. Already New York and a couple others have.

Meanwhile, I walk my woods and paddle my ponds, fingers to the pulse points, diagnosing, evaluating. It feels a little like watching a lover or a dear friend die a lingering death. Each year my woods and ponds seem a little worse, a little more anemic, a bit more toxified. I hope against hope that a remission is still possible. Yet I believe that the only effective therapy is to reduce sulfur dioxide and nitrous oxide emissions (with the accompanying toxic metals) and ozone[6] by about 70 to 80 percent.

52 No one asked my permission to kill trout and spruces. I, and they, are innocent victims. I worry. Is our bracing mountain air bad for our lungs? Is drinking lake water of pH 4.3 by the bucketful injurious to our intestines? Or brushing teeth with springwater twice a day eroding enamel? How about swimming every dawn? Will we humans, like trees, take a long time to respond to the effects of an acidified environment?

There's no way to escape those acid-bearing storm clouds that push over the mountains. It has taken fifty years to degrade my environment to its present state; it will probably take fifty years to recuperate. So even if laws were passed tomorrow, and the mechanical cleanups begun, a healthy Adirondacks would be decades away.

Imagine how many times the earth must turn until the showy white water lilies, the giant red spruces, the booming bullfrogs, and the native brook trout come back again to my woods and ponds. I've come to realize, with a pang, that I won't live to see them return.

[6]Refers to ground-level ozone, which is a pollutant that contributes to acid rain; stratospheric ozone protects against harmful ultraviolet radiation from the sun.

Understanding What You Read

1. What changes does the author notice in and around the lake where she lives in the Adirondack Mountains?
2. Where does most of the air pollution damaging the Adirondacks originate? Where does it come from in Sweden?
3. List the living things that are affected by acid rain in the order in which the damage appears.

Writing About What You Read

1. Write a letter to your representative in Congress or to the editor of a newspaper explaining the causes and effects of acid rain, and proposing specific actions to remedy the problem.
2. Do research in the library or by calling government agencies or local environmental organizations to find out about air pollution in your region and whether acid rain is a problem there. Write a report of your findings.

RITA DOVE

Born in Akron, Ohio, Dove (b. 1952) studied at Miami University in Oxford, Ohio, and the Iowa Writers Workshop. She has won numerous awards for her work, including fellowships from the National Endowment for the Arts and the Guggenheim Foundation; in 1993 she was named U.S. Poet Laureate. Dove has published a novel, *Through the Ivory Gate* (1992); a collection of stories, *Fifth Sunday* (1985); and four poetry collections: *The Yellow House on the Corner* (1980), *Museum* (1983), *Thomas and Beulah* (1986), for which she won the Pulitzer Prize, and *Grace Notes* (1989), in which "Ozone" appears.

Ozone

> . . . Does the cosmic
> space we dissolve into taste of us, then?
> —RILKE,[1] *The Second Elegy*

Everything civilized will whistle before
it rages—kettle of the asthmatic,
the aerosol can and its immaculate awl
perforating the dome of heaven.   4

We wire the sky for comfort;
we thread it through our lungs for a perfect fit.
We've arranged this calm, though it is constantly
unraveling.   8

[1]Rainer Maria Rilke (1875–1926), German poet and author of the *Duino Elegies* and *Sonnets to Orpheus*.

> *Where does it go then,*
> *atmosphere suckered up*
> *an invisible flue?*
> *How can we know where it goes?*

A gentleman pokes blue through a buttonhole.

> *Rising, the pulse*
> *sings:*
> *memento mei²*

The sky is wired so it won't fall down.
Each house notches into its neighbor
and then the next, the whole row scaldingly white,
unmistakable as a set of bared teeth.

> *to pull the plug*
> *to disappear into an empty bouquet*

If only we could lose ourselves
in the wreckage of the moment! Forget
where we stand, dead center, and
look up, look up,
track a falling star . . .

now you see it

now you don't

²Remember me.

Understanding What You Read

1. Why will "everything civilized . . . whistle before/it rages" (lines 1–2)?
2. What "comfort" is Dove referring to in line 5?
3. Why does Dove compare a row of houses to "a set of bared teeth" (line 20)?

Writing About What You Read

1. Write a paragraph explaining why the sentence "A gentleman pokes blue through a buttonhole" is (or is not) necessary to the poem.
2. Write a poem concerning another "sign of trouble"—rain-forest destruction, whale killing, or overpopulation, for example.

JAMES DAO

Dao (b. 1957), an award-winning journalist, has taken on a number of challenging assignments, such as investigating the smuggling of illegal immigrants from China to America. His coverage of the problems caused by a cluster of chemical plants around a small town won a feature writing award from the New Jersey Press Association. He was a reporter for the *Daily News* and other newspapers before becoming a metropolitan reporter for the *New York Times* in 1992. This article appeared in the *Times* on February 6, 1993.

A New, Unregulated Market: Selling the Right to Pollute

ALBANY, N.Y., Feb. 5—When Congress passed the Clean Air Act of 1990, it created something never before seen in the annals of capitalism: a free market in pollution.

If a company could clean up its emissions more than required under the new law, it could sell the right to pollute to another company. The freedom to trade pollution rights like pork bellies, and even make a profit, would give companies an incentive to upgrade dirty plants, the thinking went.

But an announcement this week that the Long Island Lighting Company was selling an option on some of its pollution rights to another company has raised fears in New York's environmental community that the Clean Air Act will not help improve air quality in New York State.

Much of Lilco's pollution drifted out to sea, but if the company that bought the rights to pollute is in, say, Ohio, the acid rain it produces could well end up over the Adirondacks, an area that the act was specifically intended to protect. 4

The problem, environmentalists and state officials say, is that the law does not regulate the pollution rights sales or require companies to provide any public information about them, at least until 1995. As a consequence, pollution could be shifted from one region to another without officials realizing it.

The Lilco transaction—among the first in the budding pollution market and the first by a New York State utility—exemplifies such concerns because the company has declined to say who has purchased the option, other than to describe it as a "non-utility energy supplier."

A Lilco spokeswoman, Suzanne Halpin, said releasing the information could damage the company's ability to negotiate future sales. She said the pollution rights had not yet been transferred because the buyer acquired an option for the rights that could be exercised in the future.

8   At the heart of New York's fears is the belief that the biggest purchasers of pollution credits will be the Midwestern coal-burning utility plants that are among the chief sources of acid rain in the East. If that were the case, there might be little or no net improvement in the acidity of the Adirondacks' numerous lakes, they say.

"The trading program didn't take into consideration where the pollution would fall after it was traded," said John F. Sheehan, a spokesman for the Adirondack Council, an environmental group. "We have Lilco, whose pollution will go out to sea, trading to the Midwest, where the pollution will fall on us."

Because there have been few sales nationwide and little information about them, it is impossible to determine who is buying pollution credits.

To some degree, the newness of the market has discouraged sales, since many utility managers do not want to invest in commodities of uncertain value.

12   But some experts expect trading to increase after the Federal Government sells at auction a stock of pollution credits in March. By raising concerns now, New York's environmental community is seeking to pressure state and Federal agencies to find ways of regulating, or at least monitoring, the trades before the market heats up.

"It's not that trading can't work, but it must also work to achieve the benefits of the law, which is acid rain abatement," said Thomas C. Jorling, the State Commissioner for Environmental Conservation.

At the request of Mr. Jorling and environmental groups, the State Public Service Commission, which oversees utilities, has begun investigating whether it can regulate pollution trades. The Assembly Environmental Committee is also considering legislation to prevent New York State utilities from selling pollution credits to plants upwind of the Adirondacks.

Federal environmental officials say New York State's concerns are unfounded for several reasons.

16   First, about half of all the sulfur dioxide produced in the nation comes from 10 states in the Midwest—10 percent from Ohio alone. Because the Clean Air Act mandates that the entire nation cut its output of sulfur dioxide in half by 2010, EPA officials believe that most of the cuts must come from the Midwest.

"The rest of the nation couldn't produce enough credits to sell to the Midwest to let it keep polluting at the same level," said Brian J. McLean, director of the EPA's Acid Rain Division.

The EPA also believes that Midwestern utility plants are likelier to sell than to buy pollution credits. Those older, coal-burning plants are so dirty that even installing the simplest, least expensive pollution control devices will substantially reduce their emissions, Mr. McLean said. Hence, they will have additional credits to trade.

"If you're going to put technology on, you're going to do it in the Midwest," he said. "That's where you get the biggest bang per buck."

But whether those reductions will be enough to help scores of Adiron- dack lakes rendered virtually lifeless by high acidity remains in doubt. About a quarter of the region's 2,800 lakes and ponds are highly acidic, most because of acid rain, according to EPA studies.

"We expect at least a substantial reduction of acid rain in the Adiron- dacks," Mr. McLean said.

What makes pollution trading difficult to predict is the newness of the market. Some analysts have estimated that pollution credits—one credit equals one ton of sulfur dioxide—are selling for between $250 and $400 each, which is considered low.

If prices remained at that level, utilities might be encouraged to buy credits rather than to install pollution control devices, or scrubbers, experts have said.

But low prices might enable environmental groups to buy up credits and then "bury them" forever, said Tim Burke, executive director of the Adiron- dack Council. "That might drive prices up, but that might also encourage companies to buy scrubbers."

In general, the notion of trading emission allowances has been praised by both environmental groups and utilities as an innovative solution to a costly problem.

In the past, the Federal Government simply set pollution levels for utility plants and then fined them if they did not meet those standards. By 2000, the Clean Air Act will have also set emission standards for most utility plants in the country.

But it will also give them more alternatives for meeting those limits: they can either invest in new equipment or buy pollution credits, whichever is cheaper. And if they fall below the level set for them they can make a profit and reduce rates for their customers.

Starting in 1995, those companies that fail to meet their limits—either by upgrading plants or by buying pollution credits—will be fined $2,000 for every ton of excess sulfur dioxide.

EPA officials said one of the reasons that Congress approved the strin- gent sulfur dioxide standards in the Clean Air Act was that it liked the idea that utilities companies could treat pollution like a commodity. Conse- quently, there might be little political support for regulating pollution trad- ing, they said.

"It is important to understand there is a real balancing point to this," said Renee Rico, chief of the Market Innovation Branch of the EPA's Acid Rain Division. "We got a larger reduction in return for flexibility."

Understanding What You Read

1. Explain how trading pollution credits gives coal-burning utility plants more flexibility in meeting environmental air quality standards.

2. Explain how selling pollution credits may defeat efforts to reduce acid rain in the Adirondack Mountains of New York.
3. How might this unintended result be avoided?

Writing About What You Read

Write a letter to the editor of the paper explaining why you think selling pollution credits is a good (or bad) idea.

WILLIAM K. STEVENS

Stevens (b. 1935) began working for the *New York Times* in 1968 as a science reporter. His positions at the *Times* include foreign correspondent in New Delhi and bureau chief in Houston, Detroit, and Philadelphia. He has written numerous articles on science and environmental topics. This article appeared on January 26, 1993.

River Life Through U.S. Broadly Degraded

TWO DECADES of Federal controls have sharply reduced the vast outflows of sewage and industrial chemicals into America's rivers and streams, yet the life they contain may be in deeper trouble than ever.

The main threat now comes not from pollution but from humans' physical and ecological transformation of rivers and the land through which they flow. The result, scientists say, is that the nation's running waters are getting biologically poorer all the time and that entire riverine ecosystems have become highly imperiled.

Dams disrupt temperature and nutrient patterns on which organisms depend. Countless river and stream channels have been straightened, eliminating the meandering course on which rivers depend for their ecological variety. Repeated diversions of water from a river's flood plain can decimate populations of fish that spawn there. Sediments from farming run into streams and suffocate many small forms of aquatic life. Vacationers who cut down trees to improve the view in front of summer homes may erode stream banks. The stream then carries more sediment and becomes wider, shallower and warmer, making the water unfit for many vital organisms.

4 "If you take a drive out into pretty, rolling farm country, nobody thinks of the farming activity as habitat destruction," says Dr. J. David Allan, a freshwater ecologist at the University of Michigan. "But the transformation

of the landscape by agriculture is taking its toll" on life in rivers and streams, as are urban and suburban development and the spread of exotic, disruptive species of aquatic life.

The transformation, says Dr. Allan, is far more destructive to aquatic life than are spills of oil or toxic chemicals. For all the one-time harm they may cause, these spills have relatively little long-term impact. And because the transformation is so much a part of deeply entrenched patterns of land and water use, it is also far harder to deal with.

Dr. Allan lays out the threat to riverine organisms and ecosystems in an article in the current issue of the journal *BioScience.*

A 1990 study by Larry Master of the Nature Conservancy found that in North America, 28 percent of amphibian species and subspecies, 34 percent of fishes, 65 percent of crayfish and 73 percent of mussels were imperiled in degrees ranging from rare to extinct. The comparable figures were 13 percent for terrestrial mammals, 11 percent for birds and 14 percent for land reptiles.

In the West, where dams and the introduction of exotic species are common, the situation is particularly acute. Of 30 species of native fish in Arizona, 25 are listed as threatened or endangered, according to Dr. W. L. Minckley, a zoologist at Arizona State University.

8

The biotic impoverishment goes beyond the loss of individual species, however. Many rivers, Dr. Allan wrote, contain few or no endangered species, yet there are so few representatives of each species present that the ecosystem's functioning is impaired. Scientists do not know at what precise point this thinning of life causes an ecosystem to disintegrate. But "it's like an airplane wing," said Dr. John Cairns Jr., an environmental biologist at Virginia Polytechnic Institute, explaining, "If you keep pulling rivets out, the wing is going to go."

Among other benefits, riverine ecosystems create breeding grounds for commercial fisheries, carry nutrients to them and support multimillion-dollar recreational activities. In concert with wetlands, they regulate the flow of water, releasing it more slowly in flood times so that more will be left for dry times.

Few if any major river systems are unaffected by the threat to ecological integrity.

Sediment from farm fields, for instance, has clouded the mighty Mississippi, making it more hostile to many organisms. Levees prevent the sediments from settling out naturally on the Mississippi Delta. Instead, they are channeled directly to the continental shelf. This contributes to a sinking of the land in southern Louisiana and releases so many river-borne nutrients into the Gulf of Mexico that plankton growth is stimulated. The plankton use up oxygen when they decay and die, and scientists fear this oxygen depletion may harm Gulf fisheries.

12

The Colorado River south of Lake Mojave has been so altered by disruption of water flow and the introduction of exotic fish species, Dr.

Minckley said, that it has become the first major river in North America with
no native fish left.

Dams on the Columbia River have so interfered with salmon migrations
that one variety of Columbia salmon has been listed by the Government as
endangered. Another has been declared threatened, and five more have been
proposed for listing.

All three of these watercourses appear on a 1992 list of North America's
10 most endangered rivers compiled by American Rivers, a Washington-
based conservation organization. Others include the Alsek and Tatshenshini
river system in Alaska and Canada, the Great Whale River in Quebec, the
Everglades, the American River in California and the Penobscot in Maine.

16   The list is rounded out by the Beaverkill and the Willowemoc, legendary
Catskill trout streams where American fly fishing was born, and Montana's
Blackfoot, the putative setting of the current hit movie *A River Runs
Through It*.

Habitat in lower stretches of the Beaverkill-Willowemoc system is threatened by developers' cutting of streamside vegetation. The Blackfoot has
become so degraded by timber cutting, agriculture, water diversions and
mining activities that the movie makers were forced to move to another
location.

Kevin Coyle, the president of American Rivers, describes "the four
horsemen of river destruction" as dams, diversion of water, alteration of
channels and land development.

Dams trap nutrients and keep them from flowing downstream. Perhaps
more devastating, they alter the temperature of downstream water, making
it either too cold or too warm and thus annihilating whole populations of
insects vital to the riverine food web. One dam might not be so bad, but
many dams on the same river, as is common in the West, repeatedly interrupt
the river's natural functioning.

20   Diversion of water for human use, also widespread in the West, has
simply dried up many rivers and streams for much of the year, with the result
that their ecosystems are, in Mr. Coyle's words, "ghosts of what they used
to be."

The straightening, diking and redirection of river channels, common
across the country to control floods and convert flood plains to cropland,
housing and highways, reduce the variety of habitats critical to biological
diversity.

Land development often denudes stream and river banks of vegetation,
eliminating the vital transition between the river and the uplands. Draining
land for farming or development causes water to flow more rapidly into the
river channel than it naturally would. This leaves less water to percolate into
the river in drier times.

If the river channel has been straightened as well, water draining from the
land moves more efficiently, producing more powerful floods. These carry

the increased sediments from farming and development farther, choking organisms and ecosystems well downstream.

On top of all this, legions of exotic species have been introduced into running waters. Some, like the zebra mussel slowly spreading across the country, have appeared by accident. Others, like fish imported to provide sport or to clean vegetation from the waters, have been introduced on purpose. Together, Dr. Allan said, they have significantly reduced biological diversity through predation, alteration of habitat, introduction of diseases or parasites and interbreeding with native organisms.

Such ecological tinkering can unexpectedly cascade through the water, onto the land and into the economy as well. In one instance, fishery managers in Montana introduced opossum shrimp into Flathead Lake and its associated river systems, hoping the shrimp would provide forage for kokanee salmon that were the basis of a thriving tourist industry.

Instead, the shrimp consumed zooplankton that were the staples of the kokanee diet. The kokanee population collapsed. Bald eagles and grizzly bears that once congregated at the rivers to feed on salmon disappeared, as did tourists who had come to see them.

Once invasive species have established themselves, said Dr. Allan, it may be impossible to eliminate them. The other main causes of biological impoverishment seem only a little less intractable. Even so, Dr. Allan, Mr. Coyle and others say much can be done.

American Rivers advocates a three-pronged strategy: saving the headwaters of the major rivers, which for the most part are already publicly owned; protecting and restoring riparian zones by replanting green strips along rivers; and working with governments to regulate water discharges from dams so they disrupt ecosystems less. Federally controlled dams are also being examined for their environmental effects as their hydroelectric licenses come up for renewal.

A number of scattered efforts to restore rivers and streams are being undertaken. Restorationists have become expert at restoring streams for game fish like trout, Dr. Allan noted. What is needed now, he said, is a comparable effort to restore habitat for the full panoply of riverine organisms.

An ambitious effort along these lines involves the Kissimmee River in Florida. To control flooding, the Army Corps of Engineers basically turned the twisting, 103-mile-long river into a straight canal, largely destroying the riverine-riparian ecosystem. Now, after a successful demonstration project, the State of Florida and the corps hope to restore the river's twists and turns—and its ecosystem.

Broader restoration of this sort is still in its infancy. But as fragile as riverine ecosystems are, Dr. Allan points out, they are also remarkably resilient. They tend to repair themselves once the causes of their impoverishment are removed.

So, he says, all is not lost.

Understanding What You Read

1. What are the four factors now considered most destructive to rivers in the United States?
2. List the ten most endangered North American rivers. Are any of these rivers near a place you have lived? What factors have damaged a particular river or efforts to support or protect that river? How can you find out more about those factors?

Writing About What You Read

Imagine taking an overnight canoe trip with a friend down an unspoiled river (perhaps one of the rivers designated as "wild and scenic" by the federal government). Tell the story of your experience, noting details and calling attention to the pleasures of a pristine river.

ELIZABETH BISHOP

Bishop (1911–1979), one of the most distinctive poets of the century, was educated at Vassar College, and spent much of her life in tropical climates, first in Key West and then in Brazil. Her first volume of poetry, *North and South,* in which "The Fish" appeared, was published in 1946 and then combined with *A Cold Spring* under the title *Poems* in 1955. That year Bishop won the Pulitzer Prize for poetry. Other works of poetry include *Questions of Travel* (1965) and *Geography III* (1976); *The Complete Poems: 1927–1979* came out in 1983. Her prose work *Brazil* was published in 1962.

The Fish

I caught a tremendous fish
and held him beside the boat
half out of water, with my hook
fast in a corner of his mouth.
He didn't fight.
He hadn't fought at all.
He hung a grunting weight.
battered and venerable

and homely. Here and there
his brown skin hung in strips
like ancient wallpaper,
and its pattern of darker brown   12
was like wallpaper:
shapes like full-blown roses
stained and lost through age.
He was speckled with barnacles,   16
fine rosettes of lime,
and infested
with tiny white sea-lice,
and underneath two or three   20
rags of green weed hung down.
While his gills were breathing in
the terrible oxygen
—the frightening gills,   24
fresh and crisp with blood,
that can cut so badly—
I thought of the coarse white flesh
packed in like feathers,   28
the big bones and the little bones,
the dramatic reds and blacks
of his shiny entrails,
and the pink swim bladder
like a big peony.
I looked into his eyes
which were far larger than mine
but shallower, and yellowed,   36
the irises backed and packed
with tarnished tinfoil
seen through the lenses
of old scratched isinglass.[1]   40
They shifted a little, but not
to return my stare.
—It was more like the tipping
of an object toward the light.   44
I admired his sullen face,
the mechanism of his jaw,
and then I saw
that from his lower lip   48
—if you could call it a lip—

[1]A semitransparent substance obtained from the swim-bladders of some freshwater fishes, used for windows.

grim, wet, and weaponlike,
hung five old pieces of fish-line,
52 or four and a wire leader
with the swivel still attached,
with all their five big hooks
grown firmly in his mouth.
56 A green line, frayed at the end
where he broke it, two heavier lines,
and a fine black thread
still crimped from the strain and snap
60 when it broke and he got away.
Like medals with their ribbons
frayed and wavering,
a five-haired beard of wisdom
64 trailing from his aching jaw.
I stared and stared
and victory filled up
the little rented boat,
68 from the pool of bilge
where oil had spread a rainbow
around the rusted engine
to the bailer rusted orange,
72 the sun-cracked thwarts,
the oarlocks on their strings,
the gunnels—until everything
was rainbow, rainbow, rainbow!
76 And I let the fish go.

Understanding What You Read

1. What does this poem suggest to you about the relationship of human beings to the natural world?
2. Is the absence of fight in this old fish a sign of trouble? If so, what kind of trouble?
3. Why in the end is everything "rainbow, rainbow, rainbow"?

Writing About What You Read

1. Consider your own response to this poem—what it makes you think or feel—and analyze how the poem evokes that response.
2. Using this poem as a model, write a poem of your own about some experience you have had with an animal.

MICHAEL G. CONEY

Coney (b. 1932) moved from England to Canada in 1972 and lives on Vancouver Island, British Columbia, where he runs his publishing company, Porthole Press. His works include *Syzygy* (1973), *Winter's Children* (1974), *Monitor Found in Orbit* (1974), a collection of short stories, *Neptune's Cauldron* (1981), and *King of the Sceptre'd Isle* (1989). "The Byrds" first appeared in an anthology, *Changes* (1983).

The Byrds

G R A N started it all.

Late one afternoon in the hottest summer in living memory, she took off all her clothes, carefully painted red around her eyes and down her cheeks, chin and throat, painted the rest of her body a contrasting black with the exception of her armpits and the inside of her wrists which she painted white, strapped on her new antigravity belt, flapped her arms and rose into the nearest tree, a garry oak, where she perched.

She informed us that, as of now, she was Rufous-necked Hornbill, of India.

"She always wanted to visit India," Gramps told us.   4

Gran said no more, for the logical reason that Hornbills are not talking birds.

"Come down, Gran!" called Mother. "You'll catch your death of cold."

Gran remained silent. She stretched her neck and gazed at the horizon.

"She's crazy," said Father. "She's crazy. I always said she was. I'll call the   8
asylum."

"You'll do no such thing!" Mother was always very sensitive about Gran's occasional peculiarities. "She'll be down soon. The evenings are drawing in. She'll get cold."

"What's an old fool her age doing with an antigravity unit anyway, that's what I want to know," said Father.

The Water Department was restricting supply and the weatherman was predicting floods. The Energy Department was warning of depleted stocks, the Department of Rest had announced that the population must fall by one-point-eight per cent by November or else, the Mailgift was spewing out a deluge of application forms, tax forms and final reminders, the Tidy Mice were malfunctioning so that the house stank. . . .

And now this.   12

It was humiliating and embarrassing, Gran up a tree, naked and painted. She stayed there all evening, and I knew that my girlfriend Pandora would be dropping by soon and would be sure to ask questions.

Humanity was at that point in the morality cycle when nudity was considered indecent. Gran was probably thirty years before her time. There was something lonely and anachronistic about her, perched there, balancing unsteadily in a squatting position, occasionally grabbing at the trunk for support then flapping her arms to reestablish the birdlike impression. She looked like some horrible mutation. Her resemblance to a Rufous-necked Hornbill was slight.

"Talk her down, Gramps," said Father.

"She'll come down when she's hungry."

He was wrong. Late in the evening Gran winged her way to a vacant lot where an ancient tree stood. She began to eat unsterilized apples, juice flowing down her chin. It was a grotesque sight.

"She'll be poisoned!" cried Mother.

"So, she's made her choice at last," said Father.

He was referring to Your Choice for Peace, the brochure which Gran and Gramps received monthly from the Department of Rest. Accompanying the brochure is a six-page form on which senior citizens describe all that is good about their life, and a few of the things which bug them. At the end of the form is a box in which the oldster indicates his preference for Life or Peace. If he does not check the box, or if he fails to complete the form, it is assumed that he has chosen Peace, and they send the Wagon for him.

Now Gran was cutting a picturesque silhouette against the pale blue of the evening sky as she circled the rooftops uttering harsh cries. She flew with arms outstretched, legs trailing, and we all had to admit to the beauty of the sight; that is, until a flock of starlings began to mob her. Losing directional control she spiraled downwards, recovered, leveled out and skimmed towards us, outpacing the starlings and regaining her perch in the garry oak. She made preening motions and settled down for the night. The family Pesterminator, zapping bugs with its tiny laser, considered her electronically for a second but held its fire.

We were indoors by the time Pandora arrived. She was nervous, complaining that there was a huge mutation in the tree outside, and it had cawed at her.

Mother said quickly, "It's only a Rufous-necked Hornbill."

"A rare visitor to these shores," added Father.

"Why couldn't she have been a sparrow?" asked Mother. "Or something else inconspicuous." Things were not going well for her. The little robot Tidy Mice still sulked behind the wainscoting and she'd had to clean the house by hand.

The garish Gran shone like a beacon in the morning sunlight. There was no concealing the family's degradation. A small crowd had gathered and people were trying to tempt Gran down with breadcrumbs. She looked none the worse for her night out, and was greeting the morning with shrill yells.

Gramps was strapping on an antigravity belt. "I'm going up to fetch her down. This has gone far enough."

I said, "Be careful. She may attack you."

"Don't be a damned fool." Nevertheless Gramps went into the toolshed, later emerging nude and freshly painted. Mother uttered a small scream of distress, suspecting that Gramps, too, had become involved in the conspiracy to diminish the family's social standing.

I reassured her. "She's more likely to listen to one of her own kind."

"Has everyone gone totally insane?" asked Mother.

Gramps rose gracefully into the garry oak, hovered, then settled beside Gran. He spoke to her quietly for a moment and she listened, head cocked attentively.

Then she made low gobbling noises and leaned against him.

He called down, "This may take longer than I thought."

"Oh, my God," said Mother.

"That does it," said Father. "I'm calling the shrink."

Dr. Pratt was tall and dignified, and he took in the situation at a glance. "Has your mother exhibited birdish tendencies before?"

Father answered for Mother. "No more than anyone else. Although, in many other ways, she was——"

"Gran has always been the soul of conformity," said Mother quickly, beginning to weep. "If our neighbours have been saying otherwise I'll remind them of the slander laws. No—she did it to shame us. She always said she hated the colours we painted the house—she said it looked like a strutting peacock."

"Rutting peacock," said Father. "She said rutting peacock. Those were her exact words."

"Peacock, eh?" Dr. Pratt looked thoughtful. There was a definite avian thread running through this. "So you feel she may be acting in retaliation. She thinks you have made a public spectacle of the house in which she lives, so now she is going to make a public spectacle of you."

"Makes sense," said Father.

"Gran!" called Dr. Pratt. She looked down at us, beady little eyes ringed with red. "I have the personal undertaking of your daughter and son-in-law that the house will be repainted in colours of your own choosing." He spoke on for a few minutes in soothing tones. "That should do it," he said to us finally, picking up his bag. "Put her to bed and keep her off berries, seeds, anything like that. And don't leave any antigravity belts lying around. They can arouse all kinds of prurient interests in older people."

"She still isn't coming down," said Father. "I don't think she understood."

"Then I advise you to fell the tree," said Dr. Pratt coldly, his patience evaporated. "She's a disgusting old exhibitionist who needs to be taught a lesson. Just because she chooses to act out her fantasies in an unusual way doesn't make her any different from anyone else. And what's *he* doing up there, anyway? Does he resent the house paint as well?"

"He *chose* the paint. He's there to bring her down."

We watched them in perplexity. The pair huddled together on the branch, engaged in mutual grooming. The crowd outside the gate had swollen to over a hundred.

48   On the following morning Gran and Gramps greeted the dawn with a cacophony of gobbling and screeching.

I heard Father throw open his bedroom window and threaten to blast them right out of that goddamned tree and into the hereafter if they didn't keep it down. I heard the metallic click as he cocked his twelve-bore. I heard Mother squeal with apprehension, and the muffled thumping of a physical struggle in the next room.

I was saddened by the strain it puts on marriages when in-laws live in the house—or, in our case, outside the window.

The crowds gathered early and it was quickly apparent that Gramps was through with trying to talk Gran down; in fact, he was through with talking altogether. He perched beside his mate in spry fashion, jerking his head this way and that as he scanned the sky for hawks, cocking an eye at the crowd, shuddering suddenly as though shaking feathers into position

52   Dr. Pratt arrived at noon, shortly before the media.

"A classic case of regression to the childlike state," he told us. "The signs are all there: the unashamed nakedness, the bright colours, the speechlessness, the favourite toy, in this case the antigravity belt. I have brought a surrogate toy which I think will solve our problem. Try luring them down with this."

He handed Mother a bright red plastic baby's rattle.

Gran fastened a beady eye on it, shuffled her arms, then launched herself from the tree in a swooping glide. As Mother ducked in alarm, Gran caught the rattle neatly in her bony old toes, wheeled and flapped back to her perch. Heads close, she and Gramps examined the toy.

56   We waited breathlessly.

Then Gran stomped it against the branch and the shattered remnants fell to the ground.

The crowd applauded. For the first time we noticed the Newspocket van, and the crew with cameras. The effect on Dr. Pratt was instantaneous. He strode towards them and introduced himself to a red-haired woman with a microphone.

"Tell me, Dr. Pratt, to what do you attribute this phenomenon?"

60   "The manifestation of birdishness in the elderly is a subject which has received very little study up to the present date. Indeed, I would say that it has been virtually ignored. Apart from my own paper—still in draft form—

you could search the psychiatric archives in vain for mention of Pratt's Syndrome."

"And why is that, Dr. Pratt?"

"Basically, fear. The fear in each and every one of us of admitting that something primitive and atavistic can lurk within our very genes. For what is more primitive than a bird, the only survivor of the age of dinosaurs?"

"What indeed, Dr. Pratt?"

"You see in that tree two pathetic human creatures who have reverted to a state which existed long before Man took his first step on Earth, a state which can only have been passed on as a tiny coded message in their very flesh and the flesh of their ancestors, through a million years of Time."

"And how long do you expect their condition to last, Dr. Pratt?"

"Until the fall. The winters in these parts are hard, and they'll be out of that tree come the first frost, if they've got any sense left at all."

"Well, thank you, Dr.—"

A raucous screaming cut her short. A group of shapes appeared in the eastern sky, low over the rooftops. They were too big for birds, yet too small for aircraft, and there was a moment's shocked incomprehension before we recognized them for what they were. Then they wheeled over the News-pocket van with a bedlam of yells and revealed themselves as teenagers of both sexes, unclothed, but painted a simple black semi-matt exterior latex. There were nine of them.

In the weeks following, we came to know them as the Crows. They flew overhead, circled, then settled all over the garry oak and the roof of our house.

They made no attempt to harass Gran or Gramps. Indeed, they seemed almost reverential in their attitude towards the old people.

It seemed that Gran had unlocked some kind of floodgate in the human unconscious, and people took to the air in increasing numbers. The manufac-turers of antigravity belts became millionaires overnight, and the skies became a bright tapestry of wheeling, screeching figures in rainbow colours and startling nakedness.

The media named them the Byrds.

"I view it as a protest against today's moral code," said Dr. Pratt, who spent most of his time on panels or giving interviews. "For more years than I care to remember, people have been repressed, their honest desires cloaked in conformity just as tightly as their bodies have been swathed in concealing garb. Now, suddenly, people are saying they've had enough. They're pleasing themselves. It shouldn't surprise us. It's healthy. It's good."

It was curious, the way the doctor had become pro-Byrd. These days he seemed to be acting in the capacity of press agent for Gran—who herself had become a cult figure. In addition, he was working on his learned paper, "The Origins and Spread of Avian Tendencies in Humans."

Pandora and I reckoned he was in the pay of the belt people.

"But it's fun to be in the centre of things," she said one evening, as the Crows came in to roost, and the garry oak creaked under the weight of a flock of Glaucous Gulls, come to pay homage to Gran. "It's put the town on the map—and your family too." She took my hand, smiling at me proudly.

There were the Pelicans, who specialized in high dives into the sea, deactivating their belts in midair, then reactivating them underwater to rocket Polaris-like from the depths. They rarely caught fish, though; and frequently had to be treated for an ailment known as Pelicans' Balloon, caused by traveling through water at speed with open mouth.

There were the Darwin's Tree Finches, a retiring sect whose existence went unsuspected for some weeks, because they spent so much time in the depths of forests with cactus spines held between their teeth, trying to extract bugs from holes in dead trees. They were a brooding and introspective group.

Virtually every species of bird was represented. And because every cult must have it lunatic fringe, there were the Pigeons. They flocked to the downtown city streets and mingled with the crowds hurrying to and fro. From the shoulders up they looked much like anyone else, only greyer, and with a curious habit of jerking their heads while walking. Bodily, though, they were like any other Byrd: proudly unclothed.

Their roosting habits triggered the first open clash between Byrds and Man. There were complaints that they kept people awake at night, and fouled the rooftops. People began to string electrified wires around their ridges and guttering, and to put poison out.

The Pigeons' retaliation took place early one evening, when the commuting crowds jammed the streets. It was simple and graphic, and well coordinated. Afterwards, people referred to it obliquely as the Great Deluge, because it was not the kind of event which is discussed openly, in proper society.

There were other sects, many of them; and perhaps the strangest was a group who eschewed the use of antigravity belts altogether. From time to time we would catch sight of them sitting on the concrete abutments of abandoned motorways, searching one another for parasites. Their bodies were painted a uniform brown except for their private parts, which were a luminous red. They called themselves Hamadryas Baboons.

People thought they had missed the point of the whole thing, somehow.

Inevitably when there are large numbers of people involved, there are tragedies. Sometimes an elderly Byrd would succumb to cardiac arrest in midair, and drift away on the winds. Others would suffer belt malfunctions and plummet to the ground. As the first chill nights began to grip the country, some of the older Byrds died of exposure and fell from their perches. Courageously they maintained their role until the end, and when daylight came they would be found in the ritualistic "Dead Byrd" posture, on their backs with legs in the air.

"All good things come to an end," said Dr. Pratt one evening as the russet leaves drifted from the trees. It had been a busy day, dozens of groups having come to pay homage to Gran. There was a sense of wrapping up, of things coming to a climax. "We will stage a mass rally," said Dr. Pratt to the Newspocket reporter. "There will be such a gathering of Byrds as the country has never known. Gran will address the multitude at the Great Coming Down."

Mother said, "So long as it's soon. I don't think Gran can take any more frosts."

I went to invite Pandora to the Great Coming Down, but she was not at home. I was about to return when I caught sight of a monstrous thing sitting on the backyard fence. It was bright green except around the eyes, which were grey, and the hair, which was a vivid yellow. It looked at me. It blinked in oddly reptilian fashion. It was Pandora.

She said, "Who's a pretty boy, then?"

88

The very next day Gran swooped down from the garry oak and seized Mother's scarf with her toes, and a grim tug-of-war ensued.

"Let go, you crazy old fool!" shouted Mother.

Gran cranked her belt up to maximum lift and took a quick twist of the scarf around her ankles. The other end was wrapped snugly around Mother's neck and tucked into her heavy winter coat. Mother left the ground, feet kicking. Her shouts degenerated into strangled grunts.

Father got a grip of Mother's knees as she passed overhead and Gran, with a harsh screech of frustration, found herself descending again; whereupon Gramps, having observed the scene with bright interest, came winging in and took hold of her, adding the power of his belt to hers.

92

Father's feet left the ground.

Mother by now had assumed the basic hanging attitude: arms dangling limply, head lolling, tongue protruding, face empurpled. I jumped and got hold of Father's ankles. There was a short, sharp rending sound and we fell back to earth in a heap, Mother on top. Gran and Gramps flew back to the garry oak with their half of the scarf, and began to pull it apart with their teeth. Father pried the other half away from Mother's neck. She was still breathing.

"Most fascinating," said Dr. Pratt.

"My wife nearly strangled by those goddamned brutes and he calls it fascinating?"

96

"No—look at the Hornbills."

"So they're eating the scarf. So they're crazy. What's new?"

"They're not eating it. If you will observe closely, you will see them shredding it. And see—the female is working the strands around that clump of twigs. It's crystal-clear what they're doing, of course. This is a classic example of nest-building."

100   The effect on Father was instantaneous. He jumped up, seized Dr. Pratt by the throat and, shaking him back and forth, shouted, "Any fool knows birds only nest in the spring!" He was overwrought, of course. He apologized the next day.

By that time the Byrds were nesting all over town. They used a variety of materials and in many instances their craftsmanship was pretty to see. The local Newspocket station ran a competition for The Nest I Would Be Happiest to Join My Mate In, treating the matter as a great joke; although some of the inhabitants who had been forcibly undressed in the street thought otherwise. The Byrds wasted nothing. Their nests were intricately woven collections of whatever could be stolen from below: overcoats, shirts, pants, clothesline, undergarments, hearing aids, wigs.

"The nesting phenomenon has a twofold significance," Dr. Pratt informed the media. "On the one hand, we have the desire of the Byrds to emulate the instinctive behavioural patterns of their avian counterparts. On the other hand, there is undoubtedly a suggestion of—how can I say it?—aggression towards the earthbound folk. The Byrds are saying, in their own way: join us. Be natural. Take your clothes off. Otherwise we'll do it for you."

"You don't think they're, uh, sexually *warped?*" asked the reporter.

104   "Sexually liberated," insisted Dr. Pratt.

The Byrds proved his point the next day, when they began to copulate all over the sky.

It was the biggest sensation since the Great Deluge. Writhing figures filled the heavens and parents locked their children indoors and drew the drapes. It was a fine day for love; the sun glinted on sweat-bedewed flesh, and in the unseasonable warmth the still air rang with cries of delight. The Byrds looped and zoomed and chased one another, and when they met they coupled. Artificial barriers of species were cast aside and Eagle mated with Chaffinch, Robin with Albatross.

"Clearly a visual parable," said Dr. Pratt. "The—"

108   "Shut up," said Mother. "Shut up, shut up, shut *up!*"

In the garry oak, Rufous-necked Hornbill mated with Rufous-necked Hornbill, then with Crow; then, rising joyously into the sky, with Skua, with Lark, and finally with Hamadryas Baboon, who had at last realized what it was all about and strapped on a belt.

"She's eighty-six years old! What is she thinking of?"

"She's an Earth Mother to them," said Dr. Pratt.

112   "Earth Mother my ass," said Father. "She's stark, staring mad, and it's about time we faced up to it."

"It's true, it's true!" wailed Mother, a broken woman. "She's crazy! She's been crazy for years! She's old and useless, and yet she keeps filling in all that stuff on her Peace form, instead of forgetting, like any normal old woman!"

"Winter is coming," said Dr. Pratt, "and we are witnessing the symbolic Preservation of the Species. Look at that nice young Tern up there. Tomorrow they must come back to earth, but in the wombs of the females the memory of this glorious September will live on!"

"She's senile and filthy! I've seen her eating roots from out of the ground, and do you know what she did to the Everattentive Waiter? She cross-wired it with the Mailgift chute and filled the kitchen with self-adhesive cookies!"

"She did?"

And the first shadow of doubt crossed Dr. Pratt's face. The leader of the Byrds crazy?

"And one day a Gameshow called on the visiphone and asked her a skill-testing question which would have set us all up for life—and she did the most disgusting thing, and it went out live and the whole town saw it!"

"I'm sure she has sound psychological reasons for her behaviour," said Dr. Pratt desperately.

"She doesn't! She's insane! She walks to town rather than fill out a Busquest form! She brews wine in a horrible jar under the bed! She was once sentenced to one week's community service for indecent exposure! She trespasses in the Department of Agriculture's fields! You want to know why the house stinks? She programmed the Pesterminator to zap the Tidy Mice!"

"But I thought . . . Why didn't you tell me before? My God, when I think of the things I've said on Newspocket! If this comes out, my reputation, all I've worked for, all . . ." He was becoming incoherent. "Why didn't you tell me?" he asked again.

"Well, Jesus Christ, it's obvious, isn't it?" snapped Father. "Look at her. She's up in the sky mating with a Hamadryas Baboon, or something very much like one. Now, that's what I call crazy."

"But it's a *Movement.* . . . It's free and vibrant and so basic, so—"

"A nut cult," said Father. "Started by a loonie and encouraged by a quack. Nothing more, nothing less. And the forecast for tonight is twenty below. It'll wipe out the whole lot of them. You'd better get them all down, Pratt, or you'll have a few thousand deaths on your conscience."

But the Byrds came down of their own accord, later that day. As though sensing the end of the Indian summer and the bitter nights to come, they drifted out of the sky in groups, heading for earth, heading for us. Gran alighted in the garry oak with whirling arms, followed by Gramps. They sat close together on their accustomed branch, gobbling quietly to each other. More Byrds came; the Crows, the Pelicans. They filled the tree, spread along the ridge of the roof and squatted on the guttering. They began to perch on fences and posts, even on the ground, all species intermingled. They were all around us, converging, covering the neighbouring roofs and trees, a great final gathering of humans who, just for a few weeks, had gone a little silly. They looked happy although tired, and a few were shivering as the afternoon shortened into evening. They made a great noise at first, a rustling and screeching and fluid piping, but after a while they quieted down. I saw Pandora amid them, painted and pretty, but her gaze passed right through me. They were still Byrds, playing their role until the end.

And they all faced Gran.

They were awaiting the word to Come Down, but Gran remained silent, living every last moment.

It was like standing in the centre of a vast amphitheatre, with all those heads turned towards us, all those beady eyes watching us. The Newspocket crew were nowhere to be seen; they probably couldn't get through the crowd.

Finally Dr. Pratt strode forward. He was in the grip of a great despondency. He was going to come clean.

"Fools!" he shouted. A murmur of birdlike sounds arose, but soon died. "All through history there have been fools like you, and they've caused wars and disasters and misery. Fools without minds of their own, who follow their leader without thought, without stopping to ask if their leader knows what he is doing. Leaders like Genghis Khan, like Starbusch, like Hitler, leaders who manipulate their followers like puppets in pursuit of their own crazy ends. Crazy leaders drunk with power. Leaders like Gran here.

"Yes, Gran is crazy! I mean certifiably crazy, ready for Peace. Irrational and insane and a burden to the State and to herself. She had me fooled at first." He uttered a short, bitter laugh, not unlike the mating cry of Forster's Tern. "I thought I found logic in what she did. Such was the cunning nature of her madness. It was only recently, when I investigated Gran's past record, that I unmasked her for what she is: a mentally unbalanced old woman with marked antisocial tendencies. I could give you chapter and verse of Gran's past misdemeanors—and I can tell you right now, this isn't the first time she's taken her clothes off in public—but I will refrain, out of consideration for her family, who have suffered enough.

"It will suffice to say that I have recommended her committal and the Peace Wagon is on its way. The whole affair is best forgotten. Now, come down out of those trees and scrub off, and go home to your families, all of you."

He turned away, shoulders drooping. It was nothing like the Great Coming Down he'd pictured. It was a slinking thing, a creeping home, an abashed admission of stupidity.

Except that the Byrds weren't coming down.

They sat silently on their perches, awaiting the word from Gran.

All through Dr. Pratt's oration she'd been quiet, staring fixedly at the sky. Now, at last, she looked around. Her eyes were bright, but it was an almost human brightness, a different thing from the beady stare of the past weeks. And she half-smiled through the paint, but she didn't utter a word.

She activated her belt and, flapping her arms, rose into the darkening sky.

And the Byrds rose after her.

They filled the sky, a vast multitude of rising figures, and Pandora was with them. Gran led, Gramps close behind, and then came Coot and Skua and Hawk, and the whole thousand-strong mob. They wheeled once over the town and filled the evening with a great and lonely cry. Then they headed off in V-formations, loose flocks, tight echelons, a pattern of dwindling black forms against the pale duck-egg blue of nightfall.

"Where in hell are they going?" shouted Dr. Pratt as I emerged from the   140
shed, naked and painted. It was cold, but I would soon get used to it.

"South," I said.

"Why the hell south? What's wrong with here, for God's sake?"

"It's warmer, south. We're migrating."

So I activated my belt and lifted into the air, and watched the house fall   144
away below me, and the tiny bolts of light as the Pesterminator hunted things. The sky seemed empty now but there was still a pink glow to the west. Hurrying south, I saw something winking like a red star and, before long, I was homing in on the gleaming hindquarters of a Hamadryas Baboon.

Understanding What You Read

1. What does Coney imply is wrong with our own world in this story?
2. What is the function of the psychiatrist? What do readers know that he fails to understand?
3. How does the antigravity belt work? What is the Peace Wagon?
4. What particular aspects of society are the "Byrds" reacting against?
5. What requirements does our own time impose on marginal citizens that resemble filling out the "Choice for Peace" form?
6. In what sense is this story about a return to nature and a reclaiming of wildness?
7. What details in this story let you know that the world is a very crowded place?

Writing About What You Read

Imagine that you are an elderly grandparent in the mid-twenty-first century. Write a fictional account of your typical day, including details about family life and news events.

PAUL R. EHRLICH AND ANNE H. EHRLICH

Paul Ehrlich (b. 1932) first came to national prominence in 1968, when he published *The Population Bomb,* a best-seller that warned of the disasters that would come with continued growth of population. He has since written other books about environmental issues, some in collaboration with others. The first book that Paul and Anne Ehrlich (b. 1933), both biologists at Stanford University, wrote together was *Population/Resources/Environment* (1970), a textbook for environmental studies. Since then they have published *Extinction* (1981) and *Healing the Planet* (1991). "Why Isn't Everyone as Scared as We Are?" is from *The Population Explosion* (1990).

Why Isn't Everyone as Scared as We Are?

IN THE early 1930s, when we were born, the world population was just 2 billion; now it is more than two and a half times as large and still growing rapidly. The population of the United States is increasing much more slowly than the world average, but it has more than doubled in only six decades— from 120 million in 1928 to 250 million in 1990. Such a huge population expansion within two or three generations can by itself account for a great many changes in the social and economic institutions of a society. It also is very frightening to those of us who spend our lives trying to keep track of the implications of the population explosion.

One of the toughest things for a population biologist to reconcile is the contrast between his or her recognition that civilization is in imminent serious jeopardy and the modest level of concern that population issues generate among the public and even among elected officials.

Much of the reason for this discrepancy lies in the slow development of the problem. People aren't scared because they evolved biologically and culturally to respond to short-term "fires" and to tune out long-term "trends" over which they had no control. Only if we do what doesn't come naturally—if we determinedly focus on what seem to be gradual or nearly imperceptible changes—can the outlines of our predicament be perceived clearly enough to be frightening.

4   Consider the *very* slow-motion origins of our predicament. It seems reasonable to define humanity as having first appeared some four million years ago in the form of australopithecines, small-brained upright creatures like "Lucy."[1] Of course, we don't know the size of this first human popula-

---

[1] Incomplete fossilized skeleton found in eastern Ethiopia in 1974 and classified as *Australopithecus asarensis.* Researchers named her Lucy for the Beatles song "Lucy in the Sky with Diamonds."

tion, but it's likely that there were never more than 125,000 australopithecines at any given time.

Our own species, *Homo sapiens,* evolved a few hundred thousand years ago. Some ten thousand years ago, when agriculture was invented, probably no more than five million people inhabited Earth—fewer than now live in the San Francisco Bay Area. Even at the time of Christ, two thousand years ago, the entire human population was roughly the size of the population of the United States today; by 1650 there were only 500 million people, and in 1850 only a little over a billion. Since there are now well past 5 billion people, the vast majority of the population explosion has taken place in less than a tenth of one percent of the history of *Homo sapiens.*

This is a remarkable change in the abundance of a single species. After an unhurried pace of growth over most of our history, expansion of the population accelerated during the Industrial Revolution and really shot up after 1950. Since mid-century, the human population has been growing at annual rates ranging from about 1.7 to 2.1 percent per year, doubling in forty years or less. Some groups have grown significantly faster; the population of the African nation of Kenya was estimated to be increasing by over 4 percent annually during the 1980s—a rate that if continued would double the nation's population in only seventeen years. That rate did continue for over a decade, and only recently has shown slight signs of slowing. Meanwhile, other nations, such as those of northern Europe, have grown much more slowly in recent decades.

But even the highest growth rates are still *slow-motion changes compared to events we easily notice and react to.* A car swerving at us on the highway is avoided by actions taking a few seconds. The Alaskan oil spill caused great public indignation, but faded from the media and the consciousness of most people in a few months. America's participation in World War II spanned less than four years. During the last four years, even Kenya's population grew by only about 16 percent—a change hardly perceptible locally, let alone from a distance. In four years, the world population expands only a little more than 7 percent. Who could notice that? Precipitous as the population explosion has been in historical terms, it is occurring at a snail's pace in an individual's perception. It is not an event, it is a trend that must be analyzed in order for its significance to be appreciated.

The time it takes a population to double in size is a dramatic way to picture rates of population growth, one that most of us can understand more readily than percentage growth rates. Human populations have often grown in a pattern described as "exponential." Exponential growth occurs in bank accounts when interest is left to accumulate and itself earns interest. Exponential growth occurs in populations because children, the analogue of interest, remain in the population and themselves have children.

A key feature of exponential growth is that it often seems to start slowly and finish fast. A classic example used to illustrate this is the pond weed that

8

doubles each day the amount of pond surface covered and is projected to cover the entire pond in thirty days. The question is, how much of the pond will be covered in twenty-nine days? The answer, of course, is that just half of the pond will be covered in twenty-nine days. The weed will then double once more and cover the entire pond the next day. As this example indicates, exponential growth contains the potential for big surprises.

The limits to human population growth are more difficult to perceive than those restricting the pond weed's growth. Nonetheless, like the pond weed, human populations grow in a pattern that is essentially exponential, so we must be alert to the treacherous properties of that sort of growth. The key point to remember is that *a long history of exponential growth in no way implies a long future of exponential growth*. What begins in slow motion may eventually overwhelm us in a flash.

The last decade or two has seen a slight slackening in the human population growth rate—a slackening that has been prematurely heralded as an "end to the population explosion." The slowdown has been only from a peak annual growth rate of perhaps 2.1 percent in the early 1960s to about 1.8 percent in 1990. To put this change in perspective, the population's doubling time has been extended from thirty-three years to thirty-nine. Indeed, the world population *did* double in the thirty-seven years from 1950 to 1987. But even if birthrates continue to fall, the world population will continue to expand (assuming that death rates don't rise), although at a slowly slackening rate, for about another century. Demographers think that growth will not end before the population has reached 10 billion or more.

12   So, even though birthrates have declined somewhat, *Homo sapiens* is a long way from ending its population explosion or avoiding its consequences. In fact, the biggest jump, from 5 to 10 billion in well under a century, is still ahead. But this does not mean that growth couldn't be ended sooner, with a much smaller population size, if we—all of the world's nations—made up our minds to do it. The trouble is, many of the world's leaders and perhaps most of the world's people still don't believe that there are compelling reasons to do so. They are even less aware that if humanity fails to act, *nature may end the population explosion for us*—in very unpleasant ways—well before 10 billion is reached.

Those unpleasant ways are beginning to be perceptible. Humanity in the 1990s will be confronted by more and more intransigent environmental problems, global problems dwarfing those that worried us in the late 1960s. Perhaps the most serious is that of global warming, a problem caused in large part by population growth and overpopulation. It is not clear whether the severe drought in North America, the Soviet Union, and China in 1988 was the result of the slowly rising surface temperature of Earth, but it is precisely the kind of event that climatological models predict as more and more likely with continued global warming. In addition to more frequent and more severe crop failures, projected consequences of the warming include coastal flooding, desertification, the creation of as many as 300 million environmental refugees, alteration of patterns of disease, water shortages, general stress on natural ecosystems, and synergistic interactions among all these factors.

Continued population growth and the drive for development in already badly overpopulated poor nations will make it *exceedingly* difficult to slow the greenhouse warming—and impossible to stop or reverse it—in this generation at least. And, even if the warming should miraculously not occur, contrary to accepted projections, human numbers are on a collision course with massive famines anyway.

Global warming, acid rain, depletion of the ozone layer, vulnerability to epidemics, and exhaustion of soils and groundwater are all, as we shall see, related to population size. They are also clear and present dangers to the persistence of civilization. Crop failures due to global warming alone might result in the premature deaths of a billion or more people in the next few decades, and the AIDS epidemic could slaughter hundreds of millions. Together these would constitute a harsh "population control" program provided by nature in the face of humanity's refusal to put into place a gentler program of its own.

We shouldn't delude ourselves: the population explosion will come to an end before very long. The only remaining question is whether it will be halted through the humane method of birth control, or by nature wiping out the surplus. We realize that religious and cultural opposition to birth control exists throughout the world; but we believe that people simply don't understand the choice that such opposition implies. Today, anyone opposing birth control is unknowingly voting to have the human population size controlled by a massive increase in early deaths.

Of course, the environmental crisis isn't caused just by expanding human numbers. Burgeoning consumption among the rich and increasing dependence on ecologically unsound technologies to supply that consumption also play major parts. This allows some environmentalists to dodge the population issue by emphasizing the problem of malign technologies. And social commentators can avoid commenting on the problem of too many people by focusing on the serious maldistribution of affluence.

But scientists studying humanity's deepening predicament recognize that a major factor contributing to it is rapidly worsening overpopulation. The Club of Earth, a group whose members all belong to both the U.S. National Academy of Sciences and the American Academy of Arts and Sciences, released a statement in September 1988 that said in part:

> Arresting global population growth should be second in importance only to avoiding nuclear war on humanity's agenda. Overpopulation and rapid population growth are intimately connected with most aspects of the current human

predicament, including rapid depletion of nonrenewable resources, deterioration of the environment (including rapid climate change), and increasing international tensions.

20   When three prestigious scientific organizations cosponsored an international scientific forum, "Global Change," in Washington in 1989, there was general agreement among the speakers that population growth was a substantial contributor toward prospective catastrophe. Newspaper coverage was limited, and while the population component was mentioned in the *New York Times*'s article, the point that population limitation will be essential to resolving the predicament was lost. The coverage of environmental issues in the media has been generally excellent in the last few years, but there is still a long way to go to get adequate coverage of the intimately connected population problem.

Even though the media occasionally give coverage to population issues, some people never get the word. In November 1988, Pope John Paul II reaffirmed the Catholic Church's ban on contraception. The occasion was the twentieth anniversary of Pope Paul's anti-birth-control encyclical, *Humanae Vitae*.

Fortunately, the majority of Catholics in the industrial world pay little attention to the encyclical or the Church's offical ban on all practical means of birth control. One need only note that Catholic Italy at present has the smallest average completed family size (1.3 children per couple) of any nation. Until contraception and then abortion were legalized there in the 1970s, the Italian birthrate was kept low by an appalling rate of illegal abortion.

The bishops who assembled to celebrate the anniversary defended the encyclical by announcing that "the world's food resources theoretically could feed 40 billion people." In one sense they were right. It's "theoretically possible" to feed 40 billion people—in the same sense that it's theoretically possible for your favorite major-league baseball team to win every single game for fifty straight seasons, or for you to play Russian roulette ten thousand times in a row with five out of six chambers loaded without blowing your brains out.

24   One might also ask whether feeding 40 billion people is a worthwhile goal for humanity, even if it could be reached. Is any purpose served in turning Earth, in essence, into a gigantic human feedlot? Putting aside the near-certainty that such a miracle couldn't be sustained, what would happen to the *quality* of life?

We wish to emphasize that the population problem is in no sense a "Catholic problem," as some would claim. Around the world, Catholic reproductive performance is much the same as that of non-Catholics in similar cultures and with similar economic status. Nevertheless, the *political* position of the Vatican, traceable in no small part to the extreme conservatism of Pope John Paul II, is an important barrier to solving the population problem. Non-Catholics should be very careful not to confuse Catholics or Catholicism with the Vatican—most American Catholics don't. Furthermore, the Church's position on contraception is distressing to many millions of Catholics, who feel it morally imperative to follow their own consciences in their personal lives and disregard the Vatican's teachings on this subject.

Nor is unwillingness to face the severity of the population problem limited to the Vatican. It's built into our genes and our culture. That's one reason many otherwise bright and humane people behave like fools when confronted with demographic issues. Thus, an economist specializing in mail-order marketing can sell the thesis that the human population could increase essentially forever because people are the "ultimate resource," and a journalist can urge more population growth in the United States so that we can have a bigger army! Even some environmentalists are taken in by the frequent assertion that "there is no population problem, only a problem of distribution." The statement is usually made in a context of a plan for conquering hunger, as if food shortage were the only consequence of overpopulation.

But even in that narrow context, the assertion is wrong. Suppose food *were* distributed equally. If everyone in the world ate as Americans do, less than half the *present* world population could be fed on the record harvests of 1985 and 1986. Of course, everyone doesn't have to eat like Americans. About a third of the world grain harvest—the staples of the human feeding base—is fed to animals to produce eggs, milk, and meat for American-style diets. Wouldn't feeding that grain directly to people solve the problem? If everyone were willing to eat an essentially vegetarian diet, that additional grain would allow perhaps a billion more people to be fed with 1986 production.

Would such radical changes solve the world food problem? Only in the *very* short term. The additional billion people are slated to be with us by the end of the century. Moreover, by the late 1980s, humanity already seemed to be encountering trouble maintaining the production levels of the mid-1980s, let alone keeping up with population growth. The world grain harvest in 1988 was some 10 percent *below* that of 1986. And there is little sign that the rich are about to give up eating animal products.

So there is no reasonable way that the hunger problem can be called "only" one of distribution, even though redistribution of food resources would greatly alleviate hunger today. Unfortunately, an important truth, that maldistribution is a cause of hunger now, has been used as a way to avoid a more important truth—that overpopulation is critical today and may well make the distribution question moot tomorrow.

The food problem, however, attracts little immediate concern among well-fed Americans, who have no reason to be aware of its severity or extent. But other evidence that could make everyone face up to the seriousness of the population dilemma is now all around us, since problems to which overpopulation and population growth make major contributions are worsening at a rapid rate. They often appear on the evening news, although the population connection is almost never made.

Consider the television pictures of barges loaded with garbage wandering like the *Flying Dutchman*[2] across the seas, and news stories about "no room at the dump." They are showing the results of the interaction between too many affluent people and the environmentally destructive technologies that support that affluence. Growing opportunities to swim in a mixture of sewage and medical debris off American beaches can be traced to the same source. Starving people in sub-Saharan Africa are victims of drought, defective agricultural policies, and an overpopulation of both people and domestic animals—with warfare often dealing the final blow. All of the above are symptoms of humanity's massive and growing negative impact on Earth's life-support systems.

32   The average person, even the average scientist, seldom makes the connection between such seemingly disparate events and the population problem, and thus remains unworried. To a degree, this failure to put the pieces together is due to a taboo against frank discussion of the population crisis in many quarters, a taboo generated partly by pressures from the Catholic hierarchy and partly by other groups who are afraid that dealing with population issues will produce socially damaging results.

Many people on the political left are concerned that focusing on overpopulation will divert attention from crucial problems of social justice (which certainly need to be addressed *in addition* to the population problem). Often those on the political right fear that dealing with overpopulation will encourage abortion (it need not) or that halting growth will severely damage the economy (it could, if not handled properly). And people of varied political persuasions who are unfamiliar with the magnitude of the population problem believe in a variety of farfetched technological fixes—such as colonizing outer space—that they think will allow the need for regulating the size of the human population to be avoided forever.

*   *   *

All of us naturally lean toward the taboo against dealing with population growth. The roots of our aversion to limiting the size of the human population are as deep and pervasive as the roots of human sexual behavior. Through billions of years of evolution, outreproducing other members of your population was the name of the game. It is the very basis of natural selection, the driving force of the evolutionary process. Nonetheless, the taboo must be uprooted and discarded.

There is no more time to waste; in fact, there wasn't in 1968 when *The*

---

[2]A phantom ship (on which a murder is committed) doomed to haunt the sea in perpetual search for harbor. A novel and an opera are based on the story.

Population Bomb was published. Human inaction has already condemned hundreds of millions more people to premature deaths from hunger and disease. The population connection must be made in the public mind. Action to end the population explosion *humanely* and start a gradual population *decline* must become a top item on the human agenda: the human birthrate must be lowered to slightly below the human death rate as soon as possible. There still may be time to limit the scope of the impending catastrophe, but not *much* time. Ending the population explosion by controlling births is necessarily a slow process. Only nature's cruel way of solving the problem is likely to be swift.

Of course, if we do wake up and succeed in controlling our population size, that will still leave us with all the other thorny problems to solve. Limiting human numbers will not alone end warfare, environmental deterioration, poverty, racism, religious prejudice, or sexism; it will just buy us the opportunity to do so. As the old saying goes, whatever your cause, it's a lost cause without population control.

America and other rich nations have a clear choice today. They can continue to ignore the population problem and their own massive contributions to it. Then they will be trapped in a downward spiral that may well lead to the end of civilization in a few decades. More frequent droughts, more damaged crops and famines, more dying forests, more smog, more international conflicts, more epidemics, more gridlock, more drugs, more crime, more sewage swimming, and other extreme unpleasantness will mark our course. It is a route already traveled by too many of our less fortunate fellow human beings.

Or we can change our collective minds and take the measures necessary to lower global birthrates dramatically. People can learn to treat growth as the cancerlike disease it is and move toward a sustainable society. The rich can make helping the poor an urgent goal, instead of seeking more wealth and useless military advantage over one another. Then humanity might have a chance to manage all those other seemingly intractable problems. It is a challenging prospect, but at least it will give our species a shot at creating a decent future for itself. More immediately and concretely, taking action now will give our children and their children the possibility of decent lives.

Understanding What You Read

1. How many people are on the planet today, and at what rate does that number increase every year?
2. What ways does nature have to end the population explosion if people do not do so voluntarily?
3. What specific environmental problems are related to population?
4. If everyone ate a vegetarian diet, how many additional people could be

fed with the grain currently fed to animals to produce milk, eggs, and meat?

5. Why, according to the Ehrlichs, have people neglected to deal with the population problem?

Writing About What You Read

Choose three environmental problems—air pollution, destruction of the rain forests, acid rain, declining biodiversity, overuse of pesticides, water scarcity, or some other issue—and explain how continued population growth might intensify the problem and how curbing population growth might reduce it.

MARK L. SCHANNON

Schannon (b. 1948) is the senior vice president and associate director for Ketchum Communications. The following speech was delivered at the Business and Environmental Ethics Conference at Wilkes-Barre, Pennsylvania, on October 11, 1990. At that time Shannon was director of public relations for the Monsanto Company, a major chemical manufacturer.

One Businessperson's View of the Ecological Crisis

GOOD AFTERNOON. Depending on the mood of this group, it's either going to be a pleasure being here, or penance—what I have to endure for having joined a chemical company some years ago. I won't know which until a little later, I suppose.

However, it is getting easier for a Monsanto employee to talk to community people about environmental issues.

Not too many years ago, the message might have been: "Hey, we're scientists, we're engineers, we're professionals. You're not. Trust us. We know what we're doing."

That message doesn't work too well anymore.

It really never did work.

Among business people, it created the illusion that the public was willing to sit back and let the professionals manage the environment.

And as the professionals managed, the public learned about ozone depletion, global warming, acid rain, Bhopal, Love Canal, Times Beach, toxic waste dumps, PCBs, Agent Orange,[1] and, for those of you who remember or saw the movie *Major League* recently, rivers on fire.

The illusion that the public would trust us did have one major effect. It hid the fact that the people were getting more and more disenchanted with the so-called experts—whether those experts lived in companies or governments. 8

Today, I think it's fair to say that the illusions have been shattered. Those of us in business, and even more problematically, in government, know too well that no one knows who to trust—or what to believe.

Think about it for a minute—the extraordinary situation where our own government is viewed with mistrust and suspicion when it makes pronouncements on environmental matters. Is it any wonder that every environmental issue becomes a crisis?

Actually, it's more complex than simple distrust.

People do believe the government when it says something is not safe. 12

However, people reject government reassurance that something is safe.

One result: The public was offered a choice when the Alar[2] controversy was launched by *60 Minutes*. Who do you trust? That well-known epidemiologist Meryl Streep?

Or do you trust virtually every governmental and scientific expert in the U.S., including the National Academy of Sciences?

The public sided with the actress. 16

In fact, at Monsanto, we recently were talking to consumers about a product we're about to introduce—to get their reaction to what we and our opponents are saying. One person said, "Hey, get Paul Newman to be your spokesperson, then we'd believe you."

He was serious. And the rest of the group agreed. Are people nuts?

When independent scientists, conducting health studies on the residents at Love Canal, found no problems associated with exposure, why did the people react with rage?

Do people enjoy being terrified? 20

I know a woman who refuses to be convinced—by her own son—that independent scientists have found America's food supply to be safe.

Is my mother crazy?

The answer, I think—I hope, is no. People aren't nuts, they don't enjoy

[1]Environmental disasters or poisons: Bhopal is a city in India where more than 3,000 people died from toxic gases accidentally released from a Union Carbide plant; Love Canal, New York, is the site of a toxic waste dump; Times Beach, Missouri, was evacuated in the mid-1980s because of dioxin contamination; polychlorinated biphenyl is a toxin used in the electrical industry, banned in the United States in 1979; Agent Orange, a defoliant used in the Vietnam War, caused health problems in people exposed to it.

[2]A petrochemical used on apples that was found to cause cancer in laboratory animals. It was taken off the market in 1989 because of public outcry.

being terrified, and my mother, despite her chemophobia, is a rational person.

24 But we don't know who to believe. We want to know that someone "out there" is acting responsibly—is looking out for us, protecting us and our families—but we get conflicting messages.

Environmental groups tell us that acid rain is destroying the world—while a reporter, Greg Easterbrook, disagrees. In the liberal journal *The New Republic,* he wrote an article called "Everything You Know About the Environment Is Wrong—a Liberal Skeptic's Guide to Earth Day."

Easterbrook wrote:

> Little-known note: in the past fifteen years, national sulfur dioxide emissions have already fallen by about one-quarter.

He goes on,

> Second note: recent studies show acid rain effects to be considerably less than theory predicts. Only high-altitude red spruce trees, not forests generally, so far display acid-rain damage; and although some enviros projected that a majority of Eastern U.S. lakes would by now be too acidic for most life, the federal study found that only four percent have crossed this threshold.

28 Then, to make sure we don't get too complacent, he finished,

> Conservative critics interpret such studies as proving acid rain is no big deal. Four percent lifelessness no big deal?

When is a deal a big deal? At what point should we be concerned? No one really knows where to turn for answers.

One final note, by way of extended introduction. In 1987, the U.S. Environmental Protection Agency issued a very courageous report, called "Unfinished Business."

They listed the pressing environmental issues of the day in two ways: one, by the amount of time and money spent on the issue by the EPA, and the second, by the degree of health risk to people.

32 They found that the things they were spending most of their money on—toxic waste dumps, for example—represented relatively low levels of risk.

The things they were spending the least amount of time on—radon and worker exposure—represented the greatest degree of risk.

Why the discrepancy? One big reason is public pressure.

The EPA is already criticized for not spending enough to clean up toxic dumps, and explaining relative risk is not going to ease the pressure on them.

36 In a very real sense, the EPA is trapped.

And so I come to the title of my talk today, "One Businessperson Looks at the Ecological Crisis."

I didn't pick the title—the Ethics Institute did. But the more I thought about it, the more appropriate it became—because there are—not is, but *are* ecological crises.

Unlike Nixon, I don't have six crises, but I do have four. The first is a crisis of communication. The second, a crisis of confidence. The third, a crisis of cooperation. And the fourth is the environmental crisis.

The crisis of communication can be maddening—for business, for the average citizen, for environmental groups and government. At times, I think we've constructed a tower of Babel[3] and God's punishment is that we neither hear nor understand one another.

The hardest step I think we at Monsanto had to face was acknowledging that we weren't effectively communicating with people about environmental issues.

It wasn't just that we didn't know how to communicate—although we really didn't.

More important, if someone's immediate response is to distrust what you say because of who you are or who you represent, then you're really left with nothing to say. You can't communicate until you work beyond that distrust.

Let me give you an example. One of our plants was having trouble with a community group that was concerned about the effect our operations were having on their health.

After much soul searching, we finally decided to have a meeting with them, but tensions were very high.

The plant manager had a two-page list of "facts" he wanted to share with these people. If only they understood the facts, he argued, they wouldn't be concerned.

I suggest a simpler goal for the first meeting. That was: to schedule a second meeting. His only objective would be to keep the discussion going. Let the community people express their feelings; acknowledge their legitimate right to be concerned; and acknowledge their right to feel secure about what's going on in the plant.

It worked. Not only was there a second meeting, but eventually, they brought in an expert of their own. (They grew more comfortable with us, but still couldn't quite trust us.) Their expert gave us very high marks for the way we were operating that facility, and, eventually, to our surprise, the local group disappeared.

They had gotten what they wanted: the level of information necessary to reassure themselves that we weren't putting them at risk.

But that was a small plant in a small town—and that tactic is awfully difficult with a quarter billion Americans—or 5 billion people in the world.

[3]Chapter 11 of Genesis tells how God punished people for attempting to raise a tower to heaven by confusing their language so they could no longer understand each other.

40

44

48

And that's why the crisis in communication is rampant.

52 News, as defined by the media, is what's unusual—out of the ordinary. Not dog bites man, but man bites dog.

Well, one problem with that is that when you report the unusual, it can be perceived as the norm.

If some chemical causes cancer and gets widespread coverage, does that mean that all chemicals cause cancer—at the same levels with the same degree of risk?

In 1988, Monsanto announced that we were cutting our toxic air emissions by 90 percent by the end of 1992, with an ultimate goal of zero effect.

56 Even that simple statement is hard to communicate. Do we mention that we mean those chemicals listed in the Superfund[4] Amendments and Reauthorization Act, Title III, Section 313? Do we mention that the law only applies to the U.S., so our ex-U.S. operations are building their own lists? What happens when the EPA takes a chemical off the list? How does that affect our progress?

At what point is too much information counterproductive?

And if that's hard to communicate, how about this: Should we try to attain zero effect? Are we truly helping the environment? Are we really reducing health risks or simply responding at great cost to public fear?

Actually, those are moot questions. We're beyond them.

60 We'll spend the money regardless of whether it makes scientific sense, because it clearly makes common sense.

And if we spend more than is necessary, that's partially because of the second crisis, the crisis of confidence.

Would any of you believe me if I said that a 50 percent reduction is all that's necessary? That the millions of tons a year we put in the air is safe?

If my mother won't believe me, I can't imagine why you would.

64 But if you don't trust me, then who? It seems that people trust no one.

A recent study found that 14 percent of Americans rate the federal government as very trustworthy when it comes to information about food safety. Fourteen percent! Thirty-five percent rate their friends and family members as very trustworthy.

Only 20 percent say the media is very trustworthy. Consumer advocacy groups get a 35 percent rating—the same as friends and family.

It will come as no surprise that 3 percent give chemical companies the nod as very trustworthy.

68 But that whole issue of trust is at the core of the crisis of confidence.

What we have learned at Monsanto is that earning the public's trust is the only way we're going to safeguard our privilege to operate.

Let me quote from our chairman, Dick Mahoney, in his speech at our last annual meeting:

---

[4]A law passed in 1980 set up this fund for cleaning up hazardous chemical dump sites.

In recent years, public concern for the environment has been growing worldwide. What were once seen as exemplary programs and policies are now viewed as the bare minimum expected by the public. Our freedom to operate will be available to us only as long as we come closer and closer to public expectations. Our response to this global public concern is basic: we are committed to being a corporate environmental leader. Our environmental program follows a long-standing theme from the time of Monsanto's founder, John Queeny—it is the right thing to do.

I want to spend a couple of minutes talking about what we have done to try and earn the public's trust.

We were the first company, back in 1985, to make available to the public what are called material safety data sheets, which describe in detail the health and safety effects associated with each of the chemicals we use.

Also in 1985, we were the first company to publicly embrace the "right to know" concept. We threw open our plant gates and invited people to see what we were doing, how we were doing it, and how we planned to do it better in the future.

We also conducted a publicized high hazard materials audit of all our sites, world wide, again launched in 1985. Led by a senior vice president, it found that, while we were good at protecting the environment, we could be better, and we made numerous improvements which we announced.

When Congress, in 1987, enacted the Superfund Reauthorization bill, which included stringent rules for making public what companies make and dispose of, we took the lead in an aggressive communications campaign to make all information easily available to the public.

And also in that year, we announced our air emissions reduction program.

Finally, earlier this year, in a speech to the National Wildlife Federation, Dick Mahoney announced the Monsanto Pledge. The pledge lays out our promise to the public of how we will discharge our environmental responsibilities.

—We pledge to reduce all toxic and hazardous emissions working towards the goal of zero effect;

—We will ensure that no Monsanto operation poses any undue risk to our employees and our communities;

—We will work to achieve sustainable agriculture through new technologies and practices;

—We will ensure the safety of our groundwater;

—We will keep our plants open to our communities and involve the community in plant operations;

—We will manage all corporate real estate, including plant sites, to benefit nature; and

—We will search worldwide for technology to reduce and eliminate waste from our operations, with the priority being not making it in the first place.

We have other specific programs, but my point in going over this rather long list of activities is that it is really only the first step in building bridges to earn the public's trust.

We know we have a long way to go.

But business alone cannot solve the crisis of confidence. Environmental groups, government, and the public have a role to play.

88 And that neatly leads into the third crisis, the crisis of cooperation.

Back in 1984, an environmental leader in an op-ed piece in the *Washington Post* criticized other environmentalists for relying on the politics of confrontation over cooperation to solve problems.

He said that real solutions to environmental issues would come only when business, government and environmentalists joined forces.

Monsanto's then chairman Lou Fernandez responded with an op-ed piece equally critical of the business community for our reliance on litigation and confrontation.

92 He proposed a meeting of the minds, which, over the past five years, has resulted in some remarkable joint efforts.

Imagine the surprise at Congress when Monsanto and the National Resources Defense Council sat on the same side of a table at a hearing, calling on Congress to increase the EPA's research budget.

But when companies like Monsanto got involved in Earth Day activities, the environmental community was split between those who welcomed our support—and those who still believe that evil money from evil people can never be put to good purpose.

There is less cooperation than there should be—or could be.

96 And that is due, I think, to the very real risks associated with any cooperative venture—and the lack of trust and difficulty in communication that makes those risks greater than they need to be.

Let's look at those risks for a bit, because until we acknowledge that they're there, and understand how they can interfere with the process, we'll continue to be trapped by them.

First, for business. Many of you are no doubt aware of the Clean Air Act which is working its way through Congress. Monsanto has an important issue we hope will be addressed in that legislation.

Remember that we announced that we would reduce air emissions by 90 percent. What happens if Congress, in this new law, calls for a 50 percent reduction? Is that on top of what we've already achieved? If not, aren't we being penalized for moving faster than other companies?

100 And if prior action is grandfathered into the law, will we be the target of environmental groups who claim a sweetheart deal between government and business?

Innovative action sometimes can result in a lose-lose situation for business—or, at least, that's what business fears.

A couple of years ago, we invited a radical environmental group to meet with us in St. Louis.

They came, we had a very cordial meeting. We provided them with loads of information—which they turned around and misrepresented to the public.

Fortunately, that kind of behavior on the part of environmentalists is not the norm—but the real possibility of that happening gives business people second thoughts when thinking about cooperative behavior.   104

Government, particularly the EPA, also faces significant risks from cooperative behavior.

Recently, Monsanto and the EPA came up with an innovative solution to a Superfund site in Texas. It was the first time a company had agreed to manage the cleanup of a site.

We were all very proud of it—the site would be cleaned up faster at less cost to the government.

Within a few months, EPA was being attacked for collusion—for abrogating their responsibility and having a too-cozy relationship with a chemical company.   108

What should have been a model program for the rest of the country has now become, to some extent, an embarrassment for the agency.

What message does that send to other EPA employees who may be considering innovative, cooperative ways to solve environmental problems?

In a world dominated by lack of trust—the crisis of confidence—the ability of a regulatory agency to be creative is sorely limited. And we all suffer the consequences.

Finally, the risk to environmental groups inherent in cooperation.   112

Let me first say that most of the environmental improvements made over the past twenty years—and, contrary to what we're often told, there have been enormous improvements—most of them are due to the pressure put on business and government by environmentalists.

But success can sometimes carry the seeds of dilemmas.

Let me quote again from Greg Easterbrook's article in *The New Republic*.

I'm quoting Easterbrook, because as a good liberal, he can say things that as a businessperson I shouldn't.   116

Here's his assessment:

> Enviros won the last twenty years by a hefty margin, but you'd never know it from their behavior. Now that their cause is mainstream, they're nervous. If Republicans call themselves environmentalists, doesn't that mean something went wrong? Of course, enviros are coded to be upset—that's their social function.
>
> Then there's the fund-raising imperative. Environmental groups now have stakes in self-preservation, and direct-mail appeals are a prime revenue source. As

the right-wing kooks have shown, scare tactics are what produce money through the mails.

Having succeeded in raising the consciousness of all of us, the environmental groups are in the strange position of having to sustain themselves in victory.

How much money would Greenpeace be able to raise, for example, if their message was: "Well, things are pretty good, but we have to remain vigilant. Most companies are coming along, but don't give up the fight now."

120   Not as stirring as "Alar Kills Children," is it?

The fault, however, lies not with the environmentalists. As much as they drive us in business crazy, we need them.

The fault, I would suggest, lies with the very nature of people. We tend to respond to shouts of "fire, fire"—no one gets a lot of attention by whispering "ember, ember."

The more environmentalists are seen as cooperating with business and government, the more people are going to think the problem is solved and direct their attention elsewhere.

124   And that makes it awfully difficult for environmentalists to admit that things are getting better.

And that leads me to the final crisis—the crisis in the environment.

Let me begin by suggesting that it is not necessarily a crisis of wills.

I think Monsanto's president, Earle Harbison, in a recent interview, spoke for most people in business when he said,

> I take nothing away from the environmentalists. They brought pressure to bear on the entire environmental picture, and I take my hat off to some of the things they did. The converse side of that is it really wasn't until lately that industry awakened to the total picture of environmental contamination that was taking place in the world. It wasn't some dark dirty secret that industry was keeping in the basement. We simply didn't understand the ramifications of it. And when we did, aided by the environmentalists, I think we have moved on it with alacrity, I think with good sense, and I know with a lot of resources.

128   I said he spoke for a lot of people in business. There are still Neanderthals out there but, like the true Neanderthals, their days are numbered. Between the environmentalists, government, citizens and a lot of business people, they're just not going to be able to ignore the issues any longer.

So it's not a matter of our willingness as a society to clean up the environment.

I think it's more that we are having trouble agreeing on what the most pressing environmental problems are and then directing our resources at those problems.

A recent study by the Roper Organization[5] asked Americans to rank environmental problems.

[5]Polling and market research organization.

The top four issues are water pollution from manufacturing plants, oil spills, hazardous waste releases and industrial air pollution.

Also recently, the EPA updated their report, "Unfinished Business."

They say that groundwater pollution and oil spills are "relatively low risk problems." On the other hand, their top four are: global climate change, habitat destruction, species extinction and ozone-layer depletion.

One high-risk issue that most experts agree on is indoor air pollution. Unfortunately, we Americans ranked it 17th of 19 items asked about.

We can't even agree on waste. People ranked the top four disposal problems as disposable diapers, plastic packaging, plastic bottles and aerosol containers. However, those four represent about 10 percent of U.S. solid waste by weight.

The four items Americans think as least important happen to represent 50 percent of solid waste: wastepaper, paper plates and paper napkins, food scraps and yard wastes.

Why the discrepancy?

To a large extent, people respond to what they've been told, and we've been told that oil spills and groundwater are major problems.

Let me conduct my own survey: How many people here have tested their homes for radon?

I have to confess that I bought a testing kit, set it up and then forgot about it until it was too late to return for analysis. Then I threw it out.

The point is that radon is a known killer—thousands of people have gotten lung cancer from exposure to radon.[6] On the other hand, most scientists agree that dioxin is not a serious health risk to humans.

But what gets the attention?

These are my four crises—it's how at least this businessperson looks at the ecological crisis. That's good news—as a society, we all agree we need to clean up the environment. But there's bad news as well: we haven't quite figured out what we should be working on.

I've given a lot of thought to so-called solutions. After all, no speech is complete without a plan to solve the critical problems of the day.

Unfortunately, I don't have any easy solutions—in fact, my fear is that what I'm going to offer is pretty general and altruistic.

First, I would suggest a moratorium on the debate about whether there *are* environmental problems.

Even if you won't grant that business believes environmental stewardship is the "right" thing to do, grant us the good sense to have realized that, like it or not, it is today's reality. And those who don't have that good sense will be getting it quickly. There simply isn't any alternative.

Second, we all need to begin doing what none of us really likes to do: pay closer attention to the issues; read more carefully, more broadly, under-

---

[6]A naturally radioactive gas in the soil that sometimes seeps into buildings contaminating the air. Repeated exposure to radon over two or three decades can cause lung cancer.

stand that we as citizens have a profound ability to influence the public policy agenda on the environment.

If Congress is going to pass laws based on what the latest Roper poll reveals, then we as citizens have a responsibility to learn more about the issue so our answers wind up directing resources to the most serious problems.

And finally, as a society we must find a way to restore trust in those federal agencies that are charged with protecting us. Discussing the implications of that is a speech in itself, but I cannot overestimate the importance of restoring a sense of confidence that good science and good public policy are in fact moving us towards a safer, cleaner world.

We have come a long way in twenty short years—our ability to continue to make progress will depend in large part on our willingness to acknowledge and address the complexity of the world around us.

152

* * *

Understanding What You Read

1. Why do businesses, government agencies, and environmental organizations have difficulty working together to solve environmental problems? What are the risks of such cooperation for all three groups?
2. In what order do Americans rank these groups as trustworthy sources of information about food safety: media, government officials, chemical companies, friends and family, and consumer advocacy groups?
3. According to a 1990 Roper poll of the American public, what were the top four environmental concerns?
4. In the same year the EPA also issued a report listing its top four environmental concerns. What are they?

Writing About What You Read

Write an essay about your top four environmental concerns, explaining why you rank them above all others and suggesting approaches we might take toward solving them.

Making Connections

1. Reread paragraph 6 of Matthiessen's "The Outlying Rocks" in Chapter 5. What particular signs of trouble does he refer to?
2. Look at your community for signs of trouble—population pressures,

pollution, toxins, excessive wastes, degrading ecosystems, species at risk, scarcities, etc. Write a paper about what you find.

3. Taking into consideration the points made in Schannon's "One Businessperson's View of the Environmental Crisis," discuss the importance of cooperative efforts among business, government, and environmental organizations to address the problems caused by pesticide use in Costa Rica.

4. In "Death from the Sky," Anne LaBastille notices signs of trouble around her cabin in the Adirondacks. Eventually she learns that the trouble is acid rain. In "The Clan of One-Breasted Women," Terry Tempest Williams also learns that death can come from the sky. Compare and contrast how these two women react to this knowledge.

5. In "The Byrds," Michael G. Coney imagines a scenario of life under increased population pressures. Write your own imaginative version of life in a world with as many people as Paul and Anne Ehrlich predict we may have twenty-five or fifty years from now.

8 ROOTS OF THE CRISIS

Man is a great blunderer going about in the woods, and there is no other except the bear makes so much noise. Being so well warned beforehand, it is a very stupid animal, or a very bold one, that cannot keep safely hid. The cunningest hunter is hunted in turn, and what he leaves of his kill is meat for some other. That is the economy of nature, but with it all there is not sufficient account taken of the works of man. There is no scavenger that eats tin cans, and no wild thing leaves a like disfigurement of the forest floor.
—MARY AUSTIN, *Land of Little Rain*

◆

And God blessed them, and God said unto them, Be fruitful and multiply, and replenish the earth and subdue it: and have dominion over the fish of the sea, and over the fowl of the air, and over every living thing that moveth upon the earth.
—Genesis 1:28

◆

We told the native peoples of North America that their relationships with the land were worthless, primitive. Now we are a culture that spends millions trying to find this knowledge, trying to reestablish a sense of well-being with the earth.
—BARRY LOPEZ, "Yukon-Charley"

◆

[The discovery of America] enabled humanity to achieve, and sanctify, the transformation of nature with unprecedented proficiency and thoroughness, to multiply, thrive, and dominate the earth as no single species ever has, altering the products and processes of the environment, modifying systems of soils and water and air, altering stable atmospheric and climatic balances, and now threatening, it is not too much to say, the existence of the earth as we have known it and the greater proportion of its species, including the human.
—KIRKPATRICK SALE, *The Conquest of Paradise: Christopher Columbus and the Columbian Legacy*

Introduction

The underlying causes of environmental degradation cannot be easily singled out. The forces that lead to the poisoning of a community, the decline of the bird and frog populations, the increase of greenhouse gases, or the erosion of our topsoil are varied, complex, and often hidden from view; they reach beyond the natural world into politics and psychology, and into our sense of individual identity. The commitment to understand these influences and to learn where and why we've gone wrong is the prerequisite to putting things right.

In *The Quiet Crisis*—published in 1963, a year after *Silent Spring*—Steward Udall, then Secretary of the Interior, looked back to the past and saw two mistaken notions that had ruled the lives of early American settlers and dictated the future for all those who came afterward. First came the Myth of Superabundance, followed by the Myth of Limitless Growth. The New World—with its wealth of forests, salmon, buffalo, and minerals—seemed inexhaustible; people couldn't imagine a day when such riches would be depleted. The New World was somehow immune to such failings of the Old as Farley Mowat recounts in "Of Men and Whales." Mowat tells how Basque whalers decimated whole populations of whales as early as the fifteenth century and how improvements in whaling techniques eventually led to the near-extermination of several whale species.

Similarly, early American industrialists assumed that there was no limit to growth—except the laws of supply and demand. In the early sixties, when Udall first called attention to the waste and destruction generated by these attitudes, most Americans were not willing to listen. Spurred on by television advertising promoting the goal of "keeping up with the Joneses," Americans acquired more things, used more energy, and perpetuated the throwaway society.

Throughout the sixties, seventies, and eighties, America exported the Myth of Superabundance to developing countries, Eastern Europe, and the former Soviet Republics, where people looked forward to the day when they too could have VCRs, cassette players, and cars of their own. Today more of us are recognizing that not only will our resources run out if consumption remains at today's levels, but the damage caused by the production and consumption of goods may bring a halt to the whole industrial enterprise. Alan Durning ("The Consumer Society") is one of those who see consumerism as a root cause of the current crisis.

Many current environmental problems are rooted in the transportation patterns of the affluent—we hop on planes and jump in cars without considering the impact of our actions. In "Clean Motion," Durning divides humanity into three classes: the walking poor, the bicycle-train-and-bus-riding middle classes, and the car-driving upper classes. It is this last group, a consumer class of some 1.1 billion members, who are responsible for most of the world's air pollution. Within this class, most people's transportation choices are made on the basis of convenience and speed. When we travel, most of us want to go as fast as possible. And usually the fastest and most convenient form of transportation is the most damaging to the environment. Ursula Le Guin's short story "Direction of the Road" reveals some of the absurdities of our attraction to cars and speed. Certainly one of the most destructive aspects of our car culture is the death toll: each year, throughout the world, 250,000 people are killed in traffic accidents.

Why is it that some problems have persisted for so long without significant efforts made to solve them? One theory is that people simply ignore or repress problems that seem overwhelming and that they don't feel they can do anything about. In "Ships in the Desert," Al Gore takes his readers on a tour of the most disturbing environmental crises today: the destruction of one of the world's largest inland seas, the thinning of the polar ice cap, the burning of the Amazon rain forests, the rapid worldwide loss of biodiversity. Both Gore and Donald Worster ("The Age of Ecology") connect the current crisis with the dawn of the nuclear age. From the moment in the 1940s that people first realized that human beings had the capacity to move beyond warfare to total destruction of the planet, there has been a strong impulse to ignore our fears and to numb ourselves to the reality of nuclear weapons.

So how did we get to this point? Several pieces in this chapter explore that question and propose various answers. Anita Gordon and David Suzuki ("How Did We Come to This?") consider some of the consequences of human arrogance and warn against the assumption that we can "manage" nature. Barry Commoner ("At War with the Planet"), who proposes that the root of the crisis lies in the battle between the ecosphere and the technosphere, raises the possibility of harmonizing the two spheres and taking what is good from each. Garrett Hardin ("The Tragedy of the Commons") examines what he sees as still deeper roots: the fundamental inclination of humans to take advantage of commonly held resources in order to maximize their own profit. Hardin's dark vision of how people behave is followed by his ideas about what will have to be done to prevent exploitation of common ground.

ALAN DURNING

A senior researcher at the Worldwatch Institute, Durning (b. 1964) specializes in the relationship between economic inequality and environmental degradation. He is the author of numerous Worldwatch papers, articles in the magazine *Worldwatch Monitor,* and articles in various national newspapers and periodicals. "The Consumer Society" and "Clean Motion" are from his book *How Much Is Enough? The Consumer Society and the Future of the Earth* (1992).

The Consumer Society

T H E W O R L D has three broad ecological classes: the consumers, the middle income, and the poor. These groups, ideally defined by their per capita consumption of natural resources, emissions of pollution, and disruption of habitats, can be distinguished in practice through two proxy measures: their average annual incomes and their life-styles. (See Table 1.)

The world's poor—some 1.1 billion people—includes all households that earn less than $700 a year per family member. They are mostly rural Africans, Indians, and other South Asians. They eat almost exclusively grains, root crops, beans, and other legumes, and they drink mostly unclean water. They live in huts and shanties, they travel by foot, and most of their possessions are constructed of stone, wood, and other substances available from the local environment. This poorest fifth of the world's people earns just 2 percent of world income.

The 3.3 billion people in the world's middle-income class earn between $700 and $7,500 per family member and live mostly in Latin America, the Middle East, China, and East Asia. This class also includes the low-income families of the former Soviet bloc and of western industrial nations. With notable exceptions, they eat a diet based on grains and water, and lodge in moderate buildings with electricity for lights, radios, and, increasingly, refrigerators and clothes washers. (In Chinese cities, for example, two thirds of households now have washing machines and one fifth have refrigerators.) They travel by bus, railway, and bicycle, and maintain a modest stock of durable goods. Collectively, they claim 33 percent of world income.

The consumer class—the 1.1 billion members of the global consumer society—includes all households whose income per family member is above $7,500. Though that threshold puts the lowest ranks of the consumer class scarcely above the U.S. poverty line, they—rather, we—still enjoy a life-style unknown in earlier ages. We dine on meat and processed, packaged foods, and imbibe soft drinks and other beverages from disposable containers. We spend most of our time in climate-controlled buildings equipped with refrigerators, clothes washers and dryers, abundant hot water, dishwashers, microwave ovens, and a plethora of other electric-powered gadgets. We travel in private automobiles and airplanes, and surround ourselves with a profusion of short-lived, throwaway goods. The consumer class takes home 64 percent of world income—32 times as much as the poor.

The consumer class counts among its members most North Americans, West Europeans, Japanese, Australians, and the citizens of Hong Kong, Singapore, and the oil sheikdoms of the Middle East. Perhaps half the people of Eastern Europe and the Commonwealth of Independent States are in the consumer class, as are about one fifth of the people in Latin America, South Africa, and the newly industrializing countries of Asia, such as South Korea.

Table 1. World Consumption Classes, 1992

Category of Consumption	Consumers (1.1 billion)	Middle (3.3 billion)	Poor (1.1 billion)
Diet	Meat, packaged food, soft drinks	Grain, clean water	Insufficient grain, unsafe water
Transport	Private cars	Bicycles Buses	Walking
Materials	Throwaways	Durables	Local biomass

SOURCE: Worldwatch Institute.

For most of us in the consumer society, the proposition that our way of life is exceptionally affluent no doubt seems farfetched. After all, we live modestly compared with the truly rich, and making ends meet is often a struggle. Just as the world's top fifth—the consumer class—makes the remainder appear impoverished, the top fifth of the consumer class—the rich—makes the lowly consumers seem deprived. In the United States, for example, the highest-paid fifth of income-earners takes home more than the remaining four fifths combined, and top corporate executives earn 93 times as much as the factory workers they employ. The relation between the rich and the consumer class is a microcosm of that between the consumer class and all people. The rich earn more, consume more natural resources, and disturb ecological systems more than average consumers do. Still, on a global scale, the rich are best taken as a subset of the consumer class, because, in terms of ecological impacts, the greatest disparities are not between the rich and the consumers but between the consumers and the middle-income class.

The emergence of the consumer society is evident in the skyrocketing consumption that has become the hallmark of our era. Worldwide, since mid-century the per capita consumption of copper, energy, meat, steel, and timber has approximately doubled; per capita car ownership and cement consumption have quadrupled; plastic use per person has quintupled; per capita aluminum consumption has grown sevenfold; and air travel per person has multiplied 33 times. Surging consumption of these things—each associated with disproportionate environmental damage—is mostly a reflection of the fortunes of the consumer class. Consumption in the middle-income class has grown more slowly, and among the poor, consumption has remained virtually unchanged.

8   The consumer society was born in the United States in the twenties, when brand names became household words, when packaged, processed foods made their widespread debut, and when the automobile assumed its place at the center of American culture. Economists and business executives, concerned that the output of mass production might go unsold when people's natural desires for food, clothing, and shelter were satisfied, began pushing mass consumption as the key to continued economic expansion. The "democratization of consumption" became the unspoken goal of American economic policy. Consumption was even painted as a patriotic duty. A business group called the National Prosperity Bureau distributed posters of Uncle Sam exhorting, "Buy what you need now!"

The Great Depression and World War II stalled the democratization of consumption temporarily, but shortly after the war's end, mass consumption came of age. In 1946, *Fortune* magazine heralded the arrival of a "dream era . . . The Great American Boom is on." By 1950, young American families were moving into 4,000 new houses each day, and filling those houses with baby carriages, clothes dryers, dishwashers, refrigerators, washing machines, and—especially—televisions. A year later, the U.S. Bureau of Labor Statistics acknowledged the rising tide of consumerism by adding televisions, electric toasters, frozen foods, canned baby foods, and do-it-yourself perm lotions to the articles tallied in its cost of living index.

In 1953, the chairman of President Eisenhower's Council of Economic Advisers canonized the new economic gospel: The American economy's "ultimate purpose," he proclaimed, was "to produce more consumer goods." Subsequent generations have faithfully pursued that aim. On average, people in the United States today own twice as many automobiles, drive two and a half times as far, use 21 times as much plastic, and cover 25 times as much distance by air as their parents did in 1950.

Since its birth in the United States, the consumer society has moved far beyond American borders, yet its most visible symbols remain American. The Disneyland near Tokyo attracts almost as many visitors each year as Mecca or the Vatican. Coca-Cola products are distributed in over 170 countries. Each day, a new McDonald's restaurant opens somewhere in the world. Singaporean youngsters can brush their teeth with the Teenage Mutant Ninja Turtle Talking Toothbrush, which says "Hey, Dudes!" in Malay. The techniques of mass marketing first perfected in the United States are now employed on every continent, teaching former East Germans, for example, to "Taste the West. Marlboro."

The consumer society's core had already expanded from the United States to Western Europe and Japan by the sixties. Taken together, France, West Germany, and the United Kingdom have almost doubled their per capita use of steel, more than doubled their intake of cement and aluminum, and tripled their paper consumption since mid-century, with the most rapid growth in the fifties and sixties. Per capita consumption of heavily packaged and processed frozen foods doubled in Europe in the eighties, and in the latter half of that decade, soft-drink consumption—mostly in disposable containers—jumped by 30 percent per person. Automobiles, too, multiplied in Europe in the eighties, surpassing households in number in 1988.

Japan started further behind the United States than Europe did in consumption, but rapidly closed the gap. Per person, the Japanese of today consume more than four times as much aluminum, almost five times as much energy, and 25 times as much steel as people in Japan did in 1950, with most of the growth occurring before the energy crises of the seventies. They also own four times as many cars per capita and, just since 1975, eat nearly twice as much meat apiece. They are flying more as well: In 1972, 1 million Japanese traveled abroad; in 1990, the number topped 11 million. Today, after four decades of consumerist expansion, West European and Japanese consumption levels are only one notch below those in the United States.

Across North America, Western Europe, and Japan, home appliances have become standard accoutrements of life. In all three regions, virtually every home has a refrigerator and a washing machine. Clothes dryers and dishwashers are spreading swiftly, and in the United States, air conditioning—which relies on ozone-depleting coolants—was standard in two thirds of homes by 1987, using 13 percent of U.S. electricity. Likewise, nearly 60 percent of Japanese homes now have at least a single-room air conditioner. Microwave ovens and video cassette recorders found their way into nearly two thirds of U.S. homes during the eighties alone.

The eighties were a decade of marked extravagance in all these core regions of the global consumer society. Laissez-faire economic policies and newly internationalized stock and bond markets created an easy-money euphoria among the well to do, which translated into a "get it while you can" binge in the middle echelons of the consumer society. In the United States, not since the Roaring Twenties had conspicuous consumption been so lauded. Over the decade, personal debt matched national debt in soaring to new heights, as consumers filled their houses and garages with third cars, motor boats, home entertainment centers, and whirlpool baths. Between 1978 and 1987, sales of Jaguar automobiles increased eightfold, and the average age of first-time buyers of fur coats fell from 50 to 26. To protect their possessions, Americans spent more on private security guards and burglar alarms than they paid through taxes for public police forces.

16   Japan also experienced a consumerist binge during the eighties. By decade's end the government was urging loyal Japanese to buy more, hoping to reduce the nation's massive and internationally resented trade surplus by inflating domestic consumption. A wave of stratospheric spending—gold-wrapped sushi and mink coats for dogs—resulted, but Japan still comes to high consumption hesitantly. Many older Japanese hold to their time-honored belief in frugality. Yorimoto Katsumi of Waseda University in Tokyo writes, "Members of the older generation . . . are careful to save every scrap of paper and bit of string for future use." Says one student, "Japanese people are materialistically well-off, but not inside. . . . We never have time to find ourselves, or what we should seek in life."

Far outpacing growth of the consumer class itself is the spread of consumerism, a cultural orientation that holds that, as British economist Paul Ekins writes, "the possession and use of an increasing number and variety of goods and services is the principal cultural aspiration and the surest perceived route to personal happiness, social status and national success." Since 1953, for example, the Institute of Statistical Mathematics has asked Japanese citizens to select the philosophy that most closely approximates their own. The share selecting "live a pure and just life" fell from 29 percent in the first survey to 9 percent in the mid-eighties, while the share opting to "live a life that suits your own taste" rose from 21 to 38 percent.

Galloping consumerism shows up even more strikingly in surveys from the United States. Between 1967 and 1990, the share of Americans entering college who believed it essential to be "very well off financially" rose from 44 to 74 percent. The share who believed it essential to develop a meaningful philosophy of life dropped from 83 to 43 percent. A student at Cornell

University in Ithaca, New York, summed up his peers' aspirations when he told *American Demographics* magazine, "My parents are happy with their life-styles. It's not enough for me."

Similarly, high school seniors polled from 1976 to 1990 displayed waning interest in "finding purpose and meaning in life," and expanding appetites for the artifacts of the consumer society. The percentage ranking "having lots of money" as "extremely important" rose from less than half in 1977 to almost two thirds in 1986, making it first on the list of life goals. More detailed survey questions confirmed consumerism's hold. Desires jumped dramatically for second cars, recreational vehicles, vacation homes, appliances, up-to-date fashions, and late-model automobiles.

The consumer class's membership includes perhaps half the citizens of the formerly socialist states of Eastern and Central Europe, and if those nations succeed in hitching their economies to the world market, they may bring most of their people into its ranks within a decade or two. A young man in a Budapest bar captured his country's consuming mood when he told a western reporter: "People in the West think that we in Hungary don't know how they live. Well, we do know how they live, and we want to live like that too." Says German banker Ulrich Ramm, "The East Germans want cars, videos and Marlboros." Seventy percent of those living in the former East Germany hope to enter the world's automobile class soon; they bought 1 million used western cars in 1991 alone.

Consumerist attitudes are also increasingly evident at the margins of the world economy, where not even elites are members of the consumer class. On the arid Deccan plateau of central India, tribal villagers who never before practiced the tradition of dowry prevalent among upper-caste Hindus are now demanding consumer goods from prospective spouses as the price of an arranged marriage.

More broadly, the emergence of an Indian middle class with about 100 million members, along with liberalization of the market and the introduction of buying on credit, has led to explosive growth in sales of everything from automobiles and televisions to frozen dinners. The streets of Indian cities are now choked with some of the world's most dangerous traffic and worst air pollution, thanks to millions of motor scooters and cars flooding onto routes formerly populated mostly by bicycles, buses, and ox carts. With 14 million televisions in Indian homes, delivering commercial messages in India's dozens of languages, the *Wall Street Journal* gloats, "The traditional conservative Indian who believes in modesty and savings is gradually giving way to a new generation that thinks as freely as it spends."

Fortune magazine is similarly excited about rapidly industrializing nations. In South Korea, it predicts: "More, of everything. More housing, and thus more telephones, appliances, TV sets, furniture, light bulbs, and toilets and toilet cleaners." In Indonesia, reports the *Far Eastern Economic Review*, "construction crews work day and night to erect vast shopping malls, air conditioned marble labyrinths where almost any local or imported luxury can be purchased—at a price." Advertising, which sows the seeds of consumerism, is one of the nation's fastest-growing industries. Mexico is also abuzz with consumerist ambitions: car sales jumped by a quarter in the first half of 1991, and shopping malls and fast food outlets are sweeping the country.

24   The wildfire spread of the consumer life-style around the world marks the most rapid and fundamental change in day-to-day existence the human species has ever experienced. Over a few short generations, we have become car drivers, television watchers, mall shoppers, and throwaway buyers. The tragic irony of this momentous transition is that the historic rise of the consumer society has been quite effective in harming the environment, but not in providing people with a fulfilling life.

Clean Motion

BEFORE the industrial age, the speeds at which fortunate and unfortunate traveled differed only as much as the average gait of horses differed from that of humans: the rich rode, the poor walked. And that dichotomy endured for centuries; as French philosopher Paul Valéry wrote early in this century, "Napoleon moved no faster than Julius Caesar." But the division has widened explosively over the past hundred years. Maximum speed soared as the affluent switched from horses to trains to automobiles to jet airplanes, adding fuel requirements with each substitution. The poor still walk, at about the same speed as always, but the affluent have accelerated from about 10 kilometers an hour, the speed of a horse, to about 1,000 kilometers per hour, the speed of a jet.

The historical progression of the affluent roughly parallels the transportation patterns of the world's economic classes: the walking poor, the bicycle-train-and-bus-riding middle-income class, and the car-driving consumer class. The richest members of the consumer class, finally, form the global jet set. With each step up this ladder, the environment suffers an order of magnitude more air pollution from burning fuels. Walking and bicycling cause virtually no ecological ills, requiring no fuel besides the person's most recent meal. For urban travel, buses, subways, and trolleys use roughly one eighth as much energy to move someone a kilometer as private cars do. For long trips, trains and buses require a tenth the energy of commercial jets—and one twenty-seventh the energy of private planes.

The walking poor, of course, have too little mobility. Many of them never go more than 100 kilometers from their birthplaces. Unable to get to jobs easily, attend school, reach health clinics, bring their complaints before government offices, or expand their horizons through the broadening experience of travel, they are severely hindered by the lack of transportation. They inhabit places such as Pilcomaya, the "River of Birds," an isolated windswept valley in the Andes. There, the necessity of traversing the expanses between the adobe huts of sheep herders and subsistence farmers on foot makes survival a struggle and social visits a rarity.

The middle-income class, particularly in China, relies on bicycles for short trips. Kilometer for kilometer, bikes are cheaper than any other vehicles, costing less than $100 new in most of the Third World. Lightweight of necessity, bikes require small amounts of materials to manufacture and their simplicity makes repair relatively easy. Indian bike repairers set up shop on street corners throughout the country by spreading a mat and laying out a few tools.

Where railways exist, the middle-income class takes longer trips by train. The Indian and Chinese rail systems, for example, move millions of people every day, allowing them to migrate for work or carry goods to market. To the consumer class, these rail systems would seem crowded and inefficient, but they function remarkably well considering their low cost. Buses, along with vans, trucks, converted jeeps, and dozens of other makeshift conveyances, carry those in the middle-income class on the rest of their journeys.

Most of these trains and buses are wasteful, polluting, and dangerous compared with models now used in industrial countries: buses with dozens of people clinging to their sides pump black diesel smoke into the streets of Lagos, Karachi, Guatemala City, and hundreds of other cities. But collectively these antiquated vehicles form transportation systems that pollute far less than would equivalent fleets of private cars, and they provide the middle-income class with affordable access to jobs, schools, and stores.

The consumer class, by contrast, employs modes of transportation—the private automobile and the jet—that all the world's people cannot use without ruining the atmosphere and coating huge areas of land in pavement. We members of the consumer class do almost all the world's driving. In 1988, per capita use of cars exceeded 4,000 kilometers in North America and Western Europe, while in the developing countries for which data were available, per person auto use was at or below 1,000 kilometers. Japan, with its excellent bicycle-and-rail-based transportation system, fell in between, with 2,510 kilometers per capita. (See Table 1.)

A car is found in nearly every household in North America and Australia, and in a large and growing share of West European ones too. In Japan, the share jumped from 20 percent in 1970 to 72 percent in 1988. The auto class is also expanding rapidly in Eastern Europe and in newly industrializing countries such as South Korea and Brazil. At the heights of the consumer class, families are adding second cars. At least two cars are already found in one fifth of French—and half of American—households. Indeed, two thirds of new houses in the United States have two-car garages.

Around the world, the great marketing achievement of the auto industry

Table 1. Automobile Use Per Capita, Selected Countries, 1988[1]	
Country	Automobile Travel (vehicle-kilometers per capita)
United States	8,870
West Germany	6,150
United Kingdom	4,730
Italy	4,030
Japan	2,510
Argentina	1,000
Poland	710
South Korea	210
Thailand	190
Cameroon	120

[1]Some countries are for earlier years.

has been to turn its machines into cultural icons. As French philosopher Roland Barthes writes, "Cars today are almost the exact equivalent of the great Gothic cathedrals . . . the supreme creation of an era, conceived with passion by unknown artists, and consumed in image if not in usage by a whole population which appropriates them as . . . purely magical object[s]."

*   *   *

Understanding What You Read

1. What are the world's broad economic (and ecological) classes? How does Durning define these three classes in terms of what people eat, how they move from place to place, and what materials they use?
2. What does Durning mean by the term "consumerism"? What does he see as the "tragic irony" of the rapid spread of this philosophy around the world?
3. Durning claims that through advertising the auto industry has turned its machines into "cultural icons." Browse through popular magazines and find examples of this phenomenon.

Writing About What You Read

Write an essay describing what the effect on the environment would be if population growth stopped somehow but all developing countries suddenly enjoyed the same standard of living enjoyed by Durning's consumer class.

URSULA K. LE GUIN

A prolific and popular writer and winner of numerous awards, Le Guin (b. 1929) is considered one of America's best storytellers. The imaginative worlds she creates often combine mythology, anthropology, psychology, and other disciplines to create a complex web of ideas and narrative. Her works include the *Earthsea* trilogy (1968–1972), *The Dispossessed* (1974), and *Always Coming Home* (1985). "Direction of the Road," from *Buffalo Gals and Other Animal Presences* (1987), imaginatively explores the connections between human beings and nonhuman life.

Direction of the Road

THEY DID NOT use to be so demanding. They never hurried us into anything more than a gallop, and that was rare; most of the time it was just a jigjog foot-pace. And when one of them was on his own feet, it was a real pleasure to approach him. There was time to accomplish the entire act with style. There he'd be, working his legs and arms the way they do, usually looking at the road, but often aside at the fields, or straight at me: and I'd approach him steadily but quite slowly, growing larger all the time, synchronizing the rate of approach and the rate of growth perfectly so that at the very moment that I'd finished enlarging from a tiny speck to my full size—sixty feet in those days—I was abreast of him and hung above him, loomed, towered, overshadowed him. Yet he would show no fear. Not even the children were afraid of me, though often they kept their eyes on me as I passed by and started to diminish.

Sometimes on a hot afternoon one of the adults would stop me right there at our meeting-place, and lie down with his back against mine for an hour or more. I didn't mind in the least. I have an excellent hill, good sun, good wind, good view; why should I mind standing still for an hour or an afternoon? It's only a relative stillness, after all. One need only look at the sun to realize how fast one is going, and then, one grows continually—especially in summer. In any case I was touched by the way they would entrust themselves to me, letting me lean against their little warm backs, and falling sound asleep there between my feet. I liked them. They have seldom lent us Grace as do the birds; but I really preferred them to squirrels.

In those days the horses used to work for them, and that too was enjoyable from my point of view. I particularly liked the canter, and got quite proficient at it. The surging and rhythmical motion accompanied shrinking and growing with a swaying and swooping, almost an illusion of flight. The gallop was less pleasant. It was jerky pounding: one felt tossed about like a sapling in a gale. And then, the slow approach and growth, the moment of looming-over, and the slow retreat and diminishing, all that was lost during the gallop. One had to hurl oneself into it, cloppety-cloppety-cloppety! and the man usually too busy riding, and the horse too busy running, even to look up. But then, it didn't happen often. A horse is mortal, after all, and like all the loose creatures grows tired easily; so they didn't tire their horses unless there was urgent need. And they seemed not to have so many urgent needs, in those days.

It's been a long time since I had a gallop, and to tell the truth I shouldn't mind having one. There was something invigorating about it, after all.

I remember the first motorcar I saw. Like most of us, I took it for a mortal, some kind of loose creature new to me. I was a bit startled, for after a hundred and thirty-two years I thought I knew all the local fauna. But a new thing is always interesting, in its trivial fashion, so I observed this one with attention. I approached it at a fair speed, about the rate of a canter, but in a new gait, suitable to the ungainly looks of the thing: an uncomfortable, bouncing, rolling, choking, jerking gait. Within two minutes, before I'd grown a foot tall, I knew it was no mortal creature, bound or loose or free. It was a making, like the carts the horses got hitched to. I thought it so very ill-made that I didn't expect it to return, once it gasped over the West Hill, and I heartily hoped it never would, for I disliked that jerking bounce.

But the thing took to a regular schedule, and so, perforce, did I. Daily at four I had to approach it, twitching and stuttering out of the west, and enlarge, loom over, and diminish. Then at five back I had to come, poppeting along like a young jackrabbit for all my sixty feet, jigging and jouncing out of the east, until at last I got clear out of sight of the wretched little monster and could relax and loosen my limbs to the evening wind. There were always two of them inside the machine: a young male holding the wheel, and behind him an old female wrapped in rugs, glowering. If they ever said anything to each other I never heard it. In those days I overheard a good many conversations on the road, but not from that machine. The top of it was open, but it made so much noise that it overrode all voices, even the voice of the song-sparrow I had with me that year. The noise was almost as vile as the jouncing.

I am of a family of rigid principle and considerable self-respect. The Quercian[1] motto is "Break but bend not," and I have always tried to uphold it. It was not only personal vanity, but family pride, you see, that was offended when I was forced to jounce and bounce in this fashion by a mere making.

The apple trees in the orchard at the foot of the hill did not seem to mind; but then, apples are tame. Their genes have been tampered with for centuries. Besides, they are herd creatures; no orchard tree can really form an opinion of its own.

---

[1]Pertaining to oak trees. *Quercus* is the genus of Oaks.

I kept my own opinion to myself.

But I was very pleased when the motorcar ceased to plague us. All month went by without it, and all month I walked at men and trotted at horses most willingly, and even bobbed for a baby on its mother's arm, trying hard though unsuccessfully to keep in focus.

Next month, however—September it was, for the swallows had left a few days earlier—another of the machines appeared, a new one, suddenly dragging me and the road and our hill, the orchard, the fields, the farmhouse roof, all jigging and jouncing and racketing along from east to west; I went faster than a gallop, faster than I had ever gone before. I had scarcely time to loom, before I had to shrink right down again.

And the next day there came a different one.

Yearly then, weekly, daily, they became commoner. They became a major feature of the local Order of Things. The road was dug up and remetalled, widened, finished off very smooth and nasty, like a slug's trail, with no ruts, pools, rocks, flowers, or shadows on it. There used to be a lot of little loose creatures on the road, grasshoppers, ants, toads, mice, foxes, and so on, most of them too small to move for, since they couldn't really see one. Now the wise creatures took to avoiding the road, and the unwise ones got squashed. I have seen all too many rabbits die in that fashion, right at my feet. I am thankful that I am an oak, and that though I may be wind-broken or uprooted, hewn or sawn, at least I cannot, under any circumstances, be squashed.

With the presence of many motorcars on the road at once, a new level of skill was required of me. As a mere seedling, as soon as I got my head above the weeds, I had learned the basic trick of going two directions at once. I learned it without thinking about it, under the simple pressure of circumstances on the first occasion that I saw a walker in the east and a horseman facing him in the west. I had to go two directions at once, and I did so. It's something we trees master without real effort, I suppose. I was nervous, but I succeeded in passing the rider and then shrinking away from him while at the same time I was still jigjogging towards the walker, and indeed passed him (no looming, back in those days!) only when I had got quite out of sight of the rider. I was proud of myself, being very young, that first time I did it; but it sounds more difficult than it really is. Since those days of course I had done it innumerable times, and thought nothing about it; I could do it in my sleep. But have you ever considered the feat accomplished, the skill involved, when a tree enlarges, simultaneously yet at slightly different rates and in slightly different manners, for each one of forty motorcar drivers facing two opposite directions, while at the same time diminishing for forty more who have got their backs to it, meanwhile remembering to loom over each single one at the right moment: and to do this minute after minute, hour after hour, from daybreak till nightfall or long after?

For my road had become a busy one; it worked all day long under almost

12

continual traffic. It worked, and I worked. I did not jounce and bounce so much any more, but I had to run faster and faster: to grow enormously, to loom in a split second, to shrink to nothing, all in a hurry, without time to enjoy the action, and without rest: over and over and over.

16 Very few of the drivers bothered to look at me, not even a seeing glance. They seemed, indeed, not to see any more. They merely stared ahead. They seemed to believe that they were "going somewhere." Little mirrors were affixed to the front of their cars, at which they glanced to see where they had been; then they stared ahead again. I had thought that only beetles had this delusion of Progress. Beetles are always rushing about, and never looking up. I had always had a pretty low opinion of beetles. But at least they let me be.

I confess that sometimes, in the blessed nights of darkness with no moon to silver my crown and no stars occluding with my branches, when I could rest, I would think seriously of escaping my obligation to the general Order of Things: of *failing to move*. No, not seriously. Half-seriously. It was mere weariness. If even a silly, three-year-old, female pussy willow at the foot of the hill accepted her responsibility, and jounced and rolled and accelerated and grew and shrank for each motorcar on the road, was I, an oak, to shrink? Noblesse oblige,[2] and I trust I have never dropped an acorn that did not know its duty.

For fifty or sixty years, then, I have upheld the Order of Things, and have done my share in supporting the human creatures' illusion that they are "going somewhere." And I am not unwilling to do so. But a truly terrible thing has occurred, which I wish to protest.

I do not mind going two directions at once; I do not mind growing and shrinking simultaneously; I do not mind moving, even at the disagreeable rate of sixty or seventy miles an hour. I am ready to go on doing all these things until I am felled or bulldozed. They're my job. But I do object, passionately, to being made eternal.

20 Eternity is none of my business. I am an oak, no more, no less. I have my duty, and I do it; I have my pleasures, and enjoy them, though they are fewer, since the birds are fewer, and the wind's foul. But, long-lived though I may be, impermanence is my right. Mortality is my privilege. And it has been taken from me.

It was taken from me on a rainy evening in March last year.

Fits and bursts of cars, as usual, filled the rapidly moving road in both directions. I was so busy hurtling along, enlarging, looming, diminishing, and the light was failing so fast, that I scarcely noticed what was happening until it happened. One of the drivers of one of the cars evidently felt that his need to "go somewhere" was exceptionally urgent, and so attempted to place his car in front of the car in front of it. This maneuver involves a

---

[2]"Nobility obliges," i.e., there are responsibilities associated with having a high rank or station in a community.

temporary slanting of the Direction of the Road and a displacement onto the far side, the side which normally runs the other direction (and may I say that I admire the road very highly for its skill in executing such maneuvers, which must be difficult for an unliving creature, a mere making). Another car, however, happened to be quite near the urgent one, and facing it, as it changed sides; and the road could not do anything about it being already overcrowded. To avoid impact with the facing car, the urgent car totally violated the Direction of the Road, swinging it round to north-south in its own terms, and so forcing me to leap directly at it. I had no choice. I had to move, and move fast—eighty-five miles an hour. I leapt: I loomed enormous, larger than I have ever loomed before. And then I hit the car.

I lost a considerable piece of bark, and, what's more serious, a fair bit of cambium layer;[3] but as I was seventy-two feet tall and about nine feet in girth at the point of impact, no real harm was done. My branches trembled with the shock enough that a last-year's robin's nest was dislodged and fell; and I was so shaken that I groaned. It is the only time in my life that I have ever said anything out loud.

The motorcar screamed horribly. It was smashed by my blow, squashed, in fact. Its hinder parts were not much affected, but the forequarters knotted up and knurled together like an old root, and little bright bits of it flew all about and lay like brittle rain.

The driver had no time to say anything; I killed him instantly.

It is not this that I protest. I had to kill him. I had no choice, and therefore have no regret. What I protest, what I cannot endure, is this: as I leapt at him, he saw me. He looked up at last. He saw me as I have never been seen before, not even by a child, not even in the days when people looked at things. He saw me whole, and saw nothing else—then, or ever.

He saw me under the aspect of eternity. He confused me with eternity. And because he died in that moment of false vision, because it can never change, I am caught in it, eternally.

This is unendurable. I cannot uphold such an illusion. If the human creatures will not understand Relativity, very well; but they must understand Relatedness.

If it is necessary to the Order of Things, I will kill drivers of cars, though killing is not a duty usually required of oaks. But it is unjust to require me to play the part, not of the killer only, but of death. For I am not death. I am life: I am mortal.

If they wish to see death visibly in the world, that is their business, not mine. I will not act Eternity for them. Let them not turn to the trees for death. If that is what they want to see, let them look into one another's eyes and see it there.

---

[3]In vascular plants, the layer that generates new growth.

Understanding What You Read

1. What clues led you to recognize that the narrator of this story is an oak tree?
2. What does the oak mean by a "making" or by a "loose creature"?
3. What does the story imply about people learning to move faster and faster?
4. What particular evidence of environmental degradation does the oak notice?
5. What human attributes does the tree ridicule in its observations about apple trees (paragraph 8)?
7. In what direction is the road going?
8. How do you interpret the oak's refusal to be eternal?

Writing About What You Read

1. What does this story suggest is wrong with the fact that humans have learned to move with increasing speed? Write about how automobiles have diminished the quality of life; or write an essay or story in which you commend automobiles and the speed they make possible.
2. Compare the oak's perspective with the anthropocentrism of some people.

FARLEY MOWAT

Mowat (b. 1921) has lived most of his life in his native Canada, but has traveled widely. High-risk expeditions—notable to the Arctic and other regions where conditions are harsh—have provided material for more than twenty-five books, some written for children. Mowat's work has been widely translated and read in many countries around the globe. His best-known books include *A Whale for the Killing* (1972) and *Sea of Slaughter* (1984). After going to the frozen tundra of the Canadian Arctic to study the impact of the wolves on the caribou population, Mowat wrote *Never Cry Wolf* (1963), which was made into a popular movie. *A Whale for the Killing* (1972) was based on his experiences living on the coast of Newfoundland. "Of Men and Whales" is from that book.

Of Men and Whales

*   *   *

THE BLOODY TALE of men and whales has its beginnings in forgotten times when a few coast-dwelling tribes began putting to sea in skin boats or dugout canoes to test their hunters' skills against the monsters they first encountered as mountains of fat and meat when dead whales washed up on their shores.

In the northern hemisphere, such primitive people were hunting the Biscayen Right Whale, and probably the now extinct Atlantic Grey Whale, off the coasts of Portugal at least as early as 2000 B.C.

In North America, Eskimoan people of the Thule culture hunted the Arctic Right Whale, while Indians on the Pacific Coast pursued the Grey Whale, and still other Indians on the Atlantic Coast took both Greys and Humpbacks.

In all cases the methods used were essentially the same. Paddlers in open boats tried to approach a whale close enough to let one of their number strike it with a barbed-bone or flint-headed harpoon, to which a rawhide line and a skin float were attached. Frequently the shallowly embedded weapon would break off or pull loose; or the boat would be swamped in the flurry as the whale sounded; or the line would part; or the float would be carried far beyond the range of the hunters to pursue it.

Rarely (and it must have been *very* rarely indeed), the hunters were able to stick with the whale, festooning it with more and more harpoons and floats until, eventually, it tired and they could pull alongside and try to kill it with thrusts from fragile lances. Since they could seldom hope to penetrate to a vital spot, they literally had to bleed it to death, a dangerous procedure during which the frenzied animal might not only crush their boats but might well crush them too. If they did succeed in killing the giant, they still had to tow it to the nearest beach, a task which, under adverse conditions of wind and tide, might take many hours or even days, or prove impossible.

Tribal traditions, together with the scarcity of whale bones in ancient kitchen middens, make it clear that any primitive whaling community which managed to kill two or three whales a year was doing rather well for itself. There was no need to kill more anyway. These people killed only to eat, and it took a long, long time for a handful of families to eat a whale. Consequently, early man posed no real threat to the continuing prosperity of the whale nation.

Nor was there much danger from modern man either until, during the 13th and 14th centuries, Europeans began building ships that could keep the sea. One of the earliest uses to which such ships were put was for pelagic, or open ocean, whaling; and, apparently, the first people to dare this chase were the Basques, who "fished" for the Biscayen Right and the Atlantic Grey

4

Whale, not only because these were common in their waters but because they were slow-moving and rather unwary and, what was essential, did not sink when killed. With luck, a Basque ship could sail close enough to a Grey or a Right Whale so that the harpooner poised in the bows could strike into it with a heavy wrought-iron harpoon made fast to the ship by a strong warp, which not even a whale could easily part. The drag of the ship would eventually exhaust the animal and it could then be lanced to death with little risk.

8 The Basques still towed dead whales to shore for disposal but there had been a momentous change in the purpose for which they were being killed. These new whalers did not catch them for food. Instead they stripped off the layers of blubber and cut out the baleen plates. Then they turned the monumental carcasses adrift into the sea.

Only the oil and baleen were wanted now; the oil to fuel the lamps of an increasingly urbanized European society, and the baleen for the manufacture of "horn" windows and utensils. Thus the whale had been transformed from edible game into an article of commerce. When that happened man ceased to be a pin-prick irritant to the whale nation and became a deadly enemy. From this time forward whales were slaughtered without quarter and with every weapon and by every method the planet's most accomplished killers could devise.

The Basques were already efficient enough. By the end of the 15th century they had so reduced the Biscayen Right Whales that the species was hardly worth the hunting, and they had evidently exterminated the eastern population of Atlantic Grey Whales. However, far to the northward lay an even larger population—the Arctic Right, Bowhead or Greenland Whale, as it was variously called. In pursuit of this immensely abundant species (it is estimated there were more than half a million Arctic Right Whales before the great hunt began), the Basques had invaded Greenland waters by 1410 and were whaling off Labrador and Newfoundland by 1440. They still relied on shore stations established on the as yet officially "unknown" coasts to which they towed their catch for "cutting-in" and rendering the blubber. However, near the end of the 15th century, the Basques made another great stride forward. They invented and perfected ship-borne tryworks so whales could now be cut-in and rendered at sea.

From that day pelagic whaling exploded into a rapacious, world-wide slaughter of all those whales which were slow enough to be caught by sailing ships, and fat enough not to sink when killed. These were primarily Sperms, Humpbacks, Greys and Rights. By the mid-1800's there were as many as two thousand ships mercilessly sweeping the North and South Atlantic, both Pacifics, and the Indian Ocean, every year. They sailed from the New England States, Holland, the Baltic States, Norway, France, England, and a score of other places. They earned huge fortunes for the money-men at home, and by 1880 they had reduced to scattered remnants the once vast population of the great whale species which they pursued.

The slaughter had been so tremendous that, as the 19th century began 12
to wane, it appeared that the hunt was coming to an end for want of
whales . . . or, more accurately, for want of whales that men could catch.

There were still—and this was something which infuriated whalers and
businessmen alike—enormous numbers of great whales in the sea. These
were the baleen whales of the group called rorquals—Blues, Fins, Seis and
a few lesser species. The rorquals included the largest, swiftest and undoubtedly the most intelligent of whales.

Quite apart from their wariness and the fact that most of them were
capable of speeds of at least twenty knots, their relatively thin blubber layer
failed to give them the positive buoyancy which had proved so fatal to the
Greys, Humpbacks, Rights and Sperms. Consequently if, by exceptional
good luck, a sailing ship managed to catch and kill one of the rorquals, the
monster promptly sank, and that was that.

For a brief time it looked as if the rorquals would remain out of man's
reach; but then the Norwegians, the most ruthless sea-marauders of all time,
and by far the most accomplished killers of marine life, stepped in and took
a hand. About 1860 they turned their hard blue eyes upon the rorquals and
put their Viking minds to work. Within ten years they had found the means
to doom, not only the rorquals, *but all surviving great whales in all the oceans
of the earth.*

They attacked with three new weapons. First was the whale gun: a 16
cannon which fired a heavy harpoon with a line attached deep into the whale's
vitals, where a bomb exploded, ripping the animal apart internally and setting
the broad barbs of the harpoon so they could not tear loose. The second was
the steam catcher: a small, steam-powered vessel of great speed and mano-
euverability which could match the rorquals' speed. The third was a hollow
lance which was thrust deep into the dead whale and through which com-
pressed air could be injected until the whale inflated and became buoyant.
With these inventions the Norwegians took virtual control of world-wide
whaling.

By the turn of the century their shore stations (for processing the carcasses) had spread like a pox along almost every coast in the world near which
whales were found. In 1904 there were eighteen such factories on the shores
of Newfoundland alone, processing an average of twelve hundred whales,
most of them rorquals, every year![1]

The world-wide slaughter was enormous and the profits even more so.
By 1912 all the great whales, including Blues, both species of Rights, Fins,

[1]Not all the hunting of rorquals was done with the newly devised harpoon gun. During
the first decade of the twentieth century Norwegians were killing Seis and Fins in a fiord near
Bergen by a method so barbarous that it is hard to credit. The whales were driven into the
long fiord by boats and the entrance was barred off with nets. The great animals were then
speared with lances whose blades had been dipped in the rotting flesh of whales killed earlier.
Infection set in and the trapped whales died horribly of septicemia or gangrene [author's
note].

Sperms and Humpbacks, had nearly vanished from the North Atlantic and, with the addition of the Greys, from the North Pacific as well.[2]

It is likely that several of these species would have become extinct in the northern hemisphere had it not been for the outbreak of the First World War, which gave the surviving whales in northern waters a brief surcease, though not enough time to recover. The remnant survivors would have been quickly finished off if the Norwegians had returned heavily to the attack after the war was over.

That they did not do so was due to the discovery by the Norwegians about 1904 of an immense and hitherto untouched population of whales in the Antarctic Ocean. Here, during the decades that had almost emptied the other oceans of great whales, a sanctuary had existed. When the Norwegians nosed it out, fleets of swift, merciless catchers swarmed southward to begin a new and even more thorough butchery of the whale nation from shore bases in the Falkland Islands and South Georgia.

Then, in 1922, a Norwegian named Carl Anton Larsen, whose name deserves to be forever remembered in equal opprobrium with that of Sven Foyn, inventor of the harpoon gun, brought about the ultimate refinement in commercial whaling. He invented the modern factory ship. In its essential form, this is a very large cargo vessel with a gaping hole in her stern through which a hundred-ton whale can be hauled up into a combined floating abattoir and processing plant. With her coming, away went the pressing need for shore stations and the long, time-wasting tows to land. Accompanied by fleets of catchers, buoy boats and tow boats, and stored for a voyage of six months or more, the factory ships could penetrate far southward to the edge of the Antarctic ice itself and could range the whole expanse of the Antarctic seas.

The ensuing slaughter of an animal population is unparalleled in human history. The combination of man's genius for destruction together with the satanic powers of his technology dyed the cold, green waters of the Antarctic crimson with the heart's blood of the whale nation. The massacre built to a crescendo in the early 1930's when as many as 80,000 great whales died each year!

The outbreak of the Second World War brought a pause to the purposeful slaughter of whales in the Antarctic, but it brought new setbacks to the slowly recovering populations of whales in the other oceans of the world. The war at sea was primarily a war between submarines and surface ships, and the submarine—which is no more than a manmade imitation of a whale, in form—came under increasingly sophisticated and sustained attack as the war went on.

Such technological marvels as sonar and Asdic were refined to detect and

[2]Grey Whales were finally exterminated in Atlantic waters sometime toward the end of the 18th century [author's note].

follow underwater objects with great accuracy, and could guide depth charges, bombs, and other deadly devices to the unseen target. Although, to my knowledge, the matter has never been investigated or even publicly discussed, there is no doubt that tens of thousands of whales were killed by the men who hunted submarines with ships or planes.

A commander in the Royal Canadian Navy who served four years in corvettes, frigates and destroyers in the North Atlantic told me he believed a high percentage of the depth-charges fired from his ships had been directed at submerged whales rather than at submarines. The drifting carcasses of bombed or depth-charged whales were a common enough sight to lookouts aboard naval and merchant ships. Wars are deadly, not only to mankind, but to those most innocent bystanders, the other forms of life which share the planet with us.

Here is as good a place as any to reply to a question I have sometimes been asked. Why is it that, if whales have such large and well-developed brains, they have not been able to avoid destruction at man's hands? The answer seems obvious. The whales never dabbled in the arcane arts of technology and so had no defence against that most deadly plague. In time they might have evolved a defence, but we gave them no time. The answer raises a counter question: Why is it, if man has such a remarkable intelligence, *he* has been unable to avoid an almost continuous acceleration of the processes of self-destruction? Why, if he *is* the most advanced of beings, has he become a threat to the survival of all life on earth?

At the end of the Second World War, despite the fact that the Antarctic whale population had shown no increase, the whalers went back to work with renewed energy and with even deadlier weapons. Sophisticated sonar gear, radar, and spotting aircraft operating from immense new floating factories (some as big as 30,000 tons) were combined with powerful new catchers that could make twenty knots with ease. This combination ensured that any whale which came within the wide-reaching electronic ken of the killer fleet stood no more than a fractional chance of survival.

By the early 1950's the Blue Whale was rapidly approaching "commercial" extinction so the hunters turned their main effort on the Fins. They were so successful that, by 1956, there were no more than 100,000 Finners left alive out of a population estimated to have been nearly a million at the turn of the century. And in 1956, 25,289 Finners—one quarter of those remaining in the seas—were slaughtered! By 1960 there *may* have been 2500 Blue Whales left in all the oceans of the world (of whom less than a thousand now survive), and perhaps 40,000 Fins in the Antarctic. They were so few, and so widely dispersed, that it hardly paid the pelagic whaling fleets to hunt them anymore, and so they turned to the lesser rorquals. They began exterminating the Seis.

Although the official whaling returns of the late 1950's made it obvious

28

that the great whales were entering their final hours on this earth, nobody took any effective action to halt the butchery. When a few worried biologists suggested that the whaling industry should establish meaningful quotas which would result in the whalers being able to make a sustained harvest indefinitely, while allowing the whale nation to at least partially recover its numbers, they were ignored. The owners of the whaling fleets made it patently clear that they were determined to hunt the whales to extinction, and the devil take the hindmost.

Hardly a voice was raised in public against this calculated policy of extermination. On the contrary, there was a spate of novels, non-fiction books and motion pictures, many of which seemed to glorify the slaughter, and all of which praised the hardihood and manliness of the whale killers.

It is true that in 1946 an organization had been formed with the publicly stated intention of giving protection to the threatened species of whales and of regulating the hunt. This was the International Whaling Commission whose headquarters were (and remain) in Norway, which also happened to be headquarters for the world's most efficient whale killers. But despite the employment of many good and dedicated men, the Commission was run for, and by, the whalers; and in such a manner that, instead of helping to preserve and conserve the vanishing whale stocks, it served as a cynical device to divert attention from the truth. It served to mask the insatiable greed which lay behind the slaughter, by promulgating regulations which appeared wise and humane but which, in fact, were useless . . . and sometimes worse than that.

32   One of the first actions of the Commission was to institute a quota system whereby each nation was allowed to kill only so many whales. It was a totally meaningless gesture since the quotas were set, and have since been consistently maintained, at levels far higher than the whale populations could support. There were regulations against the taking of undersize whales, or of cows accompanied by their calves; and these were honoured mostly in the breach. But the most hypocritical of all were the regulations, declared with great fanfare, which ultimately prohibited the killing of Blues, Humpbacks and all species of Right Whales. These were brought into effect *only after* all these species had been brought so close to extinction that they were no longer of any major commercial value and were, in fact, all threatened with *biological* extinction. These regulations were promulgated . . . but they were not enforced! The Japanese, for example, evaded them by pretending to discover a new species of whale in the Antarctic. They named it the *Pygmy* Blue Whale and, since it was outside the quota and not included in the prohibition on killing protected species, they busily cleaned up this last viable pocket which might very well have provided a nucleus for the return of the doomed Blue Whale. Furthermore, almost all pelagic whaling fleets, of whatever nationality, took protected whales upon occasion, giving the excuse that these were cases of mistaken identity. Still worse, many nations allowed their whalers to kill significant numbers of protected species for "scientific

research." Nearly 500 Greys (also a protected species) out of a world population of under 10,000 were killed under scientific permits between 1953 and 1969 by Russian, Canadian and United States whalers, with the Americans alone taking 316 of these. During the past three years whalers on Canada's east coast have killed 43 rare Humpbacks (the survivors of this once numerous species now number fewer than 2000) in the name of science. While it is true that scientists examined most of these sacrificial whales, adding presumably to their anatomical knowledge of the dead beasts, it is also true that the carcasses became the property of the whaling companies, who processed them commercially, for profit.

Because of the inestimable damage it has done by assuming the guise of champion to the beleaguered whales, and so gaining acceptance in the public eye as *the* authority on the subject, I must emphasize that the International Whaling Commission has served only to hasten the doom of most of the species it has pretended to protect, while concealing the magnitude of the crime against life which has been, and *is being,* committed by the whalers on behalf of powerful individuals, industries, and governments; and, in the last and inescapable analysis, on behalf of all of us.

Understanding What You Read

1. How did inventions made during World War II accelerate the killing of whales afterward?
2. How does Mowat distinguish *commercial* from *biological* extinction?
3. What has been the role of the International Whaling Commission?

Writing About What You Read

Mowat asks why, if humans are superior beings, they have become a threat to the survival of all life on earth. Attempt to answer his question.

DONALD WORSTER

Worster (b. 1941) is the Hall Distinguished Professor of American History at the University of Kansas. His book *Under Western Skies* is a collection of essays about the interrelations of history and culture with the American West. "The Age of Ecology" is from *Nature's Economy* (1977), a history of the idea of ecology and how the natural world has been seen from the ecological perspective.

The Age of Ecology

THE AGE OF ECOLOGY began on the desert outside Alamogordo, New Mexico, on July 16, 1945, with a dazzling fireball of light and a swelling mushroom cloud of radioactive gases. As that first nuclear fission bomb went off and the color of the early morning sky changed abruptly from pale blue to blinding white, physicist and project leader J. Robert Oppenheimer felt at first a surge of elated reverence; then a somber phrase from the *Bhagavad-Gita*[1] flashed into his mind: "I am become Death, the shatterer of worlds." Four years later, although Oppenheimer could still describe the making of the atomic bomb as "technically sweet," his worry about the consequences of that achievement had increased. Other atomic scientists, including Albert Einstein, Hans Bethe, and Leo Szilard, became even more anxiously determined to control this awesome weapon their work had made possible—a reaction eventually shared by many ordinary Americans, Japanese, and other peoples. It was increasingly feared that the bomb—however justifiable by the struggle against fascism—had put into mankind's hands a more dreadful power than we might be prepared to handle. For the first time in some two million years of human history, there existed a force capable of destroying the entire fabric of life on the planet. As Oppenheimer suggested, man, through the work of the scientist, now knew sin. The question was whether he also knew the way to redemption.

One kind of fallout from the atomic bomb was the beginnings of widespread, popular ecological concern around the globe. It began, appropriately, in the United States, where the nuclear era was launched. The devastation of Bikini atoll,[2] the poisoning of the atmosphere with strontium 90,[3] and the threat of irreversible genetic damage struck the public consciousness with an impact that dust storms and predator deaths could never have had. Here was no local problem or easily ignored issue; it was a question of the elemental survival of living things, man included, everywhere in the world. Clearly, Francis Bacon's[4] dream of extending man's empire over nature—"to the effecting of all things possible"—had suddenly taken a macabre, even suicidal, turn.

Not until 1958, however, did the ecological effects of atomic fallout become of great concern to American scientists generally. In that year the Committee for Nuclear Information was organized; its intent was to strip the secrecy from the government's weapons program and to warn their fellow citizens of the dangers in further nuclear testing. One of its members was the

---

[1]Sanskrit poem, part of the great Hindu religious epic the *Mahabharata*.

[2]A series of small islands in the west-central Pacific Ocean where the United States conducted atomic tests from 1946 to 1958. It was declared unsafe for human habitation in 1969.

[3]Radioactive substance released in atmospheric nuclear explosions.

[4]English philosopher and essayist (1561–1626), responsible for a theory of scientific classification in which human knowledge can gain power over nature.

plant physiologist Barry Commoner.[5] Other scientists began to join this campaign of information and protest, and more and more they were from the biological disciplines. It also became clear, with the publication in 1962 of Rachel Carson's *Silent Spring*,[6] that the atomic bomb was only the most obvious threat to the sanctity of life. Carson found in the new persistent pesticides a more subtle but perhaps equally devastating kind of weapon:

> Along with the possibility of the extinction of mankind by nuclear war, the central problem of our age has . . . become the contamination of man's total environment with such substances of incredible potential for harm—substances that accumulate in the tissues of plants and animals and even penetrate the germ cells to shatter or alter the very material of heredity upon which the shape of the future depends.

Six years later, another biologist, Paul Ehrlich,[7] heard yet another bomb ticking, ready to usher in chaos and mass death: the population explosion. Not technology alone, but simply man's fertility now became a factor in the rush to Armageddon.[8] By the 1970s the list of environmental threats had further expanded to include automobile emissions, solid waste, toxic metals, oil spills, even heat. It was a runaway arms race, but a thoroughly lopsided one; the enemy, or more accurately the victim, was Mother Nature, and she was virtually defenseless against the ecological arsenal devised by science.

Hard on the heels of these new technological powers, the idea of ecology flashed into the popular mind during the late 1960s, and its meaning—or mission—was unmistakable: detente, disarmament, no more war. This theme dominated the influential Reith lectures delivered in 1969 by the ecologist Frank Fraser Darling over the BBC, and in 1970 led the American media to christen the coming decade the "Age of Ecology." Early that year, the covers of news magazines were graced by a starkly beautiful image of Earth: a photograph taken from outer space, showing a cloud-enshrouded ball surrounded by endless, empty blackness. That lonely planet, we now understood in a way no previous epoch of man could have shared, was a terribly fragile place. Its film of life—man's sole means of survival—was far thinner and more vulnerable than anyone heretofore had realized. The public meaning of ecology also incorporated a revived fear of Malthusian scarcity,[9] of approaching limits. But the truly unique feature of the Age of Ecology was its sense of nature as a defenseless victim. Suddenly all the old rhetoric of conquest and power turned hollow; it was time at last, environmentalists asserted, for man to make peace with this now-vanquished adversary.

4

* * *

[5]See headnote on page 492.

[6]See headnote on page 367.

[7]See headnote on page 420.

[8]The battleground for the final struggle of good and evil at the end of the world, prophesied in the New Testament Book of Revelation.

[9]Theory proposed by the English economist Thomas Malthus (1766–1834), who argued that population would outgrow the available resources for subsistence.

Understanding What You Read

1. Worster argues that current concern with the environment actually began with the first atomic explosion as people gradually realized that it was now possible to destroy "the entire fabric of life on the planet." What specific concerns followed in the wake of this explosion?
2. Why was the Committee for Nuclear Information organized?
3. What were the next environmental concerns to reach public awareness?

Writing About What You Read

Imagine that you witnessed the first nuclear explosion in the desert of New Mexico. Research accounts of the explosion and write a diary entry in which you describe what you saw and how it affected you.

AL GORE

Gore (b. 1948) became Vice President of the United States in January 1993. He was elected to the House of Representatives from the state of Tennessee in 1976 and became that state's senator in 1984. He was a journalist for seven years before entering politics. During his sixteen years in Congress, Gore was continually learning about the environment and leading various battles to save it. His book *Earth in the Balance: Ecology and the Human Spirit* (1992) explains many aspects of the environmental crisis using up-to-date information, much of it acquired firsthand. "Ships in the Desert" is from that book.

Ships in the Desert

I WAS STANDING in the sun on the hot steel deck of a fishing ship capable of processing a fifty-ton catch on a good day. But it wasn't a good day. We were anchored in what used to be the most productive fishing site in all of central Asia, but as I looked out over the bow, the prospects of a good catch looked bleak. Where there should have been gentle blue-green waves lapping against the side of the ship, there was nothing but hot dry sand—as far as I could see in all directions. The other ships of the fleet were also at rest in the sand, scattered in the dunes that stretched all the way to the horizon.

Oddly enough, it made me think of a fried egg I had seen back in the United States on television the week before. It was sizzling and popping the way a fried egg should in a pan, but it was in the middle of a sidewalk in downtown Phoenix. I guess it sprang to mind because, like the ship on which I was standing, there was nothing wrong with the egg itself. Instead, the world beneath it had changed in an unexpected way that made the egg seem—through no fault of its own—out of place. It was illustrating the newsworthy point that at the time Arizona wasn't having an especially good day, either, because for the second day in a row temperatures had reached a record 122 degrees.

As a camel walked by on the dead bottom of the Aral Sea, my thoughts returned to the unlikely ship of the desert on which I stood, which also seemed to be illustrating the point that its world had changed out from underneath it with sudden cruelty. Ten years ago the Aral was the fourth-largest inland sea in the world, comparable to the largest of North America's Great Lakes. Now it is disappearing because the water that used to feed it has been diverted in an ill-considered irrigation scheme to grow cotton in the desert. The new shoreline was almost forty kilometers across the sand from where the fishing fleet was now permanently docked. Meanwhile, in the nearby town of Muynak the people were still canning fish—brought not from the Aral Sea but shipped by rail through Siberia from the Pacific Ocean, more than a thousand miles away.

I had come to the Aral Sea in August 1990 to witness at first hand the destruction taking place there on an almost biblical scale. But during the trip I encountered other images that also alarmed me. For example, the day I returned to Moscow from Muynak, my friend Alexei Yablokov, possibly the leading environmentalist in the Soviet Union, was returning from an emergency expedition to the White Sea, where he had investigated the mysterious and unprecedented death of several *million* starfish, washed up into a knee-deep mass covering many miles of beach. That night, in his apartment, he talked of what it was like for the residents to wade through the starfish in hip boots, trying to explain their death.

Later investigations identified radioactive military waste as the likely culprit in the White Sea deaths. But what about all of the other mysterious mass deaths washing up on beaches around the world? French scientists recently concluded that the explanation for the growing number of dead dolphins washing up along the Riviera was accumulated environmental stress, which, over time, rendered the animals too weak to fight off a virus. This same phenomenon may also explain the sudden increase in dolphin deaths along the Gulf Coast in Texas as well as the mysterious deaths of 12,000 seals whose corpses washed up on the shores of the North Sea in the summer of 1988. Of course, the oil-covered otters and seabirds of Prince William Sound[1] a year later presented less of a mystery to science, if no less an indictment of our civilization.

As soon as one of these troubling images fades, another takes its place,

---

[1]A large islanded inlet of the Gulf of Alaska, rich in wildlife and fish, much of which was destroyed when a tanker, the *Exxon Valdez*, spilled millions of gallons of crude oil in 1989.

provoking new questions. What does it mean, for example, that children playing in the morning surf must now dodge not only the occasional jellyfish but the occasional hypodermic needle washing in with the waves? Needles, dead dolphins, and oil-soaked birds—are all these signs that the shores of our familiar world are fast eroding, that we are now standing on some new beach, facing dangers beyond the edge of what we are capable of imagining?

With our backs turned to the place in nature from which we came, we sense an unfamiliar tide rising and swirling around our ankles, pulling at the sand beneath our feet. Each time this strange new tide goes out, it leaves behind the flotsam and jetsam of some giant shipwreck far out at sea, startling images washed up on the sands of our time, each a fresh warning of hidden dangers that lie ahead if we continue on our present course.

8   My search for the underlying causes of the environmental crisis has led me to travel around the world to examine and study many of these images of destruction. At the very bottom of the earth, high in the Trans-Antarctic Mountains, with the sun glaring at midnight through a hole in the sky, I stood in the unbelievable coldness and talked with a scientist in the late fall of 1988 about the tunnel he was digging through time. Slipping his parka back to reveal a badly burned face that was cracked and peeling, he pointed to the annual layers of ice in a core sample dug from the glacier on which we were standing. He moved his finger back in time to the ice of two decades ago. "Here's where the U.S. Congress passed the Clean Air Act," he said. At the bottom of the world, two continents away from Washington, D.C., even a small reduction in one country's emissions had changed the amount of pollution found in the remotest and least accessible place on earth.

But the most significant change thus far in the earth's atmosphere is the one that began with the industrial revolution early in the last century and has picked up speed ever since. Industry meant coal, and later oil, and we began to burn lots of it—bringing rising levels of carbon dioxide (CO_2), with its ability to trap more heat in the atmosphere and slowly warm the earth. Fewer than a hundred yards from the South Pole, upwind from the ice runway where the ski plane lands and keeps its engines running to prevent the metal parts from freeze-locking together, scientists monitor the air several times every day to chart the course of that inexorable change. During my visit, I watched one scientist draw the results of that day's measurements, pushing the end of a steep line still higher on the graph. He told me how easy it is—there at the end of the earth—to see that this enormous change in the global atmosphere is still picking up speed.

Two and a half years later I slept under the midnight sun at the other end of our planet, in a small tent pitched on a twelve-foot-thick slab of ice floating in the frigid Arctic Ocean. After a hearty breakfast, my companions and I traveled by snowmobiles a few miles farther north to a rendezvous point where the ice was thinner—only three and a half feet thick—and a nuclear submarine hovered in the water below. After it crashed through the ice, took on its new passengers, and resubmerged, I talked with scientists who were trying to measure more accurately the thickness of the polar ice cap, which many believe is thinning as a result of global warming. I had just negotiated an agreement between ice scientists and the U.S. Navy to secure the release of previously top secret data from submarine sonar tracks, data that could help them learn what is happening to the north polar cap. Now, I wanted to see the pole itself, and some eight hours after we met the submarine, we were crashing through that ice, surfacing, and then I was standing in an eerily beautiful snowscape, windswept and sparkling white, with the horizon defined by little hummocks, or "pressure ridges" of ice that are pushed up like tiny mountain ranges when separate sheets collide. But here too, CO_2 levels are rising just as rapidly, and ultimately temperatures will rise with them— indeed, global warming is expected to push temperatures up much more rapidly in the polar regions than in the rest of the world. As the polar air warms, the ice here will thin; and since the polar cap plays such a crucial role in the world's weather system, the consequences of a thinning cap could be disastrous.

Considering such scenarios is not a purely speculative exercise. Six months after I returned from the North Pole, a team of scientists reported dramatic changes in the pattern of ice distribution in the Arctic, and a second team reported a still controversial claim (which a variety of data now suggest) that, overall, the north polar cap has thinned by 2 percent in just the last decade. Moreover, scientists established several years ago that in many land areas north of the Arctic Circle, the spring snowmelt now comes earlier every year, and deep in the tundra below, the temperature of the earth is steadily rising.

As it happens, some of the most disturbing images of environmental destruction can be found exactly halfway between the North and South poles— precisely at the equator in Brazil—where billowing clouds of smoke regularly blacken the sky above the immense but now threatened Amazon rain forest. Acre by acre, the rain forest is being burned to create fast pasture for fast-food beef; as I learned when I went there in early 1989, the fires are set earlier and earlier in the dry season now, with more than one Tennessee's worth of rain forest being slashed and burned each year. According to our guide, the biologist Tom Lovejoy, there are more different species of birds in each square mile of the Amazon than exist in all of North America—which means we are silencing thousands of songs we have never even heard.

But for most of us the Amazon is a distant place, and we scarcely notice the disappearance of these and other vulnerable species. We ignore these losses at our peril, however. They're like the proverbial miners' canaries, silent alarms whose message in this case is that living species of animals and plants are now vanishing around the world *one thousand times faster* than at any time in the past 65 million years.

To be sure, the deaths of some of the larger and more spectacular animal species now under siege do occasionally capture our attention. I have also visited another place along the equator, East Africa, where I encountered the grotesquely horrible image of a dead elephant, its head mutilated by poachers who had dug out its valuable tusks with chain saws. Clearly, we need to change our purely aesthetic consideration of ivory, since its source is now so threatened. To me, its translucent whiteness seems different now, like evidence of the ghostly presence of a troubled spirit, a beautiful but chill apparition, inspiring both wonder and dread.

A similar apparition lies just beneath the ocean. While scuba diving in the Caribbean, I have seen and touched the white bones of a dead coral reef. All over the earth, coral reefs have suddenly started to "bleach" as warmer ocean temperatures put unaccustomed stress on the tiny organisms that normally live in the skin of the coral and give the reef its natural coloration. As these organisms—nicknamed "zooks"—leave the membrane of the coral, the coral itself becomes transparent, allowing its white limestone skeleton to shine through—hence its bleached appearance. In the past, bleaching was almost always an occasional and temporary phenomenon, but repeated episodes can exhaust the coral. In the last few years, scientists have been shocked at the sudden occurrence of extensive worldwide bleaching episodes from which increasing numbers of coral reefs have failed to recover. Though dead, they shine more brightly than before, haunted perhaps by the same ghost that gives spectral light to an elephant's tusk.

16   But one doesn't have to travel around the world to witness humankind's assault on the earth. Images that signal the distress of our global environment are now commonly seen almost anywhere. A few miles from the Capitol, for example, I encountered another startling image of nature out of place. Driving in the Arlington, Virginia, neighborhood where my family and I live when the Senate is in session, I stepped on the brake to avoid hitting a large pheasant walking across the street. It darted between the parked cars, across the sidewalk, and into a neighbor's backyard. Then it was gone. But this apparition of wildness persisted in my memory as a puzzle: Why would a pheasant, let alone such a large and beautiful mature specimen, be out for a walk in my neighborhood? Was it a much wilder place than I had noticed? Were pheasants, like the trendy Vietnamese potbellied pigs, becoming the latest fashion in unusual pets? I didn't solve the mystery until weeks later, when I remembered that about three miles away, along the edge of the river, developers were bulldozing the last hundred acres of untouched forest in the entire area. As the woods fell to make way for more concrete, more buildings, parking lots, and streets, the wild things that lived there were forced to flee. Most of the deer were hit by cars; other creatures—like the pheasant that darted into my neighbor's backyard—made it a little farther.

Ironically, before I understood the mystery, I felt vaguely comforted to imagine that perhaps this urban environment, so similar to the one in which many Americans live, was not so hostile to wild things after all. I briefly supposed that, like the resourceful raccoons and possums and squirrels and pigeons, all of whom have adapted to life in the suburbs, creatures as wild as pheasants might have a fighting chance. Now I remember that pheasant when I take my children to the zoo and see an elephant or a rhinoceros. They too inspire wonder and sadness. They too remind me that we are creating a world that is hostile to wildness, that seems to prefer concrete to natural landscapes. We are encountering these creatures on a path we have paved— one that ultimately leads to their extinction.

On some nights, in high northern latitudes, the sky itself offers another ghostly image that signals the loss of ecological balance now in progress. If the sky is clear after sunset—and if you are watching from a place where pollution hasn't blotted out the night sky altogether—you can sometimes see a strange kind of cloud high in the sky. This "noctilucent cloud" occasionally appears when the earth is first cloaked in the evening darkness; shimmering above us with a translucent whiteness, these clouds seem quite unnatural. And they should: noctilucent clouds have begun to appear more often because of a huge buildup of methane gas in the atmosphere. (Also called natural gas, methane is released from landfills, from coal mines and rice paddies, from billions of termites that swarm through the freshly cut forestland, from the burning of biomass and from a variety of other human activities.) Even though noctilucent clouds were sometimes seen in the past, all this extra methane carries more water vapor into the upper atmosphere, where it condenses at much higher altitudes to form more clouds that the sun's rays still strike long after sunset has brought the beginning of night to the surface far beneath them.

What should we feel toward these ghosts in the sky? Simple wonder or the mix of emotions we feel at the zoo? Perhaps we should feel awe for our own power: just as men tear tusks from elephants' heads in such quantity as to threaten the beast with extinction, we are ripping matter from its place in the earth in such volume as to upset the balance between daylight and darkness. In the process, we are once again adding to the threat of global warming, because methane has been one of the fastest-growing greenhouse gases,[2] and is third only to carbon dioxide and water vapor in total volume, changing the chemistry of the upper atmosphere. But, without even considering that threat, shouldn't it startle us that we have now put these clouds in the evening sky which glisten with a spectral light? Or have our eyes adjusted so completely to the bright lights of civilization that we can't see these clouds for what they are—a physical manifestation of the violent collision between human civilization and the earth?

Even though it is sometimes hard to see their meaning, we have by now all witnessed surprising experiences that signal the damage from our assault on

20

---

[2]Carbon dioxide, methane, ozone, nitrous oxide, water vapor, and other gases that trap heat near the earth's surface and thus raise the overall temperature.

the environment—whether it's the new frequency of days when the temperature exceeds 100 degrees, the new speed with which the sun burns our skin, or the new constancy of public debate over what to do with growing mountains of waste. But our response to these signals is puzzling. Why haven't we launched a massive effort to save our environment? To come at the question another way: Why do some images startle us into immediate action and focus our attention on ways to respond effectively? And why do other images, though sometimes equally dramatic, produce instead a kind of paralysis, focusing our attention not on ways to respond but rather on some convenient, less painful distraction?

In a roundabout way, my visit to the North Pole caused me to think about these questions from a different perspective and gave them a new urgency. On the submarine, I had several opportunities to look through the periscope at the translucent bottom of the ice pack at the North Pole. The sight was not a little claustrophobic, and at one point I suddenly thought of the three whales that had become trapped under the ice of the Beaufort Sea a couple of years earlier. Television networks from four continents came to capture their poignant struggle for air and in the process so magnified the emotions felt around the world that soon scientists and rescue workers flocked to the scene. After several elaborate schemes failed, a huge icebreaker from the Soviet Union cut a path through the ice for the two surviving whales. Along with millions of others, I had been delighted to see them go free, but there on the submarine it occurred to me that if we are causing 100 extinctions each day—and many scientists believe we are—approximately 2,000 living species had disappeared from the earth during the whales' ordeal. They disappeared forever—unnoticed.

Similarly, when a little girl named Jessica McClure fell into a well in Texas, her ordeal and subsequent rescue by a legion of heroic men and women attracted hundreds of television cameras and journalists who sent the story into the homes and minds of hundreds of millions of people. Here, too, our response seems skewed: during the three days of Jessica's ordeal, more than 100,000 boys and girls her age or younger died of preventable causes—mostly starvation and diarrhea—due to failures of both crops and politics. As they struggled for life, none of these children looked into a collection of television cameras, anxious to send word of their plight to a waiting world. They died virtually unnoticed. Why?

Perhaps one part of the answer lies in the perceived difficulty of an effective response. If the problem portrayed in the image is one whose solution appears to involve more effort or sacrifice than we can readily imagine, or if even maximum effort by any one individual would fail to prevent the tragedy, we are tempted to sever the link between stimulus and moral response. Then, once a response is deemed impossible, the image that briefly caused us to consider responding becomes not just startling but painful. At that point, we begin to react not to the image but to the pain it now produces, thus severing a more basic link in our relationship to the world: the link between our senses and our emotions. Our eyes glaze over as our hearts close. We look but we don't see. We hear but refuse to listen.

Still, there are so many distressing images of environmental destruction that sometimes it seems impossible to know how to absorb or comprehend them. Before considering the threats themselves, it may be helpful to classify them and thus begin to organize our thoughts and feelings so that we may be able to respond appropriately.

A useful system comes from the military, which frequently places a conflict in one of three different categories, according to the theater in which it takes place. There are "local" skirmishes, "regional" battles, and "strategic" conflicts. This third category is reserved for struggles that can threaten a nation's survival and must be understood in a global context.

Environmental threats can be considered in the same way. For example, most instances of water pollution, air pollution, and illegal waste dumping are essentially local in nature. Problems like acid rain, the contamination of underground aquifers, and large oil spills are fundamentally regional. In both of these categories, there may be so many similar instances of particular local and regional problems occurring simultaneously all over the world that the pattern appears to be global, but the problems themselves are still not truly strategic because the operation of the global environment is not affected and the survival of civilization is not at stake.

However, a new class of environmental problems does affect the global ecological system, and these threats are fundamentally strategic. The 600 percent increase in the amount of chlorine in the atmosphere during the last forty years has taken place not just in those countries producing the chlorofluorocarbons responsible but in the air above every country, above Antarctica, above the North Pole and the Pacific Ocean—all the way from the surface of the earth to the top of the sky. The increased levels of chlorine disrupt the global process by which the earth regulates the amount of ultraviolet radiation from the sun that is allowed through the atmosphere to the surface; and if we let chlorine levels continue to increase, the radiation levels will also increase—to the point that all animal and plant life will face a new threat to their survival.

Global warming is also a strategic threat. The concentration of carbon dioxide and other heat-absorbing molecules has increased by almost 25 percent since World War II, posing a worldwide threat to the earth's ability to regulate the amount of heat from the sun retained in the atmosphere. This increase in heat seriously threatens the global climate equilibrium that determines the pattern of winds, rainfall, surface temperatures, ocean currents, and sea level. These in turn determine the distribution of vegetative and animal life on land and sea and have a great effect on the location and pattern of human societies.

In other words, the entire relationship between humankind and the earth has been transformed because our civilization is suddenly capable of affecting the entire global environment, not just a particular area. All of us know that human civilization has usually had a large impact on the environment; to mention just one example, there is evidence that even in prehistoric times, vast areas were sometimes intentionally burned by people in their search for food. And in our own time we have reshaped a large part of the earth's surface with concrete in our cities and carefully tended rice paddies, pastures, wheatfields, and other croplands in the countryside. But these changes, while sometimes appearing to be pervasive, have, until recently, been relatively trivial factors in the global ecological system. Indeed, until our lifetime, it was always safe to assume that nothing we did or could do would have any lasting effect on the global environment. But it is precisely that assumption which must now be discarded so that we can think strategically about our new relationship to the environment.

Human civilization is now the dominant cause of change in the global environment. Yet we resist this truth and find it hard to imagine that our effect on the earth must now be measured by the same yardstick used to calculate the strength of the moon's pull on the oceans or the force of the wind against the mountains. And if we are now capable of changing something so basic as the relationship between the earth and the sun, surely we must acknowledge a new responsibility to use that power wisely and with appropriate restraint. So far, however, we seem oblivious of the fragility of the earth's natural systems.

This century has witnessed dramatic changes in two key factors that define the physical reality of our relationship to the earth: a sudden and startling surge in human population, with the addition of one China's worth of people every ten years, and a sudden acceleration of the scientific and technological revolution, which has allowed an almost unimaginable magnification of our power to affect the world around us by burning, cutting, digging, moving, and transforming the physical matter that makes up the earth.

32   The surge in population is both a cause of the changed relationship and one of the clearest illustrations of how startling the change has been, especially when viewed in a historical context. From the emergence of modern humans 200,000 years ago until Julius Caesar's time, fewer than 250 million people walked on the face of the earth. When Christopher Columbus set sail for the New World 1,500 years later, there were approximately 500 million people on earth. By the time Thomas Jefferson wrote the Declaration of Independence in 1776, the number had doubled again, to 1 billion. By midway through this century, at the end of World War II, the number had risen to just above 2 billion people.

In other words, from the beginning of humanity's appearance on earth to 1945, it took more than ten thousand generations to reach a world population of 2 billion people. Now, in the course of one human lifetime—mine—the world population will increase from 2 to more than 9 billion, and it is already more than halfway there.

Like the population explosion, the scientific and technological revolution began to pick up speed slowly during the eighteenth century. And this ongoing revolution has also suddenly accelerated exponentially. For example, it is now an axiom in many fields of science that more new and important discoveries have taken place in the last ten years than in the entire previous history of science. While no single discovery has had the kind of effect on our relationship to the earth that nuclear weapons have had on our relationship to warfare, it is nevertheless true that taken together, they have completely transformed our cumulative ability to exploit the earth for sustenance—making the consequences of unrestrained exploitation every bit as unthinkable as the consequences of unrestrained nuclear war.

Now that our relationship to the earth has changed so utterly, we have to see that change and understand its implications. Our challenge is to recognize that the startling images of environmental destruction now occurring all over the world have much more in common than their ability to shock and awaken us. They are symptoms of an underlying problem broader in scope and more serious than any we have ever faced. Global warming, ozone depletion, the loss of living species, deforestation—they all have a common cause: the new relationship between human civilization and the earth's natural balance.

There are actually two aspects to this challenge. The first is to realize that our power to harm the earth can indeed have global and even permanent effects. The second is to realize that the only way to understand our new role as a co-architect of nature is to see ourselves as part of a complex system that does not operate according to the same simple rules of cause and effect we are used to. The problem is not our effect *on* the environment so much as our relationship *with* the environment. As a result, any solution to the problem will require a careful assessment of that relationship as well as the complex interrelationship among factors within civilization and between them and the major natural components of the earth's ecological system.

There is only one precedent for this kind of challenge to our thinking, and again it is military. The invention of nuclear weapons and the subsequent development by the United States and the Soviet Union of many thousands of strategic nuclear weapons forced a slow and painful recognition that the new power thus acquired forever changed not only the relationship between the two superpowers but also the relationship of humankind to the institution of warfare itself. The consequences of all-out war between nations armed with nuclear weapons suddenly included the possibility of the destruction of both nations—completely and simultaneously. That sobering realization led to a careful reassessment of every aspect of our mutual relationship to the prospect of such a war. As early as 1946 one strategist concluded that

36

strategic bombing with missiles "may well tear away the veil of illusion that has so long obscured the reality of the change in warfare—from a fight to a process of destruction."

Nevertheless, during the earlier stages of the nuclear arms race, each of the superpowers assumed that its actions would have a simple and direct effect on the thinking of the other. For decades, each new advance in weaponry was deployed by one side for the purpose of inspiring fear in the other. But each such deployment led to an effort by the other to leapfrog the first one with a more advanced deployment of its own. Slowly, it has become apparent that the problem of the nuclear arms race is not primarily caused by technology. It is complicated by technology, true; but it arises out of the relationship between the superpowers and is based on an obsolete understanding of what war is all about.

The eventual solution to the arms race will be found, not in a new deployment by one side or the other of some ultimate weapon or in a decision by either side to disarm unilaterally, but rather in new understandings and in a mutual transformation of the relationship itself. This transformation will involve changes in the technology of weaponry and the denial of nuclear technology to rogue states. But the key changes will be in the way we think about the institution of warfare and about the relationship between states.

40   The strategic nature of the threat now posed *by* human civilization to the global environment and the strategic nature of the threat *to* human civilization now posed by changes in the global environment present us with a similar set of challenges and false hopes. Some argue that a new ultimate technology, whether nuclear power or genetic engineering, will solve the problem. Others hold that only a drastic reduction of our reliance on technology can improve the conditions of life—a simplistic notion at best. But the real solution will be found in reinventing and finally healing the relationship between civilization and the earth. This can only be accomplished by undertaking a careful reassessment of all the factors that led to the relatively recent dramatic change in the relationship. The transformation of the way we relate to the earth will of course involve new technologies, but the key changes will involve new ways of thinking about the relationship itself.

*   *   *

Understanding What You Read

1. List at least six examples of "humankind's assault on the earth" that Gore cites at the beginning of this selection. Can you think of examples from your own life experiences?
2. Why does Gore think that people often ignore the evidence of environmental damage?
3. Explain his classification of environmental threats as local, regional, or strategic, giving examples of each.

Writing About What You Read

Write an essay explaining the two key factors that Gore believes have changed the relationship of people to the earth, using data and examples from this and other pieces in the book.

WALLACE STEGNER

Stegner (1909–1993) wrote about the American West for decades, and he had an enormous influence on other writers, especially through the Creative Writing Program at Stanford. His numerous novels include *The Big Rock Candy Mountain* (1943); *A Shooting Star* (1961); *All the Little Live Things* (1967), winner of the Commonwealth Gold Medal; *Angle of Repose* (1971), winner of the Pulitzer Prize; and *The Spectator Bird* (1976), winner of the National Book Award. His many short stories have been widely published in periodicals and collected in individual volumes. *The Collected Stories of Wallace Stegner* appeared in 1990. Stegner was also a prolific writer of nonfiction. *Beyond the Hundredth Meridian* (1954) is a biography of John Wesley Powell, whose works on the American West inspired Stegner. *Where the Bluebird Sings to the Lemonade Springs* (1992) is a collection of essays about the West. "Land of Hope, Land of Ruin" is adapted from the introduction of that book.

Land of Hope, Land of Ruin

O N C E I said in print that the remaining Western wilderness is the geography of hope, and I have written, believing what I wrote, that the West at large is hope's native home, the youngest and freshest of America's regions, magnificently endowed and with the chance to become something unprecedented and unmatched in the world.

I was shaped by the West and have lived most of a long life in it, and nothing would gratify me more than to see it both prosperous and environmentally healthy, with a civilization to match its scenery. Whenever I return to the Rocky Mountain states, where I am most at home, or escape into the California backlands from the suburbia where I live, the smell of distance excites me, the largeness and the clarity take the scales from my eyes and I respond as unthinkingly as a salmon that swims past a river mouth and tastes the waters of its birth.

But when I am thinking instead of throbbing, I remember what history and experience have taught me about the West. Too often the Western states have been prosperous at the expense of their fragile environment, and their civilization has too often mined and degraded the natural scene while drawing most of its quality from it.

4   So I amend my enthusiasm. I say, yes, the West is hope's native home, but there are varieties and degrees of hope, and the wrong kinds, in excessive amounts, go with human failure and environmental damage as boom goes with bust.

Visionary expectation was a great energizer of the westward movement, and something like it still drives the rush to the Sun Belt. But uninformed, unrealistic, greedy expectation has been a prescription for disappointment that the West has carried to the corner drugstore too many times. Ghost towns and dust bowls, like motels, are Western inventions. All are reflections of transience, and transience in most of the West has hampered the development of stable, rooted communities and aborted the kind of communal effort that takes in everything from kindergartens to graveyards.

The deficiency of community is apparent in the cities as in the small towns. Western cities are likely to have an artificial look, and why not, since so many of them are planted in an artificial environment maintained by increasingly elaborate engineering.

In *Californians,* James Houston asks what should be a preposterous question: "Suppose 10 million people were living in a semidesert where there was not one adequate source of water closer than 200 miles?" and answers it with a further leap into the preposterous. The semidesert is the Los Angeles metropolitan area and not 10 million, but 15 million people are living there.

8   Five years of drought have not even slowed the growth. But 10 would, and 15 would stop it cold, and 20 would send people reeling back not only from Los Angeles but from San Diego, Albuquerque, Denver, Phoenix, Tucson, every artificial urban enclave. Tree rings inform us that droughts of that duration have occurred. Every Western city hell-bent for expansion might ponder the history of Mesa Verde,[1] which was abandoned after a 25-year drought.

The West, vast and magnificent, greatly various but with the abiding unity of too little water except in its extreme northwest corner, has proved fragile and unforgiving. Damaged by human rapacity or carelessness, it is more likely to go on to erosion gullies and desertification than to restore itself.

In the dry West, using water means using it *up.* What we put to municipal or industrial use is not coming back into the streams for irrigation, or if it does come back, it comes back poisoned. What is used in irrigation largely evaporates. The percentage that finds its way back to the streams is increas-

---

[1]In southwestern Colorado, the site of the cliff dwellings of the Anasazi, who abandoned them about 1300, possibly because of drought.

ingly laden with salts, fertilizers and pesticides. And everything we take out of the rivers for any purpose leaves less for trout, rafters, herons, ducks, skinny-dippers and TV cameramen photographing pristine America.

Confronted with an unavoidable shortage that is bound to get worse, many are likely to suggest ever greater engineering projects, roughly comparable to the canals of Mars, to bring water down to the dry country from the Columbia or the Snake or the Yukon, or tow it as icebergs from Glacier Bay to let San Diego expand and the desert blossom.

Pipe dreams. Arrogant pipe dreams. Why should deserts be asked to blossom? They were doing all right until we set out to reform them. Making them blossom is something we inherited from Isaiah.[2] It is an idea dear to American and especially Mormon hearts and it has had remarkable short-term successes. But it is open to all sorts of doubts when we look into the future. 12

Historically, irrigation civilizations have died, either of salinization or of accumulating engineering problems, except in Egypt, where until the Aswan Dam, the annual Nile flood kept the land sweet. And if there are no technical reasons why we cannot move water from remote watersheds, there are ecological and, I might suggest, moral reasons why we shouldn't. As a Crow Indian friend of mine said about the coal in his country: "God put it there. That's a good place for it."

From before it was even known, the West has been a land of Cockaigne[3] where every day is payday, where the handouts grow on bushes and the little streams of alcohol come trickling down the rocks. Ordinary people, making it by guess and by God, or not quite making it, are just as susceptible to dreams as the ambitious and greedy, and respond as excitedly to the adventure, the freedom, the apparently inexhaustible richness of the West. And the boosters have been there from the beginning to oversell the West as the Garden of the World.

Sometimes it is hard to tell the boosters from the suckers. They may be the same people. Many of them are deluded deluders, true believers, wishful thinkers, blindfold prophets, at once the agents, the beneficiaries and the victims of the vast speculative real estate deal that is American and Western history.

I know that historical hope, energy, carelessness and self-deception. I knew it before I could talk. My father practically invented it, though he qualified more as sucker than as booster, and profited accordingly. 16

He was a boomer at 14, always on the lookout for the big chance. As a youth he tried the Wisconsin and Minnesota woods, but found only the migratory wage slavery that has always been one payoff of the American Dream. He tried professional baseball but wasn't quite good enough. In the

[2]The Old Testament prophet Isaiah spoke of the day when God will bring rivers to the desert (Isaiah 43:20) and make the earth bloom and bear fruit (Isaiah 55:10).
[3]An imaginary land of luxury and leisure.

1890's he floated out to North Dakota on the tail end of the land rush, but found himself in the midst of a 10-year drought and ended up speculating in wheat futures and running a blind pig, an illegal beerhall.

When it became clear that Dakota's promises were indistinguishable from Siberian exile, my father dragged us out the migration route to the Northwest. His goal was Alaska, but again he was late: the Klondike rush[4] was long over. For a while he ran a lunchroom in the Washington woods where now is the Seattle suburb of Redmond. The loggers cut down the trees and left the lunchroom among the stumps. By 1914 we were up in Saskatchewan, part of another land rush, where for a change we *would* be in on the ground floor and make a killing growing wheat to feed Europe's armies.

We plowed up something over 100 acres of buffalo grass and for a while we were a wheat farm. Then, because Saskatchewan is part of the arid West, and we were in Palliser's Triangle, one of the driest parts of it, we became a tumbleweed patch and a dust bowl. Then we were on the road again, first to Montana, then to Utah, ultimately to Nevada and California.

20 Rainbows flowered for my father in every sky he looked at; he was led by pillars of fire and cloud.[5] In Salt Lake City he fell in with some men who had a doodlebug that would reveal the presence of gold and silver in the earth, and my safe-deposit box still contains, not as assets but as wry reminders, deeds to several patches of Nevada gravel and mountainside that my father firmly believed would one day make us rich.

While he waited for one of those bonanzas to pan out, he ran a gambling joint in Reno, an occupation symbolically right for him as for the West at large. Later, when he was close to down and out, he did one last desperate and damaging thing: he managed to get an option on some land in southern California, and to make his payments and a fast buck he hired a crew to cut down all its 200-year-old oaks and sell them off as firewood. Finally, like many another gambler no worse and no better, he died broke and friendless in a fleabag hotel, having in his lifetime done more human and environmental damage than he could have repaired in a second lifetime.

Out of his life I made a novel, *The Big Rock Candy Mountain,* a commentary on Western optimism and enterprise and the common man's dream of something for nothing. I took the title from the hobo ballad that Harry McClintock, "Haywire Mac," is supposed to have written in 1928 but that I heard my father sing long before that.

That vagrant's vision of beatitude, of a place where the bulldogs have rubber teeth and policemen have to tip their hats, where there's a lake of stew and of whisky, too, where the handouts grow on bushes and the hens lay soft-boiled eggs, summarized his unquenchable hope as it summarizes the

[4]The Klondike is a region of the Yukon Territory in northwestern Canada where the discovery of gold in 1886 drew thousands of people north in search of riches.

[5]In the Old Testament book of Exodus (13:21), God leads the Israelites out of captivity with a pillar of cloud by day and a pillar of fire by night.

indigenous optimism of the West. What lures many people to the West always has been, and still is, mirage.

And yet I hope that Western hopefulness is not a cynical joke. For somehow, against probability, some sort of indigenous, recognizable culture has been growing on Western ranches and in Western towns and even in Western cities. It is the product not of the boomers but of the stickers, not of those who pillage and run but of those who settle and love the life they have made and the place they have made it in.

I believe that eventually, perhaps within a generation or two, they will work out some sort of compromise between what must be done to earn a living and what must be done to restore health to the earth, air and water.

The feeling is like the feeling in a football game when the momentum changes, when helplessness begins to give way to confidence and what looked like sure defeat opens up to the possibility of victory. It has already begun. I hope I am around to see it fully arrive.

Understanding What You Read

1. What attitudes and values does Stegner see as the cause of much of the West's environmental devastation?
2. How has drought affected the development of the West?
3. How has hope—what Stegner calls the "wrong kind"—damaged the environment in the West?
4. What is wrong with efforts to make the desert bloom?
5. What about Stegner's father's dreams led him to damage the environment? Give examples.

Writing About What You Read

Write a sketch of someone you know whose attitudes, values, and behavior are inconsistent with a healthy environment.

ANITA GORDON AND DAVID SUZUKI

Gordon and Suzuki, both Canadians, collaborated on *It's a Matter of Survival* (1991), a book that grew out of a radio series in 1989 by the Canadian Broadcasting Corporation. "How Did We Come to This?" is from that book. Suzuki holds a Ph.D. from the University of Chicago and is not only a scholar but a prolific writer, a filmmaker, and the host of numerous television and radio documentaries. Gordon has produced a number of award-winning documentaries on major global issues. She is the producer of the award-winning CBC radio science series *Quirks and Quarks,* which is also carried on public radio in the United States.

How Did We Come to This?

THERE'S a strange phenomenon that biologists refer to as "the boiled frog syndrome." Put a frog in a pot of water and increase the temperature of the water gradually from 20°C to 30°C to 40°C . . . to 90°C and the frog just sits there. But suddenly, at 100°C (212°F), something happens: the water boils and the frog dies.

Scientists studying environmental problems, particularly the greenhouse effect, see "the boiled frog syndrome" as a metaphor for the human situation: we have figuratively, and in some ways literally, been heating up the world around us without recognizing the danger.

Psychologist Robert Ornstein, coauthor of *New World, New Mind,* points out that those people who have been sounding warnings receive the same response from us as would someone attempting to alert the frog to the danger of a rise in its water temperature from, say, 70° to 90°C (158° to 194°F). If the frog could talk, he would say, "There's no difference, really. It's slightly warmer in here, but I'm just as well off." If you then say to the frog, "If the heat keeps increasing at that rate, you will die," the frog will reply, "We have been increasing it for a long time, and I'm not dead. So what are you worried about?"

"Our situation is like the frog's," says Ornstein. Today, despite the fact that researchers using the most sophisticated atmospheric-monitoring equipment in the world are telling us that our future is at risk, we—as individuals and as governments—ignore or minimize the warnings.

The frog has a fatal flaw, explains Ornstein. Having no evolutionary experience with boiling water, he is unable to perceive it as dangerous. Throughout their biological evolution, frogs have lived in a medium that does not vary greatly in temperature, so they haven't needed to develop sophisticated thermal detectors in their skin. The frog in the pot is unaware of the threat and simply sits complacently until he boils.

Like the simmering frog, we face a future without precedent, and our senses are not attuned to warnings of imminent danger. The threats we face as the crisis builds—global warming, acid rain, the ozone hole and increasing ultraviolet radiation, chemical toxins such as pesticides, dioxins,[1] and poly-

---

[1]A family of some 210 chemicals. Some dioxins known to be highly toxic are emitted from trash-burning incinerators.

chlorinated biphenyls (PCBs)[2] in our food and water—are undetectable by the sensory system we have evolved. We do not feel the acidity of the rain, see the ultraviolet radiation projected through the ozone hole, taste the toxins in our food and water, or feel the heat of global warming except, as the frog does, as gradual and therefore endurable. Nothing in our evolutionary experience has prepared us for the limits of a finite world, one in which a five-degree climate change over a matter of decades will mean the end of life as we have known it on the planet.

How did we come to this? How did we plan our own obsolescence? The answer lies in millennia of human history, a surprisingly brief chapter in the chronicle of the planet. You can see just how brief if you use a standard calendar to mark the passage of time on Earth. The origin of the Earth, some 4.6 billion years ago, is placed at midnight January 1, and the present at midnight December 31. Each calendar day represents approximately 12 million years of actual history. Dinosaurs arrived on about December 10 and disappeared on Christmas Day. *Homo sapiens* made an appearance at 11:45 P.M. on December 31. The recorded history of human achievement, on which we base so much of our view of human entitlement, takes up only the last minute of that year.

The dinosaurs had a fortnight of supremacy on this planet before they were eradicated by some environmental catastrophe. We have had 15 minutes of fame. And in that short period we have transformed the world. In fact, *Homo sapiens* has managed to extinguish large parts of the living world in a matter of centuries.

For the past million years, our biological makeup has changed very little: we are essentially the same creatures as those that emerged along the Rift Valley in Africa. But culturally we are a completely different genus. Where once we lived as part of the natural world, we now seek to conscript it in the service of our ends. And the result has been that we have altered the ecosphere in which we evolved into a form that cannot ensure our survival.

Compared to that of other mammals, human physical prowess is not very impressive. We are not built for speed: a mature elephant can easily outrun the fastest sprinter in the world. We have no physical arsenal for self-defense—no claws, fangs, or horns. Our sensory acuity is limited: we can't see over great distances, as the eagle can, or at night like the owl; our hearing is not highly developed, as is the bat's; we can't sense ultraviolet light, like a bee. Indeed, our main survival strategy has been the development of a 1600-gram (3.5 lb.) brain, capable of complex thought.

Out of that brain evolved a mind possessed of self-awareness, curiosity, inventiveness, memory. It enabled us to recognize patterns and cycles in the

8

---

[2]Extremely toxic substances once used in the electrical industry, banned in 1979 in the United States.

natural world—rhythms of day and night, seasonal changes, tides, lunar phases, animal migrations, plant successions—and to make out of this predictability a mode of existence for ourselves in what we saw as our natural environment. For millions of years our ancestors shared the grassy savannahs with other mammals and birds and plant life. We learned to "read" the alarms sounded by species more attuned to danger than we were. Other living things became our "early warning system."

12   Secure in our ability to rely on the natural world to troubleshoot for us, we began to shift from passively surviving to actively seeking to improve our quality of life. We made crude tools to facilitate hunting, and even our crudest ones were sufficient to make our early forebears deadly predators. The arrival of paleolithic peoples in North America across the Bering land-bridge[3] perhaps 100,000 years ago was followed by a north-south wave of extinction of species of large mammals.

Then, between 10,000 and 12,000 years ago, a major shift in human evolution took place—*Homo sapiens* became a farmer. We learned how to domesticate and cultivate plants and in doing so made the transition from nomadic hunter-gatherer to rooted agriculturalist. Once we knew how to ensure that we would have food, settlements grew up, and we started to exploit nature to serve our needs. We began to manage the planet, and the water in our pot heated up a few degrees.

Man the farmer was far more destructive than man the hunter. Early agriculture changed the landscape of the planet. While it fostered the rise of cities and civilizations, it also led to practices that denuded the land of its indigenous flora and fauna and depleted the soil of its nutrients and water-holding capacity. Great civilizations along the Indus and Nile rivers flourished and disappeared as once-fertile land was farmed into desert. We read the devastating signs as an indication that it was time to move on. We were few in number and the world was infinite.

The Industrial Revolution stoked the fire under our pot. The replacement of muscle power by machines, driven by wood and coal, then oil and gas, and finally nuclear fission, drowned out all warning signals under the roar and clatter of a culture heading inexorably toward the new Eden of growth and progress.

16   Once it took Haida Indians in the Queen Charlotte Islands more than a year to cut down a single giant cedar. When the Europeans arrived with the technological know-how—the two-man saw and steel ax—the task was shortened to a week. Today, one man with a portable chain saw can fell that tree in an hour. It is that explosive increase in technological muscle power that has enabled us to attack the natural world and to bludgeon it into submission.

[3]Land bridge, now underwater, that once joined Siberia with Alaska. Scientists believe that ancestors of North and South American Indians traveled to America from Asia across this bridge.

The massive application of technology by industry has been accompanied by an unprecedented increase in human population. With the conquest of the major causes of early death—sepsis, infectious disease, and malnutrition—world population numbers have exploded.

We are now the most ubiquitous large mammal on Earth, and armed with technological might, we have assumed a position of dominance on the planet. We have gained the ability to destroy entire ecosystems almost overnight, with dams, fires, clearcut logging, agricultural and urban projects, and mining. And our self-awarded mandate to do so is predicated on the assumption that we possess the knowledge to manage the environment, that nature is sufficiently vast and self-renewing to absorb the shocks we subject it to, and that we have a fundamental entitlement to nature's bounty. That has been our history, but the reality is different. Our machinery, based on fossil-fuel consumption, produces carbon dioxide in quantities that exceed the ability of the natural world to absorb it, as we inject almost six billion extra tons of carbon annually into the upper atmosphere, just from the burning of fossil fuels. As well as increasing naturally occurring compounds—methane, nitrous oxide, sulfur—the chemicals industry has introduced man-made compounds such as CFCs,[4] while the pulp and paper industry generates chloroorganics such as furans and dioxins. Technology enables us to harvest previously unattainable "resources" in quantities far in excess of their regenerative capacity, and we pay no attention because, through the span of human history, we have considered those resources infinite and have believed that the human mind would always provide solutions to our problems. That belief has entrenched in us a mindless acceptance of certain truths and an equally mindless lack of comprehension of the consequences.

*   *   *

On a desolate island in the Pacific Ocean stands one of the great mysteries of the world. Archeologists speculate about the origin of the bizarre statues that loom over Easter Island. Out in the middle of nowhere, about 3200 kilometers (1988 mi.) west of Chile, on an uninhabited island, are a thousand statues, each 18,000 kilograms (18 tons) of volcanic tufa standing up to 4.5 meters (15 ft.) tall. Who carved them, and why? We may never know. The civilization that created them is gone, lost in history, but an English botanist has found that it may have been the architect of its own destruction.

The clue lies in what one finds on the island today. Just as strange as the massive statues that stand watch there is the fact that Easter Island, unlike its Pacific neighbors, is treeless. That wasn't always the case. From fossil pollen and some ancient fruit found on the island, botanist John Flenley deduced that a fruit palm had flourished there for thousands of years. By tracking the pollen record, he was able to pinpoint the decline of the tree species as beginning about 1200 years ago and continuing for several hundred years

20

---

[4]Chlorofluorocarbons, known to deplete the ozone layer.

until the tree became extinct. What cataclysm occurred that ended the millennia-long period during which the fruit palm thrived? The arrival of man.

Flenley believes that these ancient carvers arrived on the island and began to clear land for agriculture; they felled the trees to make canoes and levers for raising the statues, and for firewood; as many as 20,000 people were overusing what should have been a renewable resource. What nags at Flenley is that they were doing in microcosm exactly what we are doing to the planet today. But what nags at Flenley most is a terrible image of mindless destruction. Easter Island is so small that "if you stand on the peak of it, you can see almost all of it," says Flenley. "The man who felled the last piece of forest knew that he was felling the last piece of forest, but he did it anyway. What could he possibly have been thinking as he looked around the island, then cut down the very thing he depended on to survive?"

In 1990 the spirit of that Easter Islander hovers over the globe. And now we must ask ourselves, what can possibly be going through our minds as we threaten to destroy the very things we depend on to survive. On the western coast of North America stand the remnants of a once-magnificent temperate rain forest. Stretching from Alaska to California, these trees can trace their ancestry back more than 10,000 years. In the Carmanah Valley in British Columbia, one old giant, a Sitka spruce 90 meters (300 ft.) high and 3 meters (10 ft.) in diameter—perhaps the largest one living—towers over the surrounding trees. It began its life more than 500 years ago, long before the modern chain saw that now threatens its relatives, long before the Industrial Revolution, before a white man stepped onto the shores of North America. All along the coast, these trees are in danger, targeted to be cut—to create jobs and profit and to fill the gaping maw of corporate greed. The coastal rain forest of British Columbia is given 15 years before it is wiped out from logging. In Alaska's Tongass forest, the Sitka spruce were once prized as mainmasts for the clippers that cruised the world. Now you can buy one for the price of a cheeseburger. The U.S. forest service sells them for $1.60 apiece, mainly to Japan as pulp. Our natural heritage is being destroyed for short-term profit and short-term gain, some of it so quickly that we almost didn't even know it ever existed.

That's the way it was for Steller's sea cow. This 9 meter (30 ft.) long, 3200 kilogram (3.1 ton) marine mammal lived unknown to man on one tiny group of islands in the northernmost Pacific Ocean. It flourished on the Commander Islands of Russia in great numbers until November 4, 1741, when the Dane Vitus Bering explored the area. The sea cow was named for the only naturalist who ever saw it alive, a German named Georg Wilhelm Steller, who wrote this account of it:

> These animals love shallow and sandy places along the seashore. With the rising tide they come in so close to the shore that not only did I on many occasions prod them with a pole but sometimes even stroked their backs with my hands.

Usually entire families keep together, male and female, long-grown offspring and the little tender ones. They seem to have slight concern for their life and security, so that when you pass in the very midst of them with a boat, you can single out the one you wish to hook. When an animal caught on a hook began to move about somewhat violently, those nearest in the herd began to stir also and attempted to bring succor. To this end some of them tried to upset the boat with their backs while others tried to break the rope or strove to remove the hook from the wound by blows of their tails. It was a most remarkable proof of their conjugal affection that a male, having tried with all his might, but in vain, to free the female caught by a hook, and in spite of the beatings we gave him, neverthe-less followed her to the shore, and that several times, even after she was dead, he shot unexpectedly up to her like a speeding arrow. Even early the next morning when we came to cut up the meat to bring it to the dugout, we found the male again near the female's body, and the same thing I observed on the third day, when I went up there myself for the sole purpose of examining the intestines.

Twenty-seven years after Steller's sea cow was discovered, the last one was butchered. 24

Today we live in an era of "last ones." We're told that elephants, rhinos, and tigers will exist only in zoos within our children's lifetime. Three hundred African elephants a day are killed—for trinkets. That senseless slaughter has gone on and will go on daily until all the elephants are sacrificed. In eight brief years, Africa's elephant population has been halved through poaching from 1.2 million to just over 600,000—all to feed our consumer craving for ivory. The best projections say the elephants may last until the year 2030. The pessimistic scenario dates their demise at about 2010.

We create international laws like CITES (the Convention on Interna-tional Trade in Endangered Species)[5] to try to protect endangered species from ourselves. We mutilate animals on the verge of extinction in order to save them from our greed—for example, by cutting off the coveted horns of African rhinos so that the animals are no longer attractive to poachers. It is the unending demand for land for human use that destroys habitats and the combined forces of poverty and greed that fuel the relentless slaughter. What we don't destroy we seek to control. And through all of this we cling to the belief that science and technology are the tools that will allow us to manage the planet effectively.

Science, it has come to be believed, provides us with the knowledge and the means to transform the planet into what we need, or simply want it to be. And when Science hesitates and stops to ponder, as Francis Bacon[6] (1561–1626) did when he wrote that nature, to be commanded, must be obeyed, we dismissively call it Philosophy and plunge ahead anyway, driven

[5]Ratified in 1975, this treaty, now signed by 103 countries, prohibits commercial trading in 675 species.

[6]English philosopher and essayist (1561–1626), responsible for a theory of scientific classification in which human knowledge can gain power over nature.

by the momentum of past achievements, current needs, and a future guaranteed by our collective adherence to a body of *sacred truths.*

28   It is said that more than 90 percent of all scientists who have ever lived are still alive and publishing today. Twentieth-century science, especially since the end of the Second World War, has mushroomed, and science, when coopted by industry, medicine, and the military, has revolutionized every aspect of the way we live. An explosion in technological wizardry to aid scientists has created a sense that the knowledge gained permits us to understand and control all of nature. Experts in management of salmon, forests, and wildlife, and enforcers of quality control of air, water, and soil foster the illusion that we are capable, and entitled, to interfere in natural process.

In fact, that is a terrible delusion that anyone who understands the nature of scientific inquiry and insight understands. Scientific knowledge is fundamentally different from other ways of knowing and describing the world. A "worldview" is the sum total of a culture's insight, experience, and speculation. It is an integrated body of knowledge that incorporates values and beliefs as well as profound observational material in a holistic manner. Thus, in a worldview, the planets, a river, mountains, rocks, and so on are all interconnected, as are the past, present, and future.

Scientists examine the world in a very different way. The heart of the scientific approach is to focus on a single part of nature, whether a star, a plant, or an atom, and to try to separate and isolate it from all else. If one can bring it into the lab where it is carefully controlled, all the better. By controlling everything impinging on that fragment of nature and measuring everything within it, a scientist acquires knowledge—about that isolated fragment. But that information does not tell us about the whole, or about the interactions between the parts. Yet scientists today, with few exceptions, continue to examine the natural world in isolated fragments on the assumption that a sufficiently large inventory of pieces will yield a complete description. The picture we acquire is a vague sketch of the complex diversity that exists in nature.

Even if the reductionist assumptions were correct, it is the height of arrogance to think we are approaching a level of knowledge that enables us to manage a natural resource. Scientists don't even know the number of species on Earth because so little research money has been devoted to acquiring such a catalog. Rain-forest biologist E. O. Wilson[7] puts it more graphically: "More money is spent in the bars of New York City in two weeks than is spent annually on tropical research." And even those who have devoted their lives to such study are severely hampered by the technical difficulties.

32   We know in detail about the basic life cycle and biology of only a handful of plants and animals, and our understanding of the interaction of species in

[7]See headnote on page 151.

a diverse community is negligible. A decade ago, marine biologists based their understanding of ocean food chains and energy flow on plankton, the tiny plants and animals that can be trapped in fine-mesh nets. Then, *picoplankton,* single-celled organisms so small that they pass through the finest nets, were discovered. Today, picoplankton are thought to be so numerous that some scientists believe they are a major source of atmospheric oxygen. Yet 10 years ago, we didn't even know they existed.

Perhaps one of the species most extensively studied has been the fruit fly *Drosophila melanogaster.* The center of attention for geneticists for 80 years, the fruit fly has cost hundreds of billions of dollars in research funds, consumed millions of person-years, and earned several Nobel Prizes. Yet even the most fundamental questions—how the insects develop from an egg through larva to adult—remain mysteries. It is astonishing, therefore, to hear foresters or fisheries experts confidently speak of managing natural "resources" about which they are far more ignorant than those fruit-fly geneticists are about *Drosophila.*

Science has not provided, and will not provide in the foreseeable future, the knowledge that we need to dominate and control nature. Every practicing scientist quickly realizes the enormity of our ignorance and that it is a perversion of the scientific enterprise to turn the small gains made in the past few decades into major triumphs of human knowledge. But that has not stopped us from doing so.

Inherent in our human conviction that we can manage the planet are ideas that seem so basic and true to societies around the world that they are never questioned—nature is infinite; the biblical injunction[8] to go forth and multiply and dominate the Earth is the human mandate; pollution is the price of progress; growth is progress; all of nature is at our disposal. Yet it is these *sacred truths* that not only blind us to the reality of the environmental crisis but are the cause of it. We don't see that our current beliefs and values are right now compromising the very systems that keep us alive. Like Samson[9] blinded, we are straining at the pillars of life and bringing them down around us.

[8]See Genesis 1:28.

[9]Samson, captured by the Philistines, blinded, and chained to a pillar of the temple, had such extraordinary strength that he was able to pull down the temple, killing himself and his enemies.

Understanding What You Read

1. These writers argue that many environmental threats can't be detected by our senses and that others develop so slowly they are not even noticed. In your opinion, to what dangers does this expose us?
2. According to Gordon and Suzuki, what false assumptions threaten human dominance on the planet?

Writing About What You Read

Write a paragraph (or an essay) in which you compare the situation of the frog in boiling water with humans in specific threatening circumstances.

BARRY COMMONER

Currently director of the Center for Biology of Natural Systems at Queens College, Commoner (b. 1917) holds a Ph.D. in biology from Harvard and has been writing about the environmental costs of technology for some three decades. In 1958 he joined with physicians and other scientists to form the Committee for Nuclear Information to investigate the effects of radioactive fallout on human health. Commoner published the results of his investigations in *Science and Survival* (1966). In *The Closing Circle* (1971) he showed how human behavior had resulted in poisoned air in Los Angeles, polluted farmland in Illinois, and the contamination of Lake Erie. "At War with the Planet" is from the opening chapter of *Making Peace with the Planet* (1990).

At War with the Planet

PEOPLE LIVE in two worlds. Like all living things, we inhabit the natural world, created over the Earth's 5-billion-year history by physical, chemical, and biological processes. The other world is our own creation: homes, cars, farms, factories, laboratories, food, clothing, books, paintings, music, poetry. We accept responsibility for events in our own world, but not for what occurs in the natural one. Its storms, droughts, and floods are "acts of God," free of human control and exempt from our responsibility.

Now, on a planetary scale, this division has been breached. With the appearance of a continent-sized hole in the Earth's protective ozone layer and the threat of global warming, even droughts, floods, and heat waves may become unwitting acts of man.

Like the Creation, the portending global events are cosmic: they change the relationship between the planet Earth and its star, the sun. The sun's powerful influence on the Earth is exerted by two forces: gravity and solar radiation. Gravity is a nearly steady force that fixes the planet's path around the sun. Solar radiation—largely visible and ultraviolet light—is a vast stream of energy that bathes the Earth's surface, fluctuating from day to night and season to season. Solar energy fuels the energy-requiring processes of life; it creates the planet's climate and governs the gradual evolution and the current behavior of its huge and varied population of living things. We have been tampering with this powerful force, unaware, like the Sorcerer's Apprentice,[1] of the potentially disastrous consequences of our actions.

We have become accustomed to the now mundane image of the Earth as seen from the first expedition to the moon—a beautiful blue sphere decorated by swirls of fleecy clouds. It is a spectacularly natural object; at that distance, no overt signs of human activity are visible. But this image, now repeatedly thrust before us in photographs, posters, and advertisements, is misleading. Even if the global warming catastrophe never materializes, and the ozone hole remains an esoteric, polar phenomenon, already human activity has profoundly altered global conditions in ways that may not register on the camera. Everywhere in the world, there is now radioactivity that was not there before, the dangerous residue of nuclear explosions and the nuclear power industry; noxious fumes of smog blanket every major city; carcinogenic synthetic pesticides have been detected in mother's milk all over the world; great forests have been cut down, destroying ecological niches and their resident species.

As it reaches the Earth's surface, solar radiation is absorbed and sooner or later converted to heat. The amount of solar radiation that falls on the Earth and of the heat that escapes it depends not only on the daily turning of the Earth and the yearly change of the seasons, but also on the status of the thin gaseous envelope that surrounds the planet. One of the natural constituents of the outer layer of Earth's gaseous skin—the stratosphere—is ozone, a gas made of three oxygen atoms (ordinary oxygen is made of two atoms). Ozone absorbs much of the ultraviolet light radiated from the sun and thereby shields the Earth's surface from its destructive effects. Carbon dioxide and several other atmospheric components act like a valve: they are transparent to visible light but hold back invisible infrared radiation. The light that reaches the Earth's surface during the day is converted to heat that radiates outward in the form of infrared energy. Carbon dioxide, along with several other less prominent gases in the air, governs the Earth's temperature by holding back this outward radiation of heat energy. The greater the carbon dioxide content of the atmosphere, the higher the Earth's temperature. Glass has a similar effect, which causes the winter sun to warm a greenhouse; hence, the "greenhouse effect," the term commonly applied to global warming.

These global effects are not new; they have massively altered the condition of the Earth's surface over its long history. For example, because the early Earth lacked oxygen and therefore the ozone shield, it was once so

---

[1] In folklore, the sorcerer's apprentice accidentally flooded the sorcerer's house because he learned to make a broom fetch water but not how to make it stop.

heavily bathed in solar ultraviolet light as to limit living things to dark places; intense ultraviolet radiation can kill living cells and induce cancer. Similarly, analyses of ice (and the entrapped air bubbles) deposited in the Antarctic over the last 150,000 years indicate that the Earth's temperature fluctuated considerably, closely paralleled by changes in the carbon dioxide level.

Changes in the Earth's vegetation can be expected to influence the carbon dioxide content of the atmosphere. Thus, the massive growth of forests some 200 million to 300 million years ago took carbon dioxide out of the air, eventually converting its carbon into the deposits of coal, oil, and natural gas produced by geological transformation of the dying trees and plants. The huge deposits of fossil fuel, the product of millions of years of photosynthesis, remained untouched until coal, and later petroleum and natural gas, were mined and burned, releasing carbon dioxide into the atmosphere. The amounts of these fuels burned to provide human society with energy represent the carbon captured by photosynthesis over millions of years. So, by burning them, in the last 750 years we have returned carbon dioxide to the atmosphere thousands of times faster than the rate at which it was removed by the early tropical forests. The atmosphere's carbon dioxide content has increased by 20 percent since 1850, and there is good evidence that the Earth's average temperature has increased about 1 degree Fahrenheit since then. If nothing is done to change this trend, temperatures may rise by about 2.5 to 10 degrees more in the next fifty years. This is about the same change in temperature that marked the end of the last ice age about 15,000 years ago—an event that drastically altered the global habitat. If the new, man-made warming occurs, there will be equally drastic changes, this time endangering a good deal of the world that people have fashioned for themselves. Polar ice will melt and the warmer oceans will expand, raising the sea level and flooding many cities; productive agricultural areas, such as the U.S. Midwest, may become deserts; the weather is likely to become more violent.

Regardless of how serious the resultant warming of the Earth turns out to be, and what, if anything, can be done to avoid its cataclysmic effects, it demonstrates a basic fact: that in the short span of its history, human society has exerted an effect on its planetary habitat that matches the size and impact of the natural processes that until now solely governed the global condition.

The ozone effect leads to the same conclusion. This problem arises not from the rapid man-made reversal of a natural process, but from the intrusion of an unnatural one on global chemistry. The chief culprits are the synthetic chemicals known as CFCs or chlorofluorocarbons. Like most of the petrochemical industry's products, CFCs do not occur in nature; they are synthesized for use in air conditioners, refrigerators, and spray cans, as solvents, and as a means of producing foam plastics. CFCs readily evaporate and are extraordinarily stable; escaping from confinement in a junked air conditioner or a discarded plastic cup, they migrate upward into the stratosphere. There they encounter ozone molecules, generated by the impact of solar radiation on ordinary oxygen molecules. A complex catalytic reaction ensues, in which each CFC molecule causes the destruction of numerous ozone molecules. This chemical process has already eaten a huge hole in the protective ozone layer over Antarctica, evidence that here, too, a process recently created by human society matches in scope a natural, protective component of the Earth's global envelope. Serious damage to people, wildlife, and crops is likely if the process continues: a large increase in skin cancer; eye problems; suppression of photosynthesis. Moreover, the CFCs act like carbon dioxide toward heat radiation and, along with methane and several minor gases, contribute to global warming.

Clearly, we need to understand the interaction between our two worlds: the natural ecosphere, the thin global skin of air, water, and soil and the plants and animals that live in it, and the man-made technosphere—powerful enough to deserve so grandiose a term. The technosphere has become sufficiently large and intense to alter the natural processes that govern the ecosphere. And in turn, the altered ecosphere threatens to flood our great cities, dry up our bountiful farms, contaminate our food and water, and poison our bodies—catastrophically diminishing our ability to provide for basic human needs. The human attack on the ecosphere has instigated an ecological counterattack. The two worlds are at war.

The two spheres in which we live are governed by very different laws. One of the basic laws of the ecosphere can be summed up as "Everything is connected to everything else." This expresses the fact that the ecosphere is an elaborate network, in which each component part is linked to many others. Thus, in an aquatic ecosystem a fish is not only a fish, the parent of other fish. It is also the producer of organic waste that nourishes microorganisms and ultimately aquatic plants; the consumer of oxygen produced photosynthetically by the plants; the habitat of parasites; the fish hawk's prey. The fish is not only, existentially, a fish, but also an element of this network, which defines its functions. Indeed, in the evolutionary sense, a good part of the network—the microorganisms and plants, for example—preceded the fish, which could establish itself only because it fitted properly into the preexisting system.

In the technosphere, the component parts—the thousands of different man-made objects—have a very different relation to their surroundings. A car, for example, imposes itself on the neighborhood rather than being defined by it; the same car is sold for use on the densely packed Los Angeles freeways or in a quiet country village. It is produced solely as a salable object—a commodity—with little regard for how well it fits into either sphere: the system of transportation or the environment. It is true, of course, that all cars must have a width that is accommodated by the traffic lanes, and must have proper brakes, lights, and horn, and so on. But as every resident of Los Angeles or New York knows, in recent years their crowded streets and highways have been afflicted with longer and longer limousines, designed to

12

please the buyer and profit the producer, but hardly suitable to their habitat.

Defined so narrowly, it is no surprise that cars have properties that are hostile to their environment. After World War II, the American car was arbitrarily redefined as a larger, heavier object than its predecessors. That narrow decision dictated a more powerful engine; in turn, this required a higher engine compression ratio; in keeping with physical laws, the new engines ran hotter; at the elevated temperature, oxygen and nitrogen molecules in the cylinder air reacted chemically, producing nitrogen oxides; leaving the engine exhaust pipe, nitrogen oxides trigger the formation of the noxious smog that now envelops every major city. The new cars were successfully designed to carry people more comfortably at higher speed; but no attention was paid to an essential component in their habitat—the people themselves, and their requirement for clean, smog-free air.

Even a part of the technosphere as close to nature as the farm suffers from the same sort of clash with the environment. As a man-made object, the farm is designed for the sole purpose of producing crops. Guided by that purpose, after World War II agronomists urged the increasingly heavy application of chemical nitrogen fertilizer. Yields rose, but not in proportion to the rate of fertilizer application; year by year, less and less of the applied fertilizer was taken up by the crop and progressively more drained through the soil into groundwater, in the form of nitrate that contaminated rivers, lakes, and water supplies. Nitrogen fertilizer is a commodity sold with the narrow purpose of raising yields and manufactured with the even narrower purpose of increasing the chemical industry's profits. When inorganic nitrogen fertilizer was introduced in the 1950s, little or no attention was paid to its ecological behavior in the soil/water system or to the harmful effects of elevated nitrate levels in drinking water.

The second law of ecology—"Everything has to go somewhere"— together with the first, expresses the fundamental importance of cycles in the ecosphere. In the aquatic ecosystem, for example, the participating chemical elements move through closed cyclical processes. As they respire, fish produce carbon dioxide, which in turn is absorbed by aquatic plants and is used, photosynthetically, to produce oxygen—which the fish respire. The fish excrete nitrogen-containing organic compounds in their waste; when the waste is metabolized by aquatic bacteria and molds, the organic nitrogen is converted to nitrate; this, in turn, is an essential nutrient for the aquatic algae; these, ingested by the fish, contribute to their organic waste, and the cycle is complete. The same sort of cycle operates in the soil: plants grow, nourished by carbon dioxide from the air and nitrate from the soil; eaten by animals, the crop sustains their metabolism; the animals excrete carbon dioxide to the air and organic compounds to the soil—where microorganisms convert them into compounds such as nitrate, which nourish the crop. In such a closed, circular system, there is no such thing as "waste"; everything that is produced in one part of the cycle "goes somewhere" and is used in a later step.

The technosphere, in contrast, is dominated by *linear* processes. Crops and the animals to which they are fed are eaten by people; their waste is flushed into the sewer system, altered in composition but not in amount at a treatment plant, and the residue is dumped into rivers or the ocean as waste—which upsets the natural aquatic ecosystem. Uranium is mined, processed into nuclear fuel which, in generating power, becomes highly radioactive waste that must be carefully guarded—ineffectually thus far—from contaminating the environment for thousands of years. The petrochemical industry converts ethylene prepared from petroleum and chlorine prepared from brine into vinyl chloride, a synthetic, carcinogenic chemical. This is manufactured into the plastic, polyvinyl chloride, which is made into tile, boots, and food wrapping; sooner or later discarded, these become trash that must be disposed of. When burned in an incinerator, the polyvinyl chloride produces carbon dioxide and dioxin; both are injected, as waste, into the ecosphere where the one contributes to global warming and the other to the risk of cancer. The energy sources that now power the technosphere are mostly fossil fuels, stores that, once depleted, will never be renewed. The end result of this linear process is air pollution and the threat of global warming. Thus, in the technosphere goods are converted, linearly, into waste: crops into sewage; uranium into radioactive residues; petroleum and chlorine into dioxin; fossil fuels into carbon dioxide. In the technosphere, the end of the line is always waste, an assault on the cyclical processes that sustain the ecosphere.

The third informal law of ecology is "Nature knows best." The ecosystem is consistent with itself; its numerous components are compatible with each other and with the whole. Such a harmonious structure is the outcome of a very long period of trial and error—the 5 billion years of biological evolution. The biological sector of the ecosphere—the biosphere—is composed of living things that have survived this test because of their finely tuned adaptation to the particular ecological niche that they occupy. Left to their own devices, ecosystems are conservative; the rate of evolution is very slow, and temporary changes, such as an overpopulation of rabbits, for example, are quickly readjusted by the wolves.

The same sort of conservative self-consistency governs the chemical processes that occur in living cells. For example, there are severe constraints imposed on the variety of organic (carbon-containing) compounds that are the basic components of biochemical processes. As the physicist Walter Elsasser has pointed out, the weight of one molecule of each of the proteins that *could* be formed from the twenty different amino acids that comprise them would be greater than the weight of the known universe. Obviously, living things are constrained to produce only a very small number of the *possible* proteins. Constraints are also exercised by the enzymes, present in all living things, that catalyze the degradation of organic compounds. It is an unbroken rule that for every organic compound produced by a living thing, there is somewhere in the ecosystem an enzyme capable of breaking it down.

Organic compounds incapable of enzymatic degradation are not produced by living things. This arrangement is essential to the harmony of the ecosystem. If, for example, there were no enzymes that degrade cellulose, an otherwise very stable major constituent of plant cell walls, the Earth's surface would eventually become buried in it.

Similarly, certain molecular arrangements are shunned in the chemistry of life. Thus, very few chlorinated organic compounds, in which chlorine atoms are attached to carbons, occur in living things. This suggests that the vast number of chlorinated organic compounds that are possible chemically (many of them now produced by the petrochemical industry), have been rejected in the long course of evolution as *biochemical* components. The absence of a particular substance from nature is often a sign that it is incompatible with the chemistry of life. For example, the fact that mercury plays no biochemical role and does not normally occur in living cells—and is lethal when it does—is readily explained by the fact that it poisons a number of essential enzymes. In the same way, many man-made chlorinated organic compounds that do not occur in nature, such as DDT or dioxin[2], are very toxic.

20   In sum, the living things that comprise the biosphere, and their chemical composition, reflect constraints that severely limit their range of variation. The mermaid and the centaur are, after all, mythical animals; even the vaunted exploits of genetic engineering will never produce an elephant-sized mouse or a flying giraffe. In the same way, no natural biochemical system includes DDT, PCB,[3] or dioxin. Unfortunately, these highly toxic substances are not mythical—a fact that sharply illuminates the difference between the ecosphere and the technosphere.

In contrast to the ecosphere, the technosphere is composed of objects and materials that reflect a rapid and relentless process of change and variation. In less than a century, transport has progressed from the horse-drawn carriage, through the Model T Ford, to the present array of annually modified cars and aircraft. In a not much longer period, writing instruments have evolved from the quill pen to the typewriter and now the word processor. Synthetic organic chemistry began innocuously enough about 150 years ago with the laboratory production of a common natural substance—urea—but soon departed from this imitative approach to produce a huge array of organic compounds never found in nature and, for that reason, often incompatible with the chemistry of life. Nylon, for example, unlike a natural polymer such as cellulose, is not biodegradable—that is, there is no enzyme

---

[2]Toxic chemicals: DDT is an insecticide banned in the United States in 1972 and in some European countries in the 1960s but still used in developing countries; dioxin is a family of some 210 chemicals, some emitted from incinerators, which are thought to increase the incidence of cancer.

[3]Polychlorinated biphenyl, a toxic substance once used in the electrical industry, banned in 1979 in the United States.

in any known living organism that can break it down. As a result, when it is discarded into the ecosphere, nylon, like plastics generally, persists. Thus, oceanographers now find in their collecting nets bits of orange, blue, and white nylon and larger pieces jammed in the digestive tracts of dead turtles—the residue of nylon marine cordage. In the technosphere, nylon is a useful new commodity; in the ecosphere, nylon, untested by evolution, is a harmful intruder.

"Nature knows best" is shorthand for the view that during the several billion years in which they have evolved, living things have created a limited but self-consistent array of substances and reactions that are essential to life. The petrochemical industry has departed from these restrictions, producing thousands of new man-made substances. Since they are based on the same fundamental patterns of carbon chemistry as the natural compounds, the new ones are often readily accepted into biochemical processes. They therefore can play an insidious, destructive role in living things. For example, synthetic organic compounds may easily fit into the same reactive enzyme niches as natural molecules or may be accepted into the structure of DNA.[4] However, they are sufficiently different from the natural compounds to then disrupt normal biochemistry, leading to mutations, cancer, and in many different ways to death. In effect, the petrochemical industry produces substances that—like the fantasies of human society invaded by look-alike but dangerous aliens—cunningly enter the chemistry of life, and attack it.

Finally, it is useful to compare the ecosphere and the technosphere with respect to the consequences of failure. In the ecosphere, this is expressed by the idea that "there is no such thing as a free lunch," meaning that any distortion of an ecological cycle, or the intrusion of an incompatible component (such as a toxic chemical), leads unavoidably to harmful effects. At first glance, the technosphere appears to be extraordinarily free of mistakes—that is, a technological process or product that failed not because of some unanticipated accident but because it was unable to do what it was designed to do. Yet nearly every modern technology has grave faults, which appear not as a failure to accomplish its designed purpose but as a serious impact on the environment. Cars usually run very well, but produce smog; power plants efficiently generate electricity, but also emit dangerous pollutants; modern chemical farming is very productive but contaminates groundwater with nitrate and wildlife and people with pesticides. Even the spectacular nuclear disasters at Three-Mile Island[5] and Chernobyl were far less serious as technical failures than they were in their ecological effects. Regarded only as a failure in the plant's function, the accident at Chernobyl amounts to a serious but local fire that destroyed the plant. But the resultant release of radioactivity

---

[4]The genetic substance of all living cells that stores and replicates genetic information.

[5]Sites of nuclear disasters: Three-Mile Island, a power plant in Harrisburg, Pennsylvania, leaked radioactive material in 1979; the Chernobyl power plant, in the former Soviet Union, exploded in 1986, causing a meltdown and extensive release of radioactivity.

threatens many thousands of people all over Europe with cancer. In sum, there are numerous failures in the modern technosphere; but their effects are visited upon the ecosphere.

A free lunch is really a debt. In the technosphere, a debt is an acknowledged but unmet cost—the mortgage on a factory building, for example. Such a debt is tolerable because the technosphere is a system of production, which—if it functions properly—generates goods that represent wealth potentially capable of repaying the debt. In the technosphere, debts are repaid from within and, at least in theory, are always capable of being paid off, or, in some cases, canceled. In contrast, when the debts represented by environmental pollution are created by the technosphere and transferred to the ecosphere, they are never canceled; damage is unavoidable. The debts represented by the radioactivity disseminated from the nuclear accident at Chernobyl, and by the toxic chemicals that enveloped Bhopal,[6] have not been canceled. These debts were merely transferred to the victims, and are paid as they sicken and die.

Since they inhabit both worlds, people are caught in the clash between the ecosphere and the technosphere. What we call the "environmental crisis"—the array of critical unsolved problems ranging from local toxic dumps to the disruption of global climate—is a product of the drastic mismatch between the cyclical, conservative, and self-consistent processes of the ecosphere and the linear, innovative, but ecologically disharmonious processes of the technosphere.

Since the environmental crisis has been generated by the war between the two worlds that human society occupies, it can be properly understood only in terms of their interplay. Of course, as in a conventional war, the issues can be simplified by taking sides: ignoring the interests of one combatant or the other. But this is done only at the cost of understanding. If the ecosphere is ignored, it is possible to define the environmental crisis solely in terms of the factors that govern the technosphere: production, prices, and profits, and the economic processes that mediate their interaction. Then, for example, one can concoct a scheme, as recently proposed by President Bush, in which factories are allotted the right to emit pollutants up to some acceptable level and, in a parody of the "free market," to buy and sell these rights. But unlike the conventional marketplace, which deals in goods—things that serve a useful purpose—this scheme creates a marketplace in "bads"—things that are not only useless but often deadly. Apart from the issue of morality, it should be noted that such a scheme cannot operate unless the right to produce pollutants is exercised—hardly an inducement to eliminating them.

If the technosphere is ignored, the environmental crisis can be defined in purely ecological terms. Human beings are then seen as a peculiar species, unique among living things, that is doomed to destroy its own habitat. Thus

---

[6]City in India where in 1984 a Union Carbide plant accidentally released toxic gases that killed more than 3,000 people.

simplified, the issue attracts simplistic solutions: reduce the number of people; limit their share of nature's resources; protect all other species from the human marauder by endowing them with "rights."

This approach raises a profound, unavoidable moral question: Is the ecosphere to be protected from destruction for its own sake, or to enhance the welfare of the human beings who depend on it? This leads to a further question regarding the term "welfare." Some environmental advocates believe that human welfare would be improved if people were less dependent on the artifacts of the technosphere and lived in closer harmony with their regional ecosystem—baking bread instead of buying it; walking or pedaling a bike instead of driving a car; living in small towns instead of cities. The thrust of this approach is to deny the value to society of, let us say, a woman who uses time saved by buying bread instead of baking it in order to work as a curator in an urban museum. Nor does it allow for the possibility that time- and labor-saving technologies can be compatible with the integrity of the environment. It assumes that the technosphere, no matter how designed, is necessarily an environmentally unacceptable means of giving people access to resources that are not part of their ecological niche. But as we shall see, this assumption is wrong; although nearly every aspect of the *current* technosphere is counterecological, technologies exist that—although little used thus far—*are* compatible with the ecosphere.

The view that people are to be regarded *solely* as components of the ecosystem can lead to extreme and often inhumane proposals. Consider the global warming issue, for example. The humanist approach dictates a vigorous effort to halt the process because it is a massive threat to human society: flooded cities, drought-ridden agriculture, and prolonged heat waves. However, judged only in ecological terms, global warming can be regarded merely as a change in the structure of the global ecosystem similar to the warming that accompanied the last postglacial period, albeit more rapid. Viewed in this way, there is no more reason to oppose global warming than to be unhappy about the last ice age and the rise in global temperature that ended it. At its farthest reach, this nonhumanist position becomes antihumanist, as exemplified in an article in the publication of a group called Earth First!, which favored the spread of AIDS as a means of reducing the human population without threatening other animal species. Of course, at the other extreme is the potentially suicidal view that the enormous value of modern production technology to human society justifies whatever damage to the ecosphere it entails.

The ambiguity created by the dual habitat in which we live has led to a very wide range of responses. The extreme interpretations of the relationship between the two spheres that human society occupies—and a sometimes bewildering array of intermediate positions—is compelling evidence that we have not yet understood how the two systems have come into conflict and, as a result, are unable as yet to resolve that conflict.

This book is an effort to analyze the war between the ecosphere and the

28

technosphere, written with the conviction that understanding it—as distinct from reacting to it—is the only path to peace. It is less a lament over the war's numerous casualties than an inquiry into how future casualties can be prevented. It is not so much a battle cry for one side or the other, as a design for negotiating an end to this suicidal war—for making peace with the planet.

Understanding What You Read

1. In what two worlds do residents of industrialized countries live?
2. Why do scientists usually refer to the "threat of global warming" rather than simply "global warming"?
3. In what ways have humans already profoundly altered global conditions?
4. What is the most prominent of the greenhouse gases?
5. Explain how the ecosphere and the technosphere are at war.
6. What are Commoner's three laws of ecology?

Writing About What You Read

1. Examine your own life and note what part of it is lived in the ecosphere and what part in the technosphere. Is there always some overlap, or do you ever feel that you are totally in one or the other? Write an essay that compares your life in one sphere, or that compares the two.
2. Imagine that you are camping out in a designated wilderness area that does not allow you even to build a fire. To what extent is the technosphere present for you? Write a paper describing the experience. Be specific.
3. Think of examples, from your own experience, of Commoner's three laws of ecology. Write an essay in which you explain the three laws in your own words and illustrate them with your examples.

GARRETT HARDIN

Professor Emeritus of Human Ecology at the University of California at Santa Barbara, Hardin (b. 1915) is the author of a number of books about ecology, biology, and ethics, including *The Limits of Altruism* (1977) and *Living Within Limits: Ecology, Economics and Population Taboos* (1993), a summation of his views of overpopulation. "The Tragedy of the Commons," a frequently collected essay now considered a classic, was first published in *Science* magazine in 1968.

The Tragedy of the Commons

AT THE END of a thoughtful article on the future of nuclear war, J. B. Wiesner and H. F. York concluded that "Both sides in the arms race are . . . confronted by the dilemma of steadily increasing military power and steadily decreasing national security. *It is our considered professional judgment that this dilemma has no technical solution.* If the great powers continue to look for solutions in the area of science and technology only, the result will be to worsen the situation."[1]

I would like to focus your attention not on the subject of the article (national security in a nuclear world) but on the kind of conclusion they reached, namely, that there is no technical solution to the problem. An implicit and almost universal assumption of discussions published in professional and semipopular scientific journals is that the problem under discussion has a technical solution. A technical solution may be defined as one that requires a change only in the techniques of the natural sciences, demanding little or nothing in the way of change in human values or ideas or morality.

In our day (though not in earlier times) technical solutions are always welcome. Because of previous failures in prophecy, it takes courage to assert that a desired technical solution is not possible. Wiesner and York exhibited this courage; publishing in a science journal, they insisted that the solution to the problem was not to be found in the natural sciences. They cautiously qualified their statement with the phrase "It is our considered professional judgment. . . ." Whether they were right or not is not the concern of the present article. Rather, the concern here is with the important concept of a class of human problems which can be called "no technical solution problems," and more specifically, with the identification and discussion of one of these.

It is easy to show that the class is not a null class. Recall the game of tick-tack-toe. Consider the problem "How can I win the game of tick-tack-toe?" It is well known that I cannot, if I assume (in keeping with the conventions of game theory) that my opponent understands the game perfectly. Put another way, there is no "technical solution" to the problem. I can win only by giving a radical meaning to the word "win." I can hit my opponent over the head; or I can falsify the records. Every way in which I "win" involves, in some sense, an abandonment of the game, as we intuitively understand it. (I can also, of course, openly abandon the game—refuse to play it. This is what most adults do.)

4

[1] J. B. Wiesner and H. F. York, *Scientific American* 211 (No. 4), 27 (1964) [author's note].

The class of "no technical solution problems" has members. My thesis is that the "population problem," as conventionally conceived, is a member of this class. How it is conventionally conceived needs some comment. It is fair to say that most people who anguish over the population problem are trying to find a way to avoid the evils of overpopulation without relinquishing any of the privileges they now enjoy. They think that farming the seas or developing new strains of wheat will solve the problem—technologically. I try to show here that the solution they seek cannot be found. The population problem cannot be solved in a technical way, any more than can the problem of winning the game of tick-tack-toe.

WHAT SHALL WE MAXIMIZE?

Population, as Malthus[2] said, naturally tends to grow "geometrically," or, as we would now say, exponentially. In a finite world this means that the per-capita share of the world's goods must decrease. Is ours a finite world?

A fair defense can be put forward for the view that the world is infinite; or that we do not know that it is not. But, in terms of the practical problems that we must face in the next few generations with the foreseeable technology, it is clear that we will greatly increase human misery if we do not, during the immediate future, assume that the world available to the terrestrial human population is finite. "Space" is no escape.

A finite world can support only a finite population; therefore, population growth must eventually equal zero. (The case of perpetual wide fluctuations above and below zero is a trivial variant that need not be discussed.) When this condition is met, what will be the situation of mankind? Specifically, can Bentham's[3] goal of "the greatest good for the greatest number" be realized?

No—for two reasons, each sufficient by itself. The first is a theoretical one. It is not mathematically possible to maximize for two (or more) variables at the same time. This was clearly stated by von Neumann and Morgenstern,[4] but the principle is implicit in the theory of partial differential equations, dating back at least to D'Alembert (1717–1783).

The second reason springs directly from biological facts. To live, any organism must have a source of energy (for example, food). This energy is utilized for two purposes: mere maintenance and work. For man, maintenance of life requires about 1600 kilocalories a day ("maintenance calories"). Anything that he does over and above merely staying alive will be defined as work, and is supported by "work calories" which he takes in. Work calories are used not only for what we call work in common speech; they are also

---

[2]Thomas Malthus (1766–1834), English economist, who argued that population would outgrow the available resources for subsistence.

[3]Jeremy Bentham (1748–1832), English philosopher, political theorist, and founder of Utilitarianism, who argued that that self-interest is compatible with the general welfare.

[4]J. von Neumann and O. Morgenstern, *Theory of Games and Economic Behavior* (Princeton University Press, Princeton, N.J., 1947), p. 11 [author's note].

required for all forms of enjoyment, from swimming and automobile racing to playing music and writing poetry. If our goal is to maximize population it is obvious what we must do: We must make the work calories per person approach as close to zero as possible. No gourmet meals, no vacations, no sports, no music, no literature, no art. . . . I think that everyone will grant, without argument or proof, that maximizing population does not maximize goods. Bentham's goal is impossible.

In reaching this conclusion I have made the usual assumption that it is the acquisition of energy that is the problem. The appearance of atomic energy has led some to question this assumption. However, given an infinite source of energy, population growth still produces an inescapable problem. The problem of the acquisition of energy is replaced by the problem of its dissipation, as J. H. Fremlin has so wittily shown.[5] The arithmetic signs in the analysis are, as it were, reversed; but Bentham's goal is unobtainable.

The optimum population is, then, less than the maximum. The difficulty of defining the optimum is enormous; so far as I know, no one has seriously tackled this problem. Reaching an acceptable and stable solution will surely require more than one generation of hard analytical work—and much persuasion.   12

We want the maximum good per person; but what is good? To one person it is wilderness, to another it is ski lodges for thousands. To one it is estuaries to nourish ducks for hunters to shoot; to another it is factory land. Comparing one good with another is, we usually say, impossible because goods are incommensurable. Incommensurables cannot be compared.

Theoretically this may be true; but in real life incommensurables *are* commensurable. Only a criterion of judgment and a system of weighting are needed. In nature the criterion is survival. Is it better for a species to be small and hideable, or large and powerful? Natural selection commensurates the incommensurables. The compromise achieved depends on a natural weighting of the values of the variables.

Man must imitate this process. There is no doubt that in fact he already does, but unconsciously. It is when the hidden decisions are made explicit that the arguments begin. The problem for the years ahead is to work out an acceptable theory of weighting. Synergistic effects, nonlinear variation, and difficulties in discounting the future make the intellectual problem difficult, but not (in principle) insoluble.

Has any cultural group solved this practical problem at the present time, even on an intuitive level? One simple fact proves that none has: there is no prosperous population in the world today that has, and has had for some time, a growth rate of zero. Any people that has intuitively identified its optimum point will soon reach it, after which its growth rate becomes and remains zero.   16

Of course, a positive growth rate might be taken as evidence that a

[5]J. H. Fremlin, *New Scientist*, No. 415 (1964), p. 285 [author's note].

population is below its optimum. However, by any reasonable standards, the most rapidly growing populations on earth today are (in general) the most miserable. This association (which need not be invariable) casts doubt on the optimistic assumption that the positive growth rate of a population is evidence that it has yet to reach its optimum.

We can make little progress in working toward optimum population size until we explicitly exorcise the spirit of Adam Smith[6] in the field of practical demography. In economic affairs, *The Wealth of Nations* (1776) popularized the "invisible hand," the idea that an individual who "intends only his own gain" is, as it were, "led by an invisible hand to promote . . . the public interest." Adam Smith did not assert that this was invariably true, and perhaps neither did any of his followers. But he contributed to a dominant tendency of thought that has ever since interfered with positive action based on rational analysis, namely, the tendency to assume that decisions reached individually will, in fact, be the best decisions for an entire society. If this assumption is correct it justifies the continuance of our present policy of *laissez faire* in reproduction. If it is correct we can assume that men will control their individual fecundity so as to produce the optimum population. If the assumption is not correct, we need to reexamine our individual freedoms to see which ones are defensible.

Tragedy of Freedom in a Commons

The rebuttal to the invisible hand in population control is to be found in a scenario first sketched in a little-known pamphlet in 1833 by a mathematical amateur named William Forster Lloyd (1794–1852). We may well call it "the tragedy of the commons," using the word "tragedy" as the philosopher Whitehead[7] used it: "The essence of dramatic tragedy is not unhappiness. It resides in the solemnity of the remorseless working of things." He then goes on to say, "This inevitableness of destiny can only be illustrated in terms of human life by incidents which in fact involve unhappiness. For it is only by them that the futility of escape can be made evident in the drama."

20   The tragedy of the commons develops in this way. Picture a pasture open to all. It is to be expected that each herdsman will try to keep as many cattle as possible on the commons. Such an arrangement may work reasonably satisfactorily for centuries because tribal wars, poaching, and disease keep the numbers of both man and beast well below the carrying capacity of the land. Finally, however, comes the day of reckoning, that is, the day when the long-desired goal of social stability becomes a reality. At this point, the inherent logic of the commons remorselessly generates tragedy.

As a rational being, each herdsman seeks to maximize his gain. Explicitly

[6]Scottish economist (1823–1890), who theorized that in a laissez-faire economy the impulse of self-interest would bring about public welfare.

[7]Alfred North Whitehead (1861–1947), English mathematician and philosopher.

or implicitly, more or less consciously, he asks, "What is the utility *to me* of adding one more animal to my herd?" This utility has one negative and one positive component.

1. The positive component is a function of the increment of one animal. Since the herdsman receives all the proceeds from the sale of the additional animal, the positive utility is nearly $+1$.

2. The negative component is a function of the additional overgrazing created by one more animal. Since, however, the effects of overgrazing are shared by all the herdsmen, the negative utility for any particular decision-making herdsman is only a fraction of -1.

Adding together the component partial utilities, the rational herdsman concludes that the only sensible course for him to pursue is to add another animal to his herd. And another. . . . But this is the conclusion reached by each and every rational herdsman sharing a commons. Therein is the tragedy. Each man is locked into a system that compels him to increase his herd without limit—in a world that is limited. Ruin is the destination toward which all men rush, each pursuing his own best interest in a society that believes in the freedom of the commons. Freedom in a commons brings ruin to all.

24

Some would say that this is a platitude. Would that it were! In a sense, it was learned thousands of years ago, but natural selection favors the forces of psychological denial. The individual benefits as an individual from his ability to deny the truth even though society as a whole, of which he is a part, suffers. Education can counteract the natural tendency to do the wrong thing, but the inexorable succession of generations requires that the basis for this knowledge be constantly refreshed.

A simple incident that occurred a few years ago in Leominster, Massachusetts, shows how perishable the knowledge is. During the Christmas shopping season the parking meters downtown were covered with plastic bags that bore tags reading: "Do not open until after Christmas. Free parking courtesy of the mayor and city council." In other words, facing the prospect of an increased demand for already scarce space, the city fathers reinstituted the system of the commons. (Cynically, we suspect that they gained more votes than they lost by this retrogressive act.)

In an approximate way, the logic of the commons has been understood for a long time, perhaps since the discovery of agriculture or the invention of private property in real estate. But it is understood mostly only in special cases which are not sufficiently generalized. Even at this late date, cattlemen leasing national land on the Western ranges demonstrate no more than an ambivalent understanding, in constantly pressuring federal authorities to increase the head count to the point where overgrazing produces erosion and weed-dominance. Likewise, the oceans of the world continue to suffer from the survival of the philosophy of the commons. Maritime nations still respond automatically to the shibboleth[8] of the "freedom of the seas." Professing to believe in the "inexhaustible resources of the oceans," they bring species after species of fish and whales closer to extinction.[9]

The National Parks present another instance of the working out of the tragedy of the commons. At present, they are open to all, without limit. The parks themselves are limited in extent—there is only one Yosemite Valley—whereas population seems to grow without limit. The values that visitors seek in the parks are steadily eroded. Plainly, we must soon cease to treat the parks as commons or they will be of no value to anyone.

What shall we do? We have several options. We might sell them off as private property. We might keep them as public property, but allocate the right to enter them. The allocation might be on the basis of wealth, by the use of an auction system. It might be on the basis of merit, as defined by some agreed-upon standards. It might be by lottery. Or it might be on a first-come, first-served basis, administered to long queues. These, I think, are all objectionable. But we must choose—or acquiesce in the destruction of the commons that we call our National Parks.

POLLUTION

In a reverse way, the tragedy of the commons reappears in problems of pollution. Here it is not a question of taking something out of the commons, but of putting something in—sewage, or chemical, radioactive, and heat wastes into water; noxious and dangerous fumes into the air; and distracting and unpleasant advertising signs into the line of sight. The calculations of utility are much the same as before. The rational man finds that his share of the cost of the wastes he discharges into the commons is less than the cost of purifying his wastes before releasing them. Since this is true for everyone, we are locked into a system of "fouling our own nest," so long as we behave only as independent, rational, free-enterprisers.

The tragedy of the commons as a food basket is averted by private property, or something formally like it. But the air and waters surrounding us cannot readily be fenced, and so the tragedy of the commons as a cesspool must be prevented by different means, by coercive laws or taxing devices that make it cheaper for the polluter to treat his pollutants than to discharge them untreated. We have not progressed as far with the solution of this problem as we have with the first. Indeed, our particular concept of private property, which deters us from exhausting the positive resources of the earth, favors pollution. The owner of a factory on the bank of a stream—whose property extends to the middle of the stream—often has difficulty seeing why it is not his natural right to muddy the waters flowing past his door. The law, always

[8]A frequently used catchword or slogan.
[9]S. McVay, *Scientific American* 216 (No. 8), 13 (1966) [author's note].

behind the times, requires elaborate stitching and fitting to adapt it to this newly perceived aspect of the commons.

The pollution problem is a consequence of population. It did not much matter how a lonely American frontiersman disposed of his waste. "Flowing water purifies itself every ten miles," my grandfather used to say, and the myth was near enough to the truth when he was a boy, for there were not too many people. But as population became denser, the natural chemical and biological recycling processes became overloaded, calling for a redefinition of property rights.

How to Legislate Temperance?

Analysis of the pollution problem as a function of population density uncovers a not generally recognized principle of morality, namely: *the morality of an act is a function of the state of the system at the time it is performed.*[1] Using the commons as a cesspool does not harm the general public under frontier conditions, because there is no public; the same behavior in a metropolis is unbearable. A hundred and fifty years ago a plainsman could kill an American bison, cut out only the tongue for his dinner, and discard the rest of the animal. He was not in any important sense being wasteful. Today, with only a few thousand bison left, we would be appalled at such behavior.

In passing, it is worth noting that the morality of an act cannot be determined from a photograph. One does not know whether a man killing an elephant or setting fire to the grassland is harming others until one knows the total system in which his act appears. "One picture is worth a thousand words," said an ancient Chinese; but it may take ten thousand words to validate it. It is as tempting to ecologists as it is to reformers in general to try to persuade others by way of the photographic shortcut. But the essence of an argument cannot be photographed: it must be presented rationally—in words.

That morality is system-sensitive escaped the attention of most codifiers of ethics in the past. "Thou shalt not . . ." is the form of traditional ethical directives which make no allowance for particular circumstances. The laws of our society follow the pattern of ancient ethics, and therefore are poorly suited to governing a complex, crowded, changeable world. Our epicyclic solution is to augment statutory law with administrative law. Since it is practically impossible to spell out all the conditions under which it is safe to burn trash in the backyard or to run an automobile without smog control, by law we delegate the details to bureaus. The result is administrative law, which is rightly feared for an ancient reason—*Quis custodiet ipsos custodes?*— Who shall watch the watchers themselves? John Adams[2] said that we must

---

[1] J. Fletcher, *Situation Ethics* (Westminster, Philadelphia, 1966) [author's note].
[2] John Adams, second President of the United States (1797–1801).

margin note: 32

have a "government of laws and not men." Bureau administrators, trying to evaluate the morality of acts in the total system, are singularly liable to corruption, producing a government by men, not laws.

36   Prohibition is easy to legislate (though not necessarily to enforce); but how do we legislate temperance? Experience indicates that it can be accomplished best through the mediation of administrative law. We limit possibilities unnecessarily if we suppose that the sentiment of *Quis custodiet* denies us the use of administrative law. We should rather retain the phrase as a perpetual reminder of fearful dangers we cannot avoid. The great challenge facing us now is to invent the corrective feedbacks that are needed to keep custodians honest. We must find ways to legitimate the needed authority of both the custodians and the corrective feedbacks.

FREEDOM TO BREED IS INTOLERABLE

The tragedy of the commons is involved in population problems in another way. In a world governed solely by the principle of "dog eat dog"—if indeed there ever was such a world—how many children a family had would not be a matter of public concern. Parents who bred too exuberantly would leave fewer descendants, not more, because they would be unable to care adequately for their children. David Lack and others have found that such a negative feedback demonstrably controls the fecundity of birds.[3] But men are not birds, and have not acted like them for millenniums, at least.

If each human family were dependent only on its own resources; *if* the children of improvident parents starved to death; *if,* thus, overbreeding brought its own "punishment" to the germ line—*then* there would be no public interest in controlling the breeding of families. But our society is deeply committed to the welfare state, and hence is confronted with another aspect of the tragedy of the commons.

In a welfare state, how shall we deal with the family, the religion, the race, or the class (or indeed any distinguishable and cohesive group) that adopts overbreeding as a policy to secure its own aggrandizement? To couple the concept of freedom to breed with the belief that everyone born has an equal right to the commons is to lock the world into a tragic course of action.

40   Unfortunately this is just the course of action that is being pursued by the United Nations. In late 1967, some thirty nations agreed to the following: "The Universal Declaration of Human Rights describes the family as the natural and fundamental unit of society. It follows that any choice and decision with regard to the size of the family must irrevocably rest with the family itself, and cannot be made by anyone else."

It is painful to have to deny categorically the validity of this right; denying

[3]D. Lack, *The Natural Regulation of Animal Numbers* (Clarendon Press, Oxford, England, 1954) [author's note].

it, one feels as uncomfortable as a resident of Salem, Massachusetts, who denied the reality of witches in the seventeenth century. At the present time, in liberal quarters, something like a taboo acts to inhibit criticism of the United Nations. There is a feeling that the United Nations is "our last and best hope," that we shouldn't find fault with it; we shouldn't play into the hands of the archconservatives. However, let us not forget what Robert Louis Stevenson[4] said: "The truth that is suppressed by friends is the readiest weapon of the enemy." If we love the truth we must openly deny the validity of the Universal Declaration of Human Rights, even though it is promoted by the United Nations. We should also join with Kingsley Davis[5] in attempting to get Planned Parenthood–World Population to see the error of its ways in embracing the same tragic ideal.

CONSCIENCE IS SELF-ELIMINATING

It is a mistake to think that we can control the breeding of mankind in the long run by an appeal to conscience. Charles Galton Darwin made this point when he spoke on the centennial of the publication of his grandfather's great book.[6] The argument is straightforward and Darwinian.

People vary. Confronted with appeals to limit breeding, some people will undoubtedly respond to the plea more than others. Those who have more children will produce a larger fraction of the next generation than those with more susceptible consciences. The differences will be accentuated, generation by generation.

In C. G. Darwin's words: "It may well be that it would take hundreds of generations for the progenitive instinct to develop in this way, but if it should do so, nature would have taken her revenge, and the variety *Homo contracipiens* would become extinct and would be replaced by the variety *Homo progenitivus.*"[7]

The argument assumes that conscience or the desire for children (no matter which) is hereditary—but hereditary only in the most general formal sense. The result will be the same whether the attitude is transmitted through germ cells, or exosomatically, to use A. J. Lotka's[8] term. (If one denies the latter possibility as well as the former, then what's the point of education?) The argument has here been stated in the context of the population problem, but it applies equally well to any instance in which society appeals to an

44

---

[4]Scottish author (1850–1894) of *Treasure Island* and other novels.

[5]K. Davis, *Science* 158, 730 (1967) [author's note].

[6]The book is *On the Origin of Species by Means of Natural Selection* (1859) by Charles Darwin (1809–1882).

[7]*Homo contracipiens* refers to humans who use contraceptives to prevent pregnancies, while *Homo progenitivus* refers to those who reproduce freely.

[8]Alfred James Lotka (1880–1949), an American cyberneticist who explored how populations become stable.

individual exploiting a commons to restrain himself for the general good—by means of his conscience. To make such an appeal is to set up a selective system that works toward the elimination of conscience from the race.

PATHOGENIC EFFECTS OF CONSCIENCE

The long-term disadvantage of an appeal to conscience should be enough to condemn it; but it has serious short-term disadvantages as well. If we ask a man who is exploiting a commons to desist "in the name of conscience," what are we saying to him? What does he hear?—not only at the moment but also in the wee small hours of the night when, half asleep, he remembers not merely the words we used but also the nonverbal communication cues we gave him unawares? Sooner or later, consciously or subconsciously, he senses that he has received two communications, and that they are contradictory: 1. (intended communication) "If you don't do as we ask, we will openly condemn you for not acting like a responsible citizen"; 2. (the unintended communication) "If you *do* behave as we ask, we will secretly condemn you for a simpleton who can be shamed into standing aside while the rest of us exploit the commons."

Everyman then is caught in what Bateson has called a "double bind." Bateson and his co-workers have made a plausible case for viewing the double bind as an important causative factor in the genesis of schizophrenia.[9] The double bind may not always be so damaging, but it always endangers the mental health of anyone to whom it is applied. "A bad conscience," said Nietzsche,[1] "is a kind of illness."

To conjure up a conscience in others is tempting to anyone who wishes to extend his control beyond the legal limits. Leaders at the highest level succumb to this temptation. Has any president during the past generation failed to call on labor unions to moderate voluntarily their demands for higher wages, or to steel companies to honor voluntary guidelines on prices? I can recall none. The rhetoric used on such occasions is designed to produce feelings of guilt in noncooperators.

For centuries it was assumed without proof that guilt was a valuable, perhaps even an indispensable, ingredient of the civilized life. Now, in this post-Freudian world, we doubt it.

Paul Goodman speaks from the modern point of view when he says: "No good has ever come from feeling guilty, neither intelligence, policy, nor compassion. The guilty do not pay attention to the object but only to themselves, and not even to their own interests, which might make sense, but to their anxieties."[2]

---

[9]G. Bateson, D. D. Jackson, J. Haley, J. Weakland, *Behavioral Science* 1, 251 (1956) [author's note].

[1]Friedrich Wilhelm Nietzsche (1844–1900), German philosopher who imagined an unscrupulous "superman," exempt from ordinary morality.

[2]P. Goodman, *New York Review of Books* 10 (8), 22 (23 May 1968) [author's note].

One does not have to be a professional psychiatrist to see the consequences of anxiety. We in the Western world are just emerging from a dreadful two-centuries-long Dark Ages of Eros that was sustained partly by prohibition laws, but perhaps more effectively by the anxiety-generating mechanisms of education. Alex Comfort has told the story well in *The Anxiety Makers;*[3] it is not a pretty one.

Since proof is difficult, we may even concede that the results of anxiety may sometimes, from certain points of view, be desirable. The larger question we should ask is whether, as a matter of policy, we should ever encourage the use of a technique the tendency (if not the intention) of which is psychologically pathogenic. We hear much talk these days of responsible parenthood; the coupled words are incorporated into the titles of some organizations devoted to birth control. Some people have proposed massive propaganda campaigns to instill responsibility into the nation's (or the world's) breeders. But what is the meaning of the word conscience? When we use the word responsibility in the absence of substantial sanctions, are we not trying to browbeat a free man in a commons into acting against his own interest? Responsibility is a verbal counterfeit for a substantial quid pro quo. It is an attempt to get something for nothing.

If the word responsibility is to be used at all, I suggest that it be in the sense Charles Frankel uses it.[4] "Responsibility," says this philosopher, "is the product of definite social arrangements." Notice that Frankel calls for social arrangements—not propaganda.

Mutual Coercion Mutually Agreed Upon

The social arrangements that produce responsibility are arrangements that create coercion, of some sort. Consider bank robbing. The man who takes money from a bank acts as if the bank were a commons. How do we prevent such action? Certainly not by trying to control his behavior solely by a verbal appeal to his sense of responsibility. Rather than rely on propaganda we follow Frankel's lead and insist that a bank is not a commons; we seek the definite social arrangements that will keep it from becoming a commons. That we thereby infringe on the freedom of would-be robbers we neither deny nor regret.

The morality of bank robbing is particularly easy to understand because we accept complete prohibition of this activity. We are willing to say, "Thou shalt not rob banks," without providing for exceptions. But temperance also can be created by coercion. Taxing is a good coercive device. To keep downtown shoppers temperate in their use of parking space we introduce parking meters for short periods, and traffic fines for longer ones. We need not actually forbid a citizen to park as long as he wants to; we need merely

---

[3]A. Comfort, *The Anxiety Makers* (Nelson, London, 1967) [author's note].

[4]C. Frankel, *The Case for Modern Man* (Harper & Row, New York, 1955), p. 203 [author's note].

make it increasingly expensive for him to do so. Not prohibition, but carefully biased options are what we offer him. A Madison Avenue man[5] might call this persuasion; I prefer the greater candor of the word coercion.

Coercion is a dirty word to most liberals now, but it need not forever be so. As with the four-letter words, its dirtiness can be cleansed away by exposure to the light, by saying it over and over without apology or embarrassment. To many, the word coercion implies arbitrary decisions of distant and irresponsible bureaucrats; but this is not a necessary part of its meaning. The only kind of coercion I recommend is mutual coercion, mutually agreed upon by the majority of the people affected.

To say that we mutually agree to coercion is not to say that we are required to enjoy it, or even to pretend we enjoy it. Who enjoys taxes? We all grumble about them. But we accept compulsory taxes because we recognize that voluntary taxes would favor the conscienceless. We institute and (grumblingly) support taxes and other coercive devices to escape the horror of the commons.

An alternative to the commons need not be perfectly just to be preferable. With real estate and other material goods, the alternative we have chosen is the institution of private property coupled with legal inheritance. Is this system perfectly just? As a genetically trained biologist I deny that it is. It seems to me that, if there are to be differences in individual inheritance, legal possession should be perfectly correlated with biological inheritance—that those who are biologically more fit to be the custodians of property and power should legally inherit more. But genetic recombination continually makes a mockery of the doctrine of "like father, like son" implicit in our laws of legal inheritance. An idiot can inherit millions, and a trust fund can keep his estate intact. We must admit that our legal system of private property plus inheritance is unjust—but we put up with it because we are not convinced, at the moment, that anyone has invented a better system. The alternative of the commons is too horrifying to contemplate. Injustice is preferable to total ruin.

It is one of the peculiarities of the warfare between reform and the status quo that it is thoughtlessly governed by a double standard. Whenever a reform measure is proposed it is often defeated when its opponents triumphantly discover a flaw in it. As Kingsley Davis has pointed out,[6] worshipers of the status quo sometimes imply that no reform is possible without unanimous agreement, an implication contrary to historical fact. As nearly as I can make out, automatic rejection of proposed reforms is based on one of two unconscious assumptions: (1) that the status quo is perfect; or (2) that the choice we face is between reform and no action; if the proposed reform is imperfect, we presumably should take no action at all, while we wait for a perfect proposal.

[5]Madison Avenue is associated with advertising.
[6]See J. D. Roslansky, *Genetics and the Future of Man* (Appleton-Century-Crofts, New York, 1966), p. 177 [author's note].

But we can never do nothing. That which we have done for thousands of years is also action. It also produces evils. Once we are aware that the status quo is action, we can then compare its discoverable advantages and disadvantages with the predicted advantages and disadvantages of the proposed reform, discounting as best we can for our lack of experience. On the basis of such a comparison, we can make a rational decision which will not involve the unworkable assumption that only perfect systems are tolerable.

RECOGNITION OF NECESSITY

Perhaps the simplest summary of this analysis of man's population problems is this: the commons, if justifiable at all, is justifiable only under conditions of low-population density. As the human population has increased, the commons has had to be abandoned in one aspect after another.

First we abandoned the commons in food gathering, enclosing farmland and restricting pastures and hunting and fishing areas. These restrictions are still not complete throughout the world.

Somewhat later we saw that the commons as a place for waste disposal would also have to be abandoned. Restrictions on the disposal of domestic sewage are widely accepted in the Western world; we are still struggling to close the commons to pollution by automobiles, factories, insecticide sprayers, fertilizing operations, and atomic energy installations.

In a still more embryonic state is our recognition of the evils of the commons in matters of pleasure. There is almost no restriction on the propagation of sound waves in the public medium. The shopping public is assaulted with mindless music, without its consent. Our government has paid out billions of dollars to create a supersonic transport which would disturb 50,000 people for every one person whisked from coast to coast 3 hours faster. Advertisers muddy the airwaves of radio and television and pollute the view of travelers. We are a long way from outlawing the commons in matters of pleasure. Is this because our Puritan inheritance makes us view pleasure as something of a sin, and pain (that is, the pollution of advertising) as the sign of virtue?

Every new enclosure of the commons involves the infringement of somebody's personal liberty. Infringements made in the distant past are accepted because no contemporary complains of a loss. It is the newly proposed infringements that we vigorously oppose; cries of "rights" and "freedom" fill the air. But what does "freedom" mean? When men mutually agreed to pass laws against robbing, mankind became more free, not less so. Individuals locked into the logic of the commons are free only to bring on universal ruin; once they see the necessity of mutual coercion, they become free to pursue other goals. I believe it was Hegel[7] who said, "Freedom is the recognition of necessity."

[7]German philosopher (1770–1831) who argued that self-realization comes through self-denial.

The most important aspect of necessity that we must now recognize is the necessity of abandoning the commons in breeding. No technical solution can rescue us from the misery of overpopulation. Freedom to breed will bring ruin to all. At the moment, to avoid hard decisions many of us are tempted to propagandize for conscience and responsible parenthood. The temptation must be resisted, because an appeal to independently acting consciences selects for the disappearance of all conscience in the long run, and an increase in anxiety in the short.

The only way we can preserve and nurture other and more precious freedoms is by relinquishing the freedom to breed, and that very soon. "Freedom is the recognition of necessity"—and it is the role of education to reveal to all the necessity of abandoning the freedom to breed. Only so can we put an end to this aspect of the tragedy of the commons.

Understanding What You Read

1. Give at least three examples of how people have misused "the commons."
2. Explain what Hardin means when he says that the pollution problem is the consequence of population density.
3. At the point that the commons has an optimum number of cows, what behavior does Hardin say is to the advantage of the individual herdsman? Do you agree with this? Why or why not?
4. Explain what Hardin means when he says that "freedom in a commons brings ruin to all."
5. Hardin suggests that limiting the freedom to breed can be accomplished by some form of mutually agreed-upon coercion. What does he mean? Propose a specific example.
6. "The Tragedy of the Commons" is a demanding, formal essay first published in a scientific journal. If you were to edit this piece for a popular audience—say, a reader of *Newsweek*—, which details would you leave out? Which would you emphasize?

Writing About What You Read

1. In a society with limited resources that attempts to meet basic human needs such as education, housing, and medical care, should people be permitted to have as many children as they like? Write a paper in which you argue either side of this issue.
2. If you believe that population should be limited, write a paper about how you would accomplish this goal.

Making Connections

1. Le Guin's "Direction of the Road" and Durning's "Clean Motion" use very different methods to show how overdependence on the automobile is one of the roots of the environmental crisis. Compare and contrast these two pieces.

2. Gore ("Ships in the Desert") makes the statement that "until our lifetime, it was always safe to assume that nothing we did or could do would have any lasting effect on the global environment." Explain why this is no longer the case, citing several examples taken from other pieces in this book.

3. Gordon and Suzuki ("How Did We Come to This?") argue that the roots of the environmental crisis lie in the massive application of technology combined with an unprecedented increase in human population. What other writer in this chapter reaches the same conclusion?

4. Compare Gore's view of why people often ignore the evidence of environmental damage to that of Gordon and Suzuki's.

9 THE FUTURE:

The fateful challenge facing tomorrow's environmentalists is to reach across the artificial barriers erected by nation states, languages, and cultures and become earthkeepers who steadfastly use their talents to nourish all causes that promote life on this planet. That, for the next generation, is the ultimate message of ecology.

—STEWART L. UDALL, *The Quiet Crisis and the Next Generation*

◆

Ecofeminism is a movement of women who understand the connection between the war against women and the war against nature. . . . We fight for the freedom and self-determination of all oppressed peoples as well as for a harmonious relationship with nature: We realize that until we are all free from social and ecological exploitation, no one is free.

—CHAIA HELIER, *Earth Day Wall Street Action Handbook*

◆

Shall I not have intelligence with the earth? Am I not partly leaves and vegetable mould myself?

—HENRY D. THOREAU, *Walden*

◆

Politics properly understood is not simply human affairs; it involves the standing of each and every element making up the one world, the biosphere we partake of. Democracy properly understood gives the vote to trees . . . and to hawks, worms, aquifers, coal seams, wolves, bats, and the life-sustaining atmosphere.

—JOHN LYON, *This Incomperable Lande*

◆

Dead power is everywhere among us—in the forest, chopping down the songs; at night in the industrial landscape, wasting and stiffening the new life; in the streets of the city, throwing away the day. We wanted something different for our people: not to find ourselves an old, reactionary republic, full of ghost-fears, the fears of death and the fears of birth. We want something else.

—MURIEL RUKEYSER, *The Life of Poetry*

Paris Street Scene
(Billy Howard)

Introduction

Where do we go from here? This is the question that people all over the planet are asking and that the selections in this chapter attempt to answer. We now know something about the kind of world we live in, its dangers and its possibilities. We know that we cannot turn back the clock and undo the damage we've done, but we also know that we can do things differently in the future. "A Fable for Tomorrow," the first selection in this chapter, is Rachel Carson's vision of the future, written more than thirty years ago. While some bird populations are declining from acid rain and other pollutants, the grim scenario that Carson paints has not materialized. In fact, the bird populations that were threatened by DDT are recovering. People can change in response to warnings.

George Mitchell's vision of the future in the twenty-first century ("Two Children in a Future World") is also a warning of what could happen if we don't address two of our most talked-about problems: air pollution and ozone depletion. In both cases we know what to do. This vision of a future world is preventable.

One team of writers represented here thinks that the real problem is environmentalists themselves. In "Environmentalism and the Future," Dixy Lee Ray and Lou Guzzo argue that while there are some "real and widely recognized problems," environmentalists create their own difficulties by exaggerating problems and by being adversarial. In "Green Guilt and Ecological Overload," Theodore Roszak examines the psychological impact of the doomsday warnings and images of destruction used to further environmentalist causes. Other selections look at what may happen if we continue to live as we do, and how to fashion a different future.

Environmental solutions depend on a number of things: the activities of environmental organizations, government policies, the creative initiatives of industry, and effective legislation, among others. The success of these, however, in turn depends on the acts of millions of individuals as they join organizations, vote and write their legislators, choose what to buy and what not not to buy.

You may be wondering, like many other people, what you can do to help create a healthy environment for all living things. There is, of course, much that you can do, but making a difference can also involve *not* doing. For example, every time you walk or take public transportation instead of getting in a car, you are choosing not to contribute to the accumulation of greenhouse gases. Every time you make a purchase and refuse a paper or a plastic bag, you are reducing by a tiny fraction the number of trees that must be cut down for pulp or the amount of petroleum used to make plastic. Reading the newspaper in the library instead of buying your own, turning off the lights after you leave a room, lowering the thermostat in the winter, doing without air conditioning in the summer, taking your own cup into fast-food restaurants instead of using Styrofoam ones—these are only a few of the many "little" actions that, if more of us did more of them, could make a difference.

Two pieces in this chapter are about ways to reduce environmental pollution by changing our transportation habits. At present, there are more than half a billion cars and trucks in the world—more than a third of them in the United States. Collectively these motorized vehicles account for a substantial percentage of our air pollution, greenhouse gases, and acid rain. There are twice as many bicycles as there are cars in this country, yet most of the bicycles are used only occasionally, for recreation. In "Pedaling into the Future" Marcia Lowe explores some of the things that could be done to integrate bicycles into the transportation systems of more countries. Noel Perrin ("Have Plug, Will Commute") tells about his own experiences driving an electric car and explains the potential advantages of this nonpolluting vehicle.

We all know about the importance of recycling bottles, cans, and paper, but we may not stop to think about the global implications of participating in a throwaway society. In "Reusing and Recycling Materials," Lester Brown, Christopher Flavin, and Sandra Postel explain the magnitude of the problems caused by wasted resources.

There are many opportunities to become directly involved in solving environmental problems—for example, by joining local or national organizations, volunteering for conservation projects, or helping to clean up or restore degraded environments in your own community. Linda Leuzzi ("Eagles") relates her own experiences when she volunteered to work on an Earthwatch project to help save the bald eagle, an endangered species whose population is now growing in Michigan. Leuzzi paid to participate in the eagle project and thus contributed both time and money, but there is much that can be done that doesn't cost anything.

Small businesses as well as large corporations have been challenged around the world to develop technologies and policies that are friendly to the environment. While many look for ways to avoid the legal consequences of practices that are damaging to the environment, others see new opportunities in the growing public demand for products that are produced without creating significant waste and pollution. In "The Challenge to Companies," Frances Cairncross explores some of the opportunities available to companies that accept the challenge to be responsible for the environment, and she explains why government must create ways to encourage industries to meet the challenge.

Finally, imagining the future means imagining a new way of thinking. When North Americans have seen the future in terms of the kind of life they want five, ten, or twenty-five years from now, some do so in terms of financial security and material possessions—the kind of house, car, boat, wardrobe, or even jewelry they expect to own—or in terms of the adventures they seek. Now many people are reconsidering these choices, and the cost they exact on the environment. In *Reading the Environment*'s final selection, Bill McKibben examines his "whole material life" and imagines a "humbler world" where people live closer to their work and food supply and use technological and natural resources to sustain a healthy environment.

RACHEL CARSON

Carson (1907–1964) was a marine biologist and writer. Awarded an M.A. degree from Johns Hopkins in 1932, a time when few women earned advanced degrees, she went on to write highly acclaimed books on sea life and wetlands: *Under the Sea Wind* (1941), *The Sea Around Us* (1951), and *The Edge of the Sea* (1954). During these years, Carson had worked full-time for the U.S. Fish and Wildlife Service, but in 1958 royalties from her books made it possible for her to give up her job to begin *Silent Spring*. Published in 1962, this influential book exposed the dangers of widespread use of pesticides, particularly DDT. At first attacked by the chemical industry, Carson was later vindicated by a panel of experts appointed by President John F. Kennedy. Because of the enormous influence of *Silent Spring*, Rachel Carson is considered by many to be the founder of the modern environmental movement. "A Fable for Tomorrow" is the opening passage of *Silent Spring*.

A Fable for Tomorrow

THERE WAS once a town in the heart of America where all life seemed to live in harmony with its surroundings. The town lay in the midst of a checkerboard of prosperous farms, with fields of grain and hillsides of orchards where, in spring, white clouds of bloom drifted above the green fields. In autumn, oak and maple and birch set up a blaze of color that flamed and flickered across a backdrop of pines. Then foxes barked in the hills and deer silently crossed the fields, half hidden in the mists of the fall mornings.

Along the roads, laurel, viburnum and alder, great ferns and wildflowers delighted the traveler's eye through much of the year. Even in winter the roadsides were places of beauty, where countless birds came to feed on the berries and on the seed heads of the dried weeds rising above the snow. The countryside was, in fact, famous for the abundance and variety of its bird life, and when the flood of migrants was pouring through in spring and fall people traveled from great distances to observe them. Others came to fish the streams, which flowed clear and cold out of the hills and contained shady pools where trout lay. So it had been from the days many years ago when the first settlers raised their houses, sank their wells, and built their barns.

Then a strange blight crept over the area and everything began to change. Some evil spell had settled on the community: mysterious maladies swept the flocks of chickens; the cattle and sheep sickened and died. Everywhere was a shadow of death. The farmers spoke of much illness among their families. In the town the doctors had become more and more puzzled by new kinds of sickness appearing among their patients. There had been several sudden and unexplained deaths, not only among adults but even among children, who would be stricken suddenly while at play and die within a few hours.

There was a strange stillness. The birds, for example—where had they gone? Many people spoke of them, puzzled and disturbed. The feeding stations in the backyards were deserted. The few birds seen anywhere were moribund; they trembled violently and could not fly. It was a spring without voices. On the mornings that had once throbbed with the dawn chorus of robins, catbirds, doves, jays, wrens, and scores of other bird voices there was now no sound; only silence lay over the fields and woods and marsh.

On the farms the hens brooded, but no chicks hatched. The farmers complained that they were unable to raise any pigs—the litters were small and the young survived only a few days. The apple trees were coming into bloom but no bees droned among the blossoms, so there was no pollination and there would be no fruit.

The roadsides, once so attractive, were now lined with browned and withered vegetation as though swept by fire. These, too, were silent, deserted by all living things. Even the streams were now lifeless. Anglers no longer visited them, for all the fish had died.

In the gutters under the eaves and between the shingles of the roofs, a white granular powder still showed a few patches; some weeks before it had fallen like snow upon the roofs and the lawns, the fields and streams.

No witchcraft, no enemy action had silenced the rebirth of new life in this stricken world. The people had done it themselves.

This town does not actually exist, but it might easily have a thousand counterparts in America or elsewhere in the world. I know of no community that has experienced all the misfortunes I describe. Yet every one of these disasters has actually happened somewhere, and many real communities have already suffered a substantial number of them. A grim specter has crept upon us almost unnoticed, and this imagined tragedy may easily become a stark reality we all shall know.

What has already silenced the voices of spring in countless towns in America? This book is an attempt to explain.

Understanding What You Read

1. Rachel Carson's "A Fable for Tomorrow" was published more than thirty years ago as the opening of *Silent Spring*. What part of her description of the idyllic rural scene seems dated today?
2. What details of the scenes of blight seem exaggerated? What places that you have read about are like that spoiled community?

Writing About What You Read

Describe a place you know that has been destroyed by human activity or one that seems to have escaped environmental damage.

GEORGE J. MITCHELL

Mitchell (b. 1933) has served in the United States Senate as Democrat from Maine since 1980 and as Senate majority leader since 1988. He worked for the passage of the Clean Air Act and other environmental legislation. "Two Children in a Future World" is from Mitchell's second book, *World on Fire: Saving an Endangered Earth* (1991).

Two Children in a Future World

J O U R N E Y with me for a moment into the twenty-first century and meet two children, Luisa and Eric. Luisa lives in Mexico City sometime in the next century, about fifty years from now. She looks up at a polluted sky in this future world and sees no sun at all. In all her young life—she is now nine—she has rarely seen the sun.

She has heard that Mexico City was once a beautiful place to live. There was plenty of sun once and a lot more room.

There was plenty of sun on the cool, clear November day in the year 1519, some six centuries before Luisa was born, when the Spaniard Diego de Ordaz stood in a high mountain pass and looked down on the Valley of Mexico for the first time. It was one of the most spectacular sights on earth and he was the first European to see it.

The valley was an elevated plain a mile and a half above sea level, surrounded by rugged snow-capped mountain ranges and covering an area of nearly a thousand square miles. Near its center lay five large interconnected lakes. On a small island in one of those lakes sat the city of Tenochtitlán, then the seat of the Aztec Empire, and the future center of Mexico City.

Ordaz and his coterie of Spanish soldiers and their commander, Hernán Cortés,[1] were near the end of a three-month march from Vera Cruz to the Aztec capital. In a short time they would complete the conquest of the Aztecs and change forever the history of Central and South America. They also

4

[1](1485–1547), Spanish conqueror of Mexico.

would set in motion events that would transform the magnificent valley they now entered.

In Ordaz's day the Valley of Mexico was a place of great natural beauty. Even in Luisa's century it remains a spectacular setting. But it was also a setting for a man-made disaster, of a type and magnitude that neither the Aztecs nor their Spanish conquerors could have foreseen.

Much has happened in the valley since the sixteenth century. By the 1990s, fifty years before Luisa was born, nearly twenty million people lived in the metropolitan Mexico City area, working at thirty-six thousand industrial facilities and driving over three million motor vehicles, which they kept an average of twelve years. Mexico hadn't required any emission control devices on motor vehicles until 1992. The combustion of gasoline is only two-thirds as efficient at Mexico City's mile-and-a-half elevation as it is at sea level. The combination of no control devices and the high elevation began devastating Mexico City's air.

8 Toward the end of the twentieth century five and a half million tons of contaminants were being emitted into the atmosphere above the city each year. Regularly, and especially in the cool winter months, warm air passing over the surrounding mountains trapped the cooler air in the valley. There, stagnant and close to the ground, the pollution sickened people and sometimes killed them.

Lead, hydrocarbons, nitrogen oxides, and sulfur dioxide poisoned the air. All were unhealthy, but lead was the most dangerous. It killed some people. It slowed mental development in others. Although the level of lead in Mexican gasoline was gradually reduced, it continued to remain dangerously high.

Many people began experiencing dizziness, drowsiness, shortness of breath, irritation of the eyes and lungs, and a wide range of respiratory ailments. And it was hardest of all on the narrow airways of young children.

Bad as it was before the turn of the century, Mexico City's air only got worse in the years before Luisa was born. The government's efforts to control air pollution—improved gasoline, reduced use of motor vehicles, some emission controls—were simply overwhelmed by growth. The population of Mexico had begun exploding in the twentieth century, and as it continued to grow the air over its capital city became more and more polluted. In 1910 there had been about 15 million Mexicans. By 1950 there were 25 million. By 1990 there were more than 85 million. Very soon there were 100 million, then 150 million. Much of that growth was centered in Mexico City.

12 By the year 2000—the dawn of Luisa's century—there were more than thirty million people driving nine million motor vehicles in the Valley of Mexico. The valley of the Aztecs, that high plateau of such surpassing beauty, had become a valley of death.

It was not alone. By then the metropolitan areas of Tokyo and São Paulo also had populations of more than thirty million; New York, Seoul, and

Bombay had reached twenty million. Inexorably the number of motor vehicles on the streets of these cities increased with the population, and so did the pollution.

In the decade before the year 2000 there were five billion people in the world. Sometime in Luisa's century, the ten-billionth person would be born. Most of this jump in population had taken place in the less-developed countries. And so had the biggest increase in the number and use of motor vehicles. There were about five hundred million registered motor vehicles on earth late in the twentieth century. Their numbers continued increasing twice as fast as the numbers of people. When the population of the world reaches ten billion the number of motor vehicles will hit two billion.

Now, near the middle of Luisa's century, a dark, gray-brown shroud hanging low over Mexico City is a fact of daily life. It makes each breath an irritating effort and it shuts out the sun.

Luisa's world is not only without sun but without hope. There are now 16 too many people crammed into her city, living too close together. It is doubtful in this teeming environment that she will live to be thirty-five. Two of her brothers and many of her friends have already died. It doesn't seem fair to her that people should be dying so young and that the sky should be so dark.

But this is the twenty-first century, and that's the way the world is.

Half a continent away in this world of the twenty-first century, in the United States in a place called North Dakota, a boy of Luisa's age named Eric has a quite different kind of problem with the sun.

The summer will come and Eric, too, will see little of it. He will have to stay indoors again, where he has spent all of his nine summers.

It isn't at all like it was when his grandfather was growing up, when boys 20 lived out in the sun all summer long, from the minute school let out in June until it started again in September.

Even Eric's father and mother had been able to play outside on summer days, down by the creek or along the railroad tracks, when they were growing up. And they hadn't had to wear protective clothing. Pictures in old magazines showed kids in the twentieth century out under the sun with no shirts on at all. They thought nothing of going out in the middle of the day. They didn't even care what they wore and often as not wore hardly anything. In Eric's world that would be unthinkable.

To him life in North Dakota doesn't seem any more fair than it does to Luisa in Mexico City. Unlike her, he has about everything else he could wish for. His parents don't lack for money. He has his own room and plenty of things to play with. His parents have been very successful. But even they don't go outdoors in the summer anymore without their protective clothing and sunglasses.

And it is all because of a hole in the sky.

24   The scientists had detected the hole more than fifty years ago, late in the twentieth century. It had appeared first in the ozone layer of the stratosphere over the Antarctic, and it was bigger than the continent itself. Then a big ozone loss was discovered in the Northern Hemisphere centered on a hole over the North Pole. Now rifts in the ozone layer have spread over the more inhabited parts of the globe.

As every kid in North Dakota now knows, when there is no ozone layer in the stratosphere there is nothing to keep out the sun's ultraviolet radiation. Its rays, unfiltered by the ozone, beam down to earth and cause skin cancer. It wasn't long after the turn of the century that people began getting cancer and dying in epidemic numbers. Since then, kids like Eric just don't spend their summers under the sun.

But this is the twenty-first century, and that's the way the world is.

Is such a future world possible? Yes.
28   Can it be averted? Yes.
Will it be averted? That depends on us.

Understanding What You Read

1. What is the function of Mitchell's description of the Valley of Mexico when the first Spaniards arrived?
2. In what parts of the world is it already dangerous for children to play in the sun?

Writing About What You Read

While George Mitchell's predictions about future population, automobile use, and ozone destruction are likely scenarios, they are not certainties. Do you think we should act now to avert such catastrophes, or should we wait until there is more certainty before taking action? Write a letter to your congressman arguing for one course of action or the other.

DIXY LEE RAY AND LOU GUZZO

Ray (1914–1994) and Guzzo (b. 1919) coauthored *Trashing the Planet* (1992), a book subtitled *How Science Can Help Us Deal with Acid Rain, Depletion of the Ozone, and Nuclear Waste*. Ray was governor of the state of Washington from 1977 to 1981 and has chaired the

Atomic Energy Commission. Guzzo, who served as policy counselor to Governor Ray, has worked as a reporter, TV commentator, teacher, and editor. His books include a biography of Dixy Lee Ray. "Environmentalism and the Future" is from *Trashing the Planet*.

Environmentalism and the Future

A s w e approach the twenty-first century, we're given more than ever to reflecting upon what our society is all about, what our country means, what modern civilization has achieved, and, most of all, what the future promises to bring.

Our nation, which, to me, is the greatest the human race has conceived, is just a bit more than 200 years old. We can expect an endless supply of problems; some people have doubts about our science, our technology, and the way we use our knowledge. We have some hopes and many fears. We must wonder a little about our age. How old are we, anyway?

Human society has been around a long time, but recorded history goes back only about 6,000 years. The earth has been around between four and five billion years, and every generation of human beings that lives on it thinks its problems are the worst and that humankind has never faced such difficulties before. Most of us believe that unless we solve our problems now, all will be lost.

It's sobering to dwell upon how long humans have survived in a frequently hostile environment. We don't have claws, talons, or fangs. We have no barbs or poison glands to protect ourselves. We don't even have any fur or feathers to keep us warm when the ambient temperature drops; indeed, in our birthday suits, we are ill-adapted to live anywhere, except in the rather warm tropics. Our eyesight is not so good as that of most birds; our hearing is less keen than that of almost all of the higher animals; and our sense of smell is nothing compared to that of most fish and mammals. We can be outrun on land and outswum in the seas. 4

Yet, with all these difficulties, we've made it somehow. We have managed to penetrate every ecological niche, and we are able to survive in every environmental climate and condition anywhere on earth.

No other species of higher life can do so. You don't find polar bears swimming in a tropical sea; cactus does not grow in a rain forest. Plants and animals have their own ecological and environmental niches, and they are restricted to them. What, then, are our advantages?

First, we have a brain—a brain the likes of which is not seen in any other higher animal. That brain is capable of abstract thought; that brain can solve problems. We have developed a means of communication through human language that so far exceeds communication among other animals as to be in a completely different category. We are learning a good deal more about animal language and animal communication, but to compare even that of the higher primates or of whales and dolphins to the language capabilities of human beings is to overlook the enormous diversity of expression, the implications and nuances of words in the thousands of languages that exist among human beings. Abstract thought and language lead to systema- tized thinking, which leads to learning, the highest activity human beings engage in.

8   Learning and teaching, the buildup of knowledge, the questioning of truth, the development of philosophical systems, the practical applications of ideas—these are the things that distinguish humans from all other living things. When we join thoughts, speech, and learning to the peculiar capability to walk on two legs—thus freeing our arms—and the development of dextrous hands, we have a physical form that is truly remarkable in the animal kingdom. These gifts give us the ability to manufacture tools and gadgets of all kinds. They give us the ability to create engines and machines that utilize nonliving energy, making the muscle power of slaves and beasts of burden unnecessary in modern society.

It is through our technology that we have been able to fly far away from earth to learn, in truth, how precious it is. It is no coincidence that our awakening to the special nature of our world and to its uniquely balanced environment and its limitations coincided with our first glimpse of earth from outer space, through the eyes of astronauts, television cameras, and photo- graphic equipment. It was through technology that we saw ourselves as we really are, alone on one living, precious globe in space, a human family dependent on the resources of our minds and of our home planet, Earth.

Considering what we humans have accomplished, what we've done to build the modern high-tech society in which we live, and how we've swarmed across the land and changed its face—at least in the temperate region—some critics appear to be fearful that we are now about to destroy nature itself.

Are they right?

12   Without doubt, humans have been hard on the environment in many discrete places. Whenever mankind has cleared land to build a city or to farm or to manufacture something, the naturalness of nature has been changed. From a longer perspective, civilizations have come and gone since antiquity. Sometimes, in areas that were once inhabited and then abandoned, nature has taken over. On a shorter time scale, it has been demonstrated again and again that areas once despoiled by pollutants can return to being a healthy abode for many species.

True, humans can be and have been destructive, but humans also learn. The ways to live in harmony with nature while maintaining a comfortable, even high-tech, life-style are far better understood today. And more and more they are being practiced. There is no reason to believe that, inevitably, everything will get worse.

But activist environmentalists charge that man has gone beyond having an effect on the immediate vicinity of his activities and is now damaging the entire planet. They say man's industrial activities are changing the composition of the atmosphere, presumably irreversibly, through increased production of CO_2 and other greenhouse gases. As already pointed out, until the predictions of human-caused, global atmospheric alterations can be accepted as certain, there must be a satisfactory explanation for the increases in greenhouse gases 300 years ago, 150,000 years ago, and in the geological past. And it must be established that the ozone-destroying chloride ion really does, in fact, come from CFC[1] and not from any of a number of natural sources.

In the light of the enormous size of the atmosphere and the hydrosphere, and the colossal natural forces involved, it would appear that man's puny activities are being vastly exaggerated.

The fact is that weather will be what it is and that man's influence, if any, is trivial and relatively local. In the long term, climates, too, will change, as they have done in the past, determined not by man but by immense natural forces. Neither the sun nor the earth is immortal. Each will grow old and die. Inevitably, the sun will burn itself out, slipping first into that stage called a "red giant," where its size will become so huge that it will encompass the inner planets. Our earth will be swallowed up and cease to exist. Fortunately for us, the time scale for this is fairly long—about two billion years or so from now. That gives us a pretty good cushion of time to become better stewards of the environment. We are not ever going to control it on a worldwide scale.

Still, there are those who believe that we are threatening earth with intolerable stresses, born of just exactly those same things that have made us unique—human knowledge and technology. This belief finds expression in the modern environmental movement.

Now, aside from unrivaled success in obtaining favorable publicity for its positions, how is it that environmentalism became so successful? Part of the answer is fairly clear. There were two essential ingredients. One was national legislation that gave the activists access to the federal courts and standing before the law (the National Environmental Protection Act). In the last 15 years, more than 100 environmental laws have been passed. The other was the creation of many governmental agencies, including the Environmental Protection Agency, the Occupational Safety and Health Administration (OSHA), and the Nuclear Regulatory Commission.

Environmentalism, as we have come to know it in the waning years of the twentieth century, is a new and complex phenomenon. It is new in the sense that it goes far beyond the traditional conservation movement—be kind to animals, support good stewardship of the earth, and so on—a philosophy of nature that we have known from the past. It is complex in that it incorporates a strongly negative element of anti-development, anti-progress, anti-technol-

[1]Chlorofluorocarbons.

ogy, anti-business, anti-established institutions, and, above all, anti-capitalism. Its positive side, if that is what it can be called, is that it seeks development of a society totally devoid of industry and technology.

20   As a movement, it is activist, adversarial, punitive, and coercive. It is quick to resort to force, generally through the courts or through legislation, although some of its more zealous adherents engage in physical violence (Earth First! and Greenpeace,[2] for example). Finally, the environmentalist movement today has an agenda that goes far beyond a mere concern for nature, as shown by its links to and common cause with other leftist radical movements—such as are incorporated in the Green parties[3] of Europe.

This is not to suggest that everyone who supports more responsible policies for cleaner air and water, who believes in restraining pollution, and who cares about how the earth's resources are used is a wild-eyed extremist. Far from it. The great majority of those who make up the membership of the Audubon Society, Sierra Club, National Wildlife Federation, Wilderness Society, Nature Conservancy, and countless other groups are fine, decent citizens. They are honest, honorable supporters of a good, clean environment and responsible human actions. However, the leaders of some of their organizations—such as the Natural Resources Defense Council, Friends of the Earth, Earth First!, Greenpeace, Government Accountability Project, Institute for Policy Studies, and many others—are determinedly leftist, radical, and dedicated to blocking industrial progress and unraveling industrial society.

These activist leaders and spokesmen are referred to as "political environmentalists" to distinguish them from the rest of us, who believe that using scientific data, not scare tactics, is the correct way to deal with environmental issues.

Modern environmentalism arose in response to real and widely recognized problems, among them: growing human pressures on natural resources, accumulation of wastes, and increased pollution of land, air, and water. Remember, for example, accounts from Cleveland about the alarming condition of the Cuyahoga River, which flows through the heart of Cleveland's industrial corridor into Lake Erie and was once called the world's most polluted river. So many gallons of industrial and chemical waste, oil, and other flammables had been dumped into it over the years that the river actually caught fire and blazed for a time. The Cuyahoga has since been cleaned up, and so has Lake Erie.

24   Without question, by the 1960s it was time to curb the excesses of a

[2]Environmental organizations: Earth First! uses aggressive tactics against machinery but adheres to strict principles of nonviolence in its dealings with people; Greenpeace is the world's largest environmental group, some of whose activist members risk their lives to stop environmental abuse.

[3]In Western Europe, environmentalists have succeeded in forming political parties (Green parties) that have enough support to send representatives to several European parliaments.

throwaway society. It was time to face up to the fact that there simply wasn't any "away" to throw things any more; "vacant" land and open space were limited. It was also time to recognize that there is a human tendency to overuse a good product, whether it's a vitamin, antibiotic, fertilizer, pesticide, or wilderness. It was time to redress many environmental wrongs. But, perhaps inevitably, the movement has gone beyond correcting past abuses and now poses real obstacles to industrial and technological progress.

Under the slogan of protecting the environment, political environmentalists now oppose and cause delay in the construction of important facilities, even those that are obviously necessary and have wide support. It is now next to impossible and certainly far more expensive than in the past to build a sewage treatment plant, garbage incinerators, a power plant, a dam, or to open a new landfill. Industrial facilities, even when they are expected to produce useful commodities, hardly fare better. Liability for anything that might go wrong and the threat of litigation are effective deterrents used by political environmentalists against industry.

After achieving so much—establishing government agencies with oversight authority and regulatory power, armed with such laws as the National Environmental Protection Act, the Clean Air Act, the Clean Water Act, the Waste Management Act, and more than 100 other environmental laws—environmentalist groups apparently cannot leave well enough alone. They seem to be unable to let these laws and statutory agencies work to continue the significant progress of the last two decades. Instead, they press for ever more stringent and punitive controls. They continue to push for and insist on an unachievable pristine perfection, whatever the cost. Never mind that humans never survived without altering nature.

It is a fact that effluents no longer pour unchecked from the stacks and chimneys and waste pipes of industry. Open hearth furnaces and other industrial processes that depend on burning fuel have been largely replaced by electric furnaces and much of our foundry and smelting capacity has been shut down. Open burning of garbage no longer occurs and discharge of untreated sewage and waste water is becoming rare. It is certainly illegal.

Responsible timber companies have revised their logging practices and more trees are growing now than 50 years ago, an increase of more than three and a half times since 1920. Reforestation is a usual, not an occasional, practice. Coupled with modern agricultural procedures that require less land for food production, we now have at least as much wooded and forested acreage in America as existed in Colonial times, and probably more.

So what do the political environmental extremists want? Instant ecological perfection? A return to the Garden of Eden? To be in control? To exercise power? To remake society according to their political philosophy?

Activist environmentalists are mostly white, middle to upper income, and predominantly college-educated. They are distinguished by a vocal do-good mentality that sometimes successfully cloaks their strong streak of elitism,

28

which is often coupled with a belief that the end justifies the means and that violence and coercion are appropriate tactics. Political environmentalists are adept at publicizing their causes, at exerting pressure on elected officials and government agencies, and at using the courts of law to achieve their aims.

They also tend to believe that nature is sacred and that technology is a sacrilege. Some environmentalists appear to be in favor of taking mankind back to pantheism or animism.

32   The idea that nature is "pure" and the almost religious awe with which it is held seems to be a part of the attraction, the drawing power of the movement. This attitude appears to permeate the thinking of a great many persons who are members of the Sierra Club, Audubon Society, Wilderness Society, Friends of the Earth, and other groups. We can look upon it as a very sincere, if somewhat sophomoric, emotional response to legitimate worries about the environment.

*   *   *

Understanding What You Read

1. Which two widely discussed environmental problems do Ray and Guzzo insist must be established as certain before they are taken seriously?
2. Which environmental problems do they admit are "real and widely recognized"?
3. What language do they use to belittle people they call "activist environmentalists"?

Writing About What You Read

Write a response to Ray and Guzzo's assessment of environmental issues, either agreeing with them, debating with them, or engaging in a dialogue about what they say.

THEODORE ROSZAK

A professor of history and general studies at California State University, Hayward, Roszak (b. 1933) has published four novels as well as several works of nonfiction, including *The Making of the Counterculture* (1969), which gave a name to the sixties and a national reputation to its author. In *The Voice of the Earth* (1992), Roszak examines the psychological ramifications of environmental problems and suggests that how human beings treat nature affects their mental health. "Green Guilt and Ecological Overload" was published as an editorial in the *New York Times* (June 9, 1992).

Green Guilt and Ecological Overload

I AM listening to a lecture by Helen Caldicott,[1] the environmental activist. Dr. Caldicott is in top form, holding forth with her usual bracing mixture of caustic wit and prophetical urgency. All around me, an audience of the faithful is responding with camp-meeting fervor, cheering her on as she itemizes a familiar checklist of impending calamities: acid rain, global warming, endangered species.

She has even come up with a fresh wrinkle on one of the standard environmental horrors: nuclear energy. Did we know, she asks, that nuclear energy is producing scores of anencephalic[2] births in the industrial shantytowns along the Mexican border? "Every time you turn on an electric light," she admonishes us, "you are making another brainless baby."

Dr. Caldicott's presentation is meant to instill unease. In my case, she is succeeding, though not in the way she intends. She is making me worry, as so many of my fellow environmentalists have begun to make me worry—not simply for the fate of the Earth, but for the fate of this movement on which so much depends. As much as I want to endorse what I hear, Dr. Caldicott's effort to shock and shame just isn't taking. I am as sympathetic a listener as she can expect to find, yet rather than collapsing into self-castigation, as I once might have, I find myself going numb.

Is it possible that green guilt, the mainstay of the movement, has lost its ethical sting?   4

Despite my reservations, I do my best to go along with what Dr. Caldicott has to say—even though I suspect (as I think most of her audience does) that there is no connection between light bulbs and brainless babies. The increase in anencephalic births around the U.S.-dominated maquiladoras[3] on the Mexican border probably has more to do with the dumping of toxic wastes. And isn't that bad enough?

Still, I remind myself that the important thing is to spread the alarm. And Dr. Caldicott is an inspired alarmist. I try to bear with her habit of moral hyperbole because I know what she is up against—especially in the U.S. She is struggling to move a mountain of official complacency.

Judging by the leisurely pace at which the world's political and corporate leaders seem prepared to "phase in" such reforms as emissions controls and

---

[1]Leader of antinuclear and environmental organizations and author of *If You Love This Planet* (1992).

[2]Without a brain.

[3]Factories on the Mexican side of the border.

"phase out" such dangers as ozone-depleting chemicals, it is clear that they do not share my sense of urgency—even when it comes to such biospheric imperatives as the greenhouse effect.

8   But if politicians and corporate leaders have been remiss in registering the emergency, the public at large may not share their insouciance. Over the past two decades, environmentalists have done a good job of scaring and shaming people. They have been so effective that the movement may be in danger of crippling the public's capacity to take action.

If we were to compile all the warnings of all the ecology groups, there would be little that we in the industrial world could do that would not be either lethal, wicked, or both. From the dioxin-laced[4] coffee filters we use in the morning to the electric blankets we cover ourselves with at night, we are besieged by deadly hazards.

Worse still, many of those hazards make us unwitting accessories to crimes against the biosphere. My eyeglasses, for example. How could I have guessed that the frames are made from an endangered species, the hawksbill turtle?

There is no question in my mind that these problems are as serious as environmentalists contend. It is simply that there are so many of them and each comes at us crying, "Me first! Me first!" In part, the ecological overload arises from the haphazard way in which the movement operates. The pattern too much resembles those "disease of the month" telethons that leave us wondering if there is anybody still alive out there.

12   Only a few groups, like the Worldwatch Institute,[5] deal with the planetary habitat as a whole, seeking to assign the issues some priority. Otherwise, the biosphere has been Balkanized into a landscape of disaster areas. Scores of groups compete for public attention and funds, each fixed on a single horror. Hunger, pollution, the ozone layer, the topsoil, the rain forests, the whales, the wolves, the spotted owls. In politics, a thousand people each demanding that we do a different right thing may add up to one big bad thing: public rejection.

That result is all the more likely when environmentalists take to scolding their audience. As Jeremy Burgess, a science writer and supporter of environmentalism, asks: "Is it just me, or does everyone else feel guilty for being alive too? . . . Eventually, and probably soon, we shall all be reduced to creeping about in disgrace, nervous of our simplest pleasures."

Environmentalists are not unaware of the problem. One group has tried to make light of the matter, calling itself the Voluntary Human Extinction Movement. Under the slogan "The Answer to All Our Problems," its founder observes that "the extinction of *Homo sapiens* would mean survival for millions, if not billions, of other Earth-dwelling species."

[4]Dioxin is a family of some 210 chemicals thought to increase the incidence of cancer in people exposed to sufficient amounts.

[5]A research team that reports on environmental issues in its annual publication, *State of the World*, among others.

The humorous touch is welcome, but it may come too late. As we enter the 1990s, environmentalists are beginning to see who is reaping the political benefit of the guilty frustration they have so diligently disseminated. A fanatical anti-environmental backlash now under way is stripping away the ecologists' most important asset: their claim to public virtue.

Until now, the business community has been forced to handle the movement with care. Rather than confront it directly, they resorted to "greenwashing," trying to take the side of the angels. They redefined their products in eco-friendly terms, ran advertisements featuring frisky animals and edenic landscapes and claimed, usually deceptively, to be defending the biosphere at every turn. 16

But now a new tactic has emerged: environmental hardball. Corporations are sponsoring citizens' groups that purport to speak for hikers, hunters, fishermen and dirt-bike riders who merely want to enjoy the simple, God-given pleasures of nature. The Big Three automakers, for example, have created the Coalition for Vehicle Choice. Through the Alliance for America, lumber and mining corporations portray ecologists as bullying spoilsports, and hasten to champion the little guys, helpless victims of the elitist environmental organizations.

For conservatives, a green scare is replacing the red menace. The Competitive Enterprise Institute, which promotes "free market ecomanagement," announces, "There is an intellectual war taking place between pro-market and anti-market forces to which business should be contributing a vigorous defense of its social role." The institute claims that "antihuman" ecologists believe that "every consumer product and every consumer action is inherently anti-environmental."

At its extreme, this rhetoric can be venomous. Ron Arnold, a lobbyist for one group, the Alliance for America, describes the environmental movement as "the perfect bogyman" and admits that his goal is to "destroy" it. Another critic, George Reisman, a professor of economics at Pepperdine University, condemns environmentalism as every bit as menacing to capitalism as Bolshevism or Nazism. The movement's contention that nonhuman nature possesses intrinsic value is a thin cover for its true goal, Mr. Reisman has written, which is "nothing less than *the undoing of the Industrial Revolution,* and the return to the poverty, filth and misery of earlier centuries."

It is clearly time for the environmental movement to draw up a psychological impact statement. Have we pushed scare tactics and guilt trips as far as they can take us? At the least, the problem is one of effective public relations. Shame has always been one of the worst and most unpredictable motivators in politics; it too easily laps over into resentment. Call people's entire way of life into question and what you are apt to get is defensive rigidity. 20

Jan Beyea of the National Audubon Society wisely cautions: "Environmentalists need to be very careful to watch their own psychological state. Many of my friends . . . get such a psychological reward from being in the battle, the good guys against the bad guys, that they lose sight of what they are trying to do." Mr. Beyea wants to replace the "politics of blame" with what he calls the "politics of vision," by which he means "showing people practical ways that they can do better."

The popularity of John Javna's "50 Simple Things You Can Do to Save the Earth" stems from the fact that the book provides its readers with some small chance to act—though hardly enough to satisfy more radical environmentalists.

The response of "Earth Island Journal" was to catalogue 50 difficult things. The list begins:

1. Dismantle your car.
2. Become a total vegetarian.
3. Grow your own vegetables.
4. Have your power lines disconnected.
5. Don't have children.

24   The intention is not entirely humorous.

But there is a philosophical issue here that goes deeper than public relations. Every political movement is grounded in a vision of human nature. What do people need, what do they fear, what do they love? The question of motivation determines everything that follows in a political program. Start from the assumption that people are greedy brutes, and the tone of all you say will be one of contempt.

Issues like these become all the more pertinent for a movement that requires such sweeping change. Environmentalism may not require the total "undoing of the Industrial Revolution," but it does involve inventing new concepts of wealth and well-being that challenge many of the values on which Western politics has been based for two centuries.

The agenda for change on this scale will be the work of generations. But here and now something basic has to be decided. In its task of saving life on Earth, does this movement believe it has anything more to draw on than the ethical resolution of a small group of overworked, increasingly vituperative activists who feel they may have to be entrusted with more and more domineering control over the conduct of daily life? Or is there an ecological dimension to the human personality that is both "natural" and universal?

28   I believe there is: a sense of connectedness with nature as rooted in the psyche as Freud once believed the libido to be. When we experience this shared identity person to person, we call it love. More coolly and distantly felt between the human and not-human, it is called compassion. In either case, the result is spontaneous loyalty.

Those of us who presume to act as the planet's guardians must decide if we believe such a bond exists between ourselves and the planet that gives us life. There have been few movements as internally diverse and contentious as environmentalism.

Meanwhile, on the world scene, as the Earth Summit[6] in Rio de Janeiro is demonstrating by the day, environmentalism is fast becoming the catch-all for every form of third world discontent. The movement runs the risk of disintegrating into an angry chaos of conflicting agendas. In the nasty give-and-take of daily politics, it is sometimes difficult to realize that the essential motivation of most environmentalists is a spontaneous love of the natural beauties.

On the far side of the Earth Summit, we might do well to begin asking what environmental politics connects with in people that is generous, joyous, freely given and noble.

[6]This article was published during the United Nations Conference on Environment and Development, known as the Earth Summit or UNCED, in June 1992.

Understanding What You Read

What does Roszak mean when he says that the environmental movement "may be in danger of crippling the public's capacity to take action"?

Writing About What You Read

Some environmental groups are assigning priorities to environmental problems. List the three environmental issues that you think require the most urgent action in order of priority; explain your reasoning. Then list others that in your opinion are much less urgent.

MARCIA D. LOWE

A senior researcher at the Worldwatch Institute, Lowe (b. 1961) specializes in transportation and land-use issues. She is the author of several Worldwatch papers and has been coauthor of the annual *State of the World* reports since 1990. "Pedaling into the Future" is from Lester Brown, ed., *The Worldwatch Reader On Global Environmental Issues* (1991).

Pedaling into the Future

TRAFFIC NOISE in Beijing means the whirring of bicycle wheels and tinkling of bells. The streets of New Delhi come alive with thousands of bicycle commuters each day. Office workers in New York City depend on bicycle messengers to cruise past bumper-to-bumper traffic and deliver parcels on time. And police officers in Seattle often find bicycles better than squad cars for apprehending criminals on gridlocked downtown streets.

Outside the city, bicycles also play a vital role. Kenyan dairy farmers cycle through remote regions with milk deliveries, and Nicaraguan health workers on bikes now reach four times as many rural patients as they did on foot.

Whether a cycle rickshaw in Jakarta or a ten-speed in Boston, pedal power plays a key role in transportation. The bicycle is fast becoming the only way to move quickly through congested urban traffic and the only affordable personal transport in the developing world—where an automobile may cost more than a worker earns in a decade.

Despite its demonstrated utility, the bicycle has been formally neglected by transit planners in almost every country on the globe. Only China and a few Western European nations collect transportation data that count bicycles among forms of transport. In the case of the U.S. Department of Commerce, neglect might be a promotion in status for the bicycle; the department refers inquiries on bicycle trade to its Division of Toys and Games.

The World Bank, the main source of urban transit investment in the developing world, published a 1985 study on the Chinese transport sector that does not even mention the word bicycle, although the overwhelming majority of trips in China's cities are made by bike. This is sadly typical of a policy environment in which only motor vehicles are taken seriously.

HIGH PRICE FOR MOBILITY

The automobile has long been considered the vehicle of the future. Indeed, it has brought industrial society into the modern age with a degree of individual mobility and convenience not known before. But overreliance on the car is backfiring as too many cars clutter city streets and highways, bringing rush-hour traffic to a standstill. The side effects of massive oil use show up not only in economy-draining import bills but in deadly air pollution in cities, acid rain in dying lakes and forests, and hastened global warming.

In their enthusiasm for engine power, transit planners have overlooked the value of human power. With congestion, pollution, and debt threatening both the industrial and developing worlds, the vehicle of the future clearly rides on two wheels rather than four.

The bicycle's ascent would not eliminate automobiles, or any other vehicle, but would instead integrate bicycles with cars and mass transit. A well-balanced, diverse transport system could help save precious oil and other resources, reduce pollutants, and provide mobility to people with few or no alternatives to walking. Before this can happen, though, a shift in attitudes must take place.

*   *   *

Planning Makes a Difference

Like the United States, most other industrial countries have all but abandoned the bicycle for the automobile. Suburbanization has sprawled jobs, homes, and services over such long distances that automobiles are less a convenience than a necessity. Several North American cities have extensive bike paths, but many cities have become nearly bicycleproof: their roadways and parking facilities are designed with only motor vehicles in mind.

Three outstanding models of nationwide bicycle planning are the Netherlands, West Germany, and Japan. Local governments in these countries—spurred by traffic jams and air pollution—are demonstrating how public policy can be used to make cycling a safe and convenient alternative to the car.

The Netherlands has more than 9,000 miles of bicycle paths, more than any other country. In some Dutch cities, half of all trips are made by bike. The German town of Erlangen has completed a network of paths covering 100 miles, about half the length of the city's streets. Bicycle use has more than doubled as a result.

Bicycle-oriented cities in Europe and Japan have boosted both bicycle   12

Table 1. Bicycles and Automobiles in Selected Countries, circa 1985

Country	Bicycles Autos (millions)		Cycle/ Auto Ratio
China	270.0	0.5	540.0
India	45.0	1.5	30.0
South Korea	6.0	0.3	20.0
Egypt	1.5	0.5	3.0
Mexico	12.0	4.8	2.5
Netherlands	11.0	4.9	2.2
Japan	58.0	27.8	2.1
West Germany	45.0	26.0	1.7
Argentina	4.5	3.4	1.3
Brazil	12.0	10.0	1.2
Tanzania	0.5	0.5	1.0
United States	95.0	132.1	0.7

Sources: Bicycle Federation of America, Motor Vehicle Manufacturers Association, and International Trade Centre UNC TAD/GATT.

and public transit ridership with facilities for carrying bicycles on buses and trains, and for parking them safely at stations. So many Japanese commuters take advantage of this bike-to-rail option that train stations need parking towers. The city of Kasukabe now has a twelve-story structure that uses cranes to park more than 1,500 bicycles.

*   *   *

URBAN BANE

In 1983, a unique experiment began to unfold in the streets of Bogotá, Colombia. Every Sunday morning 37 miles of arterial roads were closed to motor traffic and half a million city dwellers took to the streets to bicycle, roller skate, and stroll. Now in its sixth year, the weekly ritual transforms a cityscape dominated by smog and honking cars into a tranquil, clean environment.

The world's automobile-bound cities, though, are a far cry from Bogotá on Sunday. Dependence on the car exacts a toll on human health, environment, and quality of life in urban areas.

Industrial-world cities typically relinquish at least one-third of their land—two-thirds in Los Angeles—to roads and parking lots. In the United States, this totals 38.4 million acres—more area than the entire state of Georgia. That, say researchers George Work and Lawrence Malone, is more than necessary. According to their calculations, for a bridge of a given size to accommodate 40,000 people in one hour would require 12 lanes for cars, 4 lanes for buses, 2 for trains, and 1 for bicycles.

With mounting pressures on Third World countries to house and feed their swelling populations, they have little room to spare for roads and parking lots. Where people and good cropland are concentrated in a relatively small area of a country, as in China, choices are narrow. If China paved over as much land per capita as the United States has (about 0.15 acres), it would have to give up a total of 158 million acres—equivalent to more than 40 percent of the country's cropland.

The automobile is very much the victim of its own success: it jams urban centers and suburbs alike. Traffic congestion is eroding the quality of life in urban areas, and the amount of time wasted in traffic continues to expand in the world's cities. London rush-hour traffic crawls at an average of 8 miles an hour. In Los Angeles, motorists waste 100,000 hours a day in traffic jams. Traffic engineers estimate that by the turn of the century Californians will lose almost two million hours daily.

Urban residents from Sao Paulo to London face eye, nose, and throat irritation, asthma, headaches, and chest discomfort brought on by car-produced smog. Emissions from gasoline and diesel fuel use are annually linked to as many as 30,000 deaths in the United States alone.

It is short automobile trips—precisely the ones bike-riding could replace—that create the most pollution, because a cold engine does not fire effectively and releases unburnt hydrocarbons into the air. In the United States, where an estimated 40 percent of urban commuters drive less than 4 miles, pedaling to work would have a dramatic effect on air quality.

Both city and country dwellers are endangered in other ways by the automobile. Some 100,000 people in North America, Western Europe, Japan, and Australia died in traffic accidents in 1985. Developing countries—with fewer automobiles but more pedestrian traffic and no provisions for separating the two—have fatality rates as much as 20 times higher than industrial countries.

Bicycle riding is not without its risks. Bicycle accidents do account for many traffic injuries, particularly in Asia, but are unlikely to kill people unless motor vehicles are involved. That is small consolation for would-be bicyclists who are intimidated off the road. Latin America has its urban cyclists—including young boys delivering newspapers and craftspeople hauling goods—but many potential riders are deterred by dangerous traffic conditions. Some Nairobi streets that once were full of bicycles now are only safe for cars.

Where it can be done safely, cycling improves public health. The popularity of stationary exercise bikes is proof that people enjoy cycling to keep fit; the irony is that so many people drive to the health club in order to ride them. Cyclists are less vulnerable to heart attacks or coronary disease than sedentary commuters, and they arrive at work more alert and less stressed by rush-hour traffic.

*   *   *

SUBSIDIZED AUTO DEPENDENCY

The economic and environmental consequences of automobile overdependence may eventually necessitate bicycle use, even without government help. But for now, public policies that ignore bicycles perpetuate private attitudes against using them. Thus, the transport planner's office seems the best place for the philosophical reordering to start.

A major barrier to bicycling is the fact that drivers are in effect paid to use automobiles. Drivers in the United States may receive as much as $300 billion in subsidies each year in the form of public funds for road repair and construction, police and fire services, and health care.

In the private sector, free parking provided by many employers in effect pays the gasoline costs of commuting. The U.S. Environmental Protection Agency has concluded that if employees were directly handed this subsidy, public transit ridership and bicycle use would go up, while auto traffic would decline by 25 percent.

Several cities have made motorists pay for the privilege of driving automobiles. Singapore charges private cars carrying fewer than four occupants "congestion fees" for entering the downtown area during rush hours, a decade-old scheme that has raised downtown traffic speeds by 20 percent and reduced traffic accidents by 25 percent.

Inconvenience—a general absence of safe parking and locker room facilities—keeps many commuters from bicycling to work, but there are precedents for dealing with this. In China, bicycle parking lots are guarded against theft by attendants. Palo Alto, California, has passed a number of innovative regulations requiring builders of large offices to provide showers and bicycle parking.

All that aside, commuters are still not likely to choose bicycling when it means taking their lives into their hands on busy city streets. Effective bicycle promotion calls for bike paths separate from roads and space on regular roadways devoted to bicycles. Perhaps even more important, cars and bikes should be treated equally in enforcing traffic laws. Along with bicycle safety campaigns, these steps can elevate bicycling to the status of real transportation in the public's mind.

PEDALING INTO THE FUTURE

In terms of sheer number of vehicles, the world is well equipped to let bicycles take on a larger share of the transportation burden. Around the world, nearly 100 million bicycles are made each year—three times the number of automobiles. The big bicycle producers, especially in Asia, are sure to keep upping their capacities.

With or without bike-oriented planning, financial imperatives may force a shift to the bicycle. For starters, most people in the world will never be able to buy an automobile, and public transit systems in many cities cannot keep pace with explosive population growth. When the next oil crunch hits, even those who can now afford to drive will be looking for alternatives. With relatively modest public investment in parking and road space for bicycles, transportation choices would multiply quickly.

Environmental degradation may also change planners' thinking. The by-products of fossil-fuel combustion—deadly urban air pollution, acid rain on lakes and forests, and global warming—as well as the paving of valuable land, point to the need for an alternative to engines. The bicycle is the only vehicle that can help address all of these problems and still provide convenient and affordable personal transportation.

While transport planners remain fixated on the auto, congestion and commuting costs are already spurring people to switch to bicycling. The number of bicycle commuters in the United States reached 1.8 million in 1985, which is still less than 2 percent of all commuters, but represents a quadrupling in one decade. This happened with virtually no public policy push, and this suggests that official encouragement could inspire a more dramatic changeover.

Just how rapidly the bicycle will expand transport options, check environmental damage, and restore urban quality of life depends on how quickly its use moves from individual preference onto the public agenda.

Understanding What You Read

1. In what developing countries does the bicycle play a major role in transportation?
2. Name three industrial countries that have carefully planned how to integrate bicycles into the transportation system.
3. What is the social cost of overdependence on the automobile?
4. What are the deterrents to cycling?
5. What needs to be done to encourage cycling?

Writing About What You Read

Write a letter to the mayor of your community explaining the advantages of using the bicycle for public transportation and requesting that the local government take action to facilitate the shift from cars to bicycling for some commuters. Be specific about your requests.

LESTER R. BROWN, CHRISTOPHER FLAVIN, AND SANDRA POSTEL

Brown (b. 1934), Flavin (b. 1955), and Postel (b. 1956) are all on the staff of the Worldwatch Institute. Brown, a recipient of the prestigious MacArthur Foundation award, is president and the author of a dozen books. Flavin is vice president for research, and he specializes in energy resource, technology, and policy issues. He is the author of numerous Worldwatch papers and coauthor of the annual *State of the World* report. Postel is also a vice president for research; during her years there she has written many Worldwatch papers and served as associate project director for several *State of the World* reports. She is the author of *Last Oasis: Facing Water Scarcity* (1992). Brown, Flavin, and Postel are coauthors of *Saving the Planet: How to Shape an Environmentally Sustainable Global Economy* (1991), from which "Reusing and Recycling Materials" is taken.

Reusing and Recycling Materials

THE THROWAWAY society that has emerged in western societies during the late twentieth century uses so much energy, emits so much carbon, and generates so much air pollution, acid rain, water pollution, toxic waste, and rubbish that it is strangling itself. Rooted in the industrial concept of planned obsolescence and appeals to convenience at almost any cost, it may be seen by historians as an economic aberration. In an environmentally sustainable economy, waste reduction and recycling industries will replace the garbage collection and disposal companies of today.

In such an economy, materials use will be guided by a hierarchy of options. The first priority, of course, is to avoid using any nonessential item. Second is to directly reuse a product—for example, refilling a glass beverage container. The third is to recycle the material to form a new product. Fourth, the material can be burned to extract whatever energy it contains, as long as this can be done safely. The option of last resort is disposal in a landfill.

Most materials used today are discarded after one use—roughly two thirds of all aluminum, three fourths of all steel and paper, and an even higher share of plastic. Society will become dramatically less energy-intensive and less polluting only if the throwaway economy is replaced by one that reuses and recycles. Steel produced entirely from scrap requires only one third as much energy as that produced from iron ore. Newsprint from recycled paper takes 25–60 percent less energy to make than that from virgin wood pulp. And recycling glass saves up to a third of the energy embodied in the original product.

4   Reuse brings even more dramatic gains. For example, replacing a throwaway beverage bottle with one made from recycled glass reduces energy use by roughly a third, but replacing it with a refillable glass bottle can cut energy use by nine tenths. Although the relative energy savings from reusing versus recycling vary from product to product, these numbers reflect the environmental advantages of reuse.

Recycling is also a key to reducing land, air, and water pollution. For example, steel produced from scrap reduces air pollution by 85 percent, cuts water pollution by 76 percent, and eliminates mining wastes altogether. Making paper from recycled material reduces pollutants entering the air by 74 percent and the water by 35 percent, as well as lowering pressures on forests in direct proportion to the amount recycled.

Although the focus in recent years has been on wastes at the consumer end of the production cycle, far more is wasted in the mining and processing of both materials and fossil fuels. For example, nonfuel mining in the United States produces, at conservative estimates, 1 billion tons per year of waste material in the form of slag, mine tailings, and other discarded materials—at least six times as much as the garbage produced by U.S. municipalities in 1988.

With most minerals now being produced from surface mines rather than from underground, the land disruption is extensive. A worldwide estimate by the U.S. government for 1976 showed that over a half-million hectares were disrupted by surface mining. Of this, roughly two thirds was from the mining of nonfuel minerals and one third was from coal. Although some countries have strict regulations on land restoration after strip mining, the more common result is wasteland of the sort that can now be seen in the brown coal mining regions of eastern Germany. Once the mining is completed, the devastated landscape is reminiscent of the surface of the moon.

The first check on the worldwide rush to a throwaway society came during the seventies as oil prices and environmental consciousness climbed. Rising energy costs made recycling more attractive, slowing the trend toward tossing out even more metal, glass, and paper. The second boost came during the eighties as many urban landfill sites filled, forcing municipal governments to ship their garbage to faraway places for disposal. For example, in many U.S. cities, garbage disposal costs during the last decade increased several-fold, making it cost-effective for them to help establish recycling industries. 8

During the nineties, this trend will be reinforced by the need to reduce carbon emissions, air pollution, acid rain, and toxic waste. In the early stages, countries will move toward comprehensive, systematic recycling of metal, glass, paper, and other materials, beginning with source separation at the consumer level. Many communities in Europe, Japan, and, more recently, the United States have already taken steps in this direction.

Steady advances in technologies are speeding the transition. Electric arc furnaces produce high-quality steel from scrap metal using far less energy than an antiquated open-hearth furnace does. In the United States, a leader in this technology, roughly a third of all steel is already produced from scrap in such furnaces. They can operate wherever there is electricity and a supply of scrap metal, and they can be built on a scale adapted to the volume of locally available scrap. Feeding on worn-out automobiles, household appliances, and industrial equipment, their geographic distribution will reflect that of population. Further, they will provide local jobs and revenue, while eliminating a source of waste.

In the sustainable economy of the future, the principal source of materials for industry will be recycled goods. Most of the raw material for the aluminum mill would come from the local scrap collection center, not from the bauxite mine. Paper and paper products would be produced at recycling mills, with recycled paper moving through a hierarchy of uses, from high-quality bond through newsprint and, eventually, into cardboard boxes. When the recycled fibers are finally no longer reusable, they can be composted or burned as fuel in a cogenerating plant. In a paper products industry that continually uses recycled materials, wood pulp will play a minor role. In mature industrial societies with stable populations, industries will feed largely on what is already within the system, turning to virgin raw materials only to replace any losses in use and recycling.

12   Although solid waste generation is on the rise in most industrial nations, some countries are now attempting to move beyond the throwaway society. Germany is taking the lead by putting pressure on manufacturers and retailers to assume responsibility for waste from their products and packaging. One response has been that German automobile manufacturers—including BMW, Daimler-Benz, and Volkswagen—are working to make disassembly and reuse of vehicle components much easier, and have set up pilot recycling programs.

In the recycling of household appliances such as refrigerators, Germany is a pioneer in reusing all the materials they contain, including chlorofluorocarbons (CFCs). With a typical refrigerator containing more than a kilogram of CFCs, the family of chemicals that is both depleting the stratospheric ozone layer that protects us from ultraviolet radiation and accounting for roughly one fifth of the rise in greenhouse gases, this is a major advance. The German technology recaptures CFCs both from the compressor and from the foam insulation used in the refrigerator.

Not only is this technology helping protect the future habitability of the planet, it is also yielding economic benefits. As other countries, most immediately Sweden and Switzerland, decide to recycle refrigerators, they are importing the CFC reclamation equipment developed in Germany.

With beverage containers, which account for a substantial share of the garbage flow from a typical household, Denmark has moved to the forefront. In 1977, it banned the use of throwaway containers for soft drinks, and in 1981 it did the same for beer containers. With these bans, Denmark was accused of discriminating against beverages from other countries and charged with protectionism by the other members of the European Community. Fortunately, its argument that environmental protection took precedence over trade policy was sustained in the European Court of Justice.

16   Although early moves away from the throwaway society are concentrating on recycling, substainability over the long term depends more on eliminating waste flows. One of the most obvious places to reduce the volume of waste generated is in industry, where a restructuring of manufacturing processes can easily slash wastes by a third or more. A trailblazer in this field, the 3M Company halved its hazardous waste flows within a decade of launching a corporation-wide program, boosting its profits in the process and leading other companies to re-examine their manufacturing technologies.

Scientists at AT&T's Bell Laboratories, for example, are redesigning their manufacturing operations to eliminate waste generation. Early successes have led to a set of corporate goals for AT&T's worldwide operations, employing some 275,000 workers. Prominent among these are the phaseout of all CFC use by the end of 1994, a 95-percent reduction in toxic air emissions by the end of 1995, a reduction in waste from manufacturing processes of 25 percent by the end of 1994, a reduction in paper use of 15 percent by 1994, and a 35-percent paper recycling rate by the end of 1994. Conspicuously absent from the list are goals for reducing carbon emissions and toxic wastes. Including these would permit the comprehensive restructuring of industrial processes that holds the key to building an environmentally sustainable global economy.

Another major potential source of waste reduction lies in the simplification of food packaging. In the United States, consumer expenditures on food packaging now routinely approach or even exceed the net income of farmers. In the interest of attracting customers, items are sometimes buried in three or four layers of wrappings. For the final trip from supermarket to home, yet another set of materials is used in the form of paper or plastic bags, also typically discarded after one use. In an environmentally sustainable world, excessive packaging is likely to be eliminated, either by consumer resistance, a packaging tax, or governmental regulations, and throwaway grocery bags will have been replaced by durable, reusable bags of canvas or other material.

Societies may also decide to replace multisized and -shaped beverage containers with a set of standardized ones made of durable glass that can be reused many times. These could be used for most if not all beverages, such as fruit juices, beer, milk, and soft drinks. Bottlers will simply clean the container, steam off the old label, and add a new one. Containers returned to the supermarket or other outlet might become part of an urban or regional computerized inventory, which would permit their efficient movement from supermarkets or other collection centers to local dairies, breweries, and soft drink bottling plants as needed.

Such a system would save an enormous amount of energy and materials. Going to refillable glass bottles that are used an average of 10 times can reduce the energy use per container by 90 percent. (See Table 1.) The Canadian province of Ontario, where 84 percent of beer is sold in standardized refillable glass bottles, is already moving in this direction. With a stiff deposit, 98 percent of these refillable bottles are returned for reuse. If the goal is to satisfy human needs as fully as possible without disrupting the earth's ecosystem, then the attraction of refillable glass bottles for the marketing of beverages is obvious.

In addition to reusing and recycling metal, glass, and paper, a sustainable society also recycles nutrients. In nature, one organism's waste is another's sustenance; in urban societies, however, human sewage has become a troublesome source of pollutants in rivers, lakes, and coastal waters. The nutrients in human wastes can be reused safely as long as the process includes measures to prevent the spread of disease.

Cities in Japan, South Korea, and China have long demonstrated this kind of nutrient recycling. Human waste is systematically returned there to the land in vegetable-growing greenbelts around cities. Intensively farmed cropland surrounding some urban areas produces vegetables year-round using greenhouses or plastic covering during the winter to extend the growing season. Perhaps the best model is Shanghai: after modestly expanding its

Table 1. Energy Consumption Per Use for 12-Ounce Beverage Containers

Container	Energy Use (Btus)
Aluminum can, used once	7,050
Steel can, used once	5,950
Recycled steel can	3,880
Glass beer bottle, used once	3,730
Recycled aluminum can	2,550
Recycled glass beer bottle	2,530
Refillable glass bottle, used 10 times	610

urban political boundaries to facilitate sewage recycling, the city now produces a surplus of vegetables that are exported to other cities in China.

Some cities will probably find it more efficient to use treated human sewage to fertilize aquacultural operations. A steady flow of nutrients from human waste into ponds can supply food for a vigorously growing population of algae that in turn are consumed by fish. In Calcutta, a sewage-fed aquaculture system now provides 20,000 kilograms of fresh fish each day for sale in the city. In a society with a scarcity of protein, such an approach, modeled after nature's nutrient recycling, can both eliminate a troublesome waste problem and generate a valuable food resource.

Strong community recycling programs will include composting of food and yard wastes, which now make up one fourth of U.S. garbage. People will have the option of composting at home or, if they are unable to do so, putting such wastes out for curbside pickup. A lost art in many communities, household composting is being fostered in Seattle, Washington, by a volunteer network of "master composters." Composting not only reduces garbage flows, it provides a rich source of humus for gardening, lessening the need to buy chemical fertilizers to maintain lawn and garden fertility.

By systematically reducing the flow of waste and reusing or recycling most remaining materials, the basic needs of the planet's growing number of human residents can be satisfied without destroying our very life-support systems. Moving in this direction will not only create a far more livable environment with less air and water pollution, it will also eliminate the unsightly litter that blights the landscape in many industrial societies today.

Understanding What You Read

1. Explain the difference between reusing and recycling materials. Which option saves the most energy? What would be a better option than either of these?
2. What two conditions of the 1970s and 1980s stimulated interest in recycling and reusing?

3. What concerns are likely to accelerate this trend in the 1990s?
4. What are the advantages and disadvantages of using refillable glass bottles of standard sizes for beverages?

Writing About What You Read

Write a proposal for a recycling program for your school or community, explaining in detail how it would work and why it should be adopted.

NOEL PERRIN

A professor of environmental studies at Dartmouth College, Perrin (b. 1927) is the author of many books, including *First Person Rural* (1978), *Giving Up the Gun: Japan's Reversion to the Sword* (1979), *Second Person Rural* (1980), and *Third Person Rural* (1983). *Solo: Life with an Electric Car* (1992) is about a cross–country trip in the car he named Solo and about its subsequent life as a commuter vehicle. "Have Plug, Will Commute" is an article about the experience published in the *Washington Post* (August 21, 1991).

Have Plug, Will Commute

I AM driving my new electric car through northern California. In the little farm town of Ignacio, two men who work for a feed company come up to check us out. "I've seen 'em on TV," one of them says, "but I never seen a real one before. How fast will it go?"

Now I'm in Wyoming, at a big motel in Laramie. I have just taken out the 50-foot extension cord I keep in back and am plugging in for the night. Summoned by his wife, the motel's maintenance man comes over to examine my solar panels. "That's what I need," he says. "That's what we *all* need."

Now I'm stopping to look at the courthouse in Albion, Ind. A small crowd gathers to look at the car. One joker asks me if I can drive on rainy days. (I can.)

Once upon a time, 90 years ago, half the cars in America were electric. Electrics were clean, quiet and much easier to drive than the early gas models. Someday in the future, electrics will again comprise half of all U.S. cars. Maybe even 100 percent. That will be because they don't use gas, don't use oil, don't pollute.

Right now, however, electrics are scarce. Not a single one is registered

4

in the District of Columbia. There are nine in Maryland. Virginia doesn't know how many it has. Counting mine, Vermont has two. Only in California do you find a significant number—and even there the number is just barely significant. Out of 16 million California cars, maybe 200 are electrics.

I have been one of the small band of electric car owners for four months now. I've been using it to commute to work. Already I understand why electrics began to fade out 80 years ago; they have serious faults.

I bought my car in Santa Rosa, Calif.—picked it up at the factory for $17,500. Solar Electric Engineering of Santa Rosa is one of the three small companies in the United States now making electrics, usually adapting them from gasoline cars. Next year the number of such companies will jump to five or six. By 1995 there will be at least a dozen companies in the business, including Ford and GM.

8   Unlike the mostly plastic solar vehicles you see on TV, my car is as mainstream as they come; it began life as a 1985 Ford Escort station wagon. Solar Electric bought it last spring and converted it. It was their 56th car.

First they stripped out all the gasoline stuff, such as the motor, the exhaust system and radiator. Then they installed a little 23-horsepower electric motor, made by General Electric. This is a sealed unit and is said to require no maintenance for the first 300,000 miles.

Next they put in about half a ton of batteries. Eight went in front where the old gas engine used to be, 10 in the rear. Then they installed an on-board charger. The early electrics back in 1910 didn't have on-board chargers; to get power you had to take your car to a special charging station.

Today, I can charge my car anyplace there's electricity. Once I plugged my long orange cord into a reading lamp in a dingy motel room in Citrus Heights, Calif. Usually I just plug into my own garage.

12   The car is mounted with a special set of Goodyear tires, inflated to a pressure of 60 pounds. These are designed both to handle the terrible weight of all those batteries and to reduce rolling resistance. Also, there are four solar panels on the roof and two more smaller ones on the hood, an option that cost me an extra $1,800; plenty of electric cars don't have solar panels. People think the car's power comes entirely from these, and they love to make cracks such as "So I guess you stay home after dark, huh?" Who do they think I am, Cinderella? With 18 batteries, I can drive just fine at night. The panels need sunlight, yes, but they generate only 5 or 6 percent of the power the car uses. Their real job is to keep the batteries trickle-charged full, and thus to prolong their life.

I drove my electric part of the way from Santa Rosa to my home in New England, and towed it the rest (people usually assumed I was taking it to a meet). It's been a joy as a commuting car. I live 13 miles from where I work, in Hanover, N.H. I can and do cruise along the interstate at 65 mph, hills and all. When I'm headed up the steep hill into Hanover without a running start, however, I couldn't possibly go over 35. No problem. The speed limit there is 30.

Once in town, the car does even better. Twice a day, at rush hour, long lines of gasoline cars "idle" at the lights, kicking out clouds of hydrocarbons. Not mine. Electric cars don't idle. When I'm waiting at a light, my engine simply shuts off. When the light turns green, I step on the accelerator and off I go.

Driving across the country is quite another matter. So is any long trip— or even a medium-length one. The two things that killed electrics back in 1910 were the low speed and the short range. A typical electric vehicle 80 years ago had a top speed of about 18 mph and a driving range of perhaps 40 miles. That was fine as long as the competition was horses.

As I've said, the speed problem is mostly solved. As for range, there has been some improvement, but it is still a problem. When I was driving east, I could regularly go 57 or 58 miles on the level roads of Illinois and Indiana before I had to stop and recharge. Even at home in Vermont, where there is no such thing as a level road, I can count on 45 miles. But if I wanted to meet a friend at Burlington Airport, 90 miles away? I'd have to take the little farm pickup. It runs on gas.

What's been needed since the first electrics were built in 1895 is a better battery. Manufacturers used the standard lead-acid battery back then; they still do. The Electric Power Research Institute in Palo Alto, Calif., is busy testing new kinds of batteries right now. Ford, Chrysler and GM have jointly formed a research group called the Advanced Battery Consortium. This year they'll spend $35 million on battery development. But so far, all the alternatives are either too expensive or too unreliable for ordinary consumer use.

There seems little doubt that a better battery will soon be along. (Thomas Edison, I admit, said the same thing in 1903—adding that he would be the one to bring it along.) Until it appears, though, electric cars will remain suitable only for commuter use. You can't solve the distance problem just by adding more lead-acid batteries, because the lead weighs so much. The 18 batteries in my car are all it can take. Add two more, and you'd have to redesign the suspension system. Besides, even if you could keep adding lead-acid batteries, you'd *still* have a problem. They are horribly slow to charge.

So where do the advantages of the electric car lie? They lie in its relation to the environment. Every day, thousands of gallons of used motor oil get dumped into fields and streams all over the United States. Not one pint comes from electrics. Every day, several hundred million gallons of gasoline get turned into exhaust fumes. Not one whiff of this bad air comes from an electric.

Ah, but electrics do have to get their electricity from somewhere. Are *those* places pollution-free? Sometimes yes. My car draws nearly all its power from an array of big solar panels on the roof of my house, plus its own six little ones.

Solar arrays are not, of course, convenient for everybody—not if you live in an apartment, for example. Besides, they're expensive. Suppose there were to be a million electric cars by 1995. Where would most of them get their electricity? Wouldn't it have to be from power plants? And not just clean, safe hydro, but also coal, oil and nuclear? Yes, it would. Pollution might be reduced; it certainly wouldn't be eliminated.

And yet, there's an answer to that too. Many utilities have surplus capacity between midnight and dawn, when demand for electricity is low. Whole power plants lie idle.

But night is just when you plug in your commuter car. It has been estimated that *20 million* electric cars could charge up every night without any need to build one additional generating plant in the United States. Better yet, they would be charging cleanly. According to studies done at the University of Southern California, making power for those 20 million cars would produce at most 10 percent of the pollution caused by 20 million gasoline cars traveling the same number of miles. On the road, electrics are, of course, zero-emission.

24
I'm hoping in three or four years to have a set of batteries that will enable me to drive freely to the airport. I'm hoping that as the volume of electric-car production rises, prices will drop. Meanwhile, it's a good feeling to be driving silently and harmlessly in to work.

Understanding What You Read

1. What are the advantages of an electric car?
2. What are the disadvantages?

Writing About What You Read

1. Someone you know is about to buy a new car that will be used mainly for commuting to work and for weekend errands. Write a persuasive letter explaining why he or she should buy an electric car. Make sure that you mention the disadvantages, which you will argue are outweighed by the advantages.
2. Someone you know is about to buy an electric car. Write a letter warning of the problems of an electric car and persuading that person to buy a conventional gasoline–powered car instead.

LINDA LEUZZI

Leuzzi (b. 1947), a free-lance writer who lives in New York City, has written numerous articles for periodicals. "Eagles" was published in the November 1991 *New Woman*.

Eagles

"THIS IS what I'd like for an anniversary present," I said, pointing to the glossy magazine. My husband planned to give me a diamond wedding band, but the magazine touted a 12-day trip to Michigan's Huron-Manistee National Forest that included bunking out in a no-frills cabin, cooking meals for a group, and hiking through miles of woods and swampy areas to help save bald eagles, an endangered species. Most husbands wouldn't understand a wife who would choose a wash-and-wear adventure over perfectly cut diamonds, but my man did. He rolled his eyes and acquiesced.

I've lived about 15 miles from Manhattan's canyons most of my life. I'd never even gone to camp. So why did this city girl, who carefully applies red lipstick before going anywhere, opt to help save a bird I never met? I'd been feeling so angry and helpless for a long time about all the wildlife and environmental disasters stacking up that the bald eagles' plight triggered an emotional last straw for me. More than 40,000 once graced our skies; now there are less than 4,000 in the continental United States. Maybe playing it safe just wouldn't cut it anymore. I wanted to turn 70 one day without a lot of regrets about the things I could have done. So I signed up with Earthwatch, an international organization whose volunteers pay to work side by side with scientists on environmental, wildlife, and cultural research projects around the world. Twenty-three thousand volunteers, some with no experience (like me), had already taken the plunge.

My friends were excited, or at least intrigued ("You always did strange things," said my glamorous executive friend Sandy). My mother despaired that I would be swallowed by some abominable creature in the woods. My mate wasn't exactly tap dancing. But I wanted adventure.

I got it pronto. On the second night of my wildlife foray in the Great Lakes region, four guys and I shared a cabin that had a bathroom door that wouldn't close. We rose at sunrise, took quick showers, made our lunch, and bolted out the door for early morning assignments. There I was, recording on a clipboard habitat information about eagle perches while listing at a 45-degree angle on steep inclines loaded with aspen, white pine, and birch trees, grabbing onto anything that would anchor me to the ground so I wouldn't plunge into the Alcona Dam Pond.

There were times my thighs screamed and times when I prayed to quell my fear of heights. But I found the work absorbing and sometimes exhilarat-

4

ing. And the forest—well, it was spectacular. One night I tracked eagles with Ed, a strapping college student who took me through bogs and marshy areas where we balanced on fallen trees, trying to avoid the muddy water that threatened to slosh through our shoes. In the twilight, we thrashed through some of the most beautiful vegetation I'd ever seen.

But why were we there? Around 40 percent of the bald eagles breeding in the lower peninsula of Michigan nest along the Au Sable, Manistee, and Muskegon rivers. Because of the eagles' threatened status, a major power company had to submit a report on how the eagles were affected by 11 hydroelectric dams on those rivers. As part of the study, 12 volunteers like myself would track eagles along the Manistee and Au Sable rivers, recording the characteristics of the birds and their perching sites. Several eagles had already been trapped and released wearing tiny transmitters.

The adventure began with an afternoon crash course, where we met the dozen young Earthwatch staffers and interns who taught us the ropes. We learned that although the overall bald eagle population in Michigan had improved, it still wasn't great. Our project leader, Bill Bowerman, a 30-year-old research biologist with Michigan State University's Department of Fisheries and Wildlife and Pesticide Control Center who had worked with the birds for six years, filled us in on the statistics. There are 177 breeding pairs of eagles living in the wilds of Michigan this year, he said, an upswing from the late 1970s when the count was only 88. He attributed the resurgence to the banning of DDT and PCBs,[1] which make their way into the food chain, causing eagles to lay thinner-shelled, more fragile eggs and weakening the birds' immune systems.

8   The young scientist was pleased about their comeback but still uneasy. Bald eagles are federally listed as "endangered" in most of the United States, except for six states including Michigan, where eagles are considered "threatened." Bowerman felt that the downgrading from endangered to threatened left room for lax enforcement. And bald eagles that nest near the Great Lakes have six times the contaminants in their bodies of inland-nesting birds, he said. Chemicals like DDT and PCBs continue to contaminate food and water sources for years after they're used. So the Michigan eagles already had two strikes against them. What's more, 90 percent of these birds don't make it to adulthood, which occurs around their fifth or sixth year. Some eaglets fall out of their nests and don't survive. Some just never catch on when it comes to foraging their own food. Modern living drives in the final stake. Adult eagles will abandon their nesting and feeding sites when human activity comes too near. Poaching, accidental shooting, and electrocution from power wires used as perches are also major enemies.

[1]Toxic chemicals: DDT is an insecticide banned in the United States in 1972 and in some European countries in the 1960s, still used in developing countries; PCB refers to polychlorinated biphenyl, a toxic substance once used in the electrical industry, banned in 1979 in the United States.

Onto this scene arrived our band of Earthwatch volunteers, determined to play a role, however small, in the eagles' survival. Our group—made up of teachers, psychologists, an administrative assistant, an entrepreneur, an accountant, a high school student, a wildlife activist, and a writer—ranged in age from 17 to 59. When there was time to spare, we sat at the kitchen table, talking about who we were and what had brought us to Michigan.

Our anything-can-happen schedules were mostly fun. But I did question what I was doing there once or twice. Like the day spent sitting on a flatbed truck in an open field, plotting locations on a map while about 30 black flies bit my face and neck.

But then there were those special moments, when the reason we were there exploded before us like a fireworks display. When we least expected it, we would observe an eagle soaring above us in all its proud toughness. Or on peaceful silvery mornings, when we shoved our motorboats out at sunrise and slowly cruised the shoreline and nature put on a show. Watching a beaver pop his head up to make a V in the water, swinging around an irregular bend to spy a pretty, tiny island of cattails, watching an eagle land in a red oak tree less than 200 feet away—I thought, it just couldn't get much better.

I also learned a great deal—and not just about bald eagles. Terry Grubb, a research wildlife biologist with the Rocky Mountain U.S. Forest Service in Tempe, Arizona, joined us for a few days. Tapped by Exxon, Grubb had spent June and July of 1989 cleaning up 100 bald eagles in Prince William Sound after the *Valdez*[2] oil-spill debacle. Scores of eagles had died in the woods, he told us. But they had not been the only wildlife tragedy: we also heard about the seals, covered with gunk, swimming around lethargically before they died and their bodies sank, making it difficult, if not impossible, to estimate the number dead.

As part of our project we helped Grubb test a net launcher, a radio-controlled device that catapults a 30 × 30-foot string net over eagles while they're on the ground. The birds, lured in by food, are immobilized by the net. Their feet are grabbed first so the deadly talons don't lash out. Then blood samples are taken and the birds are fitted with a transmitter, backpack-style, and banded. Unfortunately, we didn't get a chance to help trap the birds. That job remained for the next team of volunteers.

Before I knew it, our departure day arrived. How did I feel overall about my bald eagle experience? Pretty wonderful. I wasn't great at field work but I found I was tougher than I thought. And more flexible. The experience with my comrades, people I'd never met before who looked after and encouraged me, reaffirmed my trust in human nature. I also felt better about the future. The project's young interns and staffers were pursuing careers like avian toxicology and wildlife management. It was empowering to see self-

12

---

[2]The *Exxon Valdez* went aground in Prince William Sound in Alaska in 1989, spilling vast amounts of oil.

reliant, attractive women in their early 20s scramble nimbly up and down inclines. This new generation wants to preserve the green things and the creatures they grew up with as well as earn a living.

And then there was the importance of the project itself. The habitat work we did, marking and determining what kinds of trees the eagles preferred, will help national parks and protected wildlife areas maintain the right type of perch trees. And our tracking will help establish how far a bird's territory goes. That is valuable information land-management services need in order to allocate space for the eagles. The birds will need lots of it if they are to survive.

16   I'm back home now where life is pretty predictable. When I want to get around, I hop into my car instead of a pickup truck or van. My dogs and cats are the only "wildlife" I see, and I look out on rows of neatly kept homes instead of stands of trees. My recycling efforts have increased dramatically, however. Paper towels are out; dishrags and sponges are in. I have swapped plastic for waxed paper, bought a string bag for local shopping, and choose biodegradable products whenever I can. Do I ever dream of leaving New York and going off to track eagles? Frankly, no. But I don't feel helpless anymore; collectively what my group did will help more eagles endure and prosper. That's a powerful feeling—beats getting diamonds any day.

Understanding What You Read

1. Why are eagles increasing in number in Michigan?
2. List several major hazards that eagles face.

Writing About What You Read

In concluding, the writer expresses hope that what she has done will help more eagles endure and prosper. If you have ever faced down feelings of helplessness in the face of environmental problems, explain how you addressed them.

FRANCES CAIRNCROSS

Cairncross (b. 1944) is a journalist who specializes in making economic issues accessible to general readers. Since 1989 she has been the environmental editor of the *Economist,* and she is especially skilled in explaining how economics and the environment are connected.

"The Challenge to Companies" is from her book *Costing the Earth: The Challenge for Governments, the Opportunities for Business* (1992).

The Challenge to Companies

FOR MOST COMPANIES, the outbreak of environmentalism that began in the late 1980s is either a threat or an irrelevance. The managers who have been packing conferences on environmental law, pollution technology, and green auditing have been driven more by anxiety about the costs of getting an environmental decision wrong—an expensive lawsuit, a planning application refused, angry customers, or worried workers—than the opportunities from getting it right. Only in marketing departments has the advent of the green consumer caused a quiver of excitement.

Beyond a doubt the new greenery will impose costs on companies. Yet it also represents an extraordinary opportunity, perhaps the biggest opportunity for enterprise and invention the industrial world has ever seen. Those who spot how to make the most of this will flourish.

The impact will be immense within companies. The demand for cleaner products and processes will change the way they think about innovation. Prodded by green consumers, companies will ask their suppliers quite new questions about the origins of their raw materials and the way they are handled; cornered by regulations, companies will give growing attention to ways of disposing of waste. When a new product is conceived, an early question will be "But what happens at the end of its life?"

The costs of green policies will be an extra burden on industry. Often, indeed, governments will load onto industry costs that they feel unwilling to impose directly on voters. Companies investing in the reduction of emissions will have less cash to spend on developing new products; management time spent monitoring environmental performance is time not available for corporate growth. To that extent, industry can become greener only by growing more slowly.

But this is an inadequate and dispiriting account of what is likely to happen. At a conference on sustainable development in Bergen in May 1990, Björn Stigson, head of ABB Fläkt, a Swedish engineering firm, produced an intriguing analogy. "We treat nature like we treated workers a hundred years ago," he said. "We included then no cost for the health and social security of workers in our calculations, and today we include no cost for the health and security of nature." Environmental protection may be to the next 50 years what government-financed public services have been to the past 50: a drag on growth, true, and a large burden on corporate costs; but also an enormous and hard-to-quantify source of increased human well-being.

It will also be the source of a radical shift in consumer tastes. Developing products that use nature most frugally at both ends of their lives will call forth whole new generations of technology. The change will be more pervasive than those that followed the invention of the steam engine or of the computer. Fortunes await those who devise less expensive ways to dispose of plastics or to clean up contaminated soil. The great engineering projects of the next century will not be the civil engineering of dams or bridges, but the bio-engineering of sewage works and waste tips. Industry has before it that most precious of prospects: a spur to innovate.

The world will not grow cleaner without the cooperation of industry; for only through industry can technologies be developed which will satisfy human needs while making fewer demands on the environment. The challenge for government and for environmentalists is to spot ways of creating the right incentives so that industry finds it profitable to be clean and unprofitable to be dirty.

8   Many environmentalists wince at the very mention of industry. As they rightly see it, industrial activity is the immediate cause of most environmental damage. It is industry that spews gases into the atmosphere, dumps poison in rivers, builds factories on open fields, and digs mines in rain forests. It is industry, too, that makes the products that pollute: the packaging and plastics, the cars, and the disposables. Much environmentalism is a new version of the old hatred of business by the utopian left. Many of the policies promoted by radical greens are more concerned with stopping companies from doing whatever makes money than with making the world a cleaner, greener place.

Such utopianism is foolish. Perhaps in the Middle Ages there was a time when human activity had little lasting impact on nature's balance. That day is gone for good. Today, 5.6 billion people live on the earth; within a century that number will climb past 10 billion, perhaps to 15 billion. Even in the poorest countries, where the lives of millions are barely touched by industry as the developed world knows it, the impact on the environment is already immense. Sheer numbers will inevitably make that impact greater still. And that even without the universal desire for the fruits of development. Bringing water supplies and electricity to villages are sure ways of increasing the demands the third world makes on the environment; yet they save women hours of walking to fetch water and find wood. These saved hours mean healthier mothers, better nourished children, and improved hygiene.

It is utopian, too, to think that the fairly poor will not want the trappings of Western wealth. Top of the shopping list of every liberated East European is a family car. A senior official of Britain's Friends of the Earth recalls with pain the hostile reception he got when he delivered his standard green lecture on the environmental damage done by cars to an audience of trade union officials. Many of the products that harm the environment have made life easier for people who can still remember that life was less pleasant before. Washing machines use more water than hand washing but mean less work;

plastic packaging preserves food longer and means fewer shopping trips; chemical herbicides kill bugs more quickly than hoeing.

Above all, disposable products—be they diapers, plastic cups, or hospital gowns—have frequently brought huge increases in convenience, at the cost of extra pressure on the environment. Disposables save labor, and labor is a resource that will be increasingly scarce in rich countries if population growth does not revive. As labor costs go up, disposable products of all kinds will become more attractive. However much the greenest greens may bemoan the "throw-away" society, powerful economic forces will continue to encourage it.

ROLE OF TECHNOLOGY

It is important for environmentalists to understand these forces. Rather than yearning for a world that can never be recreated, they need to help develop incentives for industry to support human needs in the least polluting way. The best hope for the environment lies in accepting what Paul Gray, former president of the Massachusetts Institute of Technology, has called "the paradox of technological development." The industrial economy causes environmental damage, but it also offers ways to repair that damage.

From its earliest days technology has enabled mankind to use the earth's resources more frugally. The wheel requires less energy to shift a heavy weight than does the sledge. The closed stove delivers the same amount of heat as the open fire with far less fuel. Domesticated grain produces more protein from an acre of land than does wild grass.

Technology can still perform such ancient conjuring tricks. Indeed, the ability of technology to find ways of squeezing more and more output from the same volume of input, especially if given the right price signals, helps explain why pessimists, who prophesied environmental catastrophe through the exhaustion of a vital raw material, have so frequently turned out to be wrong. Consider, for instance, these words, delivered by President Theodore Roosevelt in 1905 when America's railways were gobbling wood for sleepers: "Unless the vast forests of the United States can be made ready to meet the vast demands which this [economic] growth will inevitably bring, commercial disaster, that means disaster to the whole country, is inevitable. The railroads must have ties. If the present rate of forest destruction is allowed to continue with nothing to offset it, a timber famine in the future is inevitable."

Within a matter of years, the voracious demand for wooden sleepers by American railways had been slowed by the development of techniques for treating wood with creosote, then by the replacement of wooden ties with concrete ones.

President Roosevelt was not uniquely alarmist. Forty years earlier, a British economist, W. S. Jevons, had published a book called *The Coal Question* in which he expressed deep fears for the future for British industry:

I draw the conclusion that I think anyone else would draw, that we cannot long maintain our present rate of consumption; that we can never advance to the higher amounts of consumption supposed . . . the check to our progress must become perceptible considerably within a century from the present time; that the cost of fuel must rise, perhaps within a lifetime, to a rate threatening our commercial and manufacturing supremacy; and the conclusion is inevitable; that our happy progressive condition is a thing of limited duration.

That was in 1865, only five years after oil, now the world's largest single source of primary energy, was discovered. Calculations for 1968 reckoned that at current annual rates of demand, enough fossil fuels (coal, oil, and gas) remained for the next 2,500 years.

The erroneous pessimism of Roosevelt and Jevons ought to be a reminder to those who now forecast environmental catastrophe. It is, of course, extremely hard to guess correctly the course of technology. (Partha Dasgupta defends economists from charges of unique myopia by citing the proceedings of a gathering of British scientists in 1876: "Although we cannot say what remains to be invented, we can say that there seems no reason to believe that electricity will be used as a practical mode of power."[1]) But we need to be reminded that technologies have cycles, and that public alarm at their side effects may frequently coincide with the arrival of a new technology that does not have those side effects but may well have others. Technology tends to solve one environmental problem by creating another. But it retains the ability to deliver unexpected solutions to apparently insoluble dilemmas.

The past century has seen two particularly remarkable examples of the ability of technology to make more from less. The first is energy. Between 1900 and the 1960s, the quantity of coal needed to generate a kilowatt-hour of electricity fell from nearly 7 pounds to less than 1 pound. More striking still, the entire world's per head demand for commercial energy in the ten years to 1987, a period of fast population growth, did not change, while wealth per head rose by 12% in real terms.

20 A glance at car technology suggests there could be even more efficiency ahead, given the right price signals. Renault has already built a prototype of a car that can do 100 kilometers on 3 liters of gas in town, 2.2 liters on the open road; Toyota is developing one that will do the same distance on 2.6 liters of diesel in the city, 2.1 liters on the open road. At present, the sales-weighted fuel economy of new cars in America is 8.4 liters per 100km. Remember that those prototypes were developed at a time when oil prices in real terms were declining worldwide. Calculations by General Motors suggest that the fuel price in America per vehicle mile, in 1989 prices, fell from 4 cents at the start of the 1980s to 2 cents by the end.

The increased ability of the world to feed itself has been even more striking. Anyone who looked at the terrifying projections for global popula-

[1]From Partha Dasgupta's essay "Exhaustible Resources," in *The Fragile Environment*, 1989, edited by Laurie Friday and Ronald Laskey.

tion growth in the early 1960s found it unimaginable that the world could escape a devastating famine in the next three decades. There have indeed been some famines, although most, like the one in Ethiopia in the mid-1980s, have been partly linked to political disorder. But the appalling catastrophes that might have taken place have not. Instead, food output more than doubled in the world's poor countries between 1965 and 1988, well ahead of their soaring populations. The world's two most populous countries, China and India, have become self-sufficient in grain. The proportion of the world's people suffering from malnutrition has fallen (although the absolute number has increased). To a large extent, this transformation has been the accomplishment of the "green revolution," the breeding of new high-yielding strains of cereals, especially of rice. One reason for Africa's growing hunger is that there has been no green revolution[2] in its staple food crops of cassava, millet, and corn.

The message is clear, and repeated often throughout history. It is that technology can often be environmentally helpful, finding substitutes for scarce natural resources or allowing existing resources to be stretched further. The task for government is to encourage industry to develop such technologies. One of the primary difficulties with this simple precept is the law of unintended consequences. Time and again, an apparently benign technology has turned out to have a sting in its tail.

Nothing sums up this point more poignantly than the life of Thomas Midgeley. A self-taught chemist on the research staff of General Motors, Midgeley and his team solved the problem of engine knock by discovering tetraethyl lead in 1921. This breakthrough led to the development of high-octane gas, which in turn made feasible more fuel-efficient high-compression gas engines.

Then in the late 1920s, Midgeley was given the task of finding a non-toxic, nonflammable substitute for the refrigerants in commercial use at the time. These were ammonia, methyl chloride, and sulphur dioxide, whose unpleasant characteristics made them unsuitable for use in the home. Midgeley came up with a compound called dichlorofluoromethane (freon 12). He demonstrated its safety to a meeting of the American Chemical Society in 1930 by inhaling a lungful of the gas, then using it to blow out a lighted candle. The product ensured the success of the Frigidaire division of General Motors and became invaluable in the Second World War as an aerosol propellant for insecticides such as DDT.

The life of the man who put lead into gas and chlorofluorocarbons into the ozone layer ended in 1944. In 1940, he had been crippled by an attack of polio. He developed a pulley and harness contraption to help himself in and out of bed but strangled himself with the harness. It was a peculiarly

24

[2]A radical change in farming practices, beginning in the 1950s, to increase food production by intensive use of fertilizers, pesticides, irrigation, and high-yield grains.

appropriate demonstration of the unintended and malign consequence of even the most benign technological innovation.

Once a substance proves malign, moreover, it may be extremely difficult to get it out of the system. A side effect of the green revolution has been a large increase in world use of chemical pesticides and fertilizers. Yet the world cannot easily afford to return to the old varieties of grain that needed less of both, at least not without the development of new, genetically engineered varieties that may have other drawbacks. Even when industry agrees to get rid of a harmful product, the alternative may be much less convenient. Manufacturers of vacuum pumps voluntarily agreed to get rid of poly-chlorinated benzyls (PCBs), used in vacuum-pump oil, in 1971. Yet a suitable substitute has not been found. A small quantity of mercurials in emulsion paint provided excellent protection against mold. The alternative has been to use several different compounds in much higher concentrations, without being entirely sure about the ways in which those compounds react on each other.

Often, one environmental gain may be possible only if accompanied by a loss. Put a catalytic converter on a car and its fuel efficiency declines: the engine emits less nitrous oxide and sulphur dioxide but more global-warming carbon dioxide. Ban CFCs, and it becomes harder to insulate refrigerators and buildings. The ozone layer is protected but at the expense of higher greenhouse gas emissions. Biotechnology will pose many more questions of the same sort; for instance, is it better to have genetically engineered crops that require no pesticides, or may the environmental costs ultimately exceed the benefits?

28   Yet with all these reservations, the fact remains that industry has the ability to squeeze more output from natural resources. Inventive industry can find new ways of achieving the same impact on its market: to provide people with warmth, for instance, it may be more sensible to sell them better home insulation than more electricity. Increasingly, value is added by design, infor-mation, and quality; people spend more on attributes of a product that have nothing to do with the quantity of material in its manufacture and everything to do with the application of human ingenuity.

As manufacturing processes become better controlled, waste is reduced. As products from Coke cans to calculators become lighter, it takes less raw material and less energy to make them. Government needs to find ways of encouraging industry to use raw materials frugally. Such frugality brings double benefits. For every pound of raw material used is ultimately a pound of waste: use less water and there will be less dirty water; use less packaging and landfills will not be full of discarded paper and plastic.

The best way of ensuring that industry applies technology to solving environmental problems, rather than creating new ones, is to give the right price signals. Only if prices reflect the true cost of using environmental resources will companies start to value them as they value labor and capital, and aim to improve their productivity in the use of the environment as they strive for higher productivity of labor and capital.

A study by Robert Repetto of the WRI[3] developed a measure of productivity for the American electricity industry which tries to take account of environmental productivity. Making assumptions about the damage caused by power-station emissions, he reckoned that the cost of these unpriced outputs from the electricity industry in the mid-1980s was almost as great as the value of labor or the fuel the industry used. If the electricity industry had accounted for its success in cutting emissions, especially in the 1970s, when measuring its overall productivity, its performance would have been between two and three times as good as it appears from conventional estimates.

Setting price signals, along with devising regulations or standards, is government's job. The green revolution is underpinned by governmental intervention. But industry and government have a common interest in making sure that such intervention leads to the greatest possible increase in the quality of the environment at the lowest possible cost. Companies want to try to make sure that environmental standards are set at levels they can reach but their competitors cannot; governments want to make sure that companies put cash and inventive energy into devising environmentally benign technologies. Once a company comes up with a green technology that allows it to meet a higher environmental standard than its competitors, government can insist that the higher standard become universal.

This is not what has happened in the past. Managers at environmental conferences are there because they have been trained to think of government regulation as a nuisance, not an opportunity. Yet when government intervenes, through regulation or through setting price signals, it creates new markets. Suddenly, electric cars become profitable; waste-management shares boom; desulphurization plants are in demand.

Both industry and government need to realize how far the market for environmental technology will be created and sustained by government intervention. Consumers' taste for green products will boom and fade, although always returning to a higher level of environmental consciousness from every trough. In the recession years of the mid-1990s, the green consumer will be replaced, at least at the mass market level, by the penny-pincher. Only the wealthier, trend-setting shoppers will pay a premium for green goods.

But the market for environmentally friendlier products will remain. It will be sustained by a number of things: by the rising legal penalties for polluting accidents, by the difficulty of persuading local communities to accept new factories that may pollute, and above all, by ever-tighter regulations about waste disposal. Governments, harried by voters, will continue to press for tighter standards for wastewater, for dirty air, and above all for solid rubbish,

[3]World Resources Institute, an organization that researches and publishes information on sustainable growth.

both hazardous and harmless. As these pressures will fall directly on companies (and on waste-disposal authorities), they will be largely hidden from voters, who will assume that they are being offered a free ride to greenery.

36   In fact, government regulations will raise the returns on all kinds of environmentally friendly investments. A water-treatment plant, uneconomical in the early 1980s, will look like a much better buy once the cost of sewage discharges goes up and the insurance premiums for an accidental spill become astronomical. A precipitator in the smokestack, once ridiculed by the finance director, will seem a bargain when the alternative is an entirely new plant.

For governments the trick will be to devise controls that foster green technology. That will be difficult. The temptation will be to regulate pollution by double-guessing companies: laying down the technologies they must use, instead of setting targets for the output of pollution and leaving corporate ingenuity to come up with answers. If governments seek the cooperation of the greenest companies, they will have to avoid protecting a particular technological solution to a given environmental problem.

There are dangers, of course, in relying on a confluence of interest between government and industry to raise environmental standards. Companies will always be tempted to press government to set standards in terms of a technology that they have devised, rather than in terms of its impact; and for government it will often be easier to do things that way. Large companies with political clout will see the alternative to, say, CFCs in terms of another chemical; or the alternative to cars running on leaded gas as cars running on lead-free gas.

But standards set in terms of specific technologies discourage innovation. That often comes not from the politically weighty giants, but from the minnows; environmental innovation, like many other kinds, tends to come from "outsiders," like small companies, suppliers, and foreign firms.

40   These are the companies for whom the environment presents the greatest opportunity. The new technologies that they invent are the world's best hope of enjoying a continued rise in living standards without putting greater pressure on the environment. The cleanest countries will be those whose environmental rules make it easiest for such companies to flourish. The most successful companies will be those that best turn such green rules to their own advantage.

Understanding What You Read

1. List several opportunities for business resulting from the demands of green consumers.
2. Cairncross says that in 1968 it seemed that there was enough fossil fuel to last for the next 2,500 years. What factors may limit the use of that fuel?

3. List several trade-offs of the green revolution.
4. Give several examples of how government regulations and intervention can create new markets. Explain why the author believes that standards should not be set in terms of specific technologies.

Writing About What You Read

Cairncross quotes the head of a Swedish engineering firm in paragraph 5. Write an essay explaining the statement and give specific examples of business practices that might improve "the health and security of nature."

BILL MCKIBBEN

McKibben (b. 1961) has published in *The New Yorker, The New York Review of Books,* the *New York Times, Rolling Stone,* and other national publications. His first book, *The End of Nature,* in which "Change the Way We Think: Actions Will Follow" appears, was published in 1989. *The Age of Misinformation* (1992) compares the kind of knowledge available from television with that available from nature.

Change the Way We Think: Actions Will Follow

A HALF HOUR'S hike brings my dog and me to the top of the hill behind my house. I know the hill well by now, each gully and small creek, each big rock, each opening around the edges. I know the places where the deer come, and the coyotes after them. It is no Bald Mountain,[1] no unlogged virgin forest with trees ten feet around, but it is a deep and quiet and lovely place all the same.

Only the thought of what will happen as the new weather kicks in darkens my view: the trees dying, the hillside unable to hold its soil against the rainfall, the gullies sharpening, the deer looking for ever-scarcer browse. And, finally, the scrub and brush colonizing the slopes, clinging to what soil remains. Either that or the cemetery rows of perfect, heat-tolerant genetically improved pines.

[1]In Russian folklore, a wild place where witches congregate, made famous by the Russian composer Modest Mussorgsky in his symphonic tone poem *Night on Bald Mountain.*

From the top of the hill, if I stand on a certain ledge, I can see my house down below, white against the hemlocks. I can see my whole material life—the car, the bedroom, the chimney above the stove. I like that life, I like it enormously. But a choice seems unavoidable. Either that life down there changes, perhaps dramatically, or this life all around me up here changes—passes away.

4   That is a terrible choice. Two years ago, when I got married, my wife and I had the standard hopes and dreams, and their fulfillment seemed not so far away. We love to travel; we had set up our lives so that work wouldn't tie us down. Our house is nice and big—it seemed only a matter of time before it would fill with the racket of children.

As the consequences of the greenhouse effect have become clearer to us, though, we've started to prune and snip our desires. Instead of taking long vacation trips in the car, we ride our bikes on the road by the house. Instead of building a wood-fired hot tub for the backyard (the closest I've ever come to real decadence), we installed exciting new thermal-pane windows. Most of our other changes have been similarly small. We heat with our wood, and we try to keep the house at 55 degrees. We drive much less frequently; we shop twelve times a year, and there are weeks when we do not venture out at all. Though I'm a lousy gardener, I try to grow more and more of our food.

Still, those are the easy things, especially if you live in the country. And they're as much pleasure as sacrifice. It may be icy in most of the house but it's warm cuddled by the stove. I like digging in the garden, though it makes me more nervous than it did when it was pure hobby: if a storm knocks down a tomato plant, I feel slightly queasy. If we don't travel great distances and constantly see new sights, we have come to know the few square miles around us in every season and mood.

But there are harder changes, too, places where the constricting world has begun to bind and pinch. It is dawning on me and my wife that the world we inhabit is not the world we grew up in, the world where our hopes and dreams were formed. That responsibility may mean something new and sad. In other words, we try very hard not to think about how much we'd like a baby.

8   And it may take even more. Sometimes I stand on top of the hill and wonder if someday we'll need to move away, perhaps live closer to other people. Probably that would be more energy-efficient. Would I love the woods enough to leave them behind? I stand up there and look out over the mountain to the east and the lake to the south and the rippling wilderness knolls stretching off to the west—and to the house below with the line of blue smoke trailing out of the chimney. One world or the other will have to change.

And if it is the human world that changes—if this humbler idea begins to win out—what will the planet look like? Will it appeal only to screwballs, people who thrive on a monthly shower and no steady income?

It's hard to draw a detailed picture—it's so much easier to picture the defiant future, for it is merely the extension of our current longings. I've spent my whole life wanting more, so it's hard for me to imagine "less" in any but a negative way. But that imagination is what counts. Changing the way we think is at the heart of the question. If it ever happens, the actions will follow.

For example, to cope with the greenhouse problem, people may need to install more efficient washing machines. But if you buy such a machine and yet continue to feel that it's both your right and your joy to have a big wardrobe, then the essential momentum of our course won't be broken. For big wardrobes imply a world pretty much like our own, where people pile up possessions, and where human desire is the only measure that counts. Even if such a world somehow licks the greenhouse effect, it will still fall in a second for, say, the cornucopia of genetic engineering. On the other hand, you could slash your stock of clothes to a comfortable (or even uncomfortable) minimum and then chip in with your neighbors to buy a more efficient washing machine to which you would lug your dirty laundry. If we reached that point—the point where great closetfuls of clothes seemed slightly absurd, *unnatural*—then we might have begun to climb down from the tottering perch where we currently cling.

"Absurd" and "unnatural" are different from "wrong" or "immoral." This is not a moral argument. There are plenty of good reasons having to do with aesthetics or whimsy to own lots of sharp clothes. (And many more and much better reasons to, say, drive cars or raise large families.) But those reasons may be outweighed by the burden that such desires place on the natural world. And if we could see that clearly, then our thinking might change of its own accord.

In this particular example, the thinking is more radical than the action. If we decided against huge wardrobes (which is to say, against a whole way of looking at ourselves) and against every family's owning a washer (which is to say, against a pervasive individual consumerism), then taking your clothes down the street to wash them would be the most obvious idea in the world. If people *hadn't* changed their minds about such things, these would be obnoxious developments—you'd need to employ secret police to make sure they weren't washing in private. It wouldn't be worth it, and it wouldn't work. But if we had changed our minds, our current ways of life might soon seem as bizarre as the six thousand shoes of Imelda Marcos.[2]

It's normal to imagine that this humbler world would resemble the past. Simply because the atmosphere was cleaner a century ago, though, there's no call to forget all that's been developed since. My wife and I just acquired a fax machine, for instance, on the premise that it makes for graceful, environmentally sound communication—an advanced way to do with less. But if

12

---

[2]Wife of Ferdinand Marcos, former president of the Philippines; her extravagances included buying thousands of pairs of shoes.

communication prospered in a humbler world, transportation might well wither, as people began to live closer not only to their work but to their food supply. Oranges all year round—oranges at any season in the northern latitudes—might prove ambitious beyond our means, just as the tropics might have to learn to do without apples. We—or, at least, our grandchildren—might come to use the "appropriate technologies" of "sustainable development" that we urge on peasants through organizations like the Peace Corps—bicycle-powered pumps, solar cookstoves, and so on. And, as in a less developed country (a phrase that would probably turn into a source of some pride), more Westerners might find their work connected directly with their supper. That is to say, they would farm, which begins to sound a little quaint, a little utopian.

But conventional utopian ideas are not much help, either. Invariably they are designed to advance human happiness, which is found to be suffering as the result of crowding or stress or lack of meaningful work or not enough sex or too much sex. Machinery is therefore abolished, or cities abandoned, or families legislated against—but it's all in the name of man. Dirt under your nails will make you happier!

16 The humbler world I am describing is just the opposite. Human happiness would be of secondary importance. Perhaps it would be best for the planet if we all lived not in kibbutzes or on Jeffersonian farms, but crammed into a few huge cities like so many ants. I doubt a humbler world would be one big happy Pennsylvania Dutch colony.[3] Certain human sadnesses might diminish; other human sadnesses would swell. But that would be beside the point. This is not an attempt at a utopia—as I said, I'm happy now. It's a stab at something else—an "atopia," perhaps—where our desires are not the engine.

The ground rules for such an atopia would be few enough. We would have to conquer the desire to grow in numbers; the human population would need to get gradually smaller, though how much smaller is an open question. Some deep ecologists[4] say the human population shouldn't exceed a hundred million, others a billion or two—roughly our population a century ago. And those people would need to use less in the way of resources—not just oil, but wood and water and chemicals and even land itself. Those are the essentials. But they are practical rules, not moral ones. Within them, a thousand cultures—vegetarian and hunter, communal and hermitic—could still exist.

A pair of California professors, George Sessions and Bill Devall, listed what they saw as some of the principles of deep ecology in a book (*Deep*

---

[3]Utopian communities: kibbutzes are communal farms in Israel; Thomas Jefferson (1743–1826) advocated self-sufficient farms as the building blocks of American society; the Pennsylvania Dutch are tight-knit German-speaking settlers of eastern Pennsylvania, who have prospered as farmers by avoiding outside influences.

[4]Ecologists who believe that human beings should be on equal footing with other creatures and should live simply and appropriately.

Ecology) they published several years ago. Although the work shows its West Coast origins at times (there is some discussion of how this philosophy could give us "joyous confidence to dance with the sensuous harmonies discovered through spontaneous, playful intercourse with the rhythms of our bodies, the rhythms of flowing water"), it is frank about the sharp contrast between the current worldview and their proposed replacement: instead of material and economic growth, "elegantly simple" material needs; instead of consumerism, "doing with enough." It is frank, too, in its acknowledgment that deep ecology—that humility—is an infant philosophy, with many questions yet to be asked, much less answered: Exactly how much is enough? Or, what about poor people?

Those are hard questions—but perhaps not beyond our imagination. When we decided that accumulation and growth were our economic ideals, we invented wills and lending at interest and puritanism and supersonic aircraft. Why would we come up with ideas less powerful in an all-out race to do with less?

The difficulty is almost certainly more psychological than intellectual— less that we can't figure out major alterations in our way of life than that we simply don't want to. Even if our way of life has destroyed nature and endangered the planet, it is so hard to imagine living in any other fashion. The people whose lives may point the way—Thoreau, say, or Gandhi[5]—we dismiss as exceptional, a polite way of saying there is no reason we should be expected to go where they pointed. The challenge they presented with the physical examples of their lives is much more subversive than anything they wrote or said: if they could live those simple lives, it's no use saying we could not. I could, I suppose, get by on half the money I currently spend. A voluntary simplification of life-styles is not beyond our abilities, but it is probably outside our desires. 20

*   *   *

[5]Henry David Thoreau (1817–1862): American philosopher, essayist, naturalist, and poet; Mohandas Gandhi (1869–1948): political and spiritual leader of India, who abandoned materialism for the ascetic life of the Hindus.

Understanding What You Read

1. What is the "terrible choice" McKibben describes at the beginning of this selection?
2. What changes have McKibben and his wife already made?
3. What more might they change to reduce their negative impact on the natural world?
4. What distinction does McKibben make between "utopia" and "atopia"?
5. What distinction does he make between the current worldview and that proposed by "deep ecologists"?

Writing About What You Read

1. Examine how you live: how often you use a private automobile to go from place to place, how much waste you generate in a week, how many clothes you have that you rarely wear and don't need. Then consider how you would like to live after you've graduated from college. What possessions—clothes, appliances, automobiles, luxury items—do you want? What kind of transportation do you expect to use? How much travel do you plan? How many children? Based on what you have learned, analyze what you will have to do to live that desired life and what impact this will have on the earth.

2. Imagine living in a way that does minimum harm to the environment. Consider what this means for your work, daily habits, diet, possessions, and leisure activities. Write an essay describing this life.

Making Connections

1. Compare Rachel Carson's idyllic village ("A Fable for Tomorrow") with George Mitchell's description of the pristine valley of Mexico ("Two Children in a Future World").

2. Reread the newspaper article about Mexico City in Chapter 1 ("Mexico City Family Oppressed by Pollution") and compare the lives of that contemporary Mexican family with that of Luisa ("Two Children in a Future World") in the twenty-first century.

3. Write a short essay expressing your ideas about the most effective—and least effective—ways to motivate people to take action to solve environmental problems, using and responding to ideas from Roszak ("Green Guilt and Ecological Overload"), Hardin ("The Tragedy of the Commons," paragraphs 36–40), and Gore ("Ships in the Desert," paragraphs 20–22).

4. Frances Cairncross ("The Challenge to Companies") argues that as labor costs go up, disposable products will become more attractive. Brown, Flavin, and Postel ("Reusing and Recycling Materials") maintain that using throwaway materials just to save labor costs is shortsighted, and that in the long run businesses gain from reducing the amount of waste they produce. Whose view do you agree with? Write an essay defending it.

5. Write an essay comparing Marcia D. Lowe's ideas about alternative transportation with those of Noel Perrin.

acid rain   Precipitation composed of water particles, sulfuric acid, and/or nitric acid. These acids are formed from sulfur dioxides from the smoke-stacks of power plants that burn coal and oil and from nitrogen oxides emitted by motor vehicles. They change the chemistry of healthy soils and waters, making them unfit to support life.

anthropocentric   A human-centered view of life that interprets all other elements of the natural world in terms of human significance.

aquifer   Underground reservoirs of permeable rock, sand, or gravel that store and channel groundwater. Some aquifers, like the Ogallala in the U.S. high plains, have been depleted to dangerously low levels.

biodiversity   The full array of living things, ranging from the smallest single-celled organism to large mammals and giant trees and including the genetically dictated variations within single species as well as ecosystems made up of many independent species.

biomass   The amount of living matter in a given habitat or the total mass of a particular species or groups of species in a specified area, such as the total weight of ants in a rain forest.

biophilia   A word E. O. Wilson defines in his book *Biophilia* as "the innate tendency to focus on life and lifelike processes."

bioregion   One of the many natural divisions of the planet, defined by flora, fauna, water, climate, soil, and land formations, as well as by human additions such as farms, buildings, and even golf courses. Boundaries of bioregions are determined by natural phenomena rather than political domi-nance.

bioregionalism   A movement to decentralize large societies and to develop ecologically defined regions in which people cooperate and live in ways consistent with the resources of their region.

biosphere   The parts of the earth (air, earth, or water) where living things dwell.

Brundtland Commission   An international body established by the United Nations in 1983 and headed by Gro Harlem Brundtland, prime minister of Norway, to study the relationship between economic development and protection of the environment.

carbon dioxide   The most common greenhouse gas, put into the atmo-sphere primarily by fossil-fuel burning and deforestation. The increase of carbon dioxide enhances the greenhouse effect (the earth's natural heat trap) and may contribute to global warming.

carcinogen   A substance that causes cancer, such as radon and asbestos.

chlorinated hydrocarbons   Compounds such as DDT and PCBs made of carbon, hydrogen, and chlorine atoms. Once released into the environment, these chemicals become biologically amplified as they move up the food chain; that is, as minnows eat zooplankton, larger fish eat minnows, and seabirds eat the larger fish, the concentration of these chemicals is greatly increased.

chlorofluorocarbons (CFCs)   Chemical compounds made of carbon, chlorine, and fluorine that are used in air conditioners and refrigerators and in foam plastics such as Styrofoam. CFCs are known to deplete the ozone layer as the chlorine atoms react with ozone molecules.

clear-cutting   The practice of cutting all the trees of a forest at once.

coevolution   The development of two species that are interdependent and that adapt to each other's needs. For example, many species of flowering plants and their insect pollinators have coevolved in a way that makes the relationship more effective.

Convention on International Trade in Endangered Species in Wild Flora and Fauna (CITES)   International agreement, reached in 1975 and eventually ratified by 103 nations, that lists 675 species that cannot be traded as live specimens or as wildlife products.

DDT   A chlorinated hydrocarbon widely used as a pesticide in the United States until Rachel Carson's *Silent Spring* (1962) raised questions about its safety. Although use of DDT was banned in the United States in 1972, it is still produced there and exported to other countries.

debt-for-nature swaps   An agreement by which one nation forgives the debts of another in exchange for that nation's agreeing to protect and preserve environmentally sensitive areas such as rain forests.

deep ecology   A philosophical approach to nature that assumes humans are only part of the natural world and other species have rights of their own, independent of human needs or desires. It respects the biological integrity of the earth and living things.

deforestation   Removal of trees in an area without replanting and in such a way that the forest will not regenerate. Deforestation results in the loss not only of trees, but of the myriad forms of life that live in forests.

desertification   The transformation of forests, farms, or grasslands to unusable desert. This process may be caused by overgrazing, excessive irrigation, clearing of vegetation, natural soil erosion, or climate change.

dioxin   A family of some 210 chemicals. Some dioxins known to be highly toxic are emitted from trash-burning incinerators and are thought to increase the incidence of cancer in humans.

ecofeminism   A social movement reinforced with diverse philosophical and theoretical positions, including many different approaches to how women can repair the earth and restore health to the biosphere.

ecology   The study of how living things interact with each other and with their physical environment.

ecosystem   A community of species interacting with each other and with the physical environment.

ecotage   The practice of preventing environmental damage by radical measures that include sabotaging equipment and tree-spiking construction (driving large nails into trees to hinder logging operations). While proponents of ecotage advocate civil disobedience that may damage large machinery, they do not advocate harming people.

ecotourism   Tourism focused primarily on natural beauty and environmental awareness.

environment   All the factors that act upon an organism or community of organisms, including climate, soil, water, chemicals, radiation, and other living things.

Environmental Assessment   A brief description of environmental consequences required for small federally funded or federally approved projects or actions. Environmental Assessments either result in a more thorough Environmental Impact Study or in a document explaining that there is no significant environmental impact.

environmental ethics   The study of the moral principles and issues inherent in the ways that humans relate to the environment.

Environmental Impact Statement   A comprehensive description of environmental consequences required of proposed federally funded or federally permitted projects or actions. The Statement must detail the effects on the whole environment (human, animal, plant, mineral) and lay out a spectrum of alternatives. Environmental Impact Statements must be made public through the federal registry.

Environmental Protection Agency (EPA)   A federal agency, established in 1970, concerned with air and water quality, radiation, pesticides, and solid-waste disposal. It is responsible for enforcing most federal environmental laws and for administering the Superfund cleanup.

environmental racism   The practice of locating hazardous waste dumps, incinerators, and other environmentally contaminating facilities in minority neighborhoods.

erosion   The processes that wear away the earth, breaking up particles and moving them from one place to another.

food chain   A progression of organisms, each feeding on the preceding one.

food web   A complex system of interconnected food chains and feeding relationships.

fossil fuel   Coal, petroleum, and natural gas that have been formed over millions of years from decomposing plants and animals. Fossil fuel resources are finite in that they require such long periods to develop. The pollution caused by burning fossil fuels is a major destructive force in the environment.

Gaia hypothesis   Idea that the earth and all its systems functioned as a single self-regulating living organism, keeping its various components in balance, until the unprecedented activity of industrial societies disrupted that balance.

gene pool   All the genes in all the organisms belonging to an interbreeding population.

global warming   A widely held belief that the buildup of greenhouse gases will result in the earth's atmosphere retaining more and more heat until the overall temperature rises, causing significant climatic changes which will in turn disrupt agriculture, cause sea levels to rise, and make some parts of the planet uninhabitable.

grasslands   Areas of low rainfall around the world, including the prairies and plains of North America, the pampas of South America, the steppes and plains of Eurasia, and the veldt of Africa. The fruit of grasses is called grain. Cultivated wheat, rice, corn, oats, barley, and rye provide the staple food for most humans and domesticated animals, while wild grasses are important for wildlife and many range-fed animals.

greenbelt movement   A project in Kenya founded by Wangari Maathai, who has enlisted women all over her country to plant millions of trees.

greenhouse effect   Retention of heat in the earth's atmosphere by carbon dioxide and other gases that trap infrared radiation from the sun and prevent it from escaping into space.

greenhouse gases   Carbon dioxide, methane, ozone, nitrous oxide, water vapor, and other gases that contribute to trapping heat near the earth's surface.

green revolution   A radical change in agricultural practices that took place from around 1950 through the mid-1980s. Extensive use of fertilizers, pesticides, and irrigation to grow hybrid corn and high-yield grains resulted in a dramatic increase in food production, but also in loss of topsoil and water, contamination of soil and water by pesticides and chemical fertilizers, and loss of genetic diversity, resulting in increased vulnerability to pests.

gross national product (GNP)   The basic measure of a nation's economic performance, arrived at by calculating the value of all goods and services produced during a year. This method of determining the GNP fails to take into account the loss of natural resources such as topsoil, water, and forests.

habitat   Place where an organism or community of organisms lives.

habitat disruption   Destruction or alteration of a habitat by cutting across or establishing barriers to migration routes or destroying breeding areas or food sources. Loss of habitat is the primary cause of loss of biodiversity.

hunter-gatherers   People who live by gathering wild plants and insects, hunting animals, and fishing. Gathering and hunting was the dominant way of life for most humans throughout their history of some 100,000 years. Today, few remnants of the traditional hunter-gatherer cultures remain.

incinerators   Facilities for burning solid waste. Some incinerators produce energy in the process of burning trash. Advantages include destroying disease-carrying organisms and reducing the amount of land needed for dumping trash. Incinerating solid waste has the disadvantage of producing significant air pollution and toxic ash.

intercropping   Growing two or more different crops at the same time on the same piece of land to maintain healthy soil chemistry. A farmer might choose to alternate rows of a grain that depletes nitrogen with those of a legume that adds nitrogen to the soil.

intergenerational equity   A concept established by the Brundtland Commission of being fair to future generations by insisting that the present generation consider their needs.

megafauna   The largest animals, weighing over ten kilograms; these include wolves, deer, bear, the big cats, and elephants.

metals, toxic   Some fifty of the eighty elemental metals used in industry, many of which (such as cadmium, lead, mercury and zinc) are toxic to humans and are primarily absorbed into the body by inhalation or ingestion.

methane gas   A greenhouse gas caused by bacteria that decompose organic matter in oxygen-poor environments, such as landfills, burning forests and grasslands, and the digestive tracts of cows and other livestock.

monoculture   The practice, increasingly used in world agriculture, of growing a single crop over a vast area to increase productivity. Monoculture has been shown to reduce biodiversity.

NIMBY syndrome   The tendency to reject unpleasant additions to one's own neighborhood. NIMBY means "not in my backyard."

nitrous oxide   A greenhouse gas released into the atmosphere from the breakdown of nitrogen fertilizers in soil, livestock wastes, nitrate-contaminated groundwater, and biomass burning.

overconsumption   The tendency in affluent societies to consume more than is needed to live, causing an imbalance that leaves others without enough for a decent life—and in some cases without enough to survive.

overgrazing   The practice of allowing so many grazing animals in an area that they destroy the vegetation, leaving the rangeland impoverished.

overpopulation   The condition of more people living in an area than can live there in comfort and decency without depleting resources needed by themselves or their descendants.

ozone   An important part of the stratosphere that protects the earth's surface by absorbing harmful ultraviolet radiation. At ground level, ozone is a greenhouse gas and an element in air pollution.

ozone layer   The thin layer of ozone in the stratosphere that absorbs harmful ultraviolet radiation from the sun.

perennial   Plants that persist year after year. In areas where plants die with cold weather, perennials grow back from root stock that survives the winter or dormant period.

petrochemicals   A large group of chemicals derived from petroleum or natural gas and used in producing industrial products, including plastics, synthetic fibers, fertilizers, and pesticides.

pollutants, degradable   Environmental wastes such as paper, organic garbage, and manure that can be broken down into harmless components.

pollutants, nondegradable   Environmental wastes such as lead and mercury that are permanent and likely to cause problems for all time.

polychlorinated biphenyls (PCBs)   Group of more than two hundred chlorinated toxic hydrocarbon compounds that can be amplified, that is, spread and increased, in food chains and webs.

polyculture   The practice of growing many different crops in the same area.

population explosion   A term used by Paul R. Ehrlich and Anne Ehrlich to refer to the exponential rate of growth of the human population, which, at current rates, will double in thirty-nine years.

predator   An organism that preys on another for food.

prey   An organism that serves as a food source for another.

radioactive waste   Produced by nuclear power plants, weapons production, and other processes involving nuclear reactions.

rain forests, tropical   Equatorial forests, in some thirty-seven countries around the globe, that receive extremely high annual rainfall, ranging from 160 to 400 inches a year, and have an average temperature of 80 degrees Fahrenheit. Altitude and relationship to the sea dictate variations in temperature and rainfall. Farther north and south are forests still in tropical climes that receive somewhat less rain. Tropical rain forests, now making up less than 8 percent of the earth's landmass, have the greatest diversity of species on the planet and are rapidly being destroyed.

resources, nonrenewable   Materials such as copper, aluminum, coal, and oil that exist in fixed amounts that can be created only over hundreds of millions of years.

resources, perpetual   Resources, such as solar energy, that can be used without being depleted.

resources, renewable   Materials, plants, and animals that theoretically can be replenished at the rate that they are used. Examples are trees, wildlife, fish, oxygen, and soil. Renewable resources, however, can be exhausted if they are used faster than they are restored or if the conditions necessary for renewal are destroyed.

scrubbers   Machines designed to eliminate the emission of sulfur dioxide and sulfur trioxide, chemical compounds that produce sulfurous and sulfuric acid, two components of acid rain, from power plants that burn coal or oil. There are two kinds of scrubbers. Wet scrubbers are large structures through which gases containing sulfur dioxide and sulfur trioxide are forced and subjected to a shower of water and limestone that neutralizes the sulfur compounds and makes a new compound, calcium sulfate, which is chemically inert. Dry scrubbers, used on smaller units, work on the principle of burning limestone with coal to produce an essentially neutral gas.

shifting cultivation A practice common in tropical areas where cultivators clear land and plant crops in the exposed thin layer of topsoil, only to abandon it a few years later when the soil nutrients are depleted.

slash-and-burn cultivation A practice common in tropical forests of cutting down vegetation, leaving it to dry, and then burning it to prepare land for cultivation. Such land is usually arable for two to five years.

smog A general term which once referred to a mixture of fog and smoke, but which has evolved to include various mixtures of industrial pollutants with atmospheric gases.

soil The surface layer of earth made of inorganic materials—clay, silt, sand, stones—as well as decomposed plant and animal material, microorganisms, water, and air.

solar energy Radiation from the sun that can be used to heat buildings or water or to generate electricity using photovoltaic cells. Indirect solar energy includes wind, falling and flowing water, biomass, and even fossil fuels.

species A group of living things that can reproduce fertile offspring.

species, alien or immigrant Species that migrate or are carried by animals and humans into ecosystems where they have not been found before. Winds in storms, floating logs, boats, the droppings of migrating birds, the fur of animals, and the hands of human beings are among the means by which species are transported from one ecosystem to another.

species, endangered Animal and plant species whose survival is jeopardized by human activities such as logging, hunting, trapping, and mining. Equally threatening are practices such as high-tech whaling, driftnet fishing, burning or clear-cutting of forests, and spraying with certain pesticides.

species, endemic Species that are found in a particular area and nowhere else.

species extinction Extinction, which is irreparable, occuring when the last member of a species dies. It is inevitable when members of the species lose their power to reproduce.

species, generalist Those species, such as humans and cockroaches, that can live in a variety of environments, eat diverse kinds of foods, and tolerate a wide range of weather conditions.

species, threatened A wild species that is declining and likely to become endangered.

stratosphere Second layer of the earth's atmosphere above the troposphere, beginning seven to ten or more miles above the earth.

strip logging The removal of timber in narrow strips and along contours, allowing for rapid regrowth, sustained yield, and protection of native plants and animals.

strip mining Process of retrieving minerals from the earth by removing large sections of the earth's surface in strips, thereby scarring the landscape.

succession Process by which a living community or biosphere is altered through time. For example, a pine forest that is destroyed by a storm might be replaced by a mixed hardwood forest if the seedlings are in place, or by briers and brambles if not.

Superfund program A multibillion-dollar fund financed by federal and state governments and taxes on chemical and petrochemical industries for cleaning up hazardous-waste dump sites and leaking underground tanks.

sustainable economic development Economic activities that use natural resources without depleting them so that comparable resources will be available for future generations.

sustainable yield The use of a renewable resource at a rate that leaves the available supply constant.

symbiotic relationship Two species living together for mutual benefit.

technosphere A term introduced by Barry Commoner that encompasses the objects, processes, and institutions created by humans—such as cars, factories, computers, space stations, flashlights, mines, synthesized chemical reactions.

topsoil A loose soil made of partially decomposing organic matter, minerals, and living organisms. Topsoil is essential to farming; if lost faster than it is replaced, the land may become barren.

toxic waste Discarded material that is capable of causing serious injury, illness, or death.

troposphere The atmospheric layer nearest earth extending up to ten or so miles.

UNCED The United Nations Conference on Environment and Development, held in Rio de Janeiro, Brazil, in June 1992, attended by world leaders, delegates, and journalists. Simultaneously, representatives from nongovernmental organizations, tribal leaders, and activists held a separate meeting to explore solutions to the environmental crisis.

wetlands Areas, such as swamps, marshes, and bogs, with enough surface or ground water to support a complex chain of life, including microorganisms, vegetation, reptiles, fish, and amphibians. Wetlands usually border larger bodies of water such as rivers, lakes, bays, and the open sea, and may serve as breeding grounds for many species.

A SELECTED LIST OF BOOKS FOR FURTHER READING

Abbey, Edward. *Desert Solitaire*. 1968 (McGraw Hill). New York: Ballantine, 1971. A beautifully written book about Abbey's experiences as a seasonal park ranger in Arches National Monument near the town of Moab in southeast Utah.

———. *The Monkey Wrench Gang*. 1975 (Harper & Row). New York: Avon, 1985. A comic novel about a gang of ecological saboteurs and their adventures in the American West.

Adams, Jonathan S., and Thomas O. McShane. *The Myth of Wild Africa: Conservation Without Illusion*. New York: Norton, 1992. A provocative book exploring the complex ways, often ignored by Western conservationists, that Africans have used and depended on wildlife. Adams and McShane advocate a new approach to African/Western cooperation that ultimately returns control to African nations.

Anderson, Lorraine. *Sisters of the Earth: Women's Prose and Poetry About Nature*. New York: Vintage, 1991. A collection of stories, essays, and poems by some ninety women concerned about the relationship of humans to the natural world.

Arnold, Ron. *Ecology Wars: Environmentalism as If People Mattered*. Bellevue, Wash.: Free Enterprise, 1987. Ron Arnold has set himself in opposition to environmentalists and is the self-appointed leader of the anti-environmentalist movement known as Wise Use. To understand Arnold's thinking, read "Environmental Propaganda."

Bass, Rick. *The Deer Pasture*. 1985. New York: Norton, 1989.

———. *Wild to the Heart*. New York: Norton, 1987.

———. *Winter: Notes from Montana*. Boston: Houghton Mifflin, 1991. Bass's stories and essays celebrate nature and outdoors adventure.

Berry, Wendell. *A Continuous Harmony: Essays Cultural and Agricultural*. San Diego: Harcourt Brace Jovanovich, 1972.

———. *Home Economics*. San Francisco: North Point, 1987.

———. *What Are People For*. San Francisco: North Point, 1990. Berry writes persuasively about consumerism, the environmental movement, wilderness, nature, and numerous other topics ranging from word processors to coal mining. At the heart of his work is a concern with what it means to be at home on the planet and a conviction that to begin to reverse the damage humans have done to the planet, we will have to live more simply.

Brown, Lester R., et al. *State of the World: 1993*. New York: Norton, 1993. An annual publication of the Worldwatch Institute, this collection follows the trends affecting declining species, ozone depletion, global warming, food production, mining practices, economic development, and hazardous waste, among other concerns.

Brown, Lester R., ed. *The Worldwatch Reader on Global Environmental Issues*. New

York: Norton, 1991. A comprehensive collection of up-to-date essays on topics including soil, air, water, energy, transportation, food, and population.

Brown, Lester R., Christopher Flavin, and Hal Kane, eds. *Vital Signs 1993: The Trends That Are Shaping Our Future.* New York: Norton, 1993. An annual Worldwatch publication, using some thirty-six indicators of environmental, social, and economic health, with more than forty short reports on as many subjects, including grain production, fertilizer use, carbon emissions, population, and soil erosion.

Brown, Lester R., Christopher Flavin, and Sandra Postel. *Saving the Planet: How to Shape an Environmentally Sustainable Global Economy.* New York: Norton, 1991. Intended as a source book for the multitude that assembled in Rio de Janeiro for the United Nations Conference on Environment and Development (UNCED), this volume looks at global economic policies, political choices, energy choices, international aid, and, ultimately, what is required to create a sustainable global economy.

Cairncross, Frances. *Costing the Earth: The Challenge for Governments, the Opportunities for Business.* Boston: Harvard Business School Press, 1991. The environmental editor of the *Economist,* Cairncross explains how what is good for the environment can also be good for companies and shows how successful environmental policies can encourage inventive industrial practices.

Caldicott, Helen, M.D. *If You Love This Planet: A Plan to Heal the Earth.* New York: Norton, 1992. While Caldicott does not explore any environmental issues in depth, she does provide an accessible if somewhat polemical overview of many environmental topics, ranging from the greenhouse effect to the threat of nuclear war.

Carson, Rachel. *Silent Spring.* 1962. Boston: Houghton Mifflin, 1987. A classic of environmental writing, Carson's beautifully written book alerted many people to the dangers of widespread use of insecticides and spurred major changes in government policy toward the environment.

Caufield, Catherine. *In the Rainforest.* Chicago: U of Chicago Press, 1984. This informative book includes discussions of the structure and elements of tropical forests; the human cultures that have thrived within them; the impact of cattle raising, population expansion, and deforestation on the tropical regions; and the history of how humans have used these forests around the globe.

Colinvaux, Paul. *Why Big Fierce Animals Are Rare.* Princeton: Princeton UP, 1978. This is a collection of fascinating essays focusing on the complex interactions of species.

Commoner, Barry. *Making Peace with the Planet.* 1990. New York: New Press, 1992. This presentation of basic concepts of Commoner's thought distinguishes between biosphere and technosphere and explores the effects of technosphere on the biosphere. Commoner's notions about population are interesting and at odds with those of Paul and Anne Erhlich. The chapter "Environmental Action" focuses on prevention vs. control and suggest ways to shift to a preventive policy.

Dillard, Annie. *Pilgrim at Tinker Creek.* New York: Harper & Row, 1974. A keen observer, Dillard, in this Pulitzer-Prize winning book, records the minute details of those aspects of the natural world that intrigue her.

———. *Teaching a Stone to Talk.* New York: Harper & Row, 1982. A compelling collection of essays on topics ranging from the Amazon to her own backyard.

Douglas, Marjory Stoneman. *The Everglades: River of Grass.* 1947. St. Simons Isle, Ga.: Mockingbird, 1974. Douglas, now over a hundred years old, has been a crusader for the everglades for decades. Like *Silent Spring,* this book is important not just for what it says, but for the practical results it catalyzed.

Durning, Alan. *How Much Is Enough? The Consumer Society and the Future of the Earth.* New York: Norton, 1992. A member of the Worldwatch research staff, Durning questions how much human consumption the planet can support and challenges readers to change the way they live.

Ehrlich, Gretel. *The Solace of Open Spaces.* 1985 (Viking). New York: Penguin, 1986. Compelling, personal essays focusing on life in harsh, dry parts of Wyoming.

Ehrlich, Paul R., and Anne Ehrlich. *Healing the Planet.* New York: Addison-Wesley, 1991. An excellent overview of major issues of the environmental crisis.

————. *The Population Explosion.* New York: Simon & Schuster, 1990. An update of *The Population Bomb* (1968), a best-seller that shocked readers with predictions of mass starvations and other disasters. Since then, the world's population has grown from 3.5 billion to 5.4 billion. In this new edition Paul and Anne Ehrlich explain how population growth is related to global warming, rain forest destruction, famine, and pollution.

Foreman, Dave. *Confessions of an Eco-Warrior.* New York: Harmony, 1991. To learn about the thinking behind the actions of the radical environmental movement, read this book by the founder of Earth First! Then turn to Christopher Manes's *Green Rage* for an outsider's view (see below).

Forsyth, Adrian, and Ken Miyata. *Tropical Nature: Life and Death in the Rain Forests of Central and South America.* New York: Scribner's, 1984. These seventeen essays are an excellent introduction to the wonders of tropical biology. Killer trees, poisonous frogs, army ants, and botfly larva are some of the stars of this book, but the emphasis is on the interdependency of species.

Gore, Al. *Earth in the Balance.* New York: Houghton Mifflin, 1991. A carefully researched, interesting overview of major environmental problems with a particularly fascinating chapter on how climate has affected history.

Gould, Stephen Jay. *Eight Little Piggies.* New York: Norton, 1993. This sixth volume in a series of essays brings together a rich storehouse of information about the wonders of the species. Of particular interest are the first three essays published under the title "The Scale of Extinction."

Head, Suzanne, and Robert Heinzman. *Lessons of the Rainforest.* San Francisco: Sierra Club, 1990. This collection of some twenty essays—all by experts in various aspects of rain forest studies—examines the interrelated causes and consequences of tropical deforestation and suggests ways to reverse that process.

Hoagland, Edward. *Heart's Desire: The Best of Edward Hoagland.* New York: Simon & Schuster, 1988. This collection of thirty-five essays covers a vast array of subjects, ranging from life in the city to adventures in the wilderness. Hoagland's special interest in the peculiarities of and differences between the urban and the natural worlds is reflected throughout.

————. *Balancing Acts.* New York: Simon & Schuster, 1992. In these twenty-five essays, mainly from the late eighties and early nineties, Hoagland takes his readers on a series of adventures: to rain forests in Belize, on a pack trip along the southern edge of Yellowstone, through the Okefenokee Swamp, and into the high country of Alaska.

Hubbell, Sue. *A Country Year: Living the Questions.* 1986 (Random). New York: Harper & Row Perennial Library, 1987. Hubbell's story of how she changed and simplified her life is an inspiration to others who want to live more lightly on the planet.

Jackson, Wes. *Altars of Unhewn Stone.* San Francisco: North Point, 1987.

————. *New Roots for Agriculture.* 1980. Lincoln: Nebraska UP, 1985. Wes Jackson takes the long view in solving environmental problems and reforming agricultural practices. A recent recipient of a MacArthur award, Jackson codirects the Land Institute near Salina, Kansas. Challenging the practices of industrial agriculture, Jackson is committed to reestablishing prairie ecology as a step toward achieving sustainable agriculture.

Jackson, Wes, Wendell Berry, and Bruce Colman, eds. *Meeting the Expectations of the Land.* San Francisco: North Point, 1984. A collection of seventeen essays that provide a comprehensive treatment of the possible solutions to the agricultural crisis generated during a weekend meeting of experts organized by Wes Jackson in June 1982.

Krutch, Joseph Wood. *The Desert Year.* Tucson: U of Arizona Press, 1951. A fascinating book about one man's discovery of the wonders of the Sonoran desert.

LaBastille, Anne. *Woodswoman.* 1978 (Dutton). New York: Penguin, 1991.

————. *Beyond Black Bear Lake.* New York: Norton, 1988. LaBastille tells compelling stories about building her own Thoreau-like cabins and living alone in the Adirondack wilderness. Her implicit challenge to readers—like that of Sue Hubbell and Thoreau—is to live more simply, more authentically, and more in harmony with nature.

Le Guin, Ursula K. *Always Coming Home.* New York: Harper & Row, 1985. A fanciful novel that combines poetry, stories, poems, and visual art to create the lives of the Kesh, a people who live in peace and in harmony with nature after a nuclear disaster.

————. *Buffalo Gals and Other Animal Presences.* Santa Barbara: Capra, 1987. In this collection of one novella, ten stories, and eighteen poems, Le Guin enters the world of animals and plants. By giving voice to nonhuman living things, she forces new perspectives on the human world.

Leopold, Aldo. *A Sand County Almanac, with Essays on Conservation from Round River.* SCA 1949 (Oxford UP); RR, 1953 (Oxford UP). New York: Ballantine, 1970. Considered an environmental classic, this book describes the beauty of the natural world, explores how people have damaged it, and calls for a new respect for wilderness.

Lopez, Barry. *Crossing Open Ground.* New York: Vintage, 1989. A collection of essays published in magazines over a ten-year period. Focusing on wild places such as the deserts of southern California, the Colorado River, and the Arctic coast of Alaska, these well-crafted pieces consider the possibilities for encounters between human beings and wild places.

————. *Arctic Dreams.* 1986 (Scribner's). New York: Bantam, 1987. A detailed look at an inaccessible part of the world with its rich and diverse wildlife.

Luhan, Mabel Dodge. *Winter in Taos.* 1935 (Harcourt). Taos, N.M.: Las Palomas de Taos, 1982. A celebration of the New Mexico Luhan adopted as her home.

————. *Edge of Taos Desert: An Escape to Reality.* 1937 (Harcourt). Albuquerque:

U of New Mexico Press, 1987. The story of a privileged woman who left her life as an art patron in New York City to move to New Mexico, where she became fascinated by the art and culture of the Indians.

Manes, Christopher. *Green Rage: Radical Environmentalism and the Unmaking of Civilization*. Boston: Little, Brown, 1990. A well-written overview of radical environmental groups around the world. If you want to know what's going on in the field of global ecotage, here's the place to start.

Matthiessen, Peter. *Wildlife in America*. 1959. Rev. version. New York: Viking, 1987. This classic history of American wildlife was first published in 1959, before *Silent Spring* and before there was widespread consciousness of an environmental crisis. Updated in 1987, this book traces both the destruction of wildlife and the history of wildlife conservation. Beautifully illustrated with color plates, line drawings, black-and-white photographs, and maps.

McKibben, Bill. *The End of Nature*. 1989 (Random). New York: Anchor, 1990. Philosophical, thoughtful, and challenging, this book argues convincingly that the life we are living must change or the natural world we love will die.

McPhee, John. *The Control of Nature*. New York: Farrar, Straus & Giroux, 1989. This book consists of three extended essays: on human manipulation of the Mississippi River, on efforts to control the effects of volcanic activity, and on the attempts to control the debris flows coming from the San Gabriel Mountains into the surburban neighborhoods of Los Angeles.

————. *Encounters with the Archdruid*. New York: Farrar, Straus and Giroux, 1971. McPhee presents three narratives about confrontations and adventures between David Brower, longtime leader of the Sierra Club and militant conservationist, and three men with very different commitments: Charles Park, a mineral engineer; Charles Fraser, a resort developer; and Floyd Dominy, a builder of gigantic dams.

Merchant, Carolyn, ed. *Major Problems in American Environmental History*. Lexington, Mass.: Heath, 1993. Intended as a textbook for environmental studies or environmental history courses, this is a collection of primary documents and essays that trace the transformation of the American landscape from the days of the early European explorers to the present. In addition to exploring the ways various American environments have been "perceived, used, managed, and conserved," these essays include the history of both environmental damage and preservation efforts.

Mitchell, George J. *World on Fire: Saving an Endangered Earth*. New York: Scribner's, 1991. Mitchell highlights what he considers the dominant environmental catastrophes and their causes: the burning of fossil fuels and the consequent pollution and greenhouse effect; the industrial practices that result in acid rain; the continued use of CFCs and their impact on the ozone layer; and the destruction of the world's rain forests, resulting in massive reduction of biodiversity, degradation of land and air, climate changes, and incalculable other catastrophes.

Mowat, Farley. *Never Cry Wolf*. 1963 (Little, Brown). New York: Bantam, 1979. A fascinating story of Mowat's experiences living among the wolves of the Canadian Arctic. Sent there to study the role of wolves in depleting the herds of caribou, Mowat found instead that they are useful in culling the sick and weak and thus in keeping the herds healthy.

————. *Sea of Slaughter.* Toronto: McClelland & Stewart, 1984. This is the story of the devastation of many forms of marine life along the northeastern coast of North America.

————. *A Whale for the Killing.* Toronto: McClelland & Stewart, 1972. This moving story of the senseless killing of one eighty-ton whale trapped in a lagoon in Newfoundland becomes a plea to save all whales from extinction.

Muir, John. *The Yosemite.* 1914 (Houghton Mifflin). San Francisco: Sierra Club, 1988. Muir's account of his adventures and of this close observation of the natural wonders and living creatures of the Yosemite Valley where he spent so much of his life.

Myers, Norman. *The Primary Source: Tropical Forests and Our Future.* 1984. Rev. ed. New York: Norton, 1992. An excellent overview of issues relating to rain forest destruction and efforts to stop it.

Nash, Roderick Frazier. *The Rights of Nature: A History of Environmental Ethics.* Madison: University of Wisconsin Press, 1989. A scholarly work on the history of the idea that nature has rights.

————. *Wilderness and the American Mind.* 1967. Rev. eds. New Haven, Conn.: Yale, 1973, 1982. Essential reading about the significance of wilderness in contemporary American thought.

Neihardt, John G. *Black Elk Speaks.* 1932 (Morrow). New York: Pocket, 1973. To use Black Elk's own words, this book "is the story of all life that is holy and is good to tell, and of us two-leggeds sharing in it with the four-leggeds and the wings of the air and all green things; for these are children of one mother and their father is one Spirit."

Perrin, Noel. *Solo.* New York: Norton, 1992. An entertaining account of Perrin's experiences driving an electric car across the country and then using it to commute some thirteen miles from his farm in Vermont to Dartmouth College, where he teaches.

Pollan, Michael. *Second Nature: A Gardener's Education.* New York: Atlantic Monthly, 1991. A playful and provocative advocate for the value of gardens and gardening, Pollan widens his perspective to include history, culture, and the larger environmental issues.

Ray, Dixy Lee, with Lou Guzzo. *Trashing the Planet: How Science Can Help Us Deal with Acid Rain, Depletion of the Ozone, and Nuclear Waste.* 1990 (Regency Gateway). New York: Harper & Row, 1990. Ray and Guzzo's anti-environmentalist arguments aggressively reject environmentalist stances—extreme and moderate.

Rifkin, Jeremy. *Beyond Beef: The Rise and Fall of the Cattle Culture.* New York: Dutton, 1992. Don't read this book unless you are prepared to give up hamburgers and steaks. A brilliant indictment of the cattle culture, its impact on the earth, and how the poorer nations starve in order to feed the rich.

Roberts, Elizabeth, and Elias Amidon. *Earth Prayers from Around the World.* San Francisco: Harper & Row, 1991. A collection of prayers, poems, and invocations honoring the earth by native Americans, established poets, and non-Western writers.

Sale, Kirkpatrick. *Dwellers in the Land: The Bioregional Vision.* 1985. Philadelphia: New Society, 1991. Sale gives his own version of the bioregional vision and argues that the changes necessary to save the planet must be gradual and based on a deep understanding of and respect for one's own particular region.

————. *The Conquest of Paradise: Christopher Columbus and the Columbian Legacy.* 1990 (Knopf). New York: Plume, 1991. In the prologue of this interesting book Sale lists four ways in which the Columbian voyages altered "the cultures of the globe and the life processes on which they depend." These legacies include redistribution of life forms and domination of nature by man.

Schumacher, E. F. *Small Is Beautiful.* 1973. New York: Perennial, 1989. Schumacher expands questions of economics to include ethical, philosophical, and spiritual considerations.

Seed, John, Joanna Macy, Pat Fleming, and Arne Naess. *Thinking Like a Mountain.* Philadelphia: New Society Publishers, 1988. This book is used to facilitate the deep ecology workshops.

Snyder, Gary. *The Practice of the Wild.* Berkeley: North Point, 1990. This collection of essays encompasses Snyder's thought and work over a fifteen-year period and reflect his quest for recovery and healing through nature, poetry, and mythology.

————. *Turtle Island.* New York: New Directions, 1974. Snyder's poems challenge contemporary values and find meaning in nature and myth. They are spellbinding.

Stegner, Wallace. *Where the Bluebird Sings to the Lemonade Springs.* New York: Random, 1992. These are personal essays about Stegner's parents, powerful descriptions of the land he loved, and tributes to other nature writers.

Udall, Steward L. *The Quiet Crisis and the Next Generation.* Salt Lake: Peregrine, 1988. An update of *The Quiet Crisis* (1963), this book combines the story of the use and misuse of natural resources in North America with the history of the environmental and conservation movements.

Weiner, Jonathan. *The Next One Hundred Years: Shaping the Fate of Our Living Earth.* New York: Bantam, 1990. This well-written book provides reliable information about what is happening to the planet, along with practical suggestions about what can be done to change the current trends.

Williams, Terry Tempest. *Refuge.* New York: Pantheon, 1991. As naturalist-in-residence of the Utah Museum of Natural History, Williams observed the devastation following the rising of the Great Salt Lake beginning in 1983. This book weaves that story with the narrative of her mother's slow death by cancer. The final essay, "The Clan of One-Breasted Women," connects her mother's cancer and that of two grandmothers and six aunts with the atmospheric atomic test in nearby Nevada.

Wilson, Edward O. *Biophilia.* Cambridge: Harvard UP, 1984. Highly readable, personal accounts of this world-renowned biologist's adventures and explorations into the natural world.

————. *The Diversity of Life.* Cambridge, Mass.: Harvard UP, 1992. A lucid, powerful explanation of biodiversity that focuses on the processes by which life is created, destroyed, and restored. Specifically concerned with the current rapid decline of species caused mainly by humans, Wilson argues for changes in values, behaviors, and policies that will protect the world's biological wealth.

Wilson, Edward O., ed. *Biodiversity.* Washington: National Academy, 1988. Originally presented at the National Forum on Biodiversity in 1986, the pieces in this volume provide an excellent overview of a subject so complex that no one person can begin to be an expert in the field. Hence the importance of bringing together the perspectives of numerous scientists, many of them warning that the habitats that support diverse life forms are in jeopardy from many phenomena initiated or carried out by people.

World Commission on Environment and Development. *Our Common Future.* New York: Oxford UP, 1987. This important document is widely known as the Brundtland Report, because Gro Harlem Brundtland, prime minister of Norway, chaired the commission that produced it. A comprehensive, global examination of crucial development and environmental problems with some proposed solutions.

World Resources Institute. *World Resources 1992–93.* New York: Oxford UP, 1992. Published in collaboration with the United Nations Environment Program and the United Nations Development Program, this valuable resource is packed with data about most aspects of global natural resources and environmental problems. It includes data on population, agriculture, forests, rangelands, wildlife, energy, air, and much more.

Zwinger, Ann. *Beyond the Aspen Grove.* 1970 (Random). Tucson: U of Arizona Press, 1988. The story of Zwinger's daily life combined with a detailed description of the land, the wildlife, the plants, and the weather on a forty-acre plot called Constant Friendship where the author settled with her family in the 1960s.

ACKNOWLEDGMENTS

SELECTIONS

EDWARD ABBEY: "The Serpents of Paradise" from *Desert Solitaire*. Copyright © 1968 by Edward Abbey. Reprinted by permission of Don Cogdon Associates, Inc.

JONATHAN S. ADAMS and THOMAS O. MCSHANE: "Miles and Miles of Bloody Africa" from *The Myth of Wild Africa: Conservation Without Illusion*. Copyright © 1992 by Jonathan S. Adams and Thomas O. McShane. Reprinted by permission of W. W. Norton & Company, Inc.

WILLIAM ALLEN: "The Extinction Crisis: The World's Plants and Animals Are Vanishing at a Catastrophic Rate" from *St. Louis Dispatch,* 19 November 1991. Reprinted by permission.

WENDELL BERRY: "Mayhem in the Industrial Paradise" from *A Continuous Harmony: Essays Cultural and Agricultural*. Copyright © 1972 by Wendell Berry. Reprinted by permission of Harcourt Brace & Company.

ELIZABETH BISHOP: "The Fish" from *The Complete Poems 1927–1979*. Copyright © 1979, 1983 by Alice Helen Methfessel. Reprinted by permission of North Point Press, a division of Farrar, Straus & Giroux, Inc.

WILLIAM BOOTH: "So What If It's Getting Hot?" from *The Washington Post,* 22 September 1991. Copyright © The Washington Post. Reprinted by permission.

LESTER R. BROWN, CHRISTOPHER FLAVIN, and SANDRA POSTEL: "Reusing and Recycling Materials" from *Saving the Planet: How to Shape an Environmentally Sustainable Global Economy*. Copyright © 1991 by Worldwatch Institute. Reprinted by permission of W. W. Norton & Company, Inc.

MALCOLM W. BROWNE: "Folk Remedy Demand May Wipe Out Tigers" from *The New York Times,* 22 September 1992. Copyright © 1991/92 by The New York Times Company. Reprinted by permission.

FRANCES CAIRNCROSS: "The Challenge to Companies" from *Costing the Earth*. Copyright © 1992, 1993 by Frances Cairncross. Reprinted by permission of Harvard Business School Press from *Costing the Earth*. Boston: 1992, 1993, pp. 177–188. Copyright © 1991 The Economist Books Ltd. Text copyright © 1991 and © 1992 by Frances Cairncross. Charts and diagrams copyright © 1991 The Economist Books Ltd. Reprinted with kind permission of The Economist Books Ltd.

RACHEL CARSON: "The Obligation to Endure" and "A Fable for Tomorrow" from *Silent Spring*. Copyright © 1962 by Rachel L. Carson, © renewed 1990 by Roger Christie. Reprinted by permission of Houghton Mifflin Co. All rights reserved.

ANGELA CARTER: "The Company of Wolves" from *The Bloody Chamber and Other Adult Tales*. Copyright © 1979 by Angela Carter. Reprinted by permission of HarperCollins Publishers, Inc.

EDWARD CODY: "Mexico City Family Oppressed by Pollution" from *The Washington Post,* 26 March 1992. Copyright © The Washington Post. Reprinted by permission.

PAUL COLINVAUX: "Every Species Has Its Niche" from *Why Big Fierce Animals Are Rare*. Copyright © 1978 by Princeton University Press. Reprinted by permission of Princeton University Press.

BARRY COMMONER: "At War with the Planet" from *Making Peace with the Planet,* 1990. Reprinted by permission of The New Press.

589

MICHAEL G. CONEY: "The Byrds." Copyright © 1983 by Michael G. Coney. First appeared in *Changes*. Reprinted by permission of the author and the author's agent, Virginia Kidd.

JILL KER CONWAY: "The West" from *The Road from Coorain*. Copyright © 1989 by Jill Conway. Reprinted by permission of Alfred A. Knopf, Inc.

WILLIAM CRONON: "Kennecott Journey: The Paths Out of Town" from *Under an Open Sky: Rethinking America's Western Past*, edited by William Cronon, George Miles, and Jay Gitlin. Copyright © 1992 by William J. Cronon, George Miles, and Jay Gitlin. Reprinted by permission of W. W. Norton & Company, Inc.

JAMES DAO: "A New, Unregulated Market: Selling the Right to Pollute" from *The New York Times*, 6 February 1993. Copyright © 1992/93 by The New York Times Company. Reprinted by permission.

ANNIE DILLARD: "Land Where the Rivers Meet" from *An American Childhood*. Copyright © 1987 by Annie Dillard. Reprinted by permission of HarperCollins Publishers, Inc. "Living Like Weasels" and "Life on the Rocks: The Galápagos" from *Teaching a Stone to Talk*. Copyright © 1982 by Annie Dillard. Reprinted by permission of HarperCollins Publishers, Inc.

MARJORY STONEMAN DOUGLAS: "Life on the Rock" from *The Everglades: River of Grass* (1988 edition). Reprinted by permission of Marjory Stoneman Douglas. Published by Pineapple Press, Inc., Sarasota, Florida.

CAROLE DOUGLIS: "Banana Split" from *World Watch* magazine, Jan./Feb. 1993, Washington, D.C. Reprinted by permission.

RITA DOVE: "Ozone" from *Grace Notes*, Poems by Rita Dove. Copyright © 1989 by Rita Dove. Reprinted by permission of W. W. Norton & Company, Inc.

ALAN THEIN DURNING: "Clean Motion" from *How Much Is Enough? The Consumer Society and the Future of the Earth* Copyright © 1992 by Worldwatch Institute. Reprinted by permission of W. W. Norton & Company, Inc.

EDITORIAL: "Warning from the Stratosphere" from *The Washington Post*, 11 October 1991. Reprinted by permission of The Washington Post.

GRETEL EHRLICH: "About Men" from *The Solace of Open Spaces*. Copyright © 1985 by Gretel Ehrlich. Reprinted by permission of Viking Penguin, a division of Penguin Books USA, Inc.

PAUL R. EHRLICH and ANNE H. EHRLICH: "Why Isn't Everyone as Scared as We Are?" from *The Population Explosion*. Copyright © 1990 by Paul R. Ehrlich and Anne H. Ehrlich. Reprinted by permission of Simon & Schuster, Inc.

ANITA GORDON and DAVID SUZUKI: "How Did We Come to This?" from *It's a Matter of Survival*. Reprinted by permission of the publishers, Cambridge, Mass.: Harvard University Press. Copyright © 1990 by Anita Gordon and David Suzuki.

AL GORE: "Ships in the Desert" from *Earth in the Balance*. Copyright © 1992 by Senator Al Gore. Reprinted by permission of Houghton Mifflin Co. All rights reserved.

STEPHEN JAY GOULD: "Losing a Limpet" from *Eight Little Piggies: Reflections in Natural History*. Copyright © 1993 by Stephen Jay Gould. Reprinted by permission of W. W. Norton & Company, Inc.

GREENPEACE/PUBLIC MEDIA CENTER: "Ozone Shock" from *The New York Times*, 5 October 1992. Reprinted by permission of Greenpeace/Public Media Center.

BLAINE HARDEN: "Poland Faces Communist Legacy of Pollution" from *The Washington Post*, 15 December 1991. Copyright © The Washington Post. Reprinted by permission.

GARRETT HARDIN: "The Tragedy of the Commons" from *Science*, vol. 102. Copyright © 1968 by AAAS. Reprinted by permission.

EDWARD HOAGLAND: "Howling Back at the Wolves" from *Red Wolves and Black Bears*. Copyright © 1972, 1973, 1974, 1975, 1976 by Edward Hoagland. Reprinted by permission of Random House, Inc.

PAM HOUSTON: "A Blizzard under Blue Sky" from *Cowboys Are My Weakness: Stories*. Copyright © 1992 by Pam Houston. Reprinted by permission of W. W. Norton & Company, Inc.

SUE HUBBELL: "Mites, Moths, Bats, and Mosquitoes," originally titled "Summer," from *A Country Year*. Copyright © 1983, 1984, 1985, 1986 by Sue Hubbell. Reprinted by permission of Random House, Inc.

WES JACKSON: "Old *Salsola*" and "Living Nets in a New Prairie Sea" from *Altars of Unhewn Stone*. Copyright © 1987 by Wes Jackson. Reprinted by permission of North Point Press, a division of Farrar, Straus & Giroux, Inc.

WALLACE KAUFMAN: "Confessions of a Developer" from *Finding Home*, edited by Peter Sauer. Copyright © 1992 by The Myrin Institute. Reprinted by permission of Beacon Press.

ANNE LABASTILLE: "Death from the Sky" from *Beyond Black Bear Lake*. Copyright © 1987 by Anne LaBastille. Reprinted by permission of W. W. Norton & Company, Inc.

URSULA K. LE GUIN: "Direction of the Road." Copyright © 1974 by Ursula K. Le Guin. First appeared in *Orbit 14*. Reprinted by permission of the author and the author's agent, Virginia Kidd.

ALDO LEOPOLD: "Thinking Like a Mountain" and "Prairie Birthday" from *A Sand County Almanac, with Other Essays on Conservation from Round River* by Aldo Leopold. Copyright © 1949, 1953, 1966, renewed 1977, 1981 by Oxford University Press, Inc. Reprinted by permission.

DORIS LESSING: "No Witchcraft for Sale" from *African Stories*. Copyright © 1951, 1953, 1954, 1957, 1958, 1962, 1963, 1964, 1965 by Doris Lessing. Reprinted by permission of Simon & Schuster, Inc., and by permission of Jonathan Clowes Ltd., London, on behalf of Doris Lessing.

LINDA LEUZZI: "Eagles" from *New Woman*, November 1991. Reprinted by permission of the author, who has written over 200 articles for national newspapers and magazines. She lives with three dogs, two cats, and a husband in Queens, New York, and has just completed a children's novel.

BARRY LOPEZ: "Borders" and "The Lives of Seals" from *Crossing Open Ground*. Reprinted with the permission of Charles Scribner's Sons, an imprint of Macmillan Publishing Company. Copyright © 1988 Barry Holstun Lopez.

MARCIA D. LOWE: "Pedaling into the Future" from *The World Watch Reader*, 1991. Reprinted by permission of Worldwatch Institute.

CHARLES C. MANN and MARK L. PLUMMER: "The Butterfly Problem." First published in *The Atlantic Monthly*, January 1992, and reprinted by permission.

JESSICA MATHEWS: "Unfriendly Skies" from *The Washington Post*, 22 September 1991. Copyright © The Washington Post. Reprinted by permission.

PETER MATHIESSEN: "The Outlying Rocks" from *Wildlife in America*. Copyright © 1959, renewed 1987 by Peter Mathiessen. Reprinted by permission of Viking Penguin, a division of Penguin Books USA, Inc.

COLMAN MCCARTHY: "Still Killing Whales" from *The Washington Post*, 29 June 1991. Copyright © 1993, The Washington Post Writers Group. Reprinted by permission.

WILLIAM MCKIBBEN: "Change the Way We Think: Actions Will Follow" from *The End of Nature*. Copyright © 1989 by William McKibben. Reprinted by permission of Random House, Inc.

JOHN MCPHEE: "Los Angeles Against the Mountains" from *The Control of Nature*. Copyright © 1989 by John McPhee. Reprinted by permission of Farrar, Straus & Giroux, Inc.

DONELLA H. MEADOWS: "What Is Biodiversity and Why Should We Care About It?" Granted with permission from *The Global Citizen*. Copyright © 1991 by Donella H. Meadows. Published by Island Press, Washington, D.C., & Covelo, California.

SENATOR GEORGE J. MITCHELL: "Two Children in a Future World" from *World on Fire*. Copyright © 1991 by Senator George J. Mitchell. Reprinted with the permission of Charles Scribner's Sons, an imprint of Macmillan Publishing Company.

FARLEY MOWAT: "Of Mice and Wolves" from *Never Cry Wolf.* Copyright © 1963 by Farley Mowat Ltd. Reprinted by permission of Little, Brown and Company. "Of Men and Whales" from *A Whale for the Killing.* Copyright © 1972 by Farley Mowat Ltd. Reprinted by permission of Little, Brown and Company.

JOHN MUIR: "The Birds" from *The Yosemite.* Reprinted by permission of Sierra Club Books.

NORMAN MYERS: "Nature's Powerhouse" from *The Primary Source: Tropical Forests and Our Future.* Copyright © 1992 by Norman Myers. Copyright © 1984 by Synergisms Ltd. Reprinted by permission of W. W. Norton & Company, Inc.

RODERICK NASH: "Why Wilderness?" from *For the Conservation of the Earth,* ed. Vance G. Martin, The Wild Foundation and Fulcrum Press, 1988. Reprinted by permission.

KATHLEEN NORRIS: "Rain" from *Dakota,* 1993. Reprinted by permission of Wayland Press.

MARY OLIVER: "In the Pinewoods, Crows and Owl" and "Humpbacks" from *American Primitive.* Copyright © 1978, 1982 by Mary Oliver. "In the Pinewoods, Crows and Owl" first appeared in the *Provincetown Poetry Magazine.* "Humpbacks" first appeared in *The Country Journal.* Reprinted by permission of Little, Brown and Company.

THOMAS PALMER: "The Case for Human Beings" from *Landscape with Reptile.* Copyright © 1992 by Thomas Palmer. Reprinted by permission of Ticknor & Fields/Houghton Mifflin, Co. All rights reserved.

NOEL PERRIN: "Have Plug, Will Commute" from *The Washington Post,* 25 August 1991. Reprinted by permission of the author.

MICHAEL POLLAN: "The Idea of a Garden" from *Second Nature.* Copyright © 1991 by Michael Pollan. Used with the permission of Grove/Atlantic Monthly Press.

SANDRA POSTEL: "An Illusion of Plenty" from *Last Oasis, Facing Water Scarcity.* Copyright © 1992 by Worldwatch Institute. Reprinted by permission of W. W. Norton & Company, Inc.

DAVID QUAMMEN: "The Beautiful and Damned" from *The Flight of the Iguana.* Copyright © 1988 by David Quammen. Reprinted by permission of Dell Books, a division of Bantam Doubleday Dell Publishing Group, Inc.

DIXY LEE RAY: "Environmentalism and the Future" from *Trashing the Planet* by Dixy Lee Ray with Lou Guzzo. Copyright © 1990 by Dixy Lee Ray and Lou Guzzo. All rights reserved. Reprinted by special permission of Regnery Gateway, Inc., Washington, D.C.

ADRIENNE RICH: Part I from "Sources" is reprinted from *Your Native Land, Your Life,* Poems by Adrienne Rich, by permission of the author and W. W. Norton & Company, Inc. Copyright © 1986 by Adrienne Rich.

JEREMY RIFKIN: "Big, Bad Beef" from *The New York Times,* 23 March 1992. Copyright © 1991/92 by The New York Times Company. Reprinted by permission.

THEODORE ROSZAK: "Green Guilt and Ecological Overload" from *The New York Times,* 9 June 1992. Copyright © 1992/93 by The New York Times Company. Reprinted by permission.

MURIEL RUKEYSER: "Alloy" from *Out of Silence,* TriQuarterly Books, 1992, Evanston, Ill. Copyright © William L. Rukeyser.

W. HARRY SAYEN: "Sounding the Alarm on Threats to Earth" from *The Trenton Times,* 22 November 1992. Reprinted by permission of W. Harry Sayen, Op-Ed columnist and book reviewer, The Times of Trenton.

MARK L. SCHANNON: "One Businessperson's View of the Ecological Crisis," 1990. Reprinted by permission of Mark L. Schannon, senior vice president/associate director, Ketchum Public Relations, Washington, D.C.

MARJORIE SHOSTAK: excerpts from "Life in the Bush." Reprinted by permission of the publishers from *Nisa: The Life and Words of a !Kung Woman,* Cambridge, Mass.: Harvard University Press. Copyright © 1981 by Marjorie Shostak.

GARY SNYDER: "The Call of the Wild" from *Turtle Island.* Copyright © 1974 by Gary Snyder. Reprinted by permission of New Directions Publishing Corp. "The World Is Places" from *The Practice of the Wild.* Copyright © 1990 by Gary Snyder. Reprinted by permission of North Point Press, a division of Farrar, Straus & Giroux, Inc.

WALLACE STEGNER: "Land of Hope, Land of Ruin" from *The New York Times,* 29 March 1992, Op-Ed. Copyright © 1992/93 by The New York Times Company. Reprinted by permission.

WILLIAM K. STEVENS: "Loss of Genetic Diversity Imperils Crop Advances" from *The New York Times,* 25 June 1991. Copyright © 1991/92 by The New York Times Company. Reprinted by permission. "River Life Through U.S. Broadly Degraded" from *The New York Times,* 26 January 1993. Copyright © 1992/93 by The New York Times Company. Reprinted by permission.

JULIE TITONE: "Balance of Power: Can Endangered Salmon and Hydroelectric Plants Share the Same Rivers?" from *Earthwatch,* Sept./Oct. 1992. Reprinted by permission of Julie Titone, who reports on environmental issues for the Spokesman-Review newspaper in Spokane, Washington.

F. A. VOLGELSBERG: Letter to Melissa Walker, 18 December 1992. Reprinted by permission of F. A. Volgelsberg, environmental manager, DuPont Fluorochemicals.

ALICE WALKER: "My Heart Has Reopened to You: The Place Where I Was Born" from *Her Blue Body Everything We Know: Earthling Poems, 1965–1990.* Copyright © 1991 by Alice Walker. Reprinted by permission of Harcourt Brace & Company.

DONALD WALKER, JR.: "A Logger's Story" from *The Wall Street Journal,* 15 May 1992. Reprinted by permission of The Wall Street Journal. Copyright © 1992 Dow Jones & Company, Inc. All rights reserved.

TERRY TEMPEST WILLIAMS: "The Clan of One-Breasted Women" from *Refuge.* Copyright © 1991 by Terry Tempest Williams. Reprinted by permission of Pantheon Books, a division of Random House, Inc.

EDWARD O. WILSON: "Storm over the Amazon" and "Krakatau." Reprinted by permission of the publishers from *The Diversity of Life,* Cambridge, Mass.: The Belknap Press of Harvard University Press. Copyright © 1992 by Edward O. Wilson.

GEORGE M. WOODWELL and KILAPARTI RAMAKRISHNA: "Forests, Scapegoats and Global Warming" from *The New York Times,* 11 February 1992. Copyright © 1991/92 by The New York Times Company. Reprinted by permission.

DONALD WORSTER: "The Age of Ecology" from *Nature's Economy.* Copyright © 1977 by Donald Worster. Reprinted by permission of the author, Hall Distinguished Professor of American History at the University of Kansas.

HOWARD YOUTH: "Birds Fast Disappearing" from *Vital Signs, 1992: The Trends That Are Shaping Our Future,* edited by Linda Starke. Copyright © 1992 by Worldwatch Institute. Reprinted by permission of W. W. Norton & Company, Inc.

BENJAMIN ZUCKERMAN: "Two by Two, We'll Fill the Planet" from *Los Angeles Times,* 31 October 1991. Reprinted by permission of Benjamin Zuckerman, professor of astronomy, University of California, Los Angeles.

ANN ZWINGER: "The Lake Rock" from *Beyond the Aspen Grove.* Copyright © 1970, 1981 by Ann Zwinger. Reprinted by permission of Frances Collin, literary agent.

ILLUSTRATIONS

Cover art: "Flowering in the Canopy, Atlantic Rainforest, Brazil" by Luiz Claudio Marigo. Reprinted by permission of the photographer.

Chapter 1: L.A. Highway, Airplane Photo, State of California Department of Transportation. Reprinted by permission.

Chapter 2: Photograph of John Burroughs and John Muir by Fred Payne Clatworthy from *Odyssey: The Art of Photography at National Geographic,* edited by Jane Livingston. Copyright © National Geographic Society. Reprinted by permission.

Chapter 3: Photograph of !Kung women gathering nuts in northwestern Botswana by Marjorie Shostak, Anthro-Photo.

Chapter 4: "Leaves, Mills College, Oakland, California, 1931." Photograph by Ansel Adams. Copyright © 1993 by the Trustees of the Ansel Adams Publishing Rights Trust. All rights reserved.
Chapter 5: "Pelican, Point Lobos, 1941" by Edward Weston. Copyright © 1981 Center for Creative Photography, Arizona Board of Regents. Reprinted by permission.
Chapter 6: Photograph of a Brazilian Gold Mine by Sebastiao Salgado. Reprinted by permission of Magnum Photos.
Chapter 7: "What Have We Done?" by Paul van Peenan/UNEP/Select.
Chapter 8: Sinuous rows of tract houses in Palm City, Fla. Photograph by Alex MacLean from *Look at the Land,* text by Bill McKibben, published by Rizzoli, New York. Reprinted by permission.
Chapter 9: Photograph by Billy Howard. Reprinted by permission of the photographer.

INDEX